# Brothers & Fathers

By
## Monsignor John A. Esseff
&
## George J. Esseff, Sr.

*as told by*
### Ellen Franco

P.O. Box 24
East Stroudsburg, PA 18301
(570) 972-1133 Phone | (570) 300-1600 Fax
www.EMEpress.com
ISBN: 978-0-9842953-7-1

# Dedication

To our parents,
our grandparents, and
the generations who came before us,
all of whom originated in the mountains of Lebanon
and emerged throughout the world as members of
the Khoury family,
Beit el Khoury,
the House of Priests.

To our children
and grandchildren,
physical and spiritual,
and
to all other generations
of Esseffs
as they travel throughout the world as
parents, priests, deacons, and religious,
guided always by God the Holy Spirit
and preserving our precious heritage of
faith in God,
the loving Father of us all,
and following the example of
Jesus our Brother.

# Contents

Acknowledgements .................................................................ix

Foreword .............................................................................xi

Introduction ......................................................................xv

A Defining Moment ..........................................................1
    Father John .................................................................. 1

Under One Roof ................................................................3
    Father John .................................................................. 3

Gidue.....................................................................................7
    George ........................................................................ 7

Early Memories of Growing Up ..................................11
    Father John ................................................................ 11
    George ...................................................................... 22

Beyond Our Roof ............................................................35
    Father John ................................................................ 35

High School Memories ...................................................45
    George ...................................................................... 45

An Excursion from the Linear Path of Our Lives.....57
    Father John ................................................................ 57

Patches of Family History...............................................59
    George ...................................................................... 59

Domestic Storms................................................................61
    Father John ................................................................ 61

Dad .......................................................................................63
    George ...................................................................... 63
    John ........................................................................... 64

# Contents

REFLECTIONS .................................................................67

    GEORGE ............................................................. 67

    FATHER JOHN ..................................................... 68

    GEORGE ............................................................. 69

ON MY OWN .................................................................73

    FATHER JOHN ..................................................... 73

        St. Charles Seminary...........................................73

        Inter-Session: Camp St. Andrew ........................75

        St. Mary's Seminary ..........................................78

KING'S COLLEGE.............................................................81

    GEORGE ............................................................. 81

MEETING "MR. RIGHT".................................................91

    ROSEMARY ......................................................... 91

THEOLOGICAL COLLEGE: CATHOLIC UNIVERSITY OF AMERICA....97

    FATHER JOHN ..................................................... 97

VOICES OF DISCERNMENT .............................................101

    GEORGE .............................................................101

    FATHER JOHN .....................................................106

THE HAPPIEST DAY OF MY LIFE .................................109

    GEORGE .............................................................109

BECOMING ROSEMARY ESSEFF......................................111

    ROSEMARY .........................................................111

ARMY CORPS OF ENGINEERS LAB ...............................119

    GEORGE .............................................................119

ORDINATION: MY RITE OF PASSAGE ...........................125

    FATHER JOHN .....................................................125

# Contents

First Assignment ................................................ 129

    *Father John*................................................ 129

St. Matthew's Parish .......................................... 133

    *Father John*................................................ 133

Crossing the Threshold of Parenthood ............ 151

    *Rosemary* ................................................ 151

Changing Times ................................................ 157

    *George* ................................................ 157

Seasons of Loss.................................................. 161

    *Father John*................................................ 161

        Mae Ann's Death ................................ 161

        The Flood of '55 ................................ 169

        Going Home ................................ 173

Our Growing Family ........................................ 177

    *Rosemary* ................................................ 177

Beginning in Business ...................................... 181

    *George* ................................................ 181

Across the Continent ...................................... 193

    *Rosemary* ................................................ 193

California: Starting Over .............................. 197

    *George* ................................................ 197

Grow Where You're Planted .......................... 205

    *Rosemary* ................................................ 205

My Continuing Formation at St. Matthew's.......... 213

    *Father John*................................................ 213

# CONTENTS

**DISCOVERING DIFFERENT WORLDS** ....................221
    ROSEMARY ....................221
    GEORGE ....................224
    ROSEMARY ....................227

**MY SOUTH AMERICAN EXPERIENCE** ....................233
    FATHER JOHN ....................233
    A RETOLD STORY ....................236

**RE-ENTRY: A JOURNEY OF MANY STEPS** ....................253
    FATHER JOHN ....................253

**MINISTRY IN MY HOME DIOCESE** ....................257
    FATHER JOHN ....................257

**THE BEST-LAID PLANS** ....................263
    GEORGE ....................263

**LOSING DAD** ....................267
    ROSEMARY ....................267

**RETURN TO FAMILIAR PLACES** ....................271
    GEORGE ....................271

**THE MANY FACES OF THE POOR** ....................275
    FATHER JOHN ....................275

**THE BUSINESS OF REARING CHILDREN** ....................303
    ROSEMARY ....................303

**THE GOOD LIFE: A TIME FOR MUCH GRATITUDE** ....................315
    GEORGE ....................315
        Business ....................315
        Angels in our Lives ....................329
        Sharing Our Gifts ....................336
        The Early Eighties ....................340

# CONTENTS

**MY MISSION TO LEBANON**................................................................**343**

   *GOING BACK TO A PLACE I'D NEVER BEEN* ......................343

      Father John ................................................................343

      The End of My Mission in Lebanon ........................395

**MEMORIES OF DENISE** ................................................**401**

   *THE FAMILY* ................................................................401

**AFTER LEBANON: TRAVELING A DIFFERENT PATH**................**421**

   *FATHER JOHN* ................................................421

**A GRADUAL AND NECESSARY REASSESSMENT** ................**445**

   *GEORGE* ................................................................445

**DRASTIC CHANGES** ................................................**453**

   *ROSEMARY* ................................................................453

**MY DAD** ................................................................**457**

   *GEORGE JR.* ................................................................457

**THE ROAD TO RECOVERY** ................................................**461**

   *GEORGE* ................................................................461

**THE TURN OF THE CENTURY** ................................................**469**

   *FATHER JOHN* ................................................469

**A NEW HEART**................................................................**493**

   *GEORGE* ................................................................493

**MY JOURNEY TO LEBANON** ................................................**513**

   *GEORGE* ................................................................513

**MY JOURNEY IN A LIFE OF PRAYER** ................................**521**

   *FATHER JOHN* ................................................521

      What is Prayer and How Do We Pray?....................524

# CONTENTS

THE CONTINUATION OF MY MISSION ...................................................533

   GEORGE ...................................................................................533

MY TURN TO WRITE THE NEWS ........................................................537

   GEORGE ...................................................................................537

      You're a Republican??? ...........................................................537

COMING FULL CIRCLE ....................................................................543

   GEORGE ...................................................................................543

      The Ordinary ... ...................................................................543

      And ... The Extraordinary ......................................................544

LONGING TO GO HOME .....................................................................549

   FATHER JOHN ...........................................................................549

DEALING WITH DETAILS ...................................................................551

   GEORGE ...................................................................................551

SAFELY HOME .................................................................................555

   FATHER JOHN ...........................................................................555

EPILOGUE: LEBANON REVISITED ........................................................557

   ELLEN FRANCO .........................................................................557

INDEX ...........................................................................................571

# ACKNOWLEDGEMENTS

Recorded here is a collection of memories and feelings expressed by the Esseff brothers, John and George. Their stories are enhanced by the voices and letters of family members, friends, and acquaintances as fascinating as they are diverse, all of whose lives have been touched by either or both of the Esseffs.

I wish to express my gratitude to each of these people, some of whom I've never met. This book would never have been possible without their willingness to share their reflections of these two highly gifted men who, throughout their lives, have expressed a love of God and a love of people through prayer, a legacy of hard work, great talent, and generosity of spirit.

I wish to thank George and his wonderful wife, Rosemary, for welcoming me into their home with warmth and hospitality. I became immersed in their family, their children's families, and an extended family that was at once welcoming and hospitable, and in time embracing, warm, and open.

I wish to express my personal appreciation to all those involved in this project, for their candor about so many private and poignant moments in their lives. No matter what the topic or the feelings, I knew throughout my fact-finding mission that everything was offered in a spirit of love and gratitude.

I want to thank my own family and friends for their support and encouragement as the days turned into months and the months into years, until what became a formidable task finally came to fruition.

Finally, I want to say my own heartfelt "thank you" to the Esseff family for the privilege of recording for posterity at least a part of the exceptional histories of these two men. At times, their stories were quite distinct. At other times, they intertwined or overlapped. Sharing a unique brotherhood for more than eighty years, each in his own way has served not only his own family but the family of man as well.

Accept my gratitude for entrusting to me the amazing story of your lives.

*Ellen Franco*

# FOREWORD

Pope John Paul II once reflected on how he had often paused during the Jubilee Year to look at the large number of pilgrims waiting to walk through the Holy Door at St. Peter's Basilica. "In each of them," he said, "I tried to imagine the story of a life . . ." (*Novo Millennio Ineunte*, 8).

"The story of a life." It's a remarkable little phrase, pregnant with all the experiences, hopes, joys, trials, sufferings, and longings of every person to whom we apply it. "The story of a life"—when we take this phrase to heart, it saves us from reducing others to anonymous specimens and awakens us to a living sense that each and every human being is an unrepeatable mystery worthy of profound respect. "In reality," John Paul II told us, "the name for that deep amazement at man's worth and dignity is the Gospel, that is to say: the Good News. It is also called Christianity" (*Redemptor Hominis*, 10).

In *Brothers & Fathers*, we are graciously welcomed into the remarkable "stories" of John and George Esseff—brothers of Lebanese descent born in Depression-era America and raised in a small town in Pennsylvania. John became a Catholic priest, devoting himself to the world's poor. George married, ran a successful business, and raised four children. Journeying through these brothers' and fathers' joys and trials, we come away with that deep sense of awe at the mystery of human life that is Christianity.

The title *Brothers & Fathers* indicates an important point of Catholic theology. In different, complementary ways, we see the truth of fatherhood revealed through both George and John. Calling a priest "Father" is not merely a title. "Father" is a priest's deepest identity. For the priest becomes a living sacrament of Christ, who is the perfect revelation of God the Father. And all this happens through his body "given up for us." Like Christ, the priest "marries" the Church, and through his gift-of-self bears numerous spiritual children. To understand this is to understand why only a man can be ordained a priest. Only a man can be a father.

We're often tempted to see married life and Christian celibacy in opposition to each other. But, as John Paul II wrote in his famous *Theology of the Body*, "In the life of an authentically Christian community, the attitudes and the values proper to the one and the other state . . . complete each other and in some sense interpenetrate." For "the nature of the one as well as the other love is 'spousal,' that is, expressed through the complete gift of self" (TOB 78:4).

And that is what we witness in *Brothers & Fathers*: two men whose "complete gift of self"—one in marriage and the other through celibate priesthood—reveals for us the true nature of human love and Christian service. But one must not mistake this book for a tale of saccharine piety. I thoroughly appreciated the fact that they included unvarnished accounts of their mischief, fist-fights, and humorous pranks. These stories add a refreshing "earthiness" often lacking in biographies of "spiritual" people.

I read this book with an especially keen interest because of my personal relationship with Monsignor John—I have been privileged to have him as a trusted spiritual advisor, confessor, and retreat master over the years. I remember how uncomfortable I was when he first shared his signature phrase with me: "You are Jesus." The theologian in me kept adding qualifiers and circling through doctrinal formulations to justify the expression. But Monsignor kept insisting on the simplicity of it: "You are Jesus." Again and again he'd say it, "You are Jesus!"

I knew his spiritual director had been Padre Pio, and I knew he'd served as a confessor to Mother Teresa and lots of other famous people who sought him out for his "wise" counsel, but I couldn't help but wonder if I was getting mixed up with some wacko priest. Nobody ever told me I am Jesus. To think such a thing without an assembly line of qualifications seemed at least misguided, if not heretical. I took comfort when I found the *Catechism* quoting St. Augustine to make the same point: "[W]e have become not only Christians, but Christ himself." And Joan of Arc insisted, "About Jesus Christ and the Church, I simply know they're just one thing and we shouldn't complicate the matter" (CCC, 795).

Now, having read *Brothers & Fathers*, it seems Monsignor Esseff's insistence that we are Jesus goes back to his seminary days when he studied Pope Pius XII's encyclical *Mystici Corporis*, on the Mystical Body of Christ. Jesus has united himself with each and every one of us through the mystery of the Incarnation. Among other things, that means that, in a very real way, our life experiences are Jesus' life experiences. Our sorrows and joys are his sorrows and joys. Our life story is his life story—and his life story is our life story. We are Jesus!

Whatever we may experience, whatever "the story of our lives," we can find Christ in it. And every "story of a life" inevitably passes through tragedy, suffering, and ultimately death. But—united with Christ—the stations of our own cross lead to everlasting glory. As my friend Dr. Bob Schuchts is fond of saying, "Our story is our glory." That is the witness of *Brothers & Fathers*. George and John's story is, indeed, their glory. What a joy to share in it!

*Christopher West*
*Theology of the Body Institute*
*September 7, 2010*

# Introduction

*I* have known Monsignor John Esseff for more than thirty-five years. I met him when he came to Dunmore, Pennsylvania to serve as an assistant in the parish of Christ the King, where my five children and I were members.

I met Monsignor's brother George, his wife Rosemary, and their youngest child Denise when they were visiting Monsignor one summer. At that time, Denise was being treated for a brain tumor, which subsequently took her life. On the few occasions that I saw George after that visit, he approached me each time with the idea of writing a book about his brother John. I suggested that he write a book about himself. Neither book was written. In 2006, however, after a trip to Lebanon, both of the Esseff brothers thought that maybe, just maybe, a book could "happen." They asked me to help them put one together.

Our attempts at gathering information started off very seriously, became punctuated with a lot of laughter, and resulted in a collection of many voices. Some of those voices came from the past, some from the present. Some were new and some were old. Younger voices emerged from old letters and journals, and newspaper clippings voiced sharp details in bold print. Some stories are told here for the first time; some have been told time and time again. Many conversations are recorded as they actually occurred. Many conversations opened up treasure chests filled with memories almost forgotten and helped both George and Monsignor John to formulate new insights into old events and relationships.

In the pages that follow are the songs those voices sang in the summer of 2006.

*Ellen Franco*
*Author*

# CHAPTER I

## A DEFINING MOMENT

### *Father John*

In mid-July of 2006, an event of global importance took place in the Middle East. Israel had begun a barrage of air assaults on Lebanon in response to what it regarded as an act of war by the Lebanon-based Hezbollah. While this drama was playing out, 25,000 Americans in Lebanon were advised by the United States to evacuate. Among those Americans were my brother George, his wife Rosemary, his grandson Andrew and I. We had traveled to Lebanon for a family retreat and a wedding. These events were followed by a retreat that I gave to the sisters of Mother Teresa of Calcutta's order, the Missionaries of Charity.

The close of Sunday's 4:00 o'clock Mass marked the completion of the retreat. I was soon to be picked up and driven to the village of Hardine, the birthplace of my beloved grandfather, to meet my brother George, his wife Rosemary, and their grandson Andrew. They had come to Lebanon for a family wedding and stayed on to visit relatives in Hardine. At the same time, I was conducting the retreat for the community of the House of Joy in Becharré. Since the retreat was spent in silence, neither the sisters nor I had any contact with the outside world for the previous eight days. With the retreat over, I was eager to meet my family and get on our way back to the States. George called me and I gave him an estimated time for my arrival in Hardine. I was anxious to meet him there.

The conversation that developed came as a shock to me.

"There's no possible way for us to leave Lebanon, John." George's voice was calm, but emphatic. "The airport's been bombed. Seaports are closed. The roads in and out of the country are all closed."

I wasn't looking for details. I was just as emphatic: "That's not possible. We'll find a way. I've seen these things before. If not tomorrow, we'll get out the next day. I'm sure somewhere there's a runway still open. I have all kinds of commitments to keep. I have retreats lined up and people are expecting me. We're going to get out of here. We have to get out of here!"

"You don't get the picture, John. This is serious business. It's out of our hands. Right now, there's no way out!"

I felt impatience and frustration welling up in me. I was in no mood to change my plans. Things would have to work out. I repeated, "We're going to get out of here. I'll meet you in Hardine tonight," and I hung up the phone.

Once again, there I was in Lebanon; once again, Lebanon was under fire. But now it was 2006. It had been twenty years since my initial stay, when I served for almost two years as director of the Pontifical Mission in Beirut. This trip was decidedly different for a lot of reasons. Mostly, my brother George and his family were here with me now, and I was concerned about them. I wasn't sure just how dangerous it was to be there—or if, in fact, it was dangerous at all. I did know that I had to get home. I wanted to go home.

Home ...

... and the reverie began once more, but clearer, sharper.

And it was a defining moment.

It certainly was time to look back: not just at the latest near brush with disaster, but at our entire lives, so intertwined with Lebanon, but so much more intertwined with each other. We decided that this was a good time to pause, to remember, and to record our journey for our family—those here with us now, and those yet to come. We know our journeys may be near completion, but are keenly aware of journeys of the next generation, which are still unfolding.

In two lives filled with blessings we would consider it yet another blessing if the children of today would travel through these pages with us and take the steps we took, coming to know the hearts that formed ours as we went—sometimes on separate paths, sometimes together, but always as brothers.

This story is offered with the hope that it will foster understanding, and offer a link between the past from which we came and the future which is yet to come.

# CHAPTER 2

## UNDER ONE ROOF

### *Father John*

*F*rom the days of our earliest remembrances, we were together. I was born on June 13, 1928 in Wilkes-Barre, Pennsylvania. A year-and-a-half later, on December 21, 1929, George was born. I don't remember life without George. We were together in my grandfather's home on Prospect Street in the midst of a host of people: my grandfather and grandmother, George Abdanour Esseff and Cecelia; my father Joseph; my mother Celia; my father's brother, Uncle Tony; his sisters, Aunt Marian, Aunt Martha, Aunt Sarah, Aunt Catherine, Aunt Ann; and, eventually, Dad's brother Peter—our uncle who is seven years younger than I am.

In the nub of our little world, which had a separate life from the broader life of the family, George and I developed an intense relationship that continued throughout our entire lives. One of the earliest things that both of us remember clearly was the crib we shared in our parents' bedroom. We shared that crib until after our sister Marlene was born in 1933 and George and I went off to school. Maybe it was this arrangement that lasted until we went to school that served to create the kind of relation-

*Mom holding John*

3

ship we have even to this day. We had a place where we returned each night to share our thoughts and feelings about the world that surrounded us. It was in this crib that George and I remember having the same dream—something coming up from underneath the crib that was going to grab us. It seemed like a great big dog. We have never figured out if we dreamed the same dream or if something was really there. But we do remember screaming until someone, maybe Mom, came to save us.

In that house our lives were simple … but not really. I remember being nursed by my mother while George was nursed by my grandmother. Around the time of George's birth, Grandma had weaned Dad's sister (our Aunt Ann) and was able to nurse George. George's memories go back so far; he remembers having his diaper changed as he lay on the bed and held a blanket. As the years went by, each morning we would crawl out of the crib, kiss each other, hold each other's hand, and go down the steps. We had a dog and George, more than I, would play with him.

We hid in that same bedroom and actually saw our sister Marlene being born. That was 1933 and it was not uncommon for children to be born at home. We stayed and watched until my grandmother finally spotted us and scooted us out of the room. George remembers being scared because he saw all the blood. But after that day, no one had to tell either of us where babies came from!

*George with Sho Sho*

My grandfather's home was filled, not only with family, but also with visitors. My grandmother had a pot of coffee on the stove all the time. Anybody who entered the house—the insurance man, a cousin, a neighbor—was given a hot cup of coffee. When meals were served, George and I were included with the men, even though we were only little boys. The women sat only after all the men had been served. That was a dominant dynamic we experienced in my grand-

# Under One Roof

father's home. As family came and went, when each day was over, George and I would sit in our crib and talk about all that had happened, all that we thought, all that we felt. In spite of our young ages, we would talk about things in a manner well beyond our years. In that little house on Prospect Street in Wilkes-Barre, Pennsylvania, we learned to discern what was to be accepted and what was to be rejected in what we saw and heard and experienced. We took those choices with us as we grew into manhood, into middle age, and now into the final season of our lives.

*Gidue's house*

Under that same roof, and in the midst of all the people who were part of those years, we came to know and love the person whom we both consider to have been the biggest influence in both our lives: our grandfather. As far back as we can remember, we knew him by the Arabic word, *Gidue*.

*Gidue*

5

# CHAPTER 3

## GIDUE

### *George*

The biggest influence in my life was my grandfather, Gidue. I spent the first five years of my life living in his home. That little house was home to Gidue, my grandmother, all of their children (including my father), my mother, and my older brother John. When I return to Pennsylvania and see it today, I don't know how they ever raised such a large family there. My grandparents had nine children of their own and only one was married when my father married my mother. Dad didn't have enough money to get a place of his own and so he and my mother lived in the home of his parents. That's where John and I (and, some years later, our sister Marlene) were born. It was there that I spent my formative years, during which time I observed how my grandfather lived. He was probably in his mid-forties or early fifties. He served as a Maronite deacon and as sexton at the parish. Every day he would walk from the house to the church to tend to the fires or clean up or shovel the snow. And every Saturday night he would go to the church to see that everything was ready for Mass on Sunday morning. He also felt a tremendous obligation to be at every holyday Mass. Those tasks behind him, he would then go out on his horse and wagon to buy and sell vegetables and fruits, or to buy and sell rags and metal.

Living in that home, I developed more of a relationship with my grandfather than I did with my own father. My dad was very young—just in his early twenties. He was still going out with his friends, drinking or gambling or going to fights or ballgames. But Gidue was always there. Countless

*Gidue and Grandma Esseff*

7

evenings passed with me or John or both of us sitting on his lap as he read from the Bible and interpreted what the readings meant. Other times, he'd make a kite out of sticks and twigs and newspaper for John and me to fly. He showed me how to do carpentry work, and he would always let me work alongside him, no matter what he was doing. He had a natural affection for us.

We saw Gidue each day as he walked from our house to the church to tend the fires in the wintertime. We watched him taking care of his horse as he prepared to go out and make a living on his horse-drawn wagon. In the wintertime he would collect scrap and rags; in the summertime he sold fruits and vegetables from the back of his wagon in the many neighborhoods throughout the city. When he wasn't with us or at work or at the church, he was praying at a little altar that he had set up in the house. We knew him as a man of quiet prayer. He loved the Mass, he prayed always, and because he had a personal relationship with St. Anthony, he observed a weekly novena at the church. Mostly, he lived what he believed. As I observed him in his daily life, I developed a moral dimension that has stayed with me even until today.

In spite of its being the Depression years, Gidue's home always remained open. The house we lived in was located only about two blocks from the railroad, and it seemed that almost every hobo knew about our house! I don't know what kind of communication network they had, but they would get off the train and knock on my grandparents' door. Whatever we were eating, the hobos also ate that night. In the summer, they would eat on the porch; but in the winter, they would come inside and eat in the house. I don't remember a single time when my grandparents turned anybody away.

Gidue kept two jars in a kitchen cupboard. Every Tuesday (the day dedicated to the novena to St. Anthony), when Gidue came home from his rounds of buying and selling, he would put his earnings from that day into one of the jars. The rest of the week's earnings went into the other jar. That money was for the family's needs. I'm sure now, looking back, there must have been weeks when Tuesday's sales were the best of the week, but that's the way he did it. At that time he was raising a bunch of his own kids. We were living in his house along with his wife and children; and although my dad was working, I don't think my mother and dad did much to improve my grandfather's financial situation. Yet as I look back, I don't ever remember thinking that we were poor.

When Friday came around, my grandfather would take the money that he had put into the "Tuesday jar." He would go to the wholesale stores that sold day-old bread and he would look for bargains, filling anywhere from five to eight bags with

# Gidue

groceries. Traveling home on Friday, he would pass in front of St. Mary's School, where we went to school. I would jump onto the wagon and help him deliver everything in the bags. He delivered to orphans and to the people who were taking care of them. At that time, cousins or sisters would take over and raise the kids of parents who had died. Gidue would help those families—and widows as well. I suppose he was the equivalent of today's welfare system—but on a much more personal level. That was Fridays. On holidays, he would make a special effort to give a family a turkey or a ham, and always there was something for the kids. At the day-old store, he would buy cookies or cupcakes. He was a gentle man who worked very hard and was extremely generous. One of the things I used to love (and wait for on Friday evenings) was the dessert Gidue made out of boiled wheat and sugar. That was a great treat! Then, after dessert (as on other nights), I was content to sit on his knee and listen to his stories. I don't know how many times he told me the story about the widow woman who gave her last two pennies to charity and had nothing for herself, but I never got bored hearing it. Looking back, I wonder if he was thinking about the few Lebanese in the parish who were really wealthy. If they gave, it didn't hurt them to give; and in telling that story he was making a point he made over and over again: If you're going to give something, you have to give from your substance, not from your excess. When you give from your excess, you're not really doing anything. Unless you're giving from your need, you're really not doing anything beneficial. This is the principle Gidue taught me. As I grew up, there were times I forgot that principle; but, thank God, I always got back on track. And now, looking back at my grandfather and remembering the kind of work he was doing always fills me with love and admiration. I know now that he was working as hard then as I have ever worked in my life—and all for about five dollars a day!

Yet somehow Gidue always managed to give.

# Chapter 4

## Early Memories of Growing Up

### *Father John*

All those early years in Gidue's house (and in both of our later homes) I shared with my brother George. We went to school together, we worked at the market together, we went on vacations together, we hung out together, and generally we got in trouble together! We did a lot of stuff we shouldn't have done; but even now, as we remember some of our antics, we chuckle. We had rules. We kept some of them. We broke some of them, too. Yet, in spite of the fact that Dad was a strict disciplinarian, we took our chances and enjoyed our little adventures.

There was a lady in our neighborhood who, we thought, was always spying on us. We called her "Mrs. Snoopy." She kept an eye on everything we did. Dad always had a truck, but he also had a car. During the war years, Dad had plenty of stamps for gas, since he was allotted enough of them to make his living using his truck. But Mrs. Snoopy knew that gas was rationed and she complained that the Esseffs were always "driving somewhere". There was no end to the things she could dream up to complain about. As George said, "She was always yappin' about something." Well, we teased the hell out of her. Our porch had a little space underneath it and we would hide there. We had great pea shooters that we'd load up with rotten grapes and then shoot them at her windows. We fixed it so she was washing those windows all the time!

By 1933, when Marlene was born, staying at my grandfather's house was becoming more and more impossible. Dad bought a place on Moyallen Street—the street that sat back-to-back with Prospect Street (where my grandparents lived). Dad was spending a lot of time getting the place ready so we could move in. While he was doing that rehab, we moved out of Gidue's house and into a house Dad had rented on Hazle Street. It was located in a neighborhood in Wilkes-Barre that bordered what, at the time, might have been considered the bowery.

# Brothers & Fathers

During that time, we met some pretty rough characters, but we were thrilled to hang around with them. Some of them eventually wound up in jail. Among other things, these guys—all from Lebanese families—introduced us to smoking. We didn't actually have cigarettes, but they taught us how to smoke. We'd pick up cigarette butts, take out the tobacco that was left, and roll it up in a newspaper. Then we'd find a safe place and have our smoke. It was really raunchy. Looking back, I'd say we were a bit precocious in this area. I was probably eight and George was six-and-a-half, but men smoked and we sat at their table. We were OK with it.

One day, just hanging around with nothing to do, we decided to have a smoke. It wasn't our first. Everything was fine until we saw one of the neighbors coming by who was sure to see us. I put my cigarette in my pocket and snuffed it out. George threw his away and we went home. Maybe the next day or so, when my mother was doing the wash, she found the cigarette in the pocket of the shirt. I should mention: The shirt I had been wearing was George's shirt! Since the cigarette was in his pocket, my mother assumed that it was George who had been smoking. I should be ashamed to admit it, but in the barrage of questions that followed, I never said a word. And to his credit, George didn't rat me out.

That unhappy event happened in the summer. That night, George and I were sleeping on a pullout sofa where we were allowed to sleep on really hot summer nights. My mother obviously told Dad the story when he got home. I woke up from a sound sleep to a lot of yelling and saw Dad holding George up in the air by one leg, shaking the hell out of him and yelling, "Were you smoking?" George didn't deny it; he always told the truth. And I didn't say a word. That day George took a beating for me. And that day the dynamic was set in place. After that, if something went wrong, George did it—whether he really did or not. And so after that, in our family, I was always the one who was not in trouble. I have the feeling George still thinks he needs to protect me; and if he can't, he's still willing to take a beating on my behalf.

I remember another time George took a beating for me. We had an old-fashioned freestanding RCA radio. It was the perfect height for a lamp, and my mother had put a favorite lamp of hers on top of it. I grabbed a pillow from the sofa and threw it at George. He ducked. The pillow hit the lamp and it came crashing down. Mom heard the crash and ran into the room. George was still standing next to the lamp, broken in a million pieces. Mom started in on George right away, but he just stood there, looking innocent. The look didn't save him. I let him take a beating for me that day, too.

# Early Memories of Growing Up

Of course, we were always told, "No playing in the house." But one day George and I decided to have a little game of indoor baseball. I threw the ball to George and he brought the bat way back and whacked the wall. You guessed it: A great big hole was staring back at our disbelieving eyes. We tried to fix the wall as best we could; but in the end, we both got punished for that maneuver.

Another memorable occasion happened around that same time, when George picked up the 'F' word. One day we were outside playing and neither one of us was aware that my mother was standing on the back porch. George said 'THE WORD.' My mother heard him, threw a milk bottle crashing down, and scared the hell out of us.

I remember the way my mother told the story to my dad: "George hung around with those guys in the neighborhood and that was it! They must have taught him the word." My mother's take on things was one thing, but Dad's was another. He believed in punishments that, in his thinking, fit the crime. Dad put red pepper on George's tongue and made him stand there with his tongue sticking out. He wouldn't let him take his tongue back into his mouth. How long? Probably less time than what it seemed to George. We both still remember that—no doubt, George more vividly than I!

While we were still living on Hazle Street, our sister Mae Ann was born. That was 1936. We saw that birth, too; but that time, instead of a midwife, it was a doctor who came to the house. George and I were learning more about the facts of life.

*House on Moyallen Street*

Not long after Mae Ann was born, we moved from Hazle Street to Moyallen Street into the house that Dad had successfully renovated. We were in the house that would be our home until George and I went off on our own. It was good news for us. We could walk through our back yard, zigzag through our next door neighbor's yard, and find ourselves in Grandpa's back yard. We were back in our old neighborhood.

That neighborhood was, among other things, the home of our parish church where George and I were very involved as altar boys ... when we weren't getting into trouble! In that role at St. Anthony's, we didn't have to say anything; we just had to act. So although we were very young, we could take on the duties of altar servers.

When the church was completed in 1938, there was a great celebration planned and we were very enthusiastic about being part of it. In our starched cassocks and red ties, we were an unmistakably important part of the most meaningful rituals. There was going to be a procession and I was supposed to carry a candle. I was really focused on playing that vital role in the celebration of the first Mass in the new church. There were candles placed outside the church and, as we processed up the

*George and John as altar servers*

steps, I had the distinction of being chosen to carry one of those large candles. I can only guess how pious I tried to look as I walked with great anticipation toward the front of the church. My angelic look turned to one of disbelief when one of the other altar servers jumped in front of me and grabbed the last candle. Minutes later, there I was, at Mass, not lighting even one little candle—and cursing, not the darkness, but that wise-ass kid who took my candle! It was my first experience of being upstaged.

## GEORGE

*"John was a server before I was, but something I remember from that time happened before I was even three. When the building was still under construction and the church was in the basement, I remember being at Mass. I would get out of the pew and walk up to the altar. I would kneel down right next to Father Koury, and usually the only way he'd be able to get rid of me was to reach into his pocket and give me a nickel. When he did that, I'd turn around and run back to the pew. I remember doing that again and again. It's amazing that he ever let me near the altar after all the times I did that!"*

Another time, I was scheduled to serve at Benediction. Though this was a brief service, the altar was supposed to be ablaze with candles. It was my job to light all of the branch candles and the six large candles on the altar. I had poor vision even then, and I was having a really hard time connecting the lighted wick I was carrying with the wicks on the candles—especially the ones that were up so high. I had only just begun to make some progress when Father Koury came out of the sacristy and started the devotion. By the time I got all the candles lit, Benediction was over, and I had to begin putting all the candles out.

Candles continued to be my nemesis. Once, when I was putting the flames out, wax dripped and fell onto the carpet. Father Koury grabbed my ear and said, "Look what you've done!" That was a favorite technique in those days: grabbing kids' ears. I remember praying for his demise that day.

Hard to figure why he gave George nickels but he twisted my ears!

In spite of my difficulties, I persisted in my "service." One day, when I was serving Mass, I dropped the book containing the special readings for the day. All of the ribbon markers fell out from between the pages. Father Koury couldn't hide how upset he was. I remember looking down at the pews, and there was Mom crying.

That wasn't the only time I saw people crying in church. Crying went on at funerals. The truth be told, we had less-than-noble reasons for volunteering to serve those Masses: Families of the deceased would usually give the altar boys tips. We decided that it was OK for people to die. After all, that's how they would get to heaven, wasn't it? We were quite a bit older before we realized that propriety dictated that the "tips" were better called "stipends." Those stipends were the reasons we loved to serve at weddings, too. Weddings turned out to be even better than funerals: No one had to die and, overall, everyone seemed happier. I guess the happy couple thought they were on their way to heaven, too.

We also had an altar boy club. We used to have meetings and, along with the serious business that we did accomplish, more than once in a while we were known to help ourselves to a little bit of the altar wine in the sacristy. Eventually, at one meeting, we discovered that there was no wine. Apparently, we weren't as slick as we thought we were. After a short search, we found the wine under lock and key in another sacristy. Someone was wise to us; after that, the meetings were never the same.

Some of our other indiscretions weren't dealt with so subtly, but we didn't always get caught. When we did get caught, we had to deal with Dad and his concept of justice. As soon as he declared us guilty of various transgressions, he made us kneel on the floor until, I guess, we saw the error of our ways. One time, both George and I were being disciplined for something. It's hard to remember what; it happened so often. But on that particular occasion, we were there for such a long time that we finally realized that Dad had forgotten all about us. Because we had moved into our new house on Moyallen Street, we had our own bedroom and that was where Dad had told us to kneel. Then he left. After the longest time, I had to go to the bathroom, but I wouldn't go because Dad told us to stay there. It wasn't that I couldn't have gone. I remember making the decision that I wouldn't go. Only minutes later, George said, "I'm going to the bathroom."

## GEORGE

*When I came back there was a big puddle under John all over the linoleum floor. We had been there a really long time, and I guess we both knew that Dad completely forgot that he had left us there. When he finally came back, he saw the puddle there under John. There was no disputing the evidence. We knew Dad was bothered by the whole ordeal. But John was like that. He wanted Dad to know that he had done what he was told to do. I think he also wanted Dad to know that he hadn't done what he was supposed to. The fact that there was no puddle for me didn't pass unnoticed, but it was unimportant. John was making a statement. It wouldn't be the last time John and Dad locked horns."*

Probably one of our more dramatic brushes with Dad's wrath happened one day when George decided to pull the truck out of the garage. From the first time George ever rode in the truck with Dad, he was always watching how Dad was doing the driving. He watched him shift and he watched his feet, and he watched how Dad steered that enormous truck. Me—I wasn't watching. But George loved all that mechanical stuff, as far back as I can remember. That was early on. George was about ten at the time.

"John," he said to me, "I know how to drive Dad's truck."

I said, "You don't know how to drive Dad's truck. You stay the hell away from it!" But George had made up his mind. And that was the day I thought I'd lost George forever.

Luckily, some things were never found out. When George was almost eleven and I was a full-fledged twelve, our brother Joe was born. In those days, when a baby was born everyone would look forward to a party. George and I, being somewhat astute in matters of childbirth, knew that babies didn't just pop out. Mom was having a hard time, and Dad knew it would be a while before the baby was

# Early Memories of Growing Up

## GEORGE

*"My dad would always have produce on the truck. Whatever was left we would use at home the next day. Mom wanted some lettuce for a salad and she sent me and John over to get it from the truck that was parked in Grandpa's garage. The truck was backed right up against the wall. I said to myself, 'I can do this.' So I told John I knew how to drive the truck. And though he didn't want me to, I told him to open the door of the garage. He did. I pulled the truck up about three feet from the wall, and then I pulled it out of the garage. That I think I did with the permission of my dad. But Dad did tell me, 'Just leave it there. Don't back it up.'*

*"'I know I can do it.' I said to myself, 'I can back this up.' So I yelled to John, 'You watch the back.' I put it in reverse. Then ... Bam! I rammed the back wall of the garage. 'Oh my God!' I knew I had to get out of there. I took off as fast as I could and went to a place in the mountains that we called the Indian Chair. Anyone who might go to Moyallen Street today can see that hilly area off Dana Street. At my age, they looked like mountains to me. It took me a long time to walk up there, but I did—and I sat up there all afternoon. I could only imagine how crazy Dad would be when he saw what I did to the garage.*

*"But as the hours ticked by, I got really hungry. So I decided to go back and get it over with. When I got close to the house, I could see that the roof of the garage was falling down. When Dad finally saw me, he was still furious. That night, Dad didn't just put me on my knees. He put me on my knees on the sidewalk in front of the house, in front of everyone who went up or down the street. That's the way that day ended. Not the happiest day of my life!"*

born. He put a guy who worked for him in charge of us that day; his name was Charlie Simon. Charlie had a few jobs to do, one of which was to get some beer for the upcoming celebration. So when Charlie went to get a keg of beer, we went with him. He also got some porter beer because it was supposed to be good for a woman who had just had a baby. When we got back home, I remember helping Charlie set up the beer.

George helped himself to some of the beer.

## GEORGE

*"I remember tasting the beer and thinking, 'Oh, God, this is salty.' I remember wondering, 'Do they make beer out of salt?'"*

# Brothers & Fathers

But salty as his introduction was, it wasn't the last beer that George ever tasted!

In the midst of all our escapades, and especially as we got old enough to be off on our own, George and I could always count on some kind of excitement every Saturday. That was when Dad would give each of us a dime—to us, a small fortune. With it in hand, we would go off to the movies in the center of downtown Wilkes-Barre. Usually my cousins Billy and Eddie Harry would also get ten cents each, and we'd all go together. We'd walk to the end of Moyallen Street, take a right onto Grove, a left onto High Street, and then head down Hazle Street for blocks and blocks until we came to South Main Street, where the Family Theatre was located. We got there as early as we could because there were always loads of kids who showed up early, and long lines would form quickly down Main Street as movie time approached. We wanted to be at the head of the line so we'd be among the first to get in. As soon as we bought our tickets, got a nickel in change, passed through the lobby, and gave our tickets to the usher, we were in. We'd run as fast as we could to get as close as we could to the big screen. If we were lucky enough to sit way up front, we'd bend our necks way back and wait till galloping horses ran past us, so close that we had to duck so we wouldn't get kicked in the head! After the double feature, we would scream and yell as the "serial" began. This short feature made the cliff-hanger famous, and we never got enough of it. Each week, after fifteen minutes of uninterrupted danger and adventure, the hero would find himself in a "grave" situation. He would invariably be looking death squarely in the eye, and that was it! The episode was over. Who could blame us for being first in line on the following Saturday to see what would happen next?

When we went off to the movies, we took a lunch with us because we were pretty sure that we were going to be there all day. Most of the time, we would stay and see the double feature twice. We were our father's sons: We wanted to be sure to get our money's worth. After the movie, we'd go across the street to a place called Russell's. They had all varieties of ice cream and, for the nickel that was left over from the price of the movie ticket, we could get a triple-decker ice cream. On hot summer days, only the fastest lickers could beat the sun as it melted our precious sweet treats all over our hands. Trudging up the hills, we often wished that we could be riding one of those big stallions that galloped through the Family Theatre each Saturday. When we got home with no horses to tie to the pickets of our front porch banister, we were back to reality.

Movie time. It didn't get much better than that!

# Early Memories of Growing Up

In reality, we weren't always off on our own, but those years seem to have been a far safer time than today for kids to wander around their neighborhoods. I think most kids had the kind of freedom we had.

Grandpa used to make kites for us out of newspaper and light pieces of wood. He'd put long tails on them. There was an empty yard next to Aunt Catherine's house, and we'd take our kites there. We had plenty of room to run and get them airborne. We used to like to do that. We also had a lot of fun with our pea shooters and sling shots—though they could get us into trouble! Most of us had them because we could make them. We'd have to find the right kind of reeds to hollow out to make a pea shooter, or a Y-shaped branch and a piece of an inner tube for our sling shots. If we could find what we needed, they weren't too hard to make. But George was pretty smart when it came to improvising. I remember wanting a scooter in the worst way, but we didn't have one. I don't know where George got them, but he managed to find a pair of roller skates. He took the wheels off and somehow attached them to a board and we used to ride around on that. It was quite an engineering feat, and our makeshift scooter gave us a little more mobility.

Besides exploring the neighborhood, we also found fascination in some of the activities that went on in our home. One of those was watching the women making Lebanese bread. That would happen in the cellar—a very interesting place! We had to go down a rickety flight of stairs to get into the cellar. The furnace was down there. There was also a big table where we would sometimes have family meals. There was a coal bin and, next to it, a coal stove. There was also a wood fire that the women would use for baking. Upstairs we had a gas stove; but the baking had to be done on a really hot fire, so that was done only in the cellar. My mother, my grandmother, Aunt Catherine, Aunt Marian, and sometimes others would help. They would mix the flour and other nameless ingredients together until they had dough that they would form into a ball. The ball was about six inches in diameter. They would toss the dough back and forth with their arms to get it paper thin while still keeping it circular. Then they would put it on a large paddle, stoke the fire, and put those large circles of dough into the fire for only a minute or two. When each piece was baked, the women would fold it in half and make a semi-circle, and then fold the semi-circle in half again. They would build an enormous pile of these breads and would place a cloth sheet over all of them. This was a process that was transferred from Lebanon. Incidentally, that kind of baking can still be seen there today—usually done on red-hot outdoor fires.

Besides making bread in the cellar, the women would also prepare fresh vegetables and fruits for canning. There would be beets, okra, squash, grape leaves, and many other available fruits as well. (The produce was actually "canned" in Mason jars, which are made of glass, but the term "canning" was always used.) We would eat those canned goods throughout the cold winter months.

As children, we lived in the heart of the anthracite coal region, though working in the mines was not something most Lebanese became involved in. George and I knew little about the coal industry. Still, I'm guessing the old adage applied to us: "Keep the home fires burning." Some member of the family was usually in the home throughout the day, mostly because the fire needed tending to maintain a source for cooking, hot water, and heat. Because it was assumed that someone was always home, people came to the houses for all kinds of reasons. Men worked for the coal companies delivering coal into our cellar coal bin by means of a coal chute from the back of a coal truck. There were also men who delivered ice—not for the refrigerator, but for the ice box. We kept an insulated box on our side porch, and the men would leave the ice in it during the warm seasons; they didn't need to be as careful during

the winter months, of course. Men sometimes came to the house either selling or sharpening knives. Milk was also delivered and left on the porch early in the morning. If no one went out to get it as soon as the delivery was made, it would sometimes begin to freeze! As that hap-

*Family meal circa 1946*

pened, the frozen milk would become a white volcano, pushing the paper top off the glass bottle—a pretty standard part of winter in the Northeast.

One person who stopped at the house regularly was the insurance man. He would come to collect a weekly payment of twenty-five or thirty-five cents for a life insurance policy. That was a time when many people were beginning to understand the value of that kind of insurance, mostly because funeral expenses became very difficult for families to deal with. Sometimes, when a family didn't have insurance, that person would have to rely on friends and neighbors to chip in to help them with their expenses. Mostly everyone went to the same funeral home for services:

# Early Memories of Growing Up

McLaughlin's in Wilkes-Barre. Though the funeral director prepared the body, more often than not, the body would be waked in the home of the deceased. Generally, the family would sit for the entire time of the wake, even through the night. In the day and evening, friends and neighbors would talk of going to the house "of the corpse." This turned into an odd term that became very common. Instead of saying they were going to the wake, they would say they were going to the "corpse house." That was a term that lingered long after the tradition of home wakes, and it startled a lot of people who weren't from the area when they heard it.

Every day was a blank page that waited to have new exploits sketched on it. Sunday had a flavor of its own. In the morning, we'd go to Mass and then we'd go to the Jewish bakery on Northampton Street for hard rolls, bagels and, on occasion, sweet rolls. George always liked sweets more than I did. There was something very special about the smells and the warmth that filled that place, and George and I were always eager to go there with Dad. Sometimes in the dead of winter, when we couldn't get that far because there was so much snow on the roads, someone from the bakery would go around town in a truck and deliver fresh baked goods. By that time, most people were driving cars and trucks. I think Gidue was one of the last to work from a horse and wagon.

Another part of the ritual on Sundays was buying the Sunday paper. When we got home, we'd eat our special treats slathered in butter—or, for George, butter and jelly. Then we'd wait for our part of the paper so we could read the "funnies." (I guess the more sophisticated kids called them the "comics.") Those mornings were very special: kind of leisurely and a time for family stuff. Later in the day, all of us would pile into the truck and go to visit some of our relatives.

All things considered, we have to admit that, at times, we must have been a handful for my parents. We did our crazy kid things—sometimes unnoticed, sometimes caught and disciplined. But all in all, we had a rich variety of experiences and we enjoyed a lot of people and activities. Most often, the best came at the end of the day when George and I relived all that had happened when together we rehashed the day.

# Brothers & Fathers

## *George*

From a boy's point of view, there were a lot of happy times. In our day-to-day life in Gidue's home, I loved watching Grandpa doing carpentry work and helping him in his garage. When he wasn't around, I amused myself by taking things apart. I remember once taking our clock apart and then putting it back together. Another time, I remember taking our toaster out to see if I could fix it. (It was always wobbling because it was missing one of the feet from its base.) I found a clothes brush in the house, the kind the traveling Fuller Brush men used to sell. I sawed off about a half-inch from the handle of the brush and made a foot for the toaster. Then I glued the foot to the base. It never wobbled after that. I still have that sawed-off brush in my home in California, thanks to Aunt Sarah who gave it to me a few years ago.

I was always fascinated as I watched my father and grandfather carry on their businesses. I wanted to be like them—and eventually I came up with a plan. One of my prized possessions was my red Flyer wagon. With some wood I found in my grandfather's garage, I built an extension around the wagon to enlarge it. And when it was all done, I told Dad, "I want to sell groceries in the neighborhood." I saw my grandfather doing that in the summers and I really wanted to do it, too. Dad didn't think it was such a good idea, but I pestered him so much that he finally gave in. He'd drop off certain fruits and vegetables with me in the morning before he went off on his route, and I'd load up my wagon with corn, tomatoes, lettuce, and all the different vegetables and fruits I was going to sell.

I think Dad was kind of embarrassed because I did that selling in the neighborhood, but I wasn't embarrassed at all. In fact, I was really pleased with myself. I continued to sell for quite a long time, and I started to make some decent money. By the time I was eight-and-a-half, I was probably making as much money as my grandfather! In my head, I used the tack that the neighbors would feel sorry for me and they'd buy from me. I was a neighbor. They knew me. I wasn't a bad kid, and I figured they'd think I was cute and they'd buy from me. Looking back, I think I was right!

One day, I got home and found I had made sixteen dollars. If I had any fruit or vegetables left, my mother would take them and can them. It was as simple as that. I bought my produce from my dad and then I'd sell it. I loved the challenge of it. When something like that happens—when you're successful and you're having fun—you keep working at it. That's just what I did.

# Early Memories of Growing Up

> ## JOHN
> ⤳
>
> *"Dad sometimes had some vegetables or fruit left over. George was always saying stuff like, 'John, let's go sell these.'*
>
> *"I was confused. 'What do you mean?' My reaction said it all. I guess he knew I wasn't the least bit interested.*
>
> *"And then, some time later, I saw him fix up his wagon and go out into the neighborhood. George was always picking up a few bucks here, a few bucks there. From my perspective now, I realize that George was really watching Dad buy and sell and learning how to buy and sell, too. He was enjoying every minute of it."*

By the time we were living in our own home on Moyallen Street, John and I used to spend part of our summer vacation at the home of my mother's family, the Sahds. Mom's family included her mother and father, five sisters, and three brothers. John and I were close to Mom's brothers: Uncle Frank, Uncle Charlie, and Uncle Joe who really weren't much older than we were. Mom's dad, Grandpa Sahd, was a man who was so stern he made Dad seem mellow.

> ## JOHN
> ⤳
>
> *"Grandfather Sahd was strictly an Old Testament figure. I don't think he even heard of Jesus. He was Moses on Mt. Sinai. He was remote, austere, and severe. Even after I was a grown man, his demeanor remained the same. We were still the 'grandchildren.' One day, after I was ordained, I was walking up and down saying my office. Grandpa was saying his prayers, too. I saw him and just quietly said, 'Hello, Grandpa.'*
>
> *"'You pay attention to what you're praying. Don't you talk to me.'*
>
> *"That was my Grandfather Sahd."*

Grandpa Sahd was something of a wanderer, so the family lived in many different places over the years. I remember visiting them in the city of Philadelphia, at a farm in Uniontown, at a farm in Paxinos, and at one in Northumberland. On one of those excursions, I wanted to take home some baby chicks when we left the farm. I had to hide them, so I put them under my shirt. I was really holding them tight and now I know they were awfully scared. They started shitting all over me.

They were cute little peeps, but they were dead before we even got to leave. I guess I held them too hard and they smothered to death.

Another time, we were visiting in Northumberland. My Uncle Joe had a great big German shepherd and I would ride that dog like a horse. I don't know how old I was, but I remember how much fun it was.

Sometimes I think we must've annoyed the hell out of them. My uncles were very young, and they had a lot of fun duping us all the time. One day they told John and me what to do about the mosquitoes.

"What you really want to do if you're being bit by mosquitoes is just put mud on you and they won't bite you."

So we're out there like two city slick-ers—really two jerks! John's putting mud on me; I'm slathering mud on him. By the time my grandfather came out and saw us, we were totally covered with mud. He was furious ... and Grandpa Sahd's 'furious' was *really* 'furious.'

Grandpa Sahd

But that didn't keep us from getting into other things.

Of course, we were in farm country and there were cow turds everywhere. They sort of looked like wheels when they dried out. We amused ourselves by rolling them all over the place. My grandchildren are prob-ably thinking, "Thank God for video games and basketball!" But we really did have a lot of fun doing that.

The family that lived next door to Grandpa had a barn. One day, we were down there where they had a big mound of hay mixed with cow manure. We'd go up into the hay loft and jump off the loft and land in that—sometimes kind of fresh mix-ture—of manure and hay. We came home smelling to the high heavens. As usual, Grandpa was furious. He had a little water pump in the kitchen, but a big old jack pump outside. Needless to say, he kept us outside. There we were. He took off all our clothes and stood us underneath this pump; cars were driving by and we were so damn embarrassed. I think I was about seven at that time.

# Early Memories of Growing Up

When I was about eight, my Uncle Joe shot a copperhead snake that had almost bit him. He was a sharpshooter. He took the rifle and, without even appearing to aim it, he took the head off that snake. When he picked it up, it seemed to be about five feet long. Then we went back into the house. Inside, while I had my back to him, he came up behind me and draped the snake over my neck. When I felt that damn thing around me, I almost went crazy. But we got even.

The trouble was that we didn't really get even with him; we got even with my grandmother. We'd catch garden snakes and we'd put a string around the snake's neck. Then we'd

*Grandma Sahd with George and John*

wrapped them around the door knob. When my grandmother would go to open the door, she'd grab the snake. That's when the screaming really started.

Years later, when Grandpa and Grandma Sahd moved from the farm and lived in Philadelphia, we would go to visit them there. I remember that my grandmother had a great fear of one of us getting hurt. We knew that. She was particularly frightened that one of us would get electrocuted. One day, I took the iron and I put it in the socket in the wall. Grandma was watching. No sooner did I plug the iron in than I started to shake all over, and then I fell over. I was doing a pretty damn good imitation of being electrocuted and trying not to laugh when my grandfather came in, shouting, "What's going on in here?"

My grandmother was frantic. "Do something! I think he's dead."

"He's not dead. But he's going to be dead in a little while!"

He was really a very severe guy.

Another time, when we were in Philadelphia, we were playing in their bedroom. I don't know why, but I stuck my hand in between the mattress and the box spring and there was something there. I pulled it out and there in my hand was a revolver. They were living in a pretty rough area in Philadelphia. First, I pointed the gun at John, and then (I don't know why) I turned it to the ceiling and pulled the trigger. The bullet went right up through the ceiling.

Maybe I did deserve some of the punishments I got.

# Brothers & Fathers

There were many other kinds of experiences mixed into our early years. While John and I enjoyed the adventures and misadventures young boys often have, we were also immersed in a very prayerful home. Our early experience was probably one of extremes. Gidue, on the far side of the spectrum, was always a steady, solid, nurturing and gentle figure—a storyteller, a man at prayer. Besides observing his dedication to a prayer life, John and I also saw Gidue and Grandma create a haven for the poor. Mom was a daily communicant and, more often than not, was in prayer. We could never count the hours we saw her on her knees, praying. Even if one of us got up in the middle of the night, it was not unusual to find her at prayer. Then there was my father, the cigar-smoking, cursing, hard-working, strict disciplinarian. Dad went to Mass with us only on Sundays; he rarely ever went to Communion and, more often than not, seconds before the priest began his sermon, he stepped outside to have a smoke.

During our days as boys, and in the spectrum of our home, we knew prayer as intrinsic to our everyday life. There were prayers before and after meals, night prayers, novena devotions, rosaries, Lenten devotions, and Holy Week observances. When John and I began grade school at St. Mary's, the local Catholic school, all of these and other devotions fostered and reinforced our life of prayer at home. Prayer was even part of our play time. As long as I can remember, John wanted to become a priest. When we were very young, among our playthings were dress-up clothes. John would take a towel and place it on top of his shirt. He'd arrange it so that it looked like a chasuble, one of the vestments the priest wore at Mass. He'd set up an altar and he would "say Mass," using little Necco wafers for Communion. We did that all the time. John was always the priest; I had to be the altar boy.

As we got older, Father Peyton's rosary crusade began, and Catholics everywhere were prompted by the famous saying, "The family that prays together, stays together." We said the rosary every evening in our home. I remember, too, taking a tomato basket, inverting it, and placing a statue of the Blessed Mother on top of it. That little area in our yard became a base for our rosary devotions on summer evenings and, later on, our annual outdoor crowning of the Blessed Mother.

During those early days, Dad was not perceived by us as being involved in the prayer life of the family. He was involved in the activities of the Church, but most of those seemed to center around social events and encounters with his friends. It wasn't until years later that he experienced a conversion and a deepening prayer life; when we were little, he was on the periphery of most devotions in the family. Still, oddly enough, whenever we went astray in the area of piety, Dad was still on hand to support all necessary, corrective, and punitive measures.

## JOHN

*"Even when I was a little boy, I was attentive to the sermon that the priest gave at Mass. There was never a time when I heard one, whether it was given by our pastor, Father Koury, or some other priest who might be at St. Mary's, that I didn't experience the feeling that I could give a better sermon—that I could say what he was saying, 'better.' There was a sense of wonder of God so deep inside me that I sensed a deep desire to share that mystery. I can trace that sense of wonder as far back as one of the times when Dad took George and me to Grandpa Sahd's farm in Northumberland for a summer vacation. I was just about three-and-a-half, and one day I woke up before George did while a half-light was coming in from the moon. I got out of bed and went to the window, where I had to pull myself up on the ledge to see out the window. As I perched there, the sun began coming up, so spectacularly beautiful and yet overwhelming as it shone ever brighter, and I was filled with awe. As the sun was climbing higher into the sky, I looked around and I knew that God was making the world. He was making each blade of grass and making the droplets of rain, shining like so many diamonds catching the sun as they were sitting on each blade. A weeping willow was standing off to the right, alongside a creek that was creating a deep crevice in the ground. The beauty was startling to me. The creek was bubbling with song; the dog Namoor was running around in the wet grass and all was sunlit, with colors gleaming and vibrant. It wasn't that I saw the world that God had made; in that moment, I was seeing God making the world, keeping all things in constant creation, not forgetting anything for even a second. I don't know how long I sat there watching my little world being made, experiencing the majesty and intensity of creation. For years after, I looked for an explanation of that experience, but not until I met a great Philosophy professor at St. Mary's Seminary did I unlock a bit of the mystery of that treasure and find words to describe (even yet, inadequately) what happened to me that day."*

In spite of some early difficulties, John and I eventually began to develop a greater relationship with our dad. His greatest influence came mostly as we worked alongside him on his truck and in the market. We were very young when he decided to include us in his world of work. Dad was extremely hard-working and extremely honest in business. He was in the wholesale produce business and he had the respect of the people he dealt with day after day. He owned a truck. Mondays, Tuesdays, Thursdays, and Fridays, he would go to the market, buy his produce, load the truck, and travel throughout the many neighborhoods in and around Wilkes-Barre

# Brothers & Fathers

## JOHN

*"By 1936, George and I were full-fledged altar servers. I was eight and George was seven. Easter was fast approaching and we were commemorating the sufferings and death of Jesus. Traditionally, on Holy Thursday evening, the Blessed Sacrament was placed in a side altar, known as the Altar of Reposition. The adults of the parish followed a schedule throughout the night and into Good Friday morning, staying in church in adoration of the Blessed Sacrament. Father Koury expected the children to take over at six o'clock on the morning of Good Friday. He was looking for 'sure show' servers. That would be George and me.*

*"We had been well primed. We were going to spend an hour 'keeping Jesus company' before His crucifixion. Mom had told us the night before that she wasn't going to get up to give us breakfast. Not being one to let her children go off hungry, she gave us fifty cents. I'm guessing she took the money out of Dad's pocket. Believe me: if ten cents would get me into a double-feature movie, fifty cents was a fortune that opened a world of endless possibilities. In the morning, George and I were up and ready. There we were, soldiers of Jesus prepared to lay our lives on the line for Him. We took our black cassocks, our white surplices, our Buster Brown collars, and our red neck ties and began our fifteen-minute walk to St. Anthony's. I couldn't believe we had fifty cents, and I told George, 'After we adore Jesus for an hour, Mom said we could buy something to eat.'*

*"When seven o'clock arrived, we were relieved by two other altar servers and there wasn't much competition as to where we were going to get breakfast. It was the place where Dad took us when he wanted us to have a real treat. Without any hesitation, George and I hotfooted it to South Main Street, opened the door to Abe's Deli, climbed up on the stools with the swirling red seats, and commanded the chef to bring each of us two hot dogs with everything on them—sauce, relish, onions, mustard. When we finished our early morning feast, without a penny in our pockets, we went home.*

*"On Good Friday, morning hours were traditionally quiet, but the hours of twelve to three were spent in total silence. George and I were allowed to go out into the yard, but we were expected to maintain silence while very devoutly acknowledging the time Jesus spent suffering and dying on the cross for us.*

*"By late afternoon, we were looking forward to having dinner at Grandma's. Like every other year, she was preparing a favorite Lenten meal for the whole family: lentils with rice and yogurt. While everyone sat at the table waiting for dinner to be served, Dad asked George and me his customary, 'What'd you do today?'*

## JOHN

*"That day, pride went before the fall. I wanted to impress the whole family with our piety. 'We went to church at six o'clock and adored Jesus in the Blessed Sacrament for an hour.' I must have said that two or three times. In case they didn't know how good we were, I added, 'Father Koury picked us because he knew that we would do it even though it was so early.'*

*"'Then what did you do?'*

*"'Mom gave us fifty cents so we went up to Abe's and had hot dogs with everything on them.'*

*" Silence.*

*"Dead silence.*

*"'You what?'*

*"'We went to Abe's and had breakfast.' And only then did it dawn on us that no one was allowed to eat meat on Fridays. Good Friday—we didn't even think about that. The thought was overwhelming. George burst out crying before I did. The stares from all around the table shouted, 'Pagans! Traitors! Judases!'*

*"We were crying.*

*"Mom began to cry.*

*"Dad spoke right up. 'Get out of here. Go home. No dinner for you two tonight.'*

*"We were away from the table in an instant. Not even Grandpa could save us. Dad took us through the yard, into our own house on Moyallen Street and up to our bedroom. By the time we got there, he had had a little more time to think things over, and before he left, he handed down the final verdict.*

*"'No Easter baskets for you two this year! Now get to sleep.' And he was gone."*

selling produce. When John and I were still very young, we would go to work with Dad. We would get up around two in the morning so we could be at the market by three. Eventually, John and I became part of the process and we moved more intimately into Dad's world—a new layer of experiences for two young boys.

The market was located in the bowery, the area between where we lived and where St. Mary's School was located on Washington Avenue. As we passed through there on our way to school every day, we would first see the red bricks of the Salvation Army building just on the edge of the bowery. Past that, there were two sets of railroad tracks. The center of the bowery was between those two sets of tracks. Hobos who were passing through town always seemed to find the bowery, and other characters, some reputable, some not, could usually be seen around there. In spite of the rough atmosphere, we never felt frightened there because we had become used to it from working at the market. Some of the people in the bowery area were friends of Dad's, and they knew we were his sons. Though the area was seedy, it wasn't unfamiliar. It was something we saw every day. I remember once when we were walking to school; three or four police cars came rushing in with sirens blaring. There had been a double murder and a suicide. In today's world that doesn't seem so unusual, but John and I were all eyes and ears when we began learning about another world that existed so close to our own.

There was a guy by the name of Tony Davis who had a gambling place in the bowery. Guys would go there to bet on the horses or boxing matches or whatever they were interested in. It was a betting place for the numbers racket and lots of different kinds of gambling were very evident. Tony also ran a card game and Dad used to play there. We knew Tony and he liked us. In fact, it was his house on Hazle Street that Dad rented before we moved to Moyallen Street. Tony's place was one of many where there was gambling going on in the back of the store fronts. When all of these games were going on, the men were very free with their language. Working with Dad and being with him, I think I heard every curse word that ever existed right there in the market. It was a really rough place and bad language was all around us. We were never far from it.

Another place in the bowery where we heard a lot of coarse language was at Pat's barber shop. A lot of seedy characters hung out there too and we heard a lot of stuff when we were very young.

Dad had a very close friend, Ike, who was a barber. Ike was a good barber, but he was really more interested in talking about base-

## JOHN

"I remember being at Pat's one day when we got an earful. A guy came in who worked in the Hazard, a big machine shop in the bowery, where locomotives were made. He was making a very loud announcement to everyone in the shop about a friend of his who was somewhere or other. He proceeded to tell about the guy he knew who was sticking his 'joy stick' out the window and waving it at the girls passing by. I was only about ten or eleven years old then. We saw and heard a lot of crazy things that most kids our age remained unaware of."

ball than cutting hair. So more often than not when we left Ike's, our hair was all chopped up. Dad went to Ike's because of their friendship. But Dad was very particular about how our hair looked, so occasionally he'd have to take us down to Pat's to get a good hair cut and to undo the damage Ike had caused.

I recall one morning Dad and I were at the market. The first thing we would always do was walk the market: We were going back and forth checking the pricing before deciding what to buy from which vendors. All of a sudden, a window came crashing down from above one of the wholesale stores. I didn't know it then, but I later learned there was a whorehouse named Kitty's on top of one of the wholesale produce places. As the years went by, we heard a lot more about Kitty's, but the events of that morning sort of took my breath away. A Black woman was hanging out of the window naked, screaming that some guy was raping her. The police were there in no time because they used to patrol the market area all the time. All of the people from the market had gathered and were standing around. The police brought the woman down and one of them put his coat over her. Then some other officers brought a guy down who was also Black. There weren't many Blacks who lived in Wilkes-Barre then, so he really caught my attention. He was a real slick-looking guy: well dressed, pretty flashy, and wearing a hat cocked to one side. He not only looked slick, but when it was time for him to handle the situation, he acted slick as well. When he was being escorted out by the cops, he seemed rather pleased, looked straight at the crowd, and said, "Boy, this is a really big turnout." My eyes were as big as saucers. At the age of ten-and-a-half, it was quite an experience for me.

Those kinds of experiences were a large part of the general atmosphere we worked in. But for me, there were a lot of perks during those days in the market. I was fascinated with my dad's truck. It was an enormous vehicle, an International. It had stakes on the sides, and over the top there were rods that were covered with canvas. It was a huge piece of equipment and I remember chafing at the bit to drive it. I pestered the hell out of my dad until eventually he let me drive. When we finished with our last customer, the

*A truck like Dad's*

back of the truck would be almost empty. I'd ask him. I'd beg him. I all but forced him. He finally said, "OK." I'd sit on his lap and steer the truck on our way home. It wasn't very long after that when I began to do the shifting. And it wasn't long after that when he really let me drive. At that time, I would only drive when the truck was almost empty. During the summer, I'd scoot around the block to where the truck was kept (on Prospect). It was years before I got my license, but I would drive the truck around the block go back to our house on Moyallen and pick up Dad and John. Then Dad would drive and we'd go down to the market.

During the winter, when it was freezing cold, the truck sometimes had to be jump started. We would connect a chain from the truck to Dad's car. I'd get into Dad's car and pull the truck out of the garage while Dad drove it and got it going down the hill. We had an earlier version of that same kind of truck; that one had a crank on it, so we didn't need to jump start it like the later model.

When I was a little older, one of Dad's friends, who was a long-distance driver, made my day. In the market, trailers were being loaded and unloaded, and they had to be moved to make way for one another because space was scarce. One day, Dad's friend, the tractor-trailer driver—a guy who used to drink a lot—threw his keys to me and told me to back up his tractor trailer and get it in position to be loaded. That was a big thrill for me. After that, I would move his rig around the market area, putting it in position to be loaded or unloaded. I was fourteen at the time.

Sometimes we couldn't get what we needed at the major market so we had to go to a couple of different markets to pick up the produce we needed. I would drive from one market to another, and then Dad would take over and we'd go out on his route.

By that time, I was pretty involved in the entire operation. Among other things, Dad sold potatoes and onions. Both came in burlap bags. Those bags and bushel baskets (and a lot of other things, for that matter) were scarce in those days. During the war years, when I was a few years older, I began to collect the bags from the customers after they emptied them, and I'd collect the baskets too. I'd ask the customers to save them for me and they did. My grandfather had a four-space garage. He kept his horse in one section; the truck was in another, and then there were two empty spaces. I'd stack the empty burlap bags and the bushel baskets in the garage. One summer, just collecting baskets and burlap bags and selling them back to the farmers to put their produce in, I made six hundred dollars! It was good for me and it was good for them. They had good baskets and they were buying them for half the price they'd have to pay to buy new ones. I would do this when I went to the market with my dad.

# Early Memories of Growing Up

While I ran my little side business of selling to the farmers, John and I continued to get up around two in the morning to go down to the market with Dad. The farmers would be selling before the market opened up. Dad would always go early to pick the best produce. If he got there early enough, he could buy the best fruits and vegetables for the best price before everyone found out what the other prices were. Those prices would fluctuate, depending on how much produce was available. My dad was quite shrewd about that. He was able to figure out how to get the best fruit for the best price. And he insisted on buying the best fruit—which is why his customers were so happy. He supplied them with 'A' quality goods. I know my dad was shrewd—very shrewd—in business, but everyone in the market and all his customers respected him because, along with being so shrewd, he was also honest.

My brother John worked along with us during all this time, but he wasn't involved like I was. Though he got up each morning, went off to the market, and loaded that five-ton truck with me, he just didn't seem to get the same kick out of it that I did. Me, I loved it. I loved the challenge of it. I don't remember ever being motivated by the money. The work wasn't a chore for me. I knew how to do it, and I did it well. For me, that was fun.

I look back on those early years with amusement and, even now, some curiosity.

# CHAPTER 5

## BEYOND OUR ROOF
### *Father John*

**W**hen we were kids, ethnicity played a large part in the makeup of the neighborhoods in Wilkes-Barre. Although people were born in America (as were many of their parents), they were referred to, not as "American," but almost exclusively by their ethnic backgrounds: Polish, German, Lithuanian, Irish, or (like us), Lebanese. Many people stayed within those boundaries in much of their daily living. In that, we were different.

As Lebanese Americans, we were immersed in most Lebanese traditions and other aspects of that culture. But by the standards of the day, the neighborhood we lived in was quite diverse. That diversity was reflected in the names of our neighbors: Ray, Barbario, Novak, Sanbetti, Hahn, McCarkle, Mellon. In fact, our family was one of the few Lebanese families in the area. Most Lebanese lived in neighborhoods together; we didn't. We broadened ourselves a lot more than many Lebanese did. We did go to the "Lebanese church," St. Anthony's, which was (and is still today) on the corner of Park Avenue and Dana Street in Wilkes-Barre. For many Lebanese, activities were mostly church related. Those activities were social rather than religious and, characteristically, the Lebanese people stayed within their ethnic boundaries—some almost exclusively.

In religious matters, Lebanese Catholics follow the rite of St. Maron and are commonly known as Maronite Catholics, rather than Roman Catholics. St. Anthony's was a church that was not only defined by ethnicity but also by rite.

Other Catholics in the area (Roman Catholics, for the most part), observed the Latin rite, but also belonged to ethnic parishes. The ethnic parishes had been established for the immigrant communities that settled in the area, and many of them remain even until today. There might be an Italian parish, a Lithuanian parish, or a German parish in a small geographic area, all of which observed the Latin rite. People who belonged to the Latin rite might go, (although most never did go), to an ethnic parish other than their own, but they did not go to the Lebanese church, because the liturgy there followed a different rite. Though the liturgy was the same celebration of Eucharist, the rituals were very different, and very foreign to people of the dominant Latin rite churches.

Both George and I were part of the Lebanese church community. We both served as altar boys for all of our twelve years of school. We were used to seeing my mother washing and ironing our cassocks and surplices, which we wore when we served Mass. We spent a lot of time on the altar. Also, we would often go to the church with our grandfather when he went to do his chores there, and we would go with him on Tuesdays when he attended the novena to St. Anthony. We were used to elaborate rituals that included the burning of incense, the chanting of hymns, the carrying of candles, and the ringing of bells. George and I were part of a large group of altar boys.

For the most part, though, those boys did not become our friends—at least not our best friends. Because St. Anthony's didn't have a school, we went to one of many Catholic schools in the area, St. Mary's School on North Washington Avenue. That building is no longer there.

Dad was pretty clear about education. He had only completed the eighth grade, but he was making sure that we were going to get a really good education. He also insisted that we were going to go to a Catholic school and, without question, we were going to go to college. All matters of education were non-negotiable.

Dad didn't want us to grow up the way he grew up. He was a smart man, but he was frustrated. He could spell anything. He could add figures in his head in an unbelievable way. He was a bright man who, like his father before him, was part of an immigrant family and didn't have the education because he had to go out to work.

Growing up, Dad lived in a house that held two families: his family (the Esseffs) and the Mike family. There was just a drape between their living quarters; they couldn't afford any more than that. My father's family followed a common tradition among immigrant families: Once one family came to America and got settled, the members

*Dad as a child with the Esseff, Mike and Oblen families*

of that family brought over another family of relatives. When that family came, they were put up by the earlier immigrants until they got on their feet. That's generally how it happened. When my grandfather invested in that house at 108 Prospect Street, he moved his family out of the other place. Not long after that, Mom and Dad got married. They moved into Gidue's house, and in a matter of seven years had me, George, and Marlene there. These events were happening simultaneously with the expansion of Dad's own parents' family. We were part of a growing family in which George and I had established a relationship that remained somewhat separate and mostly unencumbered by the changing dynamics of family life.

For most people, however, family life in America did undergo significant changes. While we were still in grade school, the war broke out. On December 7, 1941, Japan attacked the American fleet in Pearl Harbor.

With the war on, many things changed. A lot of things were rationed: Butter was rationed; gas was, too. Because Dad was in the produce business, he could get stamps for gas, since his business was considered essential. He got more stamps than he needed for the truck and that's what led to the Esseffs always using the car while so many others had to walk. That didn't go unnoticed. Dad was also delivering produce to stores. Certain store owners would give him a case of butter—not a pound, a case! He might also get a one-hundred-pound bag of sugar. It was some kind of bartering that went on in exchange for his produce. To tell the truth, I was always a little embarrassed about how much we had during those years. Actually, Dad made very good money during that time.

By the time we were both in high school, George and I knew that college was the next step. Few other Lebanese people I knew or traveled with had any ambition of going to college. So for George and me, going to St. Mary's was another defining point in our lives. Those school experiences may have been our introduction to the broader world, especially in terms of peers; we met a lot of people we wouldn't have met if we hadn't

> ## GEORGE
>
>
>
> *"I remember lying on the parlor carpet and listening to the radio announcement about the bombings at Pearl Harbor. I know the bombing was on Sunday and President FDR gave his speech the next day. I remember his words painting a scary picture and I was very frightened when I heard the news that day."*
>
> *"Yesterday, December 7, 1941, a date which will live in infamy, the United States of America was suddenly and deliberately attacked by naval and air forces of the Empire of Japan."*

gone to St. Mary's. We met kids from other backgrounds, and some of them became life-long friends.

George and I did our socializing with friends from school. In many ways, we were formed by those friends. Without question, George and I were expected to do well. Evenings, we did some of our school work at the kitchen table. As we got older, we did some of that studying with friends in their homes. George and I were two out of only maybe four or five Lebanese kids in the entire school. The school included grades one through twelve, and we pretty much knew all the kids around our age. We were like most teenagers: We wanted to be with our peers and be part of the crowd. St. Mary's High School, with about only four hundred students, was much smaller than the local pub-

### GEORGE

*"I remember counting up the money one Friday, calculating on the way home how much we bought, how much we sold, and how much we made: $150 that day. That was a record high. That was a hell of a lot of money for one day! We may have been on the good end of the war economy. We did have one of the first radios in the neighborhood, and eventually we had one of the first TVs. People from the neighborhood would come to watch programs with us on that 12-inch screen."*

lic high school. George and I were in separate circles, but we knew the same people. Although I don't think we realized it at the time, we both had friends who seemed to have the same value system that we did. One of my best friends at that time was John Lavin. He was one of ten or eleven children. His dad was a doctor, and they lived in a nearby town outside of Wilkes-Barre called Swoyersville. John and I were classmates at St. Mary's. He was wholesome. He was funny. He was bright. He was a good football player and a great athlete. He eventually became a Maryknoll missionary who, years later, actually died in the foreign missions. In high school, we were good friends. We enjoyed the same things and had a lot of laughs together.

Another friend of mine was Tony Conmy, who lived in East End. I knew his family well, too. After high school, he went to the same seminary in Baltimore that I did.

Before any of us knew what was going to unfold in our lives, we all continued, day by day, in our own adolescent world. It was wonderful. When I was sixteen, I got my permit to drive. I was pretty active and my dad encouraged me to get my license. I was never interested in driving Dad's truck, but he taught me to drive his car and, after six months, I went to the State Police barracks in Wyoming, a little town not far from home, and passed my driver's test. It was 1944. And from that time on, I had a lot of independence because we had a car and Dad let me drive it.

The fact that we always had a car and the gas to keep it running was actually another line of demarcation. Much to Mrs. Snoopy's continuing dismay, Dad drove the truck and usually let me have the car. We were able to do a lot of the kinds of things that guys in high school like to do. We could go to different places, like Harvey's Lake in Dallas, a small town in the Back Mountain area, a few miles outside of Wilkes-Barre. Without a car, there would be no other way for us to get that far out of the city.

In the city, there were different groups of kids. Some guys hung out in the pool hall on Hazle Street. I remember going in there a couple times with a kid by the name of Jimmy Miller. The language was coarse, but it wasn't as though I had never heard that kind of language before. And the general atmosphere was sort of seedy. Jimmy would talk about going over to Kitty's. I knew about that place from early on, when we went to the market with my dad. But we

*John at Harvey's Lake with friends*

never went down to that area at night. We'd go bowling or maybe even drinking. We did do some drinking; we didn't think too much about it. Guys drank, but that's about as wild as it got. We'd go to dances at school or in one of the nearby towns. When it was hot, we might even skip school and go to Harvey's Lake for a swim.

---

## GEORGE

*"I do remember a close encounter when I was still in high school. A fella that I worked with at Mr. Lustig's market had gone into the service. I was still in high school and I was on my way home from the market one evening when I met him. He was home on leave. It was good to see him and, as we walked, he said he wanted to go to Kitty's. I went with him and he tried to talk me into going upstairs, but I sat downstairs and waited for him. When he came down, he still kept trying to talk me into going up; he even said he'd pay for me. I remember saying, 'No, thanks,' and leaving. I guess that was something I just couldn't do. But the opportunity certainly was there."*

# Brothers & Fathers

We were active—always busy—but we stayed out of some other kinds of activities that were out there.

Like all the other students at St. Mary's, we went to daily Mass before each school day began. That practice led us to become very familiar with the Latin rite. The academic program at St. Mary's was pretty solid, and I genuinely enjoyed my academic life. Like most of the other kids, I took four years of Latin and two years of French. I was on the debate team and was very much involved in plays and public speaking. I was never shy. I also loved to sing. Some of the best times we had in high school were the minstrel shows that we put on for the public. Those were the days of Al Jolson, and our presentations as Black-faced singers were part of the common "politically incorrect" standards at that time.

I was always ready to be onstage and to perform in any area. There was something in me that really enjoyed all that. At home, I remember looking in the mirror and practicing facial expressions to show surprise or anger. When we were kids, there was a very popular show on the radio called *Amos and Andy*; it was a big favorite of mine. I would sit and listen to the radio and imagine what each of the characters looked like. Creating faces for all of them was one of the great things about listening to stories on the radio. I could picture Andy. I could picture the Kingfish. I could picture Ruby Lips. When we were given the opportunity to be in the minstrel show, I drew on the images I had created in my mind from radio shows, and I was eager to portray my impressions. I loved doing some of the Al Jolson and Jimmy Durante routines. I was also able to sing and do some pantomime. All in all, those performances were great fun for me.

On a more serious note was the strong emphasis on oratory in those days. Each week during senior year, one student would have to give an oration. At the end of the year, the six best orators were selected—three girls and three boys—and then there'd be a final competition. I won the oratorical contest in my senior year and I remember having my picture in the paper. That kind of recognition made me very happy.

When we weren't involved in school activities or at work, George and I could always dream up something to do. When I was sixteen and George was fifteen, Dad gave us his car and we drove to Pittsburgh, where we had relatives. He had a lot of confidence in us to allow us to go that far alone! I had a license and George had a permit. As we made our way across the state, George really wanted to

*John wins oratorical contest* drive—and he was pretty good at pestering in those days.

# Beyond Our Roof

## GEORGE

*"I remember driving from Harrisburg to Pittsburgh. It was about the time that the Pennsylvania Turnpike was built out that way, and we got on it. I averaged almost 95 miles an hour for that stretch. It took us only about two-and-a-half hours to get to Pittsburgh. On the way back, the car wouldn't stay in high gear. I guess I had ground the gears off so much that the car just wouldn't stay in gear anymore!"*

Finally, by the time we got to Harrisburg, I let him drive. He burnt the hell out of the car.

That was the time we met a lot of our relatives. We had a great time getting to know cousins of ours by the name of Roman. It was great that George and I could do that together. We had become pretty self-reliant. When we got home, Dad had to get the car fixed.

Overall, academically, I was focused because I had a goal: I always knew that I was going to be a priest. I never thought of becoming anything else, and I knew that the kind of studying I was expected to do was the kind of preparation I needed to be ready for the seminary. For me, high school was just a beginning. I loved all of it.

And of course, because I knew I wanted to be a priest, I'd be careful about the girls I dated. I always looked for girls I'd call "safe." I remember being at a dance one time and there was a girl there who had a kind of questionable reputation. During the evening, she asked me if I'd give her a ride home, and I said I would. But before the dance was over, John Lavin came up to me and asked, "What are you doing after the dance?" When I told him, he said, "I don't think you should do that." And I didn't. A bunch of us went out to the lake and had a couple of beers and then we went home. There were a lot of different choices out there, and I think we were confronted with all of them.

One night, shortly before I graduated, we went to a dance at St. Nick's School auditorium. By that time, I was scheduled to go to St. Charles' Seminary in July, and I was making the most of my free time—swimming at Harvey's Lake with friends, cruising around town in the car, and taking out as many girls as I could. That particular night, a bunch of us went together: John Lavin, Billy Smith, Speedy Karas and my brother George. Remember, we were all from St. Mary's. When we got to the dance, there was a real beauty there. Her name was Joanne. I danced with her, and when I came back to the crowd, one of the guys said to me, "You just danced with my girlfriend."

"Yeah," I said, "she's pretty nice. I think I'm going to dance with her again. Just watch me."

So I went over to Joanne and asked her to dance again. And when I went back to the crowd, this same guy said, "If you dance with her again, I'm going to punch you out!"

"You're welcome to it, buddy, but I am going to dance with her again." And I did.

As soon as I finished the dance, the guy was in my face, and I was up for the challenge. We went outside to fight. Some of the guys came out too, and they stopped the fight. They were yelling, "We can't do this here!" They were afraid if we fought on the school grounds, someone might see us and think it was a skirmish between the kids from St. Mary's and the kids from St. Nick's, which was another school only a few blocks away. That might bring the cops on the scene. So we set the fight up for a few nights later. George came with me. We met across from St. Anthony's Church, way up on the hill. The guy from the dance showed up with a few of his friends, and I was ready for him. I really beat the crap out of him. Later, when I saw what I had done to him, I couldn't believe it. His face was swollen, cut, and bruised. These incidents were sporadic and I began to have a deeper awareness of my anger. They were explosions that came from an otherwise gentle, fun-loving, easygoing guy. In the years that followed, I spent a lot of time trying to figure out where those explosions came from.

But long before I gained that awareness, Joanne married the guy, bruised as he was.

When I was a junior and a senior in high school, I worked after school and on Saturdays at the local grocery store and deli owned by Julius Lustig. The deli was on North Washington Avenue, just a few blocks away from St. Mary's. I made fifteen dollars a week at the market, and I also worked with Dad—but not as much as George did. Like George,

*Father Koury with the family*

# High School Memories

I gave Dad all the money I made at Lustig's market over the years, and then he would give us our spending money.

Throughout all those years, I knew I wanted to become a priest and I had discussed my wishes with Father Koury, the pastor at our parish. When it came nearer to the time for me to go to the seminary, Father Koury came to our house to talk to Mom and Dad about practical matters. In those days, tuition for the first two years at St. Charles had to be paid by the family. Dad had money saved, and he also saved the money I had earned. Father Koury actually made up a list of people he thought should contribute. He held a meeting one night at our house and Aunt Marian gave two dollars to the fund. Aunt Sarah was working in a sewing factory and she made a contribution, too. Gidue gave, and others did too. Father Koury took collecting the money on as a project, and by the time I was to go away, we had all the money we needed for tuition at St. Charles Seminary.

With as many insights as my sixteen years and a high school education afforded me, I left for Baltimore shortly after my graduation. While George looked forward to his final two years in high school, I eagerly began a new chapter in my life, studying for the priesthood at St. Charles' Seminary in Maryland.

# Chapter 6

## High School Memories

### *George*

*J*ohn was two years ahead of me in school. While I was a freshman and sopho-more, John was with me at St. Mary's. We did know the same people, but we had our own friends too. I was good friends with Tom Lavin, who was John Lavin's brother, but my best friend was Frank Hanlon. I maintained a friendship with him through grade school, high school, college, and adulthood, and I stayed in contact with him one way or another until the time of his death.

In high school my interests were very different from John's. He loved litera-ture and languages, and anything that had to do with public speaking; I suffered through those areas, but I enjoyed math and anything scientific. Those subjects seemed to come naturally to me. Even though I was two years behind John, I used to help him with his math. But John was a bright guy and an excellent student. Be-lieve me, I suffered for that. John would have As all the time. I wasn't a bad student. I'd have Bs and some As. I did what I had to do to get by. I didn't study really hard; but the stuff I loved, I studied. I had all my high marks in math and in the sciences. Honestly, I didn't really put in any time with the subjects I didn't like. There were times when I would come home from school and my father wouldn't sign my report card. I remember him saying, "You can do better than that. You go back to your teacher and tell her I'm not signing your report card till she makes you do the work you're supposed to be doing."

The teachers got used to Dad. And as far as academics were concerned, I learned to live in John's shadow.

John and I knew how Dad felt about school and we lived with it. It didn't in-terfere with our relationship. I could always count on John, especially when I was just beginning my high school years. One of my big recollections was that we always stood up for each other, no matter what. Some big hulk of a guy picked on me one day, pushed me around and called me a "camel rider." It wasn't an unfamiliar term

## JOHN

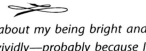

"I understand when George talks about my being bright and how much grief that brought him. I remember school vividly—probably because I enjoyed it so much. I remember loving school when I was in first grade, second grade, and third grade. Maybe I loved it so much because it gave me such satisfaction. I did well, and the success made me feel good about myself. I loved learning. I enjoyed learning all kinds of new things. I did feel, though, that Dad was always gloating over my grades when he was with his friends.

"When I went to fourth grade, I had a different experience. I thought I was doing everything the same way, but I was having a really hard time understanding the work, and the lack of understanding confused me. I went to classes, I came home, I did my homework; but when my report card came that time, Dad was furious. He carried on, screaming and yelling at me—and the words were new for me: 'How can you be so stupid, so dumb? Why aren't you trying? What's wrong with you?' I was devastated.

"This experience occurred during the one year I was at the Dodson School, a public school within walking distance of our house on Moyallen Street. I'm not sure why we were taken out of St. Mary's or why we returned there the following year, but there was a blessing in my being there when I was. One of the first things that happened was that everyone in my class was sent to the health clinic. I had an eye exam and it was determined that my vision was 20/200. I was given a note to take home. Shortly after that, I went with my dad to the office of Dr. Brown on the square in downtown Wilkes-Barre. I had an eye examination and I was fitted for glasses. When we returned about a week later and I was given the glasses to wear, we drove home. It was a spectacular trip for me. I could see every store front. I could read the marquee on the theatre in the square. I could even see signs announcing bargains and specials in the store windows.

"I returned to school and, in no time at all, I was back at the top of the class.

"I have an almost frozen image of a day some months later. At our new house that Dad had built on Moyallen Street, we had a door that had three windows in it. That day, I received my report card. When I got home, I left it on the kitchen table and went out to play. At some point, I looked up and saw Dad looking out the window. He was smiling at me, and I knew he had seen my report card.

"I felt a flush burning in my face. I was remembering how Dad treated me when he thought I was a dummy. 'I hate you,' I thought. 'I really hate you! You wouldn't be smiling at me if I weren't smart. You wouldn't be smiling if I were your dummy son. You

# High School Memories

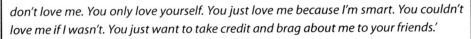
for Lebanese kids in the area. There were guys who I was friendly with who would call me that. I took the razzing from them; but this guy did more than that. He really pushed me around. John heard about it. After Mass, but before we started the school day, we had to walk down to the auditorium to go to a daily assembly. I remember walking down the steps. John was behind me. He saw the guy who had given me the hard time and John went after him. He grabbed him, got in front of him, and pushed him. The seats in the auditorium were bolted to the floor. John pushed the guy with such force that four rows of seats went down. John was beating the crap out of the guy and yelling, "You pick on my brother, I'll kill you the next time!" He really had a fierce temper in those days, and he never backed down from a fight. The news was out. We didn't have any trouble after that. During those years, John was more than my brother; he was my *big* brother, and he watched out for me. His temper served me well. But I know it was a source of confusion and pain for him.

When I was beginning my junior year in high school, John had already gone off to the seminary in Baltimore. I remember missing him during those years, though I didn't have a lot of time to be lonesome. The year that John left, Dad got sick. Probably from years of cigar smoking, he developed pyorrhea—a really painful inflammation in his gums that went through his entire system. He couldn't work and was laid up for at least eight months. At that time, I was beginning my junior year in high school. I knew I'd have to do something to help out. I was about to turn sixteen, but I already had my license. Long before he was sick, Dad was worried about how much I drove the truck, and he lied about my age. He said I was sixteen when I was only fifteen so I could get my license. I had spent so much time working with Dad that I certainly knew the routine. I explained the situation at the school, and I made a deal with my teachers: I could leave school to make my dad's deliveries as long as I kept up my school work.

# Brothers & Fathers

## JOHN

"One day when I was only about ten, I wandered down Columbus Avenue. It was not my neighborhood. I did not recognize any playmates. There were some children who were Black, and some ladies who spoke in Italian. On a corner of the street was a woman by the name of Simon. She baked bread and spoke Arabic.

"I was amusing myself with a rubber ball, enjoying my visit to a new neighborhood. I was seeing the sights, listening to the sounds, and bouncing my ball. I decided to see how high I could bounce it and catch it on the way down. Bad luck! The ball went over a neighbor's fence. Without hesitating, I opened the gate and went in search of the ball. Just as I spotted it, a huge, brown and black dog leapt on me and bit me on the shoulder.

"Without another thought, as I saw the torn shirt and the blood, I took off after the dog. I don't think I'll ever forget the terror in the dog's eyes! He had bitten the wrong kid. I feverishly grabbed a stick and tore off after him. I can still see his tail between his legs and myself in hot pursuit. I looked for him for an hour, but I didn't catch him.

"I don't remember if I got a tetanus shot or not. But it was the very first time I recall seeing this fierce side of myself. The blind fury was to show itself again and again. But it was memorable to me because the patterns of uninterrupted calm and tranquility were to be more and more subject to sporadic outbursts of fire. These outbursts would arise spontaneously, without warning. This first incident confused not only the dog, but then (and even later on), continued to confuse me too."

I was used to getting up early, so there was no problem being up and ready each morning. Before I'd leave, Dad would tell me what to buy and from which vendor. He also told me the prices I should pay. I'd be at the market about 3 a.m. I'd do the buying, finish loading up the truck, and by about 7:30, I was at school. I'd spend about an hour or so there and then I'd take off to make the deliveries. I kept up my studies reasonably well—at least enough to hold up my part of the deal.

There was part of the situation that Dad didn't find out for quite a while. I had sized up the situation pretty well, and I decided I would do it my way. At the market, I'd go to each vendor, knowing how well Dad knew them all; here I was, his young son, doing my best to keep my dad's business going while he was sick. I'd go to the guys Dad told me to, but I'd say, "You know, you're not doing me right. You can give me a better price than that." Dad didn't do that with certain guys, but I'd chisel the price down by maybe a quarter. After I left school, but before I went on the route, I'd go home. I wouldn't tell Dad what I paid, but I'd tell him what I had and he'd tell me what to charge. So then I'd go off to the customers and sell for a quarter more than what he said. I'd make an extra 50 cents a bushel on whatever I sold. When my dad found out, he was furious with me: "You're going to ruin my business!"

"No, I'm not. They love me."

Eight months later, Dad returned to his business. Lucky for both of us, he found that the business wasn't lost.

I was really proud of all the extra money I made, even though it was Dad's money; I was just working for him. I didn't get paid for that. Neither of us ever did. All the money I made at Lustig's or doing other things (like saving and selling burlap and baskets) I had to put right in the bank. Every penny of it. Dad wouldn't let me spend any of it—though he would give me spending money and money for gas. I continued to work with Dad all through high school. When I was older and able to drive, I'd come home late—sometimes as late as midnight. That didn't matter. Two o'clock, I had to be on my feet. Dad let me know it was my decision.

"It's up to you, buddy. You want to stay out till midnight, we still start at two." Working with my dad helped me to develop a lot of discipline. He was a strong man who was very energetic and worked hard. The work was back breaking, and I think John and I can trace our own back problems to those early days of lifting hundred-pound bags. Short of some back problems, though, Dad was a very healthy man. Even up until days before he died, when I shook his hand, I could feel the strength in his grip. It never lessened; it was unbelievable. I know we benefited by his insistence that we work alongside him. Even today, both John and I are very work oriented and still get by on very little sleep.

At some point in time when I was in high school, I began to think about becoming a doctor. Frank Hanlon was still my best friend, and I took advantage of the many opportunities I had to be around the hospital with him. Frank came from a family of doctors. His grandfather had been a doctor and his dad was the leading surgeon in town. He had six uncles: Five of them were doctors and one was a hospital administrator. Frank's dad even invited the two of us into surgery to watch some procedures as we got older.

Before any of those hospital experiences, and because I was thinking seriously about medicine as a possible career, I decided that I would like to do some investigating on my own in the area of anatomy. We had a cat. It wasn't a kitten and it wasn't a full grown cat; it was somewhere in between. The cat was always around—

probably security against the threat of mice. I guess you could say it was a member of the family. I thought it would be interesting to operate on the cat and see how it worked.

I got some ether—I think from the lab at the high school. Frank Hanlon was there with me for the operation. We had a gas stove down in the basement of our home and I took and sterilized all the knives I thought I would need. I put the cat to sleep with the ether and then I slit it open about three or four inches. Frank and I could actually see the cat's heart beating! We were fascinated. We thought the operation was really great. After we saw what we wanted, I sewed the cat back up. I sterilized the needle and used some plain thread that was there in the house. When the cat woke up, we let it go. It was our family cat long after that.

My sister Marlene was home at the time. She knew what we did and eventually, I guess you could say, she let the cat out of the bag. John knew the story too, but nobody else knew. Probably if it did get out, I might've been put in jail. Maybe kids who are interested in that kind of thing today have more opportunity to learn about it in school. But honestly, we were innocent. It was just something we wanted to know more about. And really—the cat was fine.

---

### MARLENE

*"When George was thinking about being a doctor, he got some ether and put our cat to sleep. He cut it open to operate on it, and he sewed it back up—and it lived! I was upstairs in the kitchen and he was down in the basement doing that. When George came up, he was eating a banana and I remember thinking, 'How can he do that? How can he cut open a cat and then eat a banana?' To me, he was fearless. Nothing bothered him. I knew he could do a lot of things. He could take a clock apart and put it back together. He could drive Dad's truck. He could fix anything. But the cat—that was very impressive!"*

---

I do remember a very surprising event that took place during my senior year. Believe it or not, I was picked as one of the six finalists in the senior oratorical contest. Like everyone else, I had written my own speech. I seem to remember it was on some phase of totalitarianism. I did practice for the contest, but the nun in charge seemed less than enthusiastic when she said to me, "I hope you get through it." Nothing like having an older brother to live up to!

The final faceoff was held in the evening. It was a big deal and the participants all had to wear caps and gowns. Well, I had forgotten to get mine. So Dad and I

# High School Memories

had to go to College Misericordia to get one. That meant we had to drive to Dallas (a town about ten miles outside of Wilkes-Barre) to get to the college. Dad complained all the way out and back into town: "We're doing all this stuff for what? You'll never be anything. Why do we need to go all the way out there?" He went on and on.

After all that, we arrived at the last minute, and I had to run into the school. Just as the contest was about to begin, I snuck onto the stage. We all gave our speeches. When we were finished, not only was I chosen as the winner, but I received a unanimous vote! Dad absolutely couldn't believe it. I guess he expected John to win things like that, but not me. I don't remember John getting anything when he won, but Dad handed me fifty dollars. (That was a lot of money at the time.) And I remember him saying, "Go out and have a good time." He was really happy that night.

*George wins oratory contest*

I remember another event that involved me and the stage—but this one didn't make Dad one bit happy. In those days, we were all expected to participate in public performances in one way or another. At the minstrel shows that we had, I wasn't as performance oriented as John, and so instead of singing or dancing, I chose to introduce some of the performers. There was a guy in my class named George Webby. He later became a well-known priest in the Maronite rite, but that night, he was just one of the guys. He had, how can I put it, a rather prominent nose. And when I introduced him, I couldn't resist. In the most serious voice, I announced loudly, "Welcome our next performer, George Webby, the man who knows all and is all nose." I just thought it was funny. Imagine that: I was telling a joke at the minstrel show. Well, George wasn't laughing; he wanted to kill me. His family was sitting in the front row. They didn't think it was funny, either; they wanted to kill me. Oh, my God, and worst of all, Dad was in the audience. He was so upset with me; it was a miracle that I survived that night.

During those high school years, I could put up with a lot of things, but I can honestly say I was a bit sensitive about ethnic slurs. In spite of the fact that I couldn't stand the way I saw my Dad lose his temper, I do remember one time in high school when I really lost my own. I was at a basketball game and I had a hat on. If you remember the Katzenjammer Kids in the comic strip, you might remember the kid with the hat. I had a hat like that. It was turned up in the front and I had put a shamrock on it. Tommy Nolan, one of the guys from school, started on me about the shamrock. He was making wise remarks about "a camel rider" wearing a shamrock. For a while, I passed it off; but he kept it up and I could feel the anger building up in me. I kept passing it off until I couldn't stand it for another minute—and then I took him outside. I really laid into him. I hit him and hit him until his face was twice its size. It took two guys to drag me off him. I put him in the hospital that day. Then and there, I decided, I didn't want to ever do that again. I didn't ever want to lose my temper. I knew I could kill someone. I was very strong—in fact, my nickname was Herky (short for Hercules). I didn't ever lose my temper again until years later when I was in California; but even then, I never got physical with anyone.

Other than that, probably the worst thing we did during those years was drink—sometimes a little too much, but never enough to get in trouble. We traveled by streetcar. At the time, we could get back and forth between Wilkes-Barre and many of the nearby towns. I remember getting on the streetcar and going to the nearby town of Sugar Notch quite a bit. The guys were so damn excited: We could get a shot and a beer there for a quarter. The drinks were so cheap; I remember having four or five of them. By the time I was sixteen I could buy drinks for the others because I looked older than I was. I think it was kind of a macho thing young guys did. But I swear: I never, ever got drunk or dizzy or acted crazy … or anything like that. Never. And I did some heavier drinking than I did in Sugar Notch. Every time I drank, I would never drink more than I knew I should. That was because, as I got older I was always the driver, and I took that seriously. I had Dad's car and I didn't want to have an accident. There were other guys in the car, and I made sure that I never drank more than I could handle. I can't say that was always true of everyone.

There were two guys in Wilkes-Barre whose last name was Guggenheim. We used to call them Little Guggi and Big Guggi. They were about two years apart in age and Little Guggi always trailed around after a crowd of us. He was only a year behind us in school, but he was a real little guy—he couldn't have been more than four feet tall. He was impossible to shake. One night, he insisted he was coming with us, and he was going to drink with us too. Well, he got blind drunk and passed out. We grabbed him by the heels and the head and he stayed stiff. A couple of us took him and put him across the streetcar tracks and waited for the car. When we saw it coming, we took him off the tracks, put him in the streetcar and took him home. A couple of the guys occupied Little Guggi's mother in front of the house while we took him into the house through the back door. Trying to sober him up, we put him in the bathtub and filled it with cold water so he would wake up. What did we know? Then we left.

Little Guggi tried to stay up with the big boys. Not a happy ending.

Tony Elias was another good friend of mine in high school. He went to GAR (one of the public schools), but he hung around with us. One time, Tony told John that I had been so drunk that I couldn't see, but I drove anyway. That was not true, and I'd like to set that story straight.

I had driven us all out to Harvey's Lake for a swim. (We did that a lot.) Sometime during the evening, I lost my glasses. When it was time to go home, one after the other the guys were all yelling, "I'll drive. I'll drive."

"Hell, no, you won't! I'm responsible for my dad's car." Enough said.

So we all piled into the car and I said, "Tell me if there's a turn coming up." I scared the crap out of them—but I could see well enough. I drove real slow, but Tony was scared shitless. The road down the Back Mountain is full of curves and I'd keep saying, "Tony, tell me when I have to make a turn." He was sure we were going to get into an accident.

Actually, that time we hadn't been drinking. There were four of us: me, Johnny Joseph and his brother, and Tony. (We traveled together sometimes.) We used to pick on Tony terribly during those days. He was really a good-natured guy, but we just couldn't resist sometimes. One time we rented a boat and I said to Tony, "You get in the boat. We're going to swim across the lake. You row next to us so that if anybody gets tired, or if anything else happens, we can climb into the boat." He didn't mind because he couldn't swim.

We swam out to the middle of the lake, and Tony was right there alongside us. The three of us swam close to the boat and started to rock it. "We're going to turn the boat over, Tony, and you can learn to swim!"

I never saw a guy row any faster than Tony did that day. He was always a scaredy cat—and we loved scaring the hell out of him.

One day we were all walking down Park Avenue near St. Anthony's Church. Well, I got this idea in my head and I said to Tony, "You look so sick. What's wrong with you?"

The other guys chimed in: "You're awfully white. You really look sick.

What's wrong with you?"

# Brothers & Fathers

We kept it up for a good while. After about fifteen minutes, he actually got physically sick. He said he was really sick, and he was going home. We were pretty tough on him. He was the butt of a lot of our jokes. But he was really good-natured.

Another night I remember, Johnny Joseph, Tony, and I went out. Johnny used to drive a guy around—a big shot who was involved in the coal industry. Every now and then, the guy would let Johnny take his car out. One night, we were out in that guy's car. I don't think it was that late, but for us it was late; it was about ten o'clock. We were driving around way the hell up in Plymouth someplace, and the car started acting funny. We stopped and got out of the car to see what was wrong. It was a flat.

Tony was scared to death: "I gotta get home! My father's going to kill me!"

We didn't have any way to change the tire. There was a lug wrench in the trunk, but no jack. So I said to Tony, "We have to stay here. We don't have a jack."

Without saying a word, Johnny Joseph took the lug wrench and went over to a parked car next to the curb and took a tire off. That was Johnny Joseph. He was like that. I don't think he even left the flat tire that we took off our car. He just put the other car up on a block. Imagine that guy coming out the next morning and finding his tire gone!

Johnny came back carrying the tire and said to Tony, "If you want to get home, you're going to have to lift up the car so we can get this tire on."

Tony was so scared about getting home late, he held up the corner of the car until we put the new tire on. He didn't give us a chance to help him. What a night!

After high school, Tony and I went our separate ways and didn't really resume our friendship until years later, when he began to date my sister Marlene. Eventually, Tony married Marlene and became part of our family.

A resurfaced letter seems to indicate that things didn't change much between us as the years went on. Tony had a loving heart, a good sense of humor, and always a need to prove himself.

During all those years, my friends and I also dated, and we looked for wholesome girls. We used to go to a dance way down on Carey Avenue. We could also get to dances in Plymouth by riding the streetcar. It makes me laugh to think of ourselves being the 'out-of-town' guys at those dances—the towns were about two miles away from each other! There were quite a few girls from Plymouth, I remember, who liked John. I remember the dance we all went to one night at St. Nick's in Wilkes-Barre and how John got into that terrible fight over a girl there. I was there

# High School Memories

a few nights later when John beat that guy to a pulp. That happened only a short time before he finished St. Mary's and went off to the seminary. He was always ready to use his fists in those days—and he was strong enough physically to win more often than not.

During my last two years of high school, and with John away, typically I'd do a lot of studying with Frank. If his family hadn't said the family rosary before I got to his house, we'd be on our knees around his dad's bed saying it. Because he was a physician, Frank's dad always got into bed early. Saying the family rosary was as common at Hanlon's as it was at my own home. The kinds of relationships I had, and the fact that my family knew the families of my friends, kept us out of a lot of real trouble.

# Brothers & Fathers

Working also kept us busy—leaving us little time to get into trouble. When John was still in high school, he worked some on the truck with Dad and me; but, as I've said, I don't think he ever got the same kick out of that work as I did. He worked less on the truck and more at Lustig's Market. When he went off to the seminary, I took over John's job there—making me pretty busy. Mr. Lustig was a great guy. Even after my dad's illness and return to working on the truck, if he knew my dad needed me, he'd say, "Go help your dad today." The next day, my job was still there. After I finished high school, and just before I began college at King's, Mr. Lustig presented me with a bank book. He said, "This is for you to have for college. As long as you've been working here, I've been taking a dollar a week out of your pay and adding two dollars to it; here's that money." There was eight hundred dollars in the bank. He was a wonderful person to work for.

Because of Dad's insistence that all of the money we earned went right into the bank, by the time I finished high school, I had almost all my money for college. Over the years, working for Mr. Lustig and doing little entrepreneurial jobs, I had earned almost four thousand dollars. That was a lot of money, back then.

I thought about being a doctor, but I also did a lot of thinking about joining the priesthood. By the time I graduated in 1947, I had made up my mind that I would go to the seminary. I had developed a strong prayer life, and I had a strong relationship with the Church. Each weekday, both John and I went to daily Mass at St. Mary's; we served as altar boys at our parish church; we said the family rosary daily; and, generally, we had a good set of values. We always lived in a home where God and religion were a vital part of each day. Mom prayed constantly, and we could find Gidue praying at his altar any time of the day or night. Because prayer was so much a part of my life, I decided to investigate the possibility of becoming a priest.

So in the early part of that first summer, I went off to St. Charles Seminary in Baltimore—the same seminary that John had attended. Father Koury drove me there and I stayed for about two weeks. After a short time, I began to realize that I was missing my brother John and I was really just chasing his vocation. We were so close; I really thought I could continue to have that closeness if I went into the seminary. By the time I got to St. Charles, John was already gone to St. Mary's on Paca Street in Baltimore. I knew I wasn't going to be with him, and somehow I didn't feel as though I wanted to stay. It wasn't long before I went back home.

My life took many turns during the years that followed.

# CHAPTER 7

## AN EXCURSION FROM THE LINEAR PATH OF OUR LIVES

### *Father John*

The day-to-day lives that George and I shared as children and young boys, and the long talks we had as we tried to understand our experiences, were a special blessing to both of us as we were growing up together. As we finished high school and began on separate paths, those early experiences—and our interpretations of them—traveled with us too. Those perceptions permeated all we did, alone or together. They help us now to understand better the kinds of responses we made as we individuated and traveled new paths without the other at our elbow. It's good now to continue to reflect, not only on the events of our early lives, but also on how we responded to the emotional ramifications of those events. It's difficult, but useful, to share what we remember—so often the same, but also occasionally different. It's good to know that we still have opportunities to grow in love and understanding. It's expanding to explore the intricacies of the human heart that hindsight so quietly reveals. Before we continue with the more easily documented events of our lives, we would like to digress for a time in order to try to capture and reveal some of the deepest, though more intangible, realities that formed us and carried us into early adulthood.

# CHAPTER 8

## PATCHES OF FAMILY HISTORY

### *George*

*W*hen we began, we shared our reflections about our early years in Wilkes-Barre. As young boys in my grandfather's home, we lived in what seemed to be a simple environment; but as we grew older, we came to understand it as a rather complicated one. In that home, very early on, we learned about our family's dynamics. In that very extended family, John and I shared a very close relationship which might be compared to the kind that often exists between twins. We had, if not a language of our own, an interpretation of our family that was our own. There was much that we embraced, but also much that we rejected. We did not have any kind of special powers. We just shared experiences, talking things over and forming opinions that did not come under anyone's scrutiny except our own. Maybe living in that private sector of our shared experiences allowed us to form what we thought were, and still are, genuine opinions. That may also be why, even today, we can talk about that family experience and name what we thought was good, or valuable, or admirable, or worthy of emulation. We can also name those things that were not good, nor valuable, nor admirable, nor worthy of emulation. To look at the past is not an opportunity to find blame, but rather an opportunity, perhaps for understanding's sake, to name those forces that helped form us and make us the men we are today.

John and I are brothers. John and I are also fathers. My fatherhood evolved in the same context as that of most people. When I was a young man, I met and married a wonderful woman, and we had a family together. We had a son and three daughters, and together we grew as parents. My brother John became a Roman Catholic priest and, as Father John, grew into that title as he ministered to the poor, the lost, and the broken.

We have emphasized many happy and positive elements in our history, but we know there were also things that loyalties sometimes kept us from sharing. I know that both of us loved, most especially (and I without qualifications) our grandfather, Gidue, with whom we lived in our most formative years. To him I give the most credit for the path my life has taken. But Gidue, as John later learned from our father, had a persona other than what we absorbed as young boys—other than what we have presented so far. What Dad told John (because he was the oldest) I eventually came to know. Both of us can now attest to the truth of that disclosure because, in all honesty, we know it was true. We accept it as part of the man we love and the man to whom we both owe so much.

# CHAPTER 9

## DOMESTIC STORMS

### *Father John*

Our story, George's and mine, has named quite clearly and concentrated on giving credit for our positive development and attitudes to someone who has grown to be an icon in our family—my grandfather, whom we called Gidue. Even as I say his name, I only want to sit on his lap and listen to him.

Gidue came to the United States from Lebanon after his first wife died. Here, he married his second wife, Cecelia Oblen, who came to be my grandmother. Like many other immigrants who didn't know the language and had limited means, he made his living as a peddler (known in our area as 'hucksters') who went around the neighborhood driving his horse and wagon. He sold produce in the summer and collected rags and junk in the winter. Aside from our own experiences with my grandfather, which George and I both remember with great affection, we were also told stories about Gidue that reinforced those earliest perceptions.

As I grew older, it was my father who told me other stories about his father, Gidue, who was generally thought of as quite inept in terms of being a provider. No matter how hard Gidue worked, he simply did not make enough money. As the years went by, and by the time six of his ten children were born, he had become so frustrated that, as my father told me, he said to my grandmother, "I'm packing up and going back to the old country." When my father, nine years old at that time, heard that, he said to my grandmother, "Don't worry. I'll take care of you. Let him go. We'll be all right."

What followed were stormy years for my grandfather—and probably for his entire family. He weathered those years in his own way; and although he didn't return to Lebanon, the family dynamic changed dramatically. It's hard to know exactly what went on during that time. Gidue might have had what today could be called a nervous breakdown, or perhaps clinical depression. We'll never know that answer. He eventually settled down and, years later (when George and I were kids), he told us the story of his going to the church, throwing himself down before the statue of St. Anthony, and making an act of total submission of himself and his entire life to God. From that time on, his life took a new direction. He took hold with a steady hand; he knew what he was going to do and, from then on, he devoted his life to what he thought God wanted of him. For George and me, it was this man of God who became the stabilizing force, and the greatest influence, in our young lives.

Nonetheless, because of that turbulence in the family, the family dynamic had changed. My dad, the oldest son, had become something of a confidante to his mother and replaced my grandfather as the seat of authority in the family. He was the one to whom all matters that demanded strong decisions were referred. When those decisions were to be made, no one looked to my grandfather anymore. If more than my father was needed to formulate a decision, that council would include not only Dad, but also my grandmother, her sister, Catherine Oblen, and maybe sometimes grandma's brother Arthur Oblen. My grandfather, though he was the patriarch, was much more of a figurehead who lacked real authority, and without the power to make decisions for the family. That power rested primarily with my father.

This set of circumstances created a lot of confusion in the family, an extended family composed of my grandparents, my father and mother, my father's siblings, and then his own children. By the time George and I came along, my father very much wanted to break that dynamic, but that break didn't occur. Everyone came to answer to my father about their report cards, their dates, the places they were going to work, and eventually even who they would be allowed to marry. All of these matters came under the jurisdiction of my father. George and I saw this operation very clearly under my grandfather's roof, and it extended to the simplest behaviors. For example, if anyone of my aunts and uncles smoked, and they weren't supposed to be smoking, they would feel all right if their father (my grandfather, Gidue) knew about it; but they didn't want my father to know about it. What had been set in motion was not a reverential fear, but an actual fear of my dad. Because of the language barrier, and because of the financial ineptness that my grandfather had exhibited, all authority went to my dad. Even when we moved out of my grandfather's home, the old dynamic continued. My grandmother consulted my dad rather than her husband who, by this time, had totally abandoned that role. All of these circumstances dramatically affected our lives.

*Dad, Grandma Esseff, Mom and John*

# CHAPTER 10

## DAD

## *George*

I remember, as I was growing up, making conscious decisions about my dad. I saw him as a radical authoritarian, and I made up my mind that I was not going to imitate him. He had a terrible temper. He sometimes made fun of people. He would verbally abuse people. He could even be cruel. It's difficult to say these things, because we love him—and, to be fair, he became quite mellow as he grew older. Yet the truth is that, when we were young, we had a stern, unapproachable father. He was a young father and he was a wild-ass guy. He was into gambling and into his friendships. He played poker with his friends; every New Year's Eve they'd play the whole night through. Dad was just too gruff to give us much nurturing. It wasn't until John was ordained that he confronted Dad on a very painful point. He told Dad, "You never once said, 'I love you' when we were growing up." And that was true. Dad did a lot of things that I'm sure he interpreted as love, but he never came across as a soft person to us. Because of the way I perceived Dad, I remember deciding, "I'm not going to do that. I'm not going to live my life that way. I will not be a force to be reckoned with like Dad is."

*Dad and John*

By the time I was planning to marry, I had very clear ideas of what I hoped to have in a marriage. I don't think I had analyzed it to the point I have at present, but at least I had looked at what I saw and objectively chose what I deemed to be worthwhile, rejecting what I did not consider worthwhile. The effect of my perceptions of Dad was that I knew, as a husband and father, I wanted to be an authority figure, but I also wanted to be a loving figure. So this may be a good time to talk about Dad a little more.

There were many times I might have reacted to Dad, but there was only one time I did. When I was in high school, maybe I was 15 or 16, he was into one of his diatribes. His language at those times always upset me; but that day I heard what I knew to be blasphemy, and without hesitation I shouted, "Don't take God's name in vain." I was so damn mad at him I wasn't only shouting; I was also shaking my fist at him. That was the only time. But I did what I did, and he backed down and didn't say anything to me.

Because that kind of language had become pretty common, I guess things had really built up inside me. Although Dad took the name of God in vain quite a bit, that day I had the courage to stand up and object. I didn't know if it was the right thing; I just reacted. I knew that he shouldn't be doing that—no one should ever take the name of the Lord in vain.

## John

Dad really had an explosive temper. When it went off, I think it bordered on insanity. He had an insane temper and it had a different effect on me than it had on George. Even as I look back at my own life, I can remember some of my own violent episodes. I wouldn't have been able to take responsibility for my own temper and eventually change it if I hadn't reflected on the turbulence Dad's temper created in my own life. As a kid and well into adulthood, I was quick to use my fists. Dad was never like that. He was never physically abusive—especially not with my mother, or with us either. But Dad was always physical in other ways and prone to violent outbreaks. He and my mother would get into arguments, and my dad would throw things and break furniture. One day I particularly remember was a day when Mom

and Dad were arguing in the kitchen. My brother Joe was little then and there was a high chair in the kitchen. It was one of those chairs that had a tray on it for the baby's food and it was really quite substantial. Well, in the midst of the argument, Dad hit the tray and smashed it. I remember that thing shattering under his fist. He seemed insane when his temper took over.

*John, Mom, Dad and George*

# Dad

Yet oddly enough, we got used to his reactions. When an argument erupted and then escalated, I'd think, "Wait till the storm passes, John. You know the storm will pass." And it always did.

My mother, prayerful and devout, was never intimidated. During those encounters she never seemed frightened, and she would talk back to Dad. As I wondered at all of it over the years, the only thing that could possibly explain her reaction to the madness was her own upbringing. She was raised in a home where everyone quivered in the presence of her father, Samuel Sahd. As I said before, compared to Grandpa Sahd, Dad seemed mellow. Probably her own dynamic with her father prepared her to deal with Dad, and she came into the marriage every bit a match for Joe Esseff. The more Dad carried on, the more she would respond. The more she did, the crazier he got. I remember one time she had the sweeper out. (She was also hard of hearing by this time.) My brother Joe was born by then, so I was in my early teens. I don't know if she really heard the pitch of the violence in what he was doing. He wanted her to listen to him, and he picked up the sweeper; when he did, I snapped. I guess I thought he was going to throw it. I actually grabbed the sweeper from him and kept shouting, "Stop it! Stop it!" And just like George, I found myself facing him and just shouting until he quieted down. I don't think he ever expected me to react that way—perhaps even less than he expected a reaction from George. I do know that, ironically, thanks to him and hauling those one-hundred pound bags, I was big enough and strong enough to back up my command physically. Thank God, he stopped.

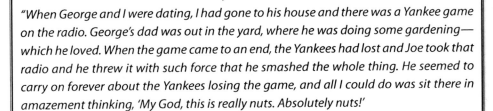

## ROSEMARY

"When George and I were dating, I had gone to his house and there was a Yankee game on the radio. George's dad was out in the yard, where he was doing some gardening—which he loved. When the game came to an end, the Yankees had lost and Joe took that radio and he threw it with such force that he smashed the whole thing. He seemed to carry on forever about the Yankees losing the game, and all I could do was sit there in amazement thinking, 'My God, this is really nuts. Absolutely nuts!'

"Another time when I was there he became angry over something so inconsequential; I can't even remember what it was. He took a kitchen chair and he threw it against the wall with such strength that the chair broke into pieces. That kind of behavior was foreign to me, and it was also really shocking because George was always soft spoken and I never saw any signs of temper in him. I thought I was in a crazy household and it was scary to me. I asked George, 'What is this all about?' George passed it off rather casually and said, 'Oh, Dad's in a sweat. It'll pass!'"

# Brothers & Fathers

Dad didn't do a lot of editing in his behavior when others were around, so it wasn't as though his temper was a family secret. This behavior persisted even as George and I grew into manhood.

Besides Dad's temper, the family had to deal with his non-negotiable opinions and the authority he could back them up with when it came to very important matters. Over the years, there were really a lot of jokes made about how everyone would have to bring whoever they were going to date or marry before the family tribunal: Uncle Art, my grandmother's sister, Aunt Catherine Khoury, Grandma and, of course, the chief, Dad. But when those events were going on, there wasn't much joking. When Dad's sister Catherine decided to marry Bill Nasser, both Bill and Catherine had to go before the board. Dad did not like Bill at all, and he used to make fun of him. Actually, I think Bill finally got himself thrown right out of the house with Catherine, and I think Catherine married Bill in spite of all that, because she wanted to. She was ready to marry him. Later, when Dad's youngest sister Ann was planning to marry Jack Kelly, the system was still in place. Although it was less effective, it was still a big deal. Jack was able to stand his ground and eventually did marry Ann. Jack worked for the NSA (National Security Administration) and maybe that explains, in part, why he was difficult to intimidate. (It's also possible that's why it seemed as though the treatment he got was less brutal than what some of the others endured.) I think by the time George had decided to marry Rosemary in 1952, Dad had mellowed some; but prior to that time, it was a baptism of fire to come into our family.

# CHAPTER 11

## REFLECTIONS

## *George*

There is much I received from my father and much that I learned from him. I know that I love him for all the good that came to us through him. I'm grateful that I have had the chance to look at him not only with the eyes of a child but also with the eyes of a man who has children of my own. Isolating and looking squarely at those areas of Dad's personality that were difficult for us to deal with has helped me to appreciate even more fully the presence of my grandfather in my life. Whatever journey he was on, whatever journey my dad was on, John and I always had a special blessing as children: a man who was gentle and caring, loving, generous, and prayerful.

The things I saw in my Dad's dad, Gidue, I needed and wanted. I took them without reservation. By the time I was about ten, I didn't agree with the way my father did things in the context of family life. My mother was a very emotional person, always ready to hug and kiss us and tell us she loved us. But not Dad. On a human level, it's important to remember that my mother was only sixteen when she married my father.

She was a complex woman. Though she had been brought up in the home of a very authoritative father, she nonetheless eloped with Dad. She had been promised, according to Lebanese tradition, to another man. When she married Dad, she left her father to explain his broken contract for the marriage of his daughter to another man. That situation was responsible for Grandfather Sahd's not coming to our home; instead we always went to his.

In our early home, it was Grandpa Esseff who did the nurturing, and Grandma Esseff was the disciplinarian—unless she turned things over to Dad. Before we reached our teens, John and I had formed our opinions. We discussed what was going on and made our own decisions about a great many things. All that we thought and did were filtered through our own perceptions and our many shared discussions over years and years.

# Brothers & Fathers

During our formative years, we lived with our mother and our father and our grandmother and grandfather. They impacted us almost like two sets of parents. In that mix, John thinks we tended to canonize my grandfather and demonize my grandmother. I wouldn't say 'demonize'; I just knew I didn't agree with the way some things were done.

In retrospect, John has clarified a lot about what we experienced.

## *Father John*

Because of the dynamic in place in our home, Grandma was the one who always had to bring up the negative stuff. There was an imbalance. Gidue, my grandfather, was able to maintain his relationship with God and the Church, but he had, in fact, given up his responsibilities to his own children. He had transferred those responsibilities (and the accompanying authority) to his wife and their eldest son, our dad. This transfer of authority overburdened my father, who had assumed it at a very young age. And he began to be the one who wore the black hat while my grandfather wore the white. I would at least like to look back and understand now how that transference could, in part, explain some of my father's gruffness.

By the time he was nineteen years old, he had his first son. At twenty, he had two sons. By the time he was twenty-five, he had three children, was holding down a job, and was functioning as the surrogate father for the entire extended family. I often heard him saying, "I don't want to be entangled in all that. I don't want to make all these decisions." But he would be sucked back into it, time and time again. So in my own demythologizing of those early years, I have had to make some distinctions. I think the myth was that my grandfather was a saint and my father and my grandmother were the demons. Now, on a human level, I can see how that dynamic developed. I don't think anyone's to blame, but I could see how practical decisions were made—many of them wrong, many of them without consultation, many of them just, "You do that because that's what we said." That dynamic really had a lot of negative consequences.

When we left the house on Prospect Street, you would think that my grandmother would have been happy. I know the girls (my aunts) were elated because they were going to have another bedroom.

*Grandma Esseff*

68

# Reflections

But it was a different story with Grandma. I remember her crying so hard when we were leaving. She was terribly upset when we left the house, although we were only moving blocks away. It was such a disorder. It was as though her surrogate husband, my dad, on whom she had depended for so many years, was leaving. The authority relationship there was really disordered and it caused a lot of suffering on a human level. My father was forced into that. And he never really got out of it.

Through all of those years, although Grandma seemed submissive, she always got what she wanted. She really ran the house. She made all the financial decisions. All my grandfather did was go to work and make the money, and he'd come home and put the money in those two jars: one for the poor and one for the rest of the family. Sometimes Grandma would complain that Tuesday had been the best day of the week, and so why did that day's money have to go to the poor? Maybe those complaints made us consider her to be less holy. But she had taken on the responsibilities of running things, and she was a very good woman. She knew what the family needed and she was concerned that everyone had what they needed. Dad did a lot of things to help Grandma with those concerns; Gidue did not take on those duties. In and through it all, as we look through our rearview mirror, we still hold that Gidue had the greatest influence on both of us.

Looking back has given us an opportunity to think about what fatherhood is on an even deeper level. It has also made us grateful for the time we have had to reflect on how each of us has affected others as we responded to the challenges and responsibilities of our own fatherhood.

## George

*Dad with Mary Ellen, Kathy and Denise*

Ironically, as Dad grew older, and especially when he was in his waning days, he spent most of his time with my children and my grandchildren. He loved doing that. He spent more time with them, in a sense, than he had spent with us. I guess it's fair to say that Dad worked with us, but he played with my children and my grandchildren.

Funny, but I do have one very early remembrance of Dad being playful. When I was probably about two years old, Dad and his friend Johnny Thomas used to throw me back and forth between them. It wasn't like they were three feet away from each other: They were throwing me across the room! (Or maybe, because I was so little, that's what I thought.) I was having a good time; I remember laughing. My mother and my grandmother were screaming. I'm sure they thought Dad was crazy. But Dad and his friends did things like that.

Looking back at all of it, it's interesting how the years progressed: Dad was 'Dad' with us, but he was 'Grandpa' with my kids and 'Great Grandpa' with their kids. He was their Gidue and their Great Gidue. The memories they have are precious to them, and as they have shared some of those memories with John and me, we are blessed and grateful for those memories, too.

*Four generations of Esseffs*

## MICHELLE SPENCER

*Daughter of Mary Ellen (Esseff) Spencer and David Spencer*

*Granddaughter of George Esseff*

*A Letter to Joe Esseff, George's Dad*

*May 1996*

*In the last few months of my young life, I have thought many times about you and what you've meant to me. I feel that, before I go to begin my 'new life,' I have to tell you, at least once, how special a place in my heart you have always held.*

*When I was younger, the first memories I had with you were the times at your old mobile home with Sithue. You would give me the Reader's Digest to take home to learn new spelling words from. I would eat all the Lebanese food Sithue could put in front of me. I'll never forget how good it was! No one could ever make Lebanese food like she could.*

*I learned to spell from those few issues, and you used to tell me that one day I was going to be the champion of the spelling bee. You would test me on the words that I told you I had learned, and if I didn't spell the word correctly, you would look me straight in* the eye and say, "Michelle, did you actually look at these, or are you guessing?" I couldn't lie to you—at least not very well, so you would send me to look at them again.

Then there were the times that I would see you at Halloween. We'd say, "Trick or treat," and you would answer by saying that we had to do a trick in order to get the desired candy. I was so shocked the first time I actually had to do something in order to get my Halloween candy, but I never minded much. I liked to show off for you because whatever I did was wonderful to you.

And how could I forget the marvelous game you played with all of your grandchildren? I can't spell it correctly in Arabic, but I always knew what it meant. "Is there anyone else like you in the world?" You would say in words familiar to me from the day that I began to comprehend things going on around me. And what is the correct answer?— "No, no, no." Always and forever!

When I began to get a little older, the famous questions you asked, always at the dinner table, at a family function, right in front of my father, were: "Aren't you going to the convent?

Dad as Gidue

"When are you going to the convent?"

"Don't you have a boyfriend?"

"You should have two boyfriends, so that you'll never be lonely on a Saturday night."

I'll never forget the look on my dad's panic-stricken face when you shot that one out!

"You know I was married at fifteen. Aren't you just about there too?"

"How is it that you can't have a boyfriend? "

"I know you have one somewhere. No? Well, that's OK, I guess."

I enjoyed every expression that popped onto my dad's face, and yours too, when I saw his reaction!

I guess what I really mean to say is that, no matter where I go and no matter where you are, I know I have had the privilege to share the time that I have with you. Of course, this is not to say that your time's up. Only God knows that date, and I wanted to make sure I told you all this before it was too late to get one last piece of advice, one last hug, or to hear one last phrase in Arabic that is all too familiar. From you I have gained an inspiration to faith in God, a sense of sarcasm and humor that only you could teach, and *a strong knowledge of integrity and courage that has given you the heart to get through the toughest of situations. These are the things that I treasure so very much in you, the things that make me proud to know that I got to know you and learn from you.*

*I never got to tell Sithue all that I wanted to because I was still young and not fully aware of the circumstances. I just had to make sure that you knew. I know that, when you go, I will not be saddened, but overjoyed to know that you will then be always with me in a form more comforting than any mortal existence could allow.*

*Lovingly always ... Your eldest granddaughter, Michelle*

Feelings have a way of spanning time in a much different way than do chronological facts. It's impossible to have one and not the other.

With a great many feelings, some quite unresolved, John and I began leaving our shared adolescence behind and forging separate paths.

# CHAPTER 12

## ON MY OWN
## *Father John*

### ST. CHARLES SEMINARY

**W**hile George was finishing high school, I began my studies for priesthood. Although everyone knew I was going to be a priest, the question of where I would actually go to begin my seminary training had to be decided. In 1945 there was no shortage of priests and the system in place mandated that each candidate for the priesthood had to have a sponsoring bishop. Also, he and his family were expected to take on the financial responsibility for the first two years of seminary training. Even though I was a member of the Maronite rite, I applied to the Diocese of Scranton, and the presiding bishop in the Latin rite at the time—Bishop Hafey—selected me as one of ten young men who would study for the priesthood. He sent me to St. Charles Seminary in Catonsville, Maryland—which, no doubt, offered the best academic preparation in the country at the time. I left for the seminary in June, shortly after I graduated from St. Mary's High School in Wilkes-Barre. While I spent the next two years at St. Charles, George finished high school at St. Mary's. At St. Charles, I received one of the most intense Latin and Greek programs presented by the Church at that time. We began with a hundred seminarians in the first year; by the end of that year, fifty had left. It was pretty clear that those in charge had a program designed to do just that sort of eliminating.

St. Mary's High School had prepared me well for my future studies, and when I went to St. Charles, I was looking forward to my studies there. I can honestly say I didn't like the place at all. I did love the scholarship, but I hated the discipline—part of which was

*John as a seminarian*

the grand silence that began each night at 7:30. The place was filled with mostly 17- and 18-year-old boys. We walked down the halls in silence going to our dormitories where fifty beds were jammed together. After a night's sleep, we were awakened at five in the morning and we were off and running all over again. If we weren't in class, we would be in study hall, where silence was also the rule. There were two priests who were in charge of seeing to it that we learned the necessity of obedience to the rules, both in the dorm and in the study hall. We called those two the North Pole and the South Pole. They were really awful! Once in study hall, there was to be complete silence. There was no talking, and we'd have to ask permission to go to the lavatory. Sometimes a guy would walk up to North Pole and say, "Father, can I go to the lavatory?" North Pole figured some guys were trying to sneak out for a smoke, so he'd give the automatic, "No!" I really wasn't into all that Mickey Mouse stuff. I was there to study to be a priest and I thought those guys were playing games. When I heard the big "No," I'd say, "Father, I really have to go."

"Put a half nelson on it, kid, and go back and sit down."

Honest to God! Piss in your pants, you know? North Pole didn't care.

"You're not getting out of here."

And so began one of the most anti-authoritarian periods of my life. I remember hating that silence so much that I got around to the guys one night when we had celery and carrots at dinner. You know—those little sticks that aren't cooked? I told the guys to save them and take them back to the dorm. When North Pole and the South Pole ordered lights out, we were supposed to maintain silence; but as soon as they turned out the lights, we all began to chew on the celery and carrots. It sounded like a herd of elephants going through the place! Either South Pole or North Pole turned the lights back on. "SILENCE!" Eventually, they'd turn the lights out and the guys would start chewing again. Dear God, they were crazy days. They never explained silence to us, so I never really got the point of it for those two years in Baltimore. They were almost inhuman with us. We were just young guys; but we learned our Latin and we learned our Greek. I really did love the study. Till today, when I meet those guys who went through that training with me, they agree that it was absolutely the most disciplined, intense time in our formation.

We had some of the old French teachers. Of course, we made fun of them all. There was a priest who was an ascetic. He was so ascetic, in fact, that it was pretty much the consensus of opinion among us seminarians that if he let his guard down for ten minutes, he would be out hugging a tree. There was also a man of German ancestry, so we called him "Torpedo Head." (No thought of political correctness going on with us during those days!) Then there were the effeminate professors, and we gave them women's names. There was Mamie, who taught us Latin and Greek. And there was Kitty, who taught us English. Well, we'd make such fun of them—walk like them, imitate them. We had all kinds of jokes about them. We were just boys—17 and 18—and as I recall, we laughed a lot … mostly at the teachers' expense. I graduated *summa cum laude*, and when I was finished there, and we were driving out, I remember saying to my dad, "I'll never be back to this place!" And I never did go back. Never! I hated it.

## GEORGE

*"I remember an incident when John was in the seminary in Baltimore and I was still in high school. We'd go down to visit him on weekends when we could. Either Dad or I would drive and, Mom and my sisters came with us. We took John out to eat. It was one of those places where you would get a table, then order the food you wanted at the counter and waiters would deliver the food to the table. We turned the chairs over and leaned them against the table to identify the table as ours. When we had finished giving our orders, and returned to the table, some other people were sitting there. There were no other tables available.*

*"John was the last to return to the table. He was wearing his collar. In an instant, he grabbed the guy at the table and was about to throttle him when Dad yelled, 'What the hell kind of a priest are you going to make?'*

*"We were going through a lot of changes. John's temper was not among them."*

### Inter-Session: Camp St. Andrew

My preparation for the priesthood began in the formal setting of the seminary. Then, with the coming of summer, along with the other seminarians from the Scranton Diocese, I was going home, but I was expected to serve as a counselor at a local camp for boys that the diocese owned. Camp St. Andrew was located in Tunkhannock, Pennsylvania, about twenty miles outside of the city of Scranton. Boys went there from all over the country for a week or two, some for the entire summer. The camp was situated in a clearing in an otherwise heavily wooded area. It included everything young boys could want in such an outdoor facility: a lake for swimming and canoeing, trails for hiking, campfires, basketball courts, sports, and somewhat rustic cabins for housing. As seminarians, we were in charge of the boys and their various activities. When I was there, I enjoyed the opportunities of being in that kind of outdoor environment; and, quite honestly, it was a welcome change from the silence and discipline of the classroom training I was having trouble adjusting to in the seminary. The summers I spent there were fun for me and I was pretty good at keeping my kids involved. Besides coaching the boys' various activities, I was able to amuse them as a storyteller. When I was in high school, I had really built up a great repertoire of stories (many from old radio and TV shows), and, of course, I loved to perform! I could tell a really great ghost story, and I developed a great following. We'd have 200 or 250 kids and I'd have them sitting around a campfire in an area that was otherwise dark as pitch. I didn't just tell a story. It was a performance: silence, sounds, shrieks—everything. The kids would be terrified; but at the same time, they loved it. One thing is for certain: Once the stories started, no one was wandering off. They stayed close to the fire and enjoyed being scared to death.

It's funny how we forget so much, but then there are people and events I remember so vividly all these decades later. There was one particular kid who came for his summer vacation at Camp St. Andrew. We called him "Boots." I guess you might call him an agitator. You know the type: The first night he was in camp, he made it very clear that he was going to "get the counselor." That would be me. He was one of those camp wise guys. He knew everything. We stayed in cabins. The counselor had a little partitioned off space, separate from the campers. One night while I was asleep, this kid got some water and threw it on me. Now remember: It was the first night of the summer season. I got up. I undid my bed. (To be honest, I forget exactly how I did it. I think maybe I slept on the springs.) But I do know I didn't go storming out—for me, that was a major accomplishment. The next day, I didn't say anything. The following day, I didn't say anything. The next day, I still didn't say anything. Overall, we were having a good time; I wanted to let the situation go unnoticed long enough to let everyone's good time continue. But always, I thought, "I'm going to get that kid." So one night, I bought a chocolate bar. We went into the cabin and I slipped the chocolate bar into his pajamas while he was asleep. It was about one o'clock in the morning. Then, I got some limburger cheese and I put it right underneath his nose. I went back to my area and waited. It was summer—and it was hot. About two hours later, I came in, banging on the floor with a great big club as loud as I could, and shouting, "Who shit in this cabin?" I woke all the kids up. Then I sniffed really loud. "Somebody shit in this cabin. I told you kids to go out to the latrine. Who shit in this cabin?"

They were all awake. One after another, I could hear, "Honest to God. I didn't."

"I didn't."

# On My Own

"Honest, I didn't."

So as I approached Boots, I said, "It smells like it's coming from here! Feel and see if it's you! He felt in his pajamas. By then, the chocolate had melted, and his fingers came out covered with it.

"Look at this! Everyone in this cabin, look at this." Then I turned to Boots and said, "Look at it. Smell it. Smell how you're stinking up this place. By then, he was crying. Then I said, "Now, I want you to taste it!" He threw up.

Well, you little sucker, I got you!

It was my hour of triumph with those kids. Without a doubt, they knew who was in charge. Remembering these days, I have to admit, I had a lot of growing to do; but at the time, I was having a ball.

Even in those days, there was a crowd of us who noticed that anybody who wanted to be a counselor would be with the kids. But then there were always the guys who wanted to be involved in administration; they really didn't like being with the kids. We thought they wanted to get away. So we were always looking to see who was sucking up to the head guy so he could get a job in the office.

Finally, we became so unpopular with the powers-that-be that they would give us (the guys in my class, that is), the worst details—I guess because we had different ideas about running the place. Every time they put up a work list, like digging ditches for drainage from Casey Hall all the way through the camp, we were out there swinging the picks.

Once, my friend Joe Conboy said to me, "Esseff, every time I get on your list, it's the shit list. We're on the shit list around here, and you got us here."

"Maybe so. But you had a good time!"

Once I painted the flag pole like a barber pole and I invited the kids up to get haircuts. There was a prissy little kid from Connecticut whose mother used to send him down on a bus. I said, "Come on. Get a haircut." With a little towel around his neck, I cut all his hair except down the center. It wasn't the days when Mohawks were the style. Trust me: When his mother came up to visit him, I disappeared!

I could always engage the guys in my schemes. I never went up to the head cabin. Instead, I'd send another friend of mine—Joe. He used to say, "Esseff, you make the bombs, but I fire them." Father Carlin, who was in charge, was always suspicious. More than once he was heard saying, "I know that Esseff's the one. Always an uprising in his cabin." And he was always threatening to take me down to 315 Wyoming Avenue (the home of the bishop), 'til I finally said to him, "I'm going to go with you, Father. Let's go down and get this over with." But, lucky for me, that never happened. Looking back on it now, it's easy to see that I was still in a state of rebellion. But I had a lot of fun. I think all of us really had a lot of fun.

George didn't come to the camp, but my younger brother Joe (who is twelve years younger than I am) came. He was a wise kid and he belonged to a wise-ass group from Wilkes-Barre. They arrived together, planning to make life miserable for the counselors. But that's a whole other story!

We certainly had stuff going on, but the kids loved the counselors. They really did. They were challenged. The counselors loved the kids. We were challenged, too. We had a lot of great times together. The program lasted for the entire summer. We had to be there for ten weeks and for that time we got one camp canteen card, which gave each

*John with Joe Jr.*

of us some cigarettes and a camp shirt. (Kind of underpaid, there!)

Those summers between seminary school years, working at that camp, were times I really enjoyed. Even now, in retrospect, I still feel those months were an integral part of my own growth and formation—and honestly, a lot of fun.

## St. Mary's Seminary

By the time I finished two years of seminary training at St. Charles, George had graduated high school, investigated the possibility of going to the seminary, and decided instead to go to King's College in Wilkes-Barre. George began his studies there, primarily in science. That same fall, armed with an associate's degree from St. Charles, I went to St. Mary's on Paca Street in Baltimore, where I continued to pursue my bachelor's degree.

My parents were crying when they left me there that fall. St. Mary's was one of those walled fortresses in a blighted area of Baltimore. I remember that there was glass on top of the walls where we used to play handball. One of the seminarians was writing about the handball court, and when he was asked why there was glass on those walls, his response was, "to keep the seminarians' balls from going over the walls." That was, without doubt, the favorite quote we had about that place.

But as much as I had hated St. Charles (which, as a physical facility, was a beautiful place), I loved St. Mary's. In that old, dingy building, I learned to read. I read and I read and I read—from morning 'til night. I loved the library. I loved philosophy, and I loved to discuss it. I also had the good fortune of having a great philosophy teacher—a priest whom we called 'Doc Harvey.' Earlier, I wrote about the experience I had at Grandpa Sahd's home when I was about three years old: I had some awareness that God was making the world, and that all I saw was being created even as I saw it. (Even then I knew it was a spectacular life experience.) Now, almost eighty years old, I still remember the sharp details of that day: the exquisite beauty of the moment and the mark it left on me. That experience was a very private one for me; at the time, I told no one about it. As the years went on, I did ask several people if they could explain it to me. I never got a satisfactory answer until I shared that experience with Doc Harvey. We discussed it and he referred me to the Summa Theologica of St. Thomas Aquinas, where I found a great explanation of that childhood experience: "Question 104: The special effects of the divine government. Article 1. Whether creatures need to be kept in being by God." Doc Harvey took me through that early experience and, not only was I grateful, but my interest in philosophy was sharpened even more. I include some of it here for anyone who might like to read more about it.

> … a thing is said to preserve another 'per se' and directly, namely, when what is preserved depends on the preserver in such a way that it cannot exist without it. In this manner all creatures need to be preserved by God. For the being of every creature depends on God, so that not for a moment could it subsist, but would fall into nothingness were it not kept in being by the operation of the Divine power. —Thomas Aquinas

That was an exceptionally profound day of learning for me. Of course, not every day was that intense. When we weren't in class, we had great opportunities to go out and visit the hospitals. One day, I was coming home from our hospital work with Father Art Kaschenbaugh, who later spent many years at the Cathedral in Scranton. It was around 5 o'clock in the evening and we were going home to have supper. We were walking by a park where people were giving witness to having been converted. There was an enormously fat, Black woman with them and she was there holding the drum with the Salvation Army, shouting her testimony at the top of her lungs.

# Brothers & Fathers

"I used to drink ... and I used to curse ... and ... I used to go with men . . . I had a fast, fast life. Then the Salvation Army came along ... and I was converted."

Her voice was at a fever pitch when she ended, "Now all I do is beat this god-damn drum!"

Art and I laughed all the way home. We never heard testimony like that—before or after. Years later, when I would see him around town, one of us would always say, "Did you have any converts lately?" And that would set us off in floods of laughter.

In Baltimore, we used to be called the drum and bugle corps. Singing at a really old cathedral in Baltimore, we wore all the traditional clerical clothes: black cassocks to our feet and square-capped birettas on our heads. On our way to the cathedral to sing, we'd pass through the red light district. What a sight we must have been! But again—we had a lot of fun. I had an absolutely wonderful two years there at St. Mary's. I did well academically, graduated, and went back to my bishop, who then determined that I would spend the next four years at Catholic University in Washington, to complete my studies. For the first two of those years at Catholic University, George was completing his studies at King's College in Wilkes-Barre.

# CHAPTER 13

## KING'S COLLEGE

### *George*

During the summer of 1947, after deciding that I wasn't going into the seminary, I enrolled in King's College, a newly founded men's college in downtown Wilkes-Barre. I was a member of the second incoming freshman class. John had already gone back to Baltimore, but to a different seminary: St. Mary's. King's proved to be a great place for me for several reasons. While I was there, I met a lot of very impressive people. One of those was Father O'Hara, the head of the Biology department. He was a Holy Cross father—a really bright guy who had written about thirty books. He had come from Notre Dame to head the department at King's, and he was a great teacher.

I didn't know that at first, and my initial encounter with him didn't go well—as a matter of fact, not well at all! The first day I was in his class, he caught me talking to someone, and he got really ticked at me. Every class after that, he would start with the expected, "In the name of the Father, and of the Son, and of the Holy Ghost. Amen." And then came an immediate addition: "George Esseff." And he'd fire a question at me about whatever we were studying. After he threw down the first gauntlet, I knew he meant business; I had to be prepared every single day. I knew that whatever the hell was going on, I had to have the material down pat for his class. That went on for a whole year. Day after day, I got used to hearing my name become a part of a very select group: "The Father, and the Son, and the Holy Ghost. Amen." Don't ask me why, but I enjoyed the way Father O'Hara challenged me. More often than not, I knew the answer. What about this? What about that? So I knew I had to be prepared—and I was. Looking back on it now, his technique as a teacher only made me sharper and more interested in knowing all that there was to know. Eventually, I earned Father O'Hara's respect, and that was very important to me.

What was important to me was important to Frank Hanlon, too. We became proctors for Father O'Hara on test days in other classes. We'd help him correct papers, and after a time we had built a solid relationship. Through our time together, he knew that both Frank and I were interested in pursuing careers in medicine. Probably for that reason, Father O'Hara gave us latitude to do things far beyond what the class required.

One day during my second year in college, Frank and I saw a dog get hit by a truck in front of the school. We witnessed the accident through the window and we knew the dog was lying in the gutter, dead. We asked Father O'Hara if we could go out and get the dog and dissect it, and he gave us permission to do that.

The study of comparative anatomy usually includes investigating a whole series of slides for whatever is under examination. Using those slides, a student can identify every part of the body and every bone. So Frank and I went out and got the dog. We skinned it—it was the first time I had ever done that. We cut it up and put it in formaldehyde. In the lab, we had access to a microtome, which is an instrument for cutting sections of organic tissues. Those slices of tissues could then be put on slides for microscopic examination. So Frank and I made up a whole series of slides for ourselves. Father O'Hara allowed us to do that. He let us use the equipment, pickle the tissue, wax it, slice it very thin, and then put each piece on a slide. So we made up our own slides and then had the whole series for ourselves. From this series of slides, we could identify certain muscle tissue, pieces of bone, and other parts of the body. That was a tremendous learning experience for us! We got to know biology really well, thanks to Father O'Hara's support.

Along with this great type of experience came the routine classroom stuff. Father O'Hara was famous for his big tests. He'd take a bunch of slides and pass them around to the class. It was our job to pass them around and identify each of the slides. Well, in his own inimitable way, one day he had put a piece of cotton on one of the slides. Cotton looks very similar to bone when it's put under the microscope. When the slide came to me, I really couldn't identify the material. I couldn't call it bone—or anything else, for that matter; so I passed it on to the next person. But as I learned later, everyone put "bone"—or some other answer.

That was the kind of stuff Father O'Hara did. He was really a bright guy and a great teacher. When I grew to know him better, I learned that he used to prepare three hours for every class. Three hours! In spite of how well he knew the material, he always prepared to meet his students, day after day. I owe a lot to him.

The great learning experiences in Father O'Hara's class were not just academic adventures. Some of them proved to be a springboard for me getting into a lot of trouble with another professor, later on. One day, in another class, we were studying the body of a cat. Each one of us had a cat that we worked on. Trust me: This study was much more involved than my earlier operation on our family cat! We studied the cat in detail: the arteries, the veins, the muscles. When we were doing this kind of work, we wore rubber gloves. They were a combination of red and orange, and the top of the glove was rolled over—it kind of looked like a round piece of vein or artery. Behind the professor's back, I cut off a piece of my glove and I buried it in a place in my cat where there shouldn't have been either a vein or an artery! Then I called him over and I said, "What's this?" pointing to the reddish-orange piece of the rubber glove. He proceeded to make up a long explanation of what the piece of rubber was. I guess he didn't want to seem baffled. Then when he pulled the "vein" out and saw what it was, he went wild! He was really furious. I knew that I knew more about the subject than he did, but I was a smart ass. Unfortunately, it was the whole class that suffered. He was so ticked at me that he announced an exam for the next day. None of us were prepared for that. He wanted us to identify the whole muscle structure, the origin, the insertion, and the action of each muscle in the cat's body. I stayed up the whole night—drinking two whole pots of coffee in the process! I studied all night. And it paid off: I scored a 98% on the test. Most of the other guys flunked, and then they were ticked at me too. There's a price to pay when you're a smart-ass kid.

Another great professor I also came to know at King's was the head of the chemistry department, Father T. J. Lane. He came to us from Notre Dame.

During the war, there was no way to get rubber. It came from one of the islands and we couldn't get it. So there was research going on to find a substitute for it. Father Lane was a man involved in that research, and he came to be one of the discoverers of neoprene—a synthetic rubber made by the polymerization of chloroprene that is characterized by superior resistance to oils. He was a really bright guy. When we first got into his chemistry class, we had about a hundred kids in our class. He made an announcement: "By the end of the semester, we're only going to have thirty-three guys here."

And that's exactly what happened.

Funny—one of the guys who was among the missing at the end of the term was Bill McGowan. He left the science department and transferred to the Business School at King's. Obviously, that was a smart move: Bill eventually became the founder of MCI.

After two years in college, Frank and I came to hear that Sister Martin had suffered a heart attack; she had been our high school teacher for calculus, trig, and both solid and plane geometry. The Mercy community didn't have a sister who could replace her. We made arrangements with Sister Martin's superior to take over her classes at St. Mary's High School. Frank and I did that for about seven months. We were really busy. We continued at the college and did our own work, but we went over to the high school to teach Sister Martin's math classes in the daytime. At a school reunion some years ago, I met a man from St. Mary's who said, "You gave me such a love for math. I carried that right through my whole life." That made me feel really good because I didn't know how good a job I had done as a teacher.

But back to Father Lane. Frank and I got to be great friends with him. We learned a lot from him and we really knew how lucky we were to have him as a professor. As time went on, we used to go and have beers with him every damn night. We got to know him well and, because of our respect for him, we studied hard. It wasn't that we ever took advantage of him or his friendship.

In August, after I had completed my sophomore year but before the fall term was to begin, I decided once again to begin seminary training in Massachusetts at the novitiate of the Holy Cross Fathers. I was there for more than a week and preparing to receive the habit. (That was the 'uniform' that was worn all through the years of study and novitiate.) The night before the reception of novitiate candidates was to take place, there was a party for the guys who were planning to enter. I was sitting and talking with the rector. John, who was then at St. Mary's in Baltimore completing his fourth year of seminary formation, had kept me up to date on what he was doing, and I said to the rector, "My brother just got his rite changed from the Maronite rite to the Latin rite. When will I have to do that?"

He threw his hands up in the air. "You're not Latin?"

*King's alumni: George, Stephanie, Kim and Michelle*

# King's College

"No, I'm Maronite."

"I didn't have any idea. Well, I'm sorry, George, but that means you can't take the habit."

I remember feeling really disappointed—but still hopeful that I would be able to continue. I sat up very late that night with the rector. We went through the canons to find some loophole so that I could accept the habit; but as it turned out, that just wasn't possible. He advised me to go back to King's, get a spiritual director, and return the following year. I couldn't begin the novitiate without the change of rite. There was a rule in place at the time that if a novice missed twenty-nine days, he would have to repeat the whole year. The rector knew it was impossible to get my rite changed in twenty nine days. The best thing for me to do was to go back to King's and not lose the whole year. So that's what I did.

I guess when I was in college, I hit my stride academically. I took a double major in biology and chemistry, because those were my greatest interests. I knew I would also need physics, so I took a minor in that too. Because I didn't want to be far behind when I returned to the novitiate, I also took a minor in philosophy. I had a packed schedule, but I loved the work and I was prepared to study hard.

I also played hard. All through the years, Frank Hanlon and I remained friends. He was bright as hell. I used to give him a little competition—but not a hell of a lot! He helped me a great deal in school and we studied together all the time. In college, his family of doctors afforded both of us great opportunities for witnessing surgical procedures.

At some point during those years, I decided I was going to try to go to med school after college. It was pretty much assumed that Frank would do the same—not because of his family, but because he was so bright. At this point in our lives, his dad would invite us into surgery; and as time went on, he'd get other doctors to invite us in too. That sort of situation has to be interpreted as a special blessing. When it came time to graduate, I had been accepted into two medical schools, and Frank had been accepted by three or four.

But life is funny.

By the time we graduated, both of us had chosen different paths. Neither of us entered the medical profession. Ironically, I became a businessman and Frank lived out his life as a Franciscan priest.

But before we knew our life's decisions, we were just enjoying college life. When we weren't studying, Frank and I could always find a way to amuse ourselves. There was a bar near the police station and we used to hang out there with the guys. One night we heard that somebody at the bar had put up a drinking challenge. Each challenger had to drink sixty shot glasses full of beer—one a minute. Drink one. Wait a minute. Drink another one. Wait a minute. The story was that, after thirty or forty drinks, guys were passing out in the bar.

I was a pretty good beer drinker at the time, and so Frank and I began to investigate the situation. The night before the next challenge, Frank and I went to a bar, but not the one where the challenge was going to take place. We set up our own challenges. The guys started betting on me. They also paid for the drinks. The bets started flying back and forth like you'd see at a fight. I drank one a minute. I didn't feel intoxicated at all. At sixty, I said, "I don't feel anything." When I stopped at seventy-five, I didn't feel anything either. It really wasn't a lot of beer. I won all the money from the betting. I remember saying, "Maybe there's something to this, Frank. Let's go up to the challenge tomorrow night."

And we did. That night, we had it made. The same thing happened as the night before. You should have seen the bets going on that night! I won—no problem. I think I stopped at about seventy. A lot of guys lost money that night. But it was a great night.

Sill, I would have to say I wasn't a heavy drinker in college. I think I drank heavier when I was in high school. Maybe I wasn't all that affected by what I drank because of all the years I had worked on the truck with Dad. I was pretty strong and had a lot of muscle. When John and I were at the market, I remember that we had made up our minds that we were going to show all the guys there that we could do all the stuff they were doing. Each of us would have to hoist those hundred-pound bags onto the truck, standing on the tip of our toes to load those heavy sacks ten feet high. We learned how to lift and how to throw those heavy bags when we were only kids. How could we not be physically developed? We got just as good a workout as any guy paying money to work out in a gym today.

In addition to that, I was a wrestler at King's. At that time I was pretty strong. But nothing I've ever done physically was more strenuous than wrestling. That

*George wrestling*

86

# King's College

training helped me the rest of my life. I was in really good shape for a long, long time because of it.

At King's I wrestled in the 'unlimited' class, not the heavyweight. I was about 180 pounds then. The heaviest guy I wrestled was 278 pounds. He was huge, but I beat him. He came lunging at me and he could have just squashed the hell out of me. I grabbed him by the shoulders and, like a guy fighting a bull, I turned sideways and grabbed him by his uniform, pulling him. I pulled him hard enough that he went off the mat, hitting his nose on the floor. He busted his nose and was bleeding all over the place. I won by default.

In terms of category, the next weight down was 175. I could never reach that—when I began college, I already weighed 196. When I started to work out, I got down to 178, but I could never get down to 175; there was no way I could ever wrestle in that class. One day the coach asked me if I'd like to wrestle in the unlimited class, and I said I would. I was in pretty good shape. The next guy I wrestled was huge, too: He was 250 pounds. I wouldn't let any of the other wrestlers pin me. A lot of times they beat me, but I know I won a few. Best of all, they didn't beat me by pinning me.

In order not to let my opponent pin me, I had to do what's called a bridge: I put down my feet and arched my back with my head on the mat so my opponent couldn't flatten me on the mat. In order to get that kind of strength in my neck muscles, I used to stand on my head with my feet against the wall. With all my weight on my head, I would roll my head back and forth to develop the muscles in my neck. I went from a 15 ½ inch neck to a 17 ½!

The coach's name was Bob Armstrong. Not long ago, he wrote to me about those days. He said he hadn't wanted to give up wrestling in any class, and he always knew he could always count on me to take on anyone. Reading his words meant a lot to me.

## BOB ARMSTRONG

*"I respect and admire what you have done with your life, particularly what you have done to help others who needed a helping hand. You planted roses where there were weeds. I really appreciate what you did to help me field a complete wrestling team back in the early days of King's. It took a lot of 'guts' to wrestle in the heavyweight division. I respected you for that. So I thank you, for helping me back then, and I congratulate you for helping others throughout your life. The world is the richer for your being here."*

*-February 28, 1991*

> ## JOHN
>
>
>
> *"I had been in the seminary a few years and George was in college. I remember one time, when I was home for a visit, we started fooling around and were wrestling in the parlor like we always did. In about three seconds, George pinned me. George had always been strong, but that day, I didn't know what hit me; in seconds I was on my back."*

Before he came to King's, Bob had been a wrestler in the Navy. When he was at King's, he not only took on the position of coach, but also became a wrestler for the college as well. He wrestled in the 145 weight class.

I remember that, during that time, I had chronic trouble with my appendix, so I had to have it taken out. During the Christmas holiday, I had the operation—that meant I couldn't wrestle. I went to watch the match, instead. Armstrong wrestled his match at 145 and won. Then he asked the opposite team if he could wrestle the heavyweight guy. He beat him as well—a guy who was over 200 pounds! When Bob came back into the locker room, he threw up blood because he had strained himself so much.

Wrestling was good for me. I kept my weight down, and I think my waist was only about 33 inches.

I can say, though, in all honesty, that college was mostly a lot of hard work. I didn't have a lot of time on my hands. I would go to Mass at 7 o'clock each morning, and then I would go to school at 8 or 8:30. I'd be in school all day, because I had a lot of classes and science labs on top of that. Some of the labs lasted three or four hours. Carrying biology, chemistry, and physics together made for a heavy load.

> ## JOHN
>
>
>
> *"I'm glad to hear about the constant study, but I heard about other stuff—some recreational stuff! What about the girl by the name of Clare? As I understood it, there were a few others, too. The way I heard it, you were pretty involved in that area of study, too! Not only did you become a 'giant,' you also developed the impressive title of 'Lover Boy' among all those nurses at Mercy."*

That's not how it was. A lot of the girls I had gone to high school with went on to study nursing. So I had kind of a girlfriend. Her name was Rita. She was a Polish girl (born, of course, in Wilkes-Barre) who was studying nursing. Through her, I met a lot of the other nurses, and I would date all of them—quite a lot. There was one that latched onto me—that was Clare. I was more her boyfriend than she was my girlfriend. She was a friend to me; I was her boyfriend, to her. And I don't know how she talked me into giving her my class ring, because I wanted to date other nurses. Clare really got ticked at me! And I do remember the night I was dropping her off and she was about to go into the nurses' quarters; but she just stood there. All of a sudden, she grabbed my ring and threw it back at me. Who could blame her? I know I was dating two or three other nurses as well.

All of that ended when I met a girl from Misericordia, the women's college in nearby Dallas. Her name was Rosemary Dorning. It was 1949. I was a junior; she was a sophomore.

> ### JOHN
>
> ⟢
>
> *"I guess you could say, at that time in his life, my brother George was seriously dating on a very casual level."*

It happened like this. When I was at King's, there was a girl at Misericordia whom I had known since high school; her name was Nancy. When it came to social events, there was usually some sort of plan for getting the guys from King's and the girls from Misery (as we called it, for short) together. One evening in November of my junior year, my friend Nancy called me and asked if I could get some of my friends together and go up to a dance on the weekend. The idea went over well with the guys I asked, so a bunch of us went up to the dance. I no sooner walked into the dance, than I spotted this beautiful girl. I announced to the guys, "That's the gal I'm dancing with!"

My buddy saw her at the same time, and he said he was going to dance with her.

"Like hell you are! I'm going to dance with her." And I danced with Rosemary all night. She and I got to talking, and I walked her back to the dorm. It was a great night—though it wasn't until some weeks later that I saw her again.

In January, I got another call from my friend Nancy. "We need some guys to come to Misery. We're having a formal dance, and some of the girls need dates."

I wasn't all that interested, but she kept after me. So finally, I said, "I'll tell you what: If Rosemary Dorning is free, I'll come up; but I'm not interested in any blind date. If she's free, I'll be there. Otherwise, count me out."

Nancy checked with Rosemary. She had a date for the formal, but the guy had called to say he couldn't go to the dance because he had to go to the funeral of his uncle, who had died unexpectedly. Nancy suggested to Rosemary that she go with me. Rosemary wasn't interested; she thought it wouldn't be right. But Nancy kept after her and after her, and finally convinced Rosemary to go with me.

That's what happened.

# Brothers & Fathers

We went to the dance together that night, and I knew that this was the gal I would spend my whole life with. She could be a companion; she could be a mother; she could be a grandmother; she could be a helpmate. I knew she could be everything I really wanted for my whole life.

At the same time that I met Rosemary, I was making plans to be a doctor. By the time I was a senior, I had been accepted at two medical schools: Georgetown University and the University of Pennsylvania. But as time went on and we became more serious, Rosemary made it clear to me that she would never marry a doctor. I knew I wanted to marry Rosemary, and so I changed the course of my life. I continued to see her. And I knew that, one day, I would marry her.

# CHAPTER 14

## MEETING "MR. RIGHT"

### *Rosemary*

I was born in the small town of Shamokin, Pennsylvania, nine years after my only sibling, my brother Bob. I graduated from the public high school in Coal Township, and I was very committed to my education by the time I went to College Misericordia. I had made up my mind to major in biology and minor in chemistry. For a time in my freshman year, I considered going into pharmacy but my dad, who was a veterinarian, said, "Forget that! You're not a math student." I respected his judgment. Ironically, the chemistry that I was most successful in as time went by was quantitative analysis—which, of course, is all math!

After my sophomore year, the opportunity available to me was to move up to Sayre Hospital in New York to continue work in the field of medical technology. Instead of doing that, though, I decided I would continue in my junior year and get my degree. My thinking was that I could always go to Sayre after I graduated—if that's what I decided I wanted to do. If I got my degree, I would have several options. I could also get certification in education and, if need be, I could go into teaching.

I knew my dad had made sacrifices for me, and I wasn't about to squander my college career. As far as my social life went, I was only interested in temporary relationships because I had definite goals—and I was going to reach them.

In December of my sophomore year, I met George at a dance at Misericordia. A month or so later, we went to another dance together. We were both studying science. There were different events that King's and Misericordia sponsored together, and I also saw him at those functions.

As George and I began dating more, my roommate Mary and I came up with a plan that would help us to get around the curfew rules at Misericordia. We were somewhat adventurous at the time, and the rules were really pretty strict. On weekdays, we had to be back on campus by 7:00 p.m; when we went out on the weekends, we had to be back by ten o'clock. Mary was the niece of one of the Mercy Sisters, Sister Joan, who was in charge of the nursing school. In order to get permission to stay off campus on a weekend, we had to have someone vouch for us and say where we would be, and essentially be responsible for our wellbeing. Mary arranged with Sister Joan that we could stay in the nurses' quarters. She assured Mary that we were welcome—and, best of all, we could stay out past our regular curfew. She said all would be fine if we got in at "a reasonable hour."

When George and I went out, he would often bring Frank or one of his other buddies to date my friend Mary. The first time we went to the nurses' living quarters to stay, Sister Joan said, "Well, who are the young men? Tell me their names." I didn't know who George was bringing for Mary, so I said, "Well, I don't know who the other fellow is, Sister, but I'm going with George Esseff."

"Oh," she said, "the Romeo of the Mercy Nursing School! Oh yes, we know him very well. You make sure you're in here by midnight—and knock on my door."

Needless to say, we did.

Early the next morning, we were on our way to the cafeteria to get some breakfast with the nurses. When we got on the elevator, there was dead silence. They knew who we were, but we didn't know any of them. We were the "Misery girls" who were staying overnight; they were the nurses. So Mary and I talked only to each other on the elevator, and then went to the dining area and ate breakfast. When we went back to our room to get our things, there was a note on the pillow on my bed.

*George Esseff belongs to the Mercy nurses.*
*HANDS OFF!*

"Oh," I said, "so this is a challenge!"

Mary piped in, "We can do this easy. It's a shoo-in."

So it became sort of a game. And we had a lot of fun with it.

As I continued to see George, I knew that the relationship couldn't be serious for me. Graduation was my goal. Come hell or high water, that was my goal.

When George graduated in 1951, I still had a year of college left. He was very serious about our relationship, but I told him that my education came first—my dad had put too much into my schooling, and so had I. If marriage was in the picture, it would be way down the line. With that settled, there was still another huge obstacle. George asked me if I would wait for him until he finished medical school.

# Meeting "Mr. Right"

My answer on that score was definite: "I'll never marry a physician. That's the long and short of it. My first love wanted medicine and I said "no" to him. He knew what he wanted, and so did I. He went his way, and I went mine. I don't want to marry into the medical profession. My dad is a veterinarian and I've watched him out morning, noon, and night on sick calls. That's not for me. I want a nine-to-five man."

Interesting how that worked out! There were a lot of other interesting moments.

No one in Shamokin knew much about the Lebanese. In Shamokin, our only reference to anything about Lebanon was a lunch meat called Lebanon bologna. If you were to ask anyone in the neighborhood, "What is Lebanese?" the answer would be, "It's a bologna."

They were about to learn that Lebanese is not a bologna; it's a nationality.

I remember the first time my brother Bob met George. Maybe because of our age difference, Bob always looked after me; he was a wonderful brother. After meeting George, he said to me, "I don't appreciate you dating this fella. You shouldn't be dating someone older than I am."

"He's not older than you, Bob."

"Oh, I think so. He looks older—and he acts older. Is he a serviceman who just got out of the service and is going to college on the GI Bill? How old is he?"

To tell the truth, I didn't really know that answer. But I assured Bob that I'd find out.

He wasn't satisfied. "What does Dad think about this? I told Dad he looks very Yiddish. He said he was from King's, and that's why he was at the dance at Misericordia; but I think he might be Yiddish and going to school at Wilkes."

Those were the concerns about George. Eventually, I discovered that he was only one year older than I was; that he was a Catholic; and that he did, in fact, go to King's College. Dad was happy as a clam about that. My mom thought he was a lovely young man: very polite, very respectful, and very, very nice to their daughter. In time, even Bob was happy.

I can't say that for all brothers.

I had met George in December. The following summer, he had made plans to take me back to Shamokin for summer vacation. He told me that his brother John was home from the seminary, where he had just finished his semester. When George picked me up at the college, his brother John was in the car. Both of them schlepped me, my boxes, and my suitcases, and we were off to Shamokin.

# Brothers & Fathers

When we stopped to get gas, I got the feeling that John was not too happy meeting me. The exact conversation has faded over the years, but I do remember John telling me that George had been to the seminary twice and there had been talk about his going back.

He was pretty direct, "Did you know that?"

"I know it now."

"Well, until he met you, he was going into the seminary."

"Well, he can still sure go to the seminary, because I have no ties to him. And don't you put all that on me! That's his doing, not mine. I'm not holding him back from anything at all."

I didn't cotton to this brother at all! I thought, "The nerve of him! He came with a chip on his shoulder. Well, that's just too bad!" That was my first encounter with John, and it certainly wasn't a good one.

---

### JOHN

"I remember as clearly as yesterday the moment when George told me about Rosemary and that he wanted to marry her.

"I always thought he was going to be a priest and that the technicalities he encountered when he went to the novitiate were only minor glitches that would eventually be worked out. I had finished third theology and I was at my parents' home. George and I were lying on our old twin beds, talking. I knew he had finished his studies at King's and that he had completed a minor in philosophy. But he wasn't talking about any of that. He was talking about Rosemary: how he met her and how they had been dating.

"He seemed in awe as he told me all about her: her beauty, her goodness. He told me about how he was very much in love with her, how much he was drawn to her. The word that seemed to capture what had happened to George was one seldom used: 'smitten.' He was surely smitten. I knew that George had dated a lot of girls. Even now, I can name some of them. I knew he dated, but I always thought that he would become a priest whenever that all worked out. I could kid him about the girls he dated and about his being a Romeo, but I knew this relationship was different. This girl was special.

"In a very real way, we had always exchanged our deepest secrets. And there he was revealing the powerful attraction he had to Rosemary. I realized at that moment that someone was now closer to my brother than I was.

# Meeting "Mr. Right"

George and I continued to have serious conversations about our relationship while I was finishing my senior year and he was working in Virginia at Fort Belvoir with the Army Corps of Engineers.

## GEORGE

"I might mention that all during the time Rosemary was still at Misericordia and I was working for the Army Corps of Engineers, I traveled to see her every weekend. I only missed one weekend in a year-and-a-half. The round trip was about 600 miles to her home in Shamokin (or a little longer to the college in Dallas. Finally, I said to her, 'I'm going to kill myself doing this.'

"'Well,' Rosemary said, 'it's your choice whether you want to keep driving up here every weekend or not.'"

My mother was pretty direct: "What is it with this young man? Enough is enough! What's going on?"

I told her, "He's really a nice fellow." But I didn't tell her that George was one of the first young men who shared with me what I considered most important: We both placed the same value on a strong spiritual life. We were on track both in spiritual matters and in what we were looking for in a spouse. He knew what he wanted in a wife. Still, I continued to go very slowly, because I was sure marriage would be way down the road. By the time I was a senior, though, George was insisting that I make a choice about whether I was going to marry him or not.

There was another complicating factor. When I was about to graduate from Misericordia, I had been awarded a scholarship to get a master's degree at Marquette University. My dad really wanted me to go in that direction; I remember him saying, "If he loves you enough, he'll wait for you and let you finish your education." I was praying non-stop to St. Jude, the saint of impossible causes, to show me the direction I should take. In May, I graduated with a degree in biology and a minor in chemistry. By the time summer came along, I received a call from Marquette wanting to know if I was going to take the scholarship or not. The caller said she would have to know within the week. If I didn't want the scholarship, it would be awarded to someone else.

When George came home that weekend, we went to Wilkes-Barre. I told him our relationship would have to be off; I was going back to school. His response was that he was going to join the Air Force. With those things said, we were going to make the best of the evening. We went to see George's sister Marlene and her date,

George's old friend, Tony Elias. When we arrived there, Tony said, "C'mon—we're going out dancing." We went along. The last hurrah. All evening, I kept thinking, "You're not making this easy, St. Jude." I couldn't shift either way. The answer wasn't coming peacefully.

At one point in the evening, George and I were dancing and I heard myself say, "George, I'll marry you on Thanksgiving Day." I shocked myself. I had spent the earlier part of that day thinking about what I had to do to get organized and make plans for going to Marquette. All I was saying in my head was "Glory be to God! I don't know where that came from." I was very amazed that I had said that.

George was somewhat shocked—but obviously delighted. "Are you serious?"

And I heard myself saying quite clearly, "Yes, I am."

I know I hadn't planned on saying what I said, but when I got home it was as though St. Jude was standing there in the room assuring me that I had made the right decision. From that moment on, I was peaceful. I got a job with a pharmaceutical firm close to home in the Danville area, and I worked there until we were married.

The night before we were married, a young man I had dated for years called me. He was planning to go into medicine and that had ended our relationship. He was about to ship out to Korea. He had heard I was getting married.

"I hope you're making the right decision. I'm going to medical school after I get home from Korea. But at the moment, I'm still here—and I'm still unattached."

"Well," I said, "I'm very much attached. Good Luck!"

George and I were married on Thanksgiving Day.

# CHAPTER 15

## THEOLOGICAL COLLEGE:
## CATHOLIC UNIVERSITY OF AMERICA

### *Father John*

The year 1949 was a pivotal one for both George and me. While my brother was finishing his last two years at King's, I began a new chapter in my preparation for priesthood when I enrolled at The Catholic University of America (CUA) in Washington, D.C. Before I arrived there, I had already decided to pursue a four-year degree in Semitics. My studies included training in Arabic and Syriac, both of which I had been somewhat familiar with since I was a little child.

Early on, I came to be well known around the Semitic library there. It was at Catholic University that I met Father Arbez, Father Ray Brown, and Father Dannemiller. Those guys all went on to be well-known scripture scholars. I also audited a class there on Comparative Religion presented by then-Monsignor Fulton Sheen. I took a minor in theology and I was exposed to marvelous understandings of theology long before Vatican II. There were outstanding scholars at the time, and we studied the works of John Courtney Murray and Henri de Lubac. I had such a rich experience there; I was meeting all kinds of great people. It was a happy and exciting time for me. I met the Archbishop of Washington—a man formerly from Scranton, Cardinal O'Boyle. He was very much in the forefront of integrating schools in Washington, and he fast became one of my heroes. At that time, Washington was about 80% Black and the city was plagued by poverty and crime. I quickly became enamored of doing work there among the urban poor. About that same time, I was also converted by my study in 2nd Theology of Mystici Corporis, an encyclical letter written by Pope Pius XII to the universal church. Many of the ideas in that encyclical completely transformed me, and helped to form me in the type of priesthood I have enjoyed for more than fifty years. It was the first time I realized that, as a Christian, I am called to be Jesus in the world.

# Brothers & Fathers

The words of that encyclical written by Pope Pius XII had a tremendous impact on me. I feel I want to include at least a few of them here.

> ... *the chief reason for Our present exposition of this sublime doctrine is Our solicitude for the souls entrusted to Us ... Our purpose is to throw an added ray of glory on the supreme beauty of the Church ... to bring out into fuller light the exalted supernatural nobility of the faithful who in the Body of Christ are united with their Head.*

> ... *a body calls for a multiplicity of members, which are linked together in such a way as to help one another. And as in the body when one member suffers, all the other members share its pain, and the healthy members come to the assistance of the ailing, so in the Church the individual members do not live for themselves alone, but also help their fellows, and all work in mutual collaboration for the common comfort and for the more perfect building up of the whole Body ... Nor must one imagine that the Body of Christ, just because it bears the name of Christ, is made up during the days of its earthly pilgrimage only of members conspicuous for their holiness, or that it consists only of those whom God has predestined to eternal happiness. It is owing to the Savior's infinite mercy that place is allowed in His Mystical Body here below for those whom, of old, He did not exclude from the banquet.*

> ... *corresponding to this love of God and of Christ, there must be love of the neighbor. How can we claim to love the Divine Redeemer, if we hate those whom He has redeemed with His precious blood, so that He might make them members of His Mystical Body? For that reason the beloved disciple warns us: "If any man say: I love God, and hateth his brother, he is a liar. For he that loveth not his brother whom he seeth, how can he love God whom he seeth not? And this commandment we have from God, that he who loveth God loveth also his brother." Rather it should be said that the more we become "members one of another," mutually careful one for another," the closer we shall be united with God and with Christ; as, on the other hand, the more ardent love that binds us to God and to our divine head, the closer we shall be united to each other in the bonds of charity.—Pope Pius XII*

As I became more and more aware that we are the Body of Christ, I joined a small group of seminarians who became intensely interested in serving the poor, and renewing diocesan priesthood. Most priests who were affiliated with a particular diocese had a lot of parish duties that kept them from serving people outside the framework of the parish. We knew that the poor were not usually part of that system. It was a period of my life when I took this work very seriously. We would do anything and everything so we could work with the poor.

# Catholic University of America

There was a place called Fides House, which was a settlement house where Blacks were our brothers and sisters. There was a lot of racial discrimination at that time, leading to horrible injustices. I became immersed in those kinds of issues during that time. I had associates and colleagues and friends in the seminary who saw it my way, others who didn't. We had a lot of theological clashes and I was very excited about new ideas about what priests could do and what seminarians (preparing to be priests) could do. What really made an impression on me was the concept that I wouldn't be a certain kind of priest unless I was that kind of seminarian. So a bunch of us used to go downtown to throw ourselves into serving the poor. I didn't go home for the holidays. I would cook for the poor and I became quite immersed in the work of Fides House. My academic studies, especially that of Mystici Corporis, were propelling a very exciting and meaningful ministry as each day I tried to "come to the assistance of the ailing ... and to work in mutual collaboration for the common comfort and for the more perfect building up of the whole Body."

The experiences of those days filled me with joy. They always bring to my mind a beautiful experience that I had had many years before, when I was an eight-year-old boy.

One Saturday morning, I was walking down South Main Street on my way to the movies. I was with a bunch of kids, but I had fallen behind and was a few feet behind them. An old woman wearing a dark babushka on her head and carrying a load of packages was coming in the opposite direction. She seemed to maneuver through the kids in front of me, heading directly towards me. She actually stopped right in front of me and said, "Little boy, will you give me a dime so I can get on the streetcar? I have to get to Nanticoke."

I had my dime for the movies and, initially, I pretended that I just didn't hear her. I took a couple of steps away from her. But then I hesitated, and I knew I had to turn around. I reached into my pocket, took out my dime, and handed it to her. When I did, I saw that her face was gleaming with joy. She turned and made her way towards the streetcar. I watched my brother and my other friends stop in front of the movie theater and get in the line to buy their tickets. I shouted to George and told him I wasn't going to the movie.

It was only a short walk from where I was to the bank of the Susquehanna River that runs right through Wilkes-Barre. I walked along the river bank for a while, and then I lay down watching the river as it coursed its way past me on its way toward the Chesapeake Bay. It was a beautiful spot and everything was peaceful. As I lay on the bank of the river, I looked at the sky and the river and the clouds.

I stayed there for hours. Time seemed to fly by. That day is a memory I have always cherished. That day was one of the happiest, most peaceful days of my childhood.

That evening, when my dad asked me what I had done that day, I didn't quite know how to tell him. I tried to. I don't think I really did. I gave away my dime and I had the happiest, most peaceful afternoon on the bank of the river. In some way, I knew I had learned something wonderful—and my Father had taught it to me. I was very young, but I knew it was my Father, God, who had let me experience the joy of giving that day. It was a very powerful lesson. Each day in the streets of Washington D.C., I knew that what I experienced by giving my dime away as a little boy was intensified. I experienced that same joy again and again.

I continued to be very much on fire with ministering to the members of the Body of Christ who were suffering from the many injustices of the 1950s, and I was especially happy to be nearing ordination.

By the time I had finished my second year at CUA, George had finished King's, and had made some very significant choices for his future. When I returned to Washington to begin my third year at CUA, George had moved to Fort Belvoir in Virginia, where he had taken a job with the Army Corps of Engineers. I wasn't the only one on fire at the time. I didn't see much of George that year, because he would travel to Pennsylvania each weekend to see Rosemary. They were quite serious, and eventually they made plans to marry in November of my last year at CUA. I was only months from ordination and can honestly say, I was disappointed that I would not officiate at the wedding. But I was happy for them.

During my last year at Catholic University, I was challenged by my ministry with the poor, as well as by my studies. I also enjoyed visits with George and Rosemary who, by that time, were married and living in Fort Belvoir, not far from Catholic University. Best of all, for me, I was approaching what I had been preparing for during the previous eight years: my ordination to the priesthood.

# Chapter 16

## Voices of Discernment

### *George*

The fifties were a time of growing individuation in the lives of my brother and me. While John was finishing his seminary training at the Catholic University of America, I was working at Fort Belvoir, Virginia, with the Army Corps of Engineers. I was not very far away from my brother geographically, but our lives were moving apart in other ways .

John and I had taken our places in the adult world, but we took much of our childhood with us. We had been born into a Lebanese–American family, but at a very early age, we began to step gradually out of what might be considered the norm in the Lebanese/Maronite tradition. John and I were pretty clear about how a Lebanese family worked—at least ours. We experienced prayer as a constant in our home and enjoyed the gentle nurturing that my grandfather showered on us. At the same time, we had been exposed to the coarse, sometimes raw atmosphere of the market, learning firsthand how the business world worked. We learned the value of knowing not only how to sell but also how to buy, and we saw our dad operate shrewdly, but honestly. We had worked with Dad, of course, and also had other jobs that demanded responsibility from us. All of these experiences gave us a pretty good idea about the adult world outside our home. By the time we were adolescents, we knew what was out there; I guess you could say we weren't naïve about life.

Still, there remained many things within the Lebanese tradition that we found troubling, and some things that we unequivocally rejected. The beauty of having John around as I was growing up was that we talked about a lot of things that were going on in the family and maybe allowed ourselves to make judgments that we might not otherwise have been able to make.

Without doubt, growing up in Wilkes-Barre, we had an identity as Lebanese. It's true that we pushed past the boundaries of that identity with school, friends, and other interests. We loved the traditional Lebanese food, the music, the card playing, and the fellowship and support of a very extended family. But there were things that disturbed both John and me. They weren't things that could be easily changed. Maybe the best way to describe them would to be to call them *attitudes*. We witnessed attitudes toward death, family feuds, education, and the choice of life's work. Some of those attitudes we came to identify as Old World, then Lebanese and, possibly later, on a broader scale, Middle Eastern. In the 1980s, when John and I first visited Lebanon, we experienced some of those same attitudes, deeply ingrained, alive and well—almost fifty years later.

Some of these attitudes were very evident in my mother's behaviors. I always measured Mom as overly scrupulous. She was a very good and holy woman, but she went far beyond that. Maybe because my dad was so aggressive, she hid behind the aura of holiness. Nevertheless, as we already said, Mom was a somewhat complex person. She was born in Clearfield, Pennsylvania, the daughter of Sadie Elia and Samuel Sahd, a very authoritative father. Her father owned a dry goods store, and was much more successful than my dad's father when it came to making a living.

When Mom was very young, her father, Samuel Sahd, heard that his father had taken a vow that he would not eat meat unless he saw his son Samuel again. Samuel's father, of course, still lived in Lebanon. Mom's dad, Samuel, hearing of the oath, packed up his entire family and went back to Lebanon. So in spite of the fact that my mother was American, she was taken back and lived for some time in Lebanon, where I guess she absorbed a lot of Lebanese culture. Her sister Mamie was actually married in Lebanon. As Samuel decided that they were able to return to America, the family left by boat and, for a while, became ensconced in France—which explains why my mother spoke French. Mom's dad became ill when they were there, and that's why they stayed in France. After a year there, the Sahd family returned to Pennsylvania, where my mother grew up. By then, she had a mixture of the old world and the new.

Mom was well aware of the old traditions and was, herself, promised in marriage by her father to a man named Jimmy. When she eloped with my dad, instead, she was responsible for her father being accused of having broken his word. That set of circumstances tells us something about this mother of ours. She was a steely character. And if there is one thing I know about my mother, it is that, once she made up her mind about something, she would not be deterred. Maybe she learned that from her father, maybe not; maybe she learned it from her mother. At any rate, John and I have surmised that the home she was reared in made her a match for Dad: No matter how tough he seemed, she was just as tough. She always stood her ground.

# Voices of Discernment

She brought many things with her from the old world. Many were good, but one of the things that we rejected totally was her response to death. It's important to note, too, that the kind of response Mom had was not exclusive to her. We saw it throughout the entire extended family.

Even our earliest experiences of death, John and I discussed. We had all of those discussions tucked inside of us as we went into the 50s. I was still at King's and John was at Catholic University in 1950 when Gidue's wife, Grandma Esseff, died. Four years after that, we suffered the death of our sister Mae Ann. And six months after that, we buried Gidue. We dealt with each of those deaths—and many later ones—through the filter of our earliest experiences with death.

## JOHN

*"One of my earliest experiences with death was the death of Dad's sister Mae. When we lived in my grandfather's home on Prospect Street, Mae was already married, and she and her husband Bill Harry were living on their own. They had children and their family would very often come to visit us. When Mae died, she was still quite young, and she left a husband and six children behind. I was only a little more than two, but I remember that day vividly. I recall being drawn down the steps by all sorts of noise. There was screaming and wailing, though I didn't even know words for what was going on; the experience was so frightening. My father was screaming, and then I saw him hitting his head on the chimney in the kitchen. He kept hitting his head over and over, and there was blood streaming down his face. My grandmother was involved in a hysterical kind of wailing. Looking back, I know she was crazy with grief; but the kind of physical reaction was terrifying to me at the time, and it still is something I reject.*

*"The behaviors we saw were in direct opposition to what our grandfather had always told us. When we die, we go to heaven. If you believe what we had learned about dying and having eternal life, there was no place for such behavior. Yes, there's a place for grief, but what we saw was different.*

*"It's good to put things in perspective. Mae was Dad's sister. She was also Grandpa's daughter. He was about to bury his daughter. When someone asked him why he wasn't crying, he said, 'She's happy.'*

*"I am sure that response came from his great awareness of the resurrection."*

# Brothers & Fathers

When Dad's cousin Eddie Oblen died, we saw all that hysteria again. Dad punched his hand right through a door that time. John and I shared our confusion with each other, and then our rejection of the model we had. My dad, my mother—neither was a good role model. Throughout our early years, we watched them (and most of our relatives) carry on about death in a way that, to us, was completely intolerable. When somebody died, you would swear the world had ended. The women, and even some of the men, would carry on with ritualistic screaming and wailing. What we saw when death occurred in the family made no sense to us at all; after all, we had been told that, when we died, we went to heaven. Every time someone died we witnessed people involved in such bizarre behavior that we could do nothing but reject that behavior. It was almost like a show was being put on. Somehow, the worth of the dead person was measured by the amount of emotion that was displayed. But then, at some point and for no apparent reason, it all got turned off. The same people who were so inconsolable moments before would simply stop and have a smoke or a drink. Then, maybe even just minutes later, if somebody new appeared in the group, the show would go back on. That's what we saw, and John and I discussed all these things between ourselves every time they happened. As far as we were concerned, there was nothing genuine about any of it.

We always thought of my mother as a great Christian. But when Dad's mother died, my mother acted like a total pagan. She was in utter despair. She wasn't crying, she was moaning.

Grandma Esseff died in 1950 while I was still in college, and John was away at Catholic University. The particulars of that event played out in a strange way. I was studying for an exam with my friend Frank Hanlon. Frank's dad was at a black-tie function when a phone call came to the house saying that his father was needed because someone at the hospital was in critical condition. Right away, Frank and I went to pick up his dad to take him to the hospital. It all seemed pretty routine to me; I was just going along with Frank. But as we were walking into the hospital, Frank said, "That call was about your grandmother." We walked into the hospital and down the hall. When I got to the room, my dad was there. My grandmother had an embolism and, even before the doctor got there, she had died. My dad went nuts! Absolutely berserk!

In the fifties, seminarians weren't usually allowed home for funerals. But John explained to the rector how he had lived in our grandparents' house for years and felt particularly close to his grandmother. They let him come home. Once again, we had an opportunity to witness reactions that we totally rejected.

## ROSEMARY

*"When Grandmother Esseff died, I went to the funeral home for the wake; I went the evening of the rosary. It was a very large wake. I didn't know a lot of the family members, because I had just been dating George for a short time. I was a senior when she died. During the months before her death, she had gall bladder surgery and I went to visit her with George. She wanted me to check her incision, which I did. She was feeling good. But later, she developed an embolism and she died suddenly. John was at school and was informed by phone. Her death was quite unexpected.*

*"At the wake, I was sitting in the back of the room, and all the women were screaming and carrying on. As I recall, they would carry out one of the mourners who seemed to have passed out, and then another would begin the same kind of wailing. I had never witnessed anything like this; I was extremely nervous and I knew I couldn't stay there too much longer. George was busy with the family. I was somewhere I had never been before. I kept thinking, 'What is going on here? This is unbelievable.' Then again, the mourners would tell stories and reminisce for a while—but then the wailing would begin again. I remember them taking out George's aunt, Catherine Nasser. She was wailing and crying, and then she passed out. Then someone else I didn't know started to cry and then to moan, and the whole thing started all over again. They were all crying hysterically. George's dad and all the relatives seemed inconsolable.*

*"Finally, I said to George, 'I have to leave.' I knew that no one expected Grandma Esseff to die. I could understand that the family was not ready for this death, and so I figured that the shock was the reason for the response I was witnessing. But in truth, I had never seen anything like it before.*

*"Gidue was sitting silently, praying his rosary. 'God bless that man,' was all I was thinking. As an outsider at the time, Gidue seemed to me to be at peace. He had lost his wife, and he was sad, but he was silent."*

Gidue was an anomaly at his wife's funeral—as well as at many other occasions of death in the family, where this kind of response always went on. From early childhood well into adulthood, we expected this kind of crazy behavior, and we were never disappointed.

John and I discussed these responses to death—and many other things. Maybe because of these negative responses, well into our adulthood we never had a desire to go to Lebanon. We didn't feel that the Lebanese culture was something we wanted to imitate. As some of our relatives sensed that rejection in us, they were not at all pleased.

Once, shortly after he was ordained, John came home for a funeral, and the carrying on began. He actually started to scream at the people: "What kind of evil people are you? What religion do you belong to? Do you believe [this person] is gone to heaven? Then why are you acting like he's gone to hell?"

Needless to say, they didn't like what he was saying at all. They criticized the hell out of him. They said everything about him—the least of which was how insensitive he was. Strangely enough, it was Dad who eventually began to change—perhaps partly in defense of John. But then others began to change too. That change, though, came only by small degrees and over a long period of time.

When my mother's brother Frank died at 58, Mom reverted to a lot of that crazy behavior. In 1955, when our own sister Mae Ann died, we had much to deal with besides our grief.

Besides the reactions to death, John and I used to talk about other things that were going on in the family. There was always a feud: with a cousin, or a brother-in-law, or someone. No matter who the person in question was, everybody was supposed to draw lines in the sand. We knew that our godfather, Bill Harry, had fallen from favor when his wife, my Dad's sister Mae, had died. My grandmother's sister, Catherine Khoury, acted as though Uncle Bill was responsible for her death, because Mae had had so many children. No one was looking for facts. The whole situation was totally illogical. John and I would discuss these never-ending emotional judgments. Those discussions brought both of us to an understanding of the family dynamics well above what our chronological years might normally have allowed.

I always got along great with one of my uncles who was more often 'out' than 'in' favor with the family. We were always advised as to who was 'in' and who was 'out' of favor at any given moment, but I never let that kind of stuff influence me; neither did John. I would always go to visit my uncle whenever I came home. We'd also visited other ones who were on the other side of the feud. And there was a lot of that; someone new was banished every month.

# Father John

You can't grow up in that kind of dynamic without understanding the pressure when someone says, "You know, you've got to be careful of [the latest person who was out of favor]." But George and I wouldn't do that. We'd say, "We like the Mikes" (our first cousins). And as we became more aware of the entire situation, we knew when we went to visit the ones on the 'outside,' we were only doing what we saw my grandfather do. In all those feuds, too numerous to mention, he was always the exception. He would visit everybody in the family, in or out of favor. There were always ins and outs. There were always arguments. We were always expected to take sides. At one point, Dad didn't want us to go to see Tommy, his good friend of so many years. Yes—even his good friend fell out of favor. Dad would tolerate our going to see him, but he did his best to make us feel that we shouldn't. George and I didn't let Dad intimidate us. Since the time we were little guys, we talked about how crazy that endless fighting was, and how irrational it was that the very one we were supposed to shun one day was the very one we were to love the next.

My grandfather, Gidue, transcended all of that; none of that stuff got in his head. He didn't hate anyone. He was such a holy guy. And it's nice now to have this time to think and to sort things out. We never said, "Hey, look what Grandpa did." If he wanted to visit the Mikes, or some other segment of the family who was on the wrong side of the current disagreement, he did. And if he wanted to visit his sister, or his neighbor, or anyone else, even in the face of his wife, her sisters, and many other people agreeing that that person was a lousy person, he would still go. If anybody was sick, he would go. If anybody needed his attention or prayer or care, he went. George and I were immersed in this man's responses, both when we were just little kids and as we grew into adults. Still today I say, "Thank you, God, for Gidue."

Another aspect of the Lebanese community that George and I rejected was the idea that we would all have to get into the junk business or go into the huckstering business. Many Lebanese did not see the value of education. Dad did. He was so focused—really focused—on us getting educated that it was a given in our lives. George and I were the only ones in the family who went to college to further our education, and we have Dad to thank for that.

We went from one phase of our lives to another, but our family dynamics always went with us—in difficult times and in happy ones as well.

# CHAPTER 17

## THE HAPPIEST DAY OF MY LIFE

### *George*

On Thanksgiving Day, November 27, 1952, Rosemary and I were married. I was 21 and would turn 22 in December; Rosemary was 20 and would turn 21 in January.

A few years ago, someone asked me if I could choose only one day that I consider my happiest, which day would it be. My answer was immediate: the day I married Rosemary. I went home that day and put down some of my thoughts on paper:

> I got to thinking about how blessed I've been, how many fantastic things have happened to me over the years. And I got to thinking about the happiest moment in my life. It's true: I've done many things and have enjoyed many blessings. I remember when I bought the first new car I ever owned. I remember when I owned a Rolls Royce, owned an airplane, owned a sports fishing boat. Many, many wonderful things have happened to me. I remember when I made my first million dollars one year. All of those things were really fantastic blessings.
>
> But what was the happiest moment?
>
> When I think about that, I recall most vividly the day I got married to Rosemary. I remember walking down the aisle after we were married and feeling like I had never before felt in my life. My heart was pounding so hard; I thought it was going to come through my chest. And still today, after more than fifty years of marriage, on top of all the other blessings that I have been given, I still feel the same way. That day was the happiest one of my life; it was and still is for me the ultimate day of happiness that I have ever had.
>
> June 25, 2003

# Brothers & Fathers

I had asked my Aunt Ann's husband, Jack Kelly to be my best man; and Rosemary had asked Agnes Dorning, her sister-in-law, to be her maid of honor. She also asked my sister Marlene to be a bridesmaid.

We were married in Rosemary's parish church, St. Joseph's in Coal Township in Shamokin. The priest who performed the ceremony was the pastor, Father Reardon. We had to get permission for me to be married in the Latin rite rather than the Maronite rite. Usually, the bride made the change and married in her husband's rite; but Rosemary and I had decided that we would get married, as was also traditional, in her parish church.

---

### JOHN

"In the fall of 1952, when I returned to Catholic University, I was ordained a deacon. I would be ordained a priest in the spring of the following year. At first, I thought George and Rosemary might wait until I could officiate at their wedding. But the intensity of what he felt for her left no possibility for that.

"In November, I went to Shamokin as an ordained deacon in the Latin rite Catholic Church. There were many thoughts in my head and many feelings in my heart. I knew my brother and I would never be priests together. He was standing next to his soon-to-be wife, and the pastor of Rosemary's parish church was about to begin the ceremony. The scene was nothing I had ever envisioned, but I knew I was privileged to be there. Looking at my brother George that day, I was aware in a new and profound way of what 'happy' truly meant."

---

# CHAPTER 18

## BECOMING ROSEMARY ESSEFF

### *Rosemary*

Once George and I decided we were going to get married in November, there were many things we had to do. Mom and Dad were very happy for me. They liked George very much, and they were pleased when they met his parents. They thought the Esseffs were a good family. Everyone seemed happy about the upcoming marriage. Then there were issues concerning the wedding that made the day memorable, but unlike anything I might have anticipated. I wanted a very small wedding, because Dad had put a lot of money into my education and I knew he was pretty well strapped by the time I got out of college. I remember saying to George, "Well, now that we know we're going to get married, you need to know it's going to be a small wedding. I don't want a big to-do."

*Rosemary's engagement*

"Well, we do have big weddings."

"Too bad. My dad will be paying for the wedding, and in my family we go by the philosophy that you get what you can afford and you don't overextend yourself."

There followed some roundtable discussions that I was not too aware of. Mom and Dad, my brother Bob and his wife Agnes came to the conclusion that we should, in fact, have a little wedding, but just somewhat bigger than I wanted. We would have a reception after the wedding for the immediate families. The Esseff family's idea of 'immediate' and the Dornings' idea of 'immediate' led to more discussion; but eventually we went along and Dad announced, "Yes, I think we should do that. We will do that." And "that" resulted in something that was not my "very little wedding," but not George's "big wedding" either.

Following on the heels of the guest list of immediate family was another issue concerning photographs. I had never been much into photographs, but I was told that it was a Lebanese tradition that each of the members of the 'immediate' family (which was, not to repeat myself, quite extensive) should receive a photograph of the bride and groom for their wall, or the piano, or wherever. So we made plans to have a photo session.

When our wedding day arrived, folks came from Wilkes-Barre. Though Wilkes-Barre isn't far from Shamokin, the interstate had not yet been constructed and the trip took probably about an hour-and-a-half or more. In spite of its being Thanksgiving Day, all of George's 'immediate' family arrived. Even his brother John was able to come in from Washington.

After the marriage ceremony, we had arranged to have a reception at the local fire house, where my brother Bob was a member. That seemed a good choice because it would be inexpensive, compared to some other options.

Before the reception began, George and I and the wedding party were to get the mandated 'traditional photos' taken. Dad came along with the wedding party to the photographer's place, which was in a nearby town. We thought we could get that commitment taken care of quickly; after all, it had been prearranged. However, when we arrived at the home of the photographer, he was eating his Thanksgiving dinner. I suppose we should have taken the holiday into consideration, but we didn't—and, obviously, the photographer didn't either! We wound up waiting and waiting for *hours*. We were pacing and trying to make little, light conversation that was going nowhere. And while we waited, the guests at the wedding reception waited and waited and waited for something to eat. No meal came.

It got to the point, as George and I learned later, that guests were calling out, "Where are you? Where are you?"

At the photographer's home, Dad was growing more and more impatient. "If he doesn't come out soon, we're gone. Whether they like it or not, there'll be no pictures."

Dad wasn't the only one who was annoyed. Our Lebanese guests at the firehouse were particularly annoyed. There was nothing served and my mother was getting very upset. She was the one who had to deal with all of the "Where are they?" inquiries—something she was also wondering, herself.

# Becoming Rosemary Esseff

With not many alternatives available, my mother kept trying to keep things quiet, and she kept announcing to anyone within earshot, "Have another glass of wine," or "Why don't you have a glass of beer?" No doubt, she wanted to scream, "Get happy, everybody! This is a happy occasion."

Well, at that point, it wasn't a very happy occasion.

Mom was a bit annoyed. And Dad was very annoyed. He was not one bit happy about spending his daughter's wedding day at the home of a photographer who obviously was not much of a businessman. Finally, Dad blurted out, "These goddamn pictures are going to be finished soon … or never!" By that time, we had been at the photographer's for about three-and-a-half hours. We were all at our wits' ends. I was trying to keep Dad from … I didn't even know what. All I could hear was his muttered comments underneath his breath: "Goddamn pictures … son of a bitch … who needs these goddamn pictures anyway?" I was accustomed to Dad's swearing—but only when he was highly agitated. And who could blame him? Dad was with us while his guests were in a firehouse in a different town!

Mom was at the firehouse with the guests. She was trying to make it clear that her daughter and her son-in-law were trying to get photos taken for the very ones who were doing the most com-plaining. Eventually, at a lot of emotional expense, the photographs were taken and we left the photographer. Dad continued his swearing until the well-known Dorning glare appeared on his face; and when that happened, Dad became quiet. There was no quick fix in situations like this. We knew the best thing to do was to let him alone until he simmered down. Of course, there was no chance of

*The long-awaited wedding photo*

that happening under the circumstances. By the time we arrived and were standing in the doorway, I can honestly say, my "Irish" was up. I was as angry and upset as I could be.

No sooner had we come into the hall than this little Lebanese man and my father-in-law came in, and all I heard were the words, "Where the hell were you? Were you out driving around town? We've been waiting and waiting. Everybody's hungry." I had known George's dad long enough to know that this was vintage Joe Esseff—saying exactly what was on his mind! Then Mr. Mike, the little man with

Joe, started yelling and flailing his arms like a bantam rooster. I didn't have any idea what he was saying (it was in Arabic, after all), but I did know he was registering a very strong complaint. My exact words I can't remember, but they weren't kind and they weren't sweet. I was about to blow this whole thing off. As the time went by ever so slowly, the Dorning stress level stayed in high gear.

By this point, I'm sure the Esseffs were wondering, "Who needs this Irish crowd and all their hostility brought into our clan?"

Then something wonderful happened. My mother looked at me and commanded, "You go over there. Sit down at that table." Then she looked at George's father and she said, "Joe, you get over there. Sit at that table—and you keep quiet! I don't want to hear another word from anybody." Then she turned to my father, and she said, "Doc, sit down and let's get this celebration started." Mother and Bob and Agnes could always turn things around. And they did—even while Dad and I were still simmering. The mood changed; finally, it was a happy day. From then on, the reception was a lot of fun.

With the formalities over, George and I went to Canada for our honeymoon. I wanted to go to Quebec, so we drove there, just missing snow storms that were always two days behind us. I enjoyed everything along the way. George was very patient, stopping at every tourist spot. I just knew when this trip was over I would become a 'hausfrau.' I was never going to get out of the kitchen and the laundry room, never have an opportunity to travel and see the country—let alone the world! God does have a great sense of humor! He must have been amused at my take on things at that time.

When we got back to Wilkes-Barre, we had a big reception at George's mom and dad's family home on Moyallen Street. All of the relatives who hadn't been invited to the "little reception" were there to greet us. We were toasted as we sat down to an elaborate Lebanese dinner. There were loads and loads of people and the toasting went on and on. They toasted the young bride. They toasted the groom. They toasted the wedding couple. My father-in-law stood up and announced, "And the first child's name will be John!" I was flabbergasted.

"Who in the hell? Where is he coming from? Where do we go from here?" Those were my thoughts. I was ready to take my place in the family: "Over my dead body. It's our child. No way! His father is George, not John. If I name a child, it'll be after his father—if the child is a boy!" Talk about pressure.

No sooner was that put to rest than Joe started to tell me (and everyone else) about what happened on wedding days years before. The wedding couple would

# Becoming Rosemary Esseff

stay their first night of marriage in the home of one of the sets of the parents. In the morning, the groom would take the sheets from the nuptial bed and toss them out to make sure that everyone knew, 'God bless her! She's a virgin!'

I said, "Oh, that's an old, old country tradition. That wasn't carried over here."

"Oh, yes, it was!" He spoke as if his memory served him well.

Old traditions die slowly—but fortunately, that was one we skipped.

All of the people who came brought wedding gifts—there were many, many, many gifts. The guests would hand me or George envelopes that I knew had money in them; and, eventually, all of the envelopes were collected and put somewhere—I guess for safe keeping. Time went by quickly while I talked to the people who were there and tried to figure out who was who. At one point, I couldn't see George, or Mom, or Marlene, and I went to find them. Well, I came upon them upstairs going through all of the cards and counting the money. I didn't know what to say, but I heard my own voice: "Be sure all of that is put back in the envelopes that they came out of so I can write 'thank you' notes to the people who gave us the gifts."

George's mom was clear enough: "Well, we wanted to know who gave what, because we have gone to many weddings over the years."

Marlene added, "We want to know who gave you gifts and what they are."

To be honest, I was a bit shaken. But I knew these kinds of experiences are all part of getting married. You don't marry just the man; you marry the man's family, too.

That was my introduction to the Esseff clan. But I knew I was now a part of the clan, too. It was all an interesting new experience for me.

After the party, George and I stayed overnight in Wilkes-Barre. We began the trip to Virginia and stopped in Shamokin, where we saw Mom and Dad. We enjoyed some family gatherings, collected our wedding gifts, and left for Virginia. George was driving his familiar route—but this time, I was with him.

While we lived at Fort Belvoir, George and I spent time with his brother John, who was still at Catholic University. Sometimes we'd go into D.C. to meet John; he'd always be in one of the most terrible parts of the city ministering to the street people. More often, John would call and say, "I'm going to bring a few guys over for dinner if that's OK." The first time, we said, "Fine! We'll put on some pasta." Then John would show up with eight or ten guys. That was quite a crowd in our one-bedroom apartment! We didn't have a pot big enough to cook two pounds of spaghetti. So all evening, we'd be boiling pots of water again and again until we had enough spaghetti cooked for everyone. They were a nice bunch of guys and we enjoyed doing that sort of thing—which is good, because we did it often! We had a lot of fun together. John and I had come a long way from our initial encounter, and we have continued to grow in love and friendship through these many years.

In fact, the difficulties and tensions that were part of our wedding day proved to be quite unlike the kinds of relationships that developed between George and me and his family as the years continued. I must say: I enjoyed the family—so full of very spirited, unique people. I had the good fortune to meet George's grandparents when we were dating. I enjoyed his grandmother, "Sithue," for the short while I knew her. God took her before I had the chance to really get to know her better. His grandfather was a very spiritual man—a kind and loving soul. What isn't always recounted about him is that he was also a wonderful storyteller, with a beautiful and ready smile for all of us. As we said, George's dad was the oldest in his family, and he had a lot of younger siblings. His sisters, though they were George's aunts, weren't that much older than us. George's Aunt Catherine and her husband Bill Nasser became close friends of ours. They lived in Scranton, and their children were close in age to ours. When we were living there, they introduced us to their many friends and included us in a very extensive network of socializing. Catherine was a very special person—very able to cheer people up, no matter how depressing things could be. George's Aunt Ann, the youngest auntie, eventually married Jack Kelly. But before that time, George and I very often double dated with Ann and Jack, and had many, many wonderful times together when we were still single. Even after we moved to the West coast, they would often come to visit, and we have had a close, lasting relationship throughout our long lives. Even though distance separated us for most of the years, we kept those close ties. Not only our children, but some of our grandchildren, visited and enjoyed the entire Kelly clan. Jack passed away in 2002. How we miss him!

We enjoyed a greater proximity to George's Aunts Sarah and Marian over the years. When we moved to California, they decided to come to the West coast, too. Both Sarah and Marian were more like older sisters to me than in-laws. George was so good to them, and they were always fun to be with.

George and I were also able to connect with his Uncle Tony and Aunt Joyce, a lovely lady from the U.K. who married Tony during World War II. And then, of course, there is George's Uncle Peter, five years George's junior. When we were young, Peter was off to the seminary, just after graduating high school. During that time, I didn't really know him well. Later, Peter left the seminary and married Mary, and as the years unfolded, we became not only family, but friends as well.

# Becoming Rosemary Esseff

And so, in spite of some tense moments, George and I began the art of becoming a family on that Thanksgiving Day in November 1952. My marriage brought me into a wonderful, warm family, who have brought a lot of happiness into my life—the kind of happiness that I wouldn't have had otherwise, because my family was small. I thought it was great to be in the middle of so many varied personalities, to experience the culture of such interesting people, and to grow in love and admiration for those older members of the family who endured great difficulties in order to come to America to make a life here for so many wonderful people.

At Fort Belvoir, long before we knew how blessed we were—and would be— the particulars of our life together began to come into place. I took an accounting job at the Officers' Club as part of settling in. Having acquired a strong background in accounting while I was in high school, I was very suited to the work. George continued his work with the Army Corps of Engineers, where very exciting things were happening. One of the multiple projects he had been working on eventually resulted in our taking a path that neither of us could have ever imagined.

# CHAPTER 19

## ARMY CORPS OF ENGINEERS LAB

## *George*

Before Rosemary and I were married, and while she stayed in Wilkes-Barre to finish her senior year at College Misericordia, I was out launching my career. I had decided I wasn't going to medical school and, after looking around at several possibilities, I decided to take a job as a chemist and metallurgist with the Army Corps of Engineers at Fort Belvoir in Virginia. I still think I would have made a damn good doctor, but that's the way it worked out. I stayed with the government for the next four years. I had great training for the different kinds of work I did there during those years, and I used every science that I had studied in college: biology, chemistry, and physics. Like everyone else, I had no idea what lay ahead.

Early on in my work with the Army Corps, I found myself back in the business of burlap. But this time, I wasn't saving it and selling it like I did when I was a kid! Burlap was needed for sandbags, and also as protection for guns. Because of the on-going Korean conflict, burlap was in very short supply and we were looking to develop a substitute for it. I was involved with a paper company, and what we did was develop a paper that would function as a sandbag. We did the research and they did the manufacturing. The paper was impregnated with plastics and, eventually, was able to be used as sandbags. That was only one of many projects. In the materials lab, we really worked on anything and everything. One time, I categorized all the Russian ballistics, from a little percussion cap to land mines. All that material was classified. I'd have a meeting with the CIA every week. They would be collecting all that stuff over in Korea and we would analyze it. When we gave them our data, they could then determine where the mines or other gathered materials were being made, and how they were being made. They wanted that information so that, if the troops were involved in a skirmish, they had enough information to cut off the supplies to the enemy. I also analyzed jet fuels and paints and other materials that were being used in one project or another. The work was interesting and I enjoyed it.

# Brothers & Fathers

During that first year, and while I was still single, I received clearance for working on classified materials, and I worked on several top-secret projects. During the ongoing Korean conflict, there were enemy soldiers who could move through the trees like monkeys and cause a lot of damage. The government wanted to develop night vision equipment to spot and eliminate those guys. Previously, after World War II, the government had captured a German scientist who had spent some time in jail. After the war ended, he accepted the option of taking a job with the Army Corps of Engineers. He brought the technology for night vision equipment to us and started a program. I worked with him. I was, more or less, his lackey—doing basic stuff. But I was part of the project.

Some of what we did was to grow crystals. We would take a crystal, each the size of one grain of sugar or one grain of salt, and we would grow it until it was the size we needed for the lenses which we were developing to use as part of a sniper scope for rifles. The crystals were growing continuously and I had to check them all the time. I would go back to the lab at night. Watching a crystal grow was like watching a seed grow. It took twenty-four days to get the crystals to the size we needed. Each crystal was very clear. We'd then slice it and make the lenses. Those lenses would be used in making sniper scopes for rifles that would allow soldiers to see at night.

As part of a daily routine while we were working on this project, I was involved in brainstorming meetings. One particular meeting in 1951 was spearheaded by some people from Crucible Steel who were presenting a new metal which had just been produced for the first time. The government bought, and gave to the Corps of Engineers, twenty tons of the material in different shapes and told us to see what we could do with it. They gave us a list of the properties of the metal. The main ones were that it was very lightweight but, at the same time, it was very strong. It also had a very high corrosion resistance. The metal was titanium.

I continued my work on the sniper scope. Once the crystals were grown and the sniper scope was made, the next step was to put the scope itself into a housing. The government wanted us to develop this housing with a jet-black, non-reflective finish so the moon wouldn't shine off the scope and give away the position of the soldier. The housing for the sniper scope was to be made of aluminum, and the aluminum had to be anodized. Over the years, I've been criticized by some of my family for not really explaining that process. For the record, I'll try to clarify it now.

Used in the laboratory, anodizing allows controlled corrosion and brings a substance to a point where it will not corrode further. When aluminum corrodes naturally, aluminum oxide results and the surface becomes porous. When aluminum is anodized, the anodizing process puts the oxide on it. Once the aluminum has the oxide on it, the aluminum becomes porous on the surface. It then has the property of absorption. The aluminum can then be put in very hot, distilled water and, by means of a chemical reaction, the aluminum gets a hydroxyl inside the pores and seals it. The aluminum will no longer corrode. However, if, before you seal it, you put it into a dye solution, the aluminum will take the color and then it can be sealed. This was the procedure I was using to dye the sniper scope black.

As I continued with the sniper scope project, I needed a rack to hold the pieces that had to be anodized. I decided to test the new metal that we had received from Crucible Steel, to see if it would be suitable as material for that rack. Each part that was to be anodized had to be placed on a rack. I put the titanium, to which I had affixed a piece of aluminum, into the anodizing solution. And when I put a current to it, the aluminum anodized beautifully, just like it would have on the aluminum rack; but nothing happened to the titanium. It just turned a little blue from the electro chemical reaction, but it didn't further erode. I could take another piece of aluminum and put it on, then put it through the anodizing process again. It would anodize the aluminum, but the titanium resisted the corrosion. Prior to that time, I was using aluminum alone. The aluminum rack would deteriorate each time it was anodized, because each time I anodized the metal a certain amount of surface came off. The metal gets thinner and thinner as you use it. However, what I discovered was that, unlike aluminum, the titanium resisted the corrosion and could, as a result, be used repeatedly in the anodizing process.

It worked so well I decided to make an adjustable rack of titanium. I came up with a concept of having T slots (little bolts) in the rack. We had a model laboratory that would make things we needed as we researched a project. I sent a drawing of the rack to the men in the lab. They sent the model back; it was about six inches wide and 18 inches long. It featured mobile contact points, which meant that the model had separate and complete units that could be moved along a track to the desired dimension, set by means of a lock-nut to provide effective and excellent electrical contact. The end result was that we had an anodizing rack that would not deteriorate and, consequently, could be used again and again. It was adaptable to many parts and I didn't have to make an individual rack to do each part, as I had had to do before. I could put any size part on the rack, and so I used one rack for all the parts—ten different parts in the assembly. I used the rack, then, to continue my work, because it saved time and money.

I didn't consider what I was doing to be much different than other things I had done previously. All projects demanded getting the job done as quickly and effectively as I could. One day, however, without my even realizing it, the course of my life changed when a patent attorney came to the lab. It was common practice for him to walk through the lab every three months or so. He stopped by my area and asked me what I was doing. I showed him the rack, and told him about the new metal.

He was quite interested. After some observation and discussion he said, "I think this is certainly an idea that should be patented. Yes—we should apply for a patent." Of course, I said "OK." He asked me to prepare a written description of the process so he could begin the procedure of applying for a patent. And honestly, it was very shortly thereafter, probably early 1953, when the patent was granted. Of course, the patent was granted to the government but, because I had done the work of developing the rack, my name was also on the patent. That fact would turn out to be very significant—though, at the time, I don't remember thinking about it too much.

I had a lab and I found my work interesting. I did all sorts of things, including anodizing and plating. Another interesting feature of the job was that the Army Corps had testing grounds for whatever project we were working on at any given time—all over the country. I used to go to Florida for high, very moist testing, or to Arizona for high, dry-climate testing. I also went to Canada whenever there was a need for deep-freeze testing.

Those many current projects were on my mind more than any one project I had worked on previously, and I enjoyed the travel and hands-on investigative work. In fact, I didn't think any more about the visit of the patent attorney until news of the patent on the rack was published in one of the metal finishing journals. Because my name was listed in the patent, I started to get a great number of calls from people requesting how and where they could get a similar rack made of titanium. Shortly afterward, I began to see the extent of the need for these racks; I knew I had to do some systematic investigatory work so I could make a better assessment of the situation. If the need was as great as it

*Invents Rack*

GEORGE ESSEFF

George J. Esseff, son of Mr. and Mrs. Joseph Esseff of 113 Moyallen Street, and a fellow chemist at the Corps of Engineers' Research and Development Laboratories, Fort Belvoir, Va., has designed and fabricated a versatile rack for anodizing aluminum and magnesium alloys.

Esseff, who attended St. Mary's High School, received his training in chemistry and biology at King's College, where he was with the 1951 graduating class. He was active in the Academy of Biological Sciences, Bowling Club, Monogram Club, Sodality, and participated in varsity wrestling.

The invention is made of aluminum and pure titanium, and is designed to accommodate jobs requiring racks of a wide variety of sizes and shapes. The rack features mobile contact points. Separate and complete units, they can be moved along a track to the desired dimension and set by means of a lock-nut to provide effective and excellent electrical contact.

Great savings have been realized in money, time, materials and storage space by the use of three of these racks at the Fort Belvoir laboratories. The three facilitated anodizing jobs which would ordinarily required as many as 60 racks of different dimensions. In common practice, it is necessary to rely upon racks that fit the dimensions of a particular job to anodize aluminum and magnesium alloys. This results in an expensive stockpiling of racks with future limited use.

*George's invention*

seemed to be, I knew I would have to negotiate for commercial rights to the rack. I was open to doing whatever needed to be done.

All of these developments took place over a long period of time and served as a backdrop for family matters. Most importantly, in the spring of 1953, Rosemary discovered that she was pregnant. We were happy to learn that we would have a baby in December. We were also looking forward to John's ordination in May. It was a great time for us, and we were looking forward to good days ahead.

# CHAPTER 20

## ORDINATION: MY RITE OF PASSAGE

### *Father John*

I was ordained to the priesthood in St. Peter's Cathedral in Scranton, Pennsylvania. On my fifty-third anniversary of priesthood, I recorded some thoughts about that day. There has been more to my life than my priesthood; but, without question, priesthood has dominated everything in my life. I would say that all my life, I wanted to be a priest.

On May 30, 1953, I was lying on the floor at St. Peter's Cathedral in Scranton. I had made a retreat at St. Anne's Monastery, and there were ten of us who were going to be ordained. I really loved my seminary career. I felt prepared. And that morning I remember thinking, "What is about to happen is the greatest thing in my life." When I first approached the Diocese of Scranton for entrance into the seminary (eight years earlier), it was Father Koury who took me to Scranton. I was still in high school at the time. Now, at last, there I was prostrate on the sanctuary floor, about to be ordained a priest.

That day, I couldn't believe my blessedness, my good fortune, my happiness, my joy at being selected. It's been said, "You have not chosen me. I have chosen you." Well, God, I thought I was choosing you, but really, you were choosing me. That day I was so full of enthusiasm, and energy, and joy. I had complete confidence that I would be a good priest. I was an ordained deacon and had come with four other candidates whom I had known in Wilkes Barre: Anthony Conmy, Dick Frank, Cyril Hudak, and Clem Markowski. They have all since gone to the Lord. Far away in Lebanon, another of my friends from St. Mary's High School was also being ordained in the Maronite rite: That was George Webby, made famous by my own brother George on that infamous night of the minstrel show, so many years before.

There I was, wearing a white robe and my deacon's stole. I still remember lying on the floor in that beautiful cathedral. Bishop Hafey was raising his hands over us and the rite of ordination had begun. I'll never forget it, because I knew that this was the moment when a transformation was taking place. When I stood up, I felt my back and my sides; I felt that a peace had fallen into place within my body. I had been really incomplete; but when I rose from that floor, an ordained Catholic priest, I knew every part I needed was finally in place. This transformation was what I had been waiting for. And when the ceremony was finished, there was an in-

ner confidence in me in knowing, "I am a Catholic priest." The dream of my whole life had come true. The rest of the ceremony was very prayerful, and I was very eager to exercise my consecratory powers for the first time. Holding up our hands, we newly ordained priests concelebrated with Bishop Hafey and changed bread into the Body of Christ and wine into His Precious Blood. I was aware that the power was going through me. As I stepped down from the altar in the cathedral, I was filled with joy: "This is who I am now." I remember blessing my parents and knowing

*John's ordination photo* the reality of that power going out from me.

After the Mass of ordination, the newly ordained had a brunch with the bishop. That was nice. I was grateful, but I was thinking, "Let's get on with this. I'm ready to get out of here. I'm a priest now. I have work to do!" That was my spirit. The ceremony's over—let's get going.

That day was powerful for me, and unlike any other in my life.

I spent that night at the rectory in Wilkes-Barre, eagerly awaiting the celebration of my first Mass. As I had changed my rite, I would celebrate the Mass according to the Latin rite; but I would celebrate that Mass in the parish church of my childhood, St. Anthony's Maronite church on Park Avenue. The Mass was scheduled to begin at ten o'clock. A friend of mine, Father Frank Wuellner from Peoria, Illinois, served as my deacon. Another friend, Father Ken Dolan, a priest from the Scranton Diocese, was my subdeacon.

I was eager for that morning to come, and I was filled with anticipation as I experienced the joy of my first Mass. The thrill of the day before had well prepared me. I remember the people—so many people. My father was one of a family of ten, and my mother one of eleven. The church was filled. There were my parents, my grandparents, my relatives, my friends, and my parents' friends and neighbors. I was a priest surrounded by so much love. I was told later that people were saying, "He looks like he's done this all his life."

# Ordination: My Rite of Passage

It was the custom, at that time, to invite a priest to speak at the first Mass. I had asked Monsignor Frank Costello, the pastor of St. Mary's Church, to give the homily; but actually, I felt bad that I didn't give it myself. I wanted to experience everything, just everything. I couldn't wait 'til I could talk to the people.

After Mass, we all went to St. Aloysius Hall on Barney Street for dinner. I had just come home from Washington, where I had spent a lot of time at Fides House. I invited many of the people whom I had worked with there to come to my first Mass. Most of them were African-Americans. I remember earlier comments from the family: "You're going to have Blacks at your Mass?" I wasn't about to get into it. "They're already invited; God willing, they're on their way."

Anyway, let's be honest: Lebanese have a little color themselves, and they probably were afraid we wouldn't know who was who! At any rate, I loved the spirit that my friends from Fides House brought with them, and it was wonderful that they could come.

The evening of my first Mass, I officiated at Benediction, also held at St. Anthony's. A reception followed that, too. Along with everyone else, I had invited the Syrian Orthodox people whom I knew to come to Benediction; I blessed them and then I preached. I spent the entire day with the people. They surrounded me. They blessed me and I blessed them. The day was a day of people praying, singing, and praising God in all His glory.

I was a very happy man.

Though in Lebanon we had come from a family of priests, there had not been a priest in our family for ninety years. Traditionally, priests of the Maronite rite did marry, and the last priest in our family was a Father Stephen Sahd. I felt that I was someone for whom my whole family had been waiting. I was eager to spend time with everyone I could. According to the aforementioned existing family tradition, I also had photos of myself taken. For me, the whole process was very simple. When I went to visit my relatives, I gave each of them a picture of me, the newly ordained priest, and I blessed each of their homes.

I remember someone had given me a fountain pen as a gift for ordination. Actually, it looked like a fountain pen, but it was really a sprinkler for holy water. It was a very handy little device. I had it in my pocket as I went from home to home. In those days, fountain pens were filled with ink, and I also had a real fountain pen in my pocket. At one of the homes, I said the blessing, I pulled out the wrong pen, and I sprinkled everything and everyone in range with black ink. It was really funny. At least, it was to me. At any rate, I was forgiven.

# Brothers & Fathers

I went to every home, blessing the homes and the people living in them. I remember a friend of Dad's came to me asking if I would hear his confession. I did and it was a beautiful experience. I had hit the ground running. The excitement was exhilarating and energizing.

During those early days following ordination, I was having a wonderful time; slowly, I became accustomed to hearing a new greeting. It filled me with wonder. As a man, I had a potential family within me, but I had chosen to give that up when I dedicated myself to the priesthood.

Each time I heard the phrase, I considered what God had in store for me.

So many people I have known for a lifetime still use that title to this day. In all honesty, it's still my favorite: "Good morning, *Father*. How are you today?"

And then I know that God has great expectations of me for yet another day.

# CHAPTER 21

## FIRST ASSIGNMENT

## *Father John*

My first assignment was to be a summer mission. I learned that I was to begin my priestly duties in one of the farthest points in the diocese. I remember Mom asking, "Where is Shohola?" This question came from a woman who had traveled all over the world. Nevertheless, we started off to find Shohola, way out in Pike County, and arrived at St. Ann's Parish—the very last parish in the diocese before the New York state border. In those days before the interstate highways, it took us—well, God only knows how long—on all of those back roads.

When we got there, I met my pastor, under whose tutelage I was to serve as assistant. He was astonished during that first meeting that I got a ride there and did not have a car of my own. "My God," he said, "you can't come out here to the country without a car! You need a car, young man. What the hell are you going to do way out here without a car? You go buy a car."

I did my best to explain to him that the bishop had told me (and the other newly ordained priests) that we were not supposed to own anything, and that's why my father and mother had driven me out to the parish. His response was perfectly clear, "I don't care what the bishop said. I'm your pastor. You go and get a car!" So I was confused. Here I was with a bishop who said you can't have a car and a pastor who said you must have a car. It was my first conflict between obedience and common sense. In my youthful arrogance, I assumed that the bishop's directive had to be followed. I'm sure I also wanted to get off the hook with my new pastor.

I remember thinking, "I'll just get a car temporarily, so I can do the job that I have to do here." I then proceeded to enlist Dad in helping me to get a car.

In Wilkes-Barre, there was a used car salesman named Ray Borek. Tony Elias, my future brother-in-law, knew him and he took my dad to see him. Dad negotiated a deal with Ray and I arranged to go to Wilkes-Barre, where I bought a 1942 Hudson for $35.00. We got tags for the car and then, ready to roll, I steamed off to my parish. I had obeyed my pastor, even though I knew I was going against the wishes of my bishop. All summer, that Hudson—a real clunker—served me well. It got me to all the places I had to go within St. Ann's parish, and it transported me to each of our two outlying missions.

Shohola. What an experience that was!

Bingo. Six nights a week. Along with the other priests, I would go to all these boarding houses, the holiday accommodations for vacationers, and we would play bingo. We also had a lot to do, helping to set up the outdoor bazaars and getting other things ready. There were three picnics that summer: one at St. Ann's in Shohola, one at Sacred Heart in Greeley, and one at the Lackawaxen mission. Throughout the whole summer, we could be found pitching tents, or taking them down, having outdoor summer picnics, and, of course, playing bingo.

My family would come to see me: my mom, my dad, my younger brother Joe, and my two sisters, Marlene and Mae Ann. George and Rosemary, of course, were in Virginia. All of them loved having a priest in the family. In fact, by this time, Marlene was planning to marry George's old friend Tony Elias. She insisted on waiting until I was ordained so I could officiate at the wedding. Eventually, I did officiate at their wedding in St. Anthony's Church in January of the following year.

I was really excited about having launched into my first parish assignment. I found my pastor to be a wonderful man with a tremendous sense of humor. He was also a gifted preacher. He had a great spirit, and his generosity was out of this world. It was easy to like him. Then one night, something happened that I was totally unprepared for. I do remember coming home with the other assistant, Father Treskauskas and finding the pastor lying on the floor, obviously passed out, drunk. I was shocked; Father Treskauskas wasn't. I asked him, "Does this happen a lot?"

"Once in a while," was all he said. He gave me a great lesson that night in how to be kind to a fellow priest who was suffering from a debilitating disease. We picked up the pastor, carried him to his room, and put him into his bed. That was the first of many episodes of the pastor's drinking that summer.

The three of us continued to work together and, for the most part, things went smoothly. The pastor's drinking episodes were intermittent, and generally, in spite of them, it became clear that the pastor loved us, and we loved him. People in the parish were aware (to varying degrees) of his drinking problem. They were very gentle with him and showed a lot of compassion. I learned a lot from them—and got over some of my brittleness.

# First Assignment

Another drinking incident happened during the church picnic on the parish grounds. We knew the pastor had been drinking, and so we locked him in his room. We were hoping he would sleep throughout the festivities. But finding himself locked in, he crawled out the window. All of his people saw him. Barely able to walk, he fell down, obviously drunk. I was so strong then. I picked him up in my arms and, with tears in my eyes, carried him into the rectory. I was weeping because I thought he had scandalized his people. I had a lot to learn.

The following Sunday, a man who was very obviously present at the picnic and saw the pastor drunk, was in the congregation waiting for Mass to begin. When no altar server showed up, I was really amazed when that same man came to the altar and served the Mass for the pastor. I understood the depth of that parishioner's capacity for compassion. At that time in my life, that man's kindness toward the pastor far exceeded mine, and he taught me a lot. It wasn't until years later that I began to learn more about the ravages of alcoholism in the lives of so many people.

My pastor eventually got sober. But, for a time, he was a very broken man. That first summer in Shohola was the first experience I had with an alcoholic priest, but it taught me that there were lessons to be learned every day, and opportunities for me to grow.

At the end of the summer, I left Shohola to spend a few days at home before I went to my next assignment. I got as far as Pittston, about eight miles from Wilkes-Barre, when the Hudson broke down; then I hitch-hiked the rest of the way home. When I got there, I made a phone call to Ray Borek, the guy who had sold me the car. I wanted to see if he could help me out. Ray bought back the Hudson he had sold me for $35.00, giving me $25.00 dollars for it. That was a business deal that even Dad could appreciate!

I did say that I was going to keep the car only until I did the job I had to do in Shohola. I could only assume that God was keeping me honest.

# CHAPTER 22

## ST. MATTHEW'S PARISH

### *Father John*

In September of that same year, 1953, I left my summer assignment at St. Ann's parish in Shohola and went to my next assignment, in East Stroudsburg, Pennsylvania. I left Pike County and moved to St. Matthew's in Monroe County.

There I shared the rectory with my pastor and one other assistant, Father Francis Barrett. St. Matthew's was a vast parish, encompassing 200 square miles, and located on the edge of the diocese. Even though there were three priests assigned to the parish, there was a lot of territory to cover and a lot of work to do. There were four different churches that were considered part of the parish: St. Matthew's, St. Mark's, St. Luke's, and St. John's, named for the four evangelists. I know my family had been hoping that I would be assigned closer to home, maybe in Wilkes-Barre or Scranton, but my bishop had other ideas. For the next fourteen years, until I went to Latin America in 1967, I served at St. Matthew's. It's difficult for me to adequately express the happiness I had during those first years of priesthood.

I can honestly say that all of the skills I needed to function as a parish priest I learned there. I learned how to deal with the aging in nursing homes. I learned how to deal with the suffering, visiting Monroe County Hospital almost every day. I learned how to deal with college students, as East Strousburg State College was located in the parish. I learned to deal with prisoners in the Monroe County Prison. All of the county institutions were located within the perimeter of that 200-square-mile area. I was eager to serve as I went from one place to another.

We had four churches and we celebrated Masses in all of them. We didn't have a lot of supervision. That changed in 1954, when Bishop Hannan came to Scranton to fill the chair left by Bishop Hafey; Bishop Hafey, the bishop who had ordained me, had died a short time earlier. Bishop Hannan soon developed a reputation for freezing people in their assignments. Every priest who had an assignment knew that he would not be relocated for years to come; very rarely did the bishop make any changes. Besides that practice, there were other things we had to get used to. We got to calling the new bishop, "Canon Hannan." He insisted that only one priest could trinate (i.e., say three Masses in a single day). That was canon law. Furthermore, the priest who was given the privilege of trination could not say all of those Masses in the same church. For all the years I was at St. Matthew's, I had the privilege and the responsibility of trination. What that meant was that, according to the rules then in effect, every Sunday I had to observe the fast from midnight until all of my Masses were celebrated. I would have Mass at St. Matthew's in East Strouds-burg. Then I would drive to St. Luke's in Stroudsburg. And, finally, I would go to St. John's in Bushkill Falls. It was mission country; and after I drove to the mission, I set up the altar, heard confessions, celebrated the Eucharist, met the people, closed the church, and made sure everything was secure when I left. Traveling from one church to another was not new for me: In Shohola, we also had mission churches. What was new at St. Matthew's was observing the fasting rules while traveling so many miles between churches. A headache generally accompanied me on Sundays as I traveled from church to church. I had nothing to eat from bedtime on Saturday night until Sunday afternoon, when I finished celebrating all three Masses. It was a challenge to drive all those miles without eating anything. I often wondered what my first pastor's response to that situation might have been. Nevertheless, whenever I had the opportunity to go home on Sunday afternoons, I accepted the additional challenge of driving more miles to Wilkes-Barre, where I enjoyed a great Lebanese meal with my family.

A little hunger or a headache was a small price to pay. I loved St. Matthew's—I loved the people there. At the time, only 10% of the people in the county were Catholic, and I had hundreds of converts during those fourteen years. What a challenge it was to teach, and to preach while I visited the hospitals and the nursing homes and the prison. When I was the Newman Club chaplain at East Strouds-burg State College, it was a time when vocations were flourishing. I saw many young college women go to the convent, and many young men join seminaries. I was also in charge of the CCD program intended for the instruction of children. We had an attendance rate of 98%. I taught the high school seniors and I also taught the other teachers. We had what we called "fishers"—those who would go out and bring the children to classes. The teachers were dedicated and enthusiastic. We all had a great time, and it was there that I acquired all the tools a parish priest would need.

Not only did I minister to the people of the parish, but I was also eager to officiate at family events. In the fall of that first year, I had been asked by my Aunt Ann and her husband, Jack Kelly, to baptize their first child, Maria. I remember it was All Saints' Day—Sunday, November 1st. Without telling the pastor, after I finished my Masses for the day, I borrowed the parish car, slipped down into Wilkes-Barre, baptized Maria, and began to make my way back to East Stroudsburg (because I had Masses the next day, All Souls' Day). When I got to the VA Hospital on the edge of Wilkes-Barre, an elderly gentleman pulled out and plowed into the side of my car. After the initial confusion, I realized that I was pretty banged up. My face was cut and bruised and my hand seemed broken. I was in a lot of pain, but I got out of the car to see if the other driver was hurt. I recognized the man: He was the owner of the amusement park at Harvey's Lake. Good news: He was uninjured. Bad news: My car was pretty smashed up. Really bad news: It wasn't my car! "What the hell is my pastor going to say to me?"

I knew my dad and the rest of the family were still at the party that followed the baby's christening. I decided to call my cousin Jake Mike, and he came to help me out. I remember we went into the VA Hospital. I did get my first medical attention there, but because I wasn't a veteran, they couldn't keep me there; I would have to go to another hospital for the kind of care I was going to need. There were also other matters, just as important. I had to call the rectory and let my pastor know what had happened. When Father Barrett answered, I told him that I had cracked up the parish car. As he relayed the message, I could hear the pastor: "You tell that young man he's got three Masses scheduled for tomorrow and he'd better get back here." That was my pastor.

Instead of taking me back to East Stroudsburg, Jake took me to Wilkes-Barre to let the family know what had happened. My dad wanted me to stay there and get some medical attention. I told him I was going back to the rectory. My dad was wild. He was ready to kill my pastor, and called him a string of names it's better not to repeat. I said, "Dad, you're not my boss; he is. I'm going back and I'm going to have those Masses. I don't care what you say."

"You need to . . ."

"I don't need to do anything but have those Masses."

It was a crisis of authority for me. Who was I to submit to? It was an instantaneous decision. My pastor told me to come back and that was what I was going to do. My father didn't want to see my pastor at all, so my cousin Jake drove me back to the rectory.

There were lots of tense moments that night. But the next day was All Souls' Day, and I was slated for three Masses. I did celebrate those Masses; but, as all the details became clearer, my hand was obviously broken, and finally the pastor got some awareness of how important it was for me to get medical attention.

My dad came up to East Stroudsburg and took me to the Monroe County Hospital. After a long while in the waiting room, it became obvious that my case wasn't getting first priority. Never a man of great patience, Dad said, "Let's get the hell out of here," and he drove me back to the Mercy Hospital in Wilkes-Barre.

When we got to the hospital, there was a Mercy Sister there who was a nurse, and initially she took care of me. "These are the hands of a priest. If your hand stays this way, you're going to have gnarled hands as you get older. I'm going to see that you get the best doctor we have." As far as I'm concerned, that's exactly what she did.

That was one of many times in my life that I had the care of a really good doctor. In fact, if I could give a tribute to another profession, it would be the medical profession. All my life I have met wonderful doctors. That day I met Dr. McNelis, an orthopedic surgeon. He rigged up something that kept the bones in my hand in the correct position to heal. It was an ingenious thing. He drilled through my fingers and hooked up a sling-like mechanism that reduced the tension. I actually looked like I was carrying a sling shot in my hand. I was able to go back to St. Matthew's the same day, November 2nd, and I was able to carry on my duties.

One of those duties involved talking to the people. I loved them and I loved talking to them. I especially loved having the opportunity to preach. In no time, the word was out that I wasn't shy about what I said from the pulpit. The rumor mill had it that some of the pastor's friends, mostly power people in the diocese, had made some comments about me. One of them had referred to me as "the hot shot new priest from Catholic University." That was OK. I was preaching the gospel. Some of them thought I was audacious, even disrespectful. Of course, what they were saying was based on hearsay. They found things to say about my manner, my casualness. They thought I seemed very much at home in the pulpit, maybe even too comfortable. But I continued to do what I had been doing. The pastor never said a word to me about my preaching.

Dad did. He and Mom used to ride out to Stroudsburg sometimes for Sunday Mass. They heard my sermons and they were pretty used to hearing things about me, because I was very involved with different groups in and out of the parish. One day, when the topic of my being quoted came up, Dad reminded me of something he had heard me say: "You people living here in Stroudsburg are so used to people on vacation, you forget that life is not a vacation, certainly not a vacation from the commandments. I go from place to place and the message I'm getting is that 'if we could put poles on the four corners of this part of the Poconos, and throw a roof on top of them, we'd have the biggest whorehouse in Pennsylvania.' Is this what your children are hearing too? Is that what you want to tell them is the way it should be? Well, it's out there!"

Dad would remind me that my language was sometimes very strong. I guess he forgot the days of the market, where I first learned those words. I thought they were accurate. Some people thought they should never be heard in a church. One of those was Josephine, a parishioner of St. Matthew's. She called the rectory one day to say, "If that young priest is going to be preaching this weekend, tell him I'm taking some friends to Mass from out of town. He needs to watch what he says."

Preaching aside, my pastor and I had some strong clashes during those early years. As time went on, I realized that there was another dimension at work, and that was the fact that this pastor came from an era of very autocratic priests. He knew I was obedient, but we went head-to-head many times during those years. I know he did get very upset with me.

One of those occasions took place in late November, just before the start of Advent. I went to the school to see the kids and to tell them that we were

> ## GEORGE
>
>
>
> *"There's another side to that coin. During that time, there was always a sermon on Sunday, but not one during the week. When John had the daily Mass, he would give a sermon. It would only be a few minutes— just some remarks about the readings for the day. He was very effective. People were hearing the beautiful things he was saying, and more and more people began to attend daily Mass. He had a message people wanted to hear."*

going to make an Advent wreath in preparation for Christmas. I had spoken to the sisters and arranged for them to meet me in the auditorium, where we could make the wreaths together. We had everything we needed, and we had plenty of room to work. The kids had never done this; I thought I was helping them to prepare for the coming of Christmas in a very significant way. We made the wreaths and the sisters took the children back to their classrooms.

Early the next morning, ready to start my day, I met my pastor in the kitchen. He blew up: "You have absolutely no respect for my authority. I heard about those wreaths. You never cleared any of that with me."

"I didn't know that I had to consult you on everything."

"You cannot run around initiating whatever you want. I am the pastor here! Today, I forbid you to go anywhere. You stay put."

That was the end of that exchange.

I knew I needed to be attentive to what my pastor was saying. I assumed that "staying put" did not mean missing morning Mass. I went over to the church. Then I returned to the rectory after Mass and had breakfast. The day loomed empty before me.

I went back to the church and I prayed there all morning.

My stomach spoke up around noon, so I went back to the rectory and had lunch. Then I returned to the church and I spent the afternoon in prayer. At 4:30, the pastor came over to the church. He was still in an autocratic mood, but the subject had shifted: "Go down to the newspaper stand and get me a paper."

That was one thing for sure: This pastor liked to read the paper. I got in the car and I started out for Carmella's Newspaper Stand, where I could buy the evening paper, The Scranton Times. We were able to get the paper in the Stroudsburg area because it was delivered by the Phoebe Snow, a train that was part of the railroad system that went through Scranton.

As I was on my way to the newspaper stand, the simplest thing happened. I stopped for a red light and, while I waited, my eyes met the eyes of a man standing on the street corner. It was a split-second in time. The light changed and I continued on my way. I got out at Carmella's, bought the paper, got back into the car, and went back to the rectory.

Later that same evening, I was upstairs in my room. I heard the doorbell ring.

Father Barrett came to tell me that someone wanted to see me. I went downstairs, and standing there was the man I had seen at the red light. He got right to the point: "I've been away from the Church for years. I saw you downtown today. The way you looked at me, I thought maybe it's time for me to come back." That was an astounding moment. Just what had brought it about? I know that, at that point, prayer wasn't the major part of my life. I would have to say that social justice was more of what I was into. Of course, when the man saw me, I was in full clerical garb—but that didn't explain anything. That day, my pastor had forbidden me to "work." I didn't. In spite of the antagonism between us, I obeyed him. Although this pastor could confine me to the parish, he could not keep me confined internally. I spent the entire day in prayer. That day, prayer did more than any work I could have done. It was a gentle, powerful lesson. God did the work that day.

# St. Matthew's Parish

That was one of the minor skirmishes I had with the pastor of St. Mathew's. Luckily, that one had a silver lining. My house arrest was over, but that was the kind of event that took place between the two of us from 1953 until the pastor died in 1960.

There were many other kinds of things that happened to me at St. Matthew's. There was a child who entered my heart in a unique way while I was there. I first heard of that child from Mother Theresa Clare. She was the superior of the IHM Sisters who taught in the school. She told me that one of the first-graders told her that she had seen the Sacred Heart of Jesus at my Mass and that she had a message for me from the Sacred Heart. I remember distinctly telling Mother Theresa Clare that I did not want to meet that child.

It was common practice for children to come into the church during recess. One day, I was making the Stations of the Cross and a little girl came up to me and said, "Jesus loves you more than me, but I'm not jealous, because I know you love me." I thought that was an odd thing for a child to say. I had never met the child. I remember that I was somewhat frightened. Was this kid kooky? She continued, "Why don't you go up and ask Jesus who He loves the most. He told me that he loved the most abandoned and the most unknown the most." That resonated with me. She reached up and took my hand, and that startled me. She began to walk toward the image of the Immaculate Conception that was in the church. "Do you know what that means?"

If this child needed information, I was there to give it.

"Mary was born free from original sin. From the moment of her coming into being in the womb of her mother, she was free of sin. The devil was unable to touch her. Therefore, she could crush the head of Satan."

"That's not what Jesus told me. He told me that we are all members of the Body of Christ. Because of her humility, Mary was the heel, the lowest part of the Body of Christ, and that is why she can crush the head of the serpent, who, of course, is Satan." I was fascinated. I continued to talk to her, and she told me her name was Marilee. Only then did I realize that this was the child Mother Theresa Clare had wanted me to meet.

One day, months later, Marilee presented me with another challenge. She came to me, and said, "You have to enthrone your home to the Sacred Heart." Obviously, she was talking about the rectory. At that very same time, Mom kept telling me about my sister Marlene's sister-in-law, Theresa Elias who had fallen off her back porch. Theresa was in an unconscious state. When she awakened from that state, she made the same request. She wanted her home enthroned to the Sacred Heart. It was all very foreign to me. "No, I'm too busy. This is my day off." Those were the kinds of responses I was making.

Marilee continued to come to me saying, "The Sacred Heart wants to be the head of the rectory. The pastor has to do it." That directive was something in me that would not go away. After a lot of resistance on my part, I gave the pastor an image of the Sacred Heart and told him, "We ought to place Jesus at the head of this house." He was open. We enthroned a picture of the Sacred Heart in the dining room over the china closet. Although I was quite unaware of the significance of those events, later experiences led me deeper into my devotion to the Sacred Heart and my dedication to enthroning the Sacred Heart in people's homes.

These events happened because of my involvement with this young child, Marilee. I learned more about her. Her mother had tuberculosis and was in a sanitarium. Her dad was alcoholic. Her parents' marriage was tumultuous, and Marilee had very little home support. As a consequence, she became very dependent on me. Sometimes, I was uncomfortable with that, and I knew my limitations in what I could be for this one child. When she got older, for a time, she was part of the Poor Clares (a Franciscan order of women religious). They sent her home. She finished high school and then expressed a desire to go into a nursing program. I paid for that training for her. By 1967 when I left St. Matthew's, Marilee was twenty years old. She came to my sister Marlene's house the night before I was leaving for South America; she wanted to say "goodbye." I never saw her after that night. But eventually, I came to know her significance in my life.

It was always busy in the parish, but Christmas was an extraordinarily busy time. I was trying to maintain a schedule to include everything that needed to be done, making sure I was carrying my weight. In the midst of a hundred things, on Christmas Eve, I got a call from a woman by the name of Margaret. She lived in the flats, the poorest area in the region, and she said she needed some money. I knew I had to hear confessions at St. Luke's and then go on to St. John's in Bushkill, where I would have midnight Mass. I remember the pressure I felt as I finished confessions a little later than I had anticipated. I had told Margaret I would stop by her house before I continued on to St. John's, and I was worried about the time. I had some money in my pocket. I would stop briefly, drop it off, and be on my way. I could feel a twinge of irritation as I hurried to the flats. When I arrived at Margaret's house, I was wearing my biretta, and a cape that someone had given me as a Christmas gift. I was so well dressed and I was walking up to the door of a house that was so shabby. There were rags stuffed into the corners of the windows, probably to keep the heat in—or maybe the cold out. I knocked on the door and Margaret answered. There was need written all over her face, and on the dark, cold atmosphere of the single room. My eyes went to a pot-bellied stove, the only source of heat in the room, and next to it, an orange crate. Instantly, I realized that there in the crate was a baby. What a moment for me! On that Christmas Eve, as I was running from one thing to another, I had almost missed Jesus. There He was in Margaret's dreary home on a cold Christmas Eve, lying in a discarded orange crate. I always remember the grace of that night. In a very short time, I would place a plastic replica of Jesus in the manger in a beautiful and warm church; but the ritual was just a ritual, how ever meaningful. And that night, once again, I was given a gentle reminder of "the supernatural nobility of the faithful, who in the Body of Christ, are united to their Head." It was a beautiful Christmas for me, and I was energized for the days that followed.

The time I spent in East Stroudsburg, especially in the late fifties and early sixties, was characteristic of a specific era in the Catholic Church. The pastor was, indeed, the pastor. He was the administrator. He made the rules. There was a school that was run by the Sisters of the Immaculate Heart of Mary; the school included kindergarten through eighth grade. There were three priests living in the parish, but there were many priests who would come to help out if the need was there. Even in Shohola, three priests lived in the rectory. That was generally the situation in most parishes; rarely was there only a pastor serving the community. But everyone had to be concerned about the pastor. There were rules to follow and obedience was expected. That's how it was. Each year after New Year's Day, the pastor and a group of his friends headed to Florida to escape the dead of winter in the mountains. They really seemed to have the life of country gentlemen. We didn't envy them. Father Barrett and I were always glad to see them go because, for about eight weeks, we had a break from total authority. With the approach of spring, the pastor would return to prepare for Lent and Easter. This practice did prevent the pastor from taking a summer vacation; he would always take some time off during the summer months. It was part of the lifestyle; there were social advantages reserved for those in the upper echelon of the hierarchy.

Though I certainly had no illusions about my place in the pecking order, I have to admit that I got to have a taste of the life of the country gentleman myself in May of 1959. Accompanied by a friend of mine, Father Bob Galligan, I went on a trip to Rome and Lourdes. Both of us had been given extraordinary gifts by our parishioners: fully paid trips to Rome and nearby sites. And during that trip, I had extraordinary experiences of grace.

# Brothers & Fathers

It was my first trip to Europe. Bob and I flew to Rome. When we got there, we were part of a papal audience with Pope Pius XII, whose writings (especially *Mystici Corporis Christi*) had such a great effect on me during my seminary years. I remember there was a soldier standing next to us, and he wanted to know what to do. I told him I had no idea; it was my first time in Rome. When Pope Pius appeared, there was a loud cry of "Viva il papa!" And in a moment we were kneeling down. Everyone else was kneeling, too. Neither the soldier, nor Bob, nor I had any idea that we'd be doing that.

Long before I got to Rome, it had been a long-standing dream of mine to visit the sites of the two great martyrs, St. Peter and St. Paul. I set aside time to do that. And when I got to Rome, I visited St. Peter's Basilica and St. Paul Outside the Walls. Only while I was on that pilgrimage did I decide to visit the other two major basilicas in Rome, St. Mary Major and the most ancient of the four, St. John Lateran—the cathedral church of Rome. As I visited each basilica, I became aware that each had a special area where the Eucharist was reserved; they were called Blessed Sacrament chapels. In turn, I went to each of those. When I entered the Blessed Sacrament chapel at St. John Lateran, I had the most overwhelming experience of prayer in my entire life. Spiritual writers speak of "consolation without previous cause." Many people talk about an experience of God which is unforgettable. Even when it is happening, the person involved knows, "I will remember this for the rest of my life." I had such an experience. I was overwhelmed by the presence, the majesty, the awe, the power of God—so overwhelming that I was unable to stand. I felt myself forced to my knees, and in an instant was prostrate on the floor in front of the Blessed Sacrament. I was seized by the awesome presence of God. I was trembling. I was crying. All I could say to God, because I knew it was God, was "What do you want, Lord?"

And I heard the Lord say, "Charity." I was unable to move, even to stir.

The state of ecstatic prayer lasted for a long time. When I got my bearings, I got up and walked closer to the Blessed Sacrament altar. I had the same experience of the presence of God and I knew that it was the Lord Jesus. Again I was crying and fearful. I remember how deeply I wept; trembling, I cried out, "What do you want, Lord?"

"Love."

I waited for the longest time to hear what more might come. I had a sense of being 'outside of myself.' The ecstasy lasted a long time. I walked before the Blessed Sacrament altar. A third similar experience began. I lay on the floor in prayer and the Lord said, "Teach the love of my Sacred Heart." Some time afterward, I heard, "Learn more about the pope buried in this chapel."

When I got up from this experience, I knew I would do whatever God wanted me to do. I remember feeling quite dazed. I knew I had entered St. John Lateran early in the morning. I was certain it was late afternoon. A tour passed by and the guide was telling the people with him that Pope Leo XIII was buried in this chapel. I looked around and saw a tomb elevated on the wall in the Blessed Sacrament chapel. I stayed there and prayed before the tomb. I knew that Pope Leo had addressed many social issues concerning the poor and the laboring classes. Much of what I did not know I learned when I returned home. I studied more about Pope Leo and was struck by a particularly curious bit of information. The last act of Leo's papacy was to enthrone the whole world to the Sacred Heart of Jesus. I was searching for direction. I thought I was supposed to join some order of the Sacred Heart. That proved untrue; but I did become involved in great devotion to the Sacred Heart, and even today that is a significant part of my ministry, wherever I am. Finally, I understood what Marilee had tried to tell me—but only because the Lord had made it clear.

Another dream I had for some time was of seeing Padre Pio while I was in Rome. I wasn't sure why that desire was so strong in my heart. At the time, I knew almost nothing about the man except that he had the stigmata, and I wasn't sure what that was all about. Everyone I had spoken to about wanting to see Padre Pio was very discouraging. Essentially, the thinking was, "Don't bother. You'll never get to see him."

Bob and I left Rome by train. Then we had to take a bus, because San Giovanni Rotondo (the monastery where Padre Pio lived) was up in the hills. We had been told that, if we got to the monastery, we should ask for a woman by the name of Mary Pyle, who was a Montessori professor. She was quite famous, because she took care of priests who went to the monastery hoping to see Padre Pio. We thought we'd take our chances and hoped she would put us into some network that might get us to see him. Bob and I were at a disadvantage: Neither one of us could speak Italian. So when we got to the monastery, I simply said "Mary Pyle." We had made no previous arrangements, but she came to see us. She invited us to go to her cottage and have something to eat. By then, it was late afternoon. At the cottage were Padre Pio's nephew, Mary Pyle, Father Galligan, and me. Mary had put some wine, some bread, and some cheese on the table for us. She also told us that she had arranged for someone in the neighborhood to give us a place to sleep that night. While those simple hospitalities were taking shape, I saw Padre Pio come into the cottage and say to me, "What are you doing here? Are you a curiosity seeker?" I was completely surprised! But I answered him, telling him what I had been thinking. I asked him why it was so important to have the stigmata. I told him that devotion to the Eucharist seemed more important. And we went from there. We talked about Jesus and the Blessed Sacrament. There was no talk of wounds. We talked for about twenty minutes and then he left. I turned to Mary Pyle and I asked her, "Does he come here often?"

Her reply was strange: "We didn't know that he was here. If he had a conversation with you, he came to see you. No one else at the table saw him here. He does that frequently. He has the gift of bilocation." I had never heard that before, but I later learned of many instances in which Padre Pio was known to be in two places at the same time. At the moment, I only knew that Padre Pio had challenged why I was there. We talked about devotion to the Eucharist, nothing about his wounds.

We were way up in the mountains. Although it was May, that night was a chilling one, and we slept in our clothes. At 2 a.m. we got up and walked to the monastery, and there we waited for the gates to open. Mary Pyle told us that, as soon as we entered, we should go right into the sacristy and sign up for an altar if we wanted to say Mass. It was pre Vatican II, and concelebration was not allowed, except during the rite of ordination. Each of us needed a private altar, so we each put our name down to reserve one. While both of us were signing up, along with many others, Padre Pio came into the sacristy to vest for his Mass. Everyone immediately knelt down. A few minutes later, he walked in my direction, stopped, and stood over me. I looked up and saw that he was looking right at me. Later, Bob told me that everyone was looking at him looking at me, and that Padre Pio stood there for ten minutes. To me, it had seemed like an hour. I also thought he seemed angry as we looked at each other. Finally, he went over and knelt on a kneeler to make his preparation for Mass. A short time later, he came back over to me. He took off his glove and I could see the hole in his hand; in fact, I could see light through the hole. He put his bare, blistered hand on my head and, smiling, he blessed me. A few minutes later, he began his Mass. When he did, blood was running from his hands and down his arms and over his vestments as his wounds bled. The Mass lasted for about three hours. At the consecration, he held the host up for at least twenty minutes.

After Mass, people dabbed up the blood that had soaked through his shoes. We learned more about Padre Pio before we left. He had been banished to the monastery where we saw him. He was forbidden to preach, but he could say Mass and hear confessions. I met with his English priests after the Mass, because they would take questions to him. I wanted to ask him about how angry he seemed to be. I wrote my questions, adding my name and address, because the priests said that I would receive an answer. Bob and I continued on our travels. We left Italy and flew to Paris, where we went to Rue de Bac—the site of the revelation of the miraculous medal to St. Catherine Labouré. We also visited the shrine of St. Therese of Lisieux, and eventually we went to Lourdes. Some time after I got home, I received a letter from the priest I had given my questions to. He had spoken to Padre Pio, who wanted him to relay a message to me. Padre Pio wanted me to know that he would be a help to me when I heard confessions. Any time I needed assistance from him during the sacrament of confession, I was to send my angel to Padre Pio and he would help me with whatever difficulty I was facing. He also told me that he would be my spiritual father.

For years, I have done just as he directed. I have had the grace of hearing many profound confessions over the years of my priesthood. I attribute those wonderful reconciliations to the assistance that Padre Pio promised—and that he has given me.

The entire journey was an experience that deeply touched my life—then and, most assuredly, now. It was such a marvelous experience for me that I was inspired to send my parents on a similar trip. They accepted my offer of sending them to Europe and, a year later, in 1960, they set off on a wonderful pilgrimage together.

When I returned from my first trip abroad, I resumed my life at St. Matthew's, where other kinds of celebrations were in the works. One of the big celebrations for men in the fraternity of the priesthood during that time was the Forty Hours devotions instituted by St. John Neumann to commemorate the Eucharistic. Many, many priests would come to St. Matthew's for that celebration in the church. After the devotion each night, great dinners and drinks were served in the rectory for those who attended the Forty Hours. That was a three-day affair, and I was first introduced to it at St. Matthew's. I remember one night, as the priests were relaxing after dinner, Father Barrett came up to me and said, "Hey, Esseff, look around at this crowd." I did. There were the fat ones, and the skinny ones, the cigar smokers, and the card players. They were all having a great time commiserating with one another. Father Barrett wasn't done. "I want you to think of this phrase of Jesus from Scripture: "I have chosen you; you have not chosen Me."

"OK," I said.

"Well then, I'm sure you'll agree, the Lord has only Himself to blame!" To say the least, Father Barrett had a very strong anti-clerical strain and wasn't afraid to express his opinions. I have to admit, I was very much influenced by him.

# Brothers & Fathers

Another priest who influenced my ministry during my years in East Stroudsburg was Monsignor Connell McHugh, the dean of the area. He was a tall man and quite elderly. To me and some of my friends, I guess he seemed ancient. We used to say that he came over with Columbus on his second voyage! He was well known and lovingly referred to as the "old man of the mountain." He was also an excellent fund-raiser. The word was, "Hang onto your wallet when you're around Monsignor McHugh." He was known for the really strong appeals he made to people who came to vacation in the Pocono Mountains in the summer. He was referred to as "Con" and, although his name was Connell, everyone knew the name fit, because he could "con" people into opening up their wallets for whatever project was in the works. But Monsignor McHugh really loved the priesthood— and he loved the priests. He took the time to know us and to care about us, and he always welcomed us at his rectory. Like so many others he, too, lived the life of a country gentleman. He was away most of the winter, but was the pastor of St. Mary's in Mount Pocono, and was known for his great pastoral skills. I remember one time, early on, when he came to St. Matthew's. He was probably checking out what we young clerics were doing. He invited me to join him as he made his rounds at the hospital.

"Young man, almost all the people in the hospital are not Catholic, but I want you to go into every room and see every patient."

That was the directive he gave me that first time I went to the hospital with him.

There were many different experiences as we went from room to room. One that I clearly remember was walking into a room where there was a lady lying in bed. He said, "All right now, get out of bed and kneel down and I'll give you my blessing."

"I'm not a Catholic."

"Well, that's OK. Your father was."

"My father was not a Catholic."

"Well, your grandfather was."

"My grandfather wasn't a Catholic. My grandfather was a Mason."

"Somewhere back there, you had a Catholic relative."

There was a moment of silence.

"Well, that's probably true."

"Well, then, get out of bed and kneel down. I'll give you a blessing."

# St. Matthew's Parish

During the whole visit, I was wondering, "What's going to happen next?"

She got out of bed and knelt down. He closed his eyes and gives her a blessing.

I had to see what effect this had, so I lingered a bit. He went out. I waited behind. She looked up at me, her face glowing, and said, "Do you know what? He gave me a blessing and I'm not even a Catholic."

From that day on, I gave everyone that I would meet my blessing. I learned the grace and the beauty of giving a blessing from that old priest, Monsignor McHugh. In house, some things needed special handling; but for the most part, I spent my time dealing with the parishioners. Early on, I became friendly with the a family of parishioners: John and Mary and their five children. John and I were about the same age and we decided to try to generate more devotions and greater involvement among the men in the parish. We encouraged the men to participate in adoration of the Blessed Sacrament, to be more attentive to Sunday Mass, and to consider daily Mass a viable option. Within myself, I was becoming more aware of my own need for growth in my prayer life. John was a great catalyst in bringing the men together and heightening their participation in the life of the parish.

About that same time, a man arrived whom I can only describe as very mysterious. He approached me and asked if I would teach him about the Catholic faith. He was a rather striking man and, in many ways, fascinating. His name was Randolph. He was bright and seemingly eager. At first, he seemed a good fit with the movement in the parish. He would come to me almost every day to learn about the faith. As I continued to see him, I began to realize how resistant he was to everything I was trying to do. When I spoke to the other men about the Mass and what it meant, and why it was important for them to be more involved, they generally responded well. One after another, they would show up at Mass, or Adoration, or Benediction. And generally, their presence became more pronounced in the life of the parish. Randolph was totally unresponsive. Though he came for instruction all the time, he was totally resistant to formation of any kind. While the other men were going to confession, attending Mass, and participating in other devotions, Randolph was never moved to do anything. This lack of responsiveness went on for a long period of time. But he persisted in showing up. One day I was talking about the apostles and discussing their role in the early church. When I had finished, he said to me, "I know Judas."

I was taken back. "What did you say?"

"I have great power." His eyes and his voice were like ice. He turned and left, and I stood frozen—wondering who or what this strange presence was.

# Brothers & Fathers

It was during this same time that my parishioner John and I had begun to develop devotion to St. Michael the Archangel. We happened to hear about a Divine Word father who had begun a ministry to spread devotion to St. Michael. The priest's name was Father Aubrey, and he was conducting a novena to St. Michael at a new shrine in upper New York state. John and I decided to attend the dedication of the shrine, along with the novena there. It was a wonderful experience. And after it was over, John and I boarded a bus to return to East Stroudsburg. When we got off at the bus stop at Eighth Street, Randolph was there waiting for us. All I could think of was that last eerie conversation I had with him and his talk of Judas and power. I knew that I needed to take the whole experience to prayer. If this person was not human, I never wanted to see him again. Prayer, once again, was the answer. That was the last time I saw Randolph.

Another night, I came home to the rectory and I had the sense of someone standing by me. I couldn't tell who. It seemed to be the presence of a man. At that time, I smoked. I reached for a cigarette and lit it. I remember saying, "If you're the devil, I'm not afraid of you"—but I knew I was terrified. "If you're a soul, I'll pray for you at my next Mass." When I got to my room, I got rid of the cigarette and took out my rosary. It was almost two o'clock in the morning. As I began to pray on each bead, the fear began to leave me. I knew I never wanted to experience that kind of fear again, and realized what a blessing the rosary was for me. There were more than a few things, however, that were puzzling. I called a priest-friend of mine from school, Clem Markowski and I asked him if he would come up to visit. When he did, we went to dinner and I shared some of my confusion with him. We talked a lot about the spiritual dimension in the world, and we realized how vulnerable we were without prayer. I certainly had experienced moments of darkness, and so had Clem. We knew we needed to enrich our prayer life and, shortly afterwards, both of us joined the Institute of the Heart of Jesus. It had members from all over the country and was designed to help diocesan priests develop and maintain a strong spiritual life. As members of the Institute, Clem and I had a community to pray with. We would join other priests for annual retreats and we enjoyed a new dedication to putting prayer at the center of our lives and our ministry. Joining the Institute was one of the most positive steps I took in focusing on the essential need I had for prayer, and it proved to be an amazing support for me and Clem for many, many years.

Many different kinds of things happened all the time at St. Matthew's. In fact, every imaginable thing that could happen to a priest came up at one time or another during those years; and, I must say, they started on day one. I was 25 years old when

# St. Matthew's Parish

I got there and 39 when I left, and all the years in between were filled with wonderful people and the incidents of their lives. They were exciting times. I was a young Father then. I was learning new things every day. I couldn't have been happier.

While I was enjoying my early years of ministry at St. Matthew's and forging my own path, George and Rosemary were miles away in Virginia. For all those years they, too, were writing new chapters in their life, not the least of which included the particulars of the coming of the next generation of Esseffs.

# CHAPTER 23

## CROSSING THE THRESHOLD OF PARENTHOOD

## *Rosemary*

The year 1952 was a happy one for George and me. Life was full and exciting and we felt doubly blessed in the early spring of 1953 to learn that we were about to have our first child. In May, we celebrated John's ordination to the priesthood and were also looking forward in early 1954 to the marriage of George's sister Marlene to his high school pal, Tony Elias. As the weeks passed, spring turned quickly into summer, and in no time, fall was approaching. In the midst of so many exciting events and upcoming plans, I realized that I was having some real difficulties with the pregnancy and, in time, they became more and more troublesome. My obstetrician advised me to quit work and to take it easy if I hoped to maintain the pregnancy.

I did as he advised and, thank God, I did maintain the pregnancy; but there were a lot of difficult moments. I knew enough about biology to know that I was experiencing circumstances that were dictating that I would not go full term. Our baby was due in mid-December. In late September, I hemorrhaged at home and was taken to the hospital. Naturally, the doctors wanted the baby to be as developed as possible and they said that I would have to stay in the hospital until it was safer for me to deliver.

One night, one week into my eighth month (and while I was still hospitalized), the doctor called George at home at 2:30 in the morning. I was hemorrhaging again and the doctors were sure they would have to take the baby. George jumped into the car and, within minutes, was on his way to the hospital.

It really wasn't a surprise that I faced a critical time during the birth.

The doctor was very honest with me, and that was such a blessing. In the early fifties, most patients weren't told anything. When he said, "I'm going to let the priest come in," I knew he knew how important that was to both of us. And I also knew things were not going well. Later, George and I found out that, up to that time, no other priest had been allowed in the operating room in that hospital.

George Jr. was born by C-section on November 4th, 1953. Both an obstetrician and a pediatrician were on hand. He was perfectly formed, but he was as gray as he could be. The priest performed an emergency baptism and then the pediatrician scooped him away.

---

### GEORGE

*"What had happened was that Rosemary had a placenta previa, a phenomenon that occurs only once in about 50,000 births. So while the birthing was actually going on, many doctors and nurses were coming into the delivery room because, even though they had studied about it, they had never seen a placenta previa themselves. Rosemary was dying giving birth and the baby was dying being born. They showed the baby to me, the priest baptized him, and then they whisked him away. He was as gray as could be, because he had swallowed so much blood during the birthing. No one on the medical staff thought that he would make it.*

*"The doctor was trying to be optimistic. He told me that, if Rosemary and the baby could live for seventy-two hours, they'd be OK. I got down on my knees that minute and offered everything up.*

*"Some time after the birth, and after they had closed up Rosemary, she was taken from the O.R. where she had had the C-section and placed into a hospital room. A short time later, she started to hemorrhage again, and they had to give her transfusions: nine pints of blood. As fast as they were putting it into her, it was coming out. The doctor said to me, 'If it doesn't stop soon, we're going to have to do a total hysterectomy, and I can't give her more than a 20% chance of surviving that.'*

*"He packed her with gauze and said that he could only leave that in for 40 or 45 minutes. If the bleeding didn't stop, they would have to take her back to surgery. The only thing we could do was pray."*

---

I consider the particulars of George Jr.'s birth one of the miracles of our early life together. I think you have to have a strong faith. And I think, too, we went into marriage well aware of the kinds of problems that could arise. During times like this one, there is so much growth, especially spiritual growth—growing together and working things out. I was always glad of the things we had discussed long before we married.

# Crossing the Threshold of Parenthood

I had a wonderful Catholic doctor, Dr. Murphy, who stayed with me until I was out of trouble. He had a bit of advice: "You know, if you were my wife, you wouldn't have any more children because of the condition of your uterus." Although both George and I were a bit in the doldrums looking at the prospect of having only one child, we were thrilled with our firstborn, who every day was growing stronger.

It took me a long time to recuperate. I stayed in the hospital for two weeks after I delivered. George Jr. stayed for at least another four weeks after I was discharged. When I was still in the hospital, my mother and dad came to help. After about two weeks, Dad felt that I was recovering nicely, and that things were going well. I was on the mend and the baby was growing. One morning he said to me, "Now, Rosemary, I have to go home."

"How come? Why can't you stay a little longer?"

"You know the Krissinger's stud bull?"

"Yeah."

"Well, I have to go home because they're going to start breeding."

"Oh, God forbid, Dad. After all, that's a $53,000 bull." I think he either missed the sarcasm, or ignored it.

"Yeah, and the stud fees for that bull are tremendously high, so I have to be there. There has to be a vet on hand. I really have to get home. You're doing fine, and your mother's going to stay here for a while."

I can't deny it. My nose was out of joint. If I hadn't had it with the veterinary practice before, at that moment, I surely did.

God forbid that I should interfere with the Krissingers' breeding program.

Anyway, that's a little sidebar I remember.

The C-section in the fifties was a very difficult thing, and I was not really well for about five months. The whole ordeal had been hard on the baby and on me; but overall, little George was a healthy baby, and a blessing in our marriage—and in the family. Everyone was happy at the birth of the first grandchild. I didn't hear even a word from Joe Esseff about the baby's name. Along with everyone else, he was just grateful that we were all OK.

## GEORGE

*"It was weeks before we were all home together. Rosemary still needed to recuperate. I was working at the lab at the time. I didn't get much sleep, but I was used to that. I'd get up and feed George during the night. He was so tiny that he required feeding every two hours. He was also a sleepy little guy, and it was difficult to keep him awake, so we could get him to eat. It might take an hour for him to take two ounces of milk.*

*"I also helped with the chores around the house. I washed the dishes or cleaned up. Dad had done those things. He would iron and do a lot of things that some might consider women's work. I'm glad I learned to do those things from him. It never bothered him and it never bothered me.*

*"I was just grateful to have my little family together."*

George as a young father

Financially, those years were tough. Without a lot of faith, they would have been even tougher. George had put me on his insurance after we were married; but because the baby wasn't full term (seven months and one week to be exact), he was born just four days before the policy went into effect. We had to take on the medical expenses in full. George sold his car to get some money, and did what he could to earn the money we needed to pay those bills. He didn't have a car for a whole year. He worked nights selling knives, sweepers, and other things that he thought were worthwhile and that people would buy. I was home with the baby. Together, we did what had to be done.

As the months went by, I stayed home with George Jr. and I seemed to be on the mend. By the time George was about eight months old, there I was finding lumps under my arms. Again, I knew enough to know this discovery could be serious. I didn't tell George about what I had found; he had so much to deal with. I made an appointment and went to see a doctor. When I did, he took a blood specimen. With that much done, I told George, who, when the results came, took me back to the doctor's office to get them. George waited outside with George Jr. while the doctor told me, "I can't deal with this. I want you to go to a specialist in Washington, D.C."

# Crossing the Threshold of Parenthood

## GEORGE

*"I was sitting with George Jr. in a car I had borrowed. Rosemary came out of the doctor's office, got into the car, and said, 'The doctor wants me to go to Washington D.C. to see a blood specialist.'*

*"I'm thinking, 'What the heck is going on?' I got out of the car and went into the doctor's office to get more information. When I finally saw him, he proceeded to tell me that he had sent the blood specimens to five hospitals and three different doctors. All came back with the same answer: Rosemary was in the late stages of leukemia and she had six weeks to live.*

*"By then, he was apologetic, 'I was going to try to call you.' Everything had been recorded. He gave me a letter spelling out the entire diagnosis to take to the specialist.*

*"'Well,' I said, 'I'm not taking her to Washington.'*

*"I knew she could get better care. I wanted her to go to Jefferson in Philadelphia, and I called to make an appointment there with a blood specialist. I was told, 'He can't see you for three months.'*

*"'Well,' I said, 'my wife doesn't have three months. I'm coming up. I don't care what you do. We'll camp on the doorstep until he sees us.' What I didn't know at the time was that Rosemary had found the letter from the doctor and read it.*

*"We didn't have a car, so we went up to Philadelphia on the train. And there I was, riding on the train next to Rosemary and thinking she didn't know.*

*"When we got to the doctor in Philadelphia, he saw us during his lunch hour. What a good man. He spent two-and-a-half hours with us."*

At this point, it was summer, and George was about eight months old. I needed a confidante. I made a decision to tell John what was going on. He was stationed at St. Matthew's in East Stroudsburg and recently had been in an accident. He had severe injuries to his hand, but he was on the job. I knew he was busy and couldn't get away. I wrote him a letter. I told him the particulars. My lifespan didn't look too great and here we had this little baby. I knew that George could really tough it out, but I was so concerned about the baby. I told John, "See to it that, if the time comes, George marries someone who will be a good mother to this child. You know how things can go with a stepchild, and that is a real big concern of mine. Watch out for this little one."

# Brothers & Fathers

With that done, I went to Philadelphia with George and the baby. I was very concerned. Because I had had so many transfusions when I was delivering George Jr., I had very strong suspicions that I had been given some contaminated blood. All I could do was hope and pray. George had called his mom and dad. I certainly didn't know what he told them, but they met us in Philadelphia and took care of George Jr. while we went where we had to go.

When we went into the doctor he said to me, "Tell me your symptoms." By now, both George and I were up front with the facts. When I listed the signs I had noticed, he said, "I don't know. Let's just see. I don't agree with the diagnosis at all."

I remember so vividly when, later, he did the sternum bone marrow test. He said, "I just feel that you don't have leukemia. It's a gut feeling, and I'd never tell you or any other patient such a thing if I weren't 99.9% certain."

We had to wait through three nights before all the tests were back and we found out the results. We prayed the whole time: Mom and Dad, and George and I. And in the midst of all this, I remember George's dad saying, "Here I am with another daughter who's sick." I was very touched that Joe Esseff had called me his daughter—though not I, nor anyone else besides him, knew just how sick his own daughter Mae Ann was.

The doctor's final diagnosis of my condition was that I had mononucleosis. Fort Belvoir had been loaded with it, and I had worked there. The doctor was sure that that was where I had picked it up. The whole situation was baffling. I couldn't imagine that I had mononucleosis and George Jr., a premature baby, didn't get it. No one whom we had been in contact with in the family got it, either.

How could five labs and three doctors all be wrong?

We're still sure to this day: It was a miracle, and we thank God for it.

While all of these things played out, George continued to work with the Army Corps of Engineers. By this time he was aware of the tremendous interest generated by the rack he had devised, he had been granted a patent, and he was beginning to chart a new course for the future of our little family.

*George, Rosemary and George Jr.*

# CHAPTER 24

CHANGING TIMES

## George

*W*hile Rosemary and I worked through health issues, financial obligations, and adjustments to parenthood, I remained with the Army Corps of Engineers. What happened there catapulted me into multiple changes that carried us through the rest of the fifties. Those years saw my family grow with the addition of two daughters, saw us make a major geographical move, and set me on a schedule that kept me away from home more than any doctor's schedule would have.

I continued to find the work I did at the Army Corps very interesting as I moved from one project to another. What came as a surprise to me was finding out that others were also interested in my work. As I said, in 1953, the government patented the work I had done on the rack, but I really didn't think much about that development. My thinking changed when news of the patent was published in one of the metal finishing journals along with a picture of the rack. Because my name was listed in the patent, I began to get a great number of calls from people requesting how and where they could get a similar rack made of titanium. At first I simply explained that I had created the rack essentially as part of a research project I was working on at the Corps, and that it couldn't be bought anywhere. The inquiries continued to come in from various industries. As they increased, I began to realize just how far reaching the interest in such a tool was. I knew I wanted to spend more time investigating the whole field, but I wanted to make sure that it would be worthwhile for me to do that. In negotiations with the government, I told them that I would like to have the commercial rights to the rack.

They gave me the rights with one stipulation: If the government ever needed such a rack or wanted to buy racks from me, I would have to give it a 20% discount. I was happy to accept those terms.

As I investigated the situation more deeply, I also began to realize from the nature of the inquiries that the initial rack I had made was not exactly what some interested parties needed. It didn't accommodate the particular parts that they were working with. By this time, Rosemary and I were back on our feet financially and I decided I would take a few months off from the government to make an honest assessment of the scope of the market that might be out there for the rack. As I met more and more interested parties, I would listen to their specific needs and then I would create a design that would fit those needs. I designed each new rack to fill their specifications. I contacted Crucible Steel, which had made the first run of titanium that I used working on the sniper scope project at the Army Corps of Engineers, and I made arrangements to buy titanium from them.

The next step was to have the racks made. I knew a fellow researcher, Sid Lavine, who was actually my assistant supervisor at work. I talked to him about what I was doing, and he decided that he would be interested in investing in the kind of work I wanted to have done. He and I formed a partnership and were engaged in what might be considered a cottage industry in the design and manufacture of titanium racks. We called the company Robe: Ro after Rosemary and Be after his wife, Bernice. I continued to develop new designs for various kinds of racks; they would be manufactured to the specs in each of my designs. As the months moved swiftly by, I knew from the continuing number of requests that it was time for me to make a major decision. By the end of 1954, I wanted to become more involved in further design and manufacture of titanium racks. If I was going to keep up with all the orders, the best road for me to follow was to quit the government job and continue in business.

I spoke to my partner and discovered that he wasn't interested in becoming involved in the risks of a new business. More to the point, he wasn't interested in leaving the security that his position with the Corps of Engineers' laboratory afforded him and his family. I understood that thinking. Working for the government in the 50s was a very secure job. There was adequate financial compensation as well as benefits, such as hospitalization, that made government work a good employment choice. The medical benefit, unfortunately, wasn't there for me when I most needed it, and maybe that's why I was less impressed with that option of security. Anyway, after a year or more of a small-but-lucrative business, I negotiated buying out my partner's interest and prepared to go into production without him. That meant I would have to find a machine shop that would make the racks for me. By that time we were well into 1955.

At home things seemed good. Rosemary's health was steadily improving and George Jr. was thriving. He had moved up from being a slow eater to reaching out to grab a chicken leg. I knew I didn't want Rosemary to work outside the home;

# Changing Times

I wanted her to raise our children. We discussed these things even before we were married, and Rosemary agreed that being a wife and mother would be her career. It was my responsibility to provide in order for her to do that. Those choices defined us as part of a different generation. As Rosemary took on the added responsibilities of motherhood, I was well aware of how supportive she was of all that I was doing during that time.

George Jr.

While these events over several years were particular to Rosemary and me, they were only part of the history that was taking shape, and came to permeate the rest of our lives. There were also events of such magnitude that they seem to have had lives of their own. These were woven into the fabric of our daily lives, but they are presented here encapsulated in the year they all occurred: 1955.

# CHAPTER 25

## SEASONS OF LOSS
### *Father John*

#### MAE ANN'S DEATH

There are many family dynamics that go into trying to explain the particulars of my sister's death. We have already talked about some of them. Mae Ann was born in 1936, when I was eight years old. During my early years, I had a friend and playmate in my brother George. My sister Marlene seemed to bond best with my Uncle Peter (Dad's brother), who was younger than both George and me, but close in age to her. Also Marlene, like us, was born while we lived with Gidue and his family. Marlene was flamboyant and enjoyed a lot of attention inside and outside of the family. Mae Ann had a quieter, more delicate nature and seemed to need less attention than Marlene. Joe, the baby of our family, was doted on by his sisters and, hands down, was the apple of my father's eye.

*Joe Jr. and Dad*

At any rate, like the rest of us, Mae Ann seemed to have "normal" high school experiences. During those years, George and Rosemary were married, I was ordained, and Marlene and Tony were married. Around the same time that I was ordained and went off to Shohola to begin my work as a priest, George and Rosemary were having their first child, and Marlene was planning her wedding. Mae Ann was planning to be—and was, in fact—the maid of honor at her sister's wedding. She was very beautiful. She had a voice even more cultivated than Marlene's. In school, she didn't have the drive to compete and seemed somewhat laissez-faire about studies. She was very interested in relationships and had a lot of friends. She valued her girlfriends; they all liked Mae Ann and enjoyed being with her. She also had a great sense of humor. She was very forthright and emotionally strong. She hated any type of deception, and liked things plain and simple. She was a real part of the many different kinds of things that were happening and overlapping in the early fifties. It all seemed normal.

What doesn't compute as normal, even now (more than fifty years later), are the details surrounding Mae Ann's death, which we still struggle to understand better.

During Mae Ann's sophomore year in high school, she had a school picture taken. When she brought the picture home, my mother noticed a swelling on Mae Ann's neck. Of course, she immediately went to my father to show him what she saw. Who knows why the photograph showed what nobody had noticed in the flesh, day after day?

After some arguments about what might be happening, Dad took Mae Ann to the family doctor, Dr. McMahon. All he could tell Dad was that he wasn't sure what the swelling indicated, but he did advise him to take Mae Ann to Jefferson Hospital in Philadelphia. Dad went along with that because he had taken Mom to Philadelphia when she had problems with her ears, and both of them were happy with the results they had gotten there.

Dad and Mom took Mae Ann to Philadelphia. After extensive testing, the doctor concluded that Mae Ann had Hodgkin's disease. It seems impossible to comprehend that, what Dad learned during those days in Philadelphia, he told no one— not his wife, not even Mae Ann. Hodgkin's disease is one of a group of cancers called lymphomas, which is a general term for cancers that develop in the lymphatic system. Hodgkin's is an uncommon lymphoma and accounts for less than 1% of all cases of cancer in America. The symptoms of Hodgkin's disease include a painless swelling in the lymph nodes in the neck, the underarm, or the groin. There can be recurrent fevers, night sweats, weight loss, or itchy skin; in fact, the symptoms can easily be mistaken for a common case of the flu. I knew none of this at the time. What we did learn initially was that Mae Ann needed treatments and one of those was blood transfusions. Looking back now, it's difficult to say what kind of symptoms became apparent in Mae Ann. She was often pale, sometimes listless and lacking in energy. We had no idea of the severity of her illness, and no one but Dad knew that Mae had a potentially life-threatening illness. We certainly didn't consider Mae Ann sickly, much less did we think she was in any danger of dying.

Totally unaware of the tragedy that had befallen her, Mae Ann continued with her "normal" life. In the midst of many suitors, she had fallen in love with Tony Roman, a guy who was considered a very eligible bachelor. He had already finished high school, had served his time in the Army, and was seriously courting Mae Ann. He was about four years older than she was.

Shortly after Marlene was married, and while I was stationed at St. Matthew's Parish, Dad came to see me. It was early 1954.

Before he told me anything, he swore me to secrecy. I look back now and I marvel at my ignorance. What Dad told me wasn't a confession; it was family stuff. He told me about Mae Ann's illness. He proceeded to confide in me that she probably had only two or three years to live. That proved not to be true. Still, no one else knew—until, eventually, Dad did tell George.

In my position then as a newly ordained priest, I knew I wanted to help Mae Ann prepare for death. Craziness at funerals was very strong in my memory, and I felt an obligation not to allow any of those behaviors to overshadow Mae Ann's death. I also remained faithful to the oath I had given my dad.

While all of this was playing out, and in spite of Mae Ann's failing health, she and Tony were making plans to marry. We were all aware of that, and still no one was dealing with the real issues. One evening when I was home, Mae Ann and I were talking. She was, by that time, a senior about to graduate, and she was filled with news of Tony and plans of marrying him. Still, just months before her death, she was unaware of what she was facing. I knew I had to address the situation. I also knew I had waited too long. "Mae Ann, you can't marry Tony."

"And why not?"

I answered her as softly as I could, but the words were harsh: "You're going to die."

How could I have been so abrupt? She screamed crying. She was filled with anger and railed out, "God is cruel!" She was true to what she felt in the moment. Her reaction was probably the most normal.

I handled that situation so poorly. I wasn't trained in dealing with death and dying. Also, as we already shared, George and I had really rejected the kinds of reactions to death that we had seen over the years. I didn't want to participate in that kind of hysterical response, but I guess I went to the other extreme.

Words, I can't remember. Logic, probably none. Here I was, a newly ordained priest, telling my sister she was going to die, and completely spiritualizing what it all meant. I remember telling Mae Ann that she should go to confession so that she would have less time to spend in purgatory. I continued to zero in on just wanting her to be at peace when she died.

# Brothers & Fathers

Anger was Mae Ann's reaction. Her disbelief was more genuine and realistic than my belief at the time. Full of life and expectations, she certainly had no reason to want to die.

Mom didn't learn of the severity of Mae Ann's situation until a short time before her death. I'm sure that keeping her unaware was not fair to Mom, but maybe Dad thought he was sparing her the pain. Or maybe he was still denying the reality, too. Mom, of course, was inconsolable when she discovered the truth. She threw herself into prayer and bargaining with God. I remember her leaving the house one day and walking on her knees from our house on Moyallen Street to St. Anthony's Church on Park Avenue to pray. She could not be stopped.

I was very strongly tested with Mae Ann. I remember when she was so sick, she still loved the joy of living. I asked her what she wanted for her birthday—what she was looking forward to. She told me she had seen a pair of pink shoes that she would love to have. I probably should have run out and bought them for her; but instead I said, "What do you want with those?"

She was very real: "I'm going to dance and I want those shoes."

I was the one who was out of touch. She probably wanted to say, "What's wrong with you, John?"

On June 24th, just five days before her death, she had her nineteenth birthday. The girls got her a beautiful dress, with flowers and those pink shoes. She was so sick and so uncomfortable, but she was stunning. She was all decked out and so beautiful—and insistent on celebrating the day she was born. That's how she responded to life, even in the face of death.

She weathered that birthday better than we did.

Five days later, Mom was still holding on as tightly as she could. Mae Ann had found her own peace and said to Mom, "I'm living because you're keeping me here."

Mom's answer was, "You're not going to die."

"If you don't let me die, I'm going to haunt you. Let me go."

Mae Ann died that day in the Mercy Hospital in Wilkes-Barre. Though Mom was sick with grief, that day I heard her utter a powerful prayer of surrender. As the church bells rang to mark the time for saying the Angelus, Mom said, "Blessed Mother, I give her into your lap."

It was a long time before my mother could really deal with the reality of that day.

Besides the grief that was a normal part of Mae Ann's death, there were other effects that were far reaching in the family, and the changing dynamics became more and more apparent.

When Mae Ann died, there was a build-up of the old kind of craziness. Dad blamed himself for calling his daughter Mae because his sister Mae had died at an early age, too. And our brother Joe had an ongoing reaction to Mae Ann's death.

## PRIEST READS SISTER'S MASS

### Final Rites Held For Mae Ann Esseff

Miss Mae Ann Theresa Esseff of 113 Moyallen street, sister of Rev. John Esseff of St. Matthew's Church, Stroudsburg, was laid to rest this morning.

The funeral was held from Mc-Laughlin Funeral Home, 142 South Washington street. Rev. Father Esseff was celebrant of the solemn high mass of requiem for his sister in St. Anthony's Maronite Church, Dana Street. Assisting were Rev. Joseph Bonner, deacon; Rev. Frank Lahout, sub-deacon; Rev. Joseph Flannery, thurifer, and Rev. Richard Frank, master of ceremonies. Acolytes were Rev. Cyril Hudak and Rev. Anthony Conmy.

A priest's choir sang for the mass, having as members Rev. Karl Monahan, Rev. E. F. Terkoski, Rev. William Wheeler, Rev. Girard F. Angelo, Rev. Joseph Doggett, Rev. Mr. William B. Healey.

Miss Mae Ann Theresa Esseff, above, of 113 Moyallen Street, sister of Rev. John Esseff of St. Matthew's Church, Stroudsburg, died yesterday afternoon at Mercy Hospital.

In ill health for almost a year and a medical patient at the hos-

*Mae Anne's obituary*

---

## GEORGE

*"Both John and I agree that the handling of Mae's death affected our brother Joe's whole life. On the morning of the day that Mae Ann died, she had asked her brother Joe to do something for her. What? No one remembers—probably nothing much. He was just a kid. He was going to the movies and said "No"; he couldn't do whatever she had asked. He had no idea that she was terminally ill, no idea at all. He was really angry that no one told him what was going on. When he came home, he found out his sister was dead. It's hard to imagine what kind of guilt came with doing something so normal— the kind of thing kids do every day.*

*"Joe couldn't let go of all of it for a really long, long time. As he went on with his adult life, he became an alcoholic and a gambler.*

*"It was a long time before he came to terms with all of it."*

---

There was a lot of residue from Dad's handling of Mae Ann's sickness and death. It was a very sad family event, but Joe's reaction was the most obvious and the most tragic. As we said, my brother Joe was the last of my father's five children.

He was pampered because of his place in the family. Anything he wanted, he got. For the first thirteen years of his life, he was the apple of my father's eye. Then Mae Ann got sick.

When that happened, Dad's attention seemed to shift away from Joe and toward Mae Ann. It's important to remember that, for a long time, no one knew the whole story. It seemed that Dad neglected Joe, who went from being the pampered pet of the family to being virtually non-existent. Joe was scarred during those years and pain became a part of his life for a long time.

---

### JOE ESSEFF

*"During the period of time in my life between fourteen and eighteen, I got in a lot of trouble. Now, psychologists can look at it and say, 'Yeah, it was because of what happened to his sister.' And it was. But the bottom line is that, after Mae Ann died, my dad lost total interest in me and in everything else that was going on around him. I felt I was invisible. See, I took it as he lost it in me. The truth is, he lost it in everything. It wasn't until I took an inventory in AA that I saw what was going on with me at the time. I stole my dad's car. I was drinking regularly. Now how do you do that in a home where there is a strict disciplinarian? I'd stagger in. Dad didn't want to see what was going on with me—and now I know that.*

*"God was not in my life. When I saw all the pain in my family I said, 'OK, God, it's not that I don't believe in you. I just don't want to have anything to do with you.' I couldn't do that physically. On Sundays, I'd have to go to church. When I got a little older and started to go to St. Mary's, I'd go to the cigar store across the street and play the pinball machine while Mass was going on. In my head, I left the Church when I was fourteen. And then, when I was nineteen, I left the Church physically when I left home. That's when I broke my father's heart—when I signed up to go in the Army. I didn't join the Army to break my father's heart; I just wanted to get away. I wanted out from what I felt was that whole thing that was crushing me. I was trying to live as a Catholic and I didn't believe any of it. I can't tell the number of events in my life when I should have died doing the crazy things I did.*

*"Because of a lot of prayer and support, I finally turned my life around. But I know that, for a lot of years, I was on a path of virtual self-destruction."*

---

Besides the emotional fallout from Mae Ann's death, there were also enormous financial problems. Because of the length and severity of Mae Ann's illness, Dad had large medical bills to pay. He was self-employed and didn't have the kind of health insurance that people might have today. For a long time, he borrowed money against his house—and I'm sure he had other bills and loans. At the time, I was still stationed at St. Matthew's in East Stroudsburg and was receiving the salary of a diocesan priest: $60.00 a month. During those years, I had come to know a very wealthy and generous person. He didn't belong to the parish, but he had relatives there. His name was Joseph. We seemed to hit it off. I don't remember why he did what he did, but once in a while, when he would be at the parish, he would hand me a hundred-dollar bill—not for the parish, but for me. That was an enormous amount of money—almost double my monthly salary.

I guess throughout my early years at St. Matthew's, I must have mentioned Joseph's great generosity. During the fifties, I was flabbergasted when, one day, Dad asked me if I would consider asking Joseph if he would lend Dad some money. I knew my Dad's finances were probably exhausted, and I would have helped him if I could; but $60 a month hardly made me a financier. I also knew that Dad was in danger of losing the house because he had borrowed against it all through Mae Ann's illness. I didn't like the idea of being put in a posture where I would ask for money for my family. I didn't feel that was my position in the family; it wasn't really something that I felt I needed to do. But after a lot of prayer, and because of Dad's extreme need, I approached Joseph. He was completely open to giving Dad the money, but he insisted that I tell no one where the money came from. And then he handed me ten one-thousand dollar bills. I gave the money to Dad—it was a life saver for him at the time. For me, it was a new and different role, but I was happy to be able to do something for my parents during that difficult time.

When Dad approached Joseph some years later to repay him, Joseph wouldn't accept the money. It was an extraordinarily generous gift. Maybe now, in the telling of this story, it can finally be acknowledged.

In the aftermath of Mae Ann's death, three years ordained, I have to admit that I still hadn't worked out some of my own issues with my dad. All of us had a lot of grief to deal with; but it would be unfair to couple what I was feeling with that loss. For many years, I was aware of my own, rather deep antagonism toward my father. When I thought about my hostility, I always traced it to the time in grade school when Dad reacted so strongly to my falling grades. That day, within myself, I knew he really didn't love me. He was proud of me only when I was successful—when he could brag about me to his friends, when he could point to me as a favorable reflection of himself. I knew that my own bouts of violent anger were rooted in that painful event so many years before. The seeds of hatred that took root in me that day stayed with me and grew over the years.

I wasn't a kid anymore. I had to take responsibility for the hostility I harbored for so many years.

One afternoon in the summer after Mae Ann's death, I went to see my parents in Wilkes-Barre. I'm not sure what day it was, but it wasn't Sunday. It was my day off. I was aware that, for some years, Dad had been trying to develop a stronger spiritual life, and he seemed to undergo some important changes. As kids, we knew that Dad, like many other people in our parish, hardly ever went to Communion. As we grew older, we did see Dad move slowly toward a greater devotional life (rather than just having a primarily social connection to the Church). Along the way, he also had a kind of conversion because of a great experience he had had at a retreat house near Philadelphia. He began to be more in touch with God. He began to go to daily Mass with Mom and, in time, he developed a devotion to the Eucharist.

In spite of all that, there was a new layer of fury growing in Dad's already explosive anger. It was the deep anger that he was experiencing with God because of Mae Ann's illness and death. He was seething with anger. But that particular day, it wasn't Dad who exploded; it was me. We were in his garden in the back yard and I gave full sway to years of anger. I told him how Mae Ann's death was about Mae Ann, not about him; how self-centered he was; how entitled he felt to tell God how things should be; how he thought everything and everyone belonged to him; how the world should reflect only what he wanted. I remember shouting, "You love no one but yourself. I know that. Even God needs to live in fear of displeasing you. You don't love me; that's for sure. You never did. I'm just a satellite in your orbit. Everyone is. Now God is! Everything and everyone belongs to you. It's you that you love. In my whole life, you never once told me you loved me. You never once hugged me. You never once said, 'I love you.' Never! Not once!"

I know I cut Dad to the quick that day. If I hit him with a hammer, he couldn't have felt the pain of those moments any more. He cried and cried and cried. He hugged me and he told me he loved me. We stayed in the garden for a long time. Much of what happened was new. Before I left, he promised that he wouldn't let a single day go by without saying, "I love you."

That was a very difficult day, but I had faced my own anger. I couldn't look at Dad's anger without looking at my own. I think we turned a corner that day. There were still rough spots to come, but we communicated that day. Change was slow and not without struggle but, as the years went by, Dad's conversion continued to grow—as did mine. As he moved into his later years, much of the rigidity that was so characteristically his began to gradually soften.

Mom continued, as we all did—but, no doubt, with a broken heart. Once in a while, she would go upstairs, where she would take out a box filled with some of Mae Ann's things, and we knew it was her precious time to spend remembering her daughter.

Eventually, we all began to adjust to the loss of Mae Ann, whose life would continue to teach us all many more things.

## The Flood of '55

Like everyone else in the family, I returned to my duties after Mae Ann's death, continuing with parish work at St. Matthew's in the weeks that followed. In early August, two hurricanes, named Connie and Diane, hit what newspapers called a one-two punch within a week of each other. Hurricane Connie left more than ten inches of rain in a 48-hour period in the Pocono mountains on August 11th; this event put the Delaware and its tributaries at flood stage. On August 18th, just one week later, Hurricane Diane brought another 11 ¼ inches in a 36-hour period. The joint events were considered the most destructive natural disaster ever to hit the Delaware Valley. The final results were, if not catasphrophic, disastrous.

In the mid fifties, people weren't as aware of upcoming weather events as we are today. We took the weather as it came. Rain was hardly a big deal; but as the time passed, I became caught up in events that my radar had no way of assessing. I do remember that it had been raining for days. I was in the parish house by myself. The pastor and the other assistant, Father Barrett, were both out, and I was taking care of things at the parish. It seemed it was raining forever, but I really had no idea of what was happening—or, more importantly, what was about to happen. I do remember it was a Friday, because I know I had made Communion calls. I went to bed at about my usual time. Sometime later, the phone rang. A parishioner named Annie was on the line. Annie was blind.

"Father," she said, "I think there's a water main break in my house. There's water up to my feet. Could you come down and help me? I don't know what to do. I'm here by myself."

I got up, dressed, jumped into the parish car, and started driving toward Annie's house.

I really had no idea of the magnitude of the problem when Annie called me. As I got closer and closer to where Annie lived, I heard the sound of water and began to understand what the tremendous roar had to mean: It was no water main break; it was some very serious flooding. As I drove on, I met a fellow by the name of Harvey. Harvey had a monstrous truck. He exchanged information with me: Brodhead Creek had dammed up and overflowed and it was sweeping away everything and anyone in its path. I left my car. I got into the truck with Harvey and we drove into the water as far as we could without causing the motor to shut off. There were cars stranded everywhere. We tried to help people who were stranded in (or on top of) their cars to get to higher ground.

Only later did I hear the disastrous particulars of a scene worse than the one we were experiencing. A 30-foot-high flood wave on Brodhead Creek disintegrated the building of a religious youth camp south of Analomink. It swept away 46 camp members, most of them children. Eight were rescued; but according to reports, 30 others perished.

Eventually, Annie's son Carl, who lived in the area, was able to evacuate his mother from her home. I was always grateful that Annie had called me, actually alerting me to what was going on without even realizing it herself.

It was reported that I saved ten lives during that flood. Most of it has blurred over the years. But I still remember a lady who was on top of one of the cars with her dog. Harvey and I threw her a rope. The woman was able to tie the rope onto the car, which was about to be swept away—and her with it. In the midst of the confusion, I could see that she was pregnant.

## Priest Saves Eucharist, 10 Persons From Flood

East Stroudsburg, Pa.—Despite torrential flood waters, a priest and a layman risked their lives to save the Blessed Sacrament in a mission church engulfed in water. Witnesses credit the priest for rescuing 10 persons, one a blind woman, endangered by the flood.

Father John A. Esseff, assistant at St. Matthew's Parish, left the rectory when flood waters rose to inspect the mission Church of St. John several miles distant in Bushkill. It was surrounded by violent, muddy waters that threatened the area.

Richard McIntyre, a parishioner and father of six children, and Father Esseff swam through the current to the church. At the time, the water had risen to the base of the tabernacle door. Father Esseff consumed the Blessed Sacrament, and the two men swam back to safety carrying the sacred vessels with them.

Father Girard Angelo, a curate at St. Matthew's, describes the heroic work of the priests to bring Holy Oils to the flood victims in the area, which was the hardest hit in Pennsylvania. At least 75 persons lost their lives.

When the flood struck, three priests of the parish were on the opposite side of Brodhead Creek, working on the other side of the creek.

Royal Brown volunteered to swim. He risked his life in two crossings in the swollen rapids, which carried along parts of houses, trees, and other debris.

Father Harold G. Durkin, pastor, and Father Francis G. Barrett, an assistant, working with the other two priests, were able to cover both sides of the creek. They gave Conditional Absolution as bodies were brought to collecting centers by helicopter and automobile.

St. Matthew's School and Rectory, undamaged by the flood, were opened as relief centers for throngs of people moving to higher ground. Rectory bedrooms were given to exhausted women and children. Sisters, Servants of the Immaculate Heart of Mary, who staff the school, aided victims until relief agencies were set up.

*Article on the flood*

As I got closer to her, I realized how concerned she was about her dog, "Oh, my dog! My dog's going to drown!"

I was screaming at her, "You and that damn dog. Let that dog go!"

"I can't."

I screamed louder, "I said let that dog go!"

By that time, I had inched my way over to her by holding onto the rope.

She still had that dog. I was pretty rough with her. I smacked her in the face. Of course, she was startled.

"What was that for?"

"If you don't let that dog go, we're all going to drown."

She loosened her grip on the dog and, with her between me and the rope, I inched us back toward the truck. Then Harvey slowly backed the truck up until we were out of the water. We put the woman in my car and I hurried her off to the hospital while Harvey stayed behind to help others. As I dashed to the hospital the woman, who was in the back seat, began to deliver her baby. By the time we arrived at the emergency room, the baby had arrived. The medical staff was on hand and they took care of the both of them. When I was on my way back to join Harvey, I found myself amazed at the miracle of having seen that baby lying on his mother's stomach, still connected by the umbilical cord. I remember thinking that, if I couldn't help anyone else, that baby made all our efforts worthwhile.

For at least the next forty-eight hours, I continued to help in any way I could. There was enormous need everywhere. Helicopters arrived and I was able to move about in one of them with the rescue teams. Many people were injured. We did what we could to get them help. Some people were close to death. Others had died. I remember anointing them. I thought that most of the people were Black until I realized that they were all covered with mud.

When the pastor and Father Barrett were able to return, we had Masses in many different places to accommodate the people. Shelters were set up all over the region to provide sleeping quarters and food. Air Force helicopters continued to bring children out of isolated areas and camp grounds. The Civil Air Patrol made food drops over affected areas.

## GEORGE

*"I was in Virginia when the flood took place in the Poconos. I went to see John as soon as I could—the day after the receding started. It wasn't until then that the authorities began to allow cars to go into the area. I drove up to Stroudsburg and I couldn't believe what I was seeing: Busses and cars were piled up ten high and looked like broken toys. I was looking at the water line when I was there. Ordinarily, the place of the pileup was a stream only about six inches deep. During the flooding, the water rose to thirty feet, becoming a force able to carry busses and cars downstream.*

*"The rain had broken a dam in the mountains, just above a religious camp full of young boys. It wiped that camp out, sweeping away 46 campers, most of them children. That group of young boys made up the greatest number of casualties among the more than one hundred who were killed.*

*"The rainfall was so rapid and intense that it took out bridges and ripped homes apart. There were dozens of people missing and hundreds left homeless. I understand that bodies were still discovered years later—and some were never found.*

*"I can't express just how much I admired John for all he did for the people during that terrible time. I never would have understood the scope of the devastation if I hadn't seen it myself.*

*"I also found out when I was in Stroudsburg that John and one of his parishioners, a man named Richard, had left East Stroudsburg and gone to the mission church of St. John's in Bushkill, where they swam through the waters surrounding the church. At the time the water had risen to the base of the tabernacle door. Entering the church, John consumed the Eucharist and then both he and Richard took the chalices from the church and swam back to safety."*

When the worst was over and a modicum of normalcy began to return, Father Barrett suggested that I go home for a few days and recuperate. With time to think, I found myself overwhelmed as I remembered the fear in the faces of children and old people, the suffering of the injured and misplaced, and the faces of the dead. I began to cry. My brother Joe came to me and put his arms around me, and I just cried and I cried and I cried. I had never before experienced tragedy of such magnitude; the suffering of so many people, so many families—it broke my heart.

# Seasons of Loss

## Going Home

As 1955 drew to a close, I got a call one night at St. Matthew's from my mother in Wilkes-Barre, telling me that my grandfather wanted to talk to me. It was Christmas day, but I hadn't gone home because Christmas was a very busy time in the parish. I was happy when Mom put him on the phone.

"John," he said to me, "could you come home and bring your oils with you? I want you to anoint me." I was somewhat taken aback. 1955 was pre-Vatican Council. In my mind, there was no such thing as anointing. 'Anointing' meant the sacrament of Extreme Unction, reserved for people who were dying. I was also sure that my understanding of the sacrament was Grandpa's understanding as well. But I respected his wish and I said, "Sure, Grandpa. I'll come. It's Christmas, so I'll have to talk to the pastor. I'll have to borrow the parish car, but I'm sure that can be arranged. I'll let you know as soon as I know when I can come."

I arranged things with the pastor and, after I celebrated the morning Mass at St. Matthew's, I drove to Wilkes-Barre; it was December 27th. I was very surprised when I got there to see my grandfather fully dressed and certainly not looking sick at all. He had on his hat and coat, and he said, "John, get back in the car. We're going to drive to St. Anthony's. I want to go to confession." So, I got back in the car and Grandpa and I rode down to St. Anthony's Church.

It was probably almost eleven o'clock by the time we arrived at the church. There was no one else there but the two of us. Grandpa went into the side confessional; I went into the center and Grandpa began a general confession. He confessed all the sins of his life. I gave him absolution and a penance to say. Then I left the confessional, walked to the back of the church, and waited in the last pew. When Grandpa finished praying, he joined me. We got back into the car and drove to his home at 108 Prospect Street, the place where I had been born and lived as a little boy. We went upstairs to the room that we lived in as children. That was his room now; his bed was there. He took his clothes off—he always wore long underwear. And then he got into bed.

With that done, he looked at me and said, "John, I want you to anoint me now."

"All right, Grandpa, I'll do that. I think I'll call Aunt Marian and Aunt Sarah (his daughters) and my mother to come up and join us." They all knew Grandpa wanted me to anoint him and they were downstairs in the kitchen. I called to them and they came up to Grandpa's room. We all stood around the bed, and I did indeed give my grandfather the sacrament of Extreme Unction, more commonly called the 'Last Rites.'

# Brothers & Fathers

When the prayers were said and the ritual of anointing was completed, the women left the room and went downstairs. I stayed with him. After a short while, he turned to me and said, "I want you to call my brother."

Grandpa had a brother by the name of Moses Esseff. My understanding of the relationship over the years was that Moses was always aggravated with his brother George or someone in George's family; I knew there were always conflicts. I called Moses, who somehow got to Prospect Street and came up to see his brother. I left them alone in the room together and they had a long visit. My guess is that they had some kind of reconciliation. Moses stayed quite a while, but I don't know how long they talked, because my grandfather was one who could be with someone in a room and not feel the need to keep talking. It seemed the two brothers spent a long time together until Moses went on his way.

I explained my plans to my grandfather: I had an overnight and would stay with Mom and Dad. In the morning, I would offer Mass in St. Anthony's and then I would bring him Communion after Mass.

Of course, Dad had been at work all day, but he came to Grandpa's when he knew I was there. He seemed really upset with Grandpa—annoyed that he had called me to come to Wilkes-Barre. "What are you bothering John for? There's nothing wrong with you."

I spoke up, "Dad, your father asked for an anointing. He didn't twist my arm or anything. I was more than happy to come." And nothing more was said on that matter.

In the morning, I did just what I had told Grandpa I would do. After Mass I returned to his room and brought him Communion. Then I sat with him for a long time. I asked if there was anything else he wanted to talk about or any more he wanted to tell me. He assured me everything was as he wanted it to be.

Shortly afterward, I said my "goodbye" and went back to East Stroudsburg.

The next morning, I offered Mass at St. Matthew's and went back to the rectory. I was only there a short time when I got a phone call and learned that my grandfather had died.

The doctor was a little vague about the cause of Grandpa's death. They really didn't know what was wrong with him; he had no symptoms. I'm guessing that wasn't all that uncommon when someone old died. I just assumed that Grandpa had some kind of foreknowledge that God was calling him home. He had led a full life. He was really a holy man. He had made his peace with God and he was ready to go home.

The response to his death was one of the most beautiful experiences that I've ever had as a priest. There were no histrionics—none of the weeping and moaning that he had watched over the years. He had had all these children, he had done his job, and he was going back with the Lord. People came and lined up to express their love and gratitude for Grandpa's care and generosity over the years. The sentiments were all similar: "He saved us from going hungry more than once. We used to look forward to his coming." And children made sure we all knew he brought them cookies, as well. People showed up in tremendous numbers and gave genuine tribute to the acts of kindness Grandpa had done all his life.

The prayers were continuous. The singing in Arabic and Aramaic was absolutely awe inspiring. The funeral Mass and the burial were filled with peace and a quiet kind of joy. That particular kind of peace lifted everyone else up and an aura of joy surrounded everyone there. When the funeral was over, it almost seemed that we all came back to earth. It was a fitting end to his generous life and his peaceful death. For me, it was one of the most significant experiences that I have had as a priest.

## GEORGE

*"When Grandpa died I was in Virginia with Rosemary and George Jr. Grandpa wasn't sick. Maybe he had a little cold. He must have known he was going to die, and that's why he called John. He did tell John, 'My work's done.' I think he was just ready to go home to God. I didn't even cry at his funeral. I can't say that I was happy, but I knew he was with God. Strange, but the thoughts of his being gone make me cry now. Maybe the tears are for us, because he's no longer here for us to enjoy."*

# Chapter 26

## Our Growing Family

### *Rosemary*

After Gidue's funeral, we all returned to our separate lives.

Early in 1956, after returning to Virginia, I discovered that I was pregnant and, as closely as could be predicted, I was due sometime in November of that same year. We had told the family and, sometime later, we went to Pennsylvania to visit our families. I remember that Dad said nothing about my pregnancy; but, at some time during the evening, he said to me, "I'm doing a C-section tomorrow morning. Eight o'clock. I want you there."

"Why do I have to be down there? Bob and Ag are there to give you a hand. I don't need to be there."

"I want you to see what happens with a C-section. No matter, animal or human, same procedure, same thing. When we have C-sections, we don't breed the animal again."

Looking back, I'm sure he had a lot of concerns, but he addressed them sort of in a backhanded way. At any rate, I must have gotten the point, because I still remember that day.

Really, though, my second pregnancy went smoothly. I didn't have the kind of complications I had with George Jr. and all seemed to be going well. George and I and young George were enjoying our little home at Fort Belvoir. By that time, George's brother John had been ordained and moved back to Pennsylvania; but also by that time, Frank Hanlon, George's class-

*Frank Hanlon*

177

mate and friend from high school and college, was living in the area. We got to see him during those years.

---

## GEORGE

*"Somewhere while finishing college and having been accepted by three or four medical schools, Frank had made up his mind: He was not going to be a doctor. He told his dad, "I'm going to enter the Franciscan seminary and become a foreign missionary." And that's exactly what he did.*

*"When we were still in Virginia, Frank was at the Franciscan monastery in Washington, D.C. When we could, Rosemary and I would visit him there. One time when we were there, Frank grabbed little George and carried him toward the doors of the cloister. He opened the door, threw a ball down the center aisle, and told George to run and get the ball. Frank hadn't changed a bit; he still loved a good laugh. We were hoping the guys in the cloister were as amused as we were."*

---

George was still in the midst of sorting out the details of possibly launching a business career. We were still living on the post then, but somewhere along the way, we had moved from our one-bedroom apartment on Knight Street to a two-bedroom apartment. Short of a month before George Jr.'s third birthday, our second child, a daughter, was born in Fort Belvoir at the Alexandria Hospital; it was October 1, 1956. Like George Jr., she was born by Caesarian section and did not go to full term. In spite of that, she was a big baby and, thank God, very healthy. I was pretty good and was certainly feeling much better than I had after George Jr.'s birth.

My mother was unable to come to Virginia to help out at the time, because she had some health issues of her own then and wasn't able to travel. Instead, my dad's sister, Aunt Lizzy, came. She was an elderly lady, but she was a big help. She took care of George Jr. and she cooked the meals; she stayed until Mom was able to come to help.

I was busy those days with the children, and George was busy too. Besides going to work each day, he was also attending night school during those early years of our marriage.

George continued to work on creating multiple designs for the rack while still working at the Army Corps of Engineers. He had always been intrigued by science, experimentation, and research but, with each new development, I began to realize that he was a scientist who was making a conscious decision to begin a business career in the design and manufacture of titanium products.

# Our Growing Family

On the home front, George and I knew we would soon have to move to a bigger place. When Mary Ellen was just about a year-and-a-half old, I received confirmation from the doctor that I was pregnant. The two children, George Jr. and Mary Ellen, were sharing a room. There was no question then: We had to move out of our two-bedroom apartment. Finding a bigger place to live was difficult then, as the area didn't have a lot of rental properties. We weren't interested in moving into Washington or Alexandria because George and his partner were making the racks in an area right off the post at Fort Belvoir, and that was convenient. We stayed on the post for a very short time until we found a place and moved to Springfield, Virginia.

In no time, we were faced with more complications. By the time my obstetrician became aware that we had moved to Springfield, he began to have some concerns about my being farther away from the hospital than I had been. George was really on the road a lot during that time and my obstetrician was in Alexandria. The doctor assured me that, as soon as it seemed prudent to take the baby, or in the event that I would have any difficulties, he would want to get me into the hospital right away. (He was well aware of my history and was taking no chances with jeopardizing either me or the baby.) The doctor also told me that I couldn't depend on ambulance service because that was not always immediately available that far out. He gave me his private phone number and said, "Anytime, night or day, you call me if you feel you might be in danger of hemorrhaging." He was fearful that this third pregnancy wouldn't work out. It was clear that he didn't approve of it, and that he really didn't think I would continue to carry. He was pretty clear when he said, "You should never have had another child after your first; that was a very difficult delivery. You know, if you were my wife, I wouldn't allow it." At any rate, the doctor was wrong and, in time, we lived to have still another blessing.

When George had to be away for any period of time, I would take George Jr. and Mary Ellen to Shamokin, where we could spend some time with my parents.

Meanwhile, George had made his final decision: He was going to quit his job with the government and go into full production. Once he shared that with his partner, we learned that the partnership was going to be dissolved. George was going to have to find a new manufacturer for the rack.

With all of these considerations, we knew we were going to have to make some significant changes in our lives.

*Grandma and Grandpa Dorning with Mary Ellen and George Jr.*

# CHAPTER 27

## BEGINNING IN BUSINESS

### *George*

My concerns about Rosemary, coupled with the knowledge that we had to relocate for business reasons, prompted me to quickly investigate which path was the best one for us to take. After many inquiries, I got a lead from my uncle Bill Nasser, who lived in Scranton, Pennsylvania. He told me about a man who had a manufacturing facility there. I followed that lead and I returned to Pennsylvania to set up manufacturing there. I would have gone anyplace; I just wanted a place where I could get the job done. Rosemary and I, with George Jr. and Mary Ellen, left Springfield in 1958.

We rented a house on Monroe Avenue in Scranton. It was a great location: Rosemary was under the care of a good obstetrician, Dr. Curtin; We were only four or five blocks from the Moses Taylor Hospital; My parents lived about 15 miles away in nearby Wilkes-Barre; I was able to continue my work—less than a mile away from our home, where I had a facility to manufacture the racks I designed.

We enrolled George in a preschool conducted at Immaculate Conception Parish, about four blocks away from our home. That gave Rosemary and Mary Ellen time together. Short of some tiredness, the pregnancy went well and, on December 6, 1958, our third child, Kathy, was born at the Moses Taylor Hospital in Scranton. The delivery went well, but Rosemary had another C-section and needed time to regain her strength. I was able to get a woman to come to the house to help Rosemary with the children and to give her more opportunity to recuperate. Kathy was baptized in St. Ann's Maronite Church in West Scranton; John was able to drive to Scranton to baptize her and we had a wonderful family celebration.

## JOHN

"I developed a great love for George and Rosemary's children. I always had a very special love for George Jr. But, I must say, I had a very special, a very tender love for Mary Ellen too. Kathy was next to steal my heart. I had the privilege of baptizing her and, as she grew up, I was always kind of aware that she had her own gifts and was very different from George and Mary Ellen. When they all lived in Scranton, I used to go to visit them. I'd stop by and we'd talk about all kinds of stuff; we'd have a lot of fun.

"We'd stay up after the three little ones were in bed, and if I wanted to stay for the night, George would put up a cot on the porch for me. One night, we stayed up talking until about one o'clock in the morning. I decided to stay the night. About three o'clock in the morning, there was a general racket going on. Young George got sick, and George and Rosemary were running around taking care of him. I could hear him throwing up. I stayed right where I was! Eventually, things quieted down. Then, no sooner was the ruckus over, than Mary Ellen woke up and she started throwing up too. I remember thinking, 'Well, that's married life—but I don't need to stay around here. I have seven o'clock Mass in the morning.'

"I got up, got dressed, got in my car, and drove to the rectory in East Stroudsburg. I had at least two hours of sleep at St. Matthew's, but I don't know if my brother or Rosemary got any sleep that night. I remember calling them the next day. There was some small talk, but the pointed message from my point of view was, 'Celibacy has assets of its own.'"

With the family settled and the manufacturing shop running, I followed the same schedule I had adopted in Virginia: I would travel to potential customers and find out what their exact needs were. I would sell the product, return to Scranton with their precise orders, create the necessary designs, and then have them fabricated in the machine shop. Once the finished product was ready, we would ship that product in whatever quantity our customers needed. That was the routine. I'd go out, sell more, take orders, create the necessary designs, have the orders manufactured according to requests, ship the racks to the customers, and then start the process all over again. The biggest downside was that I was away more than I was home.

Yet, the business seemed to be a simple operation. I would sub-contract my work to the machine shop; a secretary, my only employee, took care of all the paperwork. The business of buying titanium and selling titanium racks was extremely lucrative. When I was with the Army Corps, I was making $12,500 a year. That was a good salary in the early 50s. By 1957, with a business of my own, I made $125,000—that was ten times my former salary with the government! The following year, I made $145,000.

I was enjoying the process—introducing men in industry to titanium, creating designs, and doing business, not just in a local market, but with people all over the country. Soon, there were other areas that needed consideration. My accountant, Bill Nasser, was faced with explaining to me extenuating circumstances that came along with the financial success we were enjoying. I was now in the 90% tax bracket. Bill suggested that I invest in something so that I wouldn't have to pay so much tax. At that point, I took his advice and bought the shop from the man who was doing the manufacturing for me.

The operation that had begun in Virginia was proceeding on a much wider scope in Scranton. Unfortunately, I was naïve enough to think that the only thing I had to know was how to design what my customers wanted. As the owner of a manufacturing facility, in which I had about sixty-five people working for me, I soon learned that designing was not enough. Looking back, I realize that I made a lot of mistakes. The man who was running the shop had convinced me that, if I could buy $100,000 more worth of equipment, we could triple our sales, have a tremendous manufacturing company, and make a lot of money. I trusted him and I moved right ahead. I bought all kinds of equipment. I expanded the shop. We had two shifts working and, in no time, we had quite a thorough machine shop operation.

As time went on, I found out that the previous owner, the man from whom I had bought the shop and who had continued working for me, was doing high-specification work. He was making parts for Federal Pacific; he was also doing a big job with the Signal Corps. He was buying big blocks of copper and machining them. The men in the shop had as much work as they could handle; they were busy as could be. I wasn't familiar with the manufacture of copper or steel, and they were taking orders and doing an awful lot of work, but I eventually came to find out that we were losing money.

I wasn't sure why, but two facts were clear: We had mounting expenses and a dwindling income. Ironically, in spite of my success in selling and manufacturing titanium racks, we were still losing money. I had a wife and three children and, as far as business was concerned, we were going backwards. In time, I figured out what had been happening. I discovered that the man in charge of the shop was underbidding jobs: The shop was selling for one dollar what it was taking a dollar-and-a-half to make. All of this recklessness, of course, occurred at my expense. It didn't take long for that practice to gobble up all the money I was making in titanium sales, as well as some of the money I had made previously. I found myself losing $25,000 a month. When I investigated further and found out that some of the guys in the shop were also selling out the back door on me, I confronted them. There were no denials. I closed the doors. I didn't prosecute anyone. I just cut my losses. I had to liquidate everything to pay off my debts. Among other things, the people I had foolishly left in charge hadn't been paying Social Security for the workers and I wound up paying $40,000 to the government for just that. By the time everything was said and done, I was still $175,000 in debt.

I blamed the whole mess on myself: I wasn't paying enough attention; I relied too much on the word of others. I should have been more attentive. I used to sign checks and then go out of town for two weeks. Who the hell would sign a hundred blank checks and then leave town? That's just plain stupid, if you're running a business. I should have been more aware. I hadn't started out as a businessman and, quite frankly, I didn't know much about how to run a business on that scale. I was a researcher who was proud of his product, happy as hell that people were buying my idea and my products; I was enjoying my work and thrilled to be making money to support my growing family.

When I think about that first failure in business, I'm glad of it because it was a growth experience for me. Although what I did in Scranton seemed to have been a total failure, I'm convinced that it might have been the best decision because it taught me a lot. I lost $175,000, but I could have lost a hell of a lot more if I had been involved on an even larger scale. If I didn't lose the money at that time, I could have gone on stupidly, thinking I was smart, and could have eventually lost a lot more than I did.

On the positive side, I had had several offers of employment in Pennsylvania and I knew I could have taken any one of those jobs. Yet I knew that, if I did, I would probably make about $15,000 a year. At that rate, I would never get out of debt. In fact, I was certain that there was no salary I could have commanded working for someone else that would get me out of the kind of debt I was in. I was in a very vulnerable position and, looking back, I think that some people were more aware of that fact than I was.

When I first set up shop in Scranton, one of the outfits that began doing business with me was a group of guys who owned a family business. They had a big machining shop in a town outside of Scranton. The family had a questionable reputation and, though it was never proved, many people believed that they had ties with organized crime. I guess everyone in the area was at least familiar with the legend. I was familiar with it too, but for more than generic reasons.

Years earlier, during the war, it was alleged that some of the members of that family were selling counterfeit stamps for gasoline. I knew this because, at that time, a cousin of mine, was involved with them. They got caught and, as the story goes, my cousin took the fall for them. He served six months in the county jail in Wilkes-Barre and, because he did that, they owed him; he never had to worry again. They put him into business and helped him out a lot. I knew all of those things, but they were in a dark corner of my memory at that time.

Not long after I moved to Scranton, that same cousin introduced me to two brothers from the family that had done so much for him over the years. They had been doing business with the previous owner of the business that I bought and they immediately began doing business with me. I didn't think much of it. I assumed that their previous connection with the shop owner and their relationship with my cousin were good business connections for me. I was just happy when they sent me an order for the product right away, and really happy that they sent a check with the order! (Most people weren't paying their bills in thirty days.) I figured they paid up-front because they knew I was getting the business started and, maybe, because of their ties to my cousin. As time went on, when I was near their plant, I would often stop by and have breakfast with one of the brothers. That was my history with them.

Even before I closed the shop, and as soon as I knew there were financial problems, Rosemary and I had begun to tighten our belts. Rosemary and I each had a Cadillac; I sold both of them and bought a Buick. We were paying a lot of rent for the big house in Scranton and we knew we had to find a less expensive place to live.

It was during this time that one of the brothers from the family machine shop business approached me with an offer to work for them. They also presented several other enticing offers. It seemed that they were being really nice to me.

JOHN

*"I would stop saying that!"*

Well, anyway, at the time, it seemed that way.

They knew that Rosemary and I had to move out of the house in Scranton, and one day one of them said, "George, we're putting my mother up in another home. Bring your wife, and the both of you can look at my mother's house." He wanted to sell me that house. Because of having been awarded a great contract with Chrysler, they were flush with money. The brothers were building three homes along the Susquehanna River, and they had no need for the one they were selling.

---

### ROSEMARY

*"Poor Pop. He would come up to Scranton and he'd say, 'Is he still talking to those guys?' He didn't want George to have anything to do with them.*

---

"Yes, and now we were being offered a house down the line. George is all fired up."

Rosemary wasn't too keen on the idea, but one day we went through the house. It was full of baroque and Italian furniture. Each room we went through was very elaborately furnished. I remember saying to Rosemary, "Isn't this a great place?"

"I don't like it."

We went to the next room. "Isn't this room beautiful?"

"No, it's not something that appeals to me."

"He only wants $11,000, and that includes all the furniture."

---

### ROSEMARY

*"Our Lady of the Sacred Heart worked overtime. George's poor father and I were beside ourselves. I'll tell you honestly, there was a point when I said to George, 'Are you just pressing my buttons with all this? I don't want any part of this and I don't want to get involved. Aren't you listening to your dad? Can't you hear what he's saying?'"*

---

It was during that same time that the guys in the machine shop were fulfilling their contract with Chrysler, making turrets for the top of tanks. They were making those components for Chrysler which, in turn, was having them made for the United States Army. About six months before the deal with Chrysler went down, the family involved owned a fleet of Cadillacs. When the deal went through with Chrysler, the brothers immediately went out and bought Chrysler Imperials. They wanted to get rid of the Cadillacs and, once again, they approached me with a great deal: They asked me if I wanted to buy one of the cars. Actually, by that time, I had already sold both our cars, and Rosemary and I were sharing the replacement car. I thought it would be great if Rosemary had a car of her own again.

# Beginning in Business

"Rosemary, I got a great offer today. I can get you a new Cadillac with maybe four or five thousand miles on it for only about 10% of what the car is worth."

---

## ROSEMARY

*"I immediately knew who was selling the car. I didn't want any part of that deal, either. I agreed 100% with George's dad: He was really concerned that George would get sucked into business with those guys, now that he was deciding what to do and had so much debt to deal with. Dad kept saying, 'We don't care what they're offering. Don't ever go there. That is not an out.'*

*"But the car! That was another story. As far as the car was concerned, it was really a terrific idea. Why? It had some extras: it had bullet-proof windows. Everyone knows how important it is to have that feature when you're going to the supermarket with the kids!*

*"George and I laugh about it now. But then I was concerned as to why they were so hell bent on 'being nice' to George."*

---

I knew how strongly opposed everyone in the family was to my even considering any dealings with the two brothers, but I guess I also have to admit that I thought about all these options. I had to think about them: I was aware that the bottom had fallen out of my dream. I was worrying about feeding Rosemary and the three children. I was concerned about getting out of debt. But, all other considerations aside, to tell the truth, when I sat down and figured it out, there was no way I was going to work for that business family or, for that matter, anyone else. My gut instincts were right: I had no desire to spend the rest of my life paying off a debt on a weekly salary working for someone else.

Eventually, we moved to Forty-Fort, a small town between Wilkes-Barre and Scranton. There, Rosemary could depend on my parents for more help with the children, but I had no shop for manufacturing and no money to buy material. What I did have was a debt of $175,000.

I knew I wanted to return to the titanium industry and do what I had already successfully done. I had the design, the product, and a good customer base. I didn't have the money to do the manufacturing that would turn those key ingredients into a successful business.

During all the time I was working out of Scranton, I was pretty involved in making parts for the automotive industry and bought a lot of titanium from people in California. I knew three guys there who sold me raw material. They were well aware of what I was doing and how successful I was in selling my product. When

I stopped ordering, they called me to see what was going on, because I had been a good customer of theirs. I told them what had happened and that I had sold the shop. When they realized the kind of financial trouble I was in, they said, "We'll invest in you."

I went to California around June or July of '59 to talk to those three potential investors. When the negotiations started, all three said they'd have 25% of the business and I'd have 75%. But they were very slick and, by the time the terms were finally agreed on, I wound up with 25% and they had 75%. I didn't have much bargaining power. I was in desperate financial straits and they knew it. So when they said they would put up $70,000, I accepted what seemed to offer the greatest possibilities. The name of the company that we formed jointly was called Continental Racks.

It was late August or early September of 1959 when I arrived at their place in Hollywood to work. They gave me a desk in an office and said, "Work out of here," so that's what I did. I lived in a hotel in Hollywood and traveled home to Forty-Fort every weekend. They put up the money from the time of my arrival until January of 1960.

I had enjoyed a great deal of success working with the automotive industry and I knew that the aircraft industry also used a lot of aluminum parts. Right next door to the guys I was working with was an aircraft manufacturing company. In time, I was subcontracting my manufacturing to that firm. It wasn't much of a stretch to figure out that titanium racks could also save the people in the aircraft industry time and money. I was confident that I could sell my ideas to them just as I had to the people in the automotive industry. I knew that I could design and manufacture for them as well. If I was going to make the kind of money I needed, I knew that I had to stick with titanium.

Although the deal with the guys from Hollywood wasn't the best in the world, it gave me what I needed to get my manufacturing done. Within two weeks of joining them, I sold $30,000 worth of racks. During the next two weeks, I got another $170,000 worth of business. I was back in the business of doing what I did best— working with titanium.

Throughout all of these developments, Rosemary was always very supportive. Finances were really tight and Rosemary had a full-time job taking care of the three children. In spite of the struggle, I never heard Rosemary complain. I know a lot of wives might have said, "You're stupid. You're making a mistake." But she always stood by me. She always did what she had to do to keep the household going.

# Beginning in Business

*Mary Ellen, George Jr. and Kathy*

"George was traveling a lot during that time, trying to get the business up and running again, and figuring out how to get out of debt. Living in Forty-Fort, we were close to George's mom and dad. They would drop over, and it was really nice being so close to family. They were able to spend time with the children and I appreciated their help. George was giving me ten dollars a week to run the house. I'm not quite sure if George's dad was aware just how tight things were, but I do remember he and George's mom would bring vegetables and other kinds of food with them when they came over. That was a great help and we were able to get by.

"I could also drive to Shamokin to visit with my mom and dad, and my brother Bob and his wife Agnes. Traveling from Forty-Fort to Shamokin was certainly a lot easier for me and the children than getting there from Virginia.

"In spite of the financial crunch we were in, the children and I were enjoying the support and companionship of both our families."

While Rosemary remained settled in Pennsylvania with the kids, I went home each weekend and, on Monday mornings, returned to the West coast. With each successive week, I was getting thousands of dollars worth of orders. But on the down side, I also had thousands of dollars of debt. I was really dedicated to paying back the money I owed. At first, things remained very tight. We were very careful and Rosemary couldn't have been more encouraging. Rosemary's parents helped us out and lent us some money. They would say "down times in business are to be expected." They had a lot of faith in me and were always very positive. They kept saying that, eventually, things would perk up. We all prayed hard and worked hard, and they assured me that it was just a matter of time. Thank God, they proved to be right.

But as we approached the end of 1959, it didn't make sense that Rosemary and the kids would continue to live on the East coast while I was on the West coast.

# Brothers & Fathers

## ROSEMARY

"George was coming back each weekend and was saying, 'I think it would be good if we moved to the West coast.' I was in no way interested in doing that, partly because I liked the support I was getting from my parents and from George's parents. There were many family things that I was part of. One thing I remember happening during our stay in Forty-Fort was that George's younger brother, Joe, decided to join the army. I had hardly come to know him during our early years of marriage, partly because we lived in Virginia. Joe seemed so young, probably because he was more than ten years younger than George. His decision to join the military caused a lot of confusion— maybe even grief. I think George's parents were still trying to adjust to Mae Ann's death, and here their youngest child was going off to the Korean Conflict. I was glad that I could share that time with them.

"There were also many other matters that I was attentive to. The one that most concerned me was that I was pregnant. Because I had three children by C-section, the doctor I was seeing was cautious: 'You have to be careful if you're going to carry this baby. You're really stretching things now. I want you off your feet.'

"'Well, you know that's not possible. I have three little ones to look after.'

"I continued to say that I wasn't interested in moving. George dropped the discussion for a couple of weeks, but was sure relocating was the best way to go: 'You know, the business is doing pretty good, and I think this is going to be our way of getting out of the hole that we've gotten into.'

"I still had some reservations. The business was growing, but it was still a little if-y. We would be taking chances moving to California, where we didn't know anyone. I had a doctor that I felt confident with at the moment; he seemed to be OK with the pregnancy. Still, after dealing with the particulars of the commute to California each weekend for all of August, September, October, and November of 1959, George and I were leaning more and more toward the move. Finally, we went off to Moyallen Street to announce our plans to move.

"None of the family knew of the pregnancy, because we didn't want to tell anyone until we made up our minds about moving. Even then, we said nothing."

# Beginning in Business

Dad and Mom gave us the money to move; and in January of 1960, we traveled to California as a family. On one of my previous trips I had negotiated the rental of a house and we lived there together in a home of our own while we prayerfully looked forward to a successful pregnancy and the safe delivery of our fourth child.

# CHAPTER 28

## ACROSS THE CONTINENT

### *Rosemary*

George moved us, lock, stock and barrel, to the West coast. He had found and rented a lovely house in Van Nuys, California, in the San Fernando Valley. Thanks to his mom and dad, he was also able to buy a car when we got there. It didn't have bullet-proof windows, but it only cost $150 dollars and I could get around with the kids to wherever we needed to go.

Before I left Forty-Fort for California, I had confided in Dr. Curtin, the obstetrician in Scranton who had delivered Kathy. He knew that I was pregnant and that we were going to move to California. He was so wonderful—and so aware of my history of C-sections—that he said that he would look into the area where we were headed and would try to find me a good obstetrician. Because of my history of C-section births, he gave us the name of a top-notch doctor in California. As it turned out, that doctor's practice was in Beverly Hills, and the distance from our house to his office proved to be impractical. But I was always grateful to Dr. Curtin for his care.

When we arrived in Van Nuys, we immediately became involved in a church community, St. Elizabeth's. There we were fortunate enough to meet a couple, Bill and Helen, who had seven children. Helen told me she knew a very good Catholic doctor who had an excellent reputation for dealing in problem pregnancies. His name was Dr. Shepherd. I made an appointment to see him.

Dr. Shepherd was very thorough in learning my history of childbirth. Each of my children had to be delivered by Caesarian section, and none of them had reached full term. In those days, once a woman had had a C-section, she had to deliver all subsequent babies by C-section as well. Usually, the baby was taken before it was full term. That procedure was no longer the only option available. Dr. Shepherd was happy to announce that, although I had had three C-sections in the past, he was taking another stance. I was somewhat apprehensive. In the face of all that history, he said to me, "I want you to wait. I would like to see this baby come to full term."

I said, "I have never been advised to do that."

"Let's see how it goes."

I actually had some pain and other minor discomforts during the pregnancy, but Dr. Shepherd was like the North Star. He kept insisting that I could go full term. Each time I voiced a concern, he usually had the same response: "Well, let's just see how it goes. It's so much better for the baby to go full term."

Of course, long before this time, George and I had announced the pregnancy to both our families.

Mom came to help, as she had done with the other births. This time, she came out to help me and the children about two months before I was due. My dad, otherwise known as 'Doc Dorning,' came to join Mom, and he was furious with George: "You know, George, with the animals, we won't allow a second pregnancy when there's been a C-section. And my daughter is having a fourth?

It was a strong statement—or maybe a question, or maybe a reprimand. In any case, it wasn't as subtle a statement as he had made four years earlier when I was pregnant with Mary Ellen.

Denise was born on July 19th, 1960, and she was healthy and beautiful. It's interesting for me to think about the succession of pregnancies. My first pregnancy and birth were definitely the most difficult. But each pregnancy did get easier for me to deal with. Because C-sections are major surgery, they create limitations caused by scarring and eventual loss of the uterine wall. Moments after Denise was born, the doctor went out to tell George that he had a beautiful daughter. Denise was fine and I was fine; but my uterus wasn't fine. The doctor told George that he was going to have to do a complete hysterectomy. He proceeded immediately after Denise's delivery and performed the necessary surgery on me.

Remembering all these details has made me wonder about my own family history. Before I was married, I had no health problems at all. I do remember stories about my mother when she was young: very fun loving, vivacious, and quite a handful for Dad. She was quite a spirited lady. But as my mother got older, I remember that she had some illnesses that slowed her down. I know that she was plagued by arthritis early on, and that never left her. But she wasn't one to complain. We never heard much about the arthritis, unless she got pretty incapacitated with it. Mostly, I remember that.

# Across the Continent

But somewhere along the way, I did learn the story of my brother Bob's birth, along with that of my own. Mother had a very difficult time delivering Bob. We were never told the particulars. I do know that she was told that she probably would never have another child. I didn't remember that when George and I were pretty much told the same thing after George Jr.'s birth. I'm only remembering it now. When Bob was a little more than eight-years-old, Mother found herself not feeling all that well. She went to the doctor and he diagnosed her as having a tumor. "Definitely, Doctor, this is no tumor!"

But he insisted, "I think so."

"Well, we'll see."

It turned out Mother was right. Months later, I came into the world. Thank God, I wasn't a tumor!

I guess everyone has bumps in the road. George and I were no exception. We were well, and we had four beautiful children. We were so blessed, and always grateful for our faith—believing that the Lord would take care of us. He did. He took care of us beautifully.

# CHAPTER 29

## CALIFORNIA: STARTING OVER

### *George*

Our first home in California was the house I had rented on Califa Street in Van Nuys. I was working with the three guys who had backed me financially and given me the opportunity to move to California and continue my work at our newly created enterprise, Continental Rack. Rosemary and I were very careful and, although we had what we needed, we could never be called spendthrifts. As the weeks went by, my sales grew. I was making good money and, within six months, I was able to pay back the $70,000 my three partners had invested in me. I wanted to pay them back as fast as I could, and I did. But that wasn't the end of the story. I had borrowed a considerable amount of money when the business failed in Scranton. My dad had friends who lent me $175,000. John had a friend who had helped Dad out financially after Mae Ann's death, and he lent me money, too. I also needed to settle those affairs as quickly as I could.

At the end of that first year in business, my three partners at Continental Rack insisted that we cut the dividend from the company. I got my share of everything that was in the pot, but I wasn't in favor of the cut. I wanted to keep the money in the business to build it up. In spite of my objections, we followed that procedure of cutting the dividend each subsequent year that I stayed with the company. Even with that bad business practice, business steadily improved and, financially, everything was going well for me.

Before that first year was over, Rosemary and I were able to buy a house of our own on Delano Street, also in Van Nuys. The house cost $16,500—a bargain in California. It was an old house that had been redone. It had four bedrooms, all of which we needed. It was small, but a much nicer house than the one we had rented. I continued at Continental Rack and, after 14 months, I sold our house on Delano for $24,000. I realized that was a hell of a way to make money and, as the years went on, I continued to play my hand in similar real estate enterprises. That first venture was profitable and made it possible for me to buy another house—on

# Brothers & Fathers

Lemay Street in a very nice area of Van Nuys. I was also able to buy a duplex where we set up Mom and Dad living on one side, while I rented out the other side. That worked out well for all of us. Rosemary, the kids, and I stayed in that house for about eight years. During those years, I enjoyed a lot of success in business, but I was also paying off a lot of debt. Nevertheless, I was making a very good living and we were settled as a family. We also had the advantage of having the support of extended family from Rosemary's parents, who came often to visit, and my parents, who lived in the area for some of those years.

While Rosemary kept everything together at home, I continued with my work. I did love what I was doing, but I wasn't happy with my partners. I was always grateful for what they had done to get me back in business, but I didn't care for them and the way they did business. They were really crooked. They continued to own 75% of the business and, when it came time to report taxes at the end of the first year, they decided how much tax they were going to pay and then they'd fix the books to reflect that amount. As president of the firm, I was supposed to sign the tax return, but I refused to sign. I wouldn't put my name on it. I guess they signed my name. I don't really know what they did, but I know I didn't sign it. I really wanted to get rid of them, and I was looking for an opportunity to do just that.

By that time, I knew much more about business matters than I had in my previous venture. I knew that, if we were going to grow, we needed to build up the business. I also knew that failing to reinvest was a bad business practice that would, eventually, end up as a dead-end street. I made an assessment of the situation and decided, "I'll fix them." I put a plan into effect that demanded that I find a building that I could use. Before I joined my partners, they had built a new building in Glendale for their warehousing operation, but I didn't want to use that same plant. I found a different building and opened up a warehouse near the manufacturing company, and I started to buy a lot of inventory. The result was that, instead of having money in the bank, I had inventory. My partners didn't know much about how the business worked, and I knew firsthand how catastrophic that could be. I really had bought a hell of a lot of material, but they didn't know how much inventory I had accumulated. They were making money; they were happy. I had become a lot shrewder in terms of how to run a business, and I did what I knew was best.

During those early years, I had what I needed for my family, but Rosemary and I were really dedicated to getting out of debt. I was having a lot of success in selling my products and I was making 25% from the partnership. After three years—not a long time, all things considered—I managed to pay back all the money I owed. That was a lot of money! Rosemary and I were thrilled when we knew we were fi-

# California: Starting Over

nally debt free, and I got involved in new and challenging ways to improve the business.

I continued to work at Continental Rack but, after five years of working there, I was very aware that there was one drawback in using titanium: It was not a good conductor of electricity. And if we were going to do bigger sections and bigger parts, I really had to have something that could carry more current. I came up with the idea of drilling out the center of the titanium and either cast or put aluminum inside it for increased conductivity of current. I wanted the titanium component to continue to have the corrosion resistance on the outside, but I also wanted to have greater conductivity on the inside.

TITANIUM — Secretary of the Air Force Eugene M. Zuckert, left, studies a piece of titanium shown him by William Barcoff, executive vice president of Production Heat Treating Co., North Hollywood. Watching is metallurgist Marvin Kauffman. George Esseff, right, also helped to man the exhibit at the annual Air Force Association Convention held in Washington, D.C.

*George in Washington*

With this concept in mind, I made arrangements to go back to my alma mater, King's College in Wilkes-Barre, where the professors let me use a lab to do some conductivity tests. With my findings, I was able to create a new design. I immediately looked around for the best place to get a patent. Strangely, of all places, I got the best protection, not in the USA, but in England. There, I applied for and got a 'design' patent—not a really good, strong patent. It's somewhat common for infringement to occur in matters of design because another design can, with minor changes, still do the job, and somehow circumvent the patent. In time, people were able to infringe upon my patent and get away with it. Nevertheless, those infringements didn't matter much. Historically, I had come up with the original design and, in the long run, I did the most in sales. One of the outcomes of this new design that improved the conductivity of electricity in titanium products was that we renamed our company: Continental Rack became Ti-Core. Although it had a different name, it was the same company—though now it included newly designed products that were available to our customers. Business was going well on many fronts.

During those same years, I came to know the president of a well-known national company—a guy who was considered one of the eggheads in the United States, a top-notch entrepreneurial businessman well known throughout the country. He was, for one thing, on the President's Advisory Council. About that time, he had decided to build a little conglomerate for himself and, in no time, he owned about four companies. One of the companies he came to own happened to be a customer of mine located in Seattle, Washington. The manager of that company had stayed on to work for this man, within the newly developed private conglomerate. Seeing my product and what it did for them, the manager, on behalf of the owner, said to me, "Would you be interested in selling?" I said I'd talk to my partners to see what they thought. I went back to California, but I didn't mention the offer. Two months later, the same manager called me and asked, "Did you talk to your partners?"

"Well," I said, "if you're that interested, I'll talk to them."

If I could get them to agree, I knew we could sell the business and I'd be able to end my involvement with them. So I arranged a meeting with my three partners.

The first guy said, "I think we can sell it for $125,000."

The next guy said, "Even $100,000 would be good."

The third guy said, "Even if we get $85,000, I'd be happy."

Not a lot of surprises there. These were the same guys that wanted every available penny at the end of each year.

I was more relieved than surprised. I had their permission to sell. I explained to the guy who was buying Ti-Core what had been happening, and he understood why I had built the inventory the way I did. I arranged the deal and I sold everything for $750,000. Buying extra inventory proved to be good business, although my partners never did have any idea of how much inventory I had accumulated over the years. They bought the warehouse, the manufacturing plant, and the inventory. My partners took their 75% and I took my 25%. They couldn't have been happier, and I had almost $188,000—one-fourth of the final sale price.

I remember telling them, "This is how you do business."

With that transaction finished, the new owner immediately offered me a contract to stay on as president and work for him. I signed a five-year contract. This was the situation: In the first year, I had the proceeds from having sold my quarter of Ti-Core and, as president, I was also running the company under a new name—Futura Titanium. I had a damn good salary, great perks, and a lot of benefits. The new owner proved to be an absentee owner, but I continued to do the same thing I had been doing and the company continued to grow. I hired engineers and sales people until we had a good-sized company. Right away, I personally received a lot of recognition in the business. There was no one else selling what was proving to be

# California: Starting Over

a great product; I was the man to see for titanium anodizing racks. So in the beginning, I had everything pretty well locked up.

Throughout the years, like most businessmen, I continued to look for new products, new fields, and new sales. There had always been a finishing magazine guide in the metal industry. Through that guide, I had always been able to get in touch with a lot of people in the industry. With that network in place, during my early years, I developed a very extensive customer base. Quickly, I had distributors all over the United States.

In spite of growing competition, I still remained first in the field; and because I was spearheading so much of the growth, I was the one who reaped most of the benefits. Always looking for new products, I kept building Futura Titanium. Eventually, I got involved in many other types of manufacturing in addition to the manufacture of the original anodizing rack that I had created at the Army Corps of Engineers. I had no chemist on board, so I was doing most of the design. I also came up with quite a few other innovative concepts. We were doing a lot of very sophisticated manufacturing and, during those years, I piled up a lot of money—partly because of my broad domestic market and partly because I also began moving into the international market.

I was always looking for creative ways to continue in business and, in the early sixties, when I heard about a get-together slated to take place in London for people who were in the titanium business, I made up my mind to go. The biggest titanium company in the United States had arranged that meeting. It was highly publicized and anybody who was interested could go. I think I was the youngest person there. At that meeting, I got to speak to an executive from a firm who had interviewed a man from Holland. He couldn't say enough good things about the guy—least of all that he was pretty bright. I found out that the executive wasn't interested in hiring any new people at the time, so he was happy to give me the name of the man he had spoken about. I was quite impressed by what I heard and I was eager to meet him. I called him and made arrangements to meet in Holland. That's how I came to know Peter Wilms.

I hired Peter during that initial meeting and he became an employee at Futura. He was extremely capable. He served as our agent throughout Europe. He spoke seven languages and he could deal with anybody. He was also an engineer. He set up distributors in all of the significant manufacturing countries, including France, England, Spain, Italy, Germany, Holland, Sweden, Finland, Norway, and Israel. Peter would go to see customers and determine what they wanted. He explained to them what we were doing and how we were doing it. Because he was an engineer, he was able to design the racks that were necessary for each of their industries. Until then, I had been doing all the design work. It was great to have someone I could count on to help me with design. Because of my financial difficulties in my earliest years in business, I pretty much felt I had to watch everything. But by this time, I knew that the only way I could continue to grow on this large a scale was to hire people to do some of the things that I had always done previously. Peter Wilms was the man to assume that kind of responsibility. I had absolute confidence in him, and he stayed with me all the while I worked as president of Futura. After a brief break in my business situation, which came a little later, Peter and I resumed our business dealings and he remained with me until I went into semi-retirement in 1984. Not only did I consider Peter a great asset in the business, but he and his wife also became our good friends.

At one point in time, Peter became quite unhappy living in Holland, because the country became so socialistic. The government was taking 75% of his income, and he and his family decided to move to Belgium. Strangely enough, not too long afterward, Belgium became as socialistic as Holland. Peter and his wife would visit us once or twice a year and enjoy some vacation time in America, but they never lived in the United States. Peter was, without a doubt, a priceless business associate. As the years went by, my entire family truly came to value Peter and his family even more as wonderful friends.

In addition to my good fortune in meeting Peter Wilms and moving into the European market, I also found my way into even more widespread global territory. With the rapid expansion of the titanium industry during the 1960s, and hoping to tap the Asian market, the United States government had established an agency in Japan through which it made contacts for U.S. businesses. It was a place for people in the business to go to display the products they had for sale. People got together on an international scale to see the many products that were available. I went to Tokyo to display my products, and that proved to be a great opportunity for opening new doors in the industry for me.

Historically, it helps to remember that titanium had been made in the USA since 1951. The

*George in Tokyo*

# California: Starting Over

Japanese had a later start and, not until around 1964 did they decide to get into the titanium business. When that time came, a young man by the name of Ricky Yoshimoto was the trading company's representative for all of the manufacturing companies in Japan. When he heard about my work in the titanium industry, he came to see me at Futura, where I was still president, and offered to sell me titanium.

I didn't think much of it; I knew the Japanese were just breaking into the market. Anyway, I told him I'd buy some titanium from him. I gave him a huge order and told him, "If you can sell it to me for (x) number of dollars, I'll buy from you." I did low-ball the hell out of the price. Surprisingly, he came back with a reasonably slight markup over what I offered to pay, and so I bought a lot of titanium through him. He spoke English well, and was quite adept at representing all of the different companies in Japan. He and I struck up a good friendship, and I began to buy from him quite regularly. Because of the connection that I had with Ricky, I came to be the biggest buyer of titanium out of Japan. He had control of setting up sales; what he'd do was equalize my orders so that I was buying from all of the companies that he represented. They loved his ability to sell because they were all just breaking into the market. I had to continue to buy domestically, but I always gave Ricky a good percentage of our business. For years, all my orders were placed through him.

In time, I dealt with a protégé of Ricky's, Nissho Iwai. We really controlled the titanium business out of Japan until almost 1980. I became very highly respected in Japan as a good source of sales for titanium and I built up a relationship with the Japanese that has lasted even until today. Most of the people I dealt with initially are gone now, but my reputation has remained intact and I still enjoy red carpet treatment whenever I go there.

*Futura Titanium in Tokyo*

As the business continued to grow, I had to do more and more traveling. For a long time, I was able to get home to spend each weekend with the family, resuming travel and work on Monday mornings. By the mid sixties, with the rapid expansion of the titanium business into the international scene, I was unable to maintain that schedule of getting home each weekend. Of course, I called every day, but the responsibility of taking care of the children was mostly Rosemary's domain.

Those same years saw me move through a succession of business adventures that provided us with blessings Rosemary and I had never even dreamed of. Although those early years in business unfolded under different company names, I was always in the business of buying, selling, and/or manufacturing titanium.

In 1971, after almost a dozen successful years in the titanium business in California, my contract as president of Futura was finishing, and I told the owner that I wasn't interested in staying on. Because the owner of Futura had been pretty much absent from the daily business, he really wasn't as familiar with the business as he should have been. He decided to run the business himself. I was unaware, at that time, that he had become an alcoholic and, consequently, was not making very good decisions. Nevertheless, I went my way and got into a new company, where I was basically just selling raw material.

That was my business situation by the end of just under a dozen years in California. It didn't seem as though business could get any better. But in the years that followed, it did.

The busy-ness of the titanium industry was very consuming during those early years in California, and it demanded a lot from me—but maybe even more from Rosemary. Intertwined with business were family matters—concerns not only about our own children with their emerging personalities, but also about our parents, who were facing major decisions. During those years, Rosemary managed to meet diverse challenges on varied fronts while she continued to grow as an individual, as a wife and mother, and as a devoted daughter.

# CHAPTER 30

## GROW WHERE YOU'RE PLANTED

### *Rosemary*

*W*hen we moved to California, my role as wife and mother pretty much remained the same. George was busy with his work. George Jr. was ready to go to school. Mary Ellen and Kathy were becoming good friends and playmates. And Denise was enjoying her status as the baby of the family. I had weathered my medical storms, and George and I were enjoying having a place of our own. When we arrived in Van Nuys, we joined St. Elizabeth's, the local parish, and I began adjusting to our new surroundings. We made a lot of nice friends, mostly because of mutual interests in parish activities, in the Serra Club, and in the Knights of Columbus. George had a longstanding association with the Serrans. Before we were married, when he was just twenty-one years old, George had become a member of the Serra Club at Fort Belvoir in 1951. When we lived in Scranton, because he had heard about George's previous involvement, Bishop Hannan asked him to start a Serra Club there. He did, and he was president of the club in Scranton, eventually becoming the District Governor in Pennsylvania. When George learned about a new Serra Club starting in the San Fernando Valley, he became one of the charter members. Over the years, he was very involved and, eventually, became president of the Serrans in the Valley. We were the youngest of the group. So many of our original friends have passed away, but we still maintain friendships with the others.

With four children underfoot, I was faced with the same kinds of challenges as most mothers in similar situations. One of our immedi-

George J. Esseff, left, Serra Club of Scranton president, accepts the official club charter granted by Serra International from Joseph H. Tyson, right, past president of Philadelphia Serra Club, at a dinner-meeting last night in Hotel Casey. Looking on are the Rev. Thomas J. Carlin, second from left, club moderator, and the Most Rev. Jerome D. Hannan, second from right, bishop of Scranton Diocese.

*George as Serra Club president*

ate concerns was starting young George in kindergarten. There were a lot of people who wanted to get their kids into the parish school, and we were among them. Our friends Bill and Helen who, as soon as we arrived, had helped me find a good obstetrician, also advised us to get George's name on a rather long waiting list for the parish school. We did, and we were fortunate enough to get George into kindergarten at St.

*Denise, Kathy, Mary Ellen and George Jr.*

Elizabeth's. Eventually, the other three children went to school there, too.

We came to know many other people through George's membership in the Knights of Columbus, and we continued to be very involved in parish activities. The people in the parish were really a very nice group, and they sponsored a lot of activities for young children, so I had a lot of involvement there. We had other good friends in the valley, particularly two couples: Chip and Tillie, and John and Ann. Tillie and Ann were sisters. They were very good friends of mine and a great help with the children during those early years when George was traveling so much. Whenever I needed something or other, they were there to give me a hand. I remember having an old jalopy then, and it would break down quite a bit. Chip, John, and Bill were there and helped to keep that car on the road. Because most of the couples were older than George and I, their children were quite a bit older than ours; but we hit it off really well and remained friends for a long, long time. We still try to get together when we can. Our adult children also get together with the now-adult children of those couples, and they always have lots of fun reminiscing.

Besides our involvement with our children and our friends, we also had close relationships with our friends' parents. Helen's mother lived with them, and Tillie and Ann's parents lived close by. When my mom and dad were living with us, we would get the elderly people together as often as we could. Helen's mother converted to Catholicism and, by that time, Mom and Dad had established such a close bond with her that they acted as her sponsors when she became a Catholic. Those friendships enriched all of their lives and they all had lots of fun.

It was also a good time for the kids to enjoy their grandparents; as the years passed, the children came to know some of the history of my mother and dad. As

# Grow Where You're Planted

so often is the case, that history was the sum total of isolated facts and remembered stories repeated over the years. I guess it's natural that we want our children to know some of those tales, and I think it's good to share them. In bits and pieces, they learned that ...

*Dad was raised in the home of immigrant parents. His father, like so many other men, worked in the mines. Work was pretty much their whole lives. Everybody, including Dad, worked very hard. Times were tough and it was always hard for them to make ends meet. As a reaction to this, Dad, like so many other first-generation Americans, always had a goal of making something of himself and having a better standard of living than the one he was raised in. Still, he was always aware of the difficulty the family experienced financially. When he was nine years old, he decided that he wanted to quit school and work in the mines as a breaker boy. At that time, he was one of hundreds who made that same kind of decision. His older brothers told him he could quit and go to work if he wanted to, but assured him that, if he made that choice, he couldn't change his mind: "If you make this choice, you can't go back on it. You have to continue. If you want an education, that'll be on your own, after work."*

*So Dad did quit school. But it didn't take him too long to figure out that being a breaker boy wasn't much fun. Without anyone else knowing what was going on, his oldest sister, Julia, who was a teacher, started teaching him at night. Eventually, she was able to give him a test that would have been the equivalent of today's GED exam. He passed the test and Julia then helped him to make application to the University of Pennsylvania. He wanted to go into the field of medicine. He took an entrance exam and was accepted into the program. He later confessed to me that some of the courses, especially physics, were quite challenging; nevertheless, he stayed with the program. He worked summers as a telegrapher for the railroad. When he was away at school, he worked other small jobs. He was pretty much on his own from the time he went to the university.*

*When he was a sophomore, he became acquainted with veterinary medicine through some of his friends. After a short while, he made a decision that dealing with animals was more to his liking, and he switched to the study of veterinary medicine. After years of hard work, he finished third in his class with the title of Doctor of Veterinary Medicine.*

*After Dad graduated, he returned to Mahanoy City and worked inspecting the mules for different mining companies. He traveled by horse and buggy, going*

# Brothers & Fathers

*from one mining company to another. It was on one of these excursions that he visited a little town called Shamokin, where he had been hired to take care of the Anthracite Mining Company's mules. It was in Shamokin that he met my mother, Lillian Madara.*

*Mother and Dad married in 1917 and, because of Dad's work they did a lot of traveling. Mules were a vital part of the mining industry, and they were taken care of with great diligence. My dad continued to inspect the mules from various mining companies; but around the time of the outbreak of WWI, he and Mother went to Goshen, New York, where Dad had taken on a position with the U.S. government. He inspected mules and horses before they were shipped out to France for use by the army.*

Doc Dorning and patient

*After the war was over, and peace agreements were signed, Dad was approached by the Department of Agriculture, to work on a project that was receiving a lot of federal funding. There had been an outbreak of hog cholera in some of the southern states, and the federal government got involved with eradicating that disease in the livestock. They searched out many veterinarians to go to different states in the South. Dad took the job, and he and Mom moved to Georgia for maybe four or five years.*

*From what I heard, my parents had a really interesting marriage in those early years. Mother enjoyed going through the South, and especially enjoyed living in Atlanta with its very different lifestyle. Dad told me just what a "rascal" mother was, and that she could always get into some mischief. She was seven years younger than Dad and she had a marvelous sense of humor. Coming from the North and now living among the southern gentry, Mother soon found the lifestyle a little too sedate. She could only take so much of being the southern lady, swinging on the front porch swing and socializing at afternoon teas. All of that wasn't, by her standards, too much fun; in no time, it came to be 'old hat.'*

# Grow Where You're Planted

*So one day, she and another veterinarian's wife thought, "Well, during siesta time, let's do something fun instead of lollygagging and taking a rest. Yeah, let's do something fun." So the two of them got roller skates and went roller skating down Peach Tree Street in the heat of the afternoon.*

*One of the veterinarians who worked with Dad came into the office and repeated the news of the day. "Two crazy women were seen—can you imagine, grown women, roller skating down the middle of Peach Tree Street!"*

*It was a scandal!*

*Of course, Dad knew immediately who at least one of the women was. He came home that evening and said, "Lillian, I heard some news. Can you imagine: Two young women were seen roller skating down Peach Tree Street in the afternoon heat? It was hotter than blazes."*

*"That's terrible. Who would ever think of doing such a thing?"*

*"Well . . . I can't imagine, Lillian." And she knew ... he knew.*

*"Well, we have to have some fun now and again."*

*That was just one of the little things that she could be into. She enjoyed life to the fullest and Dad had quite a time trying to keep up with her.*

*After that adventure in the South, they came back and resettled in Shamokin. Dad did further studies at Angel Memorial Clinic in Boston for a year or so, and then he decided he would go into private practice. He went into large-and-small-animal practice in Shamokin. His practice took in a very wide area, and he did a lot of traveling, treating farmers' livestock and doing tuberculin testing of cattle. He continued doing federal inspecting of meat, which he actually continued until he was well into his 70s. Those were the earliest years.*

Another story that I remember had to do with Dad's own childhood. It was an era when the lifestyle was entirely different from what we know. It took all of the boys working simply to supply only the necessities of life.

*One year, I overheard Dad and Mother talking. It was near Christmas time and he said, "Lillian, did you get the children toys and gifts for Christmas?"*

*"Doc, you know I always take care of that. Why do you ask?"*

*"Well, I don't know. I guess I was just thinking, and remembering back to when I was a little boy. My memories of Christmas were not the happiest. But I was very happy one Christmas because I got a ball; it was very unusual, because things were always very tight financially. Usually, there were no gifts. We were just happy if we got some fresh fruit and some nuts in our stockings. That year, getting that ball made my Christmas. I suppose I always hope our kids have better memories of Christmas and receiving gifts than I did as a kid."*

I was just a little one when I heard that exchange, and it has always stuck in my mind. I guess I realize just how difficult things were, and how blessed we were as kids.

So we had our stories. And many of them were about my family. But what took most of my time was taking the children where they had to go, overseeing their schoolwork, cooking, and keeping up with the house. When George's parents or mine were visiting (or living) in California, they were also part of our everyday affairs. I never got involved in the club scene—although, for a short time, I tried to participate in a local garden club. That involvement was hit or miss. I can honestly say the only passion I pursued outside of family matters was painting. As a kid, I had dabbled in painting, and I remained fascinated by art my whole life. When I realized I could depend on George's parents, or my own, to take care of the children for a time, I participated in an oil painting class. That was my lei-

*Doc Dorning with George Jr.*

sure activity during those years. Because I saw so much talent in Mary Ellen when she was so young, I also took her to other painting classes.

Besides enjoying painting, I also had a great love for china. I like the texture of china, and the colors. Actually, it needn't be exclusively china. I like pottery, too. I do enjoy the beauty of those things and, for a time, I collected many beautiful pieces— most of which I have since given away. When I was quite young and my mother became aware of my fascination with beautiful china, she told me I probably got that love from her mother, Grandmother Madara; Mother told me that Grandmother Madara simply loved china and bought all kinds of it throughout the course of her life. I actually came to inherit some of Grandmother Madara's china, although I never knew her very well (as she died when I was only five years old).

In time, an interesting marriage resulted from those two loves of mine, painting and china. Though I had always loved painting, I had little time to pursue it when the children were very little. When we lived in Scranton, however, George and I would take the time to go to the estate sales that were popular when people were selling, not only their homes, but everything in them. At one of those sales, a young man was selling things from his mother's estate and there were a lot of old pieces which were quite beautiful. We purchased a few of them, and then I caught sight of a china hurricane lamp. The base was lovely, but the upper globe was missing. Still, it was beautiful. It was off in a corner and I thought the owner was keeping it for someone in his family. I asked him if he wanted to sell it.

"No! I just want to get rid of it." He couldn't have cared less. "I'll give it to you for fifty cents."

I bought the lamp just as it was.

We stored the lamp in our home in Scranton and, later, took it with us when we moved across the county in 1960. It remained in storage until I found an antique dealer in California who specialized in restoring old lamps to working order. He, in turn, made it possible for me to meet Marcella Wing, a very talented artist who painted antique pieces and also new lamps. She did that artwork in her studio, where she also taught china painting. It was Marcella who painted the lamp I bought in Scranton, and sparked my desire to learn more about the lovely art of china painting myself. In time, I was fortunate enough to become one of her students, and I continued to work in that medium for the next twenty years. China painting gave me the opportunity to develop my own talents and enjoy expressing my own creativity. I look back on those years with much joy.

That chance purchase of an old hurricane lamp led me to pursue an avocation that came to take its place among the many things that consumed my energies for years to come. Slowly, during those years of child rearing, china painting earned its place among the innovations in titanium, the growing international markets, the baseball games, the model airplanes, the portrait paintings, the 4H Club activities, the horseback riding, the rabbits and the goats, the paper dolls, and the jujitsu training. It was something that brought me a great deal of satisfaction and hours of enjoying my own creativity. I truly enjoyed my china painting, among so many other activities that crowded our days as the children were growing up.

# Brothers & Fathers

By the late sixties we were, as a family, well ensconced on the West coast. But in spite of our busy schedules, we stayed in touch with our East coast family. We were always eager to hear news about what everyone was doing—and especially from Father John, who was engaged in his own wonderful activities with his own "growing family" at St. Matthew's Parish in East Stroudsburg.

# CHAPTER 31

## MY CONTINUING FORMATION AT ST. MATTHEW'S

## *Father John*

Reminiscing about my life has given me new insights. I lived and ministered at St. Matthew's Parish in East Stroudsburg from 1953 until 1967. To any young person who might be reading this, my stay there may seem like a lifetime. But historically, at that time, it was very common for priests to remain stationed in a parish for years and years. What I've recently realized is the fact that I lived in that parish for nearly fourteen years. Short of about two years, that is almost the length of time I spent in the home of my parents and my grandparents. In 1945, just days after I turned 17, I went off to St. Charles' Seminary. As formative as had been the life I lived with my family for a little more than sixteen years, the years of living in St. Matthew's Parish for almost that same period of time were also formative for me.

St. Matthew's brought me into a new world of growth and development, a new kind of family—that of a priest to the people. When I arrived there, I was a kid—much as George and Rosemary were kids as they embarked on their chosen path. They knew what they knew. But they entered marriage as neophytes, and embraced what God put before them. They grew 'in wisdom and grace' as they lived their lives and had their children.

As a priest I, too, knew what I knew, and I was also a neophyte. The people who came into my life also helped me to 'grow in wisdom and grace.'

While I was functioning as a newly ordained priest in the fifties, George and Rosemary and I connected when we could. I couldn't be there when George Jr. was born. We celebrated at Marlene's wedding. We cried together when Mae Ann died. We moved out of ourselves during the flood of '55. And, only months later, we wept for ourselves as we celebrated Gidue's entrance into heaven. We celebrated the births of George and Rosemary's children, George, Mary Ellen, Kathy, and Denise.

# Brothers & Fathers

We watched them grow. We tried to support Dad and Mom as they saw Joe go off to Korea.

God was at work in me, as He was in all of us. I had many gifts, but they were not the gifts of being a biological father. Probably, as I processed it all, consciously or subconsciously, all these events and many more helped me to validate my choice of priesthood and celibacy. I think I always knew I had no gifts for parenting a child or two—not even nine or ten. Actually, nothing frightened me more than the thought of having a newborn child placed into my hands and being told, "You are responsible for this one child as long as you may live." I remember a man from the parish named Dick. He was a big guy—a fireman from Brooklyn who had moved out of New York and into the parish. He and I became very good friends. One day he was telling me what he experienced when his wife, Ellie, had a baby—his baby, his first child. I remember him saying, "When I was handed that baby, I can't tell you what happened to me. I looked at this baby and I realized I was this child's father. What a mystery!"

When he said those words, they remained with me. They expressed a realization that continued to renew itself, to repeat itself, in me. For me, it was a moment of grace. It helped me to more clearly internalize my experience with babies, with new life. It helped me to understand more deeply what I experienced when I exercised the gift of welcoming new life into the Church through the sacrament of Baptism. Every time I would take a baby and baptize that baby, I knew that I was involved in establishing a relationship with that child and God. That child became my child. Does this mean that 'I' am God? Certainly not. But I am a spiritual father to the baptized. This happens not because of any biological fatherhood, but because of the paternity of my priesthood. I become a presence—not just a person who performs a ritual, but rather, in a sense, a channel for the profound relationship that is established between God and each child through the sacrament of Baptism. That is my relationship with children in the Mystical Body of Christ. What a great mystery!

That experience was one of many that have continuously left me fascinated by the desires that God puts into the hearts of His children, and continuously grateful for the desires that He has put into my own heart.

Throughout my early years of priesthood, I loved my role in ministry. I loved administering the sacraments. Baptizing children into the faith, and giving them First Holy Communion, were especially joyful celebrations. First confessions can only be described as priceless. Experiencing the trust and joy at marriages, watching young people willing to devote a life of love to one another—those were times to celebrate the basic goodness of people. Having the power to bring peace and prayer to people facing death through the sacrament of Extreme Unction was always a blessing for me—as well as for them. It never became commonplace for me.

A parade of people appears in the rearview mirror of my mind when I think of St. Matthew's. The Sobrinskis, Joe and Mary and their ten children; the Cummings family; the Zateenys; the chiropractor, Doc Sweeney, and his wife Kathy; the MacIntyres. I could go on and on. I still meet people on occasion whom I knew there, and each one is a reminder of God's working in my life.

Another reminder of God's working in my life is a wonderful woman who got into my heart while I was at St. Matthew's. She was—and is—a sister who belonged to the Immaculate Heart of Mary congregation. A friend of mine, Father John Walsh, had asked me to assist him in giving a retreat at Pocono Catholic High School. At the school on that same day, the Vocation Director for the IHM sisters was visiting the school. When I met her, I was very attracted to her. I thought she was very beautiful. Her name was Sister Cor Immaculatum.

It was 1964. At that time, among other things, I was involved at East Stroudsburg College, primarily with the Newman Club. I knew a lot of students there, and some of them were into riding motorcycles. I had a motorcycle, too, and I often rode with them. Some weeks after I gave the retreat, I had an accident while riding my bike. I was pretty banged up; this time, it was my foot that I had smashed. I was able to limp along and get where I wanted to go. I remembered Sister Cor and I wanted to see her again, so one day I went to the convent. We had a wonderful meeting and I discovered that she was stationed at Marywood College. In the months that followed, I went there to visit her three or four times. I invited her to join a group of us socially at St. Matthew's for an ice skating party, and she did. I really began to see that I was interested in her as a person. It was easy for us to be together.

At that time, there was great unrest among college students. I tried to hang in with them, especially through the Newman Club. I was going to Newman conventions and directors were talking about new approaches with young people. Father George Hinger was a classmate of mine from Catholic University, and also a Newman Club chaplain in Wisconsin. We were very intent on trying to make the Mass (and other liturgical practices) more meaningful for students. I told George about meeting Sister Cor, and told him that I saw her as being very important. I knew young people needed both male and female perspectives. I wanted to have Sister Cor in the Newman Club—and I wanted her to be involved with me in my work. She eventually did some things with the club in existing programs, and she also functioned as a speaker on different issues.

# Brothers & Fathers

Our friendship continued to grow, and eventually I introduced Cor, as I came to call her, to my family. We would spend time together and often visited my sister Marlene, her husband Tony, and their children. I also met Cor's parents, who lived in West Chester, New York. I remember her father as quite uptight about the nature of our relationship. His concern was not difficult to understand: Many, many priests and sisters were leaving the active ministry during those years.

"My daughter chose to be a nun. She had plenty of opportunities to marry." That was pretty much his take on our relationship. I assured him that I really enjoyed his daughter's company and that I really cared for her. I also tried to assure him that I had no intentions of marrying her. I admired her and the work that she did, and I wanted to know her better. I understood in my heart of hearts that our plans were to cherish the friendship and the love that God had given us for each other. We also cherished the vocations that God had given to each of us. Neither of us saw our love and friendship and our chosen vocations as mutually exclusive. We had, by the grace of God, a wonderful friendship and intact vocations. There was also, as George would say, "a perk": We were on the same page—we wanted to be friends; we did not want to marry and we didn't want our friendship to be pushed into the darkness. I would meet Cor at her convent; she would come to my rectory. Gradually, we became more involved in ministry together, and by the grace of God, we have maintained a wonderful relationship even until today.

## SISTER COR IMMACULATUM

"In the mid-sixties, the Catholic Church was reeling from the pronouncements issued by the Second Vatican Council. The document on "The Church in the Modern World" brought the entire Catholic Church into the 20th century: hierarchically, liturgically, culturally. The role of the laity was stressed; monastic restrictions for active religious congregations were lifted; there was a sense of freedom, hope, and expanded opportunity for service. It was a time of confusion, loss of moorings, independent decision making.

"I was thirty-five and, for ten years, had been a consecrated religious in the Congregation of the Sisters, Servants of the Immaculate Heart of Mary of Scranton, Pennsylvania. My ministry was Director of Vocations and Supervisor of Art for eighty-three I.H.M. schools in thirteen states. I loved who I was and what I was doing, and I had a vision of what religious life could be for the universal Church—of the present and the future.

"I smile when I remember my second meeting with Father John at St. Matthew's in East Stroudsburg. Bandaged and recovering from a motorcycle accident, Father limped

## SISTER COR IMMACULATUM

*into the convent parlor to greet the 'Vocation Director.' He promptly told me that I was beautiful, to which I replied, 'You should see my sisters!' He then told me that I was a saint, and I promptly told him all my sins!*

*"That was a momentous occasion; somehow, I wanted him to know who I really was and he, in turn, offered a unique friendship and love. During the two years that followed, before he left for Peru, I grew to know Father John as priest and friend. He was—and is—a Roman Catholic priest of the Diocese of Scranton. Where many priests and religious during those post-Vatican II years became confused and left the active priesthood and religious life, we were never confused as to the road we each had taken. I knew that, no matter how strongly we were attracted to the goodness of the other, we would be faithful to our vows; we would hold friendship and love 'with an open hand,' careful to treasure the gift that God had so freely given us. As friends, we each knew that alone we could walk, could do God's work with energy and joy, but together we could run."*

My meeting with Sister Cor Immaculatum was then, and has remained, a special blessing throughout my life. Other people I met there while I learned priesthood at St. Matthew's were blessings as well. After the death of the pastor in 1960, Monsignor Thomas Cawley came to the parish as my new pastor. He was a very gracious man—and a very happy man. He had a much less autocratic view of the priesthood than his predecessor. Other priests in the area whom I came to know and respect were John Walsh, Bob Galligan, Vince Harrity, Mike Kennedy and, of course, the incomparable Connell McHugh.

I knew people in many different contexts, although most within the perimeters of the parish: Genevieve Zimbar, head of the Physical Education Department at East Stroudsburg College, and Sheriff Jake Altemose. Each person had his or her own story, and I was always honored to have a part in their lives. I was sad to see Father Barrett leave in 1965, but we had shared a great time of parish ministry together. He was replaced by a new assistant pastor who was a broken individual. He was a strange man who seemed to exhibit a strong attachment to young boys. After I left the parish in 1967, I learned that he was taken off the job at the parish because of sexual misconduct with young boys. History makes it clear that this was something new in the Church—a dark cloud that settled on the Church. Dark as it was, it was part of that era. On a personal level, this priest's story was the first of that kind that I had ever heard about. Unfortunately, as the years went by, it was not the last. Although, by the grace of God, it was totally foreign to me as I traveled to the foreign missions, this was a precursor of the sexual scandal that eventually wreaked so much anguish in the lives of so many people in the Catholic Church.

I'll leave all that to God. "Lord, forgive us, Lord. But thank you, God, for your great priests—loving, caring, wanting to do your will. Thank you for all of them. Thank you for preserving me. Thank you for forgiving me my own sins."

My seemingly all-inclusive experiences during those years was punctuated quite emphatically by our Holy Father, Pope John XXIII's encyclical, in which he requested that all bishops in the United States send ten percent of their priests to work in South America. Cardinal Cushing, then the Archbishop of Boston, was one of the first to respond to that request. Earlier in his ministry, Cardinal Cushing served as a director of the Propagation of the Faith and had developed a great interest in the foreign missions. His response to the papal encyclical was that he had instituted a group called the St. James Society. He then extended an open invitation to any English-speaking priest throughout the world to join the group and, as a member, serve in a South American country for five years.

The Holy Father's desire resonated in me. All my life I had longed to serve the poor. When I became aware of the Holy Father's request and the St. James Society, I sent a letter to my bishop at the time, Bishop Jerome Hannan. In that letter, I requested that he list me as a volunteer to go to Latin America. For the next five consecutive years, I continued to petition my bishop, but without success. In 1965, Bishop Hannon died and, in 1966, a new bishop arrived in Scranton: the Most Reverend J. Carroll McCormick. I immediately resubmitted my petition to join the St. James Society to Bishop McCormick. On December 12, the Feast of Our Lady of Guadalupe, patron saint of the Latin Americans, I received word that I had my bishop's permission to devote five years to the people of South America. I thought that hearing the news on the feast of Our Lady was truly prophetic.

Society of St. James

## Father Esseff Joins Missions To Work in Latin America

A PRIESTLY FAREWELL—Rev. John A. Esseff, assistant pastor of St. Matthew's Parish, East Stroudsburg, is shown in a visit with Most Reverend J. Carroll McCormick, D.D., Bishop of Scranton, prior to Father Esseff's departure for Cienacquilla, Peru, where he will serve as a Latin American Missionary for five years in the Society of St. James the Apostle, founded by Richard Cardinal Cushing, D.D., Archbishop of Boston. Members of the Society are diocesan priests who devote a term of service to the Missions in Latin America.

*Father John gets his wise*

# My Continuing Formation at St. Matthew's

I celebrated my last Mass in East Stroudsburg on a Friday evening at 7:30 in St. Matthew's Church. Mass was followed by a beautiful send-off, a wonderful farewell party in the auditorium of the school. I always remember that farewell. Even now as I think about it, I see in my mind's eye people whose lives were so involved with mine. I knew I would miss the people I had come to know and love in St. Matthew's, but I was eager to be part of the universal Church. In America at that time, there was a priest for about every 800

Father John Esseff, center, receives the 1966 Optimist Club award from Bruce Frassinelli, right, while club president, Robert Widmer, looks on.
(Photo by Arnold)

## Father Esseff wins award; makes plans for Peru

*Father John goes to Peru*

people; in South America, by contrast, there was one priest for about every 5,000 people. You know, when a priest loves his people, there's an intimacy and a love: their names, their faces, the events of their lives, marrying them, burying them, loving them, caring for them. We went through dangers together: floods, sicknesses, betrayals, all kinds of family trials. With the beauty of their lives behind and enriching me, and as a veteran of fourteen years of parish life, I began preparations to enter a new phase of my priesthood. After saying "goodbye" to the people of the parish, I went to Wilkes-Barre to say "goodbye" to my sister Marlene and her husband Tony. They invited other relatives and friends to see me there. I remember that Marilee (whom I mentioned earlier) and Sister Cor came to Wilkes-Barre to say "goodbye" to me. Before going to Boston, I went to California to say "goodbye" to George and Rosemary and their children—and to my brother Joe and Mom and Dad who, by that time, had all moved to California. With my farewells said, I left for Boston to meet the other priests who had joined the St. James Society. My journey into the world of the global Church was about to become a reality for me.

# CHAPTER 32

## DISCOVERING DIFFERENT WORLDS

## *Rosemary*

One of the exciting things that came of George's success in business was travel. At first, it wasn't exciting—at least not for me and the children. It was George who was away a lot of the time while we were home, but we knew that traveling was an absolute necessity in his work. I adjusted to his schedule very early on, and I realized that I had a good role model in my own mother, who pretty much held down the fort while my dad pursued his career in veterinary medicine. As George's business took root and then began to flourish, his travels took him to England, Europe, South America, and Asia. As the children got older and as my parents came to be more and more available, the time seemed right for me to go with George. When the opportunity first arose, I had no hesitation in deciding where I might like to go. I had always been fascinated by the stories of Padre Pio and I was sure one day he would be a saint; I just had to go to San Giovanni Rotunda to see him. When we arrived in Italy, George and I took a train from Rome to Foccia. There were a lot of people around, including many university students. We were in the heart of communist territory, and it was a dangerous place in those days. The communists were very active and Americans, especially, had to be very careful.

I should have so much to say about something I wanted to do for so long, but the truth is that, for the whole time I was there, I was sick. I was the one who really wanted to see Padre Pio, but it was George who got to go to all of his Masses. Fortunately, I did get to see Padre Pio and I did meet him; but for the most part, I was pretty sick. I had finally been able to get to Italy only to spend most of the time incapacitated.

There were many other trips over the years, some more memorable than others. Traveling seemed easier then. There weren't such large crowds as there are today. I remember when we went to Amsterdam. I do believe we went there from London. We had been in London for a titanium convention and George heard about Peter Wilms, so he wanted to go to Amsterdam to talk to him. That was the business, and this trip was not planned. We found ourselves in Amsterdam on Sunday—not a day to do business. I was delighted. I knew about wonderful art museums all over the world and I knew that, given the chance, I would visit any one of them. I'd been told that in Amsterdam there are more museums per square meter than in any other country in the world: the Rijksmuseum, the Stedelijk Museum, the Van Gogh Museum, and the Rembrandt House Museum—just to name a few. I couldn't wait to get started, so off we went to visit some of the most famous museums in the world. We arrived at the gate of the Rijksmuseum at 9:00 in the morning only to find out that the museum didn't open until noon. I was so disappointed. I turned to George and said, "Well, what are we going to do now?"

There was an English-speaking student there who was obviously listening and seemed to have sized-up the situation. He had a suggestion: "Why don't you go to the diamond-cutting factories? They're all open on Sunday mornings and you can spend some time there and then go to the museum." It sounded like a good idea. George seemed eager: The businessman faded, and the 'metallurgist' standing next to me was raring to go. So that's what we did—and we both loved it. We moved through the diamond-cutting factory and all different kinds of departments. It was quite interesting; but still, I was watching the time. The tour was ending and George was talking to someone, asking a lot of questions. We went into an area where there were showcases, and next thing I knew, the man was pulling out drawers. Then we went into an office. By then, it was a quarter to 12 and I wanted to get over to the entrance to the museum. But the man had taken out all of these trays, and was pointing out the different diamonds: "These are blue whites and these are . . ." and on and on. It got to be twelve o'clock, and I heard myself say, "Dammit, I've seen enough of this. Let's move it. I want to get to the museum, George. We don't have a long time to see all that's in there. You're letting this man go through all of this stuff and you're not going to buy any diamonds, so why are you letting him spend so much time? Let's get out of here."

I was really getting angry, and I heard George say, "No. We're staying! I'm going to buy."

I must admit: I was quite a bit more interested in staying near the diamonds with George's option on the table! "In that case, I'll sit down." We bought small diamonds, and all of them were loose. And then we decided to design a ring. George bought a pretty good-sized diamond, along with baguettes and brilliance to go around them. We hoped the diamonds we bought would develop into something beautiful.

# Discovering Different Worlds

Business finished, and with the diamonds in his pocket, George took my hand and off we went to the museum. Not much later, as were going through the museum, George said, "My feet hurt." Always it was the feet that hurt—and then the back, and then, "I can't walk anymore." We went through that museum full of masterpieces from all over the world in two hours, all because the poor boy was carrying those diamonds and his feet hurt.

But that's how I got to see the world: traveling with George when he was doing business. He didn't stay in any place too long. He would be bouncing around getting things done, so most of the trips were brief. I would get on a city tour bus for the day and would do things on my own. I was pretty independent. I'd do my thing: I loved the museums and the art galleries. George didn't. He would tour those places under duress and, for the most part, I was better off alone. Kensington Gardens, the museums, the historical places, Buckingham Palace, Windsor Castle—there was no end of things to see and places to go. Over the years, I came to know the downtown London shopping area better than I knew L.A. Harrod's! I knew that place: a million square feet of selling space, hundreds of different departments, restaurants, spas, salons. I could get lost in there for a week. It was one reason for grabbing any opportunity to go to London.

Another time we went to Detroit, where George had business. From there, we went over a bridge that led to Windsor, Canada in about twenty minutes. The man George was doing business with had brought his wife along, and she had a favorite antique store she liked to go to. George and I had a bit of history visiting antique shops, and we were happy to go with them. Among a lot of very interesting items, I saw an antique necklace and bracelet made of scarabs. They were unusual—so beautiful and so unlike anything I had ever seen before. George knew that I was impressed and he began to bargain with the guy to buy them.

## GEORGE

"We didn't go there to buy anything, but Rosemary seemed to like those pieces. I liked to bargain with sellers when I was in situations like that. For me, that was fun. So I started to bargain with the guy to buy the necklace and the bracelet. He wouldn't come down in the price. No matter what I said, he wouldn't budge. So, I took his card and we left. When I got home, I'd call him every couple of months and he still had the necklace and the bracelet.

"When I knew our wedding anniversary was coming up, I called him once again. He still had them. I tried to convince him it would be in his best interest to sell. I

**GEORGE**

*couldn't believe it, but finally he gave in and decided to bargain some. When I got him down to what I thought was a good price, I said, 'OK, it's a deal; I'll send you the money.'*

"I gave the jewelry to Rosemary for our anniversary that year, and she was genuinely thrilled. I really didn't buy the pieces for their monetary value. I bought them because Rosemary liked them; she thought they were very beautiful and unique. They didn't look like a lot of gaudy, glittery stuff. They were set very elegantly in gold and silver."

George took the necklace and bracelet to New York, years later, in 2004. He took them to two well-known auction houses, Sotheby's and Christie's. At Christie's, the saleswoman went into the back and then returned saying, "I found it." She knew when the pieces were made and who had made them. She told George the name of the jeweler that was on the pieces and traced it to the early 1800s. It was authentic. The story she told was fascinating. The scarabs were taken out of a tomb when Napoleon ransacked Egypt. He brought the jewels back to France and had a necklace and a bracelet made out of them. For Josephine? Maybe. Or maybe for his girlfriend; we weren't sure. Whoever it was got a great gift—and probably never knew it was one of the spoils of war. So that trip to Canada was more than a lot of fun; it gave us a piece of history that would stay with us for many, many years to come.

Maybe the most exotic travels of our young lives were those we took to Japan. We had many experiences there that revealed an intriguing culture unlike anything we had known in our lifetime.

# George'

I went to Japan as often as business demanded it. When I first began to go there, I stepped into a world that was very different for me. I was in and out of offices, and in and out of hotels. I was doing business in a new and interesting climate. In my earliest days of travel there, a lot of business was done in the evening. The businessmen would start with dinner. They would begin with beer, something of a ceremonial drink. Then they would drink saki with dinner. And then they would drink whiskey after dinner. Sometimes they would also have martinis. Very often, the men would order two drinks at a time. They were crazy drinkers; but drinks were paid for by the company, so most took full advantage. These meetings would start around five o'clock. After dinner, the participants would travel to four or five different bars in the course of the night. Some would get drunk every night. After so many hours of drinking, they would be bouncing off the wall—even passing out.

There was another part to the philosophy of drinking. They would see each other drunk, but that experience was closed off; they never talked about that—it was as though it didn't happen. If someone got sick, they didn't see that. When morning came, everyone 'forgot' about it. That went on every night. I would drink one ceremonial beer—or maybe just half of it. And then I would drink only scotch. I drank with them, but I know they never saw me drunk or unable to walk straight. I'd get them a bus or a taxi or a train and I'd go back to the hotel. I could drink as much as any of them, but I never got drunk. I'd be the first one up in the morning. I'd go to Mass and then go to the office. Around nine o'clock in the morning, they came into the office bleary eyed. I was already working. They couldn't figure out how I was able to do that.

### ROSEMARY

*"Obviously, none of them knew that George could drink 70 shots of beer in 60 minutes! Shades of the old days—but not exactly. When he came home from business trips in Japan, he wouldn't touch a drink for weeks."*

We'd go into these bars and there were hostesses. The typical hostess at those bars was very lovely, usually dressed in a traditional kimono. A hostess would sit next to each of the businessmen, and she would take care of him—getting him drinks and maybe feeding him cut-up fruit. The hostesses would also dance with the men. It was part of the entertainment afforded by the hosting company. There was karaoke, long before anyone here had heard of it—at that time, I knew more Japanese songs than American songs. Sometimes they would ask me to sing an American song and I wouldn't know it; but doing business there, I had learned a lot of Japanese songs.

When I started going to Japan in the 60s, I learned how open they were about sex. Anytime they were entertaining businessmen, one of the first things they would do was offer each of the men a woman. The first time I was on the opposite end of the offer, I said, "No, thanks. I don't need that." In spite of that first refusal, I had continuing offers—until after four or five offers and refusals, they finally

*Karaoke in Japan*

gave up. They gave up on me, but the practice was prevalent, part of a norm. Once, I took a guy to Japan with me. He was a customer of mine and bought a lot of titanium from the Japanese through me. He got so drunk that he took not one, but many, women—and embarrassed the hell out of me for my choice to bring him along.

Ricky Yoshimoto, my initial contact with the Japanese, knew how embarrassed I was that time and, I guess in an effort to put me at ease, he told me about a guy from Taiwan who had come to Japan to buy titanium. As usual, they offered him a woman, and they paraded ten women in front of him so he could pick. His response was, "I can't decide. I'll take them all."

Ricky told me, "I had to pay the bill for all of them."

That was when I got some insight into Ricky's position. He'd be doing fifty million dollars worth of business a month, and he'd be making three hundred dollars a month as his salary. In contrast to that conservative figure, he had an entertainment expense account of three thousand dollars a week. That was typical at the time. Since then, many things have changed.

One time, Ricky took me to dinner. We had just signed a pretty big contract—maybe two or three million dollars—and so he had made up his mind to take me to a geisha house because he knew I had never been to one. Ricky decided that the deal we had made justified the expenses. We had a business dinner that cost $450 for each of us. Just the two of us were in a small room. He and I were sitting at a table with our feet under the table. The geishas came into the room, dancing and playing instruments. They also served us our dinner. What's funny is that I was hungry when I left there. I really was! They served eight courses, but each one was miniscule compared to what Americans expect, even then. What most impressed me was the cost of the dinner. This experience was, without question, something reserved strictly for the wealthy.

During those early years, I know they tested me in many ways. Drinking was only part of it. Later, when I opened my office there, Ricky offered to help me. When it came time for me to hire people, he said, "I'll interview for you." Ricky got more than one guy drunk on purpose. He wanted to see how the men would react when they were drinking. If someone's personality changed, Ricky would say, "You don't want him!"

When I dealt with Ricky and the trading company, I was always honest. Everything I told them was 100% true. They learned to trust me and, in time, I had not only a great business relationship—but also a fine friendship with Ricky and some of the other businessmen in the firm. It was very unusual for business to overflow into family matters, but over the years I gained a place of prominence. I was invited to a wedding and was the only American there. I was asked to give a speech and I accepted what I knew was a great honor. I carefully prepared what I was going to say in Japanese and delivered my little speech at the wedding. Those kinds of things were not commonplace; I had earned the respect of the Japanese, and they had earned mine.

When I came home, I would tell Rosemary about the way things were. Once I began establishing myself in the Asian market, I knew she would love Japan. And so, as soon as it was possible, I made plans for her to come to Japan with me.

*Rosemary with sumo wrestlers in Japan*

## *Rosemary*

When they learned I was about to go to Japan with George, some of the gentlemen in the trading company asked George if he had prepared me for visiting there. That question was precipitated by a series of unfortunate events with one of the businessmen and his wife. The man's wife had no idea about Japanese life in general, and also no idea how business was carried on there. They argued all through the time they were there; and when they got home, they got a divorce. There were probably other details that went into that mix, but the men in the trading company made it clear that they didn't want to be involved in any of those kinds of personal matters. Anyone who was taking his wife along had better make sure she knew what to expect.

In the earliest days of our travels there, I must say it was still very uncommon for a wife to accompany her husband. As I did on any other trips abroad, I would go sightseeing in the day and then George and I would go out to dinner.

### GEORGE

*"On Rosemary's first visit, this gal was sitting next to me—a real pretty girl, a hostess. So she's sitting there, and she had put her hand on my leg. Then she began to peel grapes for me. So Rosemary piped up and said, "I enjoy grapes. I'd like to have some, too."*

Needless to say, I got no response. So I assumed the unspoken response was, "Peel your own." But that's the kind of thing that went on, very early on. Over the years, things did change quite a bit; but initially, travel there was quite an experience.

George had a friend who was involved in a manufacturing company in Japan, and they had become good friends. The more he thought of anyone, the more affection he had, or the more respect was translated into how much more that man entertained. In the same tradition as he followed when he was working, he would take George and me to as many bars as possible. That was how he showed his regard for George—by "kicking the doors" of as many bars as possible. He entertained us lavishly. We'd go to one bar and have a drink. And then we'd "kick the next door." (That was his expression for going to the next bar.) He was very well known in all the bars. It wasn't unusual for the hostess from one bar to go with him to another bar where she didn't work. He'd ask one or more of them to come along, and they would. It was such an unusual arrangement. I would just sit back and smile a lot, and usually nurse a drink. I was a person of interest, I guess, because they didn't see a lot of American women during those early years.

Everyone and everything I experienced was interesting to me, too. Something that I found to be exceptionally beautiful and fascinating was the kimono. I had seen kimonos on the hostesses, but I learned more about them when I visited a kimono factory in Japan. There we were shown the traditional patterns, dating back centuries. I learned that there are symbolic reasons for different flowers that are embroidered on the kimonos. The arrangement of the flowers and the choice of colors also have special meanings. Kimonos are also worn by men, most of these displaying family crests. Japan is an island country, and the people have developed a love of plants, flowers, and animals. It also enjoys the four seasons, and the designs and textiles of the kimonos reflect them. The designs are created on beautiful fabrics by the use of embroidery, painting, and dyeing. One of the ancient religions of Japan, Shintoism, teaches a strong appreciation of nature, and a respect for the coexistence of human beings and nature. There are many depictions of fertile natural scenes, seasonal flowers, the lotus, trees, cranes, tortoises, pine, bamboo, and plums. Everything pertaining to the kimono and the designs is traditional and rich with meaning. These are all inspired by Japan's culture and traditions; they are really artistic presentations that show the Japanese passion for exquisite textiles and fine art. Now they are used primarily on ceremonial occasions, and are preserved as part of the history of the country.

# Discovering Different Worlds

On another of my early trips to Japan, George and I went to a park-like area, located in front of a palace in Toyko. The area was filled with beautiful gardens which were absolutely spectacular. It was the fall of the year. In each of the gardens there were trees, and as we looked closely, we could see that there were ladders leaning against the trees. On the ladders were women wearing white uniforms, white headpieces, and white gloves; only their faces weren't covered. At first, we couldn't imagine what they were doing on those ladders, high up on the trees. They were holding big white sacks and they were putting things into them. As we continued to watch, we realized that they were picking the dead leaves off the trees before they fell to the ground. It was the job of the women to prevent a clutter of dead leaves from landing on the ground. Keeping the grounds spotless was part of the respect that was shown to the emperor, who lived in the palace there.

Besides seeing their dedication to cleanliness, George and I also experienced a similar commitment to honesty. On one occasion, George returned to the hotel and realized he had lost his wallet. He called the taxi company and was told they had found the wallet, and someone would bring it to him at the hotel. When the wallet was dropped off for him, he found that everything was in it. Another time, I left some jewelry in a hotel in Japan, and didn't realize this fact until I was on the plane. I remember thinking, "Well, that's gone!" But a short time after we got home, the jewelry arrived by mail.

Perhaps one of the most unusual, or maybe least expected, experience we had began when one of the men George had been doing business with in Nagoya left his office and went with us for a few days to show us some things he thought would be of interest to us. We went to a fertility shrine—one of many, we came to find out later, that can be found throughout Japan.

I guess we thought of a 'shrine' as our kind of shrine, so we assumed it was a place where people went to pray in hopes of having a child.

# Brothers & Fathers

There is a serious and ancient background for the festival that has a lot to do with the earth, specifically nature's power to renew and regenerate. For those who wish to pray, there are customary purification rites that should be followed. George and I knew none of this. Believe me: We were like most foreigners, hoping not to show how stunned we were, and certainly hoping not to laugh.

Another unusual experience was our opportunity to see ukai, or cormorant fishing. It has been practiced in Japan for over a thousand years. Cormorants are large birds that have very long necks, and look like very graceful geese. They have rings placed around their necks, and are held close to the boat on a leash. The boat had a lit fire on the bow. The cormorants were maneuvered by the fishermen so as not to get tied up in the leash. The cormorant could not swallow the fish it caught because of the ring around its neck. It dropped each fish it caught into the boat to the waiting fisherman. This fishing was done in the shallow water of rivers. The fishermen wore traditional kimonos and the entire operation was quite a sight. After seeing the cormorant fishing, we went out on a boat where we were served the fish that the cormorants had caught. This practice is another traditional part of Japan—though today only a handful of people are authorized to fish that way. Those who do this kind of fishing usually inherit their positions from older members of selected families.

*In Germany*

These were just a few of the many wonderful new experiences George and I had in Japan. Thanks to having had our parents to

# Discovering Different Worlds

*In Egypt*

*In Spain*

*In Hong Kong*

help with the children, we were able to enjoy these and other great opportunities for appreciating diversity all over the world. Though sometimes short lived and intermittent, those journeys were amazing experiences for George and me, and great blessings in our lives.

## GEORGE

*"When I traveled alone, I pretty much concentrated on getting the work done. When Rosemary came with me, we did do many things that were a lot of fun. I realize that, probably if Rosemary hadn't been with me, I wouldn't have had so many great experiences."*

At home, by the end of the 60s, we were involved in more immediate journeys. George began to make plans to leave Futura Titanium as his five-year contract drew to a close, and decided to continue on his own in the warehousing of titanium.

## GEORGE

*"In preparation for making that change, I designed and built a large plant in the Conejo Valley, in an area called Thousand Oaks. I had a warehouse there, as well as offices. The area was pretty rural at that time, since most of the land was still undeveloped. Rosemary and I began to think about building a home near the plant. We had seen so many beautiful places on our travels and we knew what we wanted in a home. We also knew what we needed.*

*We sat down and designed a house that we thought would be best for the family. Then we engaged an architect, drew up plans with him, and hired a contractor, and by 1970 we had built a big house on Calle Arroyo in Conejo Valley. I oversaw the construction, and that house proved to be a great place to live."*

By the time we were ready to move out of the San Fernando Valley to Calle Arroyo in the Conejo Valley, we had a houseful of teenagers and pre-teens, with unique interests and talents—and, of course, minds of their own. Also by the very late 60s, George's brother John had made important travel plans—but for reasons of his own. By 1967, his dreams of serving in the foreign missions were becoming a reality. He came to California to say "goodbye," and then left to begin his five-year mission in Peru.

# CHAPTER 33

## MY SOUTH AMERICAN EXPERIENCE

### *Father John*

*I* left my parish in East Stroudsburg and, after arriving in Boston, I went to a house there on Clark Street, where I met sixteen other men—diocesan priests like me, who had joined the St. James Society. We knew that we would be gone for the next five years, but would be expected to return to America every two years to give appeals to ask for support for our work. After a few short days of orientation, we gathered with Cardinal Richard Cushing in the cathedral in Boston and each of us received a mission cross from him. When the time came for us to leave, the cardinal, well prepared to send us off, offered us some advice in his familiar raspy voice: "Well, now, you're about to go on a mission to a country in South America. I'm sure that all of you have received much advice. My advice is, keep your eyes and your ears and your bowels open, and keep a healthy sense of humor." He was a very down-to-earth man and all of us had great affection for him. We stored his advice in memory and prepared to leave.

Our first stop was Baranco, a suburb of Lima. There I met other priests, all English speaking, who, like me, were there to begin an intensive study of Spanish. We stayed in Baranco for three months, receiving excellent language training. We were completely immersed in Spanish as we were put through daily drills. When we left, we thought we were well-equipped for the job ahead. We could speak Spanish and we had learned a little about the country and the people. From Baranco, all of us—Americans, Australians, Canadians, and Irish—were then sent to missions in three different countries: Equador, Bolivia, and various

*Father John with Cardinal Cushing*

parts of Peru—then considered the three poorest countries in Latin America. I was assigned in the Diocese of Piura to San Martin de Porres Parish in the district of Castilla—that's in northern Peru. I was eager to get to my mission and was filled with excitement as each day took me closer to it.

When I considered a mission in South America, I thought I was pretty well acquainted with inner-city poverty. My time in the blighted areas of Baltimore and Washington during my seminary days certainly gave me what I thought was a pretty graphic experience of the suffering poor. I was aware of people trapped by poverty, the welfare system, homelessness, the plague of low income, and minimal employment opportunities. Yet looking back, even with my background, I think our acculturation could have been done better before we went into our parishes. Mostly, we ultimately became involved in a 'live and learn' kind of approach as we entered our particular missions in a country that was new to each of us. I'm not saying our training wasn't good; but the grinding, grinding need, the utter misery, the disillusionment! Well, maybe that kind of unrelenting poverty isn't something you can really grasp until you live with those who live, and have always lived, in the grip of it. At any rate, I was totally unprepared for what I met in the months and years that followed my arrival.

Piura was about a thousand miles north of Lima. Even as we came in for a landing at the airport in Lima, I could see the hovels that dotted the landscape. After deplaning, I began my journey up the coast. I went through a town called Chimbote, a major Peruvian fishing port, and there I met several St. James men. One of them was Father Jim Shanahan, a priest from Pittsburgh, Pennsylvania. It was good to begin to know some of the men in the network. I was glad to enjoy a little bit of time exchanging stories of Pennsylvania with him before I had to get on my way. When I was ready to leave, Jim said, "Esseff, you're going to be stationed with Lionel Targett. He's requested a gun, and I have one here that I'd like you to take up to him. His parish has been broken into five or six times and he's had the doors shattered and the garage door broken. He's been robbed so many times that he's asked for a gun. He keeps a baseball bat next to his bed as his only defense. He wants you to take this revolver up with you."

I didn't say anything, but I remember thinking, "Oh my God, what am I getting into here?" I took the revolver that Jim put in my hand, but I felt a lot of confusion welling up in me.

I left Chimbote and Father Shanahan behind, continued up the coast by colectivo (the local taxi service), and finally arrived about ten miles outside of Piura in a place called Talarita, where the parish house was located. San Martin de Porres was

# My South American Experience

the name of the parish, and I met Lionel Targett in the rectory there. He welcomed me with great hospitality and, as we sat to talk, I was anxious to deal with the matter of the gun. I took the gun out of my belongings and said, "Lionel, I have the gun Father Shanahan sent."

Lionel was obviously pleased as I handed him the gun. "I'm going to shoot the first sonofabitch who comes through that door! I've been here with just a baseball bat for protection. They've crashed through my door so many times at night, I'm ready to shoot whoever comes through there next!"

I was taken aback. I knew it was important for both of us to understand each other as much as possible if we were going to get along. "Lionel," I said, "I don't feel comfortable with that gun. I don't think I want to be here if you're going to use it like you say."

He insisted that he was serious about keeping the gun and, if need be, using it.

I had to come up with some alternative. "I realize that this may be a dangerous mission; but if that's what you're going to do, I'm not going to stay here with you. Is there any other place that I can stay?"

So there we were on our first day, having a frank discussion about firearms. At the core of the unpleasantness of a very strong disagreement, I knew I didn't want to be in a place where someone was going to get shot.

Lionel remained hospitable, but firm. He didn't back down. Neither did I. He showed me a little place between the rectory and the church where I was welcome to stay. It was small, but there was a little place to sit and a little office-type room. I got a bed from the rectory and put it in another adjacent area. The place had no roof, but I didn't mind because I knew it hardly ever rained; and when I looked up at night, I could see the stars.

It was a bit of a rocky start, and even though I was supposed to live in the rectory, I didn't stay in the main house with Lionel for quite a few weeks. Eventually, we did get to share the rectory after he decided to put down the gun. That happened only after an experience that was recorded years ago by Ellen Franco after my return to America. What follows here is what happened in those early days of my mission in San Martin de Porres parish in Piura.

# Brothers & Fathers

## A Retold Story

*I lay on my back watching the darkness of the night grow deeper. Sleeping in a house without a roof was strange to me, though not unusual in the village. Many of the huts did not have roofs. There was little need for them; it seldom rained in Talarita and there was little inside the huts that could be hurt by a little rainwater.*

*There was a roof on the parish house, but I had decided I wouldn't stay there. I made that decision a week before, when I arrived from the States as a member of the St. James Missionary Society to begin a five-year stay. I remember how glad I had been when I finally reached the house after riding from the town of Chimbote in a jeep. The trip took pretty much the whole day. A hot bath and a soft bed would have been a king's welcome—but those, I quickly learned, were luxuries of my past. I settled for getting out of the pounding 115° heat that afternoon and strained to find enough energy to carry on a conversation with the priest I would be working with.*

*Father Lionel Targett was English and had been in South America for five years when I met him. During the weeks and months that would follow, I found a great deal to admire about the pastor. He was really very funny—dry and witty—intelligent, perceptive, and shrewd. But there was one thing that he was really definite about from the start: He insisted that he was going to keep a gun in the house—a gun that, ironically, I had brought to him. He told me about the banditos who rode the hills and robbed at will. They were dangerous men, capable of anything. The rectory had been broken into a lot; it made sense to have some protection. But I knew I wasn't about to live in a house where there was a gun. I hadn't come all this way to find someone who wound up dead in a moment of panic. As far as I was concerned, nothing could be harder for me to reconcile to the Gospel than living in a house with a gun. So I slept in the hut, secretly hoping that Father Lionel would come to his senses.*

*Each night, going to sleep became a prayer to God the Creator. I thought about the infiniteness of a God whose stars in boundless space were only pinheads of light to the naked eye. One particular night, floaters danced in my eyes as I stared into the night's shadows. The minutes between wakefulness and sleep began to merge. My eyes were heavy and not to be trusted.*

*A man?*

# My South American Experience

*Could that be a man slipping smoothly over the wall of this roofless hut, quiet and purposeful? He lowered himself with the agility of a giant tarantula and then swung just as noiselessly, shoeless, to the foot of my cot.*

*In the face of such a ridiculous interruption to my sweaty struggle with sleep, I responded in an equally ridiculous way. "Buenas noches," I said, concerned more about my pronunciation than the intruder. "Me llamo Padre Juan. Como esta ud?" I wasn't quite sure why I was talking to this man like he just showed up in my rectory in Pennsylvania.*

*That wasn't all I wasn't sure of.*

*"Padre Juan. Si, si."*

*And then I really had to pay attention, as quick Spanish came spilling out of the man's mouth, "Frederico, Padre Juan, Frederico."*

*I continued in Spanish, "What can I do for you?*

*In the absurdity of that moment, Frederico poured out his story. He was very poor. He and his wife worked very hard, but still they were poor. They had many children and his youngest daughter was sick. It broke his heart to think of her. It broke his heart to think of his wife's heart breaking, too.*

*That same story had taken place many times in my ministry at the parish I had recently left in East Stroudsburg, but never in such a setting. I strained to get the whole story, but it was clear to me that this man was broken with poverty and hardship. The details didn't matter. I gave Frederico a sandwich I had taken to the hut with me that night. Then I showed him $800 dollars in American money. It was last minute cash gifts from family and friends when I was boarding the plane in America.*

*"Frederico, you can have this money. I know it might be hard for you to exchange it. Maybe it will be enough to get some medical attention for your daughter. If not, you can come back and see me in the rectory in a few days. I'll try to get some more for you. And I'd like to meet your family."*

*Frederico smiled at me. It wasn't exactly a smile of happiness or relief; it seemed more like a smile of approval. I realized our talk was over. Frederico leaped, pulling himself up and over the same wall he had come in over.*

*"So like Jesus to come in disguise like that," I thought. And in no time, I was sound asleep.*

*Weeks passed. And our day-to-day work together seemed to be creating a genuine friendship between Lionel and me. After a few more weeks, Lionel realized that I still took the matter of the revolver very seriously—and then one afternoon, to my surprise and relief, he told me he had gotten rid of the gun. He added that he would feel better if I would give up the hut and accept his full hospitality. I was certainly ready to do that and I was thankful that I hadn't compromised the Gospel message of peace. A respect was growing out of mutual friendship.*

*As the weeks continued to pass, I moved among the people in the area of the parish and found out just how difficult, if not impossible, it was to meet their many needs. They had a deep faith—and as deep a poverty. Every day was a journey into their hearts and their sufferings, and I came home each night exhausted, but enriched by their great spirit. Father Lionel became a real friend and a genuine source of help. He seemed to have rid himself of his fear of the banditos. He said he had a good reason: Never had the parish house gone this long without being robbed. Maybe the leader of the banditos was sick; maybe he had been killed. I didn't understand; I guess I hadn't been there long enough. Anyway, Father Lionel was becoming much more relaxed about the whole matter. I insisted that it was just relief because he had thrown away the gun, but Lionel said, "We'll see. Let's just hope the bandits don't come back. And let's enjoy the peace and quiet while it lasts."*

*But the peace and quiet did end. One day, in the heat of the afternoon, one of the villagers came running to the parish house to tell us that there was excitement and much confusion in the village. The bandits had come into the center of the square. The man wanted us to go with him. When we got to the plaza, we saw one of the parents gathering up their children and taking them home. Others decided to stay to see if the story that was whispered among the villagers could be true. Were the banditos really giving gifts to the people? As Lionel and I moved among the people, I recognized a man at the edge of the crowd.*

*"I know that man over there, Lionel. One of his kids is sick and he has a lot of other troubles. I'm going to talk to him and see how his family is doing."*

*An old man near me spoke up—he had been eavesdropping, I guess. "What man, Padre Juan? You don't mean him, do you? Stay away from him. He has no children. He's the one who causes all the trouble. He's the most dangerous man around here. He's the head of the banditos. Don't waste your time on him. He's just here to play a very cruel joke on all of us. Be sure of that! They'll be no gifts.*

*I was really confused. I continued to walk through the crowd and headed toward the bandit who was smiling at me. It was Fredrico, the man who had come to the hut so many weeks before. As I drew nearer, he lifted his hand, gave me a knowing wink, and then, with the agility of a spider, disappeared into the web of the crowd.*

*I made no attempt to follow. I stood there trying to remember how long it had been since Jesus had come back to let me know that giving Him something was never a waste of time.*

*I smiled and walked back to Father Targett. "Let's go home, Lionel. Everyone here is going to be fine. Today, these people are really going to have a little holiday!"*

In many ways, I was fortunate to be with Lionel. He had been a missionary in South America for about five years before I arrived there, and he was a survivor. As we got to know each other better, I learned that he was from England. He was a convert to Catholicism. And, best of all, if you asked any of the kids about Father Targett, they thought he was great. Lionel was a magician—in the literal sense of the word. In the midst of unremitting poverty, disease, and heartache, Lionel, to the delight of us all, provided entertainment that broke into the hardships of many difficult days. Lionel would put on magic shows, and he was really terrific at his craft. He did some of the most extraordinary things. He was also an escapologist. Sometimes he'd put up a little curtain and, when we opened it, he would show everyone watching that he had manacles on his hands and on his feet. Then we'd tie a rope around him, and around the rope we'd put a chain. He'd tell us he needed fifteen minutes. Then we'd put him into a box and nail it shut; we'd close the curtain and wait. We heard hardly any noise coming from behind the curtain.

When the fifteen minutes were up, we would open the curtain and Lionel would be sitting on top of the box, the chains and the rope and the manacles sitting beside him. The kids' eyes were wild with wonder. They loved it and never ceased to be amazed as to how he got out! It was a mystery I never solved and, when Lionel left Piura, he took that secret with him.

# Brothers & Fathers

Sometimes we would get together and sing. That was something I especially liked to do. I also liked to tell stories to the kids. These were very simple kinds of play, and they were reminiscent of the kinds of things I did when I was a kid in Wilkes Barre. We used to play marbles or hide-and-seek or kick-the-can and run-the-bases. I remember a lot of those kinds of games. When I think about some of the things kids have today—video games, DVDs, computers—I realize how much more sophisticated they seem compared to us when we were kids. It also speaks to the kind of money that is available to so many Americans for gadgets and luxury toys.

In Peru, play spoke to what was available to the kids there. One of the games they played was particularly gruesome. I saw all of these things through my American eyes, of course, and I was often reminded that I was a visitor in this land and a foreigner to these people who had almost nothing, and who never knew anything else.

The children would make a circle on the ground and then they would trace over it with gasoline. In the center, they would place a centipede and a scorpion—natural enemies. Quickly, the kids would light the gasoline so that neither the scorpion nor the centipede could get out. Then, the kids would bet on which of the two would be the one to survive. Of course, the centipede wasn't able to actually kill the scorpion. The scorpion was deadly; it could whip its poisonous tail and sting its enemy. But sometimes the centipede would so wrap itself around that it would completely frustrate the scorpion with its movements. In that frenzy of frustration, the scorpion would sting and kill itself. That was the game I saw those kids play— a game bred of poverty and circumstances. The ones who "won" their bets felt the triumph of having chosen their champion wisely.

There were some other games as well, but this one in particular struck me as a sad means of amusement for kids with almost nothing.

These same children lived with their families in hovels—houses with dirt floors. They were especially vulnerable. More seemed sick than well. Many had bloated bellies, some because of prolonged periods of hunger; some for other reasons. There were great numbers of people who had had amputations. There were a tremendous number of people with tuberculosis; the Native Americans seemed extremely susceptible to it. It was so rampant that, for two years when I was there, I had to take prescribed medications because I had been exposed to so much TB.

Our population was composed of mostly Mestizoes. These people were not pure Indian. They were not Black, but rather various mixtures of many classifications of people.

240

# My South American Experience

Though there were schools, most children would go for only a short time. Mostly they would drop out after second grade. We used to go to the schools that were scattered around the area to teach the children—to get to know them better, and to try to respond to whatever needs we could.

There were hardly any roads, but we were able to get around in a pickup truck that we had. We used to bounce around on the Callimino roads that were available in our area. Most of these were dirt roads and we rode around in the dust into areas that were very remote. The Pan American Highway actually ran near the parish, but it wouldn't take us to the many out-of-the-way places where we needed to go.

We had no phone. We had no electricity, except when the municipality occasionally turned it on for us—mostly for church services.

It was intensely hot. There was nothing like a cooling system available anywhere. There were no fans. In the summer, the temperature was usually in the area of 120°. In the winter, it hovered in the 90s. Nordics generally found it very difficult to cope with the intensity of the heat, and I was no exception.

I also had a lot of difficulty with the food. Lionel was an excellent cook; but if I ever ate anything besides what we had in the rectory, I would have a bad reaction. We bought very well. There were fresh fruits and vegetables at the mercado. Fish was also plentiful. Probably the most critical of all our needs was water.

The water there was very saline and polluted, so we had to boil and filter it. Even when it was filtered, it was foul-tasting because it was so saline. Fortunately for us, we had ten-gallon cans and we would go to some distant area to fill up those cans with water. We did, thank God, have enough water to fill up the tank so we could flush the toilet a couple of times, and maybe even take a bath once in a while in the evening.

We lived on a level I had never before experienced—and yet, I knew every day that the natives had less. The extreme poverty was responsible, not only for hunger, but for various diseases. The children lived in homes with dirt floors where chickens and other animals often wandered about. Like all children, those children crawled around on the floor. But the floors were dirt floors. The fingernails of the children would become filled with dirt—along with the many kinds of bacteria that were thriving where they lived. Those children did not have the luxury of a bath in the evenings, and one day's dirt sat waiting to be covered with the next day's dirt. Many, many of the children died of dysentery simply because of the lack of sanitary conditions.

# Brothers & Fathers

There was so much that we tried to do there. I became very good friends with a Dr. Fabio Calle, a wonderful man—a Cursillista—and another man, Alfredo Abad. They were extremely helpful to me. Also, especially during my first year, there was a small Native American man, Juan Pico, who assisted me enormously by maintaining the buildings in the parish. I worked with many other wonderful, talented, skilled people who also assisted us in the parish as we tried to improve health care and teach simple hygiene and child care to the local people. We established programs and we supplied food, but there was never enough—never. Day after day, abject poverty marched pitilessly through towns and villages and left men, women, and most assuredly children, trampled in its path. We would go out and find the broken and the dead.

But even in the midst of such deprivation, there were moments of laughter. During that time, I lived in a diocese where 80% of the priests lived in concubinage. When I would make my retreats, I was used to priests who had "wives" and children. It was more common than not. The bishop was celibate, and some of the priests were celibate too, but they were much less visible, much less the norm than the others. In that environment, sixteen priests of the St. James Society also lived. They lived celibately in five missions: one in Pueblo Nuevo, one in Nigritos, one in Paita, one in Piura, and one in Talarita (outside of Piura in the district of Castilla— that's where I was).

One day, I was in the rectory and some of the young kids came around—as they often did. We had a group called the Juventud in Marcha (Young People on the Move). They were really upward-moving, good kids—young, beautiful people. One of them, Raphael Flores, a very bright, energetic kid, had gone to high school, and was in his first year at the University of Piura. That day he said to me, "Padre Juan, the kids were talking about you down in the plaza."

"What do you mean?"

"You know, they were saying stuff about you."

"Well. What are they saying about me?" I wasn't about to mention anything to Raphael, but I knew that there were a lot of anti-American feelings there. It was the time of the Vietnam War and there was a lot of tension because of the industrial complexes in Peru. I thought maybe I was guilty by association. But these kids didn't seem to be talking about anything like that.

"I don't want to tell you."

"Now I'm interested. C'mon—tell me what they're saying."

# My South American Experience

"Well," he said, "they're saying that you're a maricon, (a homosexual)."

"They are! What'd you say to that?"

"I defended you. I said that's not true at all. Padre Juan has a woman, but we don't know yet who she is."

I knew at that moment that my celibacy didn't mean very much, if anything at all, to these kids. I kept my response short: "Thanks for defending me, Raphael." There would be nothing gained by getting involved in that discussion, but I knew "I wasn't in Kansas anymore."

I did know I was in a world of terrible poverty. Yet even there, there were special places that transcended the poverty. As often as I could, I would go to one of the beaches in Peru. They were absolutely beautiful—I'm sure there are no finer beaches in the world. One day I was at the beach at Nigritos, where I had gone for a swim. I was there alone; and for a moment, when I looked up, I thought I saw a man approaching. As the figure came closer, I knew it wasn't a man. I saw wings unfolding, and a giant bird took off. It was a Peruvian condor—a huge, huge bird, unlike anything I had ever seen before. I marveled at the diverse mystery of God's creation that day; and in those few moments, the beauty of nature kept the ugliness of poverty at bay.

I would sometimes take the Juventud in Marcha for a 'paseo'—a picnic at the beach. We would take food and soft drinks and enjoy a day of swimming in the ocean. One day at the beach in Paita, after the kids spent a long time swimming and enjoyed some special foods, they were winding down and playing on the beach. I decided it was a good time for me to go out into the ocean for a swim before we left to go home. I swam out quite a way and was feeling very refreshed; I felt that I could stay there for hours. Suddenly, I began to feel a lot of movement. I wasn't swimming, but I was moving. It took me a few minutes to realize that I was caught in a current and that I was going out to sea! I needed to think. I pushed back and rested on my back. I was trying to assess the situation and decide what to do. As I looked up at the sky, I realized that I had begun to go around and around. No doubt about it: I was moving in a circular motion. There could be only one explanation—a whirlpool. I could see the shore was very far away. I knew better than to panic or to fight the movement. I didn't want to waste my strength, but I had no idea what I could do. A lot of noise began to swell around me as the water continued in a circular motion. "There's no way I can stop this. No way to get out of here." I knew the best way I could stay calm was to pray. I spun and spun, but I continued to pray. And as I prayed, I heard a voice penetrating the noise of the rushing water. It was the voice of a man. I tried to let the sound of his voice anchor his position for me. "Padrecito! Padrecito!" I strained to see over the lip of the whirlpool and saw a man approaching on a balsa raft. He was yelling, "I can't come any closer. Swim! Swim!" I knew I was going to give my best shot to breaking past the lip of the whirlpool. I turned into the ring of water and swam as hard as I could. I was still going around in a circle. I would try again. I did. I was still going around in a circle.

The next time, I gathered all the strength I had in me and barely broke past the lip of the rising water. I reached out and grabbed the foot of the man on the raft. He kept screaming, "No, no. You have to swim. Swim harder!" He was paddling as hard as he could. There was a big chance I could be caught and brought back into the spin. There was also a chance I could bring the man and his raft with me. In all my days of swimming, my hand never dug into the water as hard as it did that day; my legs never moved faster or strained harder. I paddled and paddled as hard as I could, but I never let go of the man's foot. In the midst of all kinds of motion, I could hear the man yelling, "Hang on! Swim! Swim harder!" Time wasn't registering—just the movement of my arm and my legs. Then there was no motion except gentle water flowing over me. I was on the beach. The water was warm—almost hot. It was coming from my mouth. I kept throwing up water—heaving and heaving, until I finally gave in to exhaustion. When I began to revive, still lying on the shore, I became aware of the presence of a native Indian woman, standing near me and saying, "Padrecito, Padrecito, I saw you way out in the ocean, and I sent my son to save you." The kids from Juventud in Marcha were crowding around me, pressing to see if I was ok. By the time I was able to sit up, the woman and her son, pulling his raft behind him, were far away on the beach. I never saw them again, and I never forgot her words: "I sent my son to save you."

In 1969, on August 15—the feast of the Assumption of Mary into heaven (a holy day for Catholics)—I prepared to celebrate the ten o'clock Mass at San Martin de Porres. As I did, I began to have what I later knew was an extraordinary prayer. The prayer continued and intensified throughout the Mass. My prayer was a simple one: I asked our Lord to let me share in His life, to let me be one with Him, to let me experience just a taste of the kind of sacrifice He had made for me. As I prayed the Mass—the commemoration of His suffering, death, and resurrection—I asked repeatedly to share in His life of service and sacrifice. I knew He wouldn't give me too much. It was somewhat scary to really ask for such an understanding, but I did long to know what He went through as He walked the earth, the Man who was God.

# My South American Experience

After Mass, I took off my vestments, left the church, and jumped into a beautiful jeep that had been a gift to us from a wonderful Mission Club back home in the States. I began the drive to the airport, where I would set off on my next mission. I boarded the single engine Cessna that we had been given by the Peruvian government (along with flying lessons). In no time I was in the air, on my way to say my next Mass. It was a day like many others: blistering hot. I was traveling about 70 miles an hour and grateful, as always, that I wasn't making the journey in the jeep. I was halfway to my destination when, without warning, the plane went into a dive. The sun was bright and, as the plane began to plummet to the desert floor, I could see the shadow of the tilted aircraft reflecting across on the floor of the desert. I felt my eyes closing and my head beginning to crouch as I prepared for the worst. Then, all of a sudden, the plane pulled out of the dive. I opened my eyes and realized that the plane was flying just feet above the earth. Seconds later, it hit a wall. It all happened in a flash. My head went through the windshield of the plane and then came back through when the aircraft came to an abrupt stop. My head was bleeding and people who saw me later said that it looked as though I had a crown of thorns on my head. It was numb with pain, but I could feel an excruciating pain in my left shoulder. The clock on the dashboard registered the time: It was 12 o'clock noon. The midday heat was brutal, and I don't know how long I sat there semiconscious. I do remember the arrival of some compesinos (farmers) who saw the crash and came slowly toward the plane. I think for a while they were hesitant to come too close, for fear the plane would blow up. Eventually, one of them dared to come close enough to open the door. I'm sure he was still afraid the plane would explode. I was afraid, too, but no explosion came.

When the farmer reached to pull me out of the plane, I screamed, "Don't touch me! Just please—don't touch me."

The pain was so agonizing! I couldn't stand the thought of being pulled out of the wreckage. One of the farmers asked what he could do. I said, "I'm thirsty," and minutes later they gave me a drink. It didn't even taste like water. I don't know what it was, but it tasted so bitter, I spit it out. I sat there for what seemed a lifetime in the midday heat.

Finally, a search and rescue plane came. The crew talked about taking me overland to a hospital, and when they decided what had to be done, they got me out of the plane. They took me to the Hopital Militar in Piura. I remember how every movement caused me such anguish. By the time they got me to the hospital, I was begging for something to relieve the pain. The doctor's response was, "That will cost you twenty-five dollars. I had a wallet in the pocket of my pants. I reached with my good arm, took out my wallet, and gave him the money. And I couldn't help thinking, "What if I was one of the poor? Then what would I do?" Only after I gave him the money did he give me the shot. By then it was about three o'clock and the medication set in; I felt the intense pain lessening. I heard some talk about amputating my arm. There were some people (called hueseros) who knew how to set bones. They finally put my arm in some sort of cast and I was taken from there to a hospital in Lima. When I got to Lima, I had an operation on my shoulder and then I was sent home to the States, where I went to St. Dominic's in Parsons (near Wilkes-Barre) for physical therapy. It was 1969.

## GEORGE

"During the years that John spent in Latin America, I was slated to travel there for business. When I got to Piura, I learned that John, ironically, was not there. He was in need of medical attention and therapy to treat the injuries he had suffered in a plane crash. There I was in South America, and there he was back home! I did stay for a short time; I met Lionel Targett and was able to assist him with some of physical needs of the parish.

"When that work was done, I continued to Bolivia, where I visited Frank Hanlon—by then, he was an ordained Franciscan priest serving in a parish there. We always had a lot of laughs together, and that visit was no exception. We caught up on each other's news over a bottle of scotch, and Frank told me that there were Poor Clare nuns there who ran a clinic in his compound. Two of the nuns who were there had gone to Misericordia and knew Rosemary. As soon as Frank got word that I was on my way to see him, he told the two nuns, and they were happy and wanted to see me. The nuns lived a cloistered life, so Frank took me to the cloister to meet them. Frank had made the

Frank Hanlon in Bolivia

necessary arrangements, and we waited for them in the living room. When they arrived, they were all excited and couldn't wait to hear news from home. As we sat talking, all of a sudden, there was a barrage of noise that sounded like a machine gun. (While I was on that trip, there were four different countries that had been taken over by coup, so the noise got our attention.) In a split second, the Mother Superior had jumped so high, I

# My South American Experience

*thought she was going to hit the ceiling. Who knows how or when, but when the dust settled, we learned that Father Hanlon had set up a string of Chinese firecrackers under the nuns' chairs.*

*"'He does stuff like that to us all the time. We should expect it by now!'*

*Frank hadn't changed much, as far as I could see.*

*"It was Saturday evening, and Frank prepared to have the Mass for Sunday. After Mass, he had a wedding. He called me up and invited me to stand nearby. There was a little Bolivian girl wearing the customary boler hat, and as the ceremony continued, Frank explained all the customs that were part of the marriage ritual. It was very interesting.*

*"When the wedding was over, Frank said that he had to perform a baptism, so we went to the baptismal font. By this time, everything was happening by candlelight, because there were no lights in the church and it was dark. There were also no windows, and it was stifling hot. It was a typical Latino baptism, with plenty of relatives present. In the midst of all that was going on, there was a little kid who kept running all over the place. At one point, Frank leaned over and looked down at the kid, and with a smile on his face, he said, 'You little sonofabitch, I'm gonna kick you in the ass and get you the hell out of here if you don't settle down.' And then he continued the baptism.*

*"That's the kind of guy he was. He could always make me laugh. But Frank was a saint—and a very prayerful man. After every Mass he ever said, he went into the sacristy by himself and had a private fifteen minute reflection. He didn't accept a lot of the changes that came with Vatican II, and stayed with many of the old ways, but he served the people of Bolivia until his death. He died rather young; but knowing about the kinds of conditions that existed in Latin countries through John's experiences there, I came to understand that somewhat. Frank was a good friend—and a great priest.*

*"Although I was disappointed in not seeing John on my trip, I was very glad that I had the opportunity to be with Frank there."*

When I returned to the States, I went back to the Scranton Diocese for therapy at a local facility. Nine years before, in 1960, because of financial problems and a lot of lingering grief after my sister Mae Ann's death, my parents had moved to California. Marlene and Tony hadn't yet moved to California at that time, and they gave me hospitality until I was well enough to go back to Peru. I was really run down; but I saw some family and friends. Marlene invited Sister Cor to come to see me, and she did. During that time, it was good to see people I hadn't seen for years. After three weeks of recuperation and some much-needed rest, I went back to Peru. George was long gone by the time I returned, but I was glad to hear that he had been to my parish, met Lionel, and had been able to help out.

In the summer of the following year, 1970, one of the worst natural disasters ever to hit that area occurred. On Sunday, May 31, at 3:23 p.m. local time, an earthquake of 7.9 magnitude occurred approximately fifteen miles off the coast of Peru, west of Chimbote. It was a multiple-shock earthquake. News reports estimated that the earthquake took the lives of 70,000 people, caused 50,000 injuries, destroyed roughly 200,000 homes and buildings, and left approximately 800,000 homeless. In an area of about 40,000 square miles, many villages were almost totally destroyed and several were completely swept away. The single most devastating event was the large debris huayco—a mud slide that achieved the level of an avalanche. It originated from the north peak of Huascaran, falling 12,000 feet and traveling at an average speed of about 200 mph for a distance of seven miles. It destroyed the entire village of Yungay.

We were involved in burying the dead and caring for the survivors in our area.

The town I went to initially was Hinbay, a town of 28,000 people, and the only people left were people who lived on each of the far sides of the town. A wall of mud, thirty feet high, had come down through the center of the town and swept away everything in its path. All but 3,000 people were dead, buried in the mud, and those who were still alive wished they were dead because they were so maimed by the fury of the quake.

I got six nuns, who were nurses, and a woman doctor from Ireland to come with me. We went to Hinbay to do what we could to help with the devastation that was there. On the way in, we took the jeep as far as we could, and then we took all that we had to the village by donkey. When we had done as much as we could, I set up and began to say Mass for those who were alive and able. As the Mass was just about to end, the earth began to shake again; another earthquake was underway. I couldn't believe that God was letting this happen again. I began screaming at God to stop it because 700 people in this little village had already died. I actually had my fist raised and, while I was shaking it, I kept screaming, "Stop it! Don't do this!" Though I wasn't thinking about what I was doing at the time, I realized later just how angry I was at God at that moment.

# My South American Experience

Pretty soon the earthquake quieted down. When, at last, we walked out and came down from the village, we reached the place where we had left the parish jeep. Approaching the jeep, who did we find standing at my car but Father Ed Roche, my superior.

"John, am I glad to see you!"

"Well, I'm glad to see you, too."

"Hey, I'm not just saying I'm glad. I am really glad to see you!"

"What are you talking about?" He wasn't making a whole lot of sense.

"Did you notice a helicopter over the village when you were in there?"

"No."

"That village was about to be inundated in the same way as Yungay was. We knew you were in there. When the second earthquake occurred, two of the mountains there came together and created a dam. This village was spared when the second earthquake occurred. We were hoping and praying that you'd be OK."

That was news to me. I didn't know that the second earthquake was a blessing for that little village. I was seeing what I saw, but God saw something else. In my limited vision, I was screaming at God. That day, I learned that what He does is always better than what we ask for.

The trauma of those days and weeks stayed with me for a long time.

Even before the earthquake, Lionel had gone back to England. He had already been in South America for five years when I arrived, so he was due back in his parish in England. I continued my ministry at St. Martin de Porres. After he left, there was a little fella who used to hang around the parish house. He had no home and no place to go. I'm sometimes reluctant to tell the story of this boy who came and wanted to stay in the house with me. But the climate was different then. The terrible scourge of pedophilia that has scandalized the Church in recent years was not an issue, and youngsters were always welcome in the parish. Anyway, without much thought, I gave Walter a place to stay in the rectory. He was about nine years old when he came to stay, and he stayed there for about sixteen or seventeen months. Walter was a frisky, energetic kid who was always getting into a lot of trouble. He used to drive me crazy. He loved playing tricks on people, but he was a nice kid and good company. One day when I was taking a shower, he crawled up on the top and was looking in. I didn't know he was there until I heard him yell, "Oh, Padrecito, you have pello falso." He saw my bald head. In no time he had it all around. He'd say to anyone who'd listen, "You should see Padre Juan without his hairpiece."

# Brothers & Fathers

In spite of his tricks, he proved to be a great helper. With Lionel gone, I was maintaining the rectory alone, but every so often a missionary would come to assist me. Walter would help in many ways: serving at table, helping with directions, going to the market, cleaning the church.

But those days were to become my final days in South America. Over the years, my health had failed considerably. I had some kind of illness, and very strange symptoms. I felt that I was under a general malaise. My airplane crash and the trials of the earthquake had taken a huge toll on me. It came to the point where I knew I had to go home. I didn't tell anyone that I was leaving. I was just so sick that I had to go back to America for treatment. I had signed up for five years, but I was going home after a little more than four because I was becoming more and more unable to function. I had arranged for a native missionary to take over the parish. On the day I was to leave, I made my way to the airport.

Before I was able to board, Walter showed up at the airport in Piura. I have no idea how he got there.

"You're leaving, aren't you, Padre Juan?"

"Yes, Walter. I'm leaving."

Then he looked me straight in the eye and said, "And you're never coming back, are you"?

I couldn't lie to him. "No, Walter. I'm not."

I saw the anger well up in him and he screamed at me: "I knew you never loved us, anyway." He ran out of the airport. That was his goodbye to me.

I've often thought about Walter, who probably considered me the only father he ever had; and those thoughts have often made me cry. Walter, too accustomed to need and toughened not to cave into it, probably did not cry. That's what I thought. Anyway, now I know differently. What becomes of feelings that we do not respond to?

My experience in South America was the first time that I had ever experienced such intense material and emotional poverty. I had never seen so many people in such misery. Coming from the United States, I came to know what 'culture shock' was, but even that phrase trivializes the impact of entering into a world that is so desperately poor. I don't think there's any way to soften it. The polluted water, the food, the diseases, the filth, the lack of sanitation, the vulnerability of the children, the lack of education and other social structures that could keep people from falling through the cracks—all of those deprivations made it clear every day that the

# My South American Experience

people just don't have enough. We live in this beautiful country; we live in a bubble. Living as we do gives us a sense of omnipotence. When I got out of that bubble and really lived in a Third-World country, I was stripped—and it was very real. Living in such overwhelmingly debilitating circumstances, I realized my limitations. I think everyone who has had this kind of experience also has a similar kind of realization.

During that time, a lot of the priests went 'native.' Some of them got married. After a while, bishops decided that they weren't going to send their men down there, because so many of them left the ministry—some even left the Church.

Yet, in spite of the frustration and pain, I know how grateful I am for those years, because they changed my life forever. In the people of my parish of San Martin de Porres, I met Jesus over and over again. He was hungry ... thirsty ... a stranger ... naked ... sick and imprisoned. I felt powerlessness during my years there, but I got an insight into my brothers and sisters who live in the Third World. That insight has continued to help me throughout my entire ministry. I have always been grateful for the years I spent in South America.

And I was also grateful that I was able to come home.

# CHAPTER 34

## RE-ENTRY: A JOURNEY OF MANY STEPS

### *Father John*

After my mission in Latin America, I needed a very long time to recuperate. My parents had moved back to Pennsylvania in 1970, so instead of traveling to the East coast, I went to George's home in California. I stayed there for several months, trying to recover some semblance of health.

---

### *GEORGE*

*"When John came home, he stayed with me and Rosemary and the kids for several months. Among others, I took him to my family doctor, Dr. Scribner. The doctors thought John had some strange malady, because he was really sick. They finally determined that he had Hepatitis C. In those days, the treatment included massive doses of vitamins, and that's what he got—along with other treatments. We took care of him and nursed him back to health until he was able to continue on to Scranton. The doctors also warned John that he was on the verge of emphysema and told him, 'You're going to die if you don't stop smoking.' When that diagnosis sunk in, John got scared and decided to quit smoking his pipe. Unfortunately, when he found out that he didn't have emphysema, he continued to smoke his pipe and, not until years later, did he quit smoking altogether.*

*"The whole ordeal had to have been horrific for John. When he came back to the States, he was like a zombie; he was totally wiped out. He couldn't even talk about the things that had happened. For months—almost a year, in fact—he was just not able to talk about that experience."*

---

I know those many months were very difficult for all of us. George and Rosemary were happy to have me with them, but I was on the other end of culture shock. George had visited my parish in Piura, but, unfortunately, his visit coincided with my plane crash and return to Wilkes-Barre for physical therapy. He helped Lionel to make some improvements in the parish, but I wasn't there for the visit. We had stayed in touch and George had kept me informed about family and work. I knew that, while I was away, he and Rosemary had moved several times. When I got to California, I went to their new home on Arroyo. It was spacious and very beautiful, but I had a very hard time adjusting to simple things. Seemingly little things created a lot of pain and confusion in me. There was always electricity, always hot water, always plenty of food. It wasn't because I was at George's home, although it was unlike any home I had ever lived in. I had missed my nieces and my nephew, and it was great to see them. Because George was working hard and had turned some pretty difficult times around, his family was enjoying a very comfortable home, and I was part of that home. I would find myself irritated when any of the children didn't want what was served or would express their dislike for a particular food. I'm sure wherever I went in those initial days of re-entry, my reactions would have been the same, and the transition would have been painful. I was grateful for the support I had from George and Rosemary during that time; it was something I needed very badly. Since that time, whenever I deal with people who have had similar re-entry experiences, I know what they're talking about when they tell me about their difficulties in coming home.

## ROSEMARY

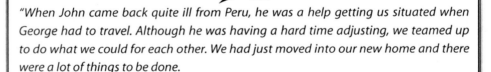

"When John came back quite ill from Peru, he was a help getting us situated when George had to travel. Although he was having a hard time adjusting, we teamed up to do what we could for each other. We had just moved into our new home and there were a lot of things to be done.

"Young George was going into his last year of high school and he wanted to finish at Crespi High School for Boys in the San Fernando Valley. To do that, he had to get his driver's license so he could drive the twenty-two miles to and from school each day. Mary Ellen was planning to start high school at La Reina High School for Girls. Kathy and Denise were enrolled in the local grade school. I had to give a lot of attention to those details. Both Mary Ellen and Kathy were very happy because they had become very involved in horseback riding. Moving to Thousand Oaks, they realized their dreams of having and riding their own horses. Denise was still young and stayed close to home. George and I were happy that our kids were content at home, because he had made sure there were a lot of activities for them to enjoy right there. They spent time swimming in the pool or golfing on the three-hole putting green that George had put

# Re-Entry: A Journey of Many Steps

Because of George's intense travel schedule, I found myself with Rosemary and the children, a new house, a lot of boxes to empty, and not too much time to lick my own wounds. George was God-knows-where, and Rosemary gave me a clipboard that had a list of things I could do to help. I can still laugh when I remember walking around that house with a clipboard as though I was the floor manager at a department store. I stepped out of my own chaos and entered into hers. One thing I remember was that she had bought some beautiful tiles on one of her travels abroad. She wanted to hang them in the kitchen and so the two of us decided exactly where each one would go. No sooner was that job about to be finished when George arrived home. Another reality check: George assured me that I was all wrong, and he had other ideas about where and how the tiles should go. Somehow, we worked through each day, and I began to regain my strength. It felt good to be useful, but there were things I had to deal with that were not easily dismissed.

Not too long after I left Piura, and while I was still in California, a fellow missionary, George Flynn, wrote to me in California. Among other bits of news, Father Flynn told me that the native priest who replaced me didn't want Walter around, so he made him leave the parish house. A short time later, Walter was found dead. It's hard to say just how grieved I was to hear that news. There were a lot of kids who just ran the streets, and doing that was a very dangerous practice. Many of them died in the streets; Walter died in the street. He wasn't much different than countless others—then and now. But I had tried to respond as 'Padre Juan' to Walter. He was just a little kid. He loved me. I cared for him. I did the best I could for as long as I could. Still, he died in the street. The news of Walter was a blaring reminder that all I had left behind was still the day-to-day life of the people who remained there.

When I felt strong enough, I went home to Wilkes-Barre, where I stayed with my parents for some time. They had moved into a different house, located at 123 Sanbourne Street in south Wilkes-Barre. By that time, my sister Marlene and her husband Tony had moved to California, where Tony was working for George. My brother Joe had also moved to the West coast. In Wilkes-Barre, many members of the family, as well as old friends, came to see me. As my health improved, I was better able to adjust to being 'home.' I resumed my friendship with Sister Cor, who would come to visit me at my parents' home. My mother, unfortunately, was somewhat suspicious as to Sister Cor's role in my life, and it wasn't unusual for her to express her worry about how a relationship with a nun appeared to anyone who was aware of it. It took years for my mother to realize that our friendship was solid and healthy and no threat to my vocation or Sister Cor's. I have to admit, though, that there were quite a few unpleasant moments with my mother as she struggled with a 'supposed threat' to my priesthood.

Without question, the truth I was most sure of at that time in my priesthood was that I wanted to work with the poor. When I began to feel strong enough to resume my ministerial duties in my home diocese, I reported to Bishop McCormick, who offered me a parish. I did not feel that I had the strength or the inclination to take on the full responsibility of parish life; I also knew that most of the poor had no parish affiliation. In that setting, I would have a difficult time seeking them out. The bishop was open to my wishes and he assigned me living quarters at an ethnic parish, St. Lucy's in west Scranton, originally established for the Italian immigrants in that area. It was the first time I had been in a parish where there was only one church and three priests—that was new. The sisters of Mother Cabrini's order lived in the parish and I celebrated Mass for them. They were wonderful to me while I was there. The other assistant was Father Maurice Raymond. My new pastor and I were, to be honest, not too good a match. I might say it was partly because I was still reeling from the impact of re-entry, but I do know I was experiencing a stark contrast in what I was being called upon to do in light of my interpretation of the Gospel. I was happy to be back in my own diocese but, because I had lived those years in South America, I was no longer the John Esseff who had left in 1967. As always, God was at work in my life.

# CHAPTER 35

## MINISTRY IN MY HOME DIOCESE

### *Father John*

The yearnings of my heart, I believe, were put there by God. He formed me in my mother's womb and continued to reveal Himself to me through human relationships within my family. Those relationships taught me about the profound connection that we have to one another and the capacity that each of us has to affect one another. I knew that, in the body called 'family'—my parents, my grandparents, my brothers and sisters—we were linked together and we were called to help one another. As I grew older, the impact of learning about the larger family, God's family, drew me as nothing else did. When, in my studies for priesthood, I came to experience the members of that larger family as the Mystical Body of Christ, my life was forever changed. Just as in every place I had ever been, when I returned to Scranton, the larger family was there reminding me once again that

> *"in the body when one member suffers, all the other members share its pain, and the healthy members come to the assistance of the ailing, so in the Church the individual members do not live for themselves alone, but also help their fellows, and all work in mutual collaboration for the common comfort and for the more perfect building up of the whole Body ... Nor must one imagine that the Body of Christ, just because it bears the name of Christ, is made up during the days of its earthly pilgrimage only of members conspicuous for their holiness, or that it consists only of those whom God has predestined to eternal happiness. It is owing to the Savior's infinite mercy that place is allowed in His Mystical Body here below for those whom, of old, He did not exclude from the banquet."*

By the grace of God, I never lost sight of my goal of serving the poor. In spite of the difficulties, my stay at St. Lucy's allowed me to build up my strength and I began to feel healthier. That was a great blessing. Another blessing was the support I received from Sister Cor, who was living with her community at St. Ann's, a nearby parish, and teaching at three high schools in Scranton. I had shared with her my desire to seek out the poor and minister to them. She told me about courses that were being offered at the University of Scranton that would be beneficial to me. Two in particular appealed to me: one on social justice and one on the papal encyclicals. I took courses at the university with two professors: Dr. Ubaldi and Dr. Benestad. With them I learned a great deal, not only about social issues, but also important data about the population of Scranton. As I became more knowledgeable and better prepared to take on the challenges of working with the local poor, I began, with the help of Sister Cor, to formulate a proposal stating my desire to work with them, and I sent it to Bishop McCormick.

Although I welcomed the opportunities of those early years back in America, they were not without challenges. St. Lucy's was the first in a succession of three parishes where I was assigned to live during the early seventies. I remained at St. Lucy's from February of 1971 until September. After those seven months, I received a response from the bishop concerning my request. He gave me authorization to minister to the poor of the city.

From that time on, that desire to work with the poor continued to grow in my heart and translated slowly, over the next thirteen years, into a kind of grassroots response that I made to the poor of Scranton, with the sanction of the bishop. Motivated by the example of Jesus, who came to do the work of His Father, I sought out those "He did not exclude from the banquet." The needs of the poor were pretty evident—not only in Scranton, but also nationwide, as many government programs were cut. As the poor were identified clearly in so many different areas of the city, many good people came forward to help me. Within a very short time, ministries evolved simultaneously to children, to prisoners, to the elderly, to alcoholics, to migrant workers, to refugees from foreign countries, to the homeless, and to just about anyone who had fallen through the cracks. For several years, I was assisted in those ministries by what came to be known as the Team Ministry. At one time or another, the team included Rev. William Walton; Jeanette Barbacane; Eleanor Shields; Sister Martha McAndrew, I.H.M.; Sister Nancy Abbott, I.H.M.; Sister Miriam Heaton, R.G.S.; Chris Ammons; Sister Patrice Kenny, R.S.M.; and Rev. Paul Gere.

## BILL WALTON

*"When I think about Father John Esseff, my friend and brother, this is what I think about, and I feel blessed.*

*"We first met shortly after Father John came home from Peru and was recuperating from hepatitis. It was like meeting a brother—another brother in exile, away from his*

# Ministry in My Home Diocese

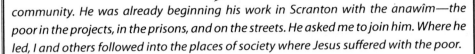

## BILL WALTON

community. He was already beginning his work in Scranton with the anawîm—the poor in the projects, in the prisons, and on the streets. He asked me to join him. Where he led, I and others followed into the places of society where Jesus suffered with the poor.

*"In the early 70s, we were in the Lackawanna County Prison one fine day when he said to me, 'Bill, I think we are going to seed.' And so we went to school: first to Marywood College for an M.S. degree, and then on to the Midwest for a doctorate at the schools of theology in Dubuque, Iowa, where three seminaries united their faculties and libraries: Wartburg Lutheran Seminary, Thomas Aquinas, and a Presbyterian seminary. There we formed what was called the Eastern group, made up of two Catholic clergymen, one Episcopalian, one Lutheran, and a Dominican woman in ministry. We critiqued each other's studies: one on poverty in the Diocese of Scranton by Father John, one on a new catechesis taught within the family, one on women in ministry, one on Jung regarding dreams as revelation, and one on the ecumenical movement. We brought our teachers to us to meet at eastern colleges, at airline terminals, and at retreat centers. Once a year we traveled to Iowa for a week of reflection and work. We all became aware of the deeper Christ within creation in His suffering people. It was a glorious time."*

The initial response of the early seventies grew—person by person, family by family—until, in 1980, it culminated in an authentic, systemic diocesan response with the establishment of the Office of Urban Ministry.

Throughout the span of all those years, my work remained the same; but as I ministered to the poor, I lived in three different parishes, and then spent a fourth, much longer period of time, living at Christ the King Parish in Dunmore (where I stayed until 1980). At that time, I moved to the Chancery in downtown Scranton and continued my work under the title of Director of the Office of Urban Ministry until 1984.

But in 1971, there was just a desire to live the Gospel and the ever-present poor. The 'poor' in Scranton had a different face than the 'poor' in Peru. They were not obvious in the same way and they usually weren't part of a parish community. Many of them could be found in the low-rent housing projects throughout the city. One of those projects, Valley View Terrace, was located within the boundaries of St. John's Parish in south Scranton. When the bishop transferred me to St. John's from St. Lucy's, I began to work at the project, spending my time with those who had little or no parish affiliation.

# Brothers & Fathers

Children and young people from 'the project' who were open to the life of the Church were invited to whatever programs or instructions were available there. Many responded and became visible in the parish. Some other people, though not affiliated with the life of the parish (maybe alcoholics, ex-prisoners, migrant workers) sometimes made their way to the parish to say "hello." As my ministry grew and time went by, it became increasingly clear that what I was trying to do while I lived at St. John's was fast becoming a thorn in the side of my new pastor. When the hordes of kids from the housing projects came down to the parish for various programs, he was overwhelmed. He said they wrecked his programs. He had a nice, little, staid parish there, and my presence was bringing "too many problems" into it. Many parishioners were unwilling to embrace the "newcomers" as members of their community, and considered my presence and that of my 'clientele' (as they called them), disruptive in the life of the parish. They weren't shy about making their feelings known.

After about a year-and-a-half, I was transferred to St. Francis' Parish, also located in south Scranton. Hilltop Manor, another housing project (much like Valley View) was situated within the perimeter of St. Francis. With my new pastor at St. Francis, the story didn't vary much from what had happened at St. John's. The people who lived in Hilltop Manor suffered the same hardships as the people in Valley View. The kinds of problems that existed among so many of them were issues many middle-class parishioners pretty much wanted to pretend didn't exist and, if they did, they didn't want to see them up-close and sitting in the pew next to them! The people I was trying to help were not the kind of people usually associated with parochial life as it was at that time. As the poor became much more visible, they found themselves in a somewhat hostile church community.

Because of the many problems, I kept petitioning the bishop to let me open a storefront kind of facility where I could receive those who were in such dire need. I thought it would be better to deal with them separately than to have them treated so poorly in the confines of a parish. The bishop wasn't open to that idea; he certainly was not going to allow a priest to live outside a rectory—no way! So I submitted to the authority of the bishop, as I always did. Feeling the same antagonism I had experienced at St. John's, I continued to live at St. Francis' Parish.

In spite of the resistance, I felt that I was making progress in living the Gospel by serving the poor. I was working hard and accepting the daily challenges. The Team Ministry was involved in the work. There were also seminarians who came forward and other volunteers who helped in particular situations where they felt they had the gifts that were needed. All were very generous. I remained committed to the challenges, wherever they took me; and, as always, the Lord was kind to me.

One day I got a call from my brother George. Living in California, he was very happy with his work and family. He was enjoying a great deal of success, and talked to me about his plans with Rosemary and all of their children. They were going on a family excursion to Europe and they wanted me to join them. I thought the time was right. My work was underway, and there were people committed to the work who would continue while I was away. I said I would go with them, and George and I began to make plans.

# City's streets are Scranton priest's parish

By MARITA LOWMAN
Staff Writer

SCRANTON — It's 9 a.m. and Monsignor John Esseff is sharing a cup of coffee with an unemployed farm laborer who came to town looking for a job but found none.

He listens to the Jamaican's story, picks up the telephone and makes arrangements to send the man to Delaware, where crops are waiting to be harvested.

**10 a.m.:** Esseff is at the Lackawanna County Jail visiting an inmate.

"This is my friend Bobby Kendricks. He's an excellent gymnast," he tells a reporter who is trailing him.

Kendricks, 23, should have been paroled three months ago.

"He's in a Catch-22 situation," Esseff explains. "He can't get out until he gets a job, but it's pretty hard to find work while you're in jail."

The two talk of job prospects and future plans. Their hands clinched together, the Catholic priest and the Baptist prisoner quietly pray.

**10:30 a.m.:** Esseff is at an alcohol abuse center a few blocks away.

"I have to check on Tommy. I brought him here the other night — he was in terrible shape. He's an al-

(See PARISH, Page 7A)

TIMES LEADER/CHUCK ZOELLER

Monsignor John Esseff prays for Anna Walsh, 82, during a visit to Valley View Apartments in Scranton

*Father John's new parishioners*

# CHAPTER 36

## THE BEST-LAID PLANS ...

### *George*

**M**y success in business brought the family many advantages. By 1970, we were living in a rather large home in Thousand Oaks. In the early sixties, when Mom and Dad decided to move to California after their return from the European trip John had given them as a gift, I was able to buy a duplex. Mom and Dad lived on one side of the house and tenants lived on the other. They lived there for ten years before returning to Wilkes-Barre, where I was able to buy them a home of their own. When Rosemary's mom and dad came to California (at first for winters and later to live with us), we always had plenty of room for them to be comfortable with us. Those years were great for the kids, because they were able to develop wonderful relationships with their grandparents. Rosemary enjoyed the company and also the support our parents provided when the kids were young.

Another great advantage of the success in business was that Rosemary and I were able to travel together as I was building the business. Since we had enjoyed traveling so much, we wanted our kids to travel, too. By the time 1972 rolled around, Denise was twelve, Kathy was fourteen, Mary Ellen was sixteen, and George Jr. was nineteen. It seemed an ideal time to take all of them on a trip to Europe with us. Hoping a little relaxation would be good for John (as he had resumed a pretty intense work schedule), we invited him to come along. He accepted the invitation and we all looked forward to having a lot of fun together. We made plans to meet in New York City and fly to England together. John was planning to meet Lionel Targett there and he wanted young George to go along with him so they could catch up on things. After that visit, the two of them would continue on to Ireland. When that was done, all of us would meet up again in Rome and continue from there. We met John as planned, traveled to Lionel's parish in Portsmouth, and had a visit with him. John and George Jr. were going to head out to Ireland, where John had made arrangements to visit the Irish missionaries he had met in South America. We were going back to stay at a hotel in London.

# Brothers & Fathers

*The Esseff kids in the '70s*

Settled in the hotel late that night, we turned on the TV to watch the news. In a moment, we were in Wilkes-Barre. There we were staring at the most amazing scenes of the city under water. It was such a disastrous event that it had made international news! We saw a shot of Handley's Diner on South Main Street in downtown Wilkes-Barre; it had been completely inundated by flood waters. No doubt, Mom and Dad's house, a few blocks away, was under water, too. Of course, we immediately tried to get some more information, but we had a difficult time finding out exactly what had happened to my parents. Finally, we were able to get in touch with my Aunt Catherine in Scranton and we found out that Mom and Dad were there. They were safe, but it was true: Their home was under water. Once we knew the situation, we had a family meeting in the hotel room. We asked each of the girls what they were thinking and they all had an opportunity to say what they wanted to do. Each of them said they thought we should go home and help Mom and Dad. Rosemary and I were really proud of how the girls reacted. They had looked forward to the trip for a long time, but it didn't have a chance compared to their affection and concern for Mom and Dad. We had a lot to do. We cancelled our plans and our reservations throughout Europe and we changed our flights. What we didn't know until we met in the Heathrow airport was that John and George had cancelled their plans, as well. Before leaving for Ireland, John had read about the flood in the morning edition of the London Times. He and George immediately changed their plans, went to Heathrow, and booked a flight back to Scranton. We flew back together on the same flight.

Eventually, the pieces of the puzzle fell into place. A tropical storm that grew into Hurricane Agnes was responsible for the major devastation that took place that summer—not only in Wilkes-Barre, but also in cities and towns throughout Pennsylvania. In Wilkes-Barre, which took the brunt of the storm, the Susquehanna River rose to a height of forty-one feet—four feet above the city's levees, leaving the downtown area flooded with nine feet of water. People were evacuated from rooftops; an estimated 25,000 homes and businesses were either damaged or destroyed; financial losses neared the billion-dollar mark. At least 200,000 people throughout the Wyoming Valley were left in need of rescue and ongoing relief. Nothing was spared. Even an historic graveyard north of Wilkes-Barre was completely flooded and there were gruesome images of caskets bobbing on the floodwaters like large corks.

By the time John and I were able to reach Wilkes-Barre, the waters had begun to recede. Not unlike most places, the water had gone up to the second floor of my parents' house. When we were able to go to the house, the water was still about three-feet high on the first floor because it had nowhere to go. I was able to swim into the murky water and unblock a floor drain in the basement so that, when the earth would take it, the water could find a way out. The cleanup was pretty tough. Everything was covered with muck. The entire area was polluted. There was a foul stench almost everywhere. An enormous number of things had to be discarded; some other things, like silverware and dishes, could be washed and disinfected and kept for use. Mom was able to take some irreplaceable things (like photos) with her when she and Dad left, but most things could not be salvaged. We all stayed in the area for about a month getting things cleaned up or replaced. John brought two seminarians with him who had been helping him in Scranton: Tom Cappelloni and Tom Stahurski. The family—and everyone else who wanted to pitch in—did a pretty thorough job of cleaning up and getting Mom and Dad's place in livable condition. Eventually, they were able to return to their home. After a month, I returned to California with Rosemary and the kids, and John continued his ministry in Scranton.

# CHAPTER 37

## LOSING DAD

## *Rosemary*

By the time we returned from Wilkes-Barre and the devastation of the flood, my parents had already been living with us on a permanent basis for some time. Mom and Dad spent the winters with us from about the time Denise was three. Each year, they would return to Shamokin so Dad could maintain his veterinary practice. Throughout those years, Dad was still quite healthy. He had to be healthy to maintain the pace his practice demanded in the care of not only small, but also large, animals. He also worked every day at the packing plant doing federal inspecting, and then took care of his large-and-small animal practice until 9 p.m. People certainly didn't take those large animals to Dad! He was called out regularly, any time of the day or night. Things changed when, at the age of 75, Dad had a very severe stroke. For a time it was uncertain whether or not he would pull through. Thank God, he did. Over the years, he had a lot of help from my brother Bob and his wife Agnes; but after his stroke, he had to start backing even further away from some of the heavy workload. It was during those years that they would come and spend winters with us. As Dad continued to get up in years, he was faced with the prospect of retirement. Once we had built the house on Calle Arroyo, it seemed the perfect time for Mom and Dad to come and stay. Dad was 80 and Mom, though seven years younger, was no longer as spry as she had been. Through all their years in Shamokin, no matter what their needs were, Bob and Agnes had always been there to support them. Faced with the choice between continuing with the practice or retiring, Dad finally decided to give up his practice, and Mother and Dad agreed to come to live with us. I was delighted. It was a wise move and I was always glad that they spent the last years of their lives with us.

Mom and Dad were great conversationalists. Always! They'd talk and talk and talk: morning, noon, and night. It was a mystery to us what they could be talking about for so many hours, but it was wonderful for us to experience their communication. They enjoyed the children, who got to know them very well. As Mom and

Dad needed more and more care, the kids were always there to help. I think that Mary Ellen's choice of becoming a nurse and Denise's choice of studying the field of geriatrics were direct results of their interactions with Mom and Dad. Learning how to give to the elderly was a good experience for our kids.

It was after our return from Pennsylvania that Dad's health began to deteriorate rapidly, and I was glad he was there with us. By that time, he was 83 and Mother was 76. Dad had colitis, an intestinal problem which had plagued him for years. When his health began to decline, we didn't know whether it was heart related or whether it was something else. No one seemed to know at that time, because those in the medical profession just couldn't diagnose as well as they can today.

When Dad and Mom initially started to stay with us for long periods of time, Dr. Scribner, an internist who was a friend of ours, took care of them whenever they needed any medical attention. Early on, both of my parents seemed rather healthy, all things considered. However, as time passed, there were instances when Dad would pass out. Those

*Doc and Diamond Lil Dorning*

events occurred generally when he took a nap in the afternoon—part of a routine he followed. When Dad was about to lie down, or sometimes while he was sleeping, he would either lose consciousness or fall out of bed. He was dead weight, but he would revive. He would not have any recollection of what had happened. Then he would sleep. He'd sleep quite a bit, get up, and feel fine. Then, there'd be no problem—at least not until the next time the same progression of events occurred. As Dad had these experiences more frequently, I took him to another very capable doctor for an opinion, but that doctor was unable to diagnose the problem. I called our friend, Dr. Bob Scribner, to bring him up to date. Dad kept saying that he had a rapid pulse, and also that he was in heart failure. At Doctor Scribner's insistence, I put Dad on the phone and he told Dr. Scribner his symptoms. When I got back on the line, the news was difficult to hear. "Your dad knows what's going on with him. He's been a vet long enough to know what's what. He is in heart failure."

# Losing Dad

All of these events occurred early in the week, and then we watched as his system slowly began to shut down. By Wednesday of that week, we noticed Dad wasn't eating properly. He seemed foggy and I remember saying to him, "I think we'll go to the hospital"; he was OK with that. We got him to a heart specialist whom he had not had before, and the specialist diagnosed Dad's condition as heart failure. After that, it was just a slow and steady decline. The following Tuesday night was election night. Richard Nixon was winning. Dad hated Richard Nixon with a passion. I remember saying to Dad that night, "Dad, it looks like Richard Nixon is going to win." The heart monitor went wild. George was so upset: "What, in the name of God, did you say that for?"

"I wanted to know if he was mentally aware—if he was aware, if he was hearing me." And he was! Forgive me, Dad, but I wanted you to know that I was there."

Those were Dad's final days. My dad, Joseph Dorning, died on November 8, 1972 at the age of 86. It was a sad day for all of us. Mom said, "I thank God that He took Doc before me; it would have been really hard for you to care for your dad without me." That was absolutely true; they were so close that Dad had learned to rely pretty exclusively on her. Mother continued to live with us until her death, twelve years later. She was a big part of our lives and the lives of the children. I have really fond memories of those days.

The years that followed were good years for us. I had my husband, my children, and my mother. I grieved the loss of my father, even as I thanked God for his long, productive life of service to all he met. George and I had wonderful years as we watched life continue to unfold for all of us. It unfolded with great successes, a good life, many celebrations—but also with an immeasurable loss.

# CHAPTER 38

## RETURN TO FAMILIAR PLACES

### *George*

**W**hen we returned from our aborted trip to Europe and our help-and-rescue mission to Wilkes-Barre, each of us journeyed on our separate paths and, as a family, we continued to work and play—whenever possible, together. We responded to the needs of Rosemary's parents, as they did to ours; and when the time came, we lay Rosemary's father to rest. Those years were a bittersweet time for Rosemary, but we had some wonderful times together. Rosemary was thrilled to have her parents living with us, and was always grateful that we could be there for her mother after Doc Dorning passed away. In spite of her loss, "Diamond Lil" (as Dr. Scribner had named Rosemary's mother), remained a "sparkler" for many years to come.

---

### DR. ROBERT SCRIBNER

*"Doc Dorning would come thirty miles to my office and was always most concerned about my physical condition. I would remind him that he came to me for help. He would say, 'Don't you know there ain't no use complaining? No one wants to hear it, and it does no good. I am on the best medicines for angina, and I won't complain. I enjoy cheering you up.' With his Irish blarney, he did just that! He really taught me, for the first time, that complaining does no good.*

*"His wife Lillian taught me to stay positive and cheerful, no matter what. She had severe, crippling arthritis, and was always cheering others up. She echoed her husband's thoughts: 'No use complaining!' My wife, Margaret, and I were honored to attend Lil's 75th birthday party. I decided that, since she was such a positive, sparkling character, and since diamonds are symbolic of 75 years, I would dub her "Diamond Lil"—just sparkling, all the time. In line with her new title, I gave her a huge, glass 'diamond' ring from the five-and-dime store. She got a big kick out of it. The Dornings were a big influence for the better in my life."*

---

## DR. ROBERT SCRIBNER

*"Rosemary learned her lessons well and is the personification of her parents' philosophy: 'Always think positive and never complain.' She lived that philosophy in her relations with George and their family. In doing so, she helped to make George the shining example of a man of God."*

In the midst of many family matters, I heard that Futura Titanium had folded and had been put up for auction. Without any hesitation, I went to the auction and bought the company—I bought all of the equipment and all of the metal. I ended up paying about ten cents on the dollar. With that done, I was not only the president, as I had been, but the owner as well. Years before, I had built Futura into a successful business, and I was confident that I could do the same again. I knew and had hired most of the important people who had stayed with the company—including Peter Wilms, of course. It was great to have him and other good people back on board. I was familiar with the entire operation and I knew the personnel. I stepped back into the company, started to manufacture again, and continued to improve and expand the business.

There was at that time, in California, a local financier whom I knew—a man who was always looking to invest in some kind of business. Eventually, I partnered up with him. We moved the business out to the Conejo Valley, where I had built a new home for our family. I had a large plant there and he also had a machine shop that had manufactured nuts and bolts. That outfit had previously collapsed and was nothing more than a shell company. We kept the location, bought the building from Cosmos Minerals, and kept the name of the company. Together we had three companies functioning under that name. One of the companies was a manufacturing division in the metal finishing industry; it made baskets, racks, and coils. Another company in the chemical/petro-chemical field made vessels, some of which were 123-feet long. We also manufactured both big heat exchangers and small heat exchangers. The fourth company, a wire company, was called Astrolite. For little more than a decade, I worked under those names and continued to prosper in the titanium business until, in 1984, I decided (for several reasons) to semi-retire.

I have already talked about establishing a great rapport with some people in Japan who were newcomers to the titanium industry. Those meetings and subsequent strong relationships took place years before I bought Futura Titanium. I was involved with a company in Nagoya and, for years, they bought my products in

# Return to Familiar Places

Japan. I met and developed very strong ties with the Japanese long before they had developed a great process called 'cladding.' When I learned about that process during the 1960s, I was very impressed. Here's the way it worked.

Cladding allows a manufacturer to make a vessel out of a large quantity of steel and then, by means of cladding, to bond a very thin layer of titanium to the inside of the existing steel vessel. The entire component is, then, mostly steel (much less expensive than titanium), and gives the vessel strength; the non corrosive titanium (much more expensive than steel) is clad to the steel and is not needed in such great quantity as before, because the steel withstands any heavy pressure or strain. The entire component gets the job done using much less titanium and, consequently, makes the product much less expensive to manufacture. The thin layer of titanium hides the greater layer of steel. Whatever is inside the vessel reacts to only the thin layer of titanium, not the heavier layer of steel. If the contents of the vessel reacted to the steel, the steel would be eaten up. Yet there is no corrosion when the contents of the vessel "see" the titanium instead of the steel.

For years, I had been involved in making vessels out of titanium which had to be strong enough to withstand intense pressures in specific operations. Some of those applications would demand three-quarters of an inch of expensive titanium to provide the necessary strength. Naturally, the expense was a drawback, and so I was searching for a way that I could lessen the cost in creating those vessels made only of titanium. For some time, I was aware of the process of cladding that would allow me to maximize the strength of a vessel while minimizing the overall cost

*George signs the cladding agreement*

of manufacturing. When the opportunity arose, I bought the use of the cladding process from the Japanese in order to be able to use it in the United States. The cost was almost a half-million dollars, but being able to use the cladding process proved to be a worthwhile investment in creating new and better products—and further broadening the market throughout the 70s and 80s. That type of transaction was one of many that helped me to continually establish my reputation as a reliable source for providing not only A-quality products, but also affordable ones.

# Brothers & Fathers

I enjoyed a lot of success as I moved into many different business ventures in the titanium industry. That success afforded us a very comfortable standard of living as Rosemary and I watched our children grow into young adults. My brother John continued his work on the east coast in his home Diocese of Scranton.

# CHAPTER 39

## THE MANY FACES OF THE POOR

### *Father John*

*I*was grateful that I had been able to be with Mom and Dad in the aftermath of the flood. Almost everyone I knew was touched by Agnes in some way or other, and it was a time of great suffering for a lot of people. When I returned from England, and when I wasn't helping Mom and Dad, I was living at St. Francis. Once back, I quickly became re-immersed in the needs of those around me. How true the words of Jesus rang in my ears, "The poor you have always with you." Immediately, I was once again caught up in the rhythm of the lives of the poor.

Early on, I saw a curious phenomenon among many of the children who lived in the so-called 'projects.' Unsupervised, maybe un-parented because of family situations, many of the children and young people became truant, and that truancy had a ripple effect. Some young people eventually dropped out of school because of a lack of interest, or a failure to keep up because of non-attendance. Others became involved in petty crimes, alcohol, or drug abuse. Whatever the cause, many were declared delinquent and sent to the House of Detention, which was located on the corner of Monroe Avenue and Linden Street, across from the University of Scranton. I would visit those kids and knew that some of them had other family members, older siblings, or possibly even parents, incarcerated at the Lackawanna County Prison. Family relationships, in those cases, took me to the prison, also located in the city, less than a few miles away.

Connecting with the prison population was one key to helping the children. I had had previous experience in the prison system when I was at St. Matthew's in East Stroudsburg. Strangely enough, my original inspiration to go to the prison there was actually connected with my sister Mae Ann. Prior to her death, I hadn't done a lot of prison ministry, although I did visit the Monroe County Jail to see anyone from St. Matthew's who was in jail. Other times, people in the parish would ask me to go to see a friend or a family member who was there. I became familiar with the system, but I didn't have a really strong prison ministry until I became involved with a woman by the name of Penny. Penny was unique. Because of the nature of her crime, she was sent, not to the Monroe County Jail, but to the Pennsylvania State Prison for Women in Muncy. When I went there to visit her, it was my first visit to a state correctional facility. That night, after the visit, I had a dream. I was going into a prison, but not to see Penny. In the dream, it was my sister Mae Ann who was in prison. As I was signing in, I could hear voices: "Oh, you're Mae Ann's brother. I haven't ever seen you here before. What kept you so long?"

I was feeling sheepish and guilty, but I continued to go deeper into the prison. As I did, I could hear the guards and the prisoners calling out, "There's Mae Ann's brother. He's never been here before."

"How come we haven't seen you before?"

With each accusation, I felt more and more guilty. I started to think about what I was going to say to Mae Ann when I saw her so I wouldn't feel so awful. I would explain to her how busy I was. I would tell her I was sorry. There were all kinds of things I was working up in my mind that I was going to tell her. After going through an extended entranceway, I finally came into one of the nicest parts of the prison, and there was Mae Ann. When she saw me, she smiled. She was so happy to see me. She never brought up the fact that I had never come to see her and I didn't need to use all the excuses that I had made up. She was just so sweet; she kept telling me just how happy she was to see me.

I still remember waking up from that dream feeling so overwhelmed with guilt. I found myself sobbing and sobbing, and wondering why I hadn't ever gone to see Mae Ann. Of course, the dream was connected with Penny, but it gave me a clearer awareness that, just like Mae Ann, Penny was my sister—she was my family, and she was in prison. The words that Jesus spoke really struck me: "I was in prison and you came to see me." It was on that occasion, years before, that I made a firm commitment to become involved in prison ministry. I continued to visit prisoners in the county jail in Monroe County and in the state facility at Muncy, but I had no idea then just how deep into that system the years would take me.

When I resumed my work in the Diocese of Scranton during the 1970s, the warden at the Lackawanna County Prison was a former state trooper whom I think was trying to do the best job he could; but, at that time, his posture was one that was prevalent and accepted. He and other wardens around the country pretty much had a mandate from the people to be very rough on prisoners. It was an era in which it was very hard to get any sympathy for the prisoners. It was almost as though you couldn't punish them enough. In the meantime, the bishops of Pennsylvania had put out a pastoral letter, Reform in the Correctional Institutions in the State of Pennsylvania. There was no doubt about the Church's concern and the bishops were ready to step into the breach. They were brave; they were bold. They made statements about pressing problems that were plaguing the correctional system of the United States, and certainly of Pennsylvania as well. In the letter, the bishops set forth some suggestions in regard to recidivism and prison rehabilitation. There was talk about overcrowded prisons, antiquated prison facilities, personnel that were ill trained, wardens who didn't have background in criminal law and who came from hard-nosed police forces. The letter presented a new way to look at prisoners and it was really a very fine document. It focused on how we could bring the spirit of the Gospel to prisoners. To this bold statement, my bishop had bravely added his name. When I read the document I felt as though I had my marching orders. This enthusiasm for helping the imprisoned, especially those whose families I knew, ate into my prayers, my mind, and my ministry. I had a great deal of hope for all prisoners, but especially for the imprisoned parents of the children I was working with in the projects.

My bishop really didn't want to hear about all the details of all the issues. God love him, his training and his background had really not prepared him for the new urban blight. I continued to work in the prisons, but also in the housing projects, meeting deprived youngsters, juvenile delinquents, criminals, and victims. There were so many views that were being propagated concerning the incarcerated, regardless of age. Two sides of the argument developed: rehabilitation or punishment. There were judges and law enforcement people who talked about bleeding hearts and those who "want to spring the crooks." What about the victims of crime? What were alternative forms of correction? Was locking up the criminal and throwing away the key the only answer?

How did prison reform relate to other ministries? How could I help? I looked around and knew there had to be a way. The children of the projects, who were exposed to violence; the sexually abused children; the child abusers; the drug addicts; the alcoholics; the prostitutes; the murderers—those were my parishioners. I really knew I couldn't go at this alone. It took some time, but I built up an ecumenical base. Prison reform was something the Catholic Church and the Protestant Churches were both interested in. I initially teamed up with a wonderful Methodist minister by the name of Gary Kuhns; I also worked with another great Baptist minister by the name of Lee Freeman. Both of these men were truly Gospel-oriented people and fine Christians. Gary Kuhns and I put together a proposal and presented it to the Methodist Mission Board. The board, eventually, awarded money to pay a minister to do full-time prison ministry. He would be free of other obligations and would be given a full salary to do work in the prison. His name was Paul Gere and he became part of the Team Ministry. Paul and I did ministry together, not only in the prison, but also at Valley View Terrace and Hilltop Manor. Another Lutheran minister, Reverend Bill Walton, was on board very early on. All of us did a lot of teaching. We did counseling with the children and we worked with other members of their families so that we could stem the tide of children moving from the delinquency program to the prison system. I also got some strong support from two very involved seminarians: Tom Cappelloni, and Tom Stahurski, who had been so helpful during the flood of '72. There were many others who came forward as problems continued to surface and the years moved quickly on.

There is no question that prisoners are people who have failed many times in using their freedom properly. As I worked with prisoners, it was very clear to me that those failures were a clear indication that prisoners (so many of whom couldn't read or write) had a need for great teachers. When prisoners were released, they were unable to get jobs; they didn't know how to identify or use their talents. The circumstances of their births, the downward slide in their families of origin, the poverty, the social deprivation, the lack of literacy and even health care—all were factors in their entering—and, more often than not, returning repeatedly to—the prison system. The needs were enormous, and I began to see that I had to agitate for courses that could be offered within the prison. If change was going to happen, prisoners needed the opportunity to learn to read and write. I needed teachers who would be willing to help. Literacy was a key component in helping to change existing conditions. It would be great if the parents of the children could foster in their children what they knew had been absent in their own lives. Maybe they could even make up some of those deficiencies in themselves and chart a new and better course for themselves.

The ecumenical apostolate that I began embraced Catholics, Protestants, and Jews. People were willing. Doctors, nurses, social workers, priests and sisters, teachers and seminarians generated great energy. I threw myself into the ministry—as did many other good people. The Church was alive, from the top to the bottom.

When we began to penetrate the jails, the courts, and the detention centers, the reaction was awesome. An explosion occurred. I suppose some thought I should have anticipated such an explosion, but I didn't. I really didn't anticipate any trouble. Wasn't everyone happy to see the changes in the fathers and mothers and children of diseased and broken families? Shouldn't we reserve for these imprisoned people our best doctors, lawyers, teachers, social workers, religious leaders? If they are the sickest, don't they need the most help? Well, such thoughts were great, but reality was reality.

As I became more and more involved with inmates at the Lackawanna County Prison, I began to develop an almost adversarial role with the warden there. He, along with many of the guards, felt that I was trying to coddle the prisoners, and saw me as one of the 'bleeding hearts.' I continued to do what I was doing.

Simultaneously, the projects continued to be a simmering pot. No one knew for sure when one area of the pot would heat up, bubble up, and finally boil over. Just when one bubble came to the top and exploded, another one was right behind. Incidences of beatings and domestic abuse were pretty common. All were pretty terrible, but several made local history. One day, I answered the phone and was told to go as fast as I could to give the Last Rites to a man by the name of Salvatore who was crippled and lived in one of the apartments there. I knew him because he was on my list for First Friday calls. I got there fast—even before the ambulance. When I went into the apartment, there was blood splattered all over the walls and all over Sal. I gave him the Last Rites, but he was obviously dead. What I came to know later was that Sal had been murdered by two prostitutes he had hired. Everyone was just so horrified, so appalled by the brutality, and once again so concerned for the kids who lived in that brutal environment.

A curious twist evolved as the case was investigated and came to trial. One of the women, who was responsible for Sal's death—Naomi— turned state's evidence against the other woman. The other woman was sent to prison; Naomi was set free. Not too long after those events, another woman by the name of Leigh Ann became notorious in the Scranton area when she fire-bombed a rooming house where she thought the man she was involved with was inside with another woman. The man she targeted was not inside, but there were two other men, along with two prostitutes, who all died in the bombing. Oddly enough, Naomi and her sister were the two women involved. After the rooming house murders, I began to minister to Leigh Ann and her family. I went through the trial with her and her mother, and her sister. She had quite a story to tell. Talk about poverty! She was put in prison and had a baby there. She escaped. She was eventually sent to Muncy State Prison for Women, where she was sentenced to serve four consecutive life sentences. Throughout all of those proceedings, there was a tremendous level of hatred that was poured out on her. She is still in prison today.

I kept Bishop McCormick pretty much informed as to what I was doing. I also continued to share my concerns with him about how prevalent the objections to the poor were during the early days of my ministry in the housing projects. He responded in 1974 by transferring me to a fourth residence, Christ the King Parish in Dunmore.

One of the first experiences that I had when I began to live in Dunmore was very indicative of who my new pastor, Father Mike Quinn, really was. I had been involved in a busy day that spilled over into night. I didn't come home until about two o'clock in the morning. Father Quinn heard me come in and came to tell me that a Black man had come to the door during the evening looking for me and he was asleep in the basement of the rectory. The man was a guy I knew as Roland, but his friends called him "Pokey." He was released from the county prison that day and had found out that I was living at Christ the King Parish (actually in walking distance from the prison). He came to the door, knocked, and asked for me.

Father Quinn had Huey Fitzpatrick, the church sexton, cook Roland something to eat. When I didn't come home, Mike told Roland that he could go downstairs to wait for me—there was a bed down there and he was welcome to stay, if it got really late. That was the first of Mike Quinn's many shows of hospitality. No matter who came to the parish—family, friends, workers in the ministry, or any of the poor—they were all welcomed. I lived there until Mike Quinn died in 1980. During my stay there, I developed a great relationship with the pastor and the parishioners of Christ the King. It was the first 'home' I had had in a long time in a welcoming parish atmosphere.

About that same time, as I found myself very well received in the parish, I found no reception by the administration in the prison. The programs, the new approach to things, and surely the disagreements caused me to butt heads with the old guard. My criticisms of some of the administrative policies at the prison, and of the physical plant of the jail, were becoming much more than an annoyance. A lot of my activity was reported in the local newspapers, and people were becoming aware of just how bad some of the conditions were. I registered many complaints on behalf of the prisoners. Not surprisingly, the warden, came to be more and more antagonistic toward me and, in November of 1974, I was denied access to the prison after one of our many disputes. A photograph of me and the story of the ban hit the paper. Strangely enough, the bishop was furious. He distanced himself from me somewhat, yet he did not remove me from my work. He was really the Church at the top. He made his statement and I made mine. Over the years, we worked things out together; but at the time, the publicity generated a lot of interest in what was happening at the prison. Some good people were surely on the side of the warden. Some good people were with the priest. Ironically, the publicity worked for the betterment of the incarcerated. After about two weeks of continuing press coverage, the prison authorities lifted the ban against me and I was able to resume my ministry inside the prison.

Many people continued to respond to that ministry. Teachers came and instructed prisoners in how to get a diploma from high school. Others offered Bible study. There were lay people, priests, ministers, and seminarians. A lot of good was brought about in the prison by many generous people. I also became involved with a wonderful Jewish lawyer, Morey Meyers—a very respected attorney in

## Warden Bars Jail Entry to Priest Who Criticized Prison's Conditions

By MITCH GROCHOWSKI

A Roman Catholic priest, who last week criticized conditions in th Lackawanna County Prison, found himself "locked out" of that institution Wednesday when h arrived there to counsel inmates.

Rev. John Esseff, diocesan chaplain for low income housing projects, was turned away by a guard at the main door when he came for his 2 p.m. weekly session with prisoners from his district. The guard told the priest h was acting on orders from Warden Louis Pizzo.

Father Esseff said he had been informed earlier he was dismissed by Pizzo from the jail's team ministry — an inter-denominational volunteer group of clergymen.

The ousted clergyman said he was told th warden's decision was made because of remarks he made on county prison reform in a forum at Temple Hesed last Friday. The priest's statements was printed in last Saturday's Tribune.

Two other clergymen waiting at the door with Father Esseff were allowed inside, they are: Rev. Paul Gens, Protestant chaplain, and Rev. Joseph Houston, Roman Catholic chaplain. Both protested th warden's action.

Fathr Esseff, who may be the first clergyman ever refused right to counsel my people and held against visitation rights at the jail, said he did not think prison officials had a legal right to deny visitations," the priest said, "but I have a moral right to counsel my people and there are a number of persons in there who come from low income housing."

Warden Pizzo, when contacted after the incident, defended his action, saying the team ministry was an arrangement he personally made with various clergymen who have

**Warden Louis Pizzo**
... ousts clergyman

caused "no problems." He said there only were "one or two" clergymen through the years besides Father Esseff who have created agitation. The warden said the move was to keep the prison "peaceful and quiet."

Pizzo denied the priest's statement that numerous destitute prisoners were unable to obtain bail. "We have only two or three who cannot afford bail," he said. "And the Father said the women here are hostile. They tell me they are not."

Father Esseff offered his own explanation of the incident.

"I had not intended for this to result in a headon confrontation with Warden Pizzo," Father Esseff said. "I am seeking only against conditions, not personalities."

The priest added, "I'm not seeking chaplains' rights . . . I am seeking prisoners' rights."

Father Esseff said his talk last Friday was to make persons aware that first-time offenders, because of lack of bail or rehabilitation programs, are

(Please Turn to Page Five)

TURNED AWAY—Rev. John Esseff, Roman Catholic chaplain for low income housing projects, is pictured leaving the entrance of the Lackawanna County Jail Wednesday after he was denied admission to counsel prisoners. Warden Louis Pizzo, who dismissed the priest from the jail's team ministry program, said the clergyman made "untrue remarks" about the institution in a recent forum on prison reform in Temple Hesed. Tribune staffer Mitch Grochowski is in background.
—(Tribune Photo—Ed Smith)

*Advocate for prisoners*

Scranton. When I was having a really hard time, I found that the greatest friend in my work for prisoners was a man like him—a good lawyer who wanted to effect social change.

Not all of the crime in Scranton originated in the projects. In 1978, a series of shootings caught the attention of everyone. A man was fatally shot in a west Scranton parking lot in February. In March, another man was also killed while he waited for the traffic light to change at North Main Avenue and the North Scranton Expressway. A third man survived being shot in the neck outside the West Side Hotel in April. There was a lot of concern about those three shootings, which seemed to have no connection to one another.

In spite of all these important matters, in May of 1978 I took time to observe the anniversary of twenty-five years of priesthood. I had two celebrations. Because I had come to know so many of the parishioners and participated in the life of Christ the King parish, I had an anniversary Mass at the parish. I had a second anniversary Mass at my other 'parish,' the Lackawanna County Jail. At first, the warden was opposed to the idea of the Mass; but in the end, he agreed to it. I considered it a great blessing to celebrate my quarter-century mark of priesthood in the prison. Along

## Prison Setting Of Mass

By FRANK SCHOLZ
Times Staff Writer

Surrounded by members of his family, more than a dozen priests and nearly 20 prisoners, the Rev. John Esseff celebrated a Mass in the exercise yard of the Lackawanna County Jail this morning commemorating his 25 years in the priesthood.

"This was his life's dream," said the father of the Roman Catholic priest following the hour-long ceremony under a warm sun behind prison walls.

Speaking to the 20 inmates invited to the Mass, Father Esseff said "for (this) one hour we are not prisoners . . . but the children of God."

Appointed to the Campaign for Human Development by Bishop J. Carroll McCormick of the Scranton Roman Catholic Diocese, Father Esseff considers the the prisoners "his parishioners" and, thus, it was his desire to mark his silver anniversary with them behind prison walls.

During the ceremony, other inmates inside the jail broke a window and set a cell on fire, but few of the people on hand paid any attention.

Father Esseff said he was "overjoyed, delighted" and privileged to celebrate his years in the priesthood here in this context."

For security reasons, attendance was limited to 50 persons. The atmosphere was cordial, almost festive, with the priest's father and mother, Joseph and Celia Essef, meeting with each of the prisoners in attendance following the ceremony.

President Judge Richard Conaboy attended the ceremony, as did Sheriff Joseph Wincovitch. Sheriff Wincovitch, who also serves as chairman of the county Prison Board, shared his hymnal and freely mixed with the inmates.

Also on hand for the Mass was Mary Scranton, wife of former Gov. William Scranton.

(Continued on Page 10)

Gothic tower at corner of Lackawanna County Prison outer wall provides backdrop for Mass marking 25th anniversary of the ordination of the Rev. John Esseff. About 20 inmates joined friends and relatives of the priest before a temporary altar set up on a blacktopped sports area of the prison yard. The priest, a member of the Team Ministry, a group of clergymen and nuns who look after the spiritual wellbeing of inmates, considers persons serving time in the jail as his parishioners. (Staff photo by Rose)

*Father John's 25th anniversary mass*

with the inmates, I was joined by my mother and dad, more than a dozen priests, and other friends and family members. For security reasons, the number in attendance was limited to fifty people. Judge Richard Conaboy, Sheriff Joseph Wincovitch (the chairman of the county Prison Board), and Mary Scranton (former first lady of Pennsylvania) also attended the celebration. The warden wasn't there because he was testifying in court that day. It was a great day for me as I prayed and gave thanks for the support of so many around me.

The shootings of the months that preceded my anniversary were eventually solved, and the story of a man and his bizarre plan of random murder was all over the news. The murderer was a former teacher and a partner in a detective agency. His plan was to kill a man whom he claimed was involved with his wife. In order to pull off the murder of that man with impunity, he had initiated a series of random murders; one victim would be the man he wanted dead while the other fatalities were tragic pawns in his plot. In spite of his ploys, the murderer was eventually caught; but by that time, three innocent people had fallen victim to his plan. Who knows how many more might have been killed if this man wasn't stopped? Who expects a teacher to be a serial killer? The murderer was sent to the Lackawanna County Prison. There, while incarcerated and awaiting trial, he staged a mock trial of a fellow inmate, Clifford Doolittle, who was also charged with murder. After sentencing Doolittle to death, this serial killer and another inmate convinced Doolittle to hang himself. That such a brutal and tragic event could

# The Many Faces of the Poor

take place in the prison became something I needed to address. Here was a man who was guilty of multiple murders; he should have been excluded from the general population. When he went to the Lackawanna County Prison, he lived in a violent place—a physical dungeon, a place resistant to reform and renewal. He found himself in a very comfortable 'psychological' place. His behaviors didn't change.

I knew I had to keep advocating for reforms, and I also knew I had to walk a tightrope. There was another incident in 1978, not nearly as riveting as this particular case, but important, nonetheless. Four prisoners overpowered a guard—just another incident in a string of escapes and attempted escapes. In 1978, I wrote a letter to *The Scranton Tribune* addressing those events:

> *I would like to make clear that I do not, in any way, find the actions of the four prisoners morally justifiable. What they have done is wrong. But when men in positions of responsibility fail to fulfill their duties and fail to respond to the constant call for improvement, then they share in the wrongdoing by what they have failed to do.*
>
> *For years now I have felt like a voice crying in the wilderness regarding the irresponsibility of the Prison Board. There has been a unanimous, universal call for change in the prison facility. The warden, the guards, the prisoners, the grand jury have all advocated increased guards, more educational programs, better health care, needed visiting facilities, etc.*
>
> *These calls for change have been made for years to the Lackawanna County Prison Board. The board turned unresponsive and deaf ears. The five judges, who continually sentence men and women to this facility, are the most powerful members of the board. The commissioners, who control the purse strings for these long-overdue improvements, are the most unresponsive members of the board.*
>
> *The track record of the board is nil. They are obliged by law to meet each month. They are obliged to publicize their meetings and report what they are doing.*
>
> *Their failure to meet, to come to grips with the issues, is obviously and absolutely uncontestable. The president of the board, Sheriff Joseph Wincovitch, has called meeting after meeting and finds no response. The grand jury has made recommendation after recommendation with no reaction. Grievance committee after grievance committee offered suggestions and recommendations—still no response. The warden and his staff continuously find a deaf ear to their requests.*

*If some incident does occur at the county prison in which someone is seriously injured or killed, I, for one, would hold the Prison Board contributory to the incident and morally indictable because of its failure to respond to the situation that now exists.*

*I have been involved in the county prison for years and the board's excuse for those years has been: Wait until we get a new jail. As far as I can determine, this new facility will not be ready for years to come. The lack of concern on the part of the board is a reason for the present state of affairs.*

Without question, ministering to prisoners in direct service at that time was very hard work. It could have been easier, however, if the climate and attitudes in our area had been different. We concentrated on helping those we could and accepting support from those who wanted to help. Thank God, I stayed in the jail long enough to show that.

I was really a member of the Church family. Many wonderful changes came into being for prisoners, prison personnel, and prison programs. In time, I saw the Lackawanna County Prison embrace an enlightened warden, a fine realistic group of trained corrections officers, and many generous and talented people willing to reach out to the broken who lived in the prison system.

*Father John's ministry to prisoners*

# The Many Faces of the Poor

The poor, especially those incarcerated, demanded a great response, but not all of the poor lived in the city. With the coming of summer, in the surrounding rural areas, signs of plenty dotted fields everywhere. It would be a rare occasion to be more than ten miles outside of the city limits and not see fields of tomatoes, squash, pumpkins, corn, and orchards of trees sprouting green apples. When the time came for harvesting those fruits and vegetables, the farmers depended on migrant workers. In our area, that was common knowledge.

When I came back from South America, one thing that I brought back with me was my ability to speak Spanish. In my diocese, I was one of very few Catholic priests who could speak Spanish at the time, and most of the migrant workers in our area were Spanish speaking—and Catholic. It seemed right that I should go out to the local migrant camps to celebrate Mass for those who had come to work in the fields. From the months of July through October (the harvest months), I would go to the camps to celebrate Mass for the workers. That involvement gave the migrants an opportunity to attend Mass and also to present their children for Baptism or for preparation for receiving Holy Communion.

There were two streams of migrant workers who came through our area; and in no time, I became aware that, on both these streams were many who were sin papeles—without documents. In its migrant programs, the state of Pennsylvania had welfare and assistance; but to receive help, migrants had to be citizens. Many were not eligible for food stamps. If a young girl who was working in the fields was pregnant but undocumented, she would not be eligible for prenatal care or for hospitalization that might be part of the outreach programs in place. There were also many children who were not eligible for programs designed for education. I began to see tremendous suffering, especially among migrants who were without papers. Crew leaders knew that those who were undocumented had no recourse under the law, and some of them tried to cheat the migrant workers out of their wages. There was tremendous potential for exploitation and, unfortunately, exploitation occurred. Each summer, the ranks of the poor swelled with the coming of the migrants. I met a woman at that time who gave tirelessly of her time and talents to improve the lot of migrant workers. Long before I met her, Mary Ellen was working with the Four County Migrant Ministry Committee, which was composed of Union, Northumberland, Montour, and Columbia Counties. Closer to home, I became involved with the Tri-County Migrant Committee, which ministered to migrants in Wyoming, Lackawanna, and Luzerne counties. According to a brochure that we created and distributed, the committee was "an ecumenical alliance devoted to improving the living conditions of the migrant farm workers ... in the hope of offering a biblical response to the 'stranger who lives in your town.'" Along with many others, I responded to the needs of the migrants. Because of continuing cutbacks in government funding at that time, there was an increased need for money for eye and dental care, emergency food, housing, and transportation for farm workers in transit, and other unforeseen emergencies that arose during the season.

I was certainly aware that Pennsylvania was not the only area that depended largely on migrant workers. On more than one occasion, I talked to my brother George about the migrants, as so many of them lived and worked in California.

## GEORGE

"I got involved with migrant workers as far back as 1963, when I opened a facility in Burbank, California. Many of the workers that I hired were illegal immigrants. As far as I was concerned, they would work as hard—or harder—than anyone. They were very faithful and I valued them as workers. What I did early on was to begin to try to get them legalized. I'd pay for their schooling to learn English. I'd pay for lawyers who helped to get them legalized. In many cases in California, when amnesty was granted, many migrant workers got green cards just because of the amnesty. As they progressed and wanted to become citizens, we helped them through the process. I have had a very happy relationship with migrants from that standpoint. Even presently, 75% of our work force is Mexican or Latin American. All of them either have green cards or are citizens. It's been a great pleasure for me through the years to see that these men now have children, who, because of a great work ethic, have become lawyers and doctors and successful members of all kinds of professions and trades.

"I paid the immigrants well. I didn't pay them any less than I paid someone else who was doing the same work. I think they appreciated that. We have many employees who have been with us for 25 or 30 years, and it has really been a great experience for me. We have three groups within some families—those who originally immigrated, then siblings, then cousins and uncles. They have been just fantastic. It seemed that they passed on what we were doing to anyone new who came in, and those who followed were equally valuable employees for us. They have served the business well. I consider them a vital part of my business family."

Besides the migrant workers, another group of people who came to our area (and other areas throughout the country) in the seventies were refugees. Many of them came from Vietnam when the Communists took over South Vietnam. Others came from Cuba. For some of them, their long journey ended near Harrisburg, Pennsylvania in the town of Indiantown Gap. At that time, I was working with the Team Ministry and we sponsored families (and individuals), relocating them in our area. I did notice that the Vietnamese were open to participating in the welfare system. Sister Martha McAndrew, a member of the Team Ministry, began to advocate for them and for others. Over the years, she dedicated her time and talents to what came to be known as the Scranton Primary Health Care Center. Among many other things, she wanted to make sure that children were immunized, and she made it her business to see that the refugees had an opportunity to achieve and maintain a healthy life. That service still exists in Scranton today and serves the needs of many.

At that time, I was still based in Christ the King parish and I sponsored three single men. Each one advanced pretty quickly in the American system. There seemed to be something about their ability to adapt and to begin to move up the socio-economic ladder. I began to look for places for each of them to stay, and I looked to the parishioners, whom I always found to be gracious when people were in need. Bob and Joan Holmes were a couple who lived in the neighborhood. Joan was a grade school teacher and she was already very involved in ministry in the prison. There were no shelters for the homeless in our area at that time, and Bob and Joan would often help out by providing temporary housing to someone I would bring who needed a place to stay. They were extraordinarily generous during those years.

## JOAN HOLMES

*"We had two extra bedrooms, because the older children were grown and had moved out. Patrick, Kathy, Karen, and Mary Beth were living in their own homes. Maureen and the two youngest, Bobby and Jeanie, were still at home. For about two or three years, Father John brought people to our home. Once, Patrick, a man who had been released from prison in Louisiana, found himself in Scranton—out of money and with no place to live. He ran into an officer who was with the Scranton police force. Patrick told the policeman that, if he didn't get some help soon, he knew he would start drinking again and would wind up in jail. The officer knew Father John well, and sent Patrick to see him. That day, Father John arrived at our door with a man who looked like he was in his early thirties. Maybe because it was almost Easter, we thought he looked a lot like Jesus: He was in his early thirties, he was tall and thin, and he had long hair. Patrick stayed with us about a week and then left to go to Canada. He did come back to town once—and when he did, he came by to thank us.*

# Brothers & Fathers

## JOAN HOLMES

"Another time, Father brought two women. One was Eileen and the other was her young daughter Susie. They were actually hiding out in a downtown hotel waiting for Susie to have her baby. The baby was late, and they had run out of money. They needed a place to stay until the baby was born and they wanted to make arrangements for the baby's adoption. Susie had the baby, and then they stayed with us for the rest of the summer.

"In 1980, Father John came to the door. A young Vietnamese man named Thanh was with him. We learned later that the two of them had come up with a plan: If, during the visit, the young man decided he would like to stay with us for the upcoming two weeks, he was supposed to nod to signify 'yes.' He was very likable. He nodded. We accepted him. He stayed with us for six years. We learned his story in bits and pieces. He had been a soldier in the South Vietnamese military. When Saigon fell in 1975, he had escaped. He piled thirty other people into a boat and the boat sank. The U.S. Seventh Fleet rescued them and airlifted them to the Philippines. He then went to Guam and later to Alaska before finally arriving in Indiantown Gap. There he met Father John, who sponsored him and two other young Vietnamese men. They all had to be relocated, so Father had to find each of them a place to live.

"When he first lived with us, Thanh worked as a mechanic at Friendship House in Scranton. It wasn't unusual to look out the window and see him and his friends crawling all over a car in front of the house. He thought Americans were wasteful: In Vietnam, people kept cars running forever, and he could do that. Among his friends, Thanh always seemed to be in a position of authority.

"My children considered Thanh their brother. Maureen, the oldest at the time, seemed the most involved. Our young guest shared his car with her. She used it in the day and he used it at night, when he took a job at St. Joseph's Hospital; there he worked as a nurse's aide. He loved working there with the babies and children who had so many challenges. He wanted to learn more and so he went to the Mercy School of Nursing, where he received his credentials as an LPN.

"This young man absolutely cherished his freedom. He would come to Robert Morris School, where I taught, and he would speak to the fourth graders about freedom. He told them about what it was like living in a place where the Communists were in control.

# The Many Faces of the Poor

Having had a home at Christ the King parish with Mike Quinn as my pastor for six years definitely made even the most difficult times tolerable. The people in the parish were very special to me, and when I could, I enjoyed much of their hospitality as well as their heartache. When Mike Quinn died in 1980, I lost a pastor, a friend, and a supporter in my work. The people loved him and we knew he was someone who could never be replaced. A good and gentle soul, ready to meet his Lord, Michael Quinn had taken his final journey home, and there was comfort in that for all of us who had grown to love him.

# Brothers & Fathers

As the parish moved into a new dynamic, there was some discussion as to where I would live next. All the while my fate was being decided, I heard talk among the upper crust in the local clergy regarding my living arrangements. The question was, "What will we do with Esseff now?" I learned that one monsignor was consulted at that time about the residency dilemma; his response was succinct and undeniably clear: "I wouldn't have him in my rectory for twenty minutes. His clientele can wreck any parish." I heard that comment and others like it. They became commonplace. Generally, I knew I was blackballed on the parochial level, and that's when Bishop McCormick stepped up to the plate. He arranged for me to live at the Chancery Building in Scranton while I manned the newly created Office of Urban Ministry on the ground floor. I found myself rubbing elbows with many of the hierarchy at the breakfast table: Bishop McCormick, Auxiliary Bishop Timlin, Monsignor (later Auxiliary Bishop) Dougherty, Father Bernie Yarrish (the bishop's secretary), Father Frank Callahan (the Propagation of the Faith director), Father Neil Van Loon (the assistant to the chancellor) and, when Bishop McCormick retired, Bishop John O'Connor (later Cardinal O'Connor of New York) who stayed with us until 1983. My brother Jesus had quite a sense of humor!

On July 1st, 1981, the warden of the Lackawanna County Prison was replaced. Things changed when the warden changed. Knowing that so many of the prisoners were in need of assistance, and as a student of criminal justice, the new warden put together a counseling program for prisoners. We were in Scranton, not Philadelphia, Chicago, or Baltimore; yet the same kind of human tragedies were being played out day by day in our city. We eventually got to the county commissioners and they began to leave some of the tough practices of the past behind and instead, to spend time on prison reform. It was about that time that a formalized ministry was established, called the St. Paul Prison Guild. It was made up of about thirty men and women who did a lot of different things in a systematic way. They made visits to the prisoners; some taught reading and writing; some conducted sessions in Bible study and created prayer groups; Some others conducted reentry courses and joined in reconciliation meetings with prisoners and their families. A system of communication through birthday cards and letters was encouraged and facilitated by some volunteers. The people in the Prison Guild were a great help, while a man named Paul and I continued to minister to prisoners in the bleakest of time—their imprisonment. I went to visit with their families and got to minister to them, too. When the prisoner's time was up, there were other things that needed to be done: trying to relocate, trying to get a job, trying to overcome the reputation that each one had so that someone would give him or her a break—just one more chance.

# The Many Faces of the Poor

While continuing to serve as Director of Urban Ministry, I was elevated to the rank of monsignor in 1983. On May 29th of that same year, I had a second celebration in the Lackawanna County Prison—this time to commemorate my investiture as a Prelate of Honor. Security throughout the service was tight, due to a brutal beating of two prisoners by two other inmates just the previous week. The celebration was planned to take place in the prison courtyard, but a rainy Sunday morning brought it indoors. Together with six other monsignors and five priests, I concelebrated the Mass. As I told reporters who were there, I felt that my elevation was not so much a personal honor but a social statement by the Catholic Church that the prison ministry is an important aspect of the Christian mission. There were about thirty prisoners who sat in the congregation, and about ninety other guests. Two guards stood beside the inmates and watched them at all times. The new warden looked down from the second level of the maximum-security wing throughout the Mass. I knew that many people condemned me because I had convicts participating in the liturgy. I also knew that I was happy to accept that condemnation because Jesus was known for His association with prisoners and outcasts.

After thirty years of being called 'Father,' I had to adjust to my new title of 'Monsignor.' Still, I'm always happy when many people, even today, call me Father.

As part of my ongoing prison ministry, I became involved in giving retreats in prison. I conducted Cursillos and, as

THE SCRANTON TIMES, TUESDAY, MAY 31, 1983

## Monsignor's Investiture Rites Attended by Prison Inmates

The maximum-security wing of the Lackawanna County Prison was the setting Sunday for the investiture of the Rev. John A. Esseff to the rank of monsignor.

The observance also marked the 30th anniversary of Monsignor Esseff's ordination to the Roman Catholic priesthood.

Monsignor Esseff, who has served 10 years as chaplain at the prison, was joined in the concelebration of the Mass by six other monsignors and five priests before the plain, cloth-covered table which served as the altar.

A few guards and prison officials looked on as female inmates walked in procession at the start of the Mass, each with a bouquet.

About 3 inmates and 90 other invited guests were present under tight security. Two of the invitees served as lectors, one of them a confessed murderer awaiting sentence.

The new monsignor thanked Bishop J. Carroll McCormick for petitioning Rome to obtain for him the title of prelate of honor.

"I had to wrestle with the title, monsignor," he said, noting that "for 30 years I've been known as 'Father'."

Asked about the setting of his investiture among the prisoners, he recalled that "Jesus was known for his association with prisoners and outcasts. These are my people and I get very defensive about them."

All entering the prison for the ceremony were checked for their credentials and invitations. The service had been planned as an outdoor service in the prison courtyard but adverse weather forced the move indoors.

Despite the security, there were no signs of tension among the prisoners. In fact, inmates joined hands with visitors as a sign of peace and all present took communion together.

Warden Ray Colleran described the event as one that "could be a first in penal history."

Lackawanna County Commissioner Robert Pettinato summed up the prison ministry of Monsignor Esseff by saying: "These people (the inmates) who have shown by their actions that they don't respect too many people, do indeed respect this man and that shows how effective he is."

Sister Adrian Barrett described Monsignor Esseff's congregation as "the prisoners and the poor."

Following the Mass, prisoners were treated to a special turkey dinner. Later, Monsignor Esseff was honored by the Lackawanna County commissioners in their office in the County Administration Building and presented with a plaque in recognition of his service as chaplain at the prison.

Monsignor Essef receives framed commission from the pope, presented by his mother, during ceremonies at prison. (Times Photo by Gallagher)

*Father John elevated to monsignor*

the years went on, my ministry went out of the local prison population. I became involved in Kairos ministry in state prisons in New Jersey and Pennsylvania. I also went to the federal prison in Lewisburg. As always, my work in prison ministry was the hardest part of all the work that I was doing at that time.

While all of these very important things were going on in the life of prisoners, there were other people in the housing projects who also had issues and concerns. When I was given the task of caring for the inner-city poor in the early seventies, I originally thought of single-parent families, the emerging Black community in a primarily White area, and second- and third-generation recipients of welfare. They were certainly there in the thousands, and I was anxious to minister to all of them. What I was very surprised to discover in my studies of the demographics of our area was that Scranton had the largest elderly population in the country outside of the city of St. Petersburg, Florida. Both Lackawanna and Luzerne Counties had an amazing number of elderly. The employment market changed drastically in the area when the coal industry ceased to function. More and more young people moved out of the area to find work. Many also took advantage of educational opportunities, became educated, and moved to other areas in New York, New Jersey, Washington, D.C., and other states where they could find suitable employment. As that exodus of the young continued, the parents remained and many, as they aged, lost the support of their children to varying degrees over time. Some of the parents remained in their own houses. Sometimes, if they lost their own properties (usually for financial reasons), they had to find more affordable housing. The Lackawanna County Housing Authority would place many of these elderly people into places like Valley View Terrace and Hilltop Manor. Their living quarters in both those places came to be known as the 'Tombs.' Most of them found the young kids marauding out on the streets to be threatening, and they were in no way equipped to deal with those threats—whether real or imagined. In those housing projects, there were usually four or five buildings. There were no elevators and, when most of the elderly went in there, they didn't come out. How to get up and down the stairs was a big problem, especially for those with arthritis or ailments of any kind. They needed groceries and medicines and all kinds of care. And so, what I began to see among those I was ministering to, was that the poorest were the elderly. They were vulnerable in the confines of their aging bodies—and also in their environment. I began to minister to them in the simplest way: by setting up a telephone. They were given a number to call when they had needs; they could telephone and someone would respond. We called our little set up, Telespond. Initially, I engaged an agoraphobic woman named Marie, who lived in her own home, and was unable to go out. Shortly after, I was able to get another young woman to help. They were

# The Many Faces of the Poor

both bright; they took messages and got the information to me or to others who would, in turn, respond. Whatever the need, whether medication or transportation or food, the elderly knew they could call. We really got a great response.

## PATTY ESSEFF

"In 1972, the Sisters of Mercy were very involved with the many people who were affected by the flood that hit Wilkes-Barre. At that time, I was Sister Patrice Kenny, a member of that order. We had hundreds of people staying in whatever beds were available in any of our facilities. During that time, the sisters were also having a big community celebration and the chapel was packed. We had gathered for a day of recollection, and a priest by the name of Father John Esseff was the presenter. I don't remember what he said exactly, but I do remember that his talk about the work he was doing caught my attention and drew me in. The next day, I called him on the phone and made plans to go to see him. It was late November or early December. One thing I remember very distinctly at that meeting was just how welcoming he was to me, an absolute stranger. I was very much in a searching mode myself and I was fascinated by the work that he was doing. Some days later, John introduced me to some of the people who were working with him. I met a young woman, "Cookie," and a young man, Chris, who were part of the Team Ministry. In time, I met Sister Martha McAndrew, I.H.M., Paul Gere, Eleanor Shields, Sister Nancy Abbott, I.H.M., Rev. William Walton, and Sister Miriam Heaton, R.G.S. The more I learned about the ministry, the more certain I was that I wanted to be involved in it. I became totally captivated by the work of the team, and by the generosity of the people who were part of it. By May of 1973, I had made arrangements with my community to work with the team for several months. I moved to Scranton and shared a place with Cookie. That was the beginning of a brand new community experience for me.

"That first summer as part of the Team Ministry was one of the sweetest summers of my life. It was as close to the Acts of the Apostles as I will ever get. All of us were involved in a patchwork of responses to all kinds of poverty. John traveled with purpose and focus, although some thought he was casual. Perhaps it was just more of a familial response: It wasn't as though he was working in the prison or with the young people or with the elderly. He was very much doing the work of 'a father'—and the work of the Father. Whichever of God's children, regardless of age, came in need on any given day, John responded to him or her in whatever brokenness was there because, in that brokenness, John saw Jesus."

# Brothers & Fathers

Telespond, our set-up to keep in touch with the elderly, seemed to be working out well. I decided to write a grant to see if there were any funds available for work with the elderly. I submitted it to the Campaign for Human Development, and they funded us to the tune of almost $80,000. Our project had started with a phone number and two volunteers to take and relay messages. All I was paying at the time was three or four dollars a month for the phone. When we got the money, one of our members on the team, Sister Patrice Kenny was put in charge of Telespond and we began to experience a real expansion of services for the elderly. Sister Patrice was very creative. Telespond was giving a significant amount of service to the community because of the volunteer base that Sister Patrice was able to put together. There were eight Vista volunteers, and people showed up from all over the place to help with that work. Once the funding came through and Sister Patrice became the director, Telespond took a whole new direction—far more structured and organized. Telespond is quite an operation even today, and buses painted with the Telespond logo are a common sight throughout the city. Today, the mission statement includes "providing high-quality community-based care to older adults and caregivers; enhancing the wellbeing of older adults by promoting independent living; providing low-cost alternatives to institutionalized care; and working cooperatively with other service providers to improve the efficient, effective delivery of needed programs." Despite any shortcomings, the program is a real success story.

## PATTY ESSEFF

"Because she became a profound teacher for me, one of the people that I most remember from my years in the Team Ministry was a young woman named Betty. She didn't look young to me. She had been in the hospital because she had overdosed, and John went to pick her up. John had someplace else to go and I was sitting and talking with Betty. When I realized that she was only a year older than I was, (I think I was 22 or 23 at the time), I was just shocked out of my shoes. This woman had been beaten and bruised and raped; she had an incredible life history of her own and her kids were running around crazy. John was really instrumental in helping Betty through a lot of stuff. What I didn't expect was that John became a help to me. I went into a fury at God over Betty's situation. It just brought up all that I perceived to be injustice, and I believed that God was doing a pretty lousy job proceeding with the job description I had worked out for Him. John was very patient with me, revisiting this issue multiple times because I was so angry and confused on multiple levels. He never said, 'Oh, just shut up.'"

# The Many Faces of the Poor

No matter what segment of the population I was dealing with, I found one problem that crossed all lines, and that was alcoholism. When I was ordained in 1953, I was very unaware of the treachery and power of alcohol to destroy individuals and families. I did not know how much of a problem it was socially, or how intimately it was woven into the fabric of society as a whole. I do know I was rather naïve when I learned about my first pastor's bouts with alcohol. While working in the prisons, I realized how much alcohol and drug addiction is related to a life of crime. The overwhelming percentage of people in institutions, prisons, and mental home care who also have trouble with either or both is staggering. Even some of the elderly and the very young struggled with alcoholism. It was—and is—the source of such terrible suffering. Years before working in the Office of Urban Ministry, when I left Shohola and went to St. Matthew's in 1953, I met a man—a daily communicant, an adult altar server. I saw him as a good practicing Catholic who was very devoted to God and to his family. What I didn't know, or couldn't detect, was that he was a severe alcoholic. It wasn't until he almost destroyed his entire family that I became aware of his wife and their seven children, almost all of whom had inherited the disease of alcoholism.

This man had been hospitalized for ailments other than alcoholism; but under close scrutiny, his problems were eventually diagnosed as byproducts of alcoholism. He and his family had made an appointment to go to a rehabilitation facility in New Jersey called Alina Lodge. I went with the man and his wife and we drove to New Jersey. We were all unaware of just how sick he was. Only after the man gained sobriety did he tell me that he manipulated stops on the way and somehow he got a couple of drinks. In spite of all that, we got him to Alina Lodge, where we met a woman by the name of Geraldine O. Delaney—she used to call herself G.O.D. I guess I knew the implication.

She was the head of the lodge, and she was the first one who began to teach me about alcoholism. "Listen, young man! This is something you really don't know much about and you really have to listen." I did. I went with the man's wife, along with another woman whose husband was also there, and the three of us began to take instructions. Later the three of us began the first AlAnon meeting in Stroudsburg. Part of understanding the program was learning about the twelve steps. What a revelation that process was to me! I could recall having been to many a retreat, having done many things in spiritual formation, but when I did my twelve steps, I made important discoveries—especially at my fourth step. It had taken me months to do the 'searching and fearless inventory.' I began to enter into the world of the alcoholic, and I was very much aware of the value of the twelve-step program. When

I got into my work in Scranton, I knew how the lives of so many people were torn apart by alcohol and I wanted to be able to minister to them in that need.

In 1972, again because of the way the government was cutting subsidies, another program that was cut was the administration of detox. When detoxification was no longer available through government-funded facilities, much more suffering entered into the already broken lives of alcoholics and their families. In response to that problem, Paul Gere and I started to think about ways that we could help. I was in touch with a fellow by the name of Dick O'Dea and we asked if he could find a place in the country where we could invite those suffering with alcoholism. He found a 67-acre farm in Dalton and worked out a deal with the owner, who was gracious enough to let us use it without paying rent if we would maintain the property. That was quite an offer!

Once word got out, we began to find crowds of people coming in to see us. I remember more than one who arrived on bicycle! We had calls from family members looking for help for someone in the family. I remember Mike who had returned from Vietnam, Ray who just got out of jail, Jerry who came to be our cook. Some came for help; others came to help. The members of the Team Ministry would help. Chris Ammons stayed at the property and Rev. William Walton and the others gave a lot of time and energy. Mary Scranton, the wife of Governor Scranton, became involved and gave us a large donation of money. Margretta Chamberlain donated animals to be cared for and we had people planting. It was a real farm experience. There was also a nice by-product: The property was so expansive that we could take some of the kids out of the summer heat in the projects to spend a day in the country. The entire enterprise was an exciting and wonderful experience, and there were many people who gained sobriety there. But the work was difficult and needed people who had specific skills. We didn't have the expertise to facilitate detoxification for everyone, and we knew people could die. We had to be on guard for anyone who could spin out and cause a lot of trouble. We did what we could for as long as we could, but eventually we closed the farm. A year later, Mary Scranton, who had been such a help to us, donated a beautiful place near that same area and Marworth, an alcohol rehabilitation facility, opened. Since 1983, thousands of people have gone through the program at Marworth and have become sober. I still go there to offer Mass whenever I'm asked, and I find that community to be one that has a deep and sustaining spirituality.

During that same time, I became acquainted with Frank Crabtree, a teacher at Marywood College, and Janie, his wife. They were very involved and started services and programs for alcoholics in prison. Those ministries took off beautifully.

# The Many Faces of the Poor

Those years of ministering to people in AA were a powerful experience for me. I began to give retreats specifically for those in the program, and I still do that today. I have given retreats in New York at the Redemptorists' Center, and at the Kirby House near Wilkes-Barre and Mountaintop. I have also given retreats at the Fatima Center in Dalton and at St. Gabriel's Retreat House. I have met hundreds of people from the program; each encounter is a time of special graces for me.

## JOE ESSEFF

*"When I was growing up, partly because of the big span in our ages, John and George seemed to be in a different family than mine. But as the years went by, I can honestly say that John became the person who helped me save my sanity. When I was getting in all kinds of trouble as a kid, the person who acted as a kind of buffer for me was John. In my view, John went from being the hard-ass to being someone who was really able to make me hear (even if not verbally), 'It's ok.' He never judged me, no matter what I did. When I was nineteen, I joined the army, and broke my father's heart. John was the one who said, 'I understand you need to do this.' He talked to my dad. As I went through all my phases, John knew I was isolated from God, but he always accepted me. As the years went on, I really started to connect with John. He was on a path of becoming more open, more gentle, more understanding. As a result, although I had removed myself from the God I was angry with, I never looked at John and said, 'How can you believe that?' I knew what he was doing was right. I knew that what he was telling people was right. I also knew he wasn't a saint: I knew he had a temper, and I knew he made mistakes—lots of them. But I also knew he was someone in my life who, when I was in trouble, I could turn to. And sometimes, I didn't even have to turn to him. He was just there. John touched my life as I got older. He touched my life in ways of understanding and acceptance.*

*"When I went into the AA program, and for the first ten years that I was sober, I believed in a higher power and I was very comfortable with a higher power. It was a higher power that I could talk to. As I was sober longer and had some things happen to me—Patty coming into my life, my boys getting older—I wanted to give them something they could hold onto. They went to the sacraments. They didn't want that. But in giving it to them, I started to reconnect with the Church. And John was always there, encouraging and understanding. I keep saying 'understanding' because, in AA we talk about 'a God of our understanding.' Sometimes priests, especially, get hung up on that. They have a God that is the Catholic God, that is the Christian God or Jesus, and therefore this is where you need to be if you're ever going to have any kind of spirituality. I had*

*JOE ESSEFF*

*spirituality in my second year of sobriety, but it wasn't 'church' spirituality. And as I stayed sober longer, and as I got more involved, John gently—ever so gently—brought me along with that. He was always there to say, 'You know what? Being comfortable and uncomfortable is a good way to look at it.' For ten, twelve years, if I'm comfortable doing something, it's ok. If I'm uncomfortable doing something, I've got to stop. That kind of thinking also connects with what I was taught in my religion. If you follow the Ten Commandments, you're going to feel good. If you break one of the commandments, you're going to feel bad. I used to think it was the 'guilt' thing—the big Catholic 'guilt' thing. And I railed at that for so long until, one day, I said, 'What am I fighting? There isn't an AA God and a Catholic God; there's a God.' I called Him 'higher power' for a long time, because I did not want to be a hypocrite like I was during those years between fourteen and eighteen. But today, I choose to call Him 'God.' I'm very comfortable with that."*

During all of the demands of the years '71, '72, and '73, the Team Ministry did wonderful things, not only at Valley View Terrace and Hilltop Manor, but also in other areas of the city where they responded to the needs of the poor. Unfortunately, by 1974, I saw some things regarding the team start to go in a direction that I did not want to go. In spite of so many successes (like the farm, work in the prisons and Telespond, health care, and countless individual interventions), the team was, in large part, imploding. We had established quite a reputation. I was meeting with the team, but I was seeing more and more and more signs of burnout among its members. I began to have serious concerns about some members of the group, and I myself was beginning to feel overwhelmed by the needs of those within the group. I saw the relationships changing among the members—in some instances, not for the good. I was very confused about my place in the group and my relationship with the members of the group. I actually began to feel trapped.

The only one I could say all that I thinking and feeling to was Sister Cor. I knew I wanted to quit—not working with the poor, but with the team. I wasn't quite sure how I could do that. I was also aware of how I trusted Sister Cor more than anyone else. She helped me to sort out a lot of things during those turbulent days and, eventually, I extracted myself from the group. When I resigned, the members of the team were really surprised, and I heard one member of the group say that I couldn't have done that without Cor's help. It's true: Cor was a great help to me in being able to sever that connection, which had been based only on my desire to work with the poor.

I was at Christ the King parish when I broke off that relationship with the team. Sister Patrice and I stayed in touch. Both of us were making changes in our lives. She, too, felt a similar need to leave the group but to continue as the director of Telespond. Eventually, she left the Team Ministry as well as Telespond.

By that time, I knew my relationship with Sister Cor was one of great trust rooted very deeply in an awareness that she was as dedicated to her religious commitment as I was to the priesthood. I knew that, when things got confused, I could trust that relationship. Once again, I was thankful for the blessing of her friendship.

## SISTER COR IMMACULATUM

*"When I first learned of the project for this book, a poem by Robert Frost came persistently to my mind: 'The Road Not Taken.' There were two brothers, John and George Esseff—two roads, and each road was specially chosen. At birth and during their early years, there was one road charted by parents, extended family, Church. And then the road diverged and one, the less traveled, became the road chosen by Father John.*

*Two roads diverged in a yellow wood,*

*And sorry I could not travel both*

*And be one traveler, long I stood*

*And looked down one as far as I could*

*To where it bent in the undergrowth;*

*Then took the other, as just as fair,*

*And having perhaps the greater claim,*

*Because it was grassy and wanted wear;*

*Though as for that the passing there*

*Had worn them really about the same,*

## SISTER COR IMMACULATUM

*And both that morning equally lay*

*In leaves no step had trodden black.*

*Oh, I kept the first for another day!*

*Yet, knowing how way leads on to way,*

*I doubted if I should ever come back.*

*I shall be telling this with a sigh*

*omewhere ages and ages hence:*

*Two roads diverged in a wood, and I—*

*I took the one less traveled by,*

*And that has made all the difference.*

*"I have witnessed Father John's ministry as both brother and father. As brother, he has responded to the needs of the poor and neglected of Scranton and the surrounding area. He began the diocesan Urban Ministry program: In the projects, he ministered to the poor and underprivileged; in the prisons he established prayer groups, retreats for prisoners, support for their families, advocacy groups; with and for the elderly, he began Telespond; for the uninsured and the sick he began the Primary Health Care Center; for those with addictions to alcohol and drugs he established The Farm in Dalton prior to the programs at Marworth; for the migrant workers and the immigrants from Vietnam and Cambodia he provided spiritual, educational, and financial assistance; ecumenically, he worked tirelessly with the Ministerium and the presbyterate.*

*"As a lover of the Sacred Heart, Father John has enthroned hundreds of homes and dedicated thousands of families to Jesus' protection. For each person, Father John is priest: healer, reconciler, intercessor, guide, spiritual leader."*

During the 1970s, because of ongoing changes in federal and state funding, mental institutions in Pennsylvania (and all over the country) were downsizing. We had the Clarks Summit State Hospital, where the mentally ill were cared for; I believe the population there was around 2,000. When the hospital administrators began to mainstream their residents around the start of the 80s, a new population became evident. There already were many homeless because of the existing economic situation in the country, but that group swelled with the addition of the great number of mentally ill who joined them. People who had lived in mental institutions were released—"mainstreamed." Authorized personnel would give former patients medications, and advise them to continue to take them as prescribed. That rarely happened, however, and downtown Scranton and Wilkes-Barre (like other cities throughout the country) were deluged with people who were homeless and living in the streets. We were faced with another growing social problem. As the director of the Office of Urban Ministry, I knew somehow we had to open shelters for men and for women. Everybody recognized that there was a problem with the homeless. The way the Salvation Army used to handle it, the way Catholic priests from the Cathedral or St. Ann's Monastery would handle it—those solutions weren't working anymore. There were just too many people who needed at least overnight shelter. The population didn't come from only Scranton and surrounding communities; there were drifters who were coming through the area from all parts of the state, and all parts of the country. There was not only a homeless population, but a transient homeless population that demanded medical attention.

Anyone or any group who hoped to establish a residence for housing the homeless ran into huge problems with zoning. Because of the severe Pennsylvania winters, there were also real conscience problems for the community when someone would freeze to death under a bridge or in the streets somewhere. With much assistance and encouragement from the then diocesan bishop, John O'Connor, I opened a shelter in Scranton where homeless men could spend the night. He didn't mind taking on the authorities; he wasn't timid about facing the zoning problems. For a time, we did push parishes to open up their auditoriums and to put up beds to house people who were out on the streets, especially during the cold winter nights. We got those shelters started, which ini-

"A Life's Fulfillment," Msgr. Essef Says

## Shelters for Homeless Need More Volunteers

Officers of the Youth Group of St. Ann's Maronite Church present T-shirts to guest speakers during celebration recently marking the 80th anniversary of the West Scranton church. From left, Marianne Michaels, Monsignor John Essef, the Rev. Kenneth Michael, pastor; Sister Adrian Barrett and Maria Deeb.

*Homeless shelter in Scranton*

tially provided overnight accommodations and a modest breakfast. It was a matter of time, but we had a very wonderful response from volunteers and donations of materials that we needed. Eventually, we also got through to those in the hard-hearted zoning areas who didn't want this kind of 'riffraff' in the area. I worked with Catholic Charities to move the homeless from shelters (which were stop-gap measures, really) to permanent housing solutions available through the existing structure. This transition continued as a big area of need, and then the diocese, through its Catholic Charities, began refurbishing and building more long-term housing for the homeless. This was a step toward independent living and specified limitations as to how long each guest could stay. Among this group, there were also some people from the prison population who needed temporary shelter as they began their return to society. We had different houses that were dedicated to that ministry. Also, a very important group that took over in this area was the Mercy sisters. They were originally founded by Mother McCauley, who had a great love for the homeless—and especially for women who were homeless. So when the need became so great in our area, there came a very strong commitment from a Sister Ann Paye and other Mercy sisters. During my time, there was a big push to do something more permanent about the problem of homeless women. That was the special ministry of the Mercy sisters. As a result, many of our ex-convents are still used as shelters for women and children and their families, and also for battered women.

My years of ministering to the poor in Scranton, years never to be duplicated, were rich in so many ways. In some ways, they were the fruition of what I wanted to accomplish in Peru; in other ways, they were training grounds for what would be my next mission.

"Here I am Lord. Is it I, Lord? I have heard you calling in the night. I will go, Lord, if You lead me. I will hold your people in my heart."

# CHAPTER 40

## THE BUSINESS OF REARING CHILDREN

### *Rosemary*

*W*hen Dad was so ill, it was a difficult time for us, but one blessing that we all had was that Mother was settled in with us; she didn't have to make any major move. After Dad died, all of the children continued to develop even stronger ties with Mom, and George and I enjoyed watching the ongoing dynamics. The kids thought that they were taking care of Mother, and she thought she was taking care of them. Denise was still quite young then, and she had a long and happy relationship with Mom. All of the children helped me in any way they could. They cooperated nicely and didn't complain when I had to take time to get Dad or Mom to doctors. Sometimes, when I look back at those years, I think it would have been nice if I could have done more with the children; but knowing how short a time Mom and Dad had left, I really wanted to make them as comfortable as possible. As they grew older, each of the children said that learning to care for the elderly was a very good experience for them.

Besides Mom, many other people were around. Often, George's Aunts Sarah and Marian would stay with us. Other members of George's family visited a lot. George's parents lived intermittently in Pennsylvania and California. Relatives from back East would often come to visit, and generally the dinner table had eight, ten, or more people at it. That practice developed early in our marriage. When the children were very young, I found it overwhelming to have business people to entertain while I needed to care for the kids and

*Grandma Dorning and the kids*

whoever else was staying with us. I shared my feelings with George and he was just fine with that. He didn't bring business people home for dinner. If he had to do business in the evening, he would take his clients to a restaurant. Most of the time, there were only men. They didn't bring their wives, and that was fortunate for me. George almost never took business people—or, for that matter, any work—home with him. When he was home, he was home. Business was separate. When we moved to the Conejo Valley, there was little or no industry there. There was a very nice restaurant in West Lake, and the owner was trying to build his business. He always accommodated George; he always had a table for him and his guests. George brought his customers and his vendors there almost every day when he was working out of the plant in the Conejo Valley. The owner was very appreciative of the business George brought there, and that was quite a bit. The arrangement worked for all of us.

So "home" was really our castle—and a busy place it was! Because George Jr. had decided to complete his senior year in the San Fernando Valley, it was pretty usual for him to have some of his high school friends from the valley stay over on weekends. There was a lot of room and there were a lot of activities for them to enjoy. Sometimes, he would spend time in the valley with his friends; but more often than not, his friends would spend time with us. It was a blessing for me that I enjoyed cooking so much, because during those years, with a house full of young people, I sure did spend a lot of time in the kitchen cooking and baking! The kids, as best they could, were usually ready to pitch in and help to get things ready. The girls and I did a lot of cooking together. They especially liked to bake, and we made a lot of cakes and cookies. Young George also liked to cook, but he was more into fancy dishes.

When he was very young, George Jr. played baseball and ran track. Although he participated in both, he didn't particularly like competitive sports. As he got older, he preferred building model airplanes to any other pastime. He and his best friend Gary would spend hours and hours building those models.

George was a good worker, and always wanted a business of his own. When he was only eight or nine years old, he wanted to start a shoe-shine business. Later, in high school, during the summer months, he'd go up to the plant and work to earn his spending money. He did all kinds of jobs, including working on the machines and sweeping up. At one point, George gave him a job cleaning the offices. The entrepreneurial streak that surfaced at eight with the shoe-shine business moved up a notch. With his office-cleaning experiences under his belt, he decided to start his own business: a cleaning company. He talked his sister Denise into working with him and, in time, also got two or three guys to work with him. They started a janitorial service in other office buildings and were pretty successful doing that. At home, George Jr. enjoyed working with our Japanese gardener, Masuda. In no time, he decided that he liked that work and decided to go to Moorpark Junior College to do some further investigation. He continued to be the gardener's helper all the time he was at Moorpark, and then he decided to go to Chico State University to get his degree in ornamental horticulture and greenhousing.

Mary Ellen had always shown a tremendous amount of artistic talent. Even when she was little, I took her to art lessons. We have wonderful portraits in our home that she has drawn over the years. Everyone who sees them is so impressed. She did most of them in hours or in a day, but she was never contented with her work. That's a good quality; it creates a desire to improve. But when she was in high school, among so many other things, she liked to draw pictures of George's model airplanes—or maybe she just liked to spend time with him.

*Mary Ellen's sketch of Father John*

*Mary Ellen's sketch of her dad*

## MARY ELLEN ESSEFF SPENCER

*"I knew there were things I could do that everyone couldn't do. I was very happy when my brother George asked me to draw models of his planes. I could do that for him. Drawing was always a part of me, and I liked to feel that I could do something for my big brother. I always wanted to feel I was important to him. I always wanted to matter to him, but I never really thought I did. "*

# Brothers & Fathers

At the time we moved out of the San Fernando Valley to the Conejo Valley, Conejo was still considered a rural area, and Mary Ellen and Kathy looked forward to doing a lot of riding. George Jr. and Denise weren't keen on riding at all.

## KATHY

*"Dad wanted to get us a horse of our own. Some friends of his in the metal business told him about a horse that he might be interested in buying. That's how we came to have Mickey. Mickey was an old horse—maybe seventeen, eighteen, even nineteen years old. He was pretty; but even better, he was an easygoing horse—such a love. Mickey was previously owned by Bing Crosby Stables, and used to be a movie horse. He was wonderful. I could walk under his belly and cinch him. My grandfather (Pop Pop) would have a fit when he saw either of us do that. Always the vet, he'd tell us, 'You do things right when you're around a big animal.' Sometimes Mickey would wander close to the house. He'd go to our covered patio, where there was a window that was usually open. He'd poke his head inside and Mom would feed him carrots. Any time he could manage, Mickey would shoot right down there and get a carrot from Mom. We were so lucky to have such a good riding horse."*

Mary Ellen wanted more of a challenge and, in time, we got her Lady, a beautiful black horse. She was a faster, 'zippier' horse, and very high-strung. Kathy and Mary Ellen didn't like "organized" riding activities; they preferred trail riding and would go down to the local canyons and ravines. There was a beautiful area below our place where they would often go. It was an arroyo about three miles from the house, and there was a bird sanctuary there. It was one of the girls' favorite places to ride.

Lady was a good horse but, unlike Mickey, she could be dangerous. She was skittish when the girls were on the road heading down to the local barranca. She had to be reined in when cars went by, and could be quite a handful. At any rate, we needed a place to keep the horses. When we had the horses, George was busy doing a lot of traveling and didn't have much free time. But with the little time he did have, and with the help of one of his friends, he started to build a stable. After two weekends, he had a two-horse stable ready for occupancy.

# The Business of Rearing Children

Sometimes, the girls went to watch local competitions. There were all types of rodeo activities going on. For a while, Mary Ellen competed in barrel racing. In any type of competition, Mickey knew exactly what to do; he needed no direction at all. He would perform and whoever was riding would win all kinds of awards. If neither Mary Ellen nor Kathy was riding, their friends used to come and borrow Mickey. Without a doubt, Mickey would be a winner and the girls would get the prize. Anyone who knew anything about riding knew that Mickey was the best way to capture a blue ribbon.

When the girls' enthusiasm for riding eventually moved to other things, I decided to use the corral for a garden. I can't tell you how big the vegetables I grew in that garden were! Everything was abundant, and I needed plenty of help from the kids when harvest time arrived. We had plenty of fresh produce for the table; and what we couldn't eat, I froze for later.

After spending her freshman year at La Reina High School, Mary Ellen decided she wanted to leave. Along with Kathy, she enrolled in Newbury Park High School. I continued to encourage them to explore all kinds of activities. All three of the girls had been in softball when they were very young. In grade school, they really loved playing, and they did well. They were also involved in swimming. Mary Ellen enjoyed the butterfly, Kathy the breast stroke, and Denise free-style. Mary Ellen also got into diving. Swimming was not a school sport at the time, and they all did that after school.

Kathy was quite a racquetball player, and was really involved in jujitsu for many years. She and Mary Ellen were invited by some of the guys who were football players at the high school to join them in some jujitsu lessons. Kathy stayed with jujitsu all during high school, and even for some years after.

# Brothers & Fathers

## KATHY

*"Mom and Dad had not really come to see me that much while I was learning jujitsu because lessons were usually early on Wednesday evenings or Fridays. We'd also work out in one of the parks on Saturday nights. I really devoted a lot of time to this discipline. When I was ready for a big test for my second-degree brown belt, Mom and Dad came to watch. Though I had started with a lot of young people, most of them had moved on to other things, so there were a lot of adults in the group. One of the adults would be my partner for the test. He was a teacher from my high school who was a very nice man, with a quiet demeanor. He was very tall. I was very nervous as I prepared to go through the twenty-five different holds and various throws. Because Mom and Dad were watching, I think I was even more nervous than I might have been otherwise. When the time came for me to do my throw, I grabbed the man and threw him. The trouble was that, when I grabbed him, I caught him a little lower than I should have and grabbed him in the groin! I was sure Mom and Dad would have some choice thoughts on this whole sport, but we lived through that night, and I persisted in jujitsu for many years after."*

In addition to all her other activities, from the time Kathy was a freshman in high school, she worked in the business. She liked secretarial work and helped out at the office whenever she could. She became more and more involved and, when she finished high school, she didn't want to go away to school. She worked in the office full time and, even after she married and had the children, she was able to arrange her schedule to stay on. Today, she is still an integral part of the business.

In addition to her softball, swimming, jujitsu, and other activities, Mary Ellen always had time for some rather unusual pursuits.

## MARY ELLEN

*"When I was little and living in the San Fernando Valley, I had a best friend who was from a family of ten. I liked to create things so that others could see what I was thinking. I liked to make my thoughts as touchable to others as they were to me, even before the creation. When my friend and I would get together, I remember not playing with dolls; she and I used to make our own paper dolls. We would make all the clothes and all of the little accessories that we would want to put on the dolls we made.*

# The Business of Rearing Children

> ## MARY ELLEN
>
> *"I had science kits. I liked putting things together. I liked thinking outside the box. I could do things. I had a good mechanical sense. That ability in me reminded me of my dad. From the time I was really little, that sense would make me try to figure things out. When I did, I would feel a great sense of achievement.*
>
> *"When I was older, the Mazda came out on the market. They had a model that showed how the rotary engine worked. I had one of those models because I wanted to see exactly how the engine worked.*
>
> *"I think I have also always tried to take care of people. I remember taking care of my grandfather, Mom's dad, when he lived with us. I remember focusing on my grandparents' health and their needs. I wanted to do whatever was needed to be done when they were sick."*

Mary Ellen had a lot of experience taking care of Mother and Dad, so it wasn't a surprise when she decided to study nursing. After finishing high school, she earned an LVN and worked for Dr. Scribner. Then, ready to go for her RN certification, her life took a turn. She was invited to be in the wedding of one of her girlfriends who was marrying the brother of David Spencer. When the wedding was over, people were socializing on the Spencer family's front lawn. All of the members of the wedding party were still dressed in their formal clothes and, at some point, the chatter turned to jujitsu. Mary Ellen was defending her expertise and prowess with David, and very emphatically said, "Well, I could throw you!" And with that, she tried to throw him and do a flip. David's shirt was ripped off, but he didn't go anywhere.

I remember her coming home and saying, "Why did I do that? Why do I do these things? I thought I knew how to do that—and do it right." She was especially upset because she really liked David. She kept muttering, "Why did I do such a thing?"

Mary Ellen knew that all of David's family had watched the whole debacle. What she didn't know was that, when it happened, David's godmother piped up and said to David's mom, Gladys, "Well, there's our next bride!"

"Oh no, no, no. He's too young!"

Young or not, love was in bloom and the wedding was planned for September 18, 1976—less than two weeks before Mary Ellen's twentieth birthday.

David and Mary Ellen Spencer

Mary Ellen had always loved to bake, and she decided she would make her own wedding cake. She created the design for a six-tier cake, and George made titanium stands for each of the tiers. In her own artistic way, she set to work creating a very elaborate and beautiful cake. It was an ambitious project, but she had the artistic talent and she could do things fast. She made the cakes not very long before the wedding. David's father had a meat market and a grocery store with a walk-in freezer. Mary Ellen stored the cakes in the freezer and then began to make five hundred roses that were needed to complete her design. She wanted to stay busy so she wouldn't get nervous. Making those roses kept her and Denise very busy. As she made them, she put them on the dining room table to dry. The table was filled with roses—that is, until our dog Sho-sho ate most of them. Sho-sho had his belly full! We could have killed that dog and hung him up to dry, but he survived for nineteen years. Mary Ellen was undaunted. Two nights before the wedding, she and Denise started all over again, making another five hundred roses. The wedding was beautiful; Mary Ellen was beautiful; and the very elaborate wedding cake with its unique design and cascading roses was, by some miracle, beautiful too. It was really a magnificent piece of art at the wedding reception.

After living on Calle Arroyo for some years, George thought we could do with less room. He decided that the house was too big for us. For what it's worth, I disagreed. Mary Ellen was married, and George was away at Chico State University where, by that time, he was getting his degree in horticulture. Kathy and Denise spent much more time together, and Mother found a great friend and caretaker in Denise who was still in high

House on Calle Yucca

# The Business of Rearing Children

school at the time. With these considerations, George decided to sell our home on Arroyo and build a new, but smaller, house on Yucca Street. At the same time, in the same area, he built three spec houses as investment properties, and then sold all three of them. When George made a mailbox of titanium and placed it in front of the house on Calle Yucca, we claimed that house as our own.

## GEORGE

*"When Rosemary and I began to make plans for our new home, there was one feature that we knew we wanted to include. When we traveled in Japan, we saw many koi ponds. We wanted this beautiful feature to be an integral part of the new property. We designed the house around an enormous boulder that became the center of the pond and the focal point of the outdoor environment. It was a very beautiful home—one that many people enjoyed."*

Around that time, George Jr. finished school at Chico. He took a job managing an orange grove in Ojai, and did that for three years. During those years, George would come back and forth from Ojai on weekends and days off to visit. Eventually, he got serious about getting married to Sherrie, the girl he had been dating, and began to have doubts as to whether or not it was wise to stay in agriculture.

During that time, George Jr. and Kathy started a youth group at St. Paschal's Church. When George Jr. was living in Ojai, he belonged to a Bible study group, and he missed that involvement when he was in the valley. Kathy was open to the idea of a youth group, and together they were successful in getting that project underway. They studied Scripture, but also socialized quite a bit.

## KATHY

*We started a youth group at St. Paschal's. We had a lot of fun with that group, and also had wonderful opportunities to talk about issues in the Church and about our faith. We were pretty organized and had a meeting every week.*

*We also started a softball team called 'Saints and Sinners' with that same group. We all played: Mary Ellen and David, Sherrie and George, and Denise and her boyfriend.*

## KATHY

*I hadn't met Mike yet. One day when we were playing, I remember Denise's boyfriend, who was a medical student, saying to Denise, 'No pregnant woman should be playing baseball.' He was talking about Mary Ellen, who was pregnant at the time. Mary Ellen didn't want to hear that.*

*About a week later, when Mary Ellen was leaving the field, she stepped in a gopher hole and broke her leg. That was shortly before she delivered.*

*"I guess you could say we were pretty dedicated to sports."*

Saints and Sinners

After three years managing the orange grove, George Jr. decided to leave that job and take his father up on his offer to work at the plant. George Jr. worked from the ground up. He was familiar with the business, since he had worked there so many summers, but his work was cut out for him. He had to understand the business at every level. He found his niche in sales and did well there. He learned the business on the job. He and Sherrie were married on November 27, 1981.

By that time, Kathy had already been on board full time at the plant for quite a while. In addition to managing her business career, she was also making significant personal choices.

George and Sherrie Esseff

# The Business of Rearing Children

> ## KATHY
>
> "I enjoyed being part of the youth group, but I knew I wanted to meet some other young people. For some time, off and on, I had dated George's best friend Gary. We used to love to go 'swing dancing.' Gary had moved away and I knew I wanted to meet some other young people. My sister Denise had a friend, Patty, who was a member of the youth group. The two of us decided we would take a class, so we went out to the junior college in Moorpark and took a ski class. The instruction took place on a plastic hill. The instructors taught us how to maneuver and master the technique. Then we would go on 'real' ski trips. That's how I met my husband, Mike McIntyre. A group of maybe fifty or sixty young people went on a ski trip; it was late 1979. I had met three really nice guys in the class and I had boarded the bus. I was looking out the window and wondering why the three of them were hovering around. They were trying to decide who was going to date me. I didn't find that out till much later. Mike won out. He said, 'I'm the one she really wants to be with.' That was true. The other two were very nice guys, but just not for me. I knew who I wanted and that's how I met Mike—on the fake ski hill. We were married two years later, on June 12, 1982."
>
>
> Mike and Kathy McIntyre

Those were wonderful years of discovery and growth for all of us. The children were no longer children, but young adults. As they married and began having children of their own, the family grew, and George and I began to share in the lives of our many grandchildren. We had wonderful, ordinary days, and very special holidays, as we continued to open our home—most especially, to our growing family. Throughout this time, George continued his work at Cosmos Minerals.

# Chapter 41

## The Good Life: A Time for Much Gratitude

### *George*

#### Business

**B**usiness in the seventies began with great possibilities coming my way. I looked forward to many new challenges and accepted many exciting opportunities for growth.

The days and weeks, months and years of family life had a rhythm of their own, which blended with other rhythms in the life of the business. Combined, they were the music of our lives. In the early seventies, after my buyout of Futura, I continued for about a decade with a partner in Cosmos Minerals in what became a very successful enterprise. At the center of my work was titanium, the metal that proved to be amazingly versatile and became a staple in the aerospace industry, the petrochemical industry, the fields of medicine and sports, and countless other areas as well.

I responded to the ongoing growth in the titanium industry and dedicated myself to multiple opportunities that presented themselves over the years. Essential to the sale and manufacture of titanium was participation in the global marketplace. Because of that necessity, from the beginning of my career, travel was an established part of business and took me away from home a lot of the time. I have a sense of what that meant in the lives of my children.

---

#### MARY ELLEN ESSEFF SPENCER

*"When I was little, I do remember watching my dad shave. That was very, very early. I remember Dad riding a bicycle. I remember him jumping rope—fast, faster than anybody else I ever saw. He was jumping rope and he was doing it very fast. I remember that so clearly.*

---

## MARY ELLEN ESSEFF SPENCER

*He was boyish. He was having fun. Dad was a lot of fun when he was there. But he wasn't there much.*

"What I remember is that I loved to be around him. I wanted so much to be around him and to matter. And I always had trouble trying to express those feelings to him in a way that he could understand. So I missed him a lot when I was a kid. I just missed having him around, because he was so much fun and was so important to me. I think my own insecurities are still wrapped around missing him so much.

"I knew that my dad was extremely gifted. I knew he could see farther than others. I knew that he was able to do things that were so very important that they were taking him to Europe and Japan, and other countries all over the world. He traveled so much; he knew so much. He

*George at home with the kids*

accomplished so many things. The things I wanted to say to him were little things. I felt that I needed to be talking about more important things. If I had really important things in my life, then I could talk about them to my dad.

"All my life it made me happy to create—to see a problem, to draw something, to make a creation, something new that wasn't there before. I think that's the thing I liked so much in myself because I saw it in my dad. I wanted to be able to help him to create. I needed to be connected to him.

"I could never seem to make him hear those feelings—or accept them, or validate them. I should know that he loves me, which, as an adult woman, I do. Intellectually. I should know from the gifts he gives me. It was Mom who first told me that, because he loved me he went and did the things he did. Mom understood Dad, but it was never enough for me. I tried to settle for a lesser relationship than I needed; but emotionally, I have never been able to do that. Of all the gifts he has to give, which are numerous, I have come to know that he can't give the gift of a fuller relationship to me. Why do I keep seeking the one thing my father can't give me?

# The Good Life: A Time for Much Gratitude

In all truthfulness, from my perspective and with my history, I felt that business opened up a world of opportunity for all of us. It was not always simple, but I felt the hand of God in each day. We always had a nice home and there was always room for people to come and stay. Rosemary had the good fortune to have her parents with her when they needed care. The children had great opportunities for having full lives and for developing their individual talents. They could invite their friends and enjoy all kinds of activities together at home, or at the beach home we owned in California. I had a plane that I didn't get to pilot, since I was always too busy to log enough hours to get my license. Rosemary and I were able to travel: We owned a condo in Japan

Cessna 142

and a condo in Hawaii, where we went as often as we could. I also kept a sport fishing boat in Hawaii. Sometimes, we would stop there on the way home from Japan and I would go fishing.

I was even able to get John, reluctant as he was, to join me there. Both of us remember one day in particular. Though there were some tense moments when it was happening, it was fun in the remembering.

A break from being a 'fisher of men'

## JOHN & GEORGE

*JOHN:*

"George invited me to go to Hawaii. I don't even remember the occasion. Anyway, he had this boat, and he was a fanatic. I really didn't want to go, but he kept insisting; finally, I went with him. He said, 'I'd like you to steer and see what life is like on the open sea.'"

*GEORGE:*

"We were just leaving the harbor. A fishing boat has a lot of lines that have to be in place if you want to bring in a big fish, so I started to prepare the rigging. I said to John, 'While I'm doing this, you steer the boat. Just head straight out.' I was working on the rigging when, all of a sudden, I heard the sound of a pretty big wave. I turned around and we were just about ready to capsize. Instead of keeping a straight course going out, John was looking at me and had turned into the wave. That wave almost sunk us! I jumped up and grabbed the wheel from him. 'What the hell is wrong with you? You can't steer?'"

*JOHN:*

"Was he ever blasting me! Anyway we got out of that. We didn't turn over. I'm thinking, I didn't want to be there in the first place. There's no stopping George. So he went way out in the ocean and said, 'Do you think you can handle it now? There's not a damn thing out here!'"

*GEORGE:*

"I said it nice. I thought I said, 'You won't have any trouble now.'"

*JOHN:*

"'NO! I don't want to touch that wheel. George, I don't want to touch that wheel.' We were way out on the ocean. And so much for my objections: I was steering again. I couldn't see that well, anyway. I looked up, and there I was heading for something sticking up out of the water. I don't even know what it's called."

*GEORGE:*

"There was a floating buoy—a fifty-five gallon can. He was ready to crash into it! We were trolling at high speed—going at a good clip because we were using lures, not live bait, so we had to go pretty fast. And he was ready to hit it. I had to jump up and take over again."

*JOHN:*

"I said, 'I'm not touching this damn boat again.' I was strictly a passenger from then on."

# The Good Life: A Time for Much Gratitude

## JOHN & GEORGE

*GEORGE:*
*"But he did catch a big fish that day."*

*JOHN:*
*"I did. I did catch a big fish. Anyway, we were out there a long time and I asked George if there was a toilet on his fancy boat. And he said, 'Go off the back—we're in the middle of the ocean. Nobody's here.'"*

*GEORGE:*
*"That's what I would do all the time, instead of using up all the sanitary equipment."*

*JOHN:*
*"Well, the wind was blowing against me and I wasn't happy. George was not sympathetic."*

*GEORGE:*
*"You should've taken care of yourself before you left."*

*JOHN:*
*"That was the sum total of my life on the open sea."*

*"I did catch a big fish!"*

When I was home, Rosemary and I could relax with the children at our beach house, not far from our home in Thousand Oaks—or, later, in Camarillo. We took mini vacations with the kids whenever we could. There were also trips abroad. I have always been especially grateful that Denise, our youngest, had wonderful trips with Rosemary and me to Japan. She was also able to study at the University of London, as well as the University of Southern California and the University of California, Northridge.

Experiencing success in business also made me acutely aware of my responsibility to develop the talents that I felt God had entrusted to me. I always tried to respond to those gifts and to take each new day with whatever challenges were in it. I also knew I wanted to share my good fortune with others. I know I am very grateful. I realize that I have benefited from many gifts. Working with my dad was a gift.

# Brothers & Fathers

From him, I learned the art of buying. If we could buy at a better price than all of our competitors, we could then sell at a price less than our competitors, still make a profit, and have satisfied customers. Following that principle has been a large part of the success of my business life.

I always had an inventive mind. Maybe, early on, I took that gift for granted—or maybe I assumed that everyone thought the way I did. Even as a kid, I always got tremendous satisfaction in coming up with innovative solutions. As a high school student and a college student, I liked the challenges of problem solving, especially under the direction of really good teachers, who were among some of the best gifts I received. I also knew that the background I had in so many different sciences was a great blessing in my life. Much of our type of manufacturing might not have materialized if I didn't have that background.

Looking back on my life and some of the gifts God has given me, I think my life ended up being remarkable because I really was an enigma in many areas. In my later years, when my son and my grandchildren were diagnosed as having ADD and ADHD, the doctor examined me and said that I have the same qualities. However, he thought that I was able to bury those debilitating qualities because of my ability to focus. I think God gave me an ability to look at a problem, and not just make a random snap decision, but to go through a thought process very quickly and then be able to come up with a solution. That ability helped me. I know I talked about my first business failure in 1958–59, and the ramifications that failure had for me financially. After that experience, when I got back into business, I became very focused on what I was doing and how I was doing it. I think I developed patience yet, paradoxically, I developed an ability to make quick decisions. If I was faced with making a decision that I did not feel comfortable with, I would not make it. On the other hand, if I was faced with a business problem or any other important choice in my life, I would very quickly come up with an answer. I often found that, when people procrastinate about making a decision, chances are they are going to make the wrong decision when they finish, because they think about it so much they actually talk themselves out of doing the proper thing. Making good choices was a pure gift I received, and I thank God for it. I'm sure it was an answer to the prayers of my grandfather, my father, and my mother. I never liked sitting on the fence. If I felt like I was sitting on the fence and not making a decision, I would take a chance or make the wrong decision.

I knew I was able to beat my competition by making rapid decisions rather than by procrastinating. I knew the value of deciding whether a particular situation demanded buying or selling. I knew the value of making a judgment on buying

# The Good Life: A Time for Much Gratitude

a piece of machinery or hiring a new person. I could make those choices readily. I don't know why God gave me the ability to see what the results would be very quickly. I went ahead and I didn't sit there on the fence. I'm sure that making those choices made my life much better. I really enjoyed solving problems. Many people, if they have a lot of decisions to make, kind of shy away from them. I never did shy away from the decision process. It was always fun for me.

I did not have that capability in business when I first started out. Because I was very idealistic about my product, I thought everybody should buy what I was selling, simply because it was a great product. That's how I did business in the first few years. I was fortunate because, honestly, the product I was selling was needed and it did have multiple uses; I was able to adapt the design into so many applications that the business grew very quickly. There were principles of business I didn't know, and I had to learn them. I decided that, in spite of the setbacks of the moment, I would stay in the titanium field and work things out. That turned out to be a good decision. After learning the principles of business, I could apply them. I had to be able to determine where a problem existed—whether it was in accounting or manufacturing or in some other phase of the business; I had to become somewhat of an industrial engineer. In time, I could go into a plant and, if they were making ten widgets an hour, I could get them to make twenty. I was willing to get the right equipment, the right people on board, or the right information that would facilitate solving the problem of the moment.

Another thing that I learned very quickly was how to turn over responsibility. I remember figuring out how much I was making an hour. It turned out to be somewhere around $800. I said to myself, "I have to get someone to do that particular job. I can hire someone who will be happy to do it for $25, $30 or whatever the skill level demands per hour." I knew that I couldn't replicate myself in every area of the business, so I learned how and when to delegate. There is a "right person" for the "right job." I hired the person I thought was the best person to get the job done, then I let him do it. If that person came up a bit short in doing the job as I would do it, I was still satisfied. If he did a bad job, I got rid of him; if, on the other hand, he was trying to fill the position in a fairly capable way, I would work with him to develop his skills. I never put the same onus on everyone else that I put on myself. I think I was generous about that because I knew God had given me gifts that a lot of people didn't have. I watched a lot of businesses fail because the people in charge could not relinquish authority. I've also watched a lot of managers struggle with decision making until, ironically, *no* decision became the catastrophic decision. When the time came, I remember teaching my son, George, the value of learning how to delegate. I knew that too many people trying to grow a business failed because they insisted on micromanaging everything.

First I made a conscious effort to solve the most difficult problems I had. After that, it seemed like everything else was much easier to decide. I remember coming back from trips many times when I had several corporations simultaneously. I had many managers, and all of them, after two weeks of my absence, would have some serious problems and some minor problems. We'd all sit down and I'd say, "I want to hear the biggest problem." I'd get that solved, then the next, then the next. Each one was easier to solve. Once I solved that big one, all the other problems seemed to melt away. They got answered very quickly.

In all my years of business, I also appreciated the importance of mutual respect. I learned that, the more people respect me, and the more I respect them by paying them properly and treating them properly, the longer they stay with me in the business. I have always felt obligated to my employees—as I am to my family; they are kind of my business family. If someone has a death in the family or if there is some kind of tragedy in a family, I am very sympathetic toward it. I got tremendous loyalty from my workers, I do believe, because I always treated them with the utmost respect. They do better work and they work as hard as I would work for someone. They are productive. They don't waste time and they don't stand around. One time, one of my employees had a death in his family (not his immediate family—maybe a cousin) and they didn't have enough money to bury her. So I bought them a coffin. That is the kind of thing I would do with my own family.

The workers I hired over the years who were immigrants appreciated having full-time work instead of seasonal work in the fields. I gave them better wages than what they would have made in the fields. I always treated them well. Those who came first would often seek employment for others in their families. Hiring several people from one family became something we did, and it's turned out very fine for our company. We have two or three family groups. They are very faithful and work very hard.

I also have to admit that I did some things just because I liked to buy cheap and sell higher. I can trace that way back to when I was a kid taking care of Dad's business when he was sick. I remember what a real kick I got doing that. That 'amusement' paid off for me more often than not.

Aside from my work with titanium, I saw the benefit of speculating in real estate and I did my share of that. Anything I bought doubled in two or three years. I kept buying real estate. At one point, Bob Scribner, our doctor friend, wanted to close his office in the valley and move out to Thousand Oaks and open an office. He asked me if I would be willing to go in on building an office complex, and I said I would. So we began looking for property and, rather quickly, I found a piece of property. Shortly before that time, MGM was thinking about moving out here and maybe opening a studio. To that end, they bought land; but afterwards they decided against building the studio and were selling the land. The parcel we were looking at was right in the center of town. MGM was selling it for $90,000 and, since they had bought it for $45,000, they were happy with the deal and the $45,000 profit. We bought the parcel and had it fixed so the escrow would close in 30 days. That kind of deal was extremely unusual. After we fixed the escrow, we put plans in for a building. As I said, that area wasn't very developed at the time. We got a permit and a design done by an architect. We also got an approval for the building. Having that approval put us way ahead. Then Doc Scribner decided he wanted to retire and he didn't want to build an office after all. We had to decide if we should build the building. That plan seemed foolish unless we had tenants. Six months later, a group of backers decided to build a shopping center for 140 stores across the street. The offer for our parcel of land, for which we had paid $90,000, was, at first, half a million, then a million-and-a-half. I turned down those offers. In the meantime, Exxon had built its West coast sales office in the area. This further development increased the worth of the property. Then General Motors came along. When GM came, they wanted our parcel for purposes of their own. We sold them three of the six acres we had for $1.4 million. We had three acres left, but there was one difficulty with that parcel: There was some concern over how much rock was under the property. An excess of rock would be very expensive to excavate. Nonetheless, we later sold the remaining three acres for $900,000. We had made in excess of $2.1 million. These deals were neither stressful nor exciting; they were lucrative, and I did enjoy buying cheap and selling high.

A buy that turned out to be not only profitable but also entertaining was a purchase I made of a Rolls Royce. It wasn't that I wanted to buy a Rolls Royce, but another doctor I knew had two Rolls Royces, a Bentley and a Mercedes. He was a nut about cars. He was building new offices and ran out of money. He called me and asked, "How would you like to buy my Rolls Royce? I really need the money to finish my building."

I told him exactly what I was thinking: "I really don't need a Rolls Royce."

But he kept after me until I offered him $45,000. The car was just six months old, and had only 3,000 miles on it. He refused. "I can't afford to lose that kind of money."

It really made no difference to me, and I figured the deal was off. Surprisingly, a week later, because he couldn't get the money from anyone, he came back and said, "If you have the money to give me, you can have the car." I had the money. I bought a Rolls Royce for $45,000 which, at that time sold for about $65,000 dollars. That was quite a bargain, and there I was with a car that I

*George's Zelten Rolls Royce*

didn't use much, because I sort of felt embarrassed to be riding around in it. Needless to say, Rosemary thought it was a bit much for trips to the supermarket!

But I can say, owning the Rolls brought us a few good laughs. One time while I had the car, my Aunt Ann and her husband Jack Kelly came to see us. Jack had had some problems with alcohol and belonged to AA. He was very faithful about going to meetings, and when he came to visit us, he found a meeting he could go to in Santa Monica. I told him I'd give him a ride there and said he should meet me out front. Minutes later, I pulled the Rolls Royce to the front of the house. It was really quite a show piece! I had locked the front door on the passenger side. I got out, went around to the other side, and I insisted that Jack get in and sit in the back seat. Then I got back in the driver's seat. As soon as we were underway, I put on a chauffeur's hat that I had picked up. We laughed all the way to Santa Monica, where a lot of well-known actors and actresses also showed up for the meeting. It was fun turning the tables, and I enjoyed playing my role as Jack's chauffeur that night.

Someone who did see me drive that car occasionally was a guy who was planning to put up the building for General Motors when I was selling my real estate. I took the car once in a while when we were negotiating that deal. One day he said to me, "I'll tell you what; the only other thing I want is to get the Rolls Royce. Do you want to sell it?"

I said, "Yeah, sure, why not." There I was getting $55,000 for a car I paid $45,000 six years earlier.

During those same years, my friend Frank Arpaia had a restaurant in Studio City. A lot of actors, producers, directors, and others associated with the motion picture industry would come into his restaurant. One of those people got Frank interested in looking into the possibility of producing a movie, which, of course, basically means putting up the money. This offer came at a time when I was doing a lot of other things.

Up to that time, my involvement with the movies was pretty much like everyone else's: I went to see them. I knew I was a little closer to the industry when we first came to California. I remember driving from our home in Van Nuys to Hollywood, where my office was located. On the way, I would sometimes see riders on horseback and, occasionally, a runaway stagecoach being filmed in the nearby hills. So, for whatever reason, when my friend talked to me about backing a movie, I said, "Yeah, let's do it."

With those few words, I became, along with Frank Arpaia, the executive producer of a sci-fi movie called *R.O.T.O.R.* It was the story of a robot that "had been programmed to combat crime and corruption." We made some money on it.

Some time later, we got talked into doing a movie with a karate theme. I'm sure most people remember the TV series, The Million Dollar Man, which starred Lee Majors. It was his son, Lee Majors II, who starred in this movie, along with a man by the name of Bruce Ly, who was a protégé of the famous karate expert and movie star Bruce Lee. The story wrapped around a Detective Warren Houston (Majors) who was teamed up with a Lieutenant John Chan (Ly). Together with a special assault team, they were responsible for crumbling a powerful crime organization that was involved with drug trafficking. The movie took place, for the most part, on a movie set. An interesting aside during the making of this movie was one other part of its filming. At the

George's first movie

time, among other things, I was also involved in a company that was making and selling mozzarella cheese. The cheese was wrapped and bundled for storing and shipping. In the movie, those bundled pieces of cheese were the "stand-ins" for packages of illegal drugs. At any rate, this was our second movie, and it hit theatres under the title *Chinatown Connection*.

Another project we were responsible for producing was a series of sex education tapes. A rather famous actor, Scott Baio (who had earlier appeared in the TV series *Happy Days* and later starred in the series *Charles in Charge*) hosted those three tape presentations. One was designed specifically to speak to the needs of preteen girls from the ages of eight to eleven, while another was aimed at boys of the same age group; the third was designed for teenagers from the ages of twelve to seventeen. All three were intended to promote abstinence among young people. We sold those tapes to a company that sold books and videos to schools. I think presently, the Discovery Channel now owns and airs those videos. We

*George's second movie*

still get residuals from all of them. Although the commercial movies we did weren't big movies, they did play—mostly on nighttime TV, and they still appear on occasion. I was told recently that they were sold to a group that intends to air them overseas and, in the future, they may be seen (among other places) in Lebanon.

During my stint in movie producing, I used to go to the set on occasion. I'd sit in a director-type chair that had my name on the back of it. That and other involvements went on for a while, but I really felt out of my element. Finally, one day, I said to myself, "What the hell am I doing here?" After we finished our third project (the series of videos), I never did any more. It was interesting in some ways, but it certainly was not my forté, and definitely not the best business for me.

These are some of the things that brought me success in varying degrees, but that does not mean that every endeavor in my life was successful. That's one of the reasons that belonging to the Serra Club throughout my adult life has been a great help to me. One of Padre Serra's famous sayings was "Never look back"—and I really didn't. I took his advice to heart. If I made a decision that cost me some money, I used it as a lesson and moved on. I didn't look back. Even now, as I'm trying to remember so many events from the past, I'm having a hard time going back and recapping a lot of things that happened because, once something was done, it was done. I was happy I got through the problem of the moment and I'm happy to be where I am today.

# The Good Life: A Time for Much Gratitude

In spite of the wonderful gifts God gave me, I was not a stranger to making bad decisions. At one point in the Vietnam era, we did move some Vietnamese families into decent living quarters—a couple of apartment houses I had bought in Oxnard. After the Vietnamese had gotten on their feet and gone off in their own directions, I decided to sell the two apartment houses. A fellow came along and I sold them to him. He made some deal with the escrow company not to record the sale for one week. During that week, he went to the Bank of America and borrowed the value of the apartments with an interest rate of 21%. That was a very, very high rate. What he did then was take the cash and walk off with it. As the payments came due, he didn't make any, and that went on for more than a year. He kept making excuses, one thing or another, as to why he couldn't make any payments, and as to how he would catch up. Well, he never did catch up and I ended up having to sue him. My lawyers' fees turned out to be about $50,000, but we finally did get a judgment against the man who bought the apartments. Unfortunately, we couldn't collect anything because of the money he owed the banks and the money that he owed to creditors. Those debts exceeded mine and my position in line was way down the list. Strangely enough, about three or four years later, I wound up getting a check for $45,000 as a settlement. The creditors had sold his properties and the government did get some money. I got $45,000 instead of the $100,000 we were originally supposed to get. But I was satisfied. At least it paid most of the lawyers' fees.

Another time, a woman came to me with a patent on the infrared ear thermometer. She asked me if I would put up the money to finish the development of this product. It was one of the first patents granted in the United States for this purpose, and I was interested. I went on to spend more money in the developing so that I could get the thermometer to market. Getting it to the market didn't happen, but I was able to sell the thermometer to a Japanese firm called Citizen Watch Company which was also involved in thermometry. They said that they had a patent two months after ours, and that patent infringed on ours. They wanted us to sell our patent to them. They offered me so little, I refused to sell.

As it turned out, I did negotiate with them later. I met the general manager in Hong Kong and had a written agreement with him to sell the thermometer to him for a million dollars. When I came back to California, I was pretty happy. About a week later, the same manager called to tell me that his supervisors and/or the board members would not approve the purchase. So we were high and dry, and we discontinued any further development. We finally wound up selling the thermometer to Beckman Dickinson, one of the big medical equipment sales outlets in the United States. They made a deal with Citizen Watch and, in a combined effort, finally made the thermometer for Wal*Mart. They put a Wal*Mart brand on it and sold it. After we sold it, the person who brought the original product to us wasn't satisfied with the results of the sale and how much money she got out of it. She tried to sue me for more than a hundred thousand dollars. I had a very good attorney; unfortunately, my attorney contracted spinal meningitis and died within four weeks. His son was in the firm. I was ready to get a more experienced attorney, but I didn't. Stan's son proved to me that I should have followed my instincts. He mismanaged the case so badly that I told my brother, Joe, just to settle the damn thing; I just wanted to get out of it. I did, but to the tune of about $100,000—not to mention $50,000 in lawyers' fees.

---

### JOE

*"When I came back from the service three years removed from my family, I tried selling life insurance for about six months; after I sold everything to my family, I starved. I went to California and George gave me a job. What I became in business came from the trust he had in me, the opportunities he gave me, and his willingness to carry me at times. Later, when I started my own business in Ohio and things went badly and I had no prospects, I was able to work for George. It was when he had a heart attack and he had a lot of things hanging in the air needing to be kept above water that I went to work for him again. I was able to do that. And I was glad that I could contribute something to George—could give back for all the times he gave to me. George touched my life as I got older, and touched it in different ways than John did.*

*I have often judged George, especially when I say, 'He looks at things as black or white.' But I have to say this, too: George never judged me. He and Rosemary were always open to me, to my wife Patty, and to my children. They always treated us with respect. I sometimes forget that, but it's true. He never judged me—and John never judged me."*

*"I love George and I am so thankful for the things he has done for me, for the things he has done for my family, and for the things he has done for a lot of people, many of whom he didn't even personally know."*

---

Another time, I had gotten into a big land development project near Fresno, California, in a place called Shaver Lake. An Armenian fellow had come to me looking for money. He told me he could buy this land very, very cheap if he could raise the cash within a week. He thought it was really a good deal. The project involved 805 acres, consisting of three-quarters of the Shaver Lake town, which included commercial real estate development. I became one of the biggest investors. The buyer indicated that, if we invested, we'd have the money back—including a one-time profit—and we'd double our money in eighteen months. Well, the poor guy contracted cancer and died in about four months. His son-in-law took over the management of the property. It was understood that those in charge would not take any money out of this property until they had satisfied all the investors. When the investors had their money back, the managers would spend the income on developing the property, but they wouldn't take any salary or any money out of the project before then. After about three or four months, I noticed they were selling only the dead wood from the property for millions of dollars. Instead of using those millions to pay off the investors, the son-in-law took the money, and was spending it on engineering water rights and all kinds of other ancillary things that were going to benefit him in the long run. Luckily, I found out about what was happening. I asked for the checkbook and I found out that the son-in-law had himself on salary for about $2,500 a week and was spending millions he had gotten from the lumber on all kinds of fancy things to further develop the property. Neither I nor any other investor would share in any of this.

I threatened to sue him, and we ended up having a stockholders meeting. I was the biggest stockholder and I had the group of investors behind me. We had a hostile takeover of the firm, and I became the general manager of the partnership. It was just prior to these events that I had had a heart attack, which left me really very sick. (I'll come to that later.) Rather than jeopardize my health further, I put my brother, Joe, in charge of liquidating everything. Joe had to take care of things like selling trees and going back-and-forth from our place to Shaver Lake a couple of times a week. Finally, we got out of the whole mess and sold the property for a darn good profit—and got all of the investors their money back. These are some of the less successful enterprises I had in my time, because I had not made good primary decisions.

## ANGELS IN OUR LIVES

Despite the fact that every decision I made over the years wasn't right, I do know that the Lord has been very generous with us. He has given us many gifts, and I really do believe he has also given us the protection of the angels. Both Rosemary and I share a very strong belief in the angels. I really believe that they have directed me and that they have taken care of the entire family. We have great devotion to the angels who have guarded us many times, and I'd like to mention just a few of the more notable occasions.

While Rosemary and the children and I were living in Scranton, I was due to take a business flight from Scranton to Detroit and then on to Midland, Michigan. During the same time, my brother-in-law's sister was going to be married and Rosemary was trying to talk me out of going on the trip so that I could stay home for the wedding instead. I had made a commitment to the meetings in Michigan; but at the last minute, due to Rosemary's urgings, I changed that meeting. The flight that I was supposed to be on from Detroit to Michigan crashed outside of Midland and everyone on board was killed. Thank God, I was saved from that fate.

Some years later, in 1965, while we were living in California, I was due to take a flight from California to Pittsburgh and then continue on to New York. When I arrived at the airport in California that morning, I decided to change my plans. It seemed to make more sense to fly directly to New York and then return home by way of Pittsburgh. That route would also eliminate a change in Cincinnati if I went to Pittsburgh first. I got in touch with the people I was supposed to see in Pittsburgh and changed the date of the meeting so I could go to New York first and then, on my return, stop in Pittsburgh before continuing home to California.

When I arrived in New York that evening, I had dinner with my customers. And when we were finished, I called home (as I usually did each night). My son George, who was about twelve at the time, answered the phone and he was crying. The flight that I originally booked was scheduled to leave Los Angeles, stop in Cincinnati, and then go on to Pittsburgh. Rosemary had heard that a plane headed for Pittsburgh had crashed in Cincinnati. She called my travel agent to see what flight I was on and, sure enough, that was the flight I was booked on. That plane went down and all 140 people on board died in the crash. Those were, I'm sure, painful hours for Rosemary and the children. I really don't know what made me change my itinerary at the airport that particular morning, except that it was an inspiration given to me by the angels. I've had many experiences like that in my lifetime, and they have convinced me that I live under a special protection from the angels.

In 1967, I was in Bogotá, Columbia on business. I had made arrangements for that trip a few months ahead of actually going there. I also had made plans to see my brother John where he was stationed in Piura, Peru. What wasn't in anyone's plans was that John would be in an airplane crash, get hurt, and return home to recuperate in Pennsylvania by the time I got to South America.

# The Good Life: A Time for Much Gratitude

I had gone to Bogotá to complete some business I had there. When I finished the business, I continued to Piura, even though I knew John had returned to the States. I met with John's associate, Father Lionel Targett and, shortly thereafter, visited my old high school pal, Frank Hanlon (who was living in Bolivia). With that visit over, I prepared to go home, and began by taking my flight back to Lima. I boarded and the plane took off. Instead of taking direction, the plane circled for about a half-hour and then, because I was sitting on the wing, I could see that the plane was dumping fuel. What was going on didn't seem to be disturbing anyone else, and I realized that no one else knew what was happening. We circled and circled and circled for about another forty-five minutes. All that time, we were dumping fuel, and then the pilot attempted to land back in Bogotá. We were just about two feet off the ground when the pilot threw the throttle forward and we took off again. As he took off, the plane pitched to the left a little bit. Since I was sitting near the window on the left, I saw the wing just miss the ground by about one foot. But once again, we recovered and then we seemed to go up. We circled around some more, and the pilot made another attempt at landing. This time, we were just a couple of feet above the runway when the pilot threw the full throttle in and took off again. By this time, everyone in the plane was screaming and some were yelling something that sounded like "*El muerto.*" I didn't understand Spanish, but I knew what they were screaming.

We continued to circle, and the screaming continued as well. Thinking that this might be where I would spend my last day, I actually wrote a note to Rosemary. However, in the minutes that followed, somehow—miraculously—the pilot was able to land the plane. I wasn't sure of the reason for my being safe at that moment, but I certainly know now.

Shortly after we landed, I found out that the landing gear was the reason for the problem. Eventually, the crew was able to crank the gear down so the pilot was able to land the plane safely. Once on the ground, it took about eight hours to get the plane fixed. At flight time, only about 20% of the passengers who should have been there showed up. I guess everyone else had found the experience too unnerving, and found another way to get where they were going.

In 1969, I was involved in still another incident. I had gone to Tokyo and, from there, I was going to Moscow to buy titanium from the Russians. I had several meetings I was scheduled to attend. We were getting ready to land in Moscow and I was starting to get all my things together when I discovered I didn't have my visa with me. I clearly remembered that I did have it at the ticket counter in Tokyo. I was on a Japan Airlines flight and I must have left my visa on the ticket counter there. I had no visa when the plane was ready to land in Moscow.

The landing itself was an interesting scenario. Before we landed, we were told, "You can't take any newspapers, no magazines. If you have a camera, and you show it, you'll have problems, so don't take a camera out. You can't take a picture of anything while you're here." When the plane landed we were surrounded by probably two hundred armed soldiers who circled the airplane, shoulder to shoulder. Because I was on a Japanese airline, that very uninviting reception was all part of normal procedure. To me, such a display of power all seemed orchestrated to scare the hell out of everyone. If so, it was successful.

On my flight into Russia, I had been riding in first class and, as I recall, there weren't too many people in first class with me. As I was ready to leave the plane, the district manager of Japan Airlines came up to me and said that I wasn't going to be allowed to stay in Russia. He wanted me to stay on the same plane, leave Russia, go on to Paris, and come back the next day after my visa was retrieved and brought to me from Tokyo by Aeroflot, the Russian airline; Aeroflot was flying the next day, but Japan Airlines flew only every other day. I explained that I had just traveled about sixteen hours and I was totally exhausted. If there was any way I could stay in Russia, I would surely prefer to do that. Even though they knew I was going to be getting my visa the next day, the answer was "No." But in time, the same district manager from the Japanese airline successfully negotiated permission for me to stay in Russia if I was willing to wait in jail until my visa arrived. I decided to opt for that. I was tired and I just didn't want to fly to Paris, turn around, and fly back the next day.

Before all this transpired, when I was going through customs in Russia, I met a fellow from India. I found out later that he was a professor at Ohio State University in Akron. He had been to some kind of bio-physical symposium in Toronto, and he had a lot of biophysical prints and documents with him. As we were waiting to get through immigration, the airport personnel started to look at his prints and, when they couldn't understand them, they insisted that he explain them. He didn't do that to their liking, so they confiscated all his work. Well, the guy went ballistic! He threw his bag at the immigration agent who, in turn, reacted by confiscating all of the professor's bags.

I had had a conversation with this professor earlier when we were both at customs. He told me he was happy that we were stopping in Russia, because he thought maybe he would be able to get into the city. He had never been to Moscow and he was hoping to see it. What he didn't know was that, first, he needed a visa to get in, and second, it was 1969: no one fooled around with the Russians. The end result: He ended up getting locked up in the same jail I was in (although I didn't learn that detail until later).

I wasn't afraid. I figured, what could they do to me? If I didn't sleep for twenty-four hours or didn't eat, it wouldn't matter. Anyway, I was staying. It was October or November, as I remember, and it was cold. There was a soldier with a gun over his shoulder who walked me to the jail. I walked through water up to my ankles and it turned out to be about almost two miles to the jail. By the time I arrived there, I was frozen.

The jail was like a big barracks. No cells, just five locked doors. (I counted them going in.) When we walked in the front door, there was a locked door. We walked through another door to get into the hall, there was another locked door. We walked down the hall and then we had to go upstairs. There was another door there, locked. We went upstairs; that was locked. I went into my bedroom; that door was locked, too. They kept locking each door behind me. In the room I stayed in, there was a cot. It was really hard. The sheet was cold. It was some sort of combination blanket and cover, but it was cold. I figured I could bear almost anything for twenty-four hours. I knew they'd let me out the next day because they said I could go as soon as my visa came.

While I stayed there, if I had to go to the bathroom, I'd knock on the door. The soldier would come, a rifle over his shoulder. He'd escort me to the bathroom, stand right there with me, and wait.

The people in charge did give me tickets to get food at the airport. (I think I still have them somewhere.) If I wanted to go back to the airport to get dinner, I could have gone back with a soldier as an escort. And if I wanted to go back in the morning for breakfast, they would've taken me back again. I opted to have neither dinner nor breakfast.

Anyway, during my stay, they did tell me I could go to the library and get a book if I wanted. So I went and, hard as it was to believe, there was a familiar face: the professor from India! So there we were—two scientists in the local lockup. He was the same guy I had seen in line and the same guy I had talked to at customs. When he was talking then, he thought the Russians were fantastic; now he was quite sure he would never come back.

The next morning, as we were about to be released, it was pretty evident that Japan Airlines had done some strong negotiations and probably paid someone a whole lot of money to appease me. I found out that the airlines had not only brought a touring bus, but had also arranged a tour. I was the only passenger. When they came to pick me up, I asked, "Do you mind if we take this professor with us?" (I was, of course, referring to my new friend from India.) "Is there any way he can come along with us? He hasn't yet seen anything in Moscow that he wants to see. Can he come along?"

"Yeah, sure, bring him along." The tourist guide didn't seem to care, so the two of us had a three-and-a-half hour tour of Moscow. We did see Moscow University and stopped in front of it. Everything we saw was described as the biggest and the best in the world. Every place we stopped, "This is the biggest. This is the best." But when we got to a hotel that had 6,000 rooms in it, I was inclined to believe the guide on that one.

We drove into downtown Moscow. We saw an absolutely enormous swimming pool that was outside and yet open all year round. We all know how cold it gets there; it was already cold and it wasn't yet December. But people swam in that pool all winter. It was heated and the steam was coming up from it; the water was warm, though it was cold outside. It turned out to be quite a tour! Really, I was happy to have gone through the whole experience. At that time in history, it was unique. That was one of the few nights that I didn't call Rosemary when I was away. She didn't know anything about what had gone on until I got home, so I like to believe she wasn't worried at all.

The next day, when I was with another businessman from Japan, he told me that all tourist guides in Russia were in the KGB. But to tell the truth, I didn't feel threatened. I didn't feel as though anyone was going to hurt me. And the Japanese agent did a hell of a favor when he hired a whole damn bus for me! I'm sure that cost him plenty.

When I was planning my trip to Russia, I had been warned that I would have to notify the authorities about every appointment I was going to have. They had to know where I was going, and what time I was going there. After I got my visa and my clearance, I was picked up by a guy from Japan who took me to the National Hotel, right in front of Red Square. I stayed there. It was one of the oldest, most beautiful hotels in Moscow.

While we were still in the car and on the way to the hotel, I was told, "Do not say anything about the government—or anything else in my office. All of my secretaries are KGB and the only place you can talk freely is in my car, because I de-bug it every morning. Your hotel room is probably going to be bugged. Your telephone

# The Good Life: A Time for Much Gratitude

will be bugged. They will probably have a video going too, so just be careful." My meeting with this gentleman and my being picked up by him had all been prearranged. It wasn't possible to do anything that wasn't prearranged—except maybe spend a night in jail! But it was 1969 and the deepest part of the Cold War was still going on. I know my angels were at work then. When I went back there in 1972, things were a little bit better, and after that things were fine.

On a business level, I really did enjoy breaking new ground. No one had been buying titanium from Russia, so I loved getting in on the ground floor (just as I had earlier in Japan). I must admit that, whenever I would leave Russia, I really wasn't afraid; but I always departed with the feeling, "Thank God! The plane's in the air."

A final incident when I felt the angels were there for us was a time in 2003 when Rosemary and I were returning from Lebanon. We left Lebanon about 2 o'clock in the morning and arrived in the Paris airport at about 6 o'clock. We were going to be leaving on a Delta flight to Los Angeles, and we had a layover of three or four hours. We walked over to the Delta gate, where there was a coffee shop right across from the gate. All they had for sale were croissants and coffee, so I said to Rosemary, "Let's go to the next coffee shop and see if they have something more to eat." And we did. We walked about two hundred feet farther, and they had juice and croissants filled with cheese, along with a few other things. We ordered and, while we were waiting to be served, we heard an enormous crash coming from the area that we had just left. This was a brand new terminal—maybe eight months old. No one could have expected what happened. The ceiling, about a hundred feet high, had big, heavy, concrete ribbons that encircled it. One of the ribbons collapsed, starting a domino effect, with each successive ribbon falling until the whole pile stopped within about a hundred feet of us. The greatest damage was right over the coffee shop, near the gate that we had just left. My first instinct was to see if I could help anyone. Rosemary grabbed me by my shirt and pulled me back. Airline personnel at the next gate started to yell to us, and to everyone in the area, telling us to get out at the other end of the terminal. We moved outside; apparently the airline personnel were afraid that the rest of the ceiling was going to start coming down. Everyone who was there was gathered outside on the tarmac. Earlier, on our way to that area, I remembered passing an Asian family of five. As we passed out of the building, I saw that they were under the rubble.

At first, everyone thought that someone had tried to bomb the place. In fact, the collapse was the result of a structural defect. I usually don't think about things like that afterward, and all my close calls have not left me afraid. I can honestly say that I don't have a fear in me. But when I do think about that event (and some of the others I have mentioned), I thank God for sparing us those tragedies.

These events were mostly things that happened as I traveled around the world, but they all pale as I think about the miracle of George Jr.'s birth and survival, coupled with the circumstances that threatened Rosemary's life over the years. I thank God every day for sending His angels to protect us.

## Sharing Our Gifts

Over the years, I feel I have also been able to help some people who were especially needy. Within the framework of business, I had many opportunities to help Latin American immigrants, first employing them and then by helping them to get documented. I have had a great deal of satisfaction watching them and their families grow into hard-working, well educated, productive members of American society in other areas of life, as well as members of my work force. I must say that connection was primarily one that was work related.

Another experience I have had with people needing help in America occurred with the tremendous exodus of people out of Vietnam, due to the war there. Those refugees were commonly referred to as the 'boat people,' and they immigrated to America in great numbers. At that time, I did bring in two Vietnamese families. They had absolutely nothing when they got here. When they first arrived, I was able to put them up temporarily with George Jr., who was managing an orange grove in Ojai. I then bought two apartment houses right next to each other. I put two of the families in those apartments, and I rented out the other units that were available. I gave the members of the families jobs at the plants and helped them to get on their feet.

There was another man, an elderly gentleman, who worked for us for about five years. During that time, he saved enough money to buy a shrimp boat in Louisiana. There were many Vietnamese families living there, and he had decided that he wanted to go there to set up a fishing business. He moved to Louisiana and became a pretty successful businessman. That was a good experience, too.

I had only one bad experience in this regard. I had hired a young Vietnamese man who really took advantage. I did what I was accustomed to doing. I paid all of them the same wage. I gave that young man a place to live; he had to pay nothing. I had also given him a car. In spite of the fact that he was earning a full paycheck from me, and with coaching from some of his friends in the area, he was able to tap into

# The Good Life: A Time for Much Gratitude

the welfare system. When I found out what he was doing, I told him how wrong he was, and how he was doing something illegal, while exploiting me, the welfare system, and other people in his position who might really have only welfare to depend on. I warned him that I would not tolerate that behavior. The matter seemed to be settled. Unfortunately, after a few more months, I learned that he was getting welfare payments again, and I fired him. That was the only bad experience I had.

One Sunday we were at Mass at St. Paschal's and there was an announcement that a Vietnamese family had been displaced from an apartment they had been in, with no place to stay. Members of the parish were working to make arrangements for the family to get some permanent housing. What they were looking for was someone who could take them for a few weeks or so until they could be permanently situated. We took in that family—a woman and her son. They lived with us for about three months and then were able to get permanent housing. They seemed to be more characteristic of most of the Vietnamese. They quickly adapted to the American system and very quickly went up the socio-economic ladder.

Another good thing that came out of these experiences was that George Jr. was involved in these situations. He was a rather young man himself then, and his involvement seemed providential. He now shares the same feelings about immigrants and others in need as we do.

In California, we had pretty much the same social start to the homeless problem as did most others places in America. We had a large psychiatric institution here in Camarillo that was serving most of southern California. Because of government cutbacks, that institution was closed in the early 80s. When it closed, many of those people went to their families, but many others went into the streets. That situation swelled the number of those living in the streets and created an additional problem with the mentally ill homeless.

I got involved with the homeless, at first as a volunteer. Seven churches here would each take one night a week and open their facility to accommodate the homeless. Each church would set up cots and they'd make arrangements to have dinner brought in. Usually dinner was brought in by one of the Jewish synagogues and the project became quite an ecumenical work, as the Protestant churches were also involved. Each facility made similar provisions. The 'drop-in shelters,' as we called them, were open from October until the end of March. The volunteers would give each guest dinner and then a place to sleep for the night. In the morning, breakfast was available, and there were packed lunches for the homeless to take with them. Many of these homeless were not derelict; and although some were mentally ill, the majority were not. There were many people who had been just one paycheck away from being evicted from their condo, apartment, or home; many of them were families with children. We used to average about 30 guests a night. I got interested in the problem and I ended up becoming involved with a group of people who were interested in doing more. We started an organization called the Canaya Homeless Assistance Program, through which we were going to try to build a permanent drop-in shelter. We worked for literally twelve or more years trying to get this done. Every time we'd find a property that could be approved by the city, we'd start proceedings to purchase the property, and then there would be a public hearing to determine what the building was going to be used for. As soon as the hearing took place, there was an uproar from the 'not in my backyard' people, and the city would back down, leaving us without a property. That went on for more than a decade.

There is a beautiful place here called Under One Roof. It's the only one like it in the country, and it was looking to expand. It has about 17 different charitable organizations located in one place, all "able to cooperate in delivering multiple services, eliminating duplications, and bridging the gaps in the system." One of those organizations is a Lutheran Social Service which had a little pantry. There is another small room with computers in it, and the homeless can use the place as their address. There was a man there who was responsible for helping individuals to get jobs. It was almost like an employment agency, and people did succeed in getting employment. There is also a thrift shop and, people going for interviews who need dresses or suits are sent to the shop with vouchers. They can get themselves dressed appropriately for their interviews. Also at Under One Roof, there is a medical facility that is open in the evening. Two doctors come in alternately to take care of the sick in either of two examination rooms. A lawyer comes in two or three times a week to help anyone with legal problems. There's also a crisis center. It is really a well equipped, beautiful center. Because we realized that we would never get a facility of our own, we decided to give our support to Under One Roof. We took all the money we had accumulated and gave it to the Lutheran Social Services, which offered the homeless many services. By giving them financial support, we helped them expand their ongoing operation. We didn't have to go to the city. We were able to put in a couple of showers, a couple of laundry rooms, and a bigger pantry. The homeless usually come there every morning and are able to get a shower, wash their clothes, get new clothes if they need them, access the Internet if they want to look for work, or go through the employment agency to help them find some work. Many homeless people have been rehabilitated and gotten into positions that enabled them to get off the streets.

# The Good Life: A Time for Much Gratitude

During the years, I also became interested in, and got on the board of directors of Many Mansions, an organization formed to supply affordable housing for needy families. When I joined the board, they were experiencing a lot of turnover within the ranks of their personnel. During my time on the finance committee, we examined the payroll structure and discovered that the organization wasn't paying its people enough money for the job they were doing. I suggested that this was probably the situation that created the turnover. Sure enough, it was. One of the members of the board was trying to get companies to pay living wages in Oxnard and I said, "If you're trying to get other people to pay a living wage, you have to do it yourself." The rules for running this organization were no different than the fair business practices that applied everywhere else.

I also got involved in the work that came to include both interim and permanent housing for the homeless. Many Mansions bought a motel to refurbish, and they got permission to go ahead with their plans. I gave a million dollars so they could rehab the motel into 50 studio units. Twenty-five of the units were intended for mentally ill homeless, and twenty-five were intended for handicapped homeless. We do have case workers who work with our people to make sure they take their medicines and get the kinds of help they need. Esseff Village, as it has been named, has been open now for six or eight years. We have many graduates from the village. There was a woman who had a mental breakdown and was living in the streets. Now, thanks to the work at Many Mansions, her mental health is restored, she's back in business, and she employs six other people. We have been able to get jobs for some handicapped people. Once someone is able to get a job, he or she graduates into our low-income housing division, where that person moves to a greater level of independence. It has been very rewarding for me to be able to do that work.

One other group I got involved with was the elderly. That involvement was the result of my daughter Denise's interest in gerontology. She had developed a love for the elderly, maybe because she had her grandparents around her almost all of her life. When the time came, she went to study gerontology at the University of Southern California. Upon completing her degree, she got involved with the head of Catholic Charities and they planned a program called Oasis, a project designed to take care of the many different needs of the elderly in the Archdiocese of Los An-

*A gift from the Esseff Village residents*

339

geles. Denise approached me about the project, and the head of Catholic Charities contacted me as well. I knew it was a worthwhile program, so I promised them I would give them starting money. I provided $100,000. With that, they were able to hire some people so they could then work with a lot of the different agencies and a lot of retirement homes. Also, if there were elderly living in inadequate housing, they'd help them get located in decent housing. They also took care of getting food to the elderly. I think it was the beginning of Meals On Wheels here. During the late 70s and early 80s, I eventually got involved with Mary, Health of the Sick, a local home for the elderly. That facility is run by a group of nuns from Puerto Rico, and we have tried to help them to broaden their capacity for taking care of the elderly.

At one point I saw an appeal in the bulletin at St. Mary Magdalene's Church. The pastor of the parish joined with a Protestant minister from Camarillo, and together they were trying to see if they could raise enough money to open a home for unwed mothers in either Camarillo or Oxnard. The closest such facility we had at the time was in downtown Los Angeles. They were having a difficult time trying to raise the money they needed. When I learned that they needed $25,000 to use as the downpayment for the home, I called the pastor and told him that I would be happy to supply that amount of money. That was my only involvement with that group at that time.

These were some of the ways that I felt I could help others by sharing the many gifts God gave me as the years unfolded. There were new paths for us to travel, and with the graces we were given, we continued to cherish each new day.

## The Early Eighties

With the eighties came several events that brought profound, far-reaching changes in all of our lives. Perhaps the one that was most like other changes I had to deal with was buying out my partner at Cosmos Minerals. I was involved in that partnership for about ten years, and business was good. There came a time, however, when my partner and I had a disagreement that left me with no choice but to make a break from him.

Years before, when I first got involved in business with the Japanese, I was able to buy quite cheaply from them and that was profitable for us. At the same time, the Japanese were grateful for the business, since they were just starting out. The relationship we established continued well into the eighties.

# The Good Life: A Time for Much Gratitude

At one point when I was with Cosmos Minerals, I made a million dollars in commissions on titanium I sold to my competitors in a single year. I had bought cheaply from Japan. Then, between the time we ordered the material until the delivery of the titanium six to eight months later, the selling prices in America escalated substantially. We sold high. My partner couldn't have been happier. About two years later, I went to Japan again to make our customary buy. We weren't getting prices anywhere near the price I had negotiated when we began, so I didn't plan to buy as huge a quantity as I had done previously; however, I did order a significant amount. Shortly afterward, the market in America started to drop, and I remained committed to a lot of orders for materials that had not yet been delivered.

Faced with the prospect of a loss, my partner said, "Cancel the orders!"

"Hell, no! How the hell can I cancel? They didn't cancel us when the prices went up here, and we made all the profit. They gave us the metal at the cheaper prices we had agreed on months before. Now the tables are turned. I'm not canceling; I'm going to follow through on our agreement!"

But every day, he was on me. He was a rich man, but he was also greedy. Every single day he was on me to cancel the orders because of the substantial drop in the domestic selling price. I held firm: "I can't cancel. I refuse." Our differing opinions shortly escalated into a big argument.

Finally, my partner said, "You cancel! If you don't cancel, I'm not going to buy the metal. If you won't cancel, then you buy it."

"Fine," I said, "I'll buy the metal."

He thought that, if he didn't back me, I would fold. He didn't think I had the money to do what I said I would do. I decided to buy him out and he gave me a price. I scraped together as much money as I could. Every time I met the price and I came up with the money, he'd push the price up so I couldn't buy him out. I had a lot of property. I sold it. I had stocks. I sold them. I went back to my partner, but again, in spite of our negotiations, he raised the price again. So much for that agreement! Each time we'd finish negotiating and I came up with the money, he'd raise his price by a half-million or a million dollars. It finally got to the point where I said to him, "What the hell do you want? You tell me, and I'm not going to pay you a penny more. You're not going to keep coming back to me and raising the price." Finally, we settled the price. I don't think he believed I would ever be able to raise the full amount. I sold everything I could get my hands on: stocks, property, real estate, everything, and he insisted that I pay him in cash. With all that I liquidated, I was still a million dollars short. I talked to my Japanese friend, Ricky Yoshimoto, and told him about my predicament. Without a minute's hesitation, he said, "We'll loan you a million dollars." I was overwhelmed, but I did accept his generous offer. I bought out my partner and became the sole owner of the company. Ricky, who was by then the vice president of Nissho-Iwai (his company in New York), was responsible for getting me the loan. I paid the firm back in six months, but was always grateful for Ricky's help. He's a great guy, and we maintained a longtime friendship.

A year or so later, I sold three of the four manufacturing companies I had. All of these sales took place within a four- or five-month period, and I let the buyers take the name Cosmos Minerals. I sold one company to Standard Oil of Ohio, which had a division in Rochester, New York. They also bought the cladding business. I sold the titanium basket business, which manufactured baskets designed to plate extremely large parts. Ironically, my former sales manager, who had been dropped from Futura years before, bought the business. The wire company Astro Lite was the last to go; I sold it to Harrisburg Steel. Since we had sold the name of Cosmos Minerals, we changed the name of the warehouse company that we kept to Supra Alloys.

By that time, I was 54 years old and I decided that it was time for me to semi-retire. We kept the warehouse business, but we sold the building. We rented a small warehouse across the freeway that was about 10,000 square feet. George Jr. took over this business and, when he did, he started growing it. In the place we had rented, there were eight people working; but as the company grew, we had to rent more warehouse space. We needed more material because we were selling more, and eventually we got to the point where we needed a third building. We added another building , giving us an additional 5,000 square feet. Finally, we decided it was crazy to have all those buildings; so in 1990, I built a building. We used it for years until George Jr. decided to sell the business and stay on as president.

As we entered the eighties, the incomprehensible happened. Our daughter, Denise, began to have some health problems that were initially diagnosed as allergy related. Her failing health became our major concern, and was one of the major reasons I relinquished most of my responsibilities to my son George. For the latter part of the eighties, our family began to face what turned out to be the saddest experience of our lives. In 1981, Denise had a grand mal seizure. We had to come to grips with the realization that we might lose her.

Around that time, I sold Cosmos Minerals. Meanwhile, my brother John had taken an assignment to serve with the Pontifical Mission for Palestine. He would be doing that work out of an office in Beirut, Lebanon.

# CHAPTER 42

## MY MISSION TO LEBANON
### *Going Back to a Place I'd Never Been*

#### FATHER JOHN

Much of what follows here is taken from tapes I made when I was in Lebanon from 1984 to 1986. I sent those tapes to America to Ellen Franco who, now, after many years, is compiling and editing the present book. The tapes were randomly sent, as it was a difficult and lengthy process to get mail out of Beirut in the mid-eighties. Unknown to me, Ellen transcribed those tapes. I didn't see the written journal, however, because when I returned to America in 1986, I was consumed by what I saw as the threat of radical Islamic fundamentalism in Lebanon. I was interested in writing about only that, and that writing took much of my energy.

There was a backdrop to my going to Lebanon. In May of 1984, I went to the Holy Land on a pilgrimage with a group from Pennsylvania. In Jerusalem, I briefly encountered a Jesuit priest from Beirut by the name of Father Martin McDermott, who was returning from Gaza after having given a retreat there to the Missionaries of Charity sisters. I had what I thought was a casual, mutually interesting conversation at the time. Father McDermott was in charge of the Oriental Library at St. Joseph's University in Beirut. He had done scholarly research on the Koran and was quite knowledgeable on the topic of Islam. Sometime after our meeting—and without my knowledge—Father McDermott recommended me to the Catholic Near East Association to fill a vacant position. After that chance encounter with Father McDermott, and through a series of other events, I learned of the recommendation, was presented with a proposal, and ultimately accepted the position of director of the Pontifical Mission for Palestine in Beirut, Lebanon. I left my work as director of Urban Ministry in Scranton and went to a place that I had heard about all my life but had never been to—the place where my grandfather was born and lived until he was a young man. My mind, my heart, my psyche had no idea what lay ahead.

Now I feel affirmed in continuing with the present book as so many actual words from the past have been preserved. Those words forbid me from denying what I thought and felt during those years, no matter how they may be judged. As I am confronted by my younger self, I feel compelled to share not only that 'me,' but also the 'me' I remember who lived in the chaos of Lebanon in the mid-1980s, and finally, the 'me' that I have become. Reading what I recorded verbally speaks to me, and it reminds me of how I felt all those many years ago.

Monsignor John Esseff, left, and Bishop James C. Timlin look over a map pinpointing an area in Lebanon, where Monsignor Esseff soon will go to work for the Catholic Near East Welfare Association based in Beirut.

## Monsignor Esseff Accepts Post At Pontifical Mission in Beirut

*Mission to Beirut*

The situation in Lebanon, a country halfway round the world, was very complex when I committed to going there. I didn't understand most of it. Like most other Americans, I was aware of the bombing of the U.S. embassy that had occurred on April 18, 1983, causing the deaths of 63 people. I also knew that, following the attack, the embassy was moved to a supposedly more secure location to the north in East Beirut. Months later, on October 23, 241 American marines lost their lives when a truck bomb struck the Marine barracks in Beirut. These tragic events were the topic of high-profile reports that dominated world news.

By the time I went to New York in September of 1984, I knew that I needed a far deeper understanding of what was happening in the Middle East. I began to study the situation as best I could. On September 20th, another car bomb exploded at the recently created embassy annex in East Beirut, killing 11 and injuring more than 50 others. As a result, my stay in New York was extended. While I waited for clearance to leave for Lebanon, I stayed in the New York Athletic Club and went each day to the local Chancery building at 1011 First Avenue. I met a lot of people there. One day, a fire alarm went off in the twenty-story-high Chancery. Everyone had to evacuate. Among the crowd that poured out of the building was a middle-aged man with a boyish face and a ready smile; he stood next to me. He was a priest. We had to stay outside for quite a while, and I introduced myself: "I'm John Esseff from Scranton, Pennsylvania. What's your name?"

# My Mission to Lebanon

"I'm Larry Jenco. I'm from Joliet, Illinois."

We began to talk, and I found out that he was the head of the Catholic Relief Services. I asked him where he was assigned, and he answered, "Beirut, Lebanon." Then with a 'try to top that one' grin, he asked, "And how about you?"

"Same place!" We roared laughing.

That chance meeting was my first encounter with Father Larry Jenco. I guess we both knew we'd be seeing more of each other in our posts in Lebanon, but neither of us knew that Father Jenco would make headlines months later when he was taken hostage by members of a radical group in Beirut.

Not knowing what lay ahead, and hoping to gain more information about my upcoming mission, I continued each day to go to the Catholic Near East office. Some of the time I spent there was quite a painful experience for me.

### Entry: October 1, 1984

*I stayed in New York until the 29th of September. My stay there was a simulation entry experience for me, a taste of what lay ahead in the battle zone known as Beirut. I found it full of power people, and many of those were ecclesiastics. The man who is the head of the Catholic Near East Welfare Association is ... a man I consider an ego-maniac. He's a very gifted man, handsome, sixty, well spoken, engaging, convincing. But he's crazy. I was his 'Exhibit A.' I was his catch. I was going to Beirut and he didn't want me to do any talking. It was his show and he orchestrated the set and the dialogue.*

*For as long as I can remember, I had always wanted to serve the poor. It's like a hunger in me. I don't understand it exactly, but all my life I have been drawn to them, The Poor. I remember as a little boy, growing up Lebanese American, sitting on my grandfather's lap, listening to him tell stories about his homeland, his dreams, his desire to "be a priest," that came to be fulfilled throughout his life without virtue of the sacrament. In his heart, there was a burning love for those who were needy. He missed his people—warm, generous, loving, hospitable, and prayerful. He would talk until he went into a reverie, and always he would cry whenever he remembered their prayerfulness. He told me in Arabic how he longed to be a priest, but had the "weakness." His was a non-celibate priesthood; he never was ordained, but he did minister. Much of how to love, I learned from him. And I have served the poor as I learned to do from him—and from his family, who were my own.*

*When I accepted the proposal to come to Lebanon, I thought it would be an opportunity to know firsthand the beauty of the people who had set my grand-*

*father's heart ablaze with love until it caught fire in me. It was my hope that, among the poor there and, in honor of my grandfather, I would serve the poor.*

*But in New York, I was not a servant. Rather, I was an accomplishment for an organization man. It was a difficult position to get filled. Maybe I was a victim to other men's ambitions. When I heard them talk, I knew I was a chess piece in their game, and the poor were not even on the board. Power was like electricity in the air.*

*No one passes through New York without scrutiny from the head man, Archbishop J. J. O'Connor. Didn't I know him? Had I been duped? Had I lost my street smarts? I didn't know. I did know that the O'Connor of New York was not the O'Connor of Scranton. In Scranton, I was impressed by his brilliance and his charisma; but more than that, his prayerful concern for the people. In New York, I'm still not sure what part of him I dealt with. He was clouded in the mystery of man's ambition and I couldn't quite sort out which kingdom was more important, who was the most powerful, and where I fit in.*

*O'Connor was illusive and short on hospitality when I arrived. I had served under him for five months in Scranton. I respected him and I felt supported by him. I thought I could look up to him, and that was something that was important to me. He was a strong leader and I remember how angry I was when he chose to go to New York, leaving behind the limping and rather obscure Diocese of Scranton to fend as best it could. It seemed that every day after he left us, he was in the news. He was a man on the move—and the moves were always upward. Archbishop in a matter of weeks, and no one doubted that the red hat would be his when an appropriate amount of time passed.*

*My visit with the Archbishop was a social one. It had very little to do with the subject of Lebanon or his knowledge of that part of the world. I didn't quite understand the kinds of concerns that he had in regard to the Palestinians, but I did read about and reflect on his expressed appraisal of the local situation. After a while, I knew I was being used. All the meetings I had after that were studies in power. And the mere fact that they were for a heavenly cause didn't obscure that truth.*

*During that extended stay in New York, I felt as though the guys at the top weren't quite sure what to do with me. I know that a lot of people think I'm an easy touch, and that was not the first time that I felt used. But when someone pushes really hard, then I stand firm. I used to push back just as hard; I've learned not to push back, but I do stand firm. And that's when some people decide to hate me and others decide to love me.*

# My Mission to Lebanon

*So the meetings continued and I grew tired of watching men center the work of the Church on themselves instead of on the people. Finally, I was totally frustrated and I said, "May I say something?"*

*"Oh, sure."*

*"I just want to say that I didn't join this outfit for Bishop O'Connor or anyone else here. I really just want to say that I joined this outfit for Jesus. I want to serve the poor for Jesus."*

*It was silent then. Some, I think, wanted to laugh. Some thought it was poor taste to bring up the name of a shabby carpenter in a mahogany-and-velvet conference room. Some few were embarrassed. And some few, I think, were quietly saying to themselves, "Yeah—why didn't I think of that?"*

*After that, I knew who wished me well and who didn't; who were disappointed that they didn't have a blob of putty to fashion, and who felt the slightest wish that they could hang up First Avenue and come to Beirut with me and meet the people.*

*The power machine kept grinding away and, one day shortly afterward, I was whisked off to Washington. By then, everything was in order. I had met the Nuncio. To describe him is to describe a retching experience in my stomach. He's of the elite—a man who knows everything, so he doesn't have to listen anymore. Meeting him was the last of my frightening encounters. He and the others said nothing and listened to nothing.*

*I longed to pray with them, but that would be too simple in the midst of top-flight strategies and high-level certainty. How isolated they have become—good men consumed with arrogance and fear. How poor they are. And in my confusion of finding so many poor men dressed in rich men's robes, I left them as poor as I found them. But I carry them in my heart and they humble me, because they test my power to love.*

Those very strong feelings were the first I recorded. Reading them, I remember how difficult it had always been for me to accept 'career men' in the priesthood. It's important for me to define what that means. Sometimes, very gifted men are given positions that place them in a myriad of duties that move them farther and farther from direct ministry to the people. Every priest, bishop, archbishop, cardinal, or nuncio is, first and foremost, "Father." True fathers have the gift of administering love with justice. In my life, I know that those gifts are a rare combination. I've seen a lot of good men make choices that furthered their moving up in the echelons of the hierarchy, who were willing to take the residual distancing from the people in stride. Thinking back to my days in Beirut, I think that some of my pain was the result of losing a lot of direct contact with the real poor. Maybe I resented moving up in the hierarchy. Maybe I wasn't willing or able to lose the contact I had always had with the poor, one person at a time.

### Entry: Friday, October 5*th*

*It's late, but so much has happened. I left New York on the 29th of September with Monsignor Ed Foster, who was assigned to help me get settled in the office in Beirut. We arrived in Rome the following day. We stayed there until yesterday and then flew to Larnaca in Cyprus. From that time on, travel for me would have been simpler if I had a Vatican passport rather than an American one. I had made an application for my Vatican passport in New York, but I didn't get it. I left without the passport, but with a promise that it would be sent to me.*

*We traveled by sea from Larnaca in Cyprus to Jounieh in Lebanon, a route that was considered safer than flying into the airport in West Beirut. It was about 4 o'clock this afternoon when we docked at Jounieh, a port north of Beirut. I was feeling somewhat apprehensive as I stood in line to reclaim my passport in the dining room of the Sun Boat. I was carrying my American passport and I was concerned about that. Americans were being told to get out of Lebanon because the threat of kidnapping or death had been steadily escalating ever since the terrorist bombing of the American embassy in Beirut two weeks ago.*

*Ed Foster had already retrieved his Vatican passport and left the ship. I could see the immigration officer checking each passport, carefully matching the face in front of him to the picture in his hand. Eventually, I found myself one of the last passengers still aboard, and I wasn't sure if the tightness in my stomach was a response to real or imagined danger. It had been a long journey from Scranton and my apprehension was high. I was only footsteps away from standing in Lebanon.*

*Finally, I was checked through. Ed Foster was watching for me and he waved. He came toward me, accompanied by a tall, attractive woman whom he introduced as Hoda Safi. She welcomed me in perfect English. She had been running the Pontifical Office for the past few months and was glad that I was there to take over. The short, slight man behind Hoda seemed somewhat intimidated. When I extended my hand, Foster introduced him to me as John Ajami, my driver.*

*I was feeling more relaxed as I became aware of the beautiful landscape around me. We were in a seaside resort area. Its white buildings were back-*

*dropped by the rugged mountains, which showed a lush green in the glare of the sunlight. The breeze, warm against my skin, reminded me of vacation days I had spent at my brother George's home in California. John, the driver, was standing silently beside the open door of a brown Mazda, waiting for me to get in. That's something I'm going to have to get used to; in Scranton, I had always opened my own doors and driven my own car. As I got into the car, the papal flag that was attached to the right fender caught my attention. I knew I was in another world.*

*We drove from the dock at Jounieh to the autobahn, a six-lane superhighway lined with movie houses, casinos, and restaurants. Road signs—in Arabic, English, and French—dotted the roadway and the tangle of traffic was distinctive in the number of Mercedes Benzes moving bumper-to-bumper toward Beirut. It wasn't until we came to our first checkpoint at the Dog River tunnel that I seemed to be in the Beirut of the American papers. We passed there slowly but uneventfully, and within a half-hour we had arrived at an eleven-story building that took up half a city block.*

*John announced that we were at the Pontifical Mission office. The red, yellow, and orange flowers potted neatly in front of the building continued to create a rather pleasant introduction to the place where I would be living and working. The car stopped. John was at my door in an instant. I stepped out of the car.*

*Finally—I'm here in Beirut.*

### Entry: October 7ᵗʰ, Sunday, the Feast of the Holy Rosary

*My first days here have been dedicated to prayer. I arrived on first Friday, October 5ᵗʰ. That day, I made a pilgrimage to Anaya, the shrine of Mar (Saint) Charbel. Then I went to visit the hermitage where he lived, way up in the mountains, and I said Mass there. Then I went to Harissa, the shrine of Our Lady of Lebanon, and asked her to bless my work. It's been good to spend the first Friday of this month in such a special way.*

*It's early morning. I'm going to have Mass soon. I did meet a man and his wife yesterday.*

*The wife's brother and his family were shot to death. It was a very confusing story as I tried to listen, but I*

*Shrine of St. Charbel*

349

# Brothers & Fathers

*did tell them I was going to have Mass here this morning and they said they'd like to come. They should be here in a few minutes ...*

*Shrine of Our Lady of Lebanon*

*The family just left. Michel and his wife came with their three children. They brought with them another child, and she is the one whose father and mother were killed in the war. She's about ten years old. She has two sisters; one is nine and the other is five. I guess I could console the sister on the death of her brother and her sister-in-law. But I guess what I really wasn't prepared for was meeting that child. She was withdrawn and didn't even want to say "hello." It was very hard for her to look at me, and that's how she was for the whole visit. I have a lingering sense of her parents being here and, yeah, I had words for Michel's wife on the death of her brother and her sister-in-law, but I didn't have any words for that child—and I still don't.*

### Evening ...

*I'm in my room. It's been a long day. I went out to dinner tonight. I don't have a cook and I just burned my finger trying to make coffee. I'm just going to have to learn to use that stove out there! I think I'll manage. I live here by myself and I'm not used to that, I guess. There's an office here and a reception room. There's a big area for my secretary, and there's the regular stuff—a Xerox machine, typewriter, desk, file cabinets. There's also a sitting room where people can wait who come to the office. There's a picture of the Holy Father on one of the walls.*

*Part of what I did in New York was to find out where our funding comes from. It will be my work here to discover needs, investigate them, write them up, send them to funding agencies, see that the funds are brought back to those who have applied for them, and then have those people who receive the funds make an accounting of how they've used them.*

*My work is to be the director of the Pontifical Mission for Palestine in Lebanon.*

*Historically, in 1948, the Palestinian refugees were a large group of people who had been put out of their homes in Israel. And for thirty-six years now, they have not had a homeland. The extremism and the fanaticism are told in the stories of the Palestinian Liberation Organization (PLO), and Arafat, and the people who do very fanatical things because of injustices that were done to them. The Palestinians were first put onto the west bank of Israel, and then were forced into Jordan; finally, they've been put into camps in Lebanon. I intend to go to visit them soon. I know that the name of my office was originally the Pontifical*

# My Mission to Lebanon

*Mission for Palestinians. Now, it is simply called the Pontifical Mission. I have been told the name change took place because, here in Lebanon, the Palestinians have caused a great deal of difficulty through a lot of political reprisals against Israel. Those reprisals have turned Lebanon into a battleground for the past ten years.*

*I continue to listen, but I know I'm in a very complicated situation.*

By Monday morning I was eager to meet my staff and begin to deal with the problems of the poor. The office had been without a director for some time, and news of my arrival had brought many to the office looking for immediate responses to their urgent needs. What transpired was nothing I expected.

Brother Joseph Lowenstein, the director of the Pontifical Mission in Jerusalem, had come to the office and insisted on seeing me—not in the office, but in an adjoining parlor. Hoda recommended that I see him first, as he had covered many of the matters of the office before I arrived and he could bring me up to date. It wasn't old or new business that concerned him. He made it clear that the most important item was not the needs of the people in the office. In fact, there was no one in the office I "should see." He told me that, before doing anything else, I had to devote myself to matters of protocol (that I had obviously not been following). I was curious, but uninformed. I told him that I would have to depend on him for his expertise. Before I could see anyone, I had to get in touch immediately with the Maronite patriarch, who resided at Bkerke, and the President of the Republic at the Presidential Palace, Amine Gemayel. Brother Lowenstein continued to add names to the list, until it eventually included some twenty people named in descending order of importance: the ranking included my own Latin rite bishop; the nuncio, Archbishop Angeloni; and several leaders of the Muslim communities. This deference to position was all new to me. The people he listed expected me to perform according to a preordained code of protocol and would consider it an offense if I did not arrive shortly after my entrance into the country in order to pay my respects. For me, protocol had always been rather stuffy, limiting, old world and, if I am to be completely honest with myself, hypocritical. But in the Middle East, nothing could be further from the truth. For me to meet a Maronite bishop before I met the Maronite patriarch was not only bad manners, but it was also an affront to the office of the patriarch. As the new director, it was my duty to meet him before anyone else. My visit was not only considered recognition of the patriarch himself, but of the Christian community in Lebanon as well. To pay my respects to the President was, in a very real sense, to pay my respects to the Republic of Lebanon and, with that, to all Lebanese.

### October 8th, Monday

*Today, the entire day was given over to making arrangements for upcoming visits. The names, the titles, the political implications that came with the religious leaders flooded in on me. My western mind was taking in facts, but having a difficult time assessing the oneness of the secular and the religious. Maybe as the titles become transformed into real people, the complex makeup of the Lebanese population and its power struggle will become clearer to me.*

*Tonight, I walked on the veranda that surrounds my living quarters, and became immersed in the calmness and beauty of the evening as the brilliant sun over Beirut began to fade. The motorized sounds coming from the autobahn below demanded my attention and somehow seemed intrusive in the sight of the distant, soundless, lapping waves that were still visible in the half-light of evening. I feel a deep confusion as I try to sort out my feelings in this new country. I can only dialogue in the quiet of my own mind. What peculiar preparation had omitted so important a concept as protocol in the East? Brother Lowenstein had been most emphatic about the necessity of all that I would have to accomplish during the coming days and yet, oddly enough, during my two-week stay in New York and Washington, nothing at all had been mentioned about the etiquette that will, no doubt, govern many other situations. I am disturbed by my confusion and I wonder if there will be other hidden agendas that I will have to deal with.*

The meetings of the following days were, for the most part, enveloped in a kind of ambassadorial elegance. On separate occasions, Brother Lowenstein, Monsignor Foster, Hoda, and I were wined and dined as we made my presence known to the political and ecclesiastical hierarchy in much-publicized meetings. Little had to do with the workings of the Pontifical Mission, and I had dealt with people long enough to know that it was I who was being studied and assessed. I wasn't thinking of myself at that moment as the man who had control over an enormous amount of funds earmarked for relief services.

Survival instincts die hard. I fell into a familiar pattern. I had always enjoyed people more than anything else; I decided to relax and enjoy myself and get to know the people, titles aside, as I met them.

We arrived at the residence of the Maronite patriarch around noon. The entrance was a large iron gate centered in a stone wall. There was a tank outside of

# My Mission to Lebanon

the wall, where there were guards posted. We were expected and we gained entrance without delay. Inside there was a large courtyard and another large door. John stopped the car and I got out. After appropriate greetings from the patriarch's nephew, Monsignor Khairche, I was introduced

*Maronite Patriarchate in Lebanon*

to several other priests. We went up two flights of stairs to the main door of the patriarchate itself. I was led to a large book, where I was directed to sign my name and indicate my position. The priests and bishops followed me and I thought it was strange that I was at the head of the line. We continued along a paneled corridor lined with potted plants and elegant paintings, into a spacious reception room where the patriarch was seated upon a throne-like chair waiting, of all things, for me to arrive. Monsignor Foster handled the introductions and I was given a seat on the right of the patriarch. He was about 5'3" tall, and was wearing a round, black hat. His face was obscured by a full beard. A pair of steel-rimmed glasses encircled eyes that smiled a warm welcome. He was hospitable and spoke of my credentials, which Monsignor Nolan had sent to him. The patriarch said he was impressed. He wanted to know where 'my' people were from. When I told him Hardine, a nearby village in the mountains, he smiled a wide smile, and somehow I thought that meant more to him than my resume. At lunch that day, scotch was served, and later, Foster said that it was the first time he could remember whiskey being served at the patriarchate. I guess my history went before me.

"Maybe they're opening up now because we have a 'Lebanese' director."

I was interested in Foster's take on things. I got the impression that I was just a kid who was born in America, but who had the good sense to 'come home' when I gained some maturity.

Our visit to President Gemayel went off on schedule. When we arrived, we were escorted by a bodyguard to a waiting room. An honor guard in a charcoal grey uniform with silver buttons stood outside the door. He reminded me of a West Point cadet.

353

# Brothers & Fathers

After a short while, we were admitted into the President's office. He seemed very western in his grey business suit and complementary tie. His handshake was strong. He was cordial and spoke in English, with only a slight trace of an accent. He spoke affectionately of Cardinal Cooke, the former Archbishop of New York, and expressed his desire to meet with Cardinal O'Connor in the near future.

The visit lasted about fifteen minutes.

I told him I was happy to be in Lebanon and was grateful for the opportunity to be of assistance to a suffering people. I assured him of my prayers and asked him if I could give him my blessing. Monsignor Foster and Brother Lowenstein seemed very uncomfortable, maybe even astonished, at my suggestion. I wasn't sure why. I offered a prayer, gave my blessing, shook the President's hand, and left, feeling a bond that surpassed formality.

Eventually, I began to sort out a lot of information. I had a meeting with the Mufti. Among other things, I learned that, what the patriarch is to Christians, the Mufti is to Muslims. He is the official head of the Sunni Muslims and has official recognition under Lebanese law. He is paid a salary by the government. Hoda accompanied me to the residence of the Mufti because he spoke only Arabic. He lived in an apartment building which had at least a half dozen bearded, gun-bearing men as guards. That was new. We were accompanied from the street to an elevator by two soldiers, and then to a waiting room. When the Mufti received us, Hoda introduced me and he welcomed me to Lebanon. I told him, again through Hoda, that I wanted to cooperate in every way I could, to bring aid to the needy and suffering of Lebanon. I explained that the Pontifical Mission hoped to work with the social agencies of the Muslim community and that my work was to relieve suffering in the name of God, and in the name of the Holy Father. He was respectful in his response, but rather distant. He brought up the question of doctrine, and eventually told me that, though the Muslims recognized Jesus as a messenger of God, they most emphatically did not recognize the cross. I knew I did not want to pursue the discussion any further at that time. Hoda expressed our gratitude and our goodbyes and we left.

I also saw the leader of the Shiite Muslims, Mohamad Mehdi Chamseddine. That visit involved traveling into West Beirut.

### Entry (no date)

*The war has blown away much of Beirut. Shelled or fallen buildings are everywhere. Burnt cars remain in the street. Eyes of suspicion are everywhere.*

# My Mission to Lebanon

*Among the squalor and the damaged buildings, young men are everywhere carrying rifles or machine guns. I learned to pronounce Sheik Chamseddine's name in preparation for my visit, and each time one of the young men approached our car, I would ask in Arabic, "Do you know where the house of Sheik Mohamed Mehdi Chamseddine is?" They would study me, but then would give me further directions, and off we would go.*

*The sheik's compound was surrounded with armed militia, and we were escorted from the moment of our arrival. When I met him, I bowed and said, "I am happy to meet you, Your Excellency."*

*We exchanged pleasantries. He asked me who I represented, and I told him, the Vatican. I also told him I was happy to be there on the occasion of Cardinal Cooke's anniversary. His expression changed with the mention of Cooke's name, and I remembered similar warmth a few days ago with President Gemayel.*

*The sheik was direct: "Catholic Relief Services demands that America be honored and thanked and recognized for its contributions." He was evidently referring to the alleged collusion between American aid and the Catholic Relief Services. He continued head-on: "What is your source and your allegiance?"*

*"Your Excellency, I am not here as an ambassador of the United States, nor of the CIA, but of God and of the Holy Father, Pope John Paul II. I hope to bring aid to all needy people of Lebanon, and it is not our purpose to use this work as propaganda. Our Lord tells us not to let the left hand know what the right hand is doing. I am here to tell you that, if there are Shiite children in need, I hope to be of service to them."*

We had tea and I told him about my family and how they had come from Lebanon, and that I was happy and honored to be able to be there. Many Shiites received help from the Pontifical Mission during the time I was there, and I was in agreement with the delivery of that aid. I began to see the value of meeting the heads of all the different communities in Lebanon. The mosaic presented in those early days and weeks was varied and intriguing. In this tiny country, not quite as large as the state of Connecticut, lived a conglomerate of peoples and ideas, a mixture of East and West, a contrast of rich and poor, a struggle for power and land. Only one constant continually emerged in situation after situation: Whether men were warm and welcoming or cold and distant, they were all surrounded by guns. By the time I had been there a little more than a week, and for all the time I stayed there, it was clear to me that Lebanon was an armed camp.

# Brothers & Fathers

With the area of protocol somewhat settled, Brother Lowenstein did what he could to try to fill me in on what he knew about requests. Leaving his own post in Jerusalem, he gave as much time as he could afford when there was no director in Beirut, and was very aware of what was going on in my office. There were many matters which he wanted expedited so that he could return to Israel. Because of that wish, he quickly explained the case of a Dr. Raheb, who was waiting for money for tuitions from the Pontifical Mission Office. Dr. Raheb was a monk who had earned his doctorate in France. Lowenstein gave me a list of some two hundred students Raheb was sponsoring for tuitions at the Lebanese school outside of the Debayeh Palestinian camp. The total amount to be paid by the Pontifical Mission was 10,000 American dollars. It was already October and the monies were overdue.

I thought this situation was a perfect opportunity for me to understand first-hand the way that the Pontifical Mission was helping the children who remained dispossessed in the Palestinian camps. I called Dr. Raheb and told him to call the principal of the school and set up a visit for us. My driver, John Ajami, and I picked up Dr. Raheb. He was an Aleppine monk and, as he joined us, I was taken by how well-groomed he looked in the confines of his elaborate clerical dress. We visited the school and met the principal, but I didn't meet any of the children from the camp. When I asked Dr. Raheb when I could see them, he explained that they might find that kind of encounter embarrassing. I was thoroughly familiar with the welfare system in Scranton, and how some felt embarrassed as part of it. I was willing to go along with Raheb's assessment, and said I would wait and meet the children in the camp. In response, Dr. Raheb said, "I'm afraid you can't go to the camp."

"Why not? That's why I'm here."

"There's too much tension there. I don't think it would be safe for you."

"I'm sure I won't be any less safe than anyone else who lives there."

Dr. Raheb was agitated and began to make a point of saying that he would be unable to arrange such a meeting at the camp because he was traveling to France the next day and wanted to allow time to come to the Mission Office to pick up the money so that he could settle the children's accounts before he left. I knew I didn't want to do that; I wanted to meet the children. Dr. Raheb seemed very reluctant to accommodate me, and was becoming strangely impatient. He said it might be better if we just postponed the visit to the children for some other day. He said he had to leave. I was somewhat suspicious, and decided to stay to visit the camp. Dr. Raheb found his own way home; I went to the camp.

# My Mission to Lebanon

John Ajami drove me past a Lebanese militia group and then to the outskirts of the camp, which was a series of unfinished buildings where people had settled in. The houses were made of cement forms that had never been completed. Vines climbed over the concrete slabs and there were some gardens where small plots of herbs and vegetables grew. Not far from all this ran open sewage. It flowed through an open conduit that took the waste from the homes to a neighboring field. The buzz of the flies and the stench created an atmosphere of disease and despair.

I met a woman in the camp who told me that her name was Grace Androlas. She was with her three children. When I asked her why they were not in school, she said that she did not have enough money to send them. I asked her to tell me the names of other children who were not in school. There were many; I wrote down all their names. The picture was coming into focus. I was eager to return to the office. I wanted to make a very careful reassessment of the needs of the children in the Palestinian camps and, of course, to see if the names I had written appeared anywhere else. I was certain they would. Intuitively, I knew that Dr. Raheb's current trip to France, and all future trips, would be not on the Pontifical Mission, but on his own purse strings. Unfortunately, that first brush with corruption was not the only one I would deal with during my stay in Beirut.

During subsequent days and weeks, the Middle East began to translate from ideas and facts into people. Beirut—like Scranton, like the Pocono mountains, like Peru—was the sum of its people. I had always loved the people, no matter where I went, and I was looking with eager anticipation to the new faces of the people who now would be my people, those who would enrich me in allowing me to serve them.

*"My people"*

## October 9th

*I'm here in my office looking out the window. It's about 10 o'clock. I've already had many visitors so far today and it just feels like a good work day. On Sunday, I went to see the patriarch and had lunch with him. Monsignor Foster and I received quite a wonderful reception from him. He's a very sweet man—very fatherly, very gentle. The patriarch's nephew, Father Albert Kreish, a Maronite diocesan priest, came and picked us up and took us there. We were given a real red carpet treatment. Maybe it's the need now of the local church to know that others are really very interested in them. I think the patriarch likes knowing that the Holy Father thinks so highly of Lebanon that he has sent an emissary to fulfill the work that needs to be done through the Pontifical Mission.*

### October 11*th*

*Even before I arrived, a cousin of mine, George El Koury, had called the Pontifical Mission and asked Hoda to have me get in touch with him as soon as I arrived. I telephoned him on Friday night and made plans to go to the village of Hardine, which is the birthplace of my grandfather. Father Daniel Deeb, another cousin of mine, would come by on Sunday and take me and Ed Foster to the village. My cousin George told me about my many relatives who were eager to meet me. I was looking forward to the visit, but part of me was feeling cautious about not allowing myself to be overwhelmed by family members who might be too insistent about my coming to see them each week. I know how Lebanese family life goes. I want to meet all of them, but I also want to make sure that they won't expect more of me than I can give. I have a ministry here and they will have to respect that. With this reservation, but also with deep expectancy, on Sunday, I am planning to go on a trip to Hardine, the village where my grandfather—Gidue—was born. I must say: I have gone inside myself, wondering if I can really appreciate the place Gidue so loved and shared with me when I was so young I could sit on his lap.*

### Sunday Morning, October 14*th*

*I suppose everyone dreams about the time that he can go back to a place that tells him about his roots. Even the words "go back" are strange words, but I find myself thinking that way about Hardine. I have never been to Lebanon before, and have only heard about Hardine from Gidue, but this morning I am very excited. In a sense I am experiencing a feeling of "returning home."*

### Sunday Night

*Life has certainly been different for me since I arrived in Lebanon. I just came back from a visit to the village of Hardine. It's a day I want to remember.*

*This morning, Monsignor Foster and I waited. Foster has been in Lebanon or other places in the Middle East for twenty years, but was never closely involved in the intimacy of a family. He was eager to go to the village with me. Father Deeb arrived to pick us up. He looks like so many members of my family in America. He's about 5'10", has dark curly hair, a ruddy complexion, and weighs about 220 pounds. In different clothes, he could be a formidable linebacker! His English is poor, but he was rich in hospitality. As we continued on the two-hour trip, we got better at communicating—his English and my Arabic, both broken.*

*As we traveled to the mountains, I became aware from both Father Deeb and Monsignor Foster that we were not on a Sunday picnic. Hardine is located very near the Syrian occupation forces, so we had to drive on roads that were not in Syrian-dominated territory. Deeb was well aware of all the checkpoints in northern Lebanon and explained that the route we were going to take was longer and wound through the hills, but he said for two American priests, it was safer than the coastal road. We passed through several checkpoints that were manned by the Lebanese forces, and I realized that Deeb knew these men well. They did not ask to see our IDs. Father Deeb was our passport through the mountains.*

*As we came near the village, there was a huge banner strung across the road in large letters:*

## WELCOME HOME: WELCOME TO YOUR HOMELAND
## MONSIGNOR JOHN ESSEFF

*It was just really touching. Father Deeb fell into tears. As we came around the next bend, there was another sign in Arabic. Father Deeb read it; it welcomed me, too. About the village square were about 200 villagers; the church bells were ringing and there was an air of festivity. Of course, I wore my red cassock, because this was a great big occasion. As I got out of the car a sense of all that Lebanon had given me welled up inside of me and I knelt down and kissed the ground. When I got up, I went to each one and said "hello." There were some who translated and made Ed and me aware of those we were meeting. They told me their names and who they were related to and how they were related. Their names were very familiar: Koury, Sahd, Assaf, Abraham. And they had so much that they wanted to share with me. One man looked like my father; another like a cousin. One woman reminded me of my sister. Family similarities were obvious everywhere I looked.*

*When the greetings ended, the ringing of the church bells began. It was the sign that Mass was about to be celebrated. The people began to leave the village square and went into the*

Mass in the Maronite rite

# Brothers & Fathers

*church. It was the Church of Mar Shina (Saint Shina). I went into the sacristy and dressed in the vestments of the Maronite rite, and I celebrated the Mass more familiar to me as a boy. Here, the words of the liturgy were in Syriac, but when it came time for the homily, I spoke in Arabic—the language I had learned in my home.*

*After Mass ended, the people from the village showed me the place where the house of Abdelnoor had stood, and all that was left was a fig tree. Abdelnoor is the man who is the first of the House of Esseff. So many of those present were eager to show me the house, and I could hear so many of them saying, "That's the house of Abdelnoor." But, of course, the house was gone and there was just the tree. One of the young boys, Leon Istambouli, climbed up and he got some figs from the tree and he gave them to me. I gave some to Monsignor Foster and we ate them. It was overwhelming to see the love and the respect and the reverence they had just for my being there. They were very genuinely touched that I had "come home."*

## LEON

"My life experience with the Esseffs began in 1984, when Father John came to Lebanon as the director of the Pontifical Mission. Since we were fourth cousins, he was related to nearly half of the village, and thus all of Hardine was preparing to meet our American cousin, who is a very important figure in Lebanon.

"The village was decorated with 'Arches of Victory (used in the old days to greet returning heroes of war). Some said, HARDINE WELCOMES ITS BELOVED SON, JOHN ESSEFF.

"It was a big deal and we were all waiting for Father Daniel Deeb (Mom's first cousin) to arrive with Father John. From the eyes of an eleven year old, I remember Monsignor getting out of the car with his black-and-dark-pink colors (colors that looked like those of an archbishop or a cardinal). I had always taken the beauty and the serenity of my village for granted, but I suddenly felt a new appreciation for my village and my heritage when I saw Father John kiss the ground in the middle of the historic village square.

"We headed down to the old house with the fig tree that grows over its roof. It was always known as the 'Abdelnoor fig tree,' but I never knew what the relationship was 'til that day. We walked down the steep hill for a hundred yards or so that leads to the house. While everyone was looking at the house, I felt the need to be noticed by this important, long-distant cousin of ours, so I ran up to the tree and picked a fig and jumped back down and handed it to Father John. And that was the beginning of our relationship. I

# My Mission to Lebanon

> ## LEON
> 
> *thought I gave him something that he had been hungry and thirsty for, for a long time. If I knew twenty-two years ago what one fig brought into my life, I would have given him a basketful! But one was enough to have Father John wake up in the middle of the night twenty years later, call me, and say, 'I felt that you needed me, so I thought I'd call you.' One fig was enough for him to be there every time I was weak, angry, or stressed and needed his spiritual guidance and direction."*

As the experiences continued, I was a bit overwhelmed. I went around the village. I saw an old man who had to be in his 80s, and when I went over to him he said, "I remember your father."

And I said, "Well, my father's Joseph Esseff.

He said, "He was here."

"No, he wasn't here. My grandfather was here."

"Oh, was his name Moses?"

"No. Moses was my grandfather's brother."

"Your grandfather was George?"

"Yes." I said.

He was so delighted. He hugged me. He told me about my grandfather and how Gidue used to give him money when he was a little boy. The man could just about walk, but he wanted me to go into his house and hear about my grandfather, who couldn't have been more than 16 or 17 years old when he cared for a little boy who was such an old man now. I can understand better why my grandfather loved people who remembered so well and so long. Now, so long after my grandfather's death, it was nice to know that the love lived on, and now it was coming back to warm me. I felt like a little boy again, sitting on my grandfather's lap.

The next place we went was the home of Nahumtalla Kassab. He was a priest and he was also born in the village of Hardine. He is about to be canonized next year. He was the teacher of St. Charbel. So we went to see the little house in which he was born; it had been made into a nice little shrine. I was really touched to discover that living in it now are displaced people who had fled one of the war zones, and the people of Hardine had taken them in and allowed them to live there. The house was built in such a way that, as we went down the steps, the house seemed to take on a cave-like effect. People must have been very poor to have been born in such primitive conditions. I saw it as a very holy place.

We left there and, as we walked around the village, the people showed me a street where about nineteen of the people who had lived there left and went to America. At the foot of the hill was the house of my Grandfather Sahd, my mother's father. This was where my grandmother used to make kibba. I got a picture of the house. My Uncle Joe would love to have it. Imagine that: Budra Sahd's house still standing!

The day passed quickly. In the midst of laughter and talking, and trying to figure out who was related and how, food appeared from everywhere and we were warmly welcomed to a great feast. Music was playing and the people of the village were dancing the Dubka. As the young men swirled, their coats flew outward and I could see that most of them were wearing guns strapped to their backs. I knew I was someplace different. I realized I was touching both a memory gone and a reality present. Hardine introduced me to Lebanon old and Lebanon new. Into the joy of family and friends intruded the terrible reality of constant watchfulness and a sense of danger.

I had much to consider as I rode down the mountain toward Beirut tonight. I am filled with wonder and uncertainty, and I'm looking forward to the days ahead.

### Entry (no date)

I've really gotten into this mission of mine and there's been a lot of growth inside of me. I've firmed up. I fired a guy I hired. That was hard. I want to say that. You have to see my desk now: It's loaded with projects. There are people coming here and asking me for all kinds of money. I have to admit, it sickens me to see some of them come in. They drive up in their Mercedes Benzes. They walk in wearing their tailored suits on return trips from Germany and other parts of Europe. I'm still in the same game, but the stakes have really escalated. A few months ago, I was in my little office in Scranton handing out a dollar or two, or maybe buying someone a pack of cigarettes or paying for a night's lodging. Now I have people coming in with requests for thousands and thousands of dollars. I find myself looking at them in total amazement and they don't even blink an eye. Well, after a few weeks here, I'm starting not to blink an eye either. I'm looking at them and I can say, "I just can't stand you. I don't like you. There is no way I will recommend your project." So, I may be fired from my position in a little while, but, I really can't stand what's going on. There are archbishops and bishops and superiors of religious groups, and I can't even put into words the things they are asking for. Then there are the real poor, and they

# My Mission to Lebanon

don't even know how to ask. So, as I see it, what's happening here in Lebanon with this war is that those people who are in love with money are using the war to line their own pockets. They come here and they expose their own love of material things so crassly that I can almost physically experience how badly they are stinking up this office. On days of this kind of greed, I have to get out of the office.

I went to Egypt. Intercontinental and exotic as it sounds, it was a trip about as long as one from Scranton to North Carolina. When I got there, I found a poor bishop who hadn't been visited in years. Nobody knew or cared about what he wanted. He's a beautiful guy. His name is Merhi, Joseph Merhi. He's 72 years old. They gave him three priests and they established a diocese over there. Can you imagine that? Three priests! One of them is Father John Hunehan. That's his name. I've got his book here. He's as husky and robust as anyone you've ever seen. He's eighty years old. He teaches every day in a school with 2,000 kids. He kind of wanders in—he doesn't shuffle yet. It's not really a stride, but he walks. When I was visiting, he walked in and gave me a copy of his book in Arabic, which I don't read too well. It was great to meet this man—a scholar, a lover of human beings. He gets up every day, says his prayers, and teaches little children.

And then there was a young guy. My God, he's like a taut wire. He's a tough little guy. He's been out on that mission for twelve years. He could put a New York taxi driver to shame, the way he drives. He's hot-tempered—a hot blooded Maronite priest who's out there working every day in Egypt. I had a nice time with them.

I never saw anything in the United States like what I saw there, so I can't compare it to anything I ever saw there, but I knew I saw something like it in Peru. Only there, had I seen the kind of catastrophe of human beings that exists in Cairo.

There were maybe several million Catholics in Cairo. They had built these cemeteries to bury their dead, and they were rather nice places. Eventually, the poor of Egypt discovered the mausoleums that had been built in the cemeteries there. The poor took the bones out of the mausoleums and they made those crypts their homes. I went there to see them and they had great dignity. I met a lady there who asked me, "What are you doing here?"

"Well, I said, I came to see you and to pray with you."

"Why?"

And I felt a sense of embarrassment. Why, indeed? I knew so many other people who were poor, but their particular circumstances were different. And she looked at me with a kind of quivering look. Her eyes seemed to go back and *forth. I think she saw the sincerity in my face. (Maybe I was just praying that she did.) And then I heard a voice that quivered like her eyes: "Welcome."*

*I think there was love then. I didn't want to embarrass her and she didn't embarrass me either. She had such a grace about her—and a swirl. And she lived in a previously occupied crypt in a cemetery. Then she introduced me to her children. Do they envy the dead their resting places? I don't know ...*

*... I am back in East Beirut. War has come to Lebanon, and has brought all kinds of injustice. I always hope war doesn't come too close to America. My experience is that, when war happens, the wealthy get wealthier. I hear the groans of the poor when I sleep and when I wake up. In my office, I most often meet the people who earn their money on the suffering of the hidden poor. I guess it's the subject that people talk about when the topic is the military or the political or industrial complex. What exists in Lebanon is not unique. It has the potential of existing anywhere in the world.*

*It's November. I am 32 or 33 days into my mission. There is so much to be done.*

Father Marty McDermott, the Jesuit I met in Jerusalem in 1984, was very instrumental in my being in Beirut. He came to see me within a week of my arrival. As time went on, he and I became good friends, and he was an invaluable source of information and genuine friendship. One of the things Marty did regularly was to minister to a group of nuns called the Missionaries of Charity, (M.C.). He and a friend of his, Father Theo Fluckt, a Jesuit from Holland, would visit them and celebrate Mass for them as often as they could. At that time, most of the English-speaking priests had left Beirut. Most priests spoke French and/or Arabic. Maronites and Melchite Latins were among those who also spoke French.

Marty told me on one occasion that the Missionaries of Charity would love for me to come to celebrate Mass for them, maybe in deference to my being the director of the Pontifical Mission. I can say that now; but at the moment, I thought they were just looking for a priest to pray with. I made up my mind I would visit them. Saying Mass for the sisters was not an

*Father John with the Missionaries of Charity*

assignment; I simply chose to make a response. Each time I went to visit them, I was showered with gratitude. As I saw the sisters more and more, I came to know more about them and their charisma. But I fell in love with the sisters before I met Mother Teresa. They spoke of her, their founder, Mother Teresa of Calcutta, and I learned a lot of wonderful things about her.

One of the first inspiring stories I heard was how Mother rescued sixty-three babies. Muslims ran an orphanage for the retarded and the abandoned in West Beirut. In the midst of intense shelling and the possibility of death, the workers left and abandoned the babies who were there. Hearing about what had happened, Mother wanted to go to West Beirut and get those babies, and she approached President Amil Gemayel for permission. He said that they could not go into West Beirut unless the shelling stopped. Mother asked Father Theo Fluckt to bring the Blessed Sacrament to the convent where they were staying. He did, and Mother and her sisters held an all-night prayer vigil. The shelling ended and President Gemayel saw to it that Mother was given ten Red Cross trucks to take into West Beirut. She rescued all 63 of the babies who had been abandoned there. This is a story Marty told me. It happened long before I got there.

I stayed in touch with the sisters. I tried to be available to hear confessions and to give them an occasional day of recollection. When time for them to travel to Rome for a retreat came, they told Mother how, at that time, it would be impossible for them to go to Rome, but they assured her that they knew a priest who could give them their retreat. They spoke to Mother about me, and in response, she said, "Tell that priest I want him to come to Rome and give a retreat for all the superiors." In time, I was able to do that. Already scheduled to be in Rome for a conference in June of 1985, I was able to arrange a retreat at the same time. I went to the Missionaries' convent in Via Casalinea, where Mother Teresa welcomed me. I gave the retreat, which Mother attended, along with all of her superiors from convents throughout the world. The theme of the retreat was the Magnificat. I realized that Mother had all of the virtues I spoke about to the sisters who were there. That was my first meeting with Mother, and our relationship grew to be an amazing

*Mother Teresa and Father John*

journey in grace. I think I connected with her because of my own love of Mary and the way in which I intertwined that love, as I understood it, with Mother's Rule of Life for her community. From that first retreat, we connected very strongly with one another, and she began to ask me if I would give retreats to her sisters who lived in various places throughout the world. After I left Beirut in 1986, I went to Calcutta from America to give Mother Teresa and her sisters a retreat. I saw her in that capacity no less than twenty-five times: in Rome, Calcutta, Albania, Mexico, and in Washington, D.C. Ironically, when she visited Scranton, she asked Bishop Timlin for me, but I was out of town. From those first encounters until the present, I have had an ongoing relationship with the Sisters of Charity.

### Entry (no date)

*I do like to visit the Missionaries of Charity sisters to offer Mass and hear confessions. I also try to get to the Palestinian camps as often as possible. On a daily basis, I'm living in what is considered the Christian sector in East Beirut. West Beirut is in the Shiite Muslim sector, and so many of the displaced people living there are the end result of the shake-up of political dominance in certain sectors. There are some Christians who live in the Muslim sector, whose lives are very difficult for them. And there are Muslims who are living in the Christian sector, whose lives are very difficult for them. In fact, this coming Tuesday, I'm going to a Palestinian camp that's here in the Christian sector. I want to go there because there has been tremendous pressure for us to assist the Palestinians, who are the 'lepers' of Lebanese society right now. This is true, in spite of the fact that my office was set up as the Pontifical Mission for Palestine. Now, the Palestinians are considered the source of all the ills and problems of this country. They are the people now who are the scapegoat for all the problems that exist here in Lebanon, and have existed for the past ten years. In fact, I have had relatives of mine who have come in here and told me in no way should I offer any assistance whatsoever to the Palestinians or to the Muslims. I'm getting an awful lot of pressure from extremist Christians, who have needs and are looking for support and help.*

*There are some 200,000 displaced people here in Lebanon, and so there are a tremendous number of Christians who have special kinds of needs for housing and other essentials. This problem exists along with the assistance that is needed for the orphanage programs and the needy children's programs. I'm beginning to see that there's also going to have to be a great deal more done for the elderly who have been displaced. These are some of my daily concerns.*

# My Mission to Lebanon

As fall turned to early winter, I met a Dutch Jesuit named Father Nicholas Kluiters. He must have impressed me, because I recorded a lot of information about him and sent those thoughts home to America. Father Kluiters had set up an appointment to come to the office to see me.

At the Pontifical Office in Beirut, part of my job was to figure out which requests for funds were real and which were self-serving. I had already met someone who had fallen prey to greed, and I knew that encounters like this one with Kluiters could quickly turn into an ugly play for power. My automatic response was caution. Just the summer before, I had been ministering to the elderly, the homeless, the families of the imprisoned, those who were living in the projects of Scranton, and the homeless in the city streets. That had been my 'basic training' for Beirut. Every day I was more and more grateful for my work in Scranton; but, in Beirut, the intrigue was so much more sophisticated or demonic, that I found myself so much more on guard.

Father Kluiters was prompt for his appointment. He talked; I listened. He was lean and taut and, as he spoke, he revealed a mind that worked with the precision of a Swiss watch. He had grown into middle age in the Bequaa Valley, immersed in service, turmoil, and intrigue. I listened to him talk for almost two hours. He was intense as he talked about the towns, the parishes, the schools, the problems—but mostly the people of the Bequaa. He was different. It was not only money that he was looking for. He wanted me to know what was really going on and he wanted me to help him to effect a genuine response to the needs of the people.

He asked me if I would go with him and visit his parish, five Christian villages in the predominantly Muslim area of the Bequaa Valley. It was easy to see that he was organized and disciplined. He was also open and warm. He was motivated by his deep commitment to a people he had adopted ten years before, when he left Holland to live as a Jesuit priest in the Bequaa. He knew the people. He knew their needs. He had come to my office to get a response to as many of them as he could. He poured information on me. He presented a clear case of need and reminded me of a lot of other Jesuits I had known who were skilled in arguing a case built on a well-defined understanding and a solid conviction.

I liked his style. One hour and fifty minutes after he arrived, I said, "OK. I'll go."

I sent all of this information in bits and pieces to Ellen Franco. Sometime later, as she was teaching writing, she chose to do what she made her students do: take an event and turn it into a story. So she became her own student. She created a story based on what I had told her. It's come to be a favorite of mine—one I often share with men in priestly formation.

---

## OUT OF LEBANON

The winter rains had made the roads slick and treacherous. The two-hour drive from Beirut had slowed into four, and the dreary day merged almost unnoticed into dusk. Negotiating sharp curves on the dark road, Father Kluiters had stopped talking and the last half-hour had been spent in silence. I was mulling over the long day and the events that had led up to it. I was tired and my eyes were burning. The darkness was a blur and I felt lost in the thickening darkness. I was trying to let my mind catch up with my body. Ever steadying circles of light intruded between the constant motion of the rain on the windows and the grey, diving floaters in my eyes.

"Just a while longer, Monsignor, and we'll be there. The village is just ahead."

I was glad to hear that news. Ten minutes later, Kluiters stopped the car. "I'll get your bags. No use coming out into this rain again."

I could feel the cold November air biting my face and neck as I climbed out of the car. I pulled my collar up and dropped my head between my hunched shoulders to shield myself from the rain. The rectory ahead was dark. Splashing through the menacing, unseen puddles, Kluiters and I quickly approached the door of the rectory. Kluiters turned the key, opened the wooden door, stepped inside, and flicked on the switch. The light hurt my eyes and I squinted.

"Welcome to the Bequaa. Make yourself at home." Kluiters was busy shaking his coat and hanging it to dry. "Let me take your coat."

I was readjusting to the light and the staccato sound of Kluiters' voice that still seemed filled with energy.

"Your room is at the top of the stairs if you want to get settled. I'm sorry it's not warmer. I'll get some supper ready."

"Sounds good to me." I reached down to get my bag when I heard a somber tone in Kluiters' voice.

"One other thing, Monsignor. I'd like to have your passport."

I felt an embarrassed tension rising up in me—and a little confusion. In Beirut, Kluiters had come courting me for favors; but now, with no lack of respect, Kluiters was assuming

# My Mission to Lebanon

*command. I reached into my pocket and pulled out my passport. I didn't take my eyes off Kluiters. I reached out and placed the booklet in his hand.*

*"This won't do you any good up here. When you're ready to leave, I'll give it back to you." He looked at the passport and then at me. He was clearly studying my face, not unlike hundreds in the village. I knew I looked darker than my picture, and a day's growth of stubble didn't help. Kluiters began to smile.*

*"Your best bet is to keep quiet and let your face do the talking. They'll be some check points when we're traveling. I know you're Lebanese American, but this week, let's forget the American part."*

*I felt a sense of relief replacing my earlier tension.*

*"Don't worry about me, brother. I'll be Lebanese all the way." I laughed for the first time all day. It was becoming much clearer to me how Kluiters had survived the last ten years in the Bequaa.*

In the midst of meeting so many self-serving people, I knew that coming to know Father Kluiters was a blessing I was given to bolster my hope."" Why

### Entry: December 11th

A lot has happened since I made an entry, but my brother George has arrived from the United States to visit me. He arrived on the feast of Our Lady, December 8th. And we've done many things together. It's really wonderful to have someone with you to share these experiences with. He's one of fewer than 100 Americans who are here right now, and we're having no big problems. I'd like to have him exposed to all of it and see it. He's a very deep man. Last night, he said to me, "I would love to have this story told." I told him that he might get to see Ellen Franco.

When he was still in New York, my brother George sponsored a group of twenty children in an orphanage in West Beirut at St. Ailey's Orphanage. He's got some candy and he would like to go to meet those kids. After that, we're going to see Mother Teresa's sisters.

## GEORGE

*"John went to Beirut in 1984. By that time, I was semi-retired after many years in business. I had traveled extensively, but I had never been to Lebanon. I cannot remember ever feeling that I wanted to go there. In 1984, I was eager to go, for no other reason but to see John and see how he was doing.*

*"I flew into the airport in West Beirut and John came with his driver, John Ajami, to pick me up. I was very happy to see John and happy that he didn't have to do any driving. We spent the ride back to his apartment catching up on all that we had been doing since we last saw each other. The trip to East Beirut was without incident.*

*"The next morning, before going anywhere, John had Mass in his apartment. He had a desk with a shelf that pulled down and served as an altar. We had done this hundreds of times before. I got the wine and the water and John vested for Mass. When it came time for communion, John placed a host in my hand. I looked at it, and I must admit, I was distracted. The bread seemed to be moving. All I could do was think, 'What kind of bread is this?' If you've ever seen wormwood, you'll have some idea what I was looking at. There were little bugs in the host; they were eating the host. I had no option; it was a consecrated host; I put it in my mouth.*

*"After Mass, I said to John, 'What kind of bread is this? What are they making these hosts out of? He had no idea. His eyesight was never really good, and I started to think it must be getting worse. 'They're all eaten up by bugs. Get rid of them. We'll go to the sisters who make them and get fresh ones. We're doing that today.' And we did.*

*"As the days went on, I also became aware that there were mice in the apartment, and ants too. I did my best to take care of those problems. There was a heater there, but John didn't know how to use it, so I got that working and did some other kinds of mechanical jobs around the place so he would be a little more comfortable.*

*"Later that day we went to an orphanage to see some children. Actually, in those first days, I just traipsed around after John, and when we returned at night we'd talk about stuff that went on in the day. I had no idea then that this trip was the first of many that I would make to Lebanon. I never knew the tapes existed, but it's been something to hear the very words that we said to each other on that first visit to Lebanon."*

# My Mission to Lebanon

**John:**

I'm here with George and we're talking about the timelessness of some stories. There's a story here that hasn't been told, and it's part of my own story and George's. Maybe the story is a part of my own self-denial, a part of my not returning to my roots until now. But maybe I wasn't ready to come back until now. And maybe these people here weren't ready to have me come back and see them until now. I like to think about Jesus and his coming to earth. You know, he came in the fullness of time, and it was the right time. When I think about my life, maybe I needed all my 33 years of priesthood and my 56 years of living before I could come back and touch some of these things. I had to be in a certain position to appreciate what I would find, and maybe too the world into which I was coming. There is a timelessness to the whole thing. And it's nice to have George here, who's confirmed what I'm going through. He, too, said he feels like he had kind of shunned—well, not shunned exactly, just didn't feel drawn to come back here. But once here, there's something very beautiful, something untold that needs telling. It's person after person.

**George:**

I agree. I think I see that your life has prepared you to come here. I really do. I think all of the things that have happened to you have happened so that you would come back here for a particular reason. I don't think you would ever have been this effective if the things didn't happen to you that have happened to you in the last five or six years, and I'm already able to see how all of this is starting to fit in. I think that just seeing what I've seen in your office and in the places we've been in the last three or four days demands so much skill and understanding. You can be so much more effective in this office than anyone else they could have sent here now. Even the fact that you were elevated to Monsignor has been a very key point to what you're going to be able to accomplish here. I see the respect that people have for status here, and you're going to be able to do so much more because of that.

**John:**

I think my own background in Arabic has helped. I think some of the people who have headed this office may have had the objectivity of the Latin Church but didn't have some of the understanding of the Maronite culture and the Lebanese family that I guess we took for granted.

**George:**

I can see that already. I had some concern about your ability to handle the Arabic language, knowing that we've been away from speaking it for so very *long. But I have been impressed with your ability to start right back into it. And when you gave your homily in Arabic at Mass on Sunday, it was very beautiful to hear—so much more than I expected so quickly.*

### Entry: December 14th

*It's the feast of St. John of the Cross, who wrote the Dark Night of the Soul. In that text, St. John of the Cross said that it's only when everything is dark, and when nothing can be heard, and nothing can be seen, that you can begin to see and to hear that God takes everything away so that we might totally rely on Him. It's kind of a very nice night. I'm here with my brother and it's been a very happy, delightful, wonderful week with him. And he's about to be leaving tomorrow to be home with his family for his birthday on the 21st—and, of course, for Christmas.*

*Do we have a story here? Aren't there so many stories? Yes. That's why I think John of the Cross talked about the quiet. You know that, somehow, all the stories end in a story. It's very interesting how they call Jesus the Word of God. There are so many words. Everybody writes words trying to communicate, and God has a Word and the Word was made flesh, and He was born of the Virgin Mary, and it was Christmas. Maybe that's what Christmas is: a very silent night in the midst of winter.*

*It's winter here and I think that, when my brother came to visit me, it was the fullness of time and the Word was made Flesh. It was really very nice that George and I could celebrate his birthday, because he too was born around this time.*

*I love the title of 'brother' when I speak of Jesus. I learned the beauty of it from my physical brother. I think he was very anxious to know where I am; he has so much common sense and is so down to earth. He is so in love with me. We did some beautiful things together. We talked. He stayed in my little room here and he slept on the couch. It opens up. It's funny: He only opened it up one night. He just slept on the couch. He used my bathroom and my shower. He monkeyed around with things here. He found out where the thermostat was. I don't know anything about those things. He just has a very practical way about him. He fixed some things here. He fixed my watch, too.*

*I want to send this final tape off to the States with George. He can mail it for me there.*

I began to make preparations for Christmas. Since my arrival in Beirut, I had many meetings with Father Jenco, the priest I met in New York, who was the di-

# My Mission to Lebanon

rector of the Catholic Relief Services in Beirut. Larry visited my quarters in East Beirut frequently, and I assured him he was welcome to have a residence there. He said he felt good living in West Beirut and he continued to live there. With George gone home, and with no community to pray with, I decided to make arrangements to concelebrate Mass on Christmas Eve with Father Jenco. John Ajami drove me to Father Jenco's in West Beirut. We visited for a while and then proceeded to St. Francis' Church on Hamra Street, where we planned to have Mass.

When I walked into the sacristy, there was a Franciscan priest attending a Sudanese student. That young man—a very tall man who, as I learned in time, was bloodied because he was wearing a cross—had been attacked, and his attackers got away.

Larry and I talked about how hostile the area was toward the cross. I remembered my first conversation with the Mufti and I began to see the depth of the antagonism that was so foreign to my American psyche.

We celebrated the Nativity—the birth of the Prince of Peace.

About two weeks later, I offered Mass at a home for the elderly. I remember talking about how much God loves us, especially those who seem so abandoned by all. I left the altar and there was a phone call for me. Father Jenco had been kidnapped. Here was news about a man who had worked with the poor and the mentally and physically handicapped in Yemen, Thailand, and India. On January 8th, 1985, while on his way to work at Catholic Relief Services in West Beirut, he was abducted by members of the radical group Islamic Holy War.

Father Jenco would be held captive for 564 days before being released and allowed to return to the U.S. Serious eye infections and other health problems continued even after his release. Larry died of cancer in 1996. Before he died, he wrote a book entitled, *Bound to Forgive: The Pilgrimage to Reconciliation of a Beirut Hostage* in which, among other things, he described how his faith sustained him through the horrors of his captivity.

In spite of the disappearance of Father Jenco, and not knowing whether he was alive or dead, we continued to do our jobs in the chaos of East Beirut, Lebanon, so less chaotic than West Beirut. How did we go on? In faith, and in hope, and most especially in love, which may be the hardest to embrace in such times of senseless violence. And I had known Father Jenco for only months. What must his family be feeling? To think about that each day was to immobilize me. I knew my own powerlessness. I took it to prayer. I am grateful to God for sustaining Father Jenco through his frightening ordeal. I wasn't tested that way, and I am grateful for that as well.

My testing came from another source. During the first week in February of 1985, I received word from Archbishop O'Connor that I had to leave Lebanon and not return for two months. After that time, he would reconsider the situation. This news came with no pre-warning. I was told that I had to go to Syria on a fact-finding mission for the Catholic Near East Association (CNEWA). I was to do that immediately; the move was non-negotiable. I had forty-eight hours to leave. Archbishop O'Connor announced to the press that he thought I was in danger of becoming a target of the same terrorist group that had taken Father Jenco and that he had ordered me out of Lebanon. He further announced that I would continue in a "safer assign-

## Americans Told to Leave Beirut

### Esseff Won't Heed Warning

*Father John ordered out of Beirut*

ment," overseeing other programs of CNEWA. I would travel, and visit dioceses and archdioceses throughout the Middle East. I wasn't happy about my situation, but I took my orders, and I went to Syria on the first leg of a tour that would take me to many other countries to check on the work of CNEWA. I continued that mission until I returned to Lebanon in March.

*Entry: March 10, 1985*

*Today is a drift day. For the first time in weeks, I can really kick back, breathe calmly, and unravel the memorabilia of nations and towns and people in my mind. I am astounded that I've gone to so many places, met so many people, listened so patiently to so many bishops, priests, and other knowledgeable people. I cannot, however, at least for the time being, make any sense out of these past two months. I can only chalk them up to a 'head office' thousands of miles away.*

*I left Lebanon, and, as ordered, went to my "safer assignment" in Syria. Upon arrival, I was hounded by the local secret service. Twice they stopped me: once to examine my notes. They wanted to know why I had come there from Lebanon (Syria and Lebanon had been at war for two-and-a-half years), why I came on*

# My Mission to Lebanon

Election Day (February 10), why I was taking so many notes, why I had my visa on a Vatican passport when I was an American. I spent some very tense and cold hours on the Syrian border.

Once situated in my office in Syria, I got to work. I found the Syrian Christians to be a really hearty lot. It was a pleasure to get to know so many of them. It was enlightening to see those who are so open to the Syrian government, and those who resist it: those Christians who are pacified, ameliorating, those who are resisting. The people endure much physical poverty: the scarcity of food, clothing, and adequate housing. And, of course, there is the cold.

When I finished my work in Syria, I got a call in Damascus that I should prepare to go to Jordan, Cairo, and Ethiopia. I bought my tickets and went to Jordan. There I prepared my report on Syria, did what had to be done, and prepared to leave for Cairo. Just before I left for Cairo, I was told, "You may go back to Beirut—if you wish." But there were certain conditions. The plot thickened. I was informed by Monsignor Nolan and Archbishop O'Connor that I was not being sent back to Beirut. I am permitted to return under certain conditions: I am not to leave East Beirut. I am to give no interviews to any newspapers. And I must agree to leave at a moment's notice, without any questions, if told to get out of Lebanon. I agreed. I definitely got the idea that the New York power team considered me self-willed, self-centered, and blind to any but my own perspective. Permission to return was just something they would go along with, but not mandate.

Meanwhile, my visa for Lebanon expired. I had to get a renewal from the Egyptian embassy. I got in touch with Bishop Joseph Merhi (the Maronite bishop of Cairo) who had many contacts, and with their help, he got me my visa. Yesterday and today I heard some news from Lebanon. There was a blast in West Beirut that killed eighty Shiites and wounded over 200 others. A great deal of anti-Israeli, anti-American reaction has developed. The Eisenhower, a naval carrier, was alerted to take Americans out of Lebanon. While those events are playing out down coast, I'm planning to enter by boat from the north at Jounieh. I was told I could not go into Lebanon through the airport.

The back route led me to Athens, Greece, and then to Larnaca , Cyprus, where I am now. Tomorrow, March 11th, I will be in Jounieh , Lebanon.

So I have the day off. I just returned from purchasing my ticket and I can give full sway to my thoughts, my confusion, my stuffed-down little snippets of feelings, and ever present dangling perplexities. These weeks, these months have been very exciting. No doubt, our Lord has brought me here. Why is it so important for me to return to Lebanon now—a mission so inconvenient, so *expensive, so disruptive to the important work I was doing, and now, apparently so dangerous?*

*I will take one of only three boats that leave Larnaca each week. Within me, I hear God telling me, "Yes." You are to be there. You are equipped to go against the tide. I am with you. That's why you can do it—not because you're so strong, or disciplined, or capable. No, only because I am with you.*

When I returned to Lebanon in those early days of spring, I heard scattered reports about Father Kluiters. On the night of March 13, 1985, after celebrating Mass with a group of nuns at the hospital in Hermel, Father Kluiters had set out to the village of Barqa where the villagers were expecting him the following morning. He never reached the village, and there seemed to be no news of him. Not until more than two weeks later was the fate of Father Kluiters to be uncovered. In every sense of the word, he was a martyr for the people he loved. He stands as a reminder of at least ten other Jesuit fathers who died during those difficult years in Lebanon. When I returned to America, I learned that Ellen had combined an eight- or nine-line item in *The Scranton Times'* recounting the death of Father Kluiters with other details she gathered from material I had sent her, and she wrote a eulogy.

## Local Priest Sought Beirut Kidnap Clue

EXCLUSIVE

MONSIGNOR JOHN ESSEFF

*Father Kluiters' kidnapping and murder*

I am happy to be a part of the preservation of a tribute to a courageous priest who did so much for a people who became his people, and whose life said so much about his priesthood. He so deserves to be immortalized.

---

### A MAN FOR THIS SEASON

*Father Nicholas Kluiters, S.J., did a great many things with and for his people. They had been adopted by him, or maybe it was he who had been adopted by them. As a young man, Nicholas Kluiters left Holland and went to Lebanon, where he became a Maronite priest of the Jesuit order. Like all priests, he celebrated the liturgy and administered*

## A MAN FOR THIS SEASON

the sacraments. He centered his life on God and dedicated his life to the service of his people. He understood how important education was, how essential that children be sent to school. But his job wasn't as simple as putting children on a school bus or giving them a book or even teaching them—because Lebanon, for ten years, had been bombarded by the destructive forces of war.

Countless lives were lost; orphans were commonplace. It wasn't a rare child who had seen his mother or father's body placed in a body bag and taken away for quick burial. Homes and buildings were destroyed, along with churches, schools, and hospitals. The land, once oozing with richness, lay scorched and untended.

Somehow, Father Kluiters had survived the war. Maybe he was shrewd enough, or lucky enough, or brave enough, or maybe his work just wasn't finished. The fighting continued even after the war had ended. Intrigue and hatred, fear and distrust were everywhere and Father Kluiters was well aware of that. His parish was strung across the Bequaa Valley—notorious then for its headline stories of terrorist activities. He served the people of five villages scattered among the winding hills. Traveling through the Bequaa was risky business. Members of the PLO, training groups of Hezbollah, proficient Syrian soldiers, and radical groups of varying persuasions had each claimed areas for themselves. They were scattered throughout the Bequaa, often setting up check points, forbidding passage, or worse.

During the war and after, Father Kluiters continued ordinary work in extraordinary circumstances. He wanted to help the people develop what they needed to build a better life, a happier life. He wanted to share with them his priestly vision of a gentler, kinder world that made every day an adventure in discovering peoples' goodness and acknowledging the many gifts they had to share. He worked tirelessly and offered all as a prayer. He wanted to empower the people to be self-sufficient. In simpler times, he might have been the priest known as an educator, developing schools and other programs wherein people could learn. In simpler times, he might have been known as an environmentalist, digging wells and developing irrigation; or he might have been known as a social worker, building a clinic where broken bodies and minds could be healed. But Lebanon did not enjoy many simple times in the 1970s and 80s. It was a country being devoured as people scurried to gain power—in any way they could, in whatever way they understood it.

# Brothers & Fathers

## A MAN FOR THIS SEASON

Yet the truth is, Nicholas Kluiters understood power. He knew that sometimes it was good, sometimes it was evil. He knew people who used it; he knew people who abused it. He knew many people who were very powerful, and he knew many who were powerless. The powerless were really the ones who intrigued him. They were the ones who made him understand himself—who he was and why he was. Maybe that's why he decided at a young age that they would be the ones that he would climb out on a limb for.

The powerless (sometimes we call them the poor) are really everywhere. They're waiting, all over the world, for someone to come and help them. They're waiting for a hero.

When Nicholas Kluiters decided to go to Lebanon, he went only to help the poor, the powerless. He had no desire to be a hero, but he was looking for an adventure. He could have stayed in Holland, but there was so much about the Middle East that fascinated him: the people, the language, the poetry, the customs, the traditions. He really had a longing to go there. And he knew that, until he went there, the people of the Middle East would always be only people in a book.

Nicholas wasn't quite sure when he realized how many gifts he had to take wherever he went. He was strong and healthy, educated and wise, clever and brave. For him, the greatest gift was knowing that the many gifts he had had come from the powerful people in his life who chose to share their gifts with him and make him, no longer poor and powerless, but able to make his own way in the world. Nicholas might have been poor and powerless, but he was not. He always thought of himself as a prince of sorts, who was so full of power because of the many gifts that he had. When he was born, like all of us, he came naked into the world. His parents clothed and fed him, they spoke to him, they taught him to pray, but most of all, they loved him. They who were so strong when he was so weak, they who had so much when he had nothing, chose to love him, and that is why they gave him so many gifts. They sent him to school. He met friends and teachers there who gave him many more gifts: gifts of knowledge and experience, and gifts of friendship and growth into manhood. He knew when it was time for him to share his gifts.

In Lebanon, Father Kluiters had hundreds of opportunities for doing that. He was a gatherer. His people clustered around him and learned from him. He became a

---

### A MAN FOR THIS SEASON

*constructive force amid tremendous destruction. As the years continued, he was responsible not for churches, or clinics, or schools, or wells or irrigation ditches, even though they too became realities. He was responsible for people—stronger people, people ever ready to try again, gifted people.*

*Not everyone understood power like Father Kluiters. Some people believe that destroying someone makes them powerful. They are afraid to let other people develop their gifts, because talented people can always be a threat.*

*One day, weeks after the disappearance of Father Kluiters, a young shepherd boy saw a suspicious horde of crows over a 300-foot-deep gorge near the village of Nabha, and he notified some people in authority about what he saw. The next day, men went and pulled the partially decomposed body of Father Kluiters from a well. His knees had been shot, his groin had been electrocuted, his fingernails had been pulled out and, finally, he was strangled.*

*The people mourned the loss of their priest. They mourned the loss of their friend, especially since each of them was richer because of him. Each one of them had new gifts and had learned that all that they were had been given to them by someone more powerful than themselves, someone loving and caring.*

*Nicholas Kluiters taught them that. It was a gift he gave them and, in some mystical way, he lives on in each of them, defying the power that amuses itself by thinking it can really destroy something as powerful and pervasive as the Spirit. Father Kluiters accomplished what he set out to do. He met his people, he shared an adventure, he gave many gifts, he remained true to what he believed in, and he gave his life for those beliefs. Some people use another name for people like that; they called them saints. Maybe he is one. It's hard to say, but when they get to storytelling, the people of the villages of the Bequaa have a tale about a favorite hero of theirs. It begins, "Once a young priest came to us whose name was Father Kluiters...*

---

Father Kluiters was buried during Holy Week, on Wednesday, April 3rd. For years previously, he had portrayed the Christus in the reenactment of the events of Holy Week. How fitting that he was taken home that Holy Week to meet the God he had served so well.

While it was still unknown what had happened to Father Kluiters, the story of another man's journey into terrorism unfolded. On March 16th, Terry Anderson, the former chief Middle East correspondent for The Associated Press, played tennis with a photographer friend of his. After the match, the two started home in Terry's car. They were accosted when a Mercedes pulled up and three bearded men jumped out of the car. Both Terry and his friend knew they were in trouble. Terry was dragged out by one of the men and pushed into the Mercedes. They drove off toward the Green Line, and that was the beginning of Terry Anderson's captivity, which lasted for almost seven years. At one point in that captivity, he shared a room with Father Jenco. Anderson was the last of more than a dozen American hostages held in Lebanon from 1982 until 1991. What better commentary on those years can there be than Anderson's own words?

## POEM BY TERRY ANDERSON, WRITTEN IN CAPTIVITY

### I

*Five men huddled close against*

*The night and our oppressors,*

*Around a bit of stale bread*

*Hoarded from a scanty meal,*

*And a candle, lit*

*Not only as a symbol*

*But to read the text by.*

*The priest as poorly clad,*

*As drawn with strain*

*As any, but his voice*

*Is calm, his face serene.*

### II

*This is the core of his existence,*

*The reason he was born.*

*Behind him I can see*

# My Mission to Lebanon

*His predecessors in their*

*Generations, back to the catacombs,*

*Heads nodding in approval,*

*Hands with his tracing*

*Out the stately ritual,*

*Adding the power of their suffering*

*And faith to his, and ours.*

*III*

*The ancient words shake off*

*Their dust, and come alive.*

*The voices of their authors*

*Echo clearly from the damp,*

*Bare walls.*

*The familiar prayers come*

*Straight out of our hearts.*

*Once again Christ's promise*

*Is fulfilled, his presence fills us.*

*The miracle is real.*

Though there is a lot of pain in these stories, there is so much to be admired in those who stood firm in their convictions even while their freedom was taken from them. I am proud of the priests and others I was privileged to know who, personally, went to the wall for what they believed. They had no desire to kill anyone. But they put themselves on the line for what they believed, and for those they loved. Doing something because you love is so different from doing something because you hate.

# Brothers & Fathers

On the heels of the tragic death of Father Kluiters, and still uncertain as to what had become of Father Jenco and Terry Anderson (and so many others), I continued my work. The country had been in chaos for more than a decade. The seeds of hate were all around: car bombings, abductions, bloody clashes between Christian and Muslim militias, random explosions, plane hijackings, and assassination attempts were commonplace. In the wake of that kind of madness, thousands were suffering. Different organizations continued to seek help for the victims from the Pontifical Mission.

But always there were the little ones who needed care—the ones who most particularly caught my attention. One such little one came into my life that late spring. One day, a Carmelite priest came to my office and told me that a baby had recently been left in their orphanage in the village of Ain Saadeh, about ten kilometers northeast of Beirut.

I thought this might be a baby I could very easily place. When I was preparing to go to Lebanon, my cousin, Darlene Sahd Terranova, told me that if I ever came to know of a baby in Lebanon who was abandoned or orphaned, she and her husband would be willing to adopt the child. So I told the Carmelite priest that I might have adoptive parents for the baby. I got in touch with the Terranovas to make sure they were still interested. They were delighted. I started to move the adoption along.

In the Lebanese legal system, the Church has the legal power to arrange adoptions, and so this adoption would have to go through the ecclesiastical court. I got in touch with the Latin rite bishop in Beirut and began to expedite the matter. Things went along well until, finally, Frank and Darlene filled out the appropriate papers and, in the midst of some other details, the time came for the baby to go to the United States. In order for the baby to be admitted into the United States, he had to go through the closest American embassy. That would be the embassy in Nicosia (in Cyprus). I planned to get the baby to Cyprus and there I would meet the new grandfather, who would transport the baby to the United States to meet his parents. By that point in the adoption plans, my brother George just happened to be in Beirut for another visit. As he heard more about the baby and the plans for adoption, he said, "You know, John, I'd be willing to take this baby with me when I return to America. I'm going anyway, and I'm sure I could meet the grandfather in New York and deliver the baby to him there instead of having him come all the way to Cyprus, then turn around and go back to America." So we discussed the matter. I had a lot of objections.

# My Mission to Lebanon

"George, this is a *baby*. Do you know what you're getting into? I know you're willing, but …"

"John, I'm a grandfather. I've taken care of my own four babies. I have grandchildren. I know how to handle this. Trust me; I can do it."

I had to admit it: I didn't have that expertise. I knew I'd be willing, but—wow—I also would be wondering, "What am I going to do with a baby on the long trip from Lebanon to New York?" But George was insistent, in spite of all my words of caution. On and on he went, and so he talked me into accepting his offer.

In a spirit of supporting my brother, I said, "Here's what I'll do. I don't think you should go by yourself. I'll go with you to Nicosia. Maybe because of my status here and because of my Vatican passport, I can be an asset to you in getting you and the baby out of here." George was willing to accept my proposal and I made arrangements to travel with him to the embassy in Nicosia.

When the time came, George and I went to the orphanage to pick up the baby. I remember the scene vividly: a nun coming down the stairs carrying a baby. I've done a lot of things. I've lived through a plane crash, an earthquake, and two floods. But when that nun came toward me and George and plunked down a baby—a living, breathing, totally dependent human being—all I could think was, "Oh, my God. Help us here!"

The sister turned over the baby. Then she handed us a bag and said, "There are enough bottles of formula here for the baby until you get to New York. There are also plenty of diapers for the whole trip."

All I could think was, "This is going to really be something!" Then George and I took the first step in our 'journey of a million' miles. We took the baby and headed out. We went to the dock in Jounieh, Lebanon, bought our tickets, and finally boarded a ship to Larnaca in Cyprus. I remember the captain of the ship was a Polish communist.

George handled all the details for getting a room on the ship. The trip was going to take about eight or ten hours. A lot of people just sat on deck chairs for that entire trip. Considering we had a baby as a traveling companion, George arranged to get a state room. He also arranged to have a crib put in the room for the baby.

# Brothers & Fathers

## GEORGE

*"We boarded, but the ship hadn't yet embarked. It was getting awfully warm in the state room, so I decided to open the hatch window. On the hatch, there was a big brass nut for opening the hatch. I unscrewed the nut, but twisted it too far, and the nut (which was pretty heavy, maybe a pound or two), dropped right down in the middle of this little guy's head, and cracked it open. Blood was squirting all over the place. I told John to get a handkerchief and put it over the cut, and told him to apply pressure. I went and got the steward of the ship, who came back with me to our state room. We were able to get the cut to stop bleeding by applying the right amount of pressure. I made a butterfly bandage and put it over the cut. Finally, the bleeding stopped.*

*"In the meantime, the baby was doing what babies do best: screaming his head off. In time, the trip wasn't too bad, because the baby was either knocked out or exhausted from screaming.*

*"We arrived in Cyprus about ten hours later, got off the boat, and jumped into a cab to start toward Nicosia, which was close to an hour's drive. When we got there, we checked into a hotel very close to the American embassy, where we planned to go in the morning. So far, we were managing.*

*"In the hotel, John and I had two single beds with a crib wedged between. It had been a long day, and we went to sleep about ten. A few hours later, maybe around midnight, the baby began to scream—really scream. I got up and went to the crib, and (for want of better words) there was shit all over the place—much more than seemed possible from this little guy! What neither John nor I knew was that the formula we had been giving him was a different brand from what he had been accustomed to since birth. The sisters gave us the formula and we went on our merry way; we had no objections. The only objections were coming from the baby's bowels.*

*"Putting a towel on the bed, I lay the baby on the towel and cleaned him up—no small job! By this time, I knew the diapers were at least two sizes too big for our little guy. Everything leaked out of the sides, all over the place, but there was nothing else I could do. I cleaned him up again and, just as I was ready to wrap him up, he shit all over the bed again.*

*"What could I do? I knew John wasn't really asleep; but, quite frankly, I also knew he wasn't going to be any help. He played possum, so I went along with it. He had never pretended to know anything about babies. I did. I filled the sink with lukewarm water. I put the baby in the warm water to comfort him. The baby proceeded to do just what*

---

### GEORGE

*he had been doing: cleaning out his bowels—endlessly. I was sure he was never going to stop. Of course, to make matters worse, all this time, he was screaming at the top of his lungs.*

*"Finally, I got the baby cleaned up and put a fresh diaper on him, but he wasn't quieting down. I needed help. I called Rosemary. 'What can I do with this baby? He's screaming like hell!' I told her about the never-ending bowel movements. She was full of suggestions. I can honestly say, I didn't want suggestions; I wanted Rosemary to appear magically and take over. That was not about to happen. So I settled for suggestions. 'Maybe he's full of gas. Start pumping his legs,' she said.*

*"By this time, John couldn't fake sleep any longer. I told him, 'Rosemary said to pump his legs.' We pumped him and pumped him and pumped him. It seemed we pumped him long enough to get oil. Then came other suggestions: rub his belly, try to get the gas out, comfort him. But all that time, we didn't know it was the formula.*

*"Somehow, we got through the rest of the night."*

---

In the morning, after George took care of the bill and we were leaving the hotel, he said, "Do you know how much that call to Rosemary cost?" Considering how long he had been on the phone, I didn't think $100 was out of line.

We moved into the day with a baby whose bowels were locked in the 'open' position!

At that point, we didn't have a lot of options. At the embassy, we completed the paperwork necessary to get George and his little charge in flight. I was there, in my cassock and my red sash. I was really playing the part of the monsignor, the person in charge of the Pontifical Mission, and hoping that persona would help us out with a ten-pound baby who was, without a doubt, calling the shots. The woman we met at the desk was also calling the shots. She quickly ascertained that neither of us was the baby's grandfather. So George began telling her the saga of his 'good deed.' She was not impressed, and at first said there was no way she could allow this. She asked us a million questions. She assured us that this type of thing was not allowed; it was against orders. We both continued to try to persuade her that we were just trying to get this baby to his adoptive family. It was not an easy task. By some miracle, finally, she said, "I'm going to let you do this, but it's against my better judgment. I'll let you take this baby, but as soon as you get to New York, you will have to call me. I'll give you the number where you can reach me and I must talk to the baby's grandfather. If that doesn't happen, there will be real trouble."

So there was my brother, holding the baby, bowels locked in the 'open' position. Some time had passed while we were under interrogation, and the baby's diaper needed to be changed again. George asked the woman (second-in-command only to the baby) where he might be able to do that.

"You'll have to do that right here. The only other place you might do that is a restroom here in the embassy, but I can't let you go in there."

If I had any influence at all, this was the time to test it.

"Couldn't you do it ... for this little baby?" Again and again, I pleaded. Finally, she acquiesced.

## GEORGE

*"I went into the bathroom and changed the baby's diaper, wrapped up the soiled one and put it in the trash. Then I went back out to the area where John was filling out a lot of papers. Our next step was to go to a doctor to have the baby undergo a complete physical. It was important to ascertain that there was nothing wrong that would prevent the baby from getting into America. Meanwhile, John continued to fill out papers. The woman at the desk said, 'When you get all of the papers filled out and you have the medical examination report filled out by the doctor, come back tomorrow morning and we'll finish processing all of the paperwork.'*

*"I was quite sure I did not want to stay another night, if there was any possible way I could avoid it. I spoke right up: 'If we're able to get all the papers filled out and get the medical examination done before the embassy closes, can we come back and finish so that I can fly out of here tonight?'*

*"'Certainly, if you can; but I don't think you'll be able to do all of that today.'*

*"I was up for the challenge. We went to the doctor and got a full examination done on the baby. We left quickly. John hailed a cab, and we went back to the embassy. As we got out of the cab and were walking up to the entrance of the embassy, a marine guard said to us, 'Man, you don't know what the hell you caused us here today!'*

*"'What do you mean?'*

# My Mission to Lebanon

It took us about an hour or more to get back to the seaport in Larnaca, where I could get a ship back to Lebanon so that George could fly out for London and then on to the United States. I knew there was a lot facing me when I returned to Beirut, but somehow, at that moment, my upcoming challenges seemed easier than what George was facing.

As wild as that experience was with little Joe Terranova, it was a happy one for me, mostly because I shared it with my brother George. It took me out of myself and gave me cause to continue to hope for other little ones.

Yet, on a-day-to-day basis, there were always the ones whose needs were not easily filled, whose pain could not be erased quickly, if ever. Each one had a story to tell, painful and gripping but untold to the world at large. I met a young seventeen-year-old girl, Maria, who spoke about the feel of a gun held to her neck by a Druze militiaman, who demanded that she deny Christ. She refused. The militiaman shot her and left her for dead on a road in her mountain village. Red Cross workers found her unconscious there the next day. The bullet, which pierced her spinal cord on that day in 1983, left Maria paralyzed from her neck down. Maria spoke of her reaction: "At first, when I was shot, I forgave him, but it wasn't really with conviction. Today, the forgiveness comes from my heart. I am a Christian, and Christ wants us to forgive others. The man who shot me didn't know what he was doing." She told me she knew why she didn't die: God wanted her to forgive her assailants and pray for them.

I met a man in a Palestinian camp. Only after talking with him did I learn that he, too, was a priest—a Greek Orthodox priest living in this camp, abandoned by his congregation. His name was Father John Hbu-Hamra. We talked for a long while. He had not received the Eucharist for a long time, so I celebrated Mass by his bedside and gave him communion. The Mass ended with two priests blessing each other.

As spring grew into summer in Lebanon, I became aware that I had to deal with some personal matters. Since I was a young boy, I had always had poor vision (as well as other difficulties with my eyes). I had had a detached retina, I suffered from glaucoma, and I had had numerous surgeries on my eyes. During my first year in Beirut, my vision had become progressively worse, partly because I was not getting the kind of routine care I had available at home. I knew I needed surgery, but the kind of laser equipment I needed was not available in Beirut. If I did not go home, I faced the prospect of a dark future. Hoping not to live the rest of my years as a blind man, I made arrangements to go to America to get the care I needed.

## Clergyman Returns from Beirut To Undergo Eye Surgery Here

By JOSEPH X. FLANNERY
Times Special Writer

Monsignor John Esseff, a Scranton Catholic Diocese priest who has been [on] assignment since last October in [Beir]ut, Lebanon, is back home to have surgery.

[Th]e 56-year-old priest said he will [und]ergo surgery at Mercy Hospital on [We]dnesday.

[A]n eye condition requiring surgery [was] detected recently by a physician in [Bei]rut, so Monsignor Esseff decided to [ret]urn here to have it done after [at]tending a meeting with church officials last week in Rome.

Last week Mrs. William Nasser, 1015 Electric St., Monsignor Esseff's aunt, revealed that his relatives and friends were expecting him to attend an Esseff family reunion here on Aug. 4.

Monsignor Esseff said his plans after his eye treatment is completed are indefinite. He said he will confer with officials of the Catholic Near East Welfare Association, an organization headed by New York Cardinal John J. O'Connor, former bishop of Scranton.

While Lebanon is a nation of great turmoil, aggravated at the present time by Shiite Moslems holding passengers of an Athens-to-Rome TWA flight as hostages in Beirut, Monsignor Esseff said he would prefer not making any public statements on events in that part of the world.

"All I can say is that I am home for eye surgery and I'm not sure yet when I will be going back," the clergyman said.

Monsignor Esseff's assignment was for a year. In addition to being in Lebanon, he also has spent time in Ethiopia, Syria, Jordan and Egypt.

Several factions of radicals in Lebanon have said they want all Americans out of that country. Seven Americans are now being held by the shadowy terroristic group, Islamic Jihad.

Monsignor Esseff's job is to carry out welfare programs of the Vatican mission in Lebanon.

*Home for surgery*

# My Mission to Lebanon

EDITOR'S NOTE: *In need of medical attention, Father John returned to America in 1985.*

*At that time his family had a reunion; people were invited to come and see their old friend, home from the war. I went to the Mass he had there that day. Many other people did, too. These were my thoughts that day. I wrote them when I returned home that evening:*

## Friends Honor Monsignor Esseff

Scranton - Monsignor John Esseff, the representative of Pope John Paul II at the Pontifical Mission in Lebanon, will be honored by his many friends at a family-type celebration at the Esseff family grove off Layton Road in Chinchilla on Sunday, August 4.

Monsignor Esseff will be principal celebrant of an outdoor Mass scheduled to begin at 10:30 a.m. A brunch will follow during which time, Msgr. Esseff will share his experience in Lebanon, the war-ravaged nation that is the homeland of his parents.

Ang Cicotti, general chairman, has announced the following committee aides: Catherine Nasser, Gladys Kellar, Plymouth; Joe Trovato, Jennie Motter, Jackie Hass, and Kay Sweeney. Tickets may be obtained from any of the committee members.

**Msgr. Esseff**

*Creating community in a field*

---

## A REFLECTION

Some drove in; others walked. Some were bumped along in wheelchairs by friends; a few managed well with canes. Curious children ran down the length of the pebbled dirt road to discover what might lie ahead. Businessmen in lightweight summer suits and high-heeled women, like misplaced pieces of city, walked awkwardly through the open field. Young men in jeans and rock concert tee-shirts bounced past them in Nike sneakers. A man in the only clothes he owned kept pace as everyone moved on towards the shaded area made dark by the thickness of the tall pines.

A pavilion roof arched protection for the early morning chefs from the rain that never came, and ceilinged in the smell of coffee, brewing robust and fresh, and sausage so savory on the outdoor grill that folks could almost taste the smell of it.

That would wait.

Several hundred people trickled into the country grove to celebrate reunion with Monsignor Esseff who, to most, was still 'Father John'—the priest who loved to pray, the priest who loved to love, the man who had been father or brother to each one

## A REFLECTION

there—briefly, but long enough and tenderly enough to heal the wounds of each one's broken heart or mind.

People alone, in twos, in small groups, even some families continued through the aromas of the covered kitchen to the open end on the far side, some twenty feet away. One step after that, each one entered a cathedral. How old it was, yet new! How simple, how majestic! Trunks of tall, sturdy trees, growing, who knew how many years? Had that growth been for today, to stand as immovable pillars blossoming in shades of lacework green? Farther on, cat-o-nine-tails stood in clusters near the rim of the silver shimmering lake amid tall, sleek reeds swayed by a warm, gentle breeze.

And a new breeze was blowing.

Father John arrived. He emerged from his car and moved toward the table set between the pillars of bark in front of the sacristy of the lake. Family and friends greeted him, detained him. He paused. He smiled. He hugged. He walked among the old, the White, the crippled, the young, the Black, the babies in their mothers' arms. He approached the altar, blazing white and warm from the sky's single candle, and within minutes began to say his familiar 'hello:'

"I greet you in the name of the Father, and of the Son, and of the Holy Spirit."

From that moment on, he was transparent in the mystery of the liturgy, and peoples' hearts were touched in a way that only Jesus could do—in and through the power and surrender of the priesthood. Every word he said loved the people; every gesture; every prayer loved and embraced them. Everything that he is was poured out for them.

Make me a channel of your peace.

We stood before the Lord—alone, broken, empty, full, cold, aching, joyful, frightened, needy, warm, content. And then Jesus allowed Father John to take his 2,000-year-old body, forever young, and break it once again, so that He could come to each of us in our separateness that day to say:

'I am with you. I love you. I know all the joys and burdens of your heart. I know even those things that you cannot find words for. I understand those, too ... even though you do not ... even though you cannot even name them. I am still unfolding in you. Be patient. I love you. I will make you whole.'

Father John rejoiced in his brother Jesus.

# My Mission to Lebanon

## A REFLECTION
~~~>

*And everyone in the cool woods was part of a family once again, because it is in a family that we are born and live, laugh and cry, hurt and heal. It is in family that we learn to love and to pray and to say 'Thank you!'*

*Everyone in that family remembered that Jesus really loved him, because He had sent Father John to say, "I love you."*

*It was hard to tell if the warmth was the sun or the love and peace that was flowing from one another—standing hungry, once again, before the table of the Lord. It was hard to tell if it was the soft morning breeze or the Spirit that moved through the fingers of the trees. It was hard to tell if it was just a little boy fishing on the makeshift dock jutting out on the lake where the dragonflies flew, or if it was Jesus, telling the story of a fisherman without using any words.*

*It was easy to know that a mystery was unfolding. It was easy to tell that there is power in prayer. And it was easy to tell, once again (because he had so dedicated his life to it), that Father John had created community in a field full of people who knew each other only in God's love.*

*It was the miracle of the Eucharist.*

*And hearts beat 'thank you' for Father John, who knows so well the love of the Lord and the joy of dedicating his life to spreading the Good News that is ours in the God of Love. Father John has revealed his brother Jesus to each one there—one by one—and now we know that He is our brother, too.*

*The day was a day of whole-ness.*

*It was a holy day.*

After several weeks, during which I underwent necessary operations on my eyes, I began making plans to return to Beirut. While I was in America, I took the opportunity to try to explain what was going on in the Middle East and to make people realize the plight of the people living there. I knew how difficult it was for them, as it had been for me, to comprehend the vast differences between the events of our lives and to interpret the ramifications of those events. When interviewed, I told the people at the local paper, *The Scrantonian*, that I was "hoping to continue to bring the message of what is most beautiful in America and in the Church. Regardless of outward circumstances of creed or culture, Americans and the Church are willing to bring all they can to help bring healing to a bleeding, war-torn nation and its people." I did take advantage of my time in Scranton to speak to many groups about what was happening in Lebanon.

I left Scranton and went to New York to see the newly elevated Cardinal O'Connor. His elevation had occurred on May 24, 1985. He had sent word for me to stop in New York to see him on my return to Beirut. During that visit, I can honestly say, I was blindsided. It took some time, but slowly I began to understand that those in command did not want me in Lebanon. In the face of so many abductions and rampant violent acts in Lebanon, most particularly in West Beruit, I could understand their concerns; but I disagreed with their thinking. That they wanted me to join them on a journey to Africa, which was next on their agenda and which slowly unfolded, completely bewildered me.

Cardinal O'Connor had made plans to go to the northern section of Ethiopia, a place called Eritrea. He wanted to make an assessment of the needs of the people there who were the victims of famine. He was taking people with him: some from the New York media, some from diocesan newspapers, representatives from Catholic Social Services, Monsignor John Nolan, and me.

We left New York and went to the capital of Ethiopia, Addis Ababa. From there, we were going to be flown to Eritrea. In the airport, everything stalled. We couldn't continue to fly to Eritrea because the area between there and Addis Ababa was ravaged by war. The dominant political power in Ethiopia was Russia, and we had to depend on getting permission from the Russians who were in charge. There were helicopters that were supposed to fly us to our destination. In no time, we learned that those helicopters were not going to take us. Why? We were Americans. There we were, a great big entourage of American dignitaries, stranded. We were nowhere near the site of the great famine area that we had come to see. Cardinal O'Connor was furious because he wanted to have a film

SCRANTON, PA. FEBRUARY 10, 1985

# Bishop, Area Priest Visit Famine Area

By TERRY BONIFANTI
Times Staff Writer

There are two things Monsignor John A. Esseff always will remember about the famine-ridden people of Ethiopia — their pain and their joy.

During a telephone interview from his office in Beirut, Lebanon, the Scranton Diocesan priest spoke of both the pain of the Ethiopian famine and of the joy with which the African natives received the former bishop of Scranton, New York Archbishop John J. O'Connor, during his visit to their nation last week.

"I think I'll always remember the pain," said Monsignor Esseff. "I don't think I'll ever forget that.

"Starvation is a terrible thing. I would go to bed at night and I couldn't sleep. I could see the faces. You know how when something happens and it's on your mind and you never forget it? I could see the scrawny limbs. I could see the sunken cheeks and the burning eyes in their faces.

"But I also could see the beauty, and the joy, and the way they would just come right up to you. And the happiness. I'll never forget those things."

Monsignor Esseff, the former Lackawanna County Prison chaplain who now is assigned to the Catholic Near East Welfare Association's Pontifical Mission in Lebanon, was one of five people representing the association on the trip.

Archbishop O'Connor is national president of Catholic Near East.

Their trip full of pain and joy was designed, Monsignor Esseff said, to bring renewed attention to the plight of the starving people as well as to

many other parts of the country is untouched by the famine, was a two-hour plane trip away.

The pain Ethiopians are enduring was evident from the moment the group's DC3 touched down at the center for famine victims near Makeley, Monsignor Esseff said.

The climate at Makeeley features 110-degree days followed by nights in which strong 50 and 60 mile per hour winds whip a chilling cold through the desert.

"One of those in our party had a thermometer on his watch," recalled Monsignor Esseff. "It was 198 the day we were there. We all got sunburned."

The residents of the relief center seem to suffer more from the climate than visitors, he said.

That cold wind and plunge in temperature each night wreaks havoc on the small bodies of the starving. Small

## Address Listed For Donations

Scrantonians wishing to donate to the Catholic Relief Services famine relief programs in Ethiopia should send their contributions to: Ethiopian Relief Services, in care of The Diocese of Scranton, 300 Archbishop John J. O'Connor Plaza, Scranton, Pa. 18503.

Donations to the Catholic Near East Welfare Association's needy child program, which is supporting about 6,000 children in orphanages and schools in Ethiopia and Lebanon

tents all most have to protect them against the night elements, Monsignor Esseff said.

The relief center with its hospital and tent city is one of the places Catholic Relief Services is distributing food and care to the famine victims.

"It was my most, most unforgettable experience," Monsignor Esseff said. "Makeeley is a town, and the famine victims come to the center outside it from all over the countryside. There was a child there, someone was holding this child in the hospital. This child looked to be about 3 with her little arms and legs, the sunken cheeks, those burning eyes, but we were told she was 12.

"So much is being done in these centers. But it's staggering. There are 7 or 8 million people starving and the programs are reaching only about 1.8 million."

The stories he has to tell of Makeeley are bittersweet.

He was overwhelmed by the spirit of those already at the center, and deeply saddened by the bewildered, abandoned look of those just wandering in.

And he was overcome with a need to find some way to assist in a brand-new problem that is developing in Ethiopia — children, the only remaining members of families wiped out by the famine.

"One of the strongest pleas I heard when I was there come from the doctor in Makeeley," the clergyman said. "He told us 70 percent of the children who come into the hospital will live. But no one visits them or asks about them

*Famine in Eritrea, Ethiopia*

made that would show the devastation of the people. There was a fellow there from Catholic Relief Services (CRS) who was supposed to have had set up all of these particulars. CRS had more people on the ground than did the Catholic Near East Welfare Association (CNEWA), of which I was a part. CRS was much larger than CNEWA and had millions of dollars for relief services.

A very curious thing occurred in the midst of the confusion. On the other side of the airport, we could see Mother Teresa and two of her sisters. While Cardinal O'Connor was reprimanding the man who had not cleared our way, Mother Teresa approached the pilots and, speaking in Russian, gave them her blessing. I guess she effected a change of heart. They boarded.

Much later, in spite of the difficulties we encountered, we finally did get to Eritrea. I stayed with Cardinal O'Connor at the nuncio's place where the Eastern Rite archbishop arranged hospitality for us. Those who were not clerics stayed in local hotels in the city. The next day, we walked in procession to the cathedral, and had Mass. In all honesty, I must admit that what struck me first was that all of the images of Jesus and Mary were Black. It gave me pause: What did American people of color think as they entered our churches?

In Eritrea, after Mass, we moved to the food distribution centers. The streams of skeletal people who came to the food centers etched a permanent picture of famine in my mind and in my heart. We stayed in the area for almost a week. People were walking in from miles away. They were looking for food and water. Some had traveled for hundreds of miles, from areas where no crops could grow. They were hoping to get bags of wheat, corn, flour. The bags had the letters 'CRS' written on them.

As the days passed, Cardinal O'Connor told me that he wanted me to leave the Beirut office and serve as director of the Catholic Near East Welfare Association there in Eritrea. I had no desire to do that. I was accustomed to buying groceries for people who had no money. The truth be told, I did not know how to begin to feed thousands who were hungry. I did not want to be in charge of an organization. I did not want to do that kind of work. I did not have the gifts that were needed for that kind of work. I hadn't signed on to do that work. After much disagreement, I left Africa, flew to Rome and then returned to Beirut. Monsignor Nolan was furious with me.

All I could do was focus on those I saw all around me who had such desperate needs.

# Brothers & Fathers

Each day, I met people who had stories to tell, and my heart longed to have those stories told. Perhaps if I could tell their stories, there were those who could help. These, the innocents, lay heaviest on my priest's heart, and I knew how powerless I was to stem the tide of all that was going on around me. An added level to all of these situations was the conflict between religious ideologies that erupted in violent acts, based on interior belief. I am grateful that I eventually did write about that phenomenon.

### Entry (no date)

*There is no scarcity of events to write about; everyday events that surround me always seem extraordinary. I had made a promise to write simply as an exercise each day. The discipline needed for that, I believe, is lacking in me, but the idea of writing a book has been growing in my mind for years. I have waited for the opportunity, and I believe that time might be now. Yet each day my energy is spent ministering to those I can. Maybe someday ...*

*In February of 1986, I attended meetings in Rome, during which I hoped to share my ideas with Cardinal O'Connor and others from the Catholic Near East Welfare Association. Unfortunately, my ideas did not prevail, and on February 28th, I was told by Monsignor Nolan that Cardinal O'Connor requested that I prepare to leave Beirut after Easter. I was hoping this order for me to leave Beirut would end as the one in 1985 had, with my return. I wrote to Cardinal O'Connor and told him of my plans:*

*I leave my post April 1, 1986. Sister Maureen Grady, recently acquired by our office, has been appointed acting interim director. At a staff meeting I simply stated that I was leaving for a period of time to perform a special assignment ... The people have no reason to believe I am not returning ... I am planning a retreat, a visit to some relatives in Australia, some fishing in Hawaii with my brother George, and back to New York by the end of May. I would be available to return to Beirut, if you so decide. I could introduce the new director when he would be assigned, acquaint him with the various aspects of the work, stay a short (but appropriate) time and give the staff and a few friends an opportunity to say 'farewell.' Asking you to consider this request, open to your decision ...*

On March 10, 1986, I received a response from Cardinal O'Connor in which he wrote, in part:

*I asked John Nolan to tell you I was and am extremely concerned about your safety and health. I told him I felt we had put you at risk too long, that we were taking advantage of your generosity, and that I would feel responsible if something happened to you.*

# My Mission to Lebanon

He understood that I did not want to leave, but he had made up his mind.

*"Whatever the case, it is ludicrous to suggest that you were fired. I have a serious problem in filling that job. It would have been easy for me to leave you there as long as you would stay—if I didn't have a conscience! You are in my Masses and prayers."*

I left Lebanon in April of 1986, just before the new Patriarch Nasrallah Pierre Sfeir was elected. Throughout this period, there was much confusion. I began to realize that a return was not part of the plan, and I suffered greatly, feeling I was being let go without cause.

I wrote much of what I was thinking as those days unfolded: some thoughts in Beirut, some as I traveled, and some after I arrived home.

## THE END OF MY MISSION IN LEBANON

### Entry (no date)

*The reality of separation is gradually sinking into my consciousness and I have many mixed feelings about "coming home." For someone who's been away for a while, coming home can be work—sometimes painful, not always smooth—because nothing ever remains the same. I have always been aware of that. Now, perhaps, it is I who no longer remain the same.*

*I went to Beirut in October of 1984 filled with expectancy and concern, and maybe even a sense of adventure and curiosity about meeting a people from whose hearts and minds I had emerged a Lebanese American. When I arrived there, I thought that I would experience firsthand the land that was gently tucked away in my heart, mostly through stories told me by my grandfather more than half-a-century before. And in spite of all the confusion, turmoil, and war, my stay in Lebanon grew very quickly into my new world: my parish, my new associates, my friends, and my ministry. Lebanon and its people had quickly become my home.*

*In retrospect, my stay there seems little more than the blinking of an eye. Eighteen months after I arrived, I was told by my superiors that I would have to leave because of the intensity of the political situation in the Middle East and the special danger to Americans. I felt embarrassed for what I thought was an irresponsible and hasty decision on the part of the Catholic Near East Welfare Association to recall me from my post at the Pontifical Mission at that time. Coupled with those feelings of embarrassment was guilt. During the previous eighteen months, only the barest skeleton of a structure had been put together. Naturally, my preference was to stay and at least complete the tasks I had begun. I had been forbidden to explain to any of the petitioners or those visiting* the office for other reasons that I would be leaving the country within weeks. I was being less than honest in allowing the people to think that I would be continuing in the job, and the guilt feelings were spilling over into my personal relationships. Those closest to me were aware of my withdrawal, my change of attitude, my lack of spontaneity. Those very subtle kinds of feelings that only friends can detect were becoming obvious. I simply avoided questions and remained silent or chose distance. I spent most of my time arranging my work and facilitating the continuance of the mission. The very last weeks, days, and hours were crowded with work. Only two days before my departure did I reveal to chosen and specific persons that I was, in fact, leaving Lebanon.

I had used a lot of energy to control all forms of anger, hidden resentment, bitterness, and sorrow. I had chosen to ignore my feelings of sadness, anxiety, loneliness, and self-pity, and tried to see each day's happenings as a new gift of God preparing me in a new direction. The final hours were so crowded with work, public appearances, and physical preparations for leaving that all of the feelings that normally would or could happen did not surface.

The night before I left, a group of friends had gathered to have an informal farewell. There were just a few, maybe twenty, very dear people—each one a life I had touched and who had touched my life in some meaningful way. Amid the pain, the tenderness, and the love, I recalled the words that so often in the past (and so powerfully in that present) gave expression to the feelings gripping me then. Once again, I had "dreamed the impossible dream." I had really "fought the unbeatable foe, borne unbearable sorrows and gone where the brave dared not go." I had tried to "right the unrightable wrong," and when my "arms were too weary," I "reached for the unreachable star." That was "my quest," and I was willing to "march into hell for a heavenly cause."

When I left for Lebanon from Scranton, I had really accepted the idea that they might even "lay me to rest, scorned and covered with scars." But I hadn't considered the possibility of the reality I lived. It was not Jihad, nor the Hezbollah, but my superiors who had laid me to rest, and the scars that I carried from Lebanon were injuries of the heart. As I readied to leave, I could almost hear people who would meet me on American soil with "Welcome home!" and I didn't know how I would explain it, because I knew in that moment that Lebanon was home. I wasn't going home; I was leaving home. ...

When we were young kids preparing for Confirmation, we learned that we were "soldiers of Christ." In those difficult last moments, I tried to console myself that way. I thought, "It's true. A priest is like a marine. You have a job to do. You do it, and when it's done, you leave. In my confusion and self-doubt, I left Lebanon on April 14th, 1986, the day before American war planes made an aerial strike on Lybia.

# My Mission to Lebanon

*Days later, I saw the joy and the welcome and the relief in my mother's face. My dad loves me and encourages me to do what I want to do, yet he knew intuitively that there was, inside of me, a poorly masked sadness. But with all that, he was also happy that I had returned. It was there, in the face of my own parents, that my deepest feelings of priesthood surfaced.*

*Just as my mother and father could not forget me, I couldn't forget my new family, the children of my promise. Even as I am looking at these words and writing them, I am feeling the pain that accompanies them. I am aware of a truth that lies deep within me, a truth I am eager to embrace.*

*One day, as I sat with my father, he told me that my mother had suffered two slight strokes and that her blood pressure was very high. I don't think he said that to make me feel guilty. I do think that my being in Lebanon caused her a great deal of anxiety, even though I tried to allay those anxieties by frequent phone calls and letters that let them know that I was well. Yet there are no ways to really control the feelings and concerns of parents. The truth is that, as I sat there, I truly knew their sacrifice in freeing me, so long ago—letting me go and always supporting me in my work. I knew that I was not the only one who paid a price. Maybe what I had forgotten was how high their price tag had been.*

*Being with them and sharing with them was much like sharing the joy and satisfaction of grandchildren. I was able to tell them, as their son, about my children, but I really never was able to explain to them that, when I was away, I was home. Even to them, I was unable to voice my deepest feelings of priesthood. I was deep inside myself. I ached with the knowledge that I was a father who had left a sick child, perhaps even a dying one. I was never really able to say it—I guess, because of my own inner discipline that wasn't allowing me to experience my own pain before I could share it with anyone else.*

*These days, when the feelings of separation are welling up in my consciousness, when I wake up and find that my bed is not in Beirut, I feel lonely and so deprived of motivation that the very center of my life—the celebration of the liturgy—is different. Each liturgy that I celebrated in Lebanon was filled with expectancy and strength, and the needs of the immediacy in the tragedy that surrounded me and in which I was immersed. Now it's not the dullness of the small talk about the Boston Celtics or the drop of enrollment in Catholic schools or what we're going to have for dessert or how my new car is running that is so deadening. It's not the absence of the bombs and the shells and the bursts of flame and the sighs and the screams of Beirut that makes the difference. It's that I, within myself, feel so useless, so ordinary, so unnecessary, that makes holding the Body and Blood of Jesus so different in my feelings. It's only in recalling what that Body and Blood really meant there that I am held to believe what that means here. There exists a central mystery of life and death. As a celebrant,*

# Brothers & Fathers

*I am not the only one who can create an atmosphere of the importance of that event. Only the community that surrounds the crucifixion and death of Jesus in a living way creates the climate that makes what liturgy is appear to be what it really is. In Lebanon that happened.*

*My re-entry is dominated also by my own inadequacies and feelings that I will no longer be able to share the suffering, the agony of the Lebanese people. Yet each day that I rise, I feel the burden of their cries and my own inadequacies as I call out for help. As I am reminded and reflect on the anguished cries of pain, I am set in contrast to the listless, preoccupied, uninterested, overindulged faces that I look at each day. The ineffectual words that I have to tell about the death of a nation get stuck in my throat. Sometimes they don't even get past my thoughts because my better judgment tells me that the hearers aren't interested and really don't give a damn, or even worse, will manage some politeness until I'm done talking and then will go on with what they want to say. I find in myself fears that tend to paralyze, anxieties that blind, and a darkness that causes me to remain motionless.*

*Yet, with all that, there is much good happening inside of me that prevents all those demons of doubt, darkness, despair, and frustration from dominating me. I have a deep sense that all of these feelings are necessary, all of these emotions are notes that eventually will play a part in a larger symphony that gains voice day by day. These feelings will carry me into new places in search of new people, new modes of expression, new avenues for telling the story.*

*Now I know I have a message for the whole world:*

*There is a child who lies ill. She is poor. She has no one to care for her. The whole world sits in judgment of her and places the sins of centuries of hate at her feet. Yet she is quite lovely, though quite needy. She looks to the world for understanding and care. She is the face of young and old. She is light and she is dark. She is Christian and Muslim. She is Jesus and she has sent me to tell you her story.*

I have no desire to rewrite history as I experienced it in Beirut. I also have no desire to argue with the feelings I recorded in the past. The mission was a difficult one, interlaced with political, religious, military, and terrorist overtones. Yet, in the midst of all that, I was privileged to have been able to serve there. In spite of the frustration that permeated so many days, each day was a gift as well as a challenge.

In Lebanon, I experienced God's amazing artistry as He touched my brother and me as we went 'home.' George and I always felt the power of God's life in each of us. He has always blessed us with gifts, very different gifts. In Lebanon, He presented us with many of the same people and events, and gave each of us opportunities to serve the poor, in and through the unique gifts He gave to each of us.

I will forever be grateful for the time I spent there, and even for the pain I endured for what I could not accomplish there. I am also grateful for the support I received from George throughout my entire mission. He didn't just visit me once, but many times; and by some grace of God, George has continued to learn about and to respond to the many needs he saw there in ways I could not: the orphans, the unschooled, the sick. He has also maintained close ties with members of our extended family there, has opened new doors for many of them, and has been a great help to many others in the Lebanese community.

I left Lebanon in June of 1986, and went home by way of Australia. I met George and Rosemary there in Sydney, and then went with them to Hawaii, where

they had a home. It was good to be with them there as I began what I knew was going to be a difficult reentry. Only days after I arrived, George and I came home from fishing. There was a phone call from California. George received the news that his youngest daughter, Denise, had suffered another grand mal seizure. We left immediately for California.

*George and Rosemary's home in Hawaii*

# CHAPTER 43

## MEMORIES OF DENISE

### *The Family*

#### ROSEMARY

Denise arrived in sunny California a happy, healthy baby on July 19, 1960. Having three older siblings to entertain, watch and learn from, she was eager to join them in their adventures. She couldn't wait to go to school. When she did join them, she worked very hard at doing well, and was always a good student. For Denise, education was all about competing with herself. School kept her challenged and never seemed to bore her.

She also enjoyed all of the socializing. Little by little, throughout her earliest years, Denise joined Mary Ellen and Kathy in their pursuits of music, art, and crafts. Later, in high school, she also joined them in sports. In the midst of so many other interests, she was really drawn to health care, and that interest began when she was very young. Denise had a lot of contact with those in the family who were aging. Mother and Dad lived with us, and George's mom and dad were close by. When Denise began college, she lived, during the week, with Aunts Sarah and Marian, whom she dearly loved. Her experiences were so positive that it seemed natural when she chose to study the field of gerontology. In high school, she did volunteer work at Mary Health of the Sick Convalescent Hospital in Thousand Oaks. She was a candy striper and that work helped form her life choices. She could see so much humor in the aging process, not the dullness and other negatives. She would come home with story after story relating so many humorous things that happened with the elderly. Many times, hearing her rendition of daily events, we would all look at each other, and think, "This girl is balmy." She and her brother George always had the same kind of "Far Side" humor which they found hysterical, but which left the rest of us feeling that perhaps they might need some professional help. All of the children were helpful in caring for my parents. Young George would take Dad wherever he needed to go, and Dad really enjoyed being around the young people. Of course, my parents enjoyed all of their stories very much. They never seemed to see themselves as elderly.

## GEORGE JR.

Denise and I were very close. She understood my sense of humor and we connected really well. She and I were appreciative of the same 'warped'-type sense of humor. While she and I laughed uncontrollably about something or other, the other members of the family looked at us in total confusion.

She was, for sure, a true social butterfly, always involved in some special activity. Her dating situation seemed to be relatively steady. I can name a few who became long-term fixtures around the house. In school, she was a scholar, but not a know-it-all. Outside of the social and school scenes, she enjoyed doing volunteer work with the sick and, most especially with the elderly.

There was a simple holiness about Denise. She had a kind of special thoughtfulness, an understanding, an insight into the interior of people, especially those who may have had difficulties. I believe she was able to help others think things out.

We also both got along well with Dad. We understood him and that also gave us a special bond.

## ROSEMARY

Denise had a very busy social life in high school. Many interesting boys from varied backgrounds were her friends. There was never a dull moment. The girls' voices were very similar and very few people could identify which of the girls was speaking on the telephone. I discovered that the different beaus, unknown to them, were being passed from one of the girls to the other for telephone conversations. The girls thought this a bit of harmless fun, which took me quite a while to figure out. I don't think the young men ever did.

## MARY ELLEN

I have to be honest. I was always envious of Denise's style, beauty, creativity, and magnetism. She was the kind of girl whom everyone noticed when she entered a room. She was meticulous about her appearance, shoes and purse (matching, of course)—and how she loved to accessorize! She could get away with things no one else could, and looked really spectacular. She had style with a capital 'S.' She had such grace and charm that, whenever she was in a room, people just wanted to be around her.

She was never without admirers. Denise always had someone pursuing her and looking for some encouragement. It took a lot of doing for her to manage all the young gentlemen in her life without hurting anyone's feelings. Whenever a 'hopeful' did not become a romantic interest for Denise, she continued to be friends with him. If anyone tried to push her to make a commitment, she would end the relationship and let things cool; but then, somehow, in her own inimitable way, she would stay in contact and continue to remain friends.

## ROSEMARY

Besides spending time with her friends, Denise was attracted to the 'broken winged' types. In high school, she was a member of a peers' hotline, set up so that students could call a peer in emergency situations or discuss a pressing or important issue. She would come home from school, and as soon as she walked in the house, the phone would start to ring off the hook. She spent many hours helping others, and then she would have to finish her school work after midnight—or even later. Finally, I had to curtail her hours by imposing an 11 p.m. curfew for incoming calls. Without that curfew, I'm sure she would have been available all night.

She didn't have a car of her own, and on occasion she would borrow mine. While she was volunteering at the local convalescent hospital, we had the infamous Rolls Royce. Denise used it to get to work when there was no other car available.

One time, a doctor made fun of her when he saw her arrive in "that great car" to do volunteer work! She understood the implication: She was a spoiled, rich kid. She came home that day very upset, very hurt. To think that he could say such a thing about her was devastating to her. She was so perplexed. She never thought of herself as a privileged type, and certainly never acted that way. She never thought she was better than anyone else. Denise never put on airs. She loved the simple things in life, and the beautiful things as well. Besides having a great sense of style, she was quite artistic in other ways. She loved holiday decorating. We deco-

*Rosemary and Denise at Halloween*

rated for every holiday on the calendar, and not just the family room but all through the house. She motivated all of us to get into the spirit of each particular season.

With so many varying interests and wonderful friends, Denise spent her high school years in a whirlwind of activity. She was in the National Honor Society and had no problem getting into the University of California, Northridge, in the San Fernando Valley after she graduated. During her freshman and sophomore years, she stayed with George's Aunts Sarah and Marian during the week and came home on the weekends. Then she made plans to transfer to the University of Southern California, which was in a high-crime area in Los Angeles. That was a concern of ours.

## GEORGE

I dealt with a Japanese firm that had an office downtown. The firm changed its personnel every five years, and generally the families lived in LA. When Denise was ready to transfer to USC, I knew the man who lived in the downtown area with his family. We worked things out so that Denise was able to rent a room in their home. Denise took Japanese courses in school. She was able to help the man's wife and children with English and, in turn, his wife taught Denise Japanese. It was a great opportunity for her to engage in conversation. She learned the feminine Japanese— the polite form that women of the upper class in Japan spoke. She became very knowledgeable, not only in reading, speaking, and writing the language, but also in the customs and traditions. It was a win–win situation. She spoke excellent Japanese and we were all impressed by her abilities. Whenever I had to make a trip to Japan, I tried to make it possible for Denise to come along. We had a condo in Japan for some time, as well as an office. It was to her advantage to go with me—or with Rosemary and me. In time, it was to our advantage to have her with us. She was able to help us out quite a bit. The men I did business with there were much taken by her. She seemed to have the same effect on them as she did on the young men at home. She was strictly interested in friendship only while she enjoyed wonderful experiences in Japan. She also considered getting an advanced degree in Japan at Sofia University in Tokyo after she finished her Bachelor's degree at USC. The Japanese were very interested in western ideas concerning the care of the elderly at that time. Denise was the only one of our four children who took those early trips to Japan with Rosemary and me. They remain as special memories for both of us.

# Memories of Denise

Denise also accompanied Rosemary and me to London. Perhaps because of her trips there, she decided to study at the Birkbeck College Summer Institute at the University of London. She spent a semester there studying art history.

## GEORGE JR.

When I returned home from college, Denise and Kathy invited me to join a young adult group that they were involved in. At the time, I thought joining would be a good chance for me to meet new people. Little did I know what trouble I was in for! That story, I'm keeping for a book of my own.

All three of us spent a lot of our free time together—group parties at the beach, dinners, and the infamous Saints and Sinners softball team. Denise was a good athlete and very competitive.

When I was managing an orange orchard in Ojai, I lived in an old ranch house. Denise would come up to visit and we would walk through the rows of trees and talk about life, about people we knew, and about our faith in God. I think we were both going through some discernment as to what God had in store for us. We were both wondering if we were going to remain single, though neither of us wanted that. We started going to a charismatic prayer group, and we enjoyed that.

When I first started working at Supra Alloys, Denise was having health issues. At the time, she was being told those conditions were related to allergies, and then later, to epilepsy. She was looking to keep herself busy without getting involved in a lot of stress, so she worked in the office answering the phone and typing test reports for orders. She always kept the mood light; she was fun to work with. She was a pretty good typist, but at one point, I remember her having difficulties doing the work, and she began to complain about her head and hands not working right. Little did we know what her problem really was.

## KATHY

When I think of my sister Denise, I remember so much more than words can capture. It never ceased to amaze me how smart she was, and how easily things came to her. From the time Denise was very young, she loved school and learning new things. I remember when she chose to study German in high school and was a member of the German Club. In case that wasn't tough enough, she began an intensive study of Japanese when that opportunity became available to her during her college years.

# Brothers & Fathers

There were so many times in the summer we enjoyed together. We would lie out in the sun on the patio and work on our California tans. We'd sip our TAB sodas while we talked about plans for the upcoming weekend, what the date situation was, and whatever countless other things young girls talk about.

Denise loved animals. When Mary Ellen and I were in our teens—fourteen and fifteen, as I recall—we really enjoyed our horses. But Denise didn't care for that big an animal. Instead, she chose for herself two beautiful bunnies. I don't remember the breed—the ones with the big droopy ears. They were cute and Denise loved them. Then our dogs discovered the bunnies and chased them all around the yard. Under those conditions, the bunnies didn't live with us very long!

Denise loved life, and sports were an important part of life for her. She was a great swimmer and a great softball player. She usually played first or second base. When she would get up to bat, she would grab the bat and flip her hips to get into a good hitting stance. The guys loved to tease her, especially at those times. She was just so pretty.

*Denise golfing*

Like so many other things, sports came easily to Denise. An exception was skiing which, at first, was frustrating for her. By the time she was eighteen, Mary Ellen and David were married and had a daughter, Michelle. I remember that winter, the three of us took Denise to Badger Pass near Yosemite. It was her first time skiing, but she was very athletic, and she assumed it would be like any other sport. (Translation: for her, easy!) She was at the top of the beginners' run and we had worked with her a while. Mary Ellen, David and I took turns helping her up the lift, and then we watched her come down the slope. She got in her snow plow stance and, very slowly, started down the hill. We watched her, and it seemed as if she was barely moving: She looked like she was operating in slow motion! Her first run must have taken her almost a half-hour. But so like Denise, by the middle of the day, all of a sudden everything clicked and she was heading down the hill with the rest of us.

A couple days later, we were coming around a corner of the intermediate run. I knew Denise was ahead of me, but when I came to the turn I couldn't see her. There was a huge drop as I came around the bend, and I thought maybe she had gone the other way. All of a sudden, I heard a noise to the side of me. I knew there were a lot of trees there and a really big snow bank. As I took another quick glance, I saw Denise plunged head-first into the soft snow. She was struggling to get out, but the harder she tried, the more difficult it became for her to get out. By the time we arrived to help her out of the bank, she was laughing so hard that none of us could do anything but join in her infectious laughter. She told us the snow was in "every place" she could imagine, and she couldn't believe we had to pay to have such fun. She became a great skier, and we enjoyed many trips together.

## SHERRIE ESSEFF

I met my husband, George Jr., through the Young Adult Group at St. Paschal's Church. Later, when I met his sisters, I realized that I had gone to school with Mary Ellen and Kathy. I didn't really know them because, at that time, we had different groups of friends. As I came to know them, I wasn't surprised to discover that they were all very close to one another as sisters, and were good friends with one another too. Because one of the things that drew me to George was how family-oriented he was, I really wasn't surprised that his sisters were also the same. It was hard to tell if Mary Ellen and Kathy were Denise's friends, which they were, or her sisters which they were. How nice that you choose your sister as your friend.

## KATHY

Denise made me feel special in the many small things she did for me. I know she also made others feel special, too. She was so well liked and had so many won-derful friends. When I began to date Michael, the man who would become my husband, Denise just loved him. She and Michael became very close. She was so happy for me. Mike had some health issues (not as severe as those of Denise) and they would talk about how they had to deal with those health concerns. They were able to relate in many ways because of what was happening at that time in both their lives.

I know that for Mike, Denise was like the sister he never had. She made us laugh and we had such a special bond with her. Finding out I was pregnant was such a joyous moment for Mike and me. When

*Big and little Dee*

our daughter was born in 1983, it was only fitting that we would name her for Denise, a young woman whom we both loved very much—a woman of courage, a woman of faith. Denise always called our daughter "little Dee," and took such great delight when she could hold our little baby in her arms. It meant so much to her. And when she came to know how short her own life would be, she told all of our children to pray to her whenever they needed help and she would be there for them always.

As Mary Ellen said, Denise had a flair for clothes, and she always looked spectacular. Just like Dad, she was always looking for a great sale. We enjoyed many shopping days when we would be gone all day hitting the malls and not getting home until early evening. Mom, Mary Ellen, Denise, and I enjoyed those excursions time and time again. Poor Dad never had a chance with all of us girls, but he never seemed to complain about any of that.

Denise loved sending funny cards to anyone at any time. We would go to Hallmark on the Oaks in Thousand Oaks. I would be done and move on to another store, leaving Denise still looking at cards. I remember one time I must have been gone for well over an hour or more and then I was trying to find her. I couldn't find her, so I thought she must have gone on to another store. All of a sudden, I heard Denise laughing very loud. She was still in the back of the card shop, picking out someone's upcoming birthday card, and enjoying every minute of it.

Denise's poetry was a help to all of us during those challenging times when she was dealing with life-and-death issues. She loved to write poetry and she loved to read the works of the Lebanese poet, Kahlil Gibran.

Besides her love of poetry, Denise had a great spiritual life, even from her youngest days. Prayer was very important to her all through her life. Everyone could perceive her spirituality and that drew so many people to her.

## SHERRIE

When I first met Denise at the Young Adult Group, we weren't really friends because she was a little younger than I was. I can remember how I admired her ability to talk with authority on so many subjects. She had a great sense of humor and she commanded a presence in any room she was in, probably without realizing it. She was a beautiful young woman with a uniquely exotic Lebanese look. She drew the young men to her like fireflies to a flame. While she was definitely pretty on the outside, she also had an inner glow—a spiritual beauty that emanated from within her, as well.

# Memories of Denise

## MARY ELLEN

Before it was determined that Denise had a brain tumor, she suffered with many things that were the unrecognized symptoms of a condition that had been completely misdiagnosed by her primary physician. She did spend a lot of time feeling "pretty lousy." In her junior year of college, Denise had her first grand mal seizure. We were at the bridal shower of her best friend Linda. Both Kathy and I were with Denise at the shower and, during the festivities, she excused herself to the ladies' room, saying she wasn't feeling well. When she was gone for what seemed too long, I went to check on her. She said she felt nauseous, and thought she was going to be sick. She said, "I hate when this happens," and then she fell backwards towards a glass shower door. I was so glad I was there with her. I caught her as she fell. Because I was a nurse, I suspected that she was having a seizure. We called 911 and rushed her by ambulance to the hospital, where we met Mom and Dad. There, I was able to tell the doctor what had happened. Prior to this event, Denise did suffer with auras, headaches, and vomiting, but what occurred that day was much more severe. Denise was kept in ICU for several days and went through many tests. The doctors worked on stabilizing her.

And so it began: neurologists, CAT scans, drugs, but still—seizures or ill effects from the medications she was taking. Denise's doctor couldn't seem to figure out why she was having seizures. All he could find was a shadowy area on the CAT scan that he could not identify at the time. His most adhered-to diagnosis was that she was having allergic reactions to something. He prescribed medicines that were generally indicated in the treatment of allergies; by and large he was practicing holistic medicine. Dad suggested to the doctor that he do an MRI, which was cutting-edge technology at the time, but the doctor kept insisting that the seizures were related to allergies—or possibly epilepsy. An onset of epilepsy did not characteristically occur in a person who was twenty, which Denise was at that time. As it turned out, the prescribed medications were not only ineffective, but contraindicated for what Denise was actually experiencing at that time.

The medicines were ineffective: either too weak to stop the continuing seizures or so strong that they created a plethora of side effects. Denise's struggles with her illness, which we eventually came to know had been egregiously misdiagnosed, continued for years. She had a difficult time with medications aimed primarily at preventing seizures. Some she couldn't tolerate because of the side effects; some had few side effects but were not strong enough to stop the seizures. It became difficult for her to maintain her college schedule. She'd go to the college, get some work, and try to keep up. She spent a lot of time seeing doctors. Eventually, she had to take a year off from her studies. She tried to stay active; she exercised, especially by swimming, something she always loved. She had wonderful friends and they also kept her busy. After a year, she went back to school and was able to resume her studies. She still had her symptoms, but she stuck with her college agenda. Denise continued forward. She graduated with honors in 1983 from the University of California with a B.S. in Gerontology.

## ROSEMARY

Throughout this time, when Denise wasn't away at school, she was living at home. The school was not a great distance from home, and she made it a practice to come home for weekends. Mother's health had failed considerably by then, and she was also with us. We were still living on Yucca Street, and all of the other children were married. In spite of their own family commitments, everyone helped with Mother when they could. George was really very attentive to her and, of course, Denise (our live-in professional in gerontology) was just so loving. She was quite young when my parents came to live with us, and so she was pretty much raised with them. Mother and Dad had their own bedroom; but otherwise, we all shared the same house. They never interfered, and they really enjoyed the kids. The feelings were mutual. They were very content. Even before Dad passed away, Mother was very arthritic, and that condition worsened over the years. Denise, from her early years, made caring for her grandparents a priority. Even when she was still in college, and even as her own health was declining, she looked forward to taking care of

'Mom Mom' (as she called her) on weekends. After a fall in June of 1983, Mother continued to become increasingly more debilitated. That year, Denise bought a small Christmas tree to put by Mother's bed. That was to be her last Christmas. On January 7th, 1984, George and I needed to go shopping to pick up some groceries. Mother had been in and out of a semi-con-

*Denise and her 'Mom Mom'*

scious state for some time. Denise assured us that everything would be fine; she would be with MomMom. We weren't gone long, but when we returned Denise told us that Mother had just passed away. Although I was saddened that I hadn't been there, it seemed fitting that Denise was. They had such a wonderful relationship; and, for both their sakes, I found comfort in knowing that it was Denise who was the one to be with Mother at the moment of her death. Another comfort for me was that Mother was not really totally aware of the gravity of Denise's illness and was spared that sorrow.

About a month after Mother passed away, Denise came to me and said, "I had this dream—or, I think it was a dream, but I felt that I was awake. I could see MomMom and I said to her, "MomMom, you look so happy."

"Yes," she said, "I'm very happy." And that experience, whether a dream or otherwise, I think was very healing for Denise in her loss. It was not the only time she had an experience like that.

## MARY ELLEN

For a long time, David and I had suspected that Denise would probably never have children of her own. In 1985, as David and I awaited the birth of our fourth child, Kimberly, we invited Denise to come into the delivery room with us when the time came for the baby to be born. We wanted Denise to share that wonderful experience with us. We have always been so glad we did that.

## SHERRIE

For some reason, my babies were all quite content to remain in utero! At the end of nine months each of them needed some gentle persuasion to make their grand entrance into the world. I always had to be induced. My doctor and I had a great rapport, and I told him I would like to pick the date of the baby's birth. George and I wanted to have our baby on Denise's birthday. It was our little secret. With the cooperation of a wonderful doctor, and the blessings of a loving Lord, Andrew John was born on July 19, 1988. Denise was in Hawaii with her parents at the time, so my husband George called to relay the happy news. Since Hawaii has a three-hour time difference from California, Denise thought Andrew had just missed her birthday. When we got all the time differences sorted out, it was clear: They shared the same birthday. Denise was so excited. It was a great birthday gift for her. Now, each year on Andrew's birthday, we have another occasion to think of Denise and keep her memory alive.

# Brothers & Fathers

## MARY ELLEN

In 1986, after more than five years of declining health, Denise had another grand mal seizure. Mom and Dad, along with Father John, rushed home from Hawaii, where they were vacationing together. Denise underwent many tests, including an MRI that showed, without question, a brain tumor—an astrocytoma, a very 'leggy' tumor that extended into many areas of her brain. It had been growing so many years that it was the size of a baseball and was, of course, life threatening. Dad was so understandably upset with Denise's primary physician that he made arrangements for her continuing care with other physicians. Dad was in a cheese business for a time with a Dr. Steve Bass, who was instrumental in organizing that care for Denise. There were other physicians involved, all working at the clinic that was owned by Dr. Lantanzi, a friend of Dad and Mom. Dr. Raphael Queones was the first neurosurgeon who said he could remove the pressure but didn't think anything else could be done. However, when he opened the port, he was able to lift out seventy-five percent of the tumor. It was really a miracle for all of us. About three hours after the surgery we were able to talk to her. She was blessed with none of the side effects that Dr. Queones said could occur, such as blindness and paralysis. We were so grateful for that news. Dr. Queones said that the residual tumor might not grow, or it might remain dormant for months or even years. That was the hope that all of us hung onto.

## KATHY

When Denise was diagnosed as having a brain tumor in 1986, I was pregnant with our second child, Clifton. Some members of the family thought it best not to tell me about Denise, because of the pregnancy. Coupled with Dad's history of having his own sister's impending death kept from him and his family for so long, and given the reality of Denise's situation, Dad told me that Denise did, in fact, have a brain tumor. My husband Michael was concerned about me hearing the news while I was home alone and due to deliver in a week or two. Nonetheless, Dad dealt with things as he thought best. In light of his own history with his sister, I can understand why he thought the way he did.

## ROSEMARY

Throughout these years, George's mom and dad lived nearby. Though living in a place of their own (unlike my own mother, who shared our home), they were very much aware of all that was happening.

# Memories of Denise

## JOHN

"I had been aware of Denise's continuing struggle with ill health for some time. When I returned from Lebanon in 1986, I traveled with George and Rosemary when they took Denise to Germany in the hopes of finding some effective medications that were available there, but not yet approved in America. As Denise's prognosis seemed more and more life threatening, George and Rosemary were willing to try procedures on the cutting edge. They were endlessly in pursuit of anything that could help her. In 1986, I went to visit George for Christmas and my mother was in the hospital. She had suffered a fall and was unable to walk. I remember Mom saying to me at that time, "I do not want to see another death. I do not want to see Denise die.

*Denise and Sithue*

"The next month, on January 21, 1987, I got a call from California. By that time, I was living at St. Theresa's parish in Shavertown (a town not far from Wilkes-Barre, where I had taken the assignment of administrator). I immediately thought of Denise. I was mistaken.

"The news was quite unexpected: It was Mom who had died. I made plans to go immediately to California. When I got there, I learned more about just how difficult Denise's illness had been for Mom to deal with. It was almost as though she had willed herself to die, unable to face the prospect of seeing her granddaughter die— just as she had seen her own daughter die so many years before.

Her words from my last visit to California were clear in my mind.

"Even as George and Rosemary continued to deal with the prospect of Denise's impending death, they opened their home to family and friends as they made arrangements for Mom's funeral, and we began to consider how best to deal with the fact that Dad was now alone."

"A cluster of sadness had come to visit us once again."

413

# Brothers & Fathers

## MARY ELLEN

In spite of the significant losses we shared as a family, along with Denise's enormous health issues, she maintained what might be described as a 'normal' schedule. She always had many boyfriends. Even when she was undergoing operations and was very sick—and bald as a Q-ball—she had two male nurses chasing her. Only Denise! But among her many suitors, the one who never gave up was Joe Ortiz. Denise dated him off-and-on for some time, but insisted she wasn't serious about him—in spite of his continual proposals. He was thirteen years older than she, and at times she expressed feelings that that age difference was too great. During their ongoing relationship, Denise went to the east coast to visit Father John and stayed there for some time. While she was there, she realized how much she missed Joe, and that "missing" was a new feeling for her. When she returned to California, she was so delighted and happy to see Joe. She continued to devote a lot of time to prayer. After a special novena to St. Theresa, she finally decided to say "yes" to the next proposal. It came when Joe got down on his knees in the vegetable department of the local grocery store and, once again, proposed. We were so happy for them. They knew what the odds were. Joe said he didn't care how much time she had; he loved her and wanted to spend whatever time she had with her. They were married on November 13, 1988. Everyone commented on how beautiful and happy they both were.

*Denise as a bride*

## GEORGE JR.

I developed a close friendship with Denise's husband Joe, especially when she was sick. We spent many hours together sitting and talking next to Denise while she was bedridden at home. It helped both of us get through that very difficult time. Even today, Joe and I are still good friends. I think our friendship would make Denise happy.

# Memories of Denise

## MARY ELLEN

Everything in Denise's life had her unique imprint on it. At the wedding, in the midst of tremendous love, great joy, and unwavering hope, there was also her touch of humor. We learned that Denise had sat four old boyfriends at the same table. None of them was aware that they had a common link! By the end of the evening, the news had finally surfaced, and there was general amusement—as well as quiet admiration for the young woman who had such a gift for nurturing friendship. I don't know anyone else who could have pulled that off. The wedding was spectacular, and Joe and Denise began their married life—a life they would share for a year-and-a-half.

## ROSEMARY

Unfortunately, Denise's tumor started to grow again within a year after her first operation. I would usually drive her to visit several doctors and the trip would register about 175 miles when we visited all three of her doctors. The radiation would leave her extremely tired, but she often wanted to stop at one of the malls so we could shop. I marveled at her ability to keep going, not to give in. As the girls often said, "She had a way of putting clothes together," and she would take every opportunity to enjoy her flair for fashion, even when she was so sick. And still, for Denise, any item was better if it had the magic word 'SALE' on the tag. We knew every store from Santa Barbara to Santa Monica to Beverly Hills. She had a favorite shoe store near UCLA where we'd go often—we would go anywhere in God's creation to get a pair of shoes at a discount! That's what made it fun for her: getting a bargain. I wonder where she got that? Shopping was a small pleasure for her—a way of feeling normal. I was happy to go on those excursions when she was still at home with us.

With the resurgence of growth in Denise's tumor, we were advised to see a Dr. Black at UCLA, a well-known neurosurgeon. He was a man of extraordinary talent who dealt with cancerous tumors.

## GEORGE

Years later, in the fall of 1997, Dr. Black's picture appeared on the front of a *TIME* magazine special issue under the title "Heroes of Medicine." Looking back, we certainly had the best in the business. According to *TIME*, Dr. Black was one of only fifty neurosurgeons who could be considered brain tumor specialists at that time. Dr. Black did operate on Denise once, but unsuccessfully. It would not be until a decade later that powerful new technology became available to doctors which, in the gifted hands of a Dr. Black, might have saved her. Denise was in the heart and hands of God.

The way Denise handled the news of her impending death led us to believe that maybe she had some foreknowledge about the shortness of her life. I remember when we first got word of the tumor which would eventually take her life, the three of us (Rosemary, me, and Denise) left the doctor's office and went to St. Paschal's Church. We prayed and had a conversation there. She didn't really seem that shaken by the news. She never lamented anything; she was remarkably accepting. I remember her saying, "Thank God it's me and not either of my sisters. They have children who need them." As I recall, she didn't cry.

## GEORGE JR.

Denise accepted her illness, as well as the suffering and pain that came with it, with a lot of grace. It wasn't that she didn't ever complain; there were times when she got frustrated and really mad, but she offered up all those difficulties. She didn't know why, but she was going to make sure her suffering wasn't wasted. I always thought there was a tremendous power in that.

What she went through in the last months of her life brought us all closer together as a family. I know that seeing her suffer was really difficult for my parents, especially Dad. He is the ultimate 'fixer,' and Denise's illness was something he couldn't fix. My family and I tried to stay close at hand. I would stop to see Denise after work, and my wife Sherrie would bring the boys to see her. Denise always loved having the boys around.

Denise's funeral Mass was a real testament to who she was. It was concelebrated by all the priests who knew her, and the church was packed. She had a great send-off. I think of her often looking down on us all. I know she is in heaven. I always ask her to keep an eye on our five boys, and to ask God to help them make good decisions, and to keep them safe.

## ROSEMARY

Denise had always had some sort of metaphysical connection with George's sister Mae Ann—although she, of course, never knew her. She did hear about her over the years, but her relationship with Mae Ann seemed to transcend just knowing simple facts. Somehow, Denise seemed to 'know' her in a deep, spiritual way. Denise had a similar type of relationship with Padre Pio and, during her final days, that relationship became quite clear to us. She told me that Padre Pio appeared to her several times while she was in the hospital. She said that she had a waking dream, and Padre Pio told her that the reason Dr. Queones was able to get so much of the tumor out was that Padre Pio held her head in his hands during the surgery. Another time, she expressed concern that Joe would have trouble accepting her death. She prayed a lot to Padre Pio whom, she said, came to her and told her that it was not yet her time. On another occasion, Joe was in a chair outside the room and heard Denise say the Spanish word for uncle, Tio. He went into the room and asked her about what he heard. "No," she said, "not Tio. I'm talking to Padre Pio. There, don't you see him, by the window—there!" Joe did not see him.

Padre Pio brought Denise a great deal of comfort during those difficult days.

## MARY ELLEN

When Denise was dying and we had the children around her, she told them that she would watch over them from heaven. She loved all of them. She had often said that, since she couldn't have children of her own, ours were hers. Also Denise told Joe that she would find him a good woman after she was gone—though she was quick to add, "She won't be quite as good as me!" In time, Joe did meet a very lovely lady whom he married. She had never been married before, and now they have two boys. What a great blessing for him.

Denise went to the Lord on August 4, 1990. I was with her when she took her last breath. She had been in a coma many hours. I knew that, after her last breath, she was no longer stuck in that body. I knew that she was high up, floating above, and I looked up expecting to see her. I didn't see her, of course, but I was able to let go of her physically, and that gave me a lot of peace. I had told her that I want to see her when I get called to heaven and that, if she could, please save me a seat next to her.

## SHERRIE

I knew Denise only a short time, but time enough to grow in admiration as she exhibited such amazing faith, grace, and dignity in the face of her own mortality. She was an inspiration to so many people—and still is. Her love for her nieces and nephews was tremendous. She promised to watch over them all from heaven and to intercede for them in all their needs. As we watched our five boys grow into manhood, George and I have no doubt that she is doing just that. It was a privilege to have had her as a sister-in-law, and I know she loved me because she knew how much I love her brother and our wonderful children.

## MARY ELLEN

Dad's brother, Father John, has always somehow been around when there were difficult times. After Denise's funeral, I was standing in the kitchen near him. I asked him how we were going to be able to continue without Denise; the void was so enormous. He told me that, when his sister Mae Ann died, he knew he couldn't be with her physically, and so he began a spiritual relationship with her—praying to

*In difficult times*

her, talking to her in his heart. I took his suggestion to heart, and that's what I have done. Anytime an emergency happens, small problems or big ones, I call upon Denise. She always solves things. An answer always comes.

## ROSEMARY

I can attest to that. Mary Ellen's children were in 4H and involved in the raising and showing of goats. Sometime after Denise's death, Mary Ellen and the children were taking their herd of goats to show—they had maybe fifteen or more goats. From the start of the day, Mary Ellen was a bit frazzled. She had a hard time getting all of the goats into the trailer so they could be on their way. The goats were running all over, and I remember her telling me, "I just about lost my mind getting started and I was afraid we would be late." At any rate, they did get to the arena and the show continued until about eleven o'clock that night. She was so exhausted. The 'kids'—both hers and the goats—were tired, too. The same kind of confusion that had dominated the morning continued throughout the whole day. Now with a long drive ahead of them, Mary Ellen was faced once again with a scattering herd of goats. She was at her wits' end and she heard herself say, "Denise, I'm calling on you right now. Get moving up there! I have to get these goats into the trailer. You have to help me if I'm going to get home at all tonight. I'm tired; everyone's tired; and if I have to run after these damn goats again, I don't know if I'll be able to keep my head on my shoulders." Mary Ellen told me all about the night and said, "Mom, can you believe it? Every one of those goats walked right into the trailer. I couldn't believe it! I banged the door closed and said in a loud voice, 'Thanks, Denise. I really needed that. Thanks. Thanks again.'"

## GEORGE

There are so many little things to remember about Denise. One of my favorites is a card she gave me on Father's Day when she was thirteen. At that time, we had no inkling of what the future held. I am glad I kept the handmade card she gave me that Sunday.

| | |
|---|---|
| *June 16, 1974*<br>*A Spritual Bouquet*<br><br><br>*2 Our Father's*<br>*10 Hail Mary's*<br>*3 Glory Be's*<br>*1 Holy Communion* | *Dear Dad,*<br>*I hope you have*<br>*a very happy Father's Day*<br>*You're the best of the best!*<br><br>*God Bless ya always*<br>*Love ya bunches and*<br>*bunches* |

## ROSEMARY

What a great blessing Denise was—and is. We thank God for the great gift she was in our lives, a source of tremendous joy to all of us. That joy turned to sadness when we lost her. We miss her laughter and her love of life. We miss her and the days that might have been. We remember with gratitude so many wonderful people who helped us through our grief, and were humbled to receive a personal note from Mother Teresa of Calcutta, in which she offered such wonderful words of comfort.

# Brothers & Fathers

The bittersweet knowledge that Denise is enjoying a new and richer life is true. Her life is "changed, not ended" (to quote one of the prayers of the funeral liturgy). With her passing, our lives changed, too. But still we have the wonderful gift of memory, an exceptional and powerful faculty which makes the past present to us. By memory, those who pass before us go on living. No one is dead until he or she is forgotten.

With great love and gratitude, we remember Denise.

# CHAPTER 44

## AFTER LEBANON: TRAVELING A DIFFERENT PATH

### *Father John*

I left Lebanon in 1986 and, after short stays in Australia and Hawaii, returned to the United States faced with enormous concern for George's youngest child, Denise. What might happen to her remained a priority for all of us as we continued on our own separate paths.

I supported George and Rosemary as they continued to look for a solution to what turned out to be Denise's insolvable physical condition. My brother George and his wife Rosemary did everything possible to help their daughter win her battle against the relentless brain tumor. With her own indomitable spirit, Denise began to make plans for her wedding to Joe Ortiz.

All I could do was be present to her, to my brother George, and to Rosemary whenever that was possible. I did accompany them to Germany soon after I returned with them to California.

---

### GEORGE

*"I took Denise to Germany, where I heard that maybe they could do something for her tumor. After three trips there, the doctor said there really wasn't anything he could do. While we tried to come to grips with that situation, Rosemary's mother died on January 7, 1984; my mother died in 1987; and Dad's sister, Aunt Sarah died on May 15, 1990. These were women who taught both my daughters, Mary Ellen and Denise, how to tend to the aging. We loved all of them, and in some way each of these women provided us with some comfort as we experienced events that fulfilled the existing notion we had of death. They had all lived long lives."*

---

# Brothers & Fathers

Rosemary and George remained committed to all of their other children, who were married and had growing families of their own. Trying to hold on to 'normal' day-to-day living, they remained very involved with grandchildren, elderly parents, friends, and business concerns.

For myself, when I returned to my diocese, I was grateful to hear that my bishop, James Timlin, was willing to give me some time to debrief, and was gracious enough to provide a residence for me in the Chancery building. Without a formal assignment, I was able to spend time doing some writing and speaking. I was concerned that the Catholic Church did not seem to be grasping the full picture of what was happening in Lebanon. I saw radical Islamic fundamentalism rampant there, and knew I wanted to raise awareness in my home diocese concerning that threat. I had seen the reality of that threat—not only in Lebanon, but throughout the world. Years later, the events of 9/11, horrific as they were, gave me affirmation that I was right to have done all I could do to raise awareness of that threat through writing and speaking about it.

Along with my attempts at writing, I also became involved with George and my brother and sister-in-law, Joe and Patty, in setting up a group called the Mission for Lebanon (MFL). It was our hope that we could respond to the egregious needs of the Lebanese people, whom I had come to know through this organization. On a personal level, perhaps the greatest gift I had during that time was having the opportunity to meet with Pope John Paul II regarding the situation in Lebanon. George had visited me many times while I lived in Lebanon, and he became keenly aware of the needs of the Lebanese people. He invested a lot of time and money in improving the situation there. Even after I left there, George continued to return to Lebanon, where he had set up an office. He did extensive work abroad while I did work for the MFL from home. I did, however, travel to Lebanon when it was important for me to do so. We continued to try to effect a necessary and caring response to the people of Lebanon, but the group met with the same kind of intrigue and corruption as I had found while I worked there at the Pontifical Mission.

*Father John with Pope John Paul II*

# After Lebanon: Traveling a Different Path

> ## PATTY ESSEFF & FATHER JOHN
>
> *PATTY ESSEFF*
> When I became executive director of the Mission for Lebanon (MFL) in July 1987, I began an intensive study of Lebanon, its [then-] current situation, history and culture, and the numerous religious sects and their interactions. We became deeply involved in responding to the needs that were identified. By November, we were able to travel to Lebanon and distribute several thousands of dollars to specific programs, clinics, and orphanages. We had gone there, however, mainly on a fact-finding mission.
>
> The destruction of villages, the relocation of large numbers of people, and the breakup of extended families were, in large part, results of the ongoing conflict. However, it was our observation that the Catholic school system in Lebanon, while weary and abused, was still reasonably intact. The goals of the MFL were clear: to bridge the needs of the schools with the available resources. We had a specific and achievable plan. We worked from 1987 until January 1989.
>
> *FATHER JOHN*
> So much of the work of those intervening months was an exercise in frustration and futility: so many details, so much work, and then such an inexplicable refusal to accept help for so many people in need. In the name of what? I do not have that answer.
>
> "On January 9, 1989, the Mission for Lebanon was unofficially, but unequivocally, informed that the local Lebanese church would not support the activities of the MFL in Lebanon. Upon further inquiry, we learned that the funding for our proposed school survey project was withdrawn. Although it was unclear who initiated this activity, we did know many people who were antagonistic towards our efforts, and who were eager to see the MFL eliminated in Lebanon. It serves no purpose to mention their names."

My involvement with MFL, my writing and speaking engagements, and my reentry into the life of the diocese were happening simultaneously. In January of 1987, Bishop Timlin asked me to administer St. Theresa's, a parish where one of the priests had been removed because of sexual 'impropriety.' On January 21ˢᵗ, shortly after I arrived in the parish, I received word of the death of my mother in California. Many people responded to Mom's death and, when I returned from the funeral, I was comforted by many notes and letters. One of those was from Monsignor Tom Cawley, my former pastor at St. Matthew's in the 1960s. He expressed sentiments like so many others who knew Mom:

# Brothers & Fathers

*John,*

*I was saddened to hear of your mother's death. However, my sadness does not extend to her. Hers was all gain. The loss is the family's and those of us who were honored in knowing her. She was a woman of deep faith and abiding love of God and her fellow man. Now she enjoys the reward He reserves for the choicest of his children. You and the entire family have my sincere sympathy.*

*Blessings, Tom.*

I had a memorial Mass at the parish and many relatives, old friends, and neighbors of Mom and Dad were able to attend. I was happy that we all had that opportunity for prayer and closure. It was also a great blessing that my dad could come and stay with me for a time in the rectory before he returned to California and to all the changes that he would have in his life as a widower.

I left St. Theresa's in Shavertown in September of 1987. Another priest came after me, and in time I learned that he, too, was removed from the parish for the same kind of sexual 'impropriety' as the former pastor. That word, that charge, was soon replaced in the civil courts by a more appropriate term: abuse.' I had left the war in Lebanon only to come home to find another war waging in America: Members of the clergy involved in cases of sexual abuse. It was a new war zone—one that took a tremendous toll on the Church, the clergy, but—most especially, and more importantly—on the victims of sexual abuse. Even after I left that parish, another priest who was assigned there was accused of sexual impropriety of another nature. That parish was reeling. The problem was all around.

I left Shavertown to begin a new assignment as the director of the Propagation of the Faith in Scranton, where I served for the next fifteen years. For me at the time, it seemed the place where I could do the most good. For the first four years of that mission, I lived at Sacred Heart Parish in the south side of Scranton with a very hospitable pastor, Monsignor Leonard Novak. While I lived there, I sponsored a baptism for the child of one of my cousins whom I had met in Lebanon.

George and Leah El Khoury had contacted me to see if I could arrange a place for them to stay while they were awaiting the birth of their first child. Because of the continuing chaos in Lebanon, they were hoping to have the child born in America. If the child was born in America, he or she would have citizenship—and, thus, a safe haven in the event of even further catastrophe in Lebanon. I arranged for them to come to America, and they lived with Ellen Franco and her family for the months preceding the birth of their daughter, Sandra. We had the christening

# After Lebanon: Traveling a Different Path

at Sacred Heart Parish. My brother George was Sandra's godfather and Ellen was her godmother.

I accepted with love the residue of my mission in Lebanon, but I was experiencing a new spirit growing in me. I was eager to take on the responsibilities of the Office of the Propagation of the Faith, in large part because it was both pontifical and global. Through that office, missionaries from all over the world were able to make their appeals to the local churches in my home diocese of Scranton. Missionaries would first make an appeal to the bishop—and there could be as many as 150 appeals for assistance in any given year. The coordination and the decisions regarding which of those appeals would be accepted were handled in our office; we could only honor about forty in any given year. The appeals would be arranged so that all of the people of the diocese could respond, but no one area or parish would be overburdened with those appeals.

I had always been very concerned about the global church, even since high school, when my classmate John Lavin decided to join the foreign missions. My work in Latin America and in Lebanon had only intensified my concerns.

On the other end of the spectrum, I also knew from my work in the diocese that the concerns of most priests were primarily for the local church. I often asked myself what so saps the energy of the diocesan clergyman that he becomes unable to look up to see the global Church, as well as the local one. To be sure, every parish priest needs to be concerned about the preaching of God's word on the parish level, and facilitating the sanctification of God's people and caring for the poor in the local area. In fact, the central act of priesthood is to lead people in the celebration of the Eucharist, the source and center of the life of the Church. Without a doubt, that celebration of Eucharist must be the major concern of the local church. Additionally, baptizing in the name of Jesus in order to extend the Kingdom of God—not only in the Diocese of Scranton or in any given parish, but also throughout the whole Church—that and other ministries are the concerns of the local priest. Yet the Catholic Church is universal and, therefore, every local church must strive to remain connected to the global Church.

When I took on the responsibilities of the director of the Propagation of the Faith, I wanted to present the needs of the universal Church to every parish in my diocese. I wanted to bring home the message that you cannot be Catholic (which means "universal,") if you are not aware of the Church throughout the world. I wanted to raise the awareness of our obligation to evangelize the whole world. I felt I had some understanding of the big picture.

# Brothers & Fathers

I had been a parish priest for the first fourteen years of my ministry—first in Shohola and then in East Stroudsbrug at St. Matthew's parish. While I worked as the director of Urban Ministry, I was able to become available to those outside the parish system. During those years, I did advanced study at the Aquinas Institute of Theology, a Roman Catholic graduate school and seminary located on the campus of the Dominican College of St. Rose of Lima in Dubuque, Iowa. My dissertation was a study of twenty-six parishes in the Scranton Diocese, exploring the *diakonia* (service) of those parishes in the Diocese of Scranton to the *anawim* (the poor). That objective study, coupled with my personal experiences in and out of the parish system in my own diocese, had given me a lot of insights into what the local, diocesan clergy face every day. I try not to forget how easy it is for diocesan clergy to get bogged down with never-ending details that draw them so deeply and exclusively into the local church. I certainly do not want to say that local clergy deliberately lack concern for people who are victims of famine or war, or migrants who are strangers in—our own country and within their own parishes. Often, however, the attention of the local clergy is diverted totally to local concerns. The parish, hoping to maintain itself, is busy with parish collections, bazaars, picnics, and bake sales, which help the parish to meet the financial demands in the maintenance of necessary parish programs. For years, I remember counting the Sunday collection, along with the money that was so generously put into the poor box. The counting of money sometimes took more time than celebrating my Masses! There were also concerns about the physical plant—maybe the furnace, maybe making sure the steps were free of snow in the winter, maybe making sure the lighting system and the audio system were working. There were baptisms and weddings that demanded responses. From the time I got up in the morning until late at night, I was faced with no end of needs in the parish. Even then, there were far fewer priests than previously, but the needs weren't any fewer.

As the director of the Propagation of the Faith, I wanted to address the needs of the global church while remaining mindful of the needs of the local church. I would go each weekend into that same system that I, myself, had lived in and ministered in. I would go to parishes throughout the diocese to plead the causes of the global Church during all the weekend Masses. I did that petitioning in the face of all that I knew were the ever-pressing needs of the local parishes. I would set down the needs of the global Church in front of the people I met. I knew what a sensitive area that was for me—and for those to whom I spoke. I begged them for prayer and for the sacrifice of some of their time to learn about the missions. I was sure that, once they grew in awareness, they would be more than generous in financially

# After Lebanon: Traveling a Different Path

supporting the missions. My early firsthand experiences in Peru made it clear to me that any parish I visited, even inner-city parishes in Williamsport that were so poor, was composed of people who still had a much better life than the people I met in Latin America. The poor people in the projects in Williamsport had their own needs, yet they needed to begin to be aware of needs even greater than theirs in other parts of the world. I felt that, because of my own experiences, I could put faces on some of those needs and the people would respond with prayer, heightened awareness, and financial support.

Even as I began that work, two wonderful, enthusiastic people were with me in the office: Sharon Warunek, my secretary and office manager, and a first cousin of mine, Miriam (Harry) Heverline, the educational coordinator. We worked together, mapped out a plan, and carried it out. We wrote and implemented a mission statement:

> *The principal aim of the Pontifical Mission Societies in the Diocese of Scranton is to promote a 'mission spirituality' and a global vision in the hearts and minds of the faithful.*

We also instituted a five-year plan, by which we would foster awareness among children from kindergarten through eighth grade by getting them involved in the Holy Childhood Association. By the time those children reached high school, they would be ready to participate in mission experiences. The oldest children could then assume leadership positions. That blueprint lasted, not five, but fifteen years. The result was that both the clergy and the laity grew into a greater sense of their own mission to spread the Gospel and to be present to people in every corner of the globe.

I kept encouraging Miriam and Sharon to be part of a firsthand mission experience. In 1991, I had plans to give a retreat to Mother Teresa's sisters in west Africa. Sharon joined me; that was her first mission. She spent time in Guinea and on the Ivory Coast, doing work among the poor.

---

### SHARON WARUNEK

*"Learning from and working with Monsignor John Esseff has impacted not only my life but that of my entire family. I embrace life now, knowing that I am not in control. That realization makes life so freeing. When I met Monsignor for the first time, he was able to look into my eyes and see what I needed to grow in my faith. He did not tell me*

---

### SHARON WARUNEK

*what I needed—he silently guided me without words. I know this sounds funny, but it is true. Going on Mission to Africa with Monsignor was a gift. I believe he knew it would give me the opportunity to value my gifts, my faith, and my ministry. I needed a little push, and he ever so gently pushed. Mission was the missing ingredient in my life. He truly is my life-long friend."*

Miriam and another woman, Helen Phillips, joined me on their first mission to Haiti in 1991. Once again, I gave the Missionaries of Charity sisters their retreat and the women worked at the Hospice St. Joseph in Port au Prince.

### MIRIAM HEVERLINE

*"During the time that Father John served as a missionary in Peru, I was busy taking care of my five young children. I would eagerly look forward to his letters telling me about his experiences in that poverty-stricken country. I had always been drawn to a missionary outlook on life. Little did I know that, after my own children were grown, I would find the perfect fit for my life's work as mission education coordinator working with Monsignor John in our diocese. My first mission experience in Haiti made me deeply aware of the difference between needs and wants. It enabled me to be more effective in teaching about people, especially the children who live in poverty; that first mission experience also prompted the beginning of our mission journeys for high school students and adults under the auspices of the Office for the Propagation of the Faith."*

Both Miriam and Sharon returned to their jobs with even more enthusiasm and so much more energy. Having a mission experience in a Third World country was really transforming for each of them. When anyone sees what a Third World country is like then, invariably, that person returns with so much more to give. As the mission plan continued to evolve, we eventually were able to coordinate the taking of juniors in high school and other volunteers, both to Third World countries and also to American missions. I knew that there were local Catholic schools that sponsored similar missions, but we did this for public school and Catholic school children alike. The excursion was not a tour and not a pilgrimage, but a mission, and we prepared the young people to go as missionaries. So it was not only their Baptism and Confirmation that went with them, but the mission itself was also a retreat experience. They began to go to Third World countries such as Mexico,

Ecuador, and Tanzania. When the first group of juniors came back to the diocese and became seniors, they were able to assume leadership responsibilities with the younger students. As with the adults, the experience was transforming. Our mission clubs and our mission groups took on a new dimension. It was really exciting.

Bishop Timlin was very supportive of all our endeavors, and keenly aware of the challenges of Pope John Paul II's encyclical letter:

*"The mission of Christ the Redeemer, which is entrusted to the Church, is still very far from completion ... an overall view of the human race shows that this mission is still only beginning and that we must commit ourselves wholeheartedly to its service."*

As early as 1996, Bishop Timlin reformulated a Diocesan Mission Board under the auspices of the Pontifical Mission for the Propagation of the Faith. The goals and objectives of the board were to be accomplished through committees set up to concentrate on education, prayer and parish life, communications, and support of local and global missionary involvement among the religious and laity of the diocese.

By 1991, as I continued as the director of the Propagation of the Faith, I moved to a new residence in Dalton (a suburb of Scranton) where I took on additional duties as formation director at the local seminary, St. Pius X. I was headed in a new direction—one that gave me great focus as the years continued. When I arrived at St. Pius X Seminary, I had a lot of interest in building greater strengths for those men engaged in the formation process for priesthood. The transition was a good one. In time, many of the seminarians I worked with at St. Pius X Seminary joined the existing mission groups that were off on Third World missions under the auspices of the Propagation office. Seminarians preparing for priesthood had come to Pius X from different dioceses, and many were eventually ordained. They served not only the Diocese of Scranton, but also the Archdiocese of Washington, the Archdiocese of Baltimore, and the Diocese of Allentown. They took their mission awareness with them wherever they went as priests.

It was a fulfilling experience to see the response of the local Church to the global Church. I always loved being a member of the presbyterate of the Diocese of Scranton. I am a Scranton priest but, by virtue of that priesthood, I know I am also a priest of the universal Catholic Church. My priesthood is always something that urges me on to service of my brothers and sisters around the world. I never offer Mass without connecting to Jesus on every altar in the world. That same Jesus is One—throughout the whole world. I know, too, that God has blessed me with opportunities that He has not given to some of my brother priests. I need to keep that in mind; I need to be always grateful; I need to hear their criticisms of me with a unique freedom in my priesthood.

Many times, as I went from place to place, I felt that my role was similar to the one of sand in the bathing suit. Diocesan clergy, of which I am a part, can become very comfortable. There are parishes that are urban and quiet, and sometimes seem remote from the problems of the rest of the world. I have lived in those parishes. There are parishes that have few financial or social problems. I have lived in those parishes too. In those environments, I (as any priest or parishioner) can develop a very cushioned vision of Jesus. The role of a true missionary (not unlike that of the diocesan priest) is to dispel that type of blurred vision of Jesus. My preaching then—as now—was intended to comfort those who are uncomfortable, and to bring discomfort to those who are too comfortable. I had to be the sand in the bathing suit; I had to agitate for justice around the world.

Those years as director of the Propagation of the Faith were productive ones in which all those who came on board were able to raise awareness of the global Church within the local Church. My staff and I would go to national conferences and meet people from Propagation of the Faith offices throughout the country. The national office began to use a new expression: There was talk of 'Scrantonizing' other dioceses of the country, doing what we had done successfully. Our mission office was really having a great impact. Those were very busy years—and ones I thoroughly enjoyed.

Each year we had a wonderful celebration of Mission Sunday at the cathedral. On those occasions, we would acknowledge the contributions and service rendered by the grade school and high school students. Each year, we would invite a prominent missionary to speak at the Mission Sunday Mass. It was a very special annual occasion.

By the time I arrived at St. Pius X Seminary, I had seen a bit of life; I knew the exquisite beauty of the Church, but I was also aware of so much that needed to be done. I knew parish life; I knew ministry to people who did not participate in parish life but who, nonetheless, longed for God. I had served the poor as a missionary in Peru, and I had experienced the devastation of a country made poor in Lebanon.

At the seminary, I became involved with many new people. My associates there included Monsignor David Bohr, the rector of the seminary and Father John Polenak, the spiritual director; another member of our formation team at that time

430

was eventually removed because of accusations of sexual abuse. During those years there were always tragic reminders of the cancer that was surfacing in the Church. I sometimes wonder how many books will be written about that era—one that demands much study. But I leave those painful chapters to someone else. During my stay at the seminary, Father Polednak left to take on the duties of pastor in the nearby parish of Nicholson; Father Jeff Walsh was named spiritual director to succeed him. Father Joseph Kopacz and Father Joe Bambera also joined us as formation advisors. I worked with all of those priests and still others as I served my tenure there; Father Bambera later went on to become the tenth Bishop of Scranton in 2010.

About that same time (the early nineties), I was invited to speak at the local Jesuit preparatory school in Scranton. On the occasion of that visit, I was introduced to a Jesuit who taught there, Father John Horn. Because of that meeting, I learned that he was looking for a time and a place to pray. I also came to know a priest who was looking for the same thing; his name was Father Leo McKernan, and he was serving as spiritual director at St. Pius X Seminary at that time. Through these men, I also came to know of Father Richard Gabuzda, a diocesan priest who was the liturgical director at St. Pius X. I believe that, by God's design, Father Leo McKernan and Father John Horn and I began to pray in my office each morning; we simply set a time as a community of priests (tiny as it was) to pray. We were very faithful to this hunger in each of us. As we traveled deeper into prayer, we began to get strong messages about how important renewal in the priesthood was. All around us, there was devastation in that priesthood. I knew that the crisis which was so apparent in the Church at that time was somehow connected to the lack of prayer. I was beginning to really see a need for priestly renewal. John and Leo also knew that renewal was essential. For many years previous, and still at that same time, I was closely working with Mother Teresa, giving her and her sisters retreats around the world. Mother was encouraging me to become involved in the renewal of men in formation for priesthood. As early as 1988, she had concretized that desire in me. She asked me if I would become the rector in Tijuana, Mexico, where she had established a seminary to form priests who wanted to participate in her work as Missionaries of Charity. There existed within me, by that time, a lot of understanding of what the Church (both the local and global) meant, what being a missionary really meant, what gifts God had given me, and where I could serve God best. I was on a road of many choices, and I knew I had to discern the will of God for me. I couldn't think of any person I would want to emulate more than Mother Teresa. I spent a lot of time in prayer, but I decided not to take the position of rector in

# Brothers & Fathers

Tijuana. I was a diocesan priest. I had felt the pain of leaving after having served as 'Father' in Peru and in Lebanon. I wanted to experience 'fatherhood' in myself, my brother priests, and the young men who aspired to priesthood. Alive and well blessed, I pledged my allegiance once again to the Diocese of Scranton and to the American priesthood. I think I always understood the power of priesthood, and I knew how essential priesthood was to my being. I had spent all but twenty-four years of my life as a priest. I knew that the priesthood was under fire; I also knew that priesthood was not defeated. So many years in my priesthood had been pure joy for me. In so many ways, priesthood had been easy for me.

This was a different time. I felt that I needed to go to the front line. How could I best serve my commander-in-chief? How could I best serve Jesus? Eventually, through prayer, I came to know that I needed to become more deeply involved in the formation of men for priesthood. I knew I wanted to do that for the American priesthood. I was certain that God would take me where He wanted me to be.

In time, He took me to many other places—both inside and outside the country. But in those early years, Fathers Rich Gabuzda, John Horn, and Leo McKernan, and I were envisioning a stronger, renewed priesthood even as we grappled with the reality that we were "dancing among the ruins." The formation system for priesthood was, in fact, in ruins; but the dance was continuing. That vision, in God's time,

---

### REV. JOHN HORN

"Responding to a call to shared prayer, I began to meet with Monsignor John Esseff and Father Leo McKernan in the early morning hours in the 1990–1991 school year. Those 6:00 a.m. gatherings for prayer took place in the office of the Propagation of the Faith. The meetings involved quiet, contemplative, Scripture-based prayer, and we were blessed with gifts of the Holy Spirit which we exercised in a discerning fashion. After several months of prayer, each of us received a word of knowledge directing us to dedicate this time together to intercede for priests and for the renewal of diocesan priesthood. Each of us also sensed a call to labor apostolically in the spiritual formation for diocesan priests.

"Father McKernan was already serving as a spiritual director for St. Pius X College Seminary in Dalton.

"Monsignor had already received from the now Blessed Mother Teresa of Calcutta and Bishop Timlin powerful confirmations of this call to serve priests.

# After Lebanon: Traveling a Different Path

## REV. JOHN HORN

*"I was commissioned by my provincial for doctoral studies in pastoral theology, which prepared me to serve in the spiritual formation of priests. This preparation was grounded in the Spiritual Exercises of St. Ignatius Loyola, and also in his teachings concerning the discernment of spirits."*

culminated in the creation of what is now known as the Institute of Priestly Formation (IPF), currently based at Creighton University in Omaha, Nebraska.

We were very much affirmed on our journey in what we were doing when, on March 25, 1992, Pope John Paul II presented his Post-Synodal Apostolic Exhortation, *Pastores Dabo Vobis* ("To Bishops, Clergy, and Faithful on the Formation of Priests in the Circumstances of the Present Day"):

> *"The new generation of those called to the ministerial priesthood display different characteristics in comparison to those of their immediate predecessors. In addition, they live in a world which in many respects is new and undergoing rapid and continual evolution. All of this cannot be ignored when it comes to programming and carrying out the various phases of formation for those approaching the ministerial priesthood."*

Pope John Paul II went on to clarify what the commitment of every seminary should be:

> *"Inasmuch as it is an educating community, the seminary and its entire life—in all its different expressions—is committed to formation: the human, spiritual, intellectual and pastoral formation of future priests."*

> *For someone like me, who was trained in a highly academic setting, I understood completely the need for spiritual formation—the need to help young men develop a solid prayer life, which is essential to their very being. In the midst of so many things to do, every priest must continually grow in his relationship to God. He must be a man of prayer.*

## REV. JOHN HORN

*"In 1994, I went on an eight-day silent retreat under Monsignor Esseff's spiritual direction. That experience was pivotal for me. During those days, a variety of inspirations coalesced in my heart to help form and found the Institute of Priestly Formation (IPF). The conception, birth, and maturation of this institute were (and are) grounded in the ministry of spiritual direction given to both me and my colleagues: Father Richard Gabuzda, Miss Kathy Kanavy, and Father George Aschenbrenner, S.J. That direction was (and still is) given by Monsignor Esseff, who serves as 'a spiritual grandfather' to each of us.*

*"Throughout this entire time, Sister Cor Immaculatum, I.H.M., became engaged as both an intercessor in prayer and an advisor in matters of formation, an area in which she had so long been involved in her own community of sisters. She was a source of strong support as she offered valuable input to the soon-to-be cofounders of the Institute for Priestly Formation."*

The time I spent in helping Father Horn, Father Gabuzda, and Kathy Kanavy discern what God was calling them to do was one of great hope for me. Throughout that entire time, I was involved in overseeing the formation of young men at St. Pius X Seminary on a daily basis. The need for renewal was something I encountered every day, and the firsthand experiences I was dealing with made my considerations much more practical, urgent, and prayerful than theoretical. I knew I was in for the long haul.

Even while that new, and very exciting, adventure into priestly formation was developing, I continued my work at the Propagation of the Faith and encouraged my bishop, James Timlin, to make a mission trip. In the midst of his many commitments, to the delight of all, he made that trip in the year 2000. From February 6th to February 11th, he immersed himself in fourteen-hour days in a Third World country. I accompanied him, along with five other priests, a deacon, and six laypeople (two of whom were journalists) on a weeklong mission to poverty-stricken Haiti, the poorest country in the western hemisphere.

*Father John in Haiti*

# After Lebanon: Traveling a Different Path

Upon the return of the group, highlights of the mission were presented in the Scranton newspaper by *Times* staff writer Marita Lowman and photographer Rich Banick, both of whom had been part of the group.

---

## BISHOP JAMES TIMLIN

*"This is life to them. The children don't know any differently. They're jammed together, living on top of one another. It's like living on top of a huge garbage heap amid animals, sewage, stench ...*

*"I always want to find a solution. I think, 'How can I fix it?' I want to roll up my sleeves and fix it. Many here are trying to do that. But the problems are immense ...*

*"The Haitians' dignity is a lesson for all. Poverty of dignity is far worse than poverty of material things. I noticed a father sitting with his wife and looking at the sunset, and somehow they're immaculately dressed. Here, people are in human misery, but in many ways they are very rich. They are blessed by God because of their spirit and dignity ...*

*"They showed us that the human spirit is resilient. The people eke out an existence. The children rise to the occasion. But they are in a prison and they can't get out ...*

*"We will remember and we will be much more sympathetic to the poor at home. We will speak more about the good works of the missions.*

Reprinted with the permission of the managing editor of *The Times–Tribune*, Lawrence K. Beaupre.

---

Some other reactions to what transpired were also recorded in the *Scranton Times* and reproduced in the diocesan newspaper, *The Catholic Light* on October 5, 2000 in celebration of the upcoming Mass for Mission Sunday that year.

## OTHER REACTIONS

*REV. EDWARD SCOTT*

*"A scene that stays with me is that poignant moment when we were driving out of the slum in Food for the Poor's van, and a woman was standing next to the van holding her baby up and asking someone to take the baby. I wanted to do something and I felt such a sense of powerlessness."*

*REV. MARTIN BOYLAN*

*"I felt overwhelmed by the number of people and the apparent chaos of the streets. There was so much noise. The kids were walking through the streets in bare feet.*

*"I wonder whether the government is intentionally letting the Church do everything. Is it malign neglect?"*

*REV. STEPHEN STAVOY*

*"The kids in the schools were immaculately clean, and I still haven't figured out how they do that.*

*"Beyond that, I played as many games with the kids as I could— with colors, and balancing tricks, and other things children do, and they reacted just like any other kids."*

*REV. MICHAEL HARRIS*

*"I feel renewed as a priest. There's a real tugging at my heart. It makes a difference in how I say the liturgy. I see the differences and gradations of poverty.*

*"I'm in reverence."*

*DEACON GENE KOVATCH*

*"This was my fourth mission experience.*

*I went twice to Mexico and once to a soup kitchen in the Bronx. This trip was much more difficult than the other three.*

*"I think of the filth, the rats in the garbage, the pigs and dogs going through the garbage, and the people rooting through the garbage. The children play in mud and dirt and garbage. There's so much destitution, but they seem to have hope.*

*"There's a brightness in their spirit, and I don't know how to account for that."*

# After Lebanon: Traveling a Different Path

Once these missionaries saw the people in Haiti and became aware of the poverty and the misery that people there endured, they all returned with an entirely different view of the global Church. And so those missions were bringing about a global awareness in my home diocese. The Propagation of the Faith does not mean collecting money for the poor; it doesn't mean throwing money over the wall or into the basket. 'Mission' means that we are one body and that we are responsible for one another, and that what's happening 'over there' is very vital to what's happening here. There is a connection to all parts of the body. It's the universality of the Church uniting all God's people into one body. It is that concept that sensitizes the people of any diocese to the plight of those outside the local Church. When I was the director of the Propagation of the Faith, there were 220 parishes in the diocese. I had the extraordinary privilege of visiting every parish twice during my time as director. I went to every parish, preaching and teaching and heightening awareness of the global vision of the Church. The work was very important—and invaluable in my own development as a priest.

I was immersed in a great many endeavors during the nineties, and each of them was very fulfilling. On a personal level, there were other events that brought shared grief and quiet acceptance. The new decade had brought with it significant losses for the family. Without question, the most difficult was the loss of Denise, and the fact that we knew her death was imminent didn't make her passing any less difficult to accept. Six years after her death, on September 11, 1996, we lost the patriarch of our family when Dad died. He had lived his last years with my brother Joe and his wife Patty, who took great care of him in their home. A formidable man, Dad was surely going to be missed by children, grandchildren and great grandchildren, relatives and friends. He had a long and fruitful life, and his legacy lives on in all that he gave us. Dad's death, as well as the deaths of my mother, Rosemary's mother and father, her daughter Denise, and others in the family were times of sadness. They also were times of reflection. We had wonderful opportunities to experience gratitude for so many loving people who had come before us, for resignation to the will of God, and for hope in the promise of the resurrection.

In the midst of those great personal losses, but also in the midst of great and wonderful days as I served the Propagation of the Faith and the community of St. Pius X Seminary, I experienced perhaps the most traumatic event in my personal life. I had conducted a pilgrimage to the Holy Land in April of 2000. On April 13, the group returned to the Fatima Center in Dalton, where we had begun our journey, and the people who had made the pilgrimage went home.

The next day, Tuesday, April 14th, I went to Scranton to resume my duties at the Propagation of the Faith office. I spent most of the day there, and then started on my way home from Scranton to the seminary in Dalton. I remember the early details quite clearly. It was late afternoon—a busy time to get through the congested boroughs of Chinchilla and Clarks Summit on my way home to Dalton. I decided to take an alternate, somewhat rural route—South Abington Road veered off from the main highway. I was very conscious about keeping the thirty-five m/p/h speed limit, because of once having been stopped there by a state trooper who gave me a sound warning about keeping that speed limit; from that time on, I was very careful on that road. Before I had gone a mile, in an instant, something came crashing through my windshield. To try to put the events together is difficult. Many times, over and over, I have thought about what happened. It seemed as though someone or something pitched into my way and then came up, crashing into the windshield before finally disappearing. I stopped the car and got out to see what had happened. I walked back to the point of impact saying in my heart as I went, "Dear God, I hope that was a deer that crashed into my windshield."

It was not.

It was a man.

He was lying there on the road, and all I could see was blood gushing from him. I leaned down. I had my oils with me and I had the presence of mind to anoint him, to pray over him, and to give him the Last Rites—because I really did believe he was dying. I stayed there praying with him and for him. Traffic, of course, was stopped. Pretty soon, I became more conscious of my surroundings. A nurse was there, trying to do whatever she could do for the man lying on the pavement. Someone had called an ambulance—I may have done that myself; I may have called

# After Lebanon: Traveling a Different Path

9–1–1. Anyway, there was a lot of confusion. The police were also there. The ambulance seemed to have gotten there within minutes. While I stood there, dazed, the man was taken in the ambulance to the hospital. This was, indeed, a human being, and I really felt that he was going to die. His bodily wounds were extensive. It is still quite a scene for me to remember. I stood there and waited to speak to the police. Having a car phone at that time, I called Monsignor Dave Bohr, the rector, who was waiting for me at the seminary to attend a meeting. I told him about the accident. It wasn't very long before he came down and was with me. When I called Monsignor Bohr, I asked him to call local pastors because I thought this man might be a parishioner in one of the local parishes. By that time, I knew the man's name: Thomas Murray. I stayed at the scene for a couple of hours while the police took the necessary information about my license number and my insurance. They were trying to ascertain how fast I had been going and whether or not there was alcohol involved. They were asking me a lot of questions and, to the degree I could, I was trying to help them piece together the entire event. I was the center of the investigation and I had to recall what had happened.

It wasn't until later, with the help of Mrs. Murray, that the whole story unfolded. Thomas Murray was 91 years old. He was sitting on his porch; it was late afternoon. Mrs. Murray said she had told her husband that she was going to pay their taxes; it was April 14. She also said that she wouldn't be gone long and that he should stay on the porch until she returned. She was concerned because her husband had recently had a hip operation and he was still recuperating.

Unfortunately, that is not what happened. Deciding to clean up some brush on the side of the road, Mr. Murray was walking down the steep embankment in front of their house when he must have lost his balance. He pitched forward and we collided. I never saw him until he hit the windshield. Such a terrible accident! Such devastating loss. Such tragedy—in an instant.

Standing there praying after I anointed the man, I heard a woman's voice: "Oh, Father, he just made the nine First Fridays, and you were there, and you sent him off to heaven." It was the man's wife. She was saying this to me. She was consoling me in the midst of her great loss. What a sweet, wonderful woman!

In the meantime, Monsignor Bohr had determined that the Murrays belonged to Our Lady of the Snows Parish, where Father McGarry was pastor. Father McGarry knew the man and, shortly afterward, he too appeared at the site. He was with Mrs. Murray when she came up to me. I didn't feel that I was the right one to minister to this widow. I realized how powerful the priesthood was, and I was so grateful for Father McGarry's presence to this woman, who was so unbelievably concerned about me in the midst of her own loss.

The next morning, I went to the chapel to have my daily Mass. I wasn't paying too much attention to who was there. I knew, as always, the seminarians were there. At one point, Monsignor Dave Bohr, who was concelebrating with me, leaned over and said, "John, do you see who's here?"

I remember calling George the evening before just to tell him what had happened, but I was amazed to look up and see him and my brother Joe right there, that very next morning! It was hard to believe that they could have gotten there so fast. For me, it was as if they were in Wilkes-Barre and I was in Scranton, fifteen or so miles away. But the fact was, they were in Dalton, Pennsylvania and to be there with me they had traveled across the entire country, at least three thousand miles from their homes in California.

## GEORGE

*"John had called me and told me that he had killed a man while he was driving home. I couldn't imagine how he must have felt. I knew I wanted to see him, and when Joe learned of what had happened, he decided he would come with me. We came into Scranton on the redeye from California, rented a car, and drove to the seminary. I knew there was Mass every morning, and it was just about that time when we arrived. Joe and I went right to the seminary chapel and found John at the altar saying Mass.*

*"After Mass and a little breakfast, the three of us went to see Mr. Murray's wife. John, Joe, and I sat and talked with her. I think we were just trying to help everyone get through that very tragic event. Of course, Mrs. Murray was experiencing tremendous grief; at the same time, I could see what a terrible toll the accident was taking on John—how devastated he was.*

*"I guess we just wanted to support John as he went through such a painful time.*

*"I went to a local nursery and bought a tree, which I got permission to plant on the seminary grounds; it was a memorial to Mr. Murray. I thought something living and long-lasting would be a more appropriate remembrance than a plaque or a stone. I hoped it would be a small comfort to the family. The tree still stands on the grounds today."*

# After Lebanon: Traveling a Different Path

After we did the best we could to give some small comfort to Mrs. Murray, George got to work seeing that the things we had to do were getting done. I was beginning to be able to think about the events of the day before. When the accident occurred, there were a lot of policemen at the scene. I had had to answer a lot of questions. There was talk of vehicular homicide, and the investigating officer was not a local policeman but a state trooper out of Harrisburg. The investigators had made chalk marks around the body of the man. They took measurements to ascertain how far away from the body the car had stopped. The entire area was treated pretty much like a crime scene. Of course, my windshield was smashed; but for other legal reasons, I could not take my car. It had been towed away from the scene for further scrutiny and was placed in a secure area in a garage on nearby Layton Road in Chinchilla. George wanted to help me deal with details: like what to do with the car. It had to be released and repaired, or possibly disposed of. He wanted those kinds of things settled before he had to leave. At some point during the day, Joe, George, and I went to the garage to check the status of the car. When we got out of his rental car, George looked around, obviously confused. "I don't see the car. Are you sure this is the right garage?" Not until that moment did I remember the car George was looking for.

Months earlier, when George was leaving his home in Florida, he decided he wanted me to have a car he had there rather than to ship it to California. I was fine with the car I had, and I told George I didn't want the car. Nevertheless, one day— George being George—the car arrived. I was flabbergasted. It was practically brand new: a red, flashy car. As the director of the Propagation office, I was going all over the diocese begging for money for the missions. The car was humongous—and fire engine red! I took it on one weekend mission, but even as I did, I knew there was something really wrong with the picture. The next day, I took the car to a local dealership and sold it, along with my own car. The proceeds from the sale covered almost the entire cost of buying a new, albeit less flashy, vehicle for myself.

The only trouble was that I never bothered to tell George any of these details.

My face was as red as the car George was looking for.

"George, I really appreciated you giving me that car, but it was too flashy for me. I got rid of it and the money I got pretty much covered the whole cost of the new one. It was a real bargain. (I was hoping he could appreciate that!) We're in the right garage. The car is here. It's not red. I'll show it to you."

And George said nothing. He just loved me.

Short of that one light moment, I was immersed in the reality that I had killed a man. In my youth, I had hurt people: I hit some guys, I got involved in fights; but I never envisioned myself killing another human being. I was never a soldier engaged in war, and I remember how strongly I had objected to Lionel's having a gun in Peru. I never wanted anything to do with killing another human being. As I recall, even when I was in Monroe County for 14 years, the game warden always wanted me to go hunting with him. I just didn't want to do that. When I was a kid, I used to go target shooting with my uncles, but I was very careful about touching a gun. And yet, there I was: responsible for another man's death. I grieved for Mrs. Murray and for her son.

I was advised that I should not go to the funeral; I prayed for Mr. Murray at my own Masses. I did know that their son was, quite understandably, angry—or maybe just sad at the death of his dad. He didn't want to see me or be in touch with me, nor for me to be in touch with them. I honored their wishes, and that is how this tragic event played out. In retrospect, I think I was very depressed about that entire event for some time. I did have a lot of support from people in the area. I was grateful for the care and concern.

## FRANCINE QUESADA

*Editor: My heart feels an incredible amount of sadness for Monsignor Esseff, who has devoted his entire life to helping others. Monsignor Esseff represents the very essence of Christ because of his loving, non-judgmental presence. While I feel heartfelt condolences for the family of Thomas Murray, who have suffered a significant loss, my sense of pain for Monsignor Esseff is profound. I am concerned for Monsignor because I know how gentle and loving he is.*

*Rarely does one live a lifetime and have the grace and blessing to meet someone as loving, spiritual, and selfless as Monsignor Esseff. I am not of the Catholic faith, but Monsignor Esseff's friendship, love, and kindness have brought me closer to God and a higher power than I had ever dreamed possible. If there were a definition in the dictionary next to 'unconditional love,' it surely would be Monsignor Esseff.*

*This kind, gentle, loving, non-judgmental soul has brought hope to thousands of people all over the world. He has helped me enormously, never expecting anything in return.*

442

# After Lebanon: Traveling a Different Path

In my own grief, I experienced as closely as I could the kind of grief my brother George might have experienced when he lost Denise. I did gain some insight into the kind of anguish he suffered, but comparisons are futile. Is there any real way to measure grief?

# CHAPTER 45

## A GRADUAL AND NECESSARY REASSESSMENT

### *George*

As soon as we were informed that Denise would die of the tumor, I decided to stop the doctor who had let her deteriorate to that point from treating any other patients. For years, her doctor had misdiagnosed and mistreated her as he kept insisting that she had just some allergies. I did everything I could to convince him that he should take an MRI, a relatively new procedure at that time, to see if she had any other problems. He kept refusing to order one. When we finally learned that the tumor was a big as a baseball and that Denise had just a short time to live, I really became furious with him. Without question, I did want him out of business—and to that end, I sued him for Denise's life and for the loss of our daughter. I won both suits in a very short time. There was a lot of damaging evidence concerning the doctor's competency and his response to what we wanted him to do. When he learned that I had taken Denise to Germany, this doctor called the doctor I had taken her to and told him not to treat Denise. He told the doctor in Germany that he hoped she would die. With so much data and with proof of that kind of rhetoric, the court ruled in favor of my suit, and the doctor lost the case.

As I said, I wanted that man out of business; but other than making sure he could not repeat what he had done to Denise, the suit didn't change the fact that Denise had died. And even though we had time to prepare, I now know I was unable to face her death. I knew it was the will of God. In time, though, I also came to know that I talked a good game, but I didn't face her death easily. I said all the right things outwardly, but I buried her loss deep in my heart. I guess I talked the talk, but I wasn't really walking the walk. As the years came and went, I came to know that some of the things that transpired in my life were intricately connected with how I dealt with the loss of Denise.

For one thing, I got into many more businesses than I had been involved in prior to Denise's death, and many of those businesses had nothing to do with titanium. I got into so many damn businesses, it wasn't funny. At one point I had a fistful of business cards naming various corporations: Infra-Temp, Inc.; Economation, Inc.; SF Properties, Inc.; Esseff-Arpaia Productions; Shaver Lake 805, LLP— and the list could go on and on, from a cheese company to a car wash. My name was listed underneath each company and usually identified as president, CEO, or general partner. Anything that came along, I jumped on board, just so I could fully occupy my mind. It got to the point where I was involved in so many things that now, thinking back, it seems crazy. I didn't leave my business (by that time, functioning under the name Supra Alloys, Inc.), even after my son George had picked up most of the responsibilities there. I went to the office all the time, and didn't officially retire until 1997. I had done some work with my brother John in Lebanon, and I continued many involvements there even after John came home. Although it may seem hard to believe, I was traveling even more than I had during my earlier years.

Returning from our place in Japan on one occasion in 1994, I stopped at a place we had in Hawaii. I went fishing for a day and I brought in a 480-pound marlin along with a 250-pound shark. After that day of fishing, I planned to head for California. I had had a great time, and I felt fantastic.

For my whole life, I had really been blessed with a very healthy body. Even in high school, I was a pretty husky guy. Coupled with the kind of work I had done for years with my dad, I was pretty strong for a young kid. In college, I continued on a pretty strict regimen because of my participation in the wrestling program at King's. The very rigorous training I did during those years put me on the road to having a good, healthy body.

I can't say I didn't ever abuse my body. I smoked cigarettes (four or five packs a day) until I finally quit when I was about forty. I was also a big coffee drinker. Traveling a lot, I never got a hell of a lot of sleep, but when I got on an airplane, I rested. A lot of business had to do with entertaining clients—taking them to dinner or being taken to dinner—so eating and drinking were part of the business world for me. Because I went to Japan so often, I was eating a lot of Kobe beef—the buttery flavored steak that the Japanese are so well known for. I ate it all the time, although I knew it was very fatty. I still felt pretty good most of the time. When I was home, I did a lot of work around the house: I'd work in the yard or in the garden. Some of the work involved pretty hard labor, hauling and lifting. We built the stable for the girls' horses in two weekends, and that was pretty rigorous. So in spite of some excesses, I felt I was in pretty good shape. I was always happy when I could enjoy a great day of fishing like the one I had had in Hawaii.

# A Gradual and Necessary Reassessment

When I returned to California, I enjoyed two days at home before leaving for Paris on another business trip. As usual, I got up in the morning and got ready for the day ahead. I remember that I finished shaving. I was ready to go to the eight o'clock Mass, but before I took a step out of the house, I felt a tremendous pain in my chest, my arm, and my shoulder. I knew immediately what was happening.

I said to Rosemary, "I'm having a heart attack. Get me to the hospital!"

We didn't call the ambulance. By that time, we had moved out of our home on Yucca Street and into a big house in the country. We were in the Santa Rosa Valley, which was at least eleven miles from the hospital. As quickly as we could, Rosemary and I jumped into the car and got to the hospital in eight minutes. She must have been going at least ninety miles an hour. We pulled up. I walked in and told the emergency personnel I was having a heart attack. They grabbed me, got me onto a gurney, and rushed me in. As soon as they began taking vital signs and doing other procedures, they knew I was in the worst possible situation. I had never had heart trouble, and so I didn't have a heart doctor. Fortunately, there was in Los Robles at that time one of the best heart doctors, a Dr. Hubert. Not only was he in the area, but he had just finished doing a procedure on an angioplasty patient in the very hospital I was in. The staff wheeled me right into the O.R. When someone asked me how bad the pain was, on a scale of one to ten, I said, "Twelve." It was the worst pain I had ever experienced. Very quickly, it was determined that my two major arteries were blocked. Dr. Hubert blew up the balloon and opened the main arteries in my heart, each of which was 100% closed. When he blew up the first one, I felt the pain, the most excruciating I had ever felt, go away. I was aware of nothing else until I woke up eighteen hours later to learn all that had happened. I had had a stroke on the table. I also learned much later that, only six months before my heart attack, one of the first clot busters had been developed. Clot busters (thrombolytics) are medications given to break up blood clots. If a patient is having a heart attack or an ischemic stroke (in which the blood supply to the brain is disrupted by a blood clot), clot busters can reduce the damage to the heart or brain and prevent death. To be most effective, they need to be administered quickly.

Fortunately for me, the recently developed clot buster was available and I was given a dose—or maybe two. When I woke up, I could hardly see; I could just barely make out Rosemary's face. I couldn't hear and I was totally paralyzed on my left side. I was put in intensive care. Our friend Dr. Bob Scribner had come to the hospital to be with Rosemary—but, of course, I had no idea of what was going on or how bad things were going for me. I also learned later that Doc Scribner was talking to the staff and telling them to do whatever they needed to do, because it was generally assumed that I might not get through the night.

Thank God, I did.

About a week later, I was able to get out of bed and stand on my feet. I needed a walker; and even with that, I was just about able to manage. But what was happening was better than the alternative. Much later, Dr. Hubert told me that, if I had arrived at the hospital eight minutes later than I did, I would have died. About three seconds after he opened me up, he saw that my aorta was full of clots. Some of those clots went to my brain and I started to mumble. That was when he knew I had suffered a stroke. They took me immediately into the CCU and did the necessary procedures.

I was pretty sick for a long time. I remember feeling that it was the end for me.

---

### ROSEMARY

*We were really concerned because the doctor hadn't told me at that time that George had had a stroke. He wasn't telling me much of anything. Dr. Scribner had come down to the hospital to stay with me while George was in the O.R. When they took George into the CCU, Mary Ellen and I saw him, and we knew things were bad.*

*"I said to the nurse, 'My husband seems comatose, is he?'*

*"'Well, hasn't your doctor told you anything?'*

*"'No. He told us nothing. Our children are out in the waiting room and are getting ready to go home.'*

*"'Oh, no, no, no! You tell them to stay. He's critical.'*

*"'Dr. Hubert never told me anything like that.'*

*"'Well, he'll be down later tonight. Maybe around eleven. You can talk to him then.'*

*"I talked to the doctor as soon as they brought George down. He said, 'Oh, he'll be OK. He had a little stroke activity, but he'll be fine.'*

*"I realized I was in the dark, so when Dr. Scribner arrived at the hospital, I filled him in: 'This man is not telling me a thing. He did say to me, "If I told you, you wouldn't understand anyway." I'm fit to be tied. Please talk to him and find out what went on.'*

---

# A Gradual and Necessary Reassessment

> ## ROSEMARY
>
> *"Dr. Scribner talked to the doctor, who explained what had happened, 'We won't know what's going on here or how bad it is for forty-eight hours. Let's see if he makes it through the night.'*
>
> *"I stayed overnight. The next night, I went home, but came back into the room early in the morning—maybe about six, when the staff was changing shifts. The commode that was in George's room was across the room from his bed. It was turned over. I asked, 'What's going on here?'*
>
> *"George was in bed. I was very concerned. 'Something has happened here.' Well, lo and behold, he had gotten out of the bed and was looking for the bathroom, wandering about the room. We never actually had a full report on all that transpired during that time."*

I have a vague remembrance of what happened. I had all kinds of needles in me, and I pulled them all out. I got out of bed in search of the bathroom, and I guess I was so disoriented that I knocked the chair over.

> ## ROSEMARY
>
> *"I just didn't feel that they were monitoring him as they should have been. I was pretty upset."*

After about five days or so, I did go home. I really wasn't good. As bad as Dad had been the day before he died, I was worse than that. I could hardly walk; I was fully dependent on the walker. Even with that aid, someone had to hold me. I really never thought I was going to be able to walk alone again. But I did get the feeling back in my left side. What I was left with was that the right side of my face dropped about an inch. I saw double for about four months. I had no peripheral vision. I couldn't close my right eye at all. Till today, I can't wink with that eye.

About a month later, as I began to think I might be back on the road to good health, I felt a pain in the center of my chest. Immediately, I went to the hospital. The doctor put me under again. When I was able to talk to the doctor, he told me, "I saw the one that was closed in the back of your heart when you were here before, but we couldn't even take the time to try to open it, for fear you would die. We were just trying to save your life." So this time, they opened the one in the back of my heart. I was in the hospital a few days before I came home that time. I actually started to do fairly well. They had me on a beta blocker and that made me just like a zombie.

Before either of those attacks occurred, Rosemary and I had made plans to go on a trip to Germany in September of that year with Bob and Margaret Scribner. I talked to my doctor about going, and I figured I'd be with a doctor and a nurse; if anything happened to me, they would probably know what to do. I felt OK to go, but I wasn't very alert. I was sluggish. We'd go someplace and I'd walk for a while, and then I'd have to sit down. In the end, we did go for a month and we had a good time.

After we came home from Europe, in November of that same year, Rosemary was driving me home from the office (because I had been advised not to drive). Once again, I felt an all-too-familiar pain in the middle of my chest. We went immediately to the hospital. I was having another heart attack.

It turns out that the blockage that had been cleared during the procedure when I had my first heart attack was back, but fortunately, with a little less vengeance. The blockage by that time was 98% rather than 100%. The doctor said he was going to do the same procedure as he had done before but more aggressively, "I'm going to blow this up bigger than I did before and try to see if we can make this thing hold." He followed his plan, and I never had another heart attack after that. Once again I had a mini stroke, but it didn't last long and I felt fairly good. However, I wasn't feeling normal. Rosemary would take me to the office but I couldn't stay as long as I wanted to; I just didn't have the stamina I needed. It was very fortunate that George Jr. had pretty much taken over running the company. Also, just before all of these events occurred, my brother Joe had come to work with me. He was a great help at the time, especially when I was involved in the big land development at Shaver Lake that I've already talked about. Joe stepped in and took care of things like that.

That land development project was the kind of thing I was involved in even after my heart attack, and it reminds me of just how extensive my activity was after Denise died. Nonetheless, at that time, I wasn't taking any time to look inside myself.

# A Gradual and Necessary Reassessment

I really didn't feel good. By the time July rolled along, I was begging my doctors to do open-heart surgery. They assured me that surgery was out of the question. In order to do that kind of surgery, the surgeon has to pinch off the main artery. My doctor was the same guy who had operated on Dad years before. He was considered one of the best surgeons in his field, so we were sure that he was giving us the best advice. He was up front: "If we do open-heart surgery on you, when I close the main artery, all those clots will go to your brain and you'll be dead in minutes." So I was not a candidate for open-heart surgery. I was disappointed because I didn't really feel good. The situation was frustrating.

The physical toll had been great, but another kind of toll was continuing to build, although I was very unaware of it. I was not unlike a lot of other people who had survived heart attacks but continued to exhibit continuing psychological repercussions. I had survived not one, but three, heart attacks that year, and I had much to be grateful for. On the other hand, there was much more I had to do. Eventually, with Rosemary's help, I took time to do what needed to be done.

# Chapter 46

## Drastic Changes

### *Rosemary*

I remember George telling the story of fighting with a kid in high school who had made a remark to him. (I think his name was Tommy.) He had seen George wearing a cap with a shamrock on it, and asked George why a 'camel rider' was wearing a shamrock. George passed off the remark at first, but when Tommy kept it up, George took him outside and gave him a really bad beating. That day, George decided that he never wanted to lose his temper again. I didn't know George at that time, of course; it was just a story he told me. The only time I ever saw George lose his temper was once when one of his business associates made some comment about the business and then went on to talk about George's relationship with me. George got furious. He didn't get physical, but he really lost his temper, and that was the only time I saw that happen in all the years I knew him. Then came George's heart surgery.

After the surgery, George seemed to be a different person from the man I had lived with for more than half my life. I saw outbursts of temper and a type of behavior that was almost a flashback of his dad. He would react to the simplest things in ways that were so foreign to all of us who knew him. One time, David and Mary Ellen, married and living on their own with children of their own, had decided that they wanted to go down to the desert. George advised them not to go. David stated his case for why they wanted to go, and George absolutely lost it. He went into a diatribe, the likes of which we had never seen. Then he walked away and went to bed. Both David and Mary Ellen were crushed. They were so hurt because of the way George had demeaned them for not agreeing with what he had said—and all about an incident that was rather inconsequential in the grand scheme of things.

All I could do was say to them, "You do as you feel you have to do. When you think the time is right, then do it." And they did just that. I was able to keep my composure, but I was every bit as confused by the incident as they were.

That was a single incident that seemed so out of character for George, but not unlike other incidents during his recovery. That recovery spanned quite a long time and was very tough on everyone, because his personality completely changed. It caused a lot of confusion in our children, who were all adults, and in their children.

This change was difficult for me, but not as baffling as it might have been. I used to take George's dad, Joe, to his doctor appointments after he had had his heart surgery. I remember the doctor asking me, "Have you seen any changes in Joe's personality?" I said, "A little, but not all that much."

"Well, expect it! All kinds of personality changes occur in coronary patients." Of course, I wasn't living in the same house as my father-in-law. I was living with George! Oddly enough, what had been predicted of George's dad was surfacing in George. I made it my business to tell the children, "This is all part of your father's heart problem, so please just try to overlook some of what's happening."

## GEORGE & JOHN

*GEORGE:*

*"The kids were not used to me expressing my opinions. I like to think it wasn't as bad as Rosemary is saying, but I have to admit it wasn't good. It wasn't that I threw stuff; I never did anything like that. But I did lose my temper."*

*JOHN:*

*"I think I hear what Rosemary is saying. I also think I know a little bit about you too, George. I know how emphatically you rejected the stormy outbursts you saw in Dad all the years we were growing up; but just like me, you experienced them. They are part of a repertoire inside our psyches. I've already said those behaviors are in me. You mentioned that yourself. I always said, if my anger was unleashed, I could kill someone. It's not as though those weaknesses ever left me. It's that I just have to continually ask God to help me control those impulses.*

*"Over all the years, it's not that you didn't have those negative feelings. You did have a very strong moral code and you chose to respond, not to the anger but to an inner discipline that governed your choices. Throughout your life, you harnessed those impulses, probably better than I did as a kid and as a young man, and you responded in discipline. There is that governing force in all of us. But in diminished circumstances— let's think about your heart attack, your three heart attacks, and your stroke— your*

# Drastic Changes

George's behavior did not go unnoticed—except, maybe, by George himself. I knew he always wanted to do the best for all of us, and it was difficult to see him so unlike himself. Especially during these difficult times, it was a blessing that George's brother Joe had already come to work for him. Joe took care of a lot of things that needed responses in George's multiple new business enterprises, leaving George Jr. free to concentrate on running Supra Alloys.

# CHAPTER 47

## My Dad

*George Jr.*

It was only after finishing college and pursuing a career in agriculture for a time that I was invited to join my father in business. That move was a major one for me, and one I am grateful for because I know I wouldn't have the relationship I have today with my dad if I hadn't become involved in the business with him.

Over the years, my respect and admiration for my dad have grown tremendously. Today, I am a successful businessman in my own right, but I stand in awe of some of the amazing qualities that I see in my dad. He is the consummate businessman and entrepreneur, with talents that many people overlook. He has the ability to see what can be. He's always thinking about the big picture. I like to call that the ability to perceive the 'grand view.' He sees things clearly, makes decisions quickly, and goes ahead confidently. He rarely looks back. Over the years, I have watched my dad and I have listened to him, and I have learned an amazing amount from him.

I think that his ability to see the 'grand view' is what makes him who he is. That's what has made him so successful. I, myself, don't have that ability, but I'm as successful as I am because I have been able to watch him and learn how to do what he's doing. He's taught me how to be a good businessman simply by being a good businessman himself and giving me the opportunity to watch him and to work with him.

His many talents and gifts of knowing have certainly served him well over the years. Yet, like so many things in life, those extraordinary talents have had a downside. His tremendous vision, his ability to see things so clearly, also affects the way that he deals with others. For all his amazing understanding in so many areas, he doesn't understand why, if he sees something, others don't. Maybe because of that quality, many people think he's a hard ass—someone who's incapable of bending. There have been times when someone asked him a question or looked for explanations and he has been very dismissive. I can attest to that. He can also be very dictatorial—my way or no way. There are many, including my children, who can attest to that.

I accept my dad as he is. I don't try to change him. I try to understand him just as he is.

Part of the challenge for me has been trying to understand who he is. A lot of that understanding has come with my own maturation, and I like to think I have a deeper perception as I grow older. My father is a great and a talented man. He's tough as nails, and I know (more than I feel, sometimes) that he loves me. The reality is always a simple truth: We are all part of the human family; we live our lives in the mixture of the perfect and the less-than-perfect. Our stories are in that striving.

As long as I have known him, my father has always had an interior motivation. When we were growing up, there were certain things he made very clear, very often. He would always say, "It's not what anyone else thinks; it's what you think, what you know—whether you're doing the right thing, whether you're happy with yourself or with what you're doing. It's inside."

I think these beliefs were true for him and he wanted them to be true for us. I think it explains why, when we were growing up, we didn't get a lot of strokes from my dad. He wanted us to experience that interior 'pat on the back.' He didn't want us to be people who were always looking for someone else's approval. He thought that, if we were, we would always be disappointed. He believed that that kind of back-slapping approval just isn't going to happen, and that life just doesn't work that way. I realize, now, that when we were looking for strokes from my father and we didn't get them, he thought he was making us stronger.

I remember years when my dad was away so much, and I have grappled with the truth about those absences. I remember being resentful about my dad's traveling and made up my mind that I would never travel like my dad had done. As a father of five young men, now I understand pretty clearly the implications of balancing work and family, and I have spent a lot of time getting to know and understand my own father better.

I have come to value what Dad gave us. And even though it wasn't always given as I would have liked it at the time, I have come to appreciate more that it was given in love. I take it as it was given—then and now, I take it as it is given. As I deal with my own children, I try to give them the kinds of strokes I think they need, but I realize that giving strokes is not something that comes easy to me, either.

# My Dad

I also have to admit that I wasn't the easiest kid in the world. There were things I did when I was growing that I'm sure drove him crazy. Maybe I was trying to get his attention. But he never responded with anger. I guess I know now that that was his way of cutting out what he saw and liked least about his own dad—a bad temper. When I did something that was out of line, he would turn and walk away. A day later, or maybe two or three, he'd reappear, and there'd be a discussion. That was the way he'd keep his emotions buttoned down.

I guess, by his standards, I'm a really emotional guy.

These are some of the things that were tough to deal with as I grew up with my dad, but even the negatives have taught me well. I don't beat my own drum. I know what's important to me and what I believe. I believe as strongly as my dad believes.

My father is the icon.

In business, I'm different from my father.

As time went on, and when I took over the business, I had to make sure that I did things on my own. I worked hard at establishing my own reputation. People know that I do things differently. There are things I can do that he can't. He's a very smart man and there seems to be nothing he can't figure out. But I know that he can't always figure out people. He doesn't understand people really well—and many people don't understand him. He might beg to differ with me on this point. And that's OK. He understands certain things about people, but he doesn't understand them in the same way that he understands things he can measure and calculate. I'm not sure why, except maybe when you deal with people, emotions creep in, and he doesn't like to admit that he operates on an emotional level. I know that, when I have a different opinion than my father has, I better have my ducks in a row. I better not be emotional and I have to be just as strong as, or stronger than, he is. I have to be strong in my own right. When I believe something, I believe strongly, and I accept the tension that the belief creates. I can't say that he likes that, and I think he still can't understand why I'm so adamant at times. Yet I know that, when I deal with my father, if I'm not solid in what I think, I'm toast. When all is said and done, I know my father respects—and expects—that kind of courage.

All of the Esseffs are passionate. What we believe, we believe strongly. We aren't lukewarm about anything, and that makes us quite formidable. Within the family itself, and among its many members, that dynamic is always a force to be reckoned with.

# Brothers & Fathers

There are a lot of us who want to get in there and turn the dials. For me, as I deal with my children, I try to be less dogmatic than I might like to be because I experienced that dogmatism as my dad dealt with me. With my dad, I try to have a greater appreciation for the many talents he has and a deeper gratitude for the understanding the years have afforded me and my family.

What I think most people don't know about 'Mr. Titanium' is how much he does out of love and concern. He has qualities that are too numerous to mention. He has always responded to the needs of the poor, even more than his recent works with the homeless and the elderly show.

My father is a man of deep faith. He has a very strong prayer life, and his greatest prayer is that he will gain heaven and all those he loves will share eternal happiness in heaven with him. He has done things throughout his life for people in need and no one has heard about them. What he did, no doubt, was done for the love of God and to honor the memory of his own grandfather, his Gidue, by emulating his love for the poor.

I have learned a great deal from my father. He is a man who casts a big shadow. He can be unbending and stern, yet he is humble and gentle. He is not comfortable in the spotlight, but he has responded so completely to developing his gifts masterfully that he often finds himself there. He is a man with a big ego, but he is a man of humility too. He doesn't need applause. He does need to feel he is pleasing God. Perhaps what most defines him as a human being as he serves God are the very things he prefers to keep private. In that paradox, I have been blessed with, and value, my father.

These few thoughts only scratch the surface of my life as the son of George Esseff.

Maybe putting all the feelings down in words will help all of us to understand better what we received and what we may, in the end, be blessed to give.

# CHAPTER 48

## THE ROAD TO RECOVERY

### *George*

In retrospect, I can say that everyone was aware of the changes in me after my series of heart attacks and strokes. One day, our friend Dr. Bob Scribner, sent a book to us about a Dr. Dean Ornish from northern California. Dr. Ornish, a research cardiologist, was the founder and president of the Preventive Medicine Research Institute in Sausalito, California. It was his contention that comprehensive lifestyle changes can begin to reverse even severe coronary heart disease without drugs or surgery. He came up with a regimen of exercising and eating properly for his cardiac patients. It was his belief that, by following his program, patients could reduce their cholesterol and increase their ability to live naturally. Rosemary and I thought the program might have some merit, and we made an appointment to go to Sausalito and participate in it for a week. It was quite an intense experience, and one that turned out to have a significant impact on my life. As expected, there was a pretty rigorous exercise program that included treadmill and bike workouts, as well as swimming. The program for proper eating was also presented. The diet included grains, fruits, vegetables, and beans. No oils whatsoever were allowed, and no fish, no chicken, no meat, no cheese. Everything had to be fat free. The attending spouses were told how to shop: Stay on the perimeter of the store. Buy everything fresh. Do not go up and down the aisles. Buy nothing canned. The staff also did more than just give out information. There were chefs there who were part of the program. They taught the spouses of the patients how to cook the kinds of foods that were included in the regimen. Rosemary, along with others, was taught how to make at least twenty different kinds of pizza—all vegetarian, and all allowed on the program.

---

### ROSEMARY

*"I knew a lot of what was presented at the workshop because Denise was put on a similar restrictive diet by the doctor in Germany. I had prepared her food for quite some time."*

---

I could eat pasta with tomato sauce and seasonings, but I had to watch the volume. I was told that I had to exercise four days a week. I asked if I could exercise every day, and the doctor said, "Sure, that would be even better."

Before we went to the workshop, I had learned that, in addition to eating right and exercising regularly, I would also have to learn how to do yoga. It was considered the necessary defense against stress. Learning how to do yoga relaxation and also yoga stretching was entirely new to me, but I was willing to participate fully. Rosemary and I stayed at the Institute for a whole week; and even before the end of that short time, for a lot of reasons, I began to feel better.

In addition to all of these facets of the program, all patients were put through a series of psychological tests and, for the first time I found out how deeply Denise's death had really affected me. With all that I disclosed to them, they were quite sure that business was not my problem. With business ruled out, they dug further. They talked to me about Denise's death and they determined that losing her was what had caused me the biggest problem. I did believe that God had taken her to heaven. I do believe she is in heaven now. How I felt about her loss was another chapter in the story.

## ROSEMARY

"Even before we went up to see Dr. Ornish, George had begun to exercise and to watch his diet—not as strictly or intensely as he did after going to the Institute, though. When we got to the workshop, Dr. Ornish made it clear, "You can do these two things, but if you don't do yoga to reduce stress, you will not get the full effect of my program. And so, included in the group of other professionals—the doctor, a cardiac nurse, and psychologists—there was also someone who taught us yoga. I had to go through the same regimen as George, but they insisted that we each participate separately, not together. The psychologists would sit with the patients in an effort to find out what the source and level of their stress was. It was a given, one way or another, that each cardiac patient there had stress. I had never heard George admit to having any stress from business, but that's where the psychologist began."

The psychologists put me through all sorts of questioning about my business habits and how I ran my business. I described those areas and gave what I felt was an accurate appraisal of my work habits. All my life, no matter how many things I was involved in, I always made it a practice to handle only one thing at a time. I never tried to deal with two things at once; I'd finish one thing and go on to the next. I gave them all kinds of details: I never took any work home. I never opened a briefcase on an airplane; I rested as much as I could when I traveled. I tried to tell them, as honestly as I could, everything they wanted to know. With all that I disclosed to them, and after many hours of discussion, they were quite sure that business was not my problem.

A case-in-point might be a situation that I had been involved in for some time, which came to a head while I was actually involved in Dr. Ornish's program. Because of the gravity of the situation, I got a telephone call from my secretary. I only include what happened because it was something that could probably be considered stress related. The problem my secretary called me about that day was something that had come to light right after I had my heart attacks. I wasn't happy about the situation that developed, but I dealt with it in pretty much the same way I dealt with all business matters.

When I received that phone call from my office, my secretary told me that I had received a bill from the IRS. The bill related to an investment I had made many years before. In 1979, I had invested $600,000 in an oil and tax shelter which was sold to us as a big profit-making venture from an outfit out of Denver. The shelter also brought with it a big tax benefit. When we got involved, we had very reputable professional advisors who told us that the deal was very sound—a good, solid investment in a time of big gas and oil shortages. However, about four years later (around 1983), the IRS discovered that there had been some shenanigans with the guys in Denver who had put the deal together. At some point, the government looked more closely at the deal and didn't approve of what they saw. They branded the guys in Denver crooks and went after them. The whole process took years. Part of the initial agreement was that the group in Denver would take care of any lawsuits that might arise concerning the deal. What actually happened was that, over the years, they used all the money they had for legal fees, and then they kept calling all the investors for more money to continue to pursue the lawsuit—which went on for years. I was one of those investors. By the time the government took the guys to court and finished with them, ten years had passed. Throughout the whole fiasco, my tax attorney was keeping tabs on the case and began to indicate to me that we were definitely going to lose the suit. In time, we did, in fact, lose the suit.

When I spoke to my secretary that day from Dr. Ornish's, she told me we had received a sixty-day letter. (A sixty-day letter means that we had 60 days to pay the whole amount we owed to the IRS.) The government was offering a settlement of 33% off if we would pay the fees to cover all the cost. I agreed to those terms. When all was said and done, between the state and the IRS, we owed the tremendous sum of $5,250,000; the interest alone was running $40,000 a month. A $600,000 investment had cost me $5,250,000. My lawyer told me that, if I didn't pay it, the IRS would start by attaching my home and business. I didn't want that to happen. I knew I had much more in assets than I owed, and so I decided I would pay it off. Of course, there was no way to do what I eventually did in the midst of Dr. Ornish's program. Because of my health, I couldn't let the situation become a great weight on me. It was much more important to concentrate on what I was doing, trying to repair myself. That's what I did.

I guess I should tell how that story ended. When I finished Dr. Ornish's program, I took care of the tax bill. In order to pay what I owed, I had to sell securities. I had to sell properties, six of which were in Hawaii. I also had to sell other properties and some homes I owned. Selling all of those things, I did raise the money in the sixty days allotted. It was a tragedy, really, and it ate up a lot of the money I had earned over the years; but it had to be done, and I did it, and I didn't look back—not until now. It was over for me when I paid the bill in sixty days.

The psychologist was well aware of my situation, and he continued to maintain that the way I responded to business was not causing my stress. He certainly had enough data to base his judgment on. And so with business ruled out, they dug further. They talked to me about Denise—her illness and the circumstances of her death. Ultimately, they determined that losing her was what had caused me the stress I obviously had, but tried to ignore. They told me, "If you have that kind of stress and it hits you that strongly, you can literally have a heart attack in a very short time. Your vessels can shrink and, along with developing plaque, blockages can occur in a very short time." They got me talking about Denise and, in no time, I broke down and cried. I don't think there was ever a time in my life that I cried the way I did that day. I cried and I cried and I cried. Finally, I had identified my grief—either denied or ignored, but certainly not gone away. The psychologist was sure that losing Denise and shelving my feelings was definitely the source of my stress.

## ROSEMARY

*When we were going through this process, the psychologists would come out of George's session and talk to me. After three sessions, one of them came to me one evening and said, "We found it. George had a breakthrough. At last, he's aware of the source of his stress. On an emotional level, he has never really fully faced what happened and how he felt when your daughter died. He never admitted his need to do that, and has never allowed himself to grieve. This is where it is; and this encounter with such intense grief is*

ROSEMARY

*what he will have to continue to work on. He can do that through yoga. Doing yoga is the key for him in reducing his stress, and if he does that (as well as everything else we've talked about), this program will work for him."*

The week we spent there was the start of a new way of life for me in many ways. For the next seven years, I exercised seven days a week. I'd start usually at 5:00 in the morning and finish about 7:30. I did yoga for 45 minutes to an hour. I also did yoga stretching and then used the treadmill and the exercise bike. I stuck with that regimen religiously. I wouldn't go anyplace on business or pleasure without calling ahead to make sure that the proper exercise equipment would be available for me. I was dedicated and I really did work out faithfully.

Of course, much of the program was centered on eating properly. Fortunately, following the eating regimen had quick initial results for me. Before we even left the Institute, I had lost nine pounds and I was feeling so much better. That initial success really motivated me to stay with the program for a lot of years. Rosemary, as always, was my support staff. She shopped carefully and was so creative in preparing meals that she made it much easier for me to stick to the plan. Though it was a diet that excluded a lot of things, Rosemary was clever enough not only to keep variety in the meals and to make meals that tasted good, but also to follow the program's strict food regimen. The clarity that I gained about the way I handled Denise's death and the opportunity to express my grief were parts of a healing process that I continued to pursue through my dedication to yoga.

ROSEMARY

*George's participation in Dr. Ornish's program proved invaluable during those years. It wasn't, however, an overnight process, or a week-long process, or even a year-long course of action. For those who were standing by and watching a series of complicated life events, the entire process was one that evolved a step at a time—with the occasional step backwards. At one point, after following Dr. Ornish's regimen for a time, George went into a depression that lasted for about two weeks. He was tired and he didn't want to get out of bed; he lost interest in just about everything. Fortunately, with the help of his doctor, he was able to find the right medication that helped him, and he began to feel better again.*

# Brothers & Fathers

## A Letter to my Sponsor

*To my Grandfather and Sponsor,*

*Through these past two years, you have been my role model and my supporter in the process of Confirmation. You've been a patient teacher and my loving grandfather. Your thoughts were always centered in what was best for me and you've shown me the righteous path in your actions and your example.*

*Even in your busy schedule and with your sudden illness, you've been there to stand by my side. This day means so much to me, and to have you here with me makes it even more special! I love you so very much. God Bless.*

*Granddaughter Michelle*

*Lovingly, Your Eldest Granddaughter,*

*Michelle Marie Michael*

During my long period of recuperating, I went on a business trip to Australia. While I was there, I had the opportunity to meet one of the leading yogis in the world. I had heard about this yoga master through Bob Scribner: A relative of Bob's was in Australia and had met her. He got me a record of hers to play for my yoga meditation and, when I got to Australia, I made arrangements to meet her. I had a two-hour session with her. Though I will always be grateful for Dr. Ornish's introduction to yoga, I have to say that this yogi taught me more in two

*Rosemary and George with Dr. Scribner in Australia*

hours than I had learned during my full week at Dr. Ornish's place. Since my heart attack and stroke, I still had some distortions in my face. Because my mouth was pulled over to one side and my eyes were still not right, she taught me yoga exercises for those areas. She also taught me other body-stretching activities that helped me get back on track and rededicate myself to my existing regimen. It took a lot of time, but I slowly improved; I generally kept feeling better and I stayed focused on enjoying a healthy lifestyle and resuming those things I wanted to continue to do.

Since the mid-eighties, I had been going to Lebanon off-and-on for a long time; I had relatives, friends, and several projects I was involved in there. About seven years after I had my heart attack, I was on a flight to Lebanon from Los Angeles. I was flying into London and then continuing to Lebanon. Three hours outside of London, I started to get a pain in my chest, arm, and shoulder. Of course, I thought I might be having another heart attack. When we landed, I immediately got in touch with the emergency personnel on the ground. I told them what I was feeling and they called an ambulance, which took me to a local hospital. I stayed there for two days. Because of my history, they were very cautious; but still they were unable to find anything. I went to pay my bill, but I wasn't charged anything because they had socialized medicine. I went back to the airport but decided not to continue to Lebanon. Instead, I boarded a plane for California, and when I got home the next day, I went to see my doctor. He listened to the whole story and was open to the possibility that my arteries were closing again. He did an angiogram and, when he put the wire in and put me under the scope there, he literally started jumping up and down with excitement, "I can't believe what I'm seeing. You've reversed your heart disease. All of the clots are gone. There's almost no plaque in your system!" All along, he had sort of dismissed my going for treatment to Dr. Ornish. "I always thought it was a crazy diet, but you've made a believer out of me. I couldn't get one patient to do what you've done."

My doctor figured out that I had a pinched nerve in my neck and that was what had caused the pain in my neck and shoulder on my way to London—and was still causing it right there in his office. I began physical therapy and, shortly, was rid of that pain. After all that I had been through, when I heard my cardiologist's take on the state of my heart and my health, I felt as though I had been given a new life. I started eating meat again, and a lot of things that I hadn't eaten in a long time. I don't suppose that was all that prudent, but I decided to indulge myself after so many disciplined years.

I think that God has always protected me. If he didn't cure me with a miracle, He cured me by helping me find the right doctors, the right medicine, and the right course of action.

Naturally, I was always happier with good health than with bad. In spite of some medical problems, I feel that I had the blessings of a generally strong body and the energy to enjoy my life. Since God decided that I had more life to live, my obligation was to figure out what that life should be focused on and dedicated to.

# CHAPTER 49

## THE TURN OF THE CENTURY

### *Father John*

I can honestly say that, as I experienced the turn of the century, I couldn't help looking backward and I couldn't help looking forward. As the century came to an end, I could look back and say that, after almost fifty years of priesthood, I knew the fullness of priesthood. I have no idea how many babies I baptized, but I would venture to say the number is somewhere in the thousands. Many adults who had experienced later conversions to the faith also swelled that number. I remember with great happiness the beautiful days when little children received Jesus in the Eucharist for the first time. It was nothing short of pure joy when I had the honor of telling them how much Jesus wants to feed and nourish them and to invite them to be Jesus in the world. Before those celebrations came their first confessions. What poured from their hearts as they prepared for First Holy Communion was a miracle of innocence and grace.

On the other end of the spectrum, perhaps there was nothing short of awe as I had the privilege of absolving those who, in spite of unimaginable pain and brokenness, responded to the grace of a good confession. Through the wonderful sacrament of reconciliation, so many good people returned to the waiting arms of God, our loving Father. Such profound moments of repentance and forgiveness have been moments of great grace and humility for me as I stood in wonder, experiencing the infinite love and mercy of God.

To think about the numberless marriages I officiated at is to recognize an almost inexpressible happiness. Meeting so many couples who were so in love and so willing to live out that love as husband and wife was certainly inspiring for me. Those celebrations of the sacrament of matrimony were testimonies to the faith men and women have in one another, the hope with which they approach the future, and the love they desire to cherish for a lifetime.

# Brothers & Fathers

When I remember how many people I was able to comfort with the so-called 'last rites' before they died, I am filled with gratitude. I was even more grateful when the Church restored Extreme Unction to its role the as sacrament of the Anointing of the Sick. The Scriptures are filled with account after account of Jesus healing the sick—not just of physical ailments but also those of the spirit. Today, people are invited to come to the communal Anointing of the Sick to be anointed on the head and the hands with holy oil as the priest prays for healing. People with illnesses can now seek healing from the Lord through that sacrament which was, for a time in the Church's history, reserved only for those who were dying.

### CAROL BURTI

*"Did I know that I had a gift for music? That music speaks to the heart? That song is a healing tool?*

*"How could I ever come to know those things to be true?*

*"As a young child, I loved to go to church and listen to the great music sung by our choir. I would always try to join in the singing. However, that singing in the pews was a little too much for our pastor. That's when I would hear my name called out from the altar: 'Carol Burti, BE STILL!' I didn't understand why my singing was so upsetting to the priest. And when I went home, I was scolded again for causing a commotion in church.*

*"At that very early age, fear, anxiety, and deep wounds had already set in. Whenever I went to church, all I could think of was, 'BE STILL!' It was a stern reprimand.*

*"Many, many years later, I was invited to Marywood College to sing at a Healing Service in the context of a Mass celebrated by Monsignor John Esseff. I was very hesitant about accepting the invitation and found myself experiencing fear—the old paralyzing anxieties concerning my singing. How could I overcome all that I was feeling?*

*"Monsignor explained to me that, when we help others to heal, we too can be healed. We can be 'wounded healers.' He encouraged me to help others through my gift of music. I very apprehensively said 'Yes.' I sang and played my guitar at that Mass and Healing Service, and I too experienced healing.*

*"Now, twenty-five years later, I am still singing a beautiful hymn taken from the Psalms. 'Be Still' is no longer a reprimand; it's a blessing."*

Be still, be still, be still and know that I am your God.

Be still, be still, and know that I am with you.

# The Turn of the Century

As I thought about the great graces that pour out from the sacraments, I was at once gladdened and saddened by stories of those who had received the sacrament of Holy Orders. Those stories, mine and those of so many others, are unique; but the history of the priesthood in the sixties and into the turn of the century is a story that tells of a great deal of brokenness.

While I was in Lebanon, I was privileged to meet the Missionaries of Charity and, through them, Blessed Mother Teresa of Calcutta who founded the order. After many encounters with Mother, she gave me great affirmation in the work I was doing with her sisters. She also identified gifts I had and, as I became comfortable with them, I knew I wanted to use those gifts in response to men in formation for the priesthood. By the start of the nineties, I knew I had grown in my ability to do that kind of work. I also knew that my insights into what needed to be done stood in sharp contrast to my earlier attempts in the 70s to make an appropriate response to men in formation in American seminaries. Let me recall that time.

After I came back from South America, I felt as though I had something that I could share with young men who were studying for the priesthood. At that time, I was invited to give two retreats: one on the east coast and another on the west coast. I conducted both of those retreats with the help of Sister Cor Immaculatum. We felt that, as a team, we could present both the masculine and the feminine perspective on issues of importance to young men in formation. The formation director in California and the rector in Maryland accepted the two of us as a viable team to conduct the retreats. In fact, the retreat in California was an ordination retreat and, as such, was extremely important. Unfortunately, my experience with both those retreats went far beyond my capacity to stay involved in the work of priestly direction and still maintain my own integrity. During both retreats, I became aware of a pervasive and accepted atmosphere of what seemed to me rampant homosexual overtones and acting out. The acting out was so extensive that I felt that I had some obligation to address the issue, but I was bewildered as to how I might do that. I got in touch with a prominent theologian I knew and asked him point blank what my obligation was. I have to admit: I was surprised at his response, but I accepted his advice. He said I had no responsibility. It seemed to him that what I had learned in a few days was something that the administration was already aware of and permitting, or maybe even participating in. Homosexuality seemed to be a major issue at that time.

With the environments that I saw and the disorders that seemed evident, I decided that I could not make any significant contribution in formation at that time. My ineffectiveness led me to discern that my gifts lay elsewhere at that time, and I devoted most of my time to the poor of the Diocese of Scranton. Those were very fruitful years.

After my mission in Lebanon, however, throughout the late eighties and early nineties, my experiences with Mother Teresa, especially those dealing with priestly formation, once again stirred in me the desire to take on the challenges that the priesthood presented, in all its variations. I studied my own diocese and recognized many aspects of the priesthood that demanded attention. Besides recognizing the present challenges of preparing men for the future, I knew that there were men who had suffered significant losses and a great deal of pain in relationship to the priesthood. Those hurts had gone on for years without any formal response from the Church. I could not fully devote myself to all of the new concerns in the priesthood unless I tended to some of the old ones.

I was painfully aware of the great exodus that had occurred in the diocesan priesthood in the late sixties and the seventies. I was also aware of the difficulties priests who had left the active ministry were experiencing as they dealt with their relationship to the Church. In some ways, many became lepers. Many left the areas in which they had lived and, consequently, the diocese for which they had been ordained. I knew many of those men, and I knew that they were good men. I also knew that many of the men who remained in the priesthood were being prosecuted for sexual impropriety. Much of that impropriety was of a disordered, even criminal nature. Along those lines, I found it curious that those who had left the priesthood were asked to articulate why they had left the active ministry. At the same time, those who stayed were not asked to articulate why they were staying. Was it to serve Jesus Christ through his people and for the glory of His Father? Was it for financial, social, or emotional security of some kind? Was there any other kind of self serving motivation? No one said— because no one was asked. It was pretty simple: Those who had left were considered traitors, and those who stayed were thought to be heroes. History has shown that was not necessarily so in every instance. The priesthood had suffered much and was still under siege. What I was witnessing was painful for me to watch, and I felt called to do something for those who, in the past, had left the active ministry.

It was a time for healing. In 1991, I invited as many inactive priests as I could locate, with the scant means available, to come to the seminary (where I was living at the time) for a day of prayer and reconciliation. That initial meeting was attended only by the men. Surrounded by prayer, it was an opportunity for the former priests to renew old acquaintances and to discuss some of their thoughts about their place in the Church. There was a lot of camaraderie among those who came, and a great interest in expanding the encounter to include wives and children of the men who had married. Eventually, with the help of those who had come to the initial encounter, I initiated a program for priests who had left the active ministry. It was called Re-Connections. I could look back on my heritage in the Maronite rite and know that I, myself, came from a family of priests. The Roman rite, however, did not include married clergy. Because of my background, I had no trouble with the idea of priests who wanted families of their own.

What I did have trouble with was within my own priesthood. I had ministered to so many who were poor: alcoholics, drug addicts, victims of abuse of one kind or another, and here were my brother priests, alienated and in need of healing. I wanted to reach out to them and minister to them as best I could. The first of these outreach programs, one just for the men, was held in the early nineties while Bishop Timlin was the bishop of Scranton. With the help of many of those who came to that first meeting, the Re-Connections experiences became possible. Beginning in 2004, a series of retreats were held at the Fatima Center on the grounds of St. Pius X Seminary; and then, after the closing of the seminary in May of 2004, one other retreat was held at St. Gabriel's Retreat House in Clarks Summit. The retreats were prepared for diocesan priests who had left the active ministry, their wives and children, and some priests from religious orders who had served in the diocese. All were invited to "Come together in the Lord" for a retreat weekend held March 12-13, 2004. Bishop Timlin, by then the bishop emeritus of the diocese, was on hand that day and gave the welcoming address.

There were well over fifty priests who had left the active ministry in the Diocese of Scranton by the turn of the century. Some had gone through the process of laicization; some had not. Many had married and had families. On our first Re-Connections encounter, as well as on the others that followed, we spent a great deal of time together. We prayed; we shared; we socialized. There were meetings for husbands and wives together. There were meetings for wives alone. There were sessions for the children whose fathers had left the active ministry. During all these group sessions, we shared our thoughts and feelings, and we discussed a great many things that needed to be addressed.

As I had planned the weekend session, I was aware of the stipulations concerning the event: There was to be no publicity, and there was to be no Eucharistic celebration. We had informal moments over meals, and those who stayed at Fatima Center for the weekend talked and shared well into the evening. The children seemed to find a community meeting other children who were raised in similar situations.

When Bishop Timlin retired and Bishop Joseph Martino assumed the leadership of the Diocese of Scranton in October 2003, there were three additional encounters. The last of those was held at St. Gabriel's Retreat House in Clarks Summit. By that time, St. Pius X Seminary had been closed. I thought then, as I do now, how difficult it is for a priest to experience forgiveness—and its precursor, understanding. I was grateful for the opportunity to meet with these men and their families, as was Bishop Timlin. During his years as bishop of the diocese, Bishop Timlin had served with most of the men who attended the Re-Connections encounters, and many of them had received Holy Orders from him. Much reconciliation took place during those encounters.

# The Turn of the Century

## DOLLY MARIE DENSEVICH

*"I married Charles "Chick" Densevich on July 18, 1974, after he left the active ministry and was laicized. He had served for seven years as a priest of the Altoona-Johnstown Diocese. After we were married, we lived in Scranton, where we raised our three children. Our son and our daughters were always aware that their dad had been a priest. We talked about it openly and participated in the life of our local parish. We knew that acknowledging the priesthood as part of the family history was not something done by everyone who had left the active ministry. We also knew that, to some degree, feelings of alienation and loss were part of the history of each man there.*

*"After more than twenty-five years of marriage, we were invited to take part in Re-Connections. We were thrilled when we heard about this response that we had so long hoped for from the Church. We were eager to participate, and to experience the touch of Jesus through it. That touch came through the efforts of Monsignor Esseff.*

*"At the Re-Connections retreat, there must have been more than fifty priests who had left the active ministry. Bishop Timlin, who had ordained 90 to 95% of those men during his episcopacy, attended the retreat. The men were so happy to be with him there because many had felt alienated for so many years. I remember one man weeping, just crying for such a long time. It was as if each tear, one at a time, was freeing him from his pain.*

*"The first retreat, under the name of Re-Connections, was held at St. Pius X Seminary, where some of the men had been trained. For them, the seminary atmosphere had been very formal. That first evening, many who had been classmates were there with their wives and children. They seemed very comfortable in the new environment. We were all having a wonderful time and experiencing healing. Each day was a wonderful opportunity for the men to express how much it meant to them to be able to talk about their priesthood and to be with others who had left the active ministry. Besides Bishop Timlin and Monsignor Esseff, there were also other priests from the diocese who joined us on the retreat. We felt that they were interested, and they welcomed us and listened to what we had to say. They respected our feelings of alienation and the sense of loss that had gone unacknowledged for so long. After so many years of having no place to go, we did, in fact, come to feel re-connected in a very beautiful way through those weekend retreats.*

*"Chick and I had a wonderful time. I remember him saying that he saw people healing right before his eyes. I met a woman on the retreat who I had gone to high school with. She and her husband lived in Virginia. She had married a man who had been a priest*

*of the Scranton diocese. It was just so wonderful to see this woman whom I had not seen in more than a quarter of a century because she, like so many others, had left the diocese with her husband. As I reflect on it now, I am reminded that my husband Chick also left his home diocese and had come to start his new life with me, not in the Altoona-Johnstown diocese, but in Scranton.*

*"From the time Chick and I first met Monsignor Esseff until Chick's death on August 3rd, 2007, Monsignor remained a source of strength and comfort for all of us. Monsignor was always very much a brother to Chick. I remember when he came to our home to anoint Chick just days before he passed away. It was a time for many graces that day. I remember how touched Chick was when Monsignor said to him, "You have taught me a great deal about fraternity and fatherhood." Although my husband Chick had been laicized, Monsignor gave him healing affirmation about the beauty of his priesthood, and the love God had for him and for me and for our children.*

*"Monsignor Esseff continues to be a source of grace and healing in my life and in the lives of my children and grandchildren. I will always be grateful to God for the blessing of Monsignor in our lives."*

Though these sessions brought a lot of healing, they also made it clear that the possibility for a married clergy in the Church was still remote, if at all feasible in the lifetimes of the men who were there. It was difficult to firm up goals for the group as a whole because there were many agendas that needed to be addressed. The encounters did give the men several opportunities to connect with one another and to know that they were not forgotten. The last of those meetings took place on Saturday, May 28, 2005, at St. Gabriel's Retreat House in Clarks Summit. By that time I had moved to Fargo, North Dakota to serve as formation director at a seminary there. I did, however, return to my diocese for that last retreat.

It is interesting to note that, in recent years, there are priests in the active ministry who were at one time married and then widowed. The children of those men had all reached adulthood by the time the men chose to dedicate their lives to the priesthood. There was also a community of people from the Episcopal Church in Scranton who recently came into the Catholic Church along with their priest. That story made headlines throughout the country. The priest of that community was given permission to enter seminary training and has since been ordained as a Catholic priest. He, too, has a family. Perhaps some of these developments have caused confusion for the laity, and no doubt they have not gone unnoticed by those priests who left the ministry to marry. None of them has been invited back, as far as I know. Without a doubt, God remains the God of surprises, and how each man's journey serves to glorify God is not ours to understand.

By the time I had assumed my duties at St. Pius X, I was much more aware of the problems that faced men who were thinking about becoming priests. Along with others on the faculty, I had the wisdom of Pastores Dabo Vobis to guide me as we took on the challenges of how to discern the suitability of men for priesthood in terms of their human, spiritual, academic and pastoral formation. It was a formidable task. There was a big range in age among the seminarians: Some were right out of high school, some were older, and some had left successful careers to pursue formation in the priesthood later in life. Working with the developing IPF and serving as formation director at St. Pius X constituted some of my most challenging and satisfying years as a priest.

Before I began to see the fruit of these endeavors, however, I think it is important to note what the early days at the seminary were like for me. One day not long after I took up residence at Pius X Seminary, I experienced what I felt was a most oppressive force in my room. There were times that I felt that someone, or some weight, was sitting on my chest. There were almost audible voices telling me, "Get out of here. We don't want you here." I was confused. I felt confined and oppressed. I didn't know what those forces were, but they were in my room. Around that time, my brother Joe and my sister-in-law Patty were making a retreat with a Jesuit priest not far away in Syracuse, New York. When they finished their retreat, I went there to meet them for dinner. As we sat together over dinner, I mentioned to the priest who had come along with them that I was stationed at St. Pius X Seminary. I wasn't expecting his response: "You have to exorcise that seminary. You have to drive the demons out of there. I've given retreats in that place and the walls are talking." As I began to hear what he was saying, and put it together with what I had been experiencing, I told him I thought I should do an exorcism. He advised me very strongly, "Do not do the exorcism by yourself." Well, I went against that advice and I used to go from place to place in the seminary performing the Rite of Exorcism. One day while I was in my room, I was actually knocked to the floor. The same force that I had experienced before was once again in my room. I crawled to the phone and called Father Rich Gabuzda, who came and found me on the floor. He took me to the hospital, where the doctor found nothing wrong with me. Only then did I put it together; only then could I name the forces that were oppressing me. I recognized them, and I knew what I had to do. This time, I took the advice of the Jesuit I had met in Syracuse, Father Joseph Neville. I gathered a group together to pray for deliverance: the three members of the team who were contemplating the formation of the IPF, Father Horn, Father Gabuzda, and Kathy Kanavy; Sister Cor Immaculatum, who had been a source of direction and prayerful support for the team; and myself. Of course, I had informed Monsignor Bohr, the rector, about what I wanted to do. He really had trepidations about my plans and asked me to wait until a time when all of the seminarians would be out of the seminary building. I did respect his request. When the time came, every one of those people who came to pray with me experienced the presence of the power of evil in the building. We went through every part of the seminary: the chapel, the administration buildings, the dormitories, even the outdoor grounds. We prayed for deliverance from any demons that were in or near the place. After that time of prayer and deliverance, a peace came to St. Pius X Seminary.

It was some time after that experience that I gave Father John Horn his retreat. After his retreat, he and the others began to concretize their plans for the formation of the IPF, and they began to search for a place where they could implement their program. After looking at various locations, they chose Creighton University in Omaha, Nebraska, where they would be free of the interference of any bishops.

Long aware of the love my brother George had for the priesthood, I began thinking that he, too, might want to be involved in making the Institute for Priestly Formation a reality. George had always had a strong interest in the priesthood. He is very happily married, but has always understood the value of the priesthood, and has remained firm in his commitment to fostering vocations. From very early on, George has had a history of praying for and encouraging young men who might have a vocation to seriously consider that call as a life choice. That involvement can be traced way back to when he was a young man and quite active in the Serra Club.

## GEORGE

"I have been involved in supporting priests and seminarians since I joined the Serra Club. The Serra Club began when a group of professional men met to discuss how their Christian values could best be lived out in their lives. Those first Serrans, who chose the Spanish missionary, Padre Junipero Serra, as their patron, quickly took on an additional focus: to promote vocations to the priesthood through prayer.

"When I went to work with the Army Corps of Engineers at Fort Belvoir in Virginia in 1951, I would go to Mass at the chapel on the post. I got to know the priest and some

*GEORGE*

of the men, mostly officers, who were instrumental in doing innovative things around the post.

"The Serra Club, which was started in 1934, was still reasonably new at that time. The priest told me that one of the officers had been requested by Serrans in West Virginia to see about starting a Serra Club at Fort Belvoir. These few men were going to be doing a kind of experimental thing to see if they could support and build a Serra Club on an Army post where men in the club would have to leave because of reassignments. Then those in leadership would have the task of acquiring other men to replace those who had left in order to keep the club going. They decided to bring in some non-military men and I asked if I could belong to it. At that time, the Serrans were usually middle-aged or older men, well established in their fields. There I was, 21, and I said I would be really eager to work with other men in Serra. They did allow me to join and I have been a member since then. At 21, I was the youngest man ever to join! It's now almost sixty years that I have been a member.

"When I lived in Scranton, I was asked by the bishop to begin a Serra Club, and I was able to form a club there. I did engage a group of about 25 men who became the first Serra Club in Scranton. When I moved to California, I asked the pastor of St. Elizabeth's parish if there was a Serra Club in the area and he told me that he knew of one being set up; he got me in touch with a man by the name of Frank Arpaia. I came to be a charter member of the new club in the San Fernando Valley club, and I remain a member there since 1959."

Father Horn, Father Gabuzda, and Kathy Kanavy continued to make tremendous progress. As they remained steadfast in developing this new and vital approach to formation in the priesthood, I realized, as they did, that there were going to be great expenses in putting together the program that they had envisioned. Around 1994, I went to George and told him about those three young people and how they had started a new organization called the IPF at Creighton University.

## GEORGE

"I had asked John throughout many of his other missions what I could do to help financially, but he would never take money. He never started to do something that depended on money, and if money was needed, he didn't come to me. When John got more and more involved with the founders of IPF and the programs they hoped to provide, they found that they did have a need for money to keep moving that organization in the direction they wanted it to go. John came to me and told me that this Institute was the first thing that ever looked like it could save the priesthood in the United States and make it viable for the 21st century. When he told me about the IPF, it seemed a natural progression for me to continue with the Serra Club and to become involved somehow with the IPF as well.

"This was the first time that John had ever come to me and asked me for money. I was very surprised, and extremely curious as to what was motivating this highly unusual request. I remember clearly what he said: 'George, we need some money to get this program started. Would you be interested in supporting it? I don't know of anyplace else where you could put your money that could help the Church more. We feel we're going to be changing the priesthood for the better. It would be great if you decide to support this worthwhile project.'

"So I did do that. On John's recommendation, I got involved in IPF and initially donated $500,000. Over the years, I have given them almost a million dollars. I feel I'd give all I have in the Esseff Foundation to see the Institute flourish because I really feel that it has tremendous merit and unlimited potential for renewal in the Church."

I am grateful that George has been able to be a part of the IPF because I know his great dedication to the Church. He has watched the program grow, along with the rest of us. His prayers, as well as his money, are greatly appreciated every day.

# The Turn of the Century

*REV. JOHN HORN, S.J.*

*"Our first program began with six seminarians who came in the summer of 1994 to Creighton University in Omaha, Nebraska. Their goal was to dedicate ten weeks to growing in relational prayer through daily prayer, retreats, and one-on-one spiritual direction according to the Spiritual Exercises of St. Ignatius Loyola. The program grew to twenty seminarians the following summer.*

*"As of 2006, over a hundred dioceses of the U.S. and beyond had been served by the Institute. Diocesan priestly formation is being impacted greatly as twenty-five percent of all future diocesan pastors are passing through one of the Institute's programs of formation. At present, over one-third of all seminary spiritual directors have received some initial training in the art of contemplative spiritual direction through IPF.*

*"International outreach includes seminary personnel in Canada, Uganda, and Malta. Future outreach to the Church in the Ukraine and the Middle East is also in the planning stages."*

Throughout my years in the priesthood, I know there were many young men whom I influenced in choosing the priesthood as their life's work. That came long before I did any work in seminaries. There are many I can name whom I met as college students: Tom Cappelloni, Carmen Perry, and Tom Stahurski, to name a few. Then there was Neil Carrigan, who became an Orthodox priest. I know I also influenced Frank Ashcroft, Dan Bastianelli, Tom McLaughlin, and Gerry Mullally. I officiated at Dave Cramer's parents' marriage, so my influence there goes back a long way. Those names come quite easily to me, although there were many more. I think what was new for George when he became involved with the IPF was that he actually knew the men he was supporting as they sought direction in their priestly formation. I think that's meant a lot to him.

## GEORGE

"I'm happy that, in some way, I have been able to help IPF go from the initial group of six in 1994 to 130 in 2006. It's really uplifting for me to be involved, and I'm sure the IPF is going to have a great impact on the priesthood.

"As long as I've been a member of Serra, I could never say I really helped that man get into the priesthood. I think we did sort of shotgun things that helped some seminarians, but never did we say we were responsible for a particular man's vocation. Of course, vocations are from God; all we do is try to help them along.

"I am pleased to say that I, myself, have sponsored about eight seminarians from the Los Angeles archdiocese who have participated in IPF's program. To hear firsthand the amazing testimonials from those men who have gone through the program has been really gratifying for me. I am happy to be a part of what I see as a truly great approach to revitalizing spirituality in men engaged in priestly formation. I'm happy for whatever support I can give."

Throughout my life, I have seen many people selected in the seminary structure who were more de-formed than formed. The womb of the Catholic Church, the seminary where the seed should grow, was diseased for a time. If a man kept rules and regulations, more often than not, he went on to ordination; that external obedience was not enough. With a program such as the IPF, a strong, healthy spiritual life becomes the hallmark of the viable candidate for priesthood. With each successive year, the IPF has continued to grow; but, more importantly, it has produced great results.

## REV. JOHN HORN, S.J.

"George and Rosemary have certainly been a tremendous support in prayer and encouragement. I am especially grateful to them and to Monsignor that I am living this dream. As a priest, I have been blessed with a wonderful opportunity to respond to a call within a call.

"Because of George's generous contribution to the IPF, we were able to expand as we serve the Church by dedicating time, personnel, and resources to further the spiritual formation of diocesan priests. The formation and the continuance of this new ministry to priests and seminarians is, in large part, the result of the Esseff brothers' prayers, benefaction, vision, and example. I am grateful for all these two men have done to make the IPF possible, and I pray each day for God's continued blessings on them."

# The Turn of the Century

And so it was that my brother and I were instrumental in bringing the IPF to fruition. On May 31, 2002, the IPF awarded Sister Cor Immaculatum and me the Guadalupe Award for our work with the IPF, and also for serving as a model of friendship and mutual support for priests and religious. George and Rosemary, for their outstanding contributions and prayerful support, have also been honored with the Lady of Guadalupe Award. These years with the IPF have been very fulfilling. We are especially grateful that we have had the opportunity to focus on the future, and to look forward with great hope to a stronger, revitalized Catholic priesthood.

George and Rosemary being honored by IPF

---

## GEORGE

*"John has been father to thousands of children. His children are priests and seminarians. They have been given the challenge to carry on his work. If they take his example, they too will take care of their children—prisoners, elderly, homeless, all who are poor in any way. John's children are all over the world. That's the way I see his fatherhood playing out. He's had a lot to do with bringing a lot of people into the 'world'—the world that truly matters, the Kingdom of God. I see his work as a huge legacy."*

---

Earlier, in 2001, I took on the additional responsibility of serving as pastor at Our Lady of the Abingtons, a parish located across the street from St. Pius X Seminary, where I had lived since 1991. I remember having a dream at that time: I hoped I could bring the seminarians into parish life and allow them to have a taste of what serving as a priest was all about. That dream never materialized—for reasons that, I guess deep inside me, I always understood.

When I was appointed pastor of Our Lady of the Abingtons, I had many obligations. I was still director of the Propagation of the Faith. I was serving as formation director at St. Pius X Seminary. I was involved in the IPF program, and I continued to conduct retreats for individuals and groups. I knew that I had a lot of responsibilities and, in conscience, I thought it best to leave the Propagation of the Faith office. I knew that there were many capable priests who could fill that position, and I had a well-versed staff working there to support the incoming director. The seminary was only a short walk away from my parish and that seemed to be very manageable. I enjoyed taking care of the needs of the parishioners, and it was a place where many other individuals and groups could come for spiritual direction and prayer. Besides the regular schedule of Masses for the parish, I also had many Healing Masses for AA groups, and opened the parish to other groups who were hungry for a place to pray. There were always people who would assist me as I tried to have meaningful liturgies. Carol Burti was always a great help in providing music. She's a woman who, for years, had supplied music in more places than I can name.

On the other side of the coin, my experience at Our Lady of the Abingtons parish was, in some ways, reminiscent of the years I spent in parishes after I had returned from South America. Some in the parish community did not respond well to the presence of people who obviously were not parishioners. Nonetheless, many who were not members of the parish community found their way there. I always assumed the Lord had sent them there.

## GEORGE CAMPBELL

*"It's very difficult to sum up my story with Monsignor Esseff or to really explain what he has meant in my life. I was one of those boys who grew up in north Jersey, basically living my life chasing the wrong things in life, and eventually getting caught up in a fast-paced lifestyle. I was doing things that I enjoyed doing at the time, but they were just destroying me morally. I got so caught up in alcohol and drugs that I was living a life of self-destruction until my life just crashed in on me. I was put into rehabs, thrown into the meetings of AA, and nothing seemed to be working for me. I would get out of one rehab and be put back into another. I was in a pattern of constant relapse. I was not listening to anybody. I had no God in my life and no understanding of what I had to do to get better, because I wouldn't listen to anyone. In the last halfway house I was at, I started praying and hoping that I would have the courage to change. I left that place; I just walked out. I was lost, totally lost. I was in a terrible place. I was losing my family, losing my wife, losing my kids. I was scared. I was lonely, and very alone. That's a dangerous place to be.*

## GEORGE CAMPBELL

*"One day I was sitting in a park near Dalton, Pennsylvania. I was praying, meditating, and this wind literally just blew me out of the park. I got in my car and drove around for a long time until finally I saw a little church. I walked in and morning Mass was going on. That was the first time I ever laid eyes on Monsignor Esseff. He was having a Mass of Healing. Some time later, he told me that he didn't normally have Healing Masses in the morning, but for some reason he had one that morning. When the time came for anointing the sick, I went up to him. I didn't say anything to him. I was praying within myself for what I wanted, what I needed. I wanted to stop doing what I was doing. I wanted to change. I wanted to be teachable. I didn't want to get high anymore.*

*"From that day on my life has changed. I continued to go back there to pray; and since that time, Monsignor has been like a father to me. I listened to the things he said about giving up my own will to God and getting out of the fear. That happened some years ago. All that I heard didn't hit me all of a sudden, but it started hitting me, and it's been a remarkable journey. How does he put it? I am not to live like Jesus; I am Jesus. He's put that in my brain and my life has changed. I wasn't perfect. There were times that I fell. But Monsignor was there to pick me up and brush me off and tell me to forgive myself and move on. For most of my life I was only thinking about me. I'm sure I'm still self-centered, but I feel I can go to sleep at night without any guilt or shame after a day that I lived trying to be Jesus in the world.*

*"Monsignor is responsible for the way I pray, when I pray, how I pray. I feel sometimes that there are days when I'm in prayer even when I'm working, even while I'm doing whatever I'm doing, for hours straight. Each day I read the gospel and try to relate it to my life. He also instilled in me a love for Mary, and a devotion to the rosary which has released me from so much of the fear and the anxiety I was dealing with. I still live in a world of temptations, but every single day I try to respond in the way Monsignor showed me.*

*"All my life, I've talked to dozens of priests, to dozens and dozens and dozens of counselors, psychiatrists, and doctors. They told me what I had to do.*

*Monsignor told me that the answer was in me. I just had to allow Jesus to come in.*

*I had to open the door of my heart and invite Him in because I had closed that door and left it closed for a big part of my life. Each day, I open that door.*

## GEORGE CAMPBELL

"I can honestly say, I don't live in fear. I don't live in anxiety, and I have a lot more compassion towards other people. It's been a beautiful experience for me, and I pray it for everyone. I pray that everyone can be Jesus.

"Monsignor is the holiest man I've ever met. I think he is a lot like me, a man like me, but he has a faith that I've never seen in anybody else—the strongest faith I've ever seen. His faith is bigger than anything else in the world. When I am in his presence, I can feel that faith, and I know that God has touched my life through him. Meeting Monsignor was a crossroad in my life, and I am grateful for the healing that has come to me through him."

In so many situations where I have met people who are searching for answers, I have found true pilgrims. Their faith is real, and they need to belong. Oftentimes, they are looking to belong, not just to a parish community, but to the family of man. They are looking for a brother, and they find him in Jesus. They are looking for a father, and Jesus leads them to His Father. It is our duty as Christians to welcome and support them as they struggle to find the love and peace that Jesus wants to give them.

## SEAN SCANLON

"There was a time when I was struggling with many things in my life, mostly going through a separation from my wife and family. I was searching for some kind of peace. I was trying to figure out when I last had that peace and, as I looked backward, I realized that the times in my life that I was most peaceful was when I went to church. I was in Clarks Summit at the time, and I remember asking people on the street where there might be Mass. Sooner or later, someone told me that there was an eight o'clock Mass at Our Lady of the Abingtons in Dalton. I had no idea where that church was located, but I did manage to get directions, and I went to the church. When I walked into the church, there was this little priest. I realized that I had seen him a few times in the restaurant that I owned, but I had never met him. He was giving a homily about how we're all called to be saints, and I was very moved because I knew he couldn't be talking to me because I was so sinful. He was saying that it might take ten years or more for us to become saints; and, as I looked around the church, I realized that in the tiny community of people at that Mass, there wasn't one person in the church besides

SEAN SCANLON

*me who was going to make another ten years! I couldn't get over the fact that this guy was really talking to me. I felt so comforted, in spite of all the pain I was in. He seemed to be saying what I needed to hear. After Mass, I thought about what he had said, and then I thought I was just crazy to think I could ever become a saint.*

*"When I woke up the next day, I thought, 'Where can I go?' I decided, 'I'm going to try that guy again,' and I drove all the way back to Dalton from Peckville. I'm sure I passed at least five other churches on the way. I found the church again and I heard this little priest, and it sounded like he was talking to me—like there was nobody else in the church. Every time I hear him preach, that's the way it is. There's a sort of mystery when he speaks, like he's speaking to everyone in their own pain, and it's as if God is speaking through him to each person in the church. After I had heard just a few more of his homilies, it was easy for me to ask him for help. I remember how warm and welcoming he was. I thought, 'This guy doesn't even know me and he's so caring.' He made me feel as if he loved me like my mother and father loved me—just immediately—but I guess really as God loves me. I couldn't experience that with anyone else in my life at the time.*

*"It was so easy for me to seek him out to hear my confession. His gifts as a confessor are something else! I was so comfortable. He never judged me or scolded me or made me feel awful about myself. He just made me feel loved, and that is probably the greatest gift I have felt from him—a love like the love of a mother or father. That love has been a great healing for me since I lost my father when I was a young boy. Monsignor has helped to fill that void in me.*

*"And he keeps calling me to a greater response to all the situations in my life. He makes me better able to look at my faults and at my sinfulness, but he is never judgmental. In all of it, he still loves me. In the loving forgiveness he grants me in confession, I truly feel the forgiveness of God and, more than anything, God's great love for me. It's easy to see how much Monsignor loves people. When I see him care for so many people, I do see Jesus in him. He has been a great teacher for me, and continues to call me to sainthood—just as the first time I heard him speak. No matter how often I fail, I know, like all good fathers, he's there for me."*

Within the parish at Our Lady of the Abingtons, an especially rewarding source of growth in prayer life became possible when, in the late months of 2001, plans were initiated to create a perpetual adoration chapel on the grounds of the parish.

# Brothers & Fathers

Wonderful people came forward to help with both the physical environment and the organization of people who had expressed a desire to participate in adoration of the Blessed Sacrament on a regular basis. There were all kinds of donations of materials and labor until, finally, that dream became a reality. Richard Cordiano was quite proficient with computers and was able to coordinate names, times, and dates for adoration. He had four team captains who compiled information for him: Sean Scanlon, Bill and Zora Velechi, George and Alice Aschenbrenner, and Bill Emanuel and his son Billy. Bill and his son also did the construction work for the chapel, a room adjacent to the rectory and they built the altar. In no time, people came forward to donate carpeting and all kinds of other items that were necessary to complete the physical plant. On January 5, 2002, Bishop Timlin came to Our Lady of the Abingtons and dedicated the chapel which is known as the St. Pio Adoration Chapel. People from the entire area came forward to make sure that there was, in fact, perpetual adoration of the Blessed Sacrament. Still today, it is a wonderful place of prayer and adoration for anyone who wants to participate.

I marked an exciting milestone in my life in 2003. That was the year that marked my having been a priest for fifty years, and I wanted to celebrate the joy I had had for so long. I began to make preparations for that celebration, which was held in the best possible place: a seminary—not the seminary where I was trained, but a seminary where the seed growing in the hear of every young man longing for priesthood is nourished and finally comes to fruition. It was a glorious day; people I hadn't seen for many, many, years came to see me. There were people from my earliest assignments in Shohola and East Stroudsburg. There were people from the inner-city projects and from local parishes where I had lived and had been part of the parish community. There were people I had met in AA and in NA. There were people I had ministered to in prison. There were people, God forgive me, whom I had forgotten, but who remembered me. At some terribly difficult place in their lives, I was there. No, that is not true—Jesus was there, in me, and some comfort, some peace, came to them through me. For me, with every person who came to see me, there was gratitude in my heart. I thanked God for my years of ministry to God through people, and also for His wonderful reminders that I must always step aside, as Mother Teresa taught me in her own prayer: "Help me to stay out of Your way." Those people who came to me that day whom I had forgotten gave affirmation that I did stay out of His way, at least on some occasions. Jesus healed his people through whatever comfort or peace or reconciliation came through me from Him.

Shortly after that celebration, I celebrated my 75th birthday on June 13th. It was time for me to retire. I really had no idea of what that meant! Nevertheless, I retired in July, simply because I was seventy-five years old. I had to give up my pastorate at Our Lady of the Abingtons, returning to live at the seminary once more.

My experience at Our Lady of the Abingtons taught me that it was not an easy task to be a good priest and an effective pastor. It is virtually impossible to succeed in pleasing everyone in the parish. I knew that there were some people there who wrote to the bishop objecting to my leadership. I think that is something I can look back on and still feel bad about, but I also think it's something that should be recorded. I can still recall the names of the people who signed that letter. Those people were talking in different terms as to what they expected me to be as their parish priest. I found solace in Scripture: "When you have done all you have been commanded, say, 'We are unprofitable servants; we have done what we were obliged to do.'"

Among so many other moments, one of the most significant events that occurred during that time was the installation of a new bishop of Scranton on October 1, 2003. His name was Bishop Joseph Martino. Shortly after he arrived, he closed St. Pius X Seminary and moved the men there to other seminaries. It was a rather abrupt closing. The priests who were living there as they served in priestly formation had to relocate; I was one of those priests. It seemed almost instantaneous. I had given up my pastorate; the seminary was closed; the rector, Monsignor Bohr, was assigned to Rome; and I was given no further direction. I took it as a mandate when, that very same day, I got a call from the Vicar of Priests, Father Kopacz, asking me if I would take a temporary assignment administering Ss. Peter and Paul parish in west Scranton. From that day to this, I don't remember anyone saying, "You did a great job at Pius X"; but again, I was reminded of the Scripture, "We have done what we were obliged to do." I said I would take the position at Ss. Peter and Paul, and I made plans to leave the seminary that same day. A group of people who used to come to AA meetings and retreats came with a truck. I had to collect what I wanted to take with me and decide what I wanted to give away. After almost thirteen years of living there, I was out of St. Pius X and moved into Ss. Peter and Paul within a span of about four or five hours. It was quite dramatic. I stayed in west Scranton for several months, until my services were no longer required and a new pastor came in.

When the new pastor was assigned to Ss. Peter and Paul, I turned everything over to him. Just prior to that transition, I had received a call from Bishop Aquila of Fargo, North Dakota. He and I had become acquainted through the IPF program. The summer before, I had given him guidance and spiritual direction on his own retreat at Creighton. The day he called he said to me, "It came to me in prayer that maybe God wants you to help us here in Fargo." I told him I was open to whatever God wanted of me; but I remember saying, "If that's what God wants, could you please ask Him to let me know."At that time, I was also doing half-week-long periods of spiritual direction in Sioux Falls as part of an outreach program. While I was there on one of those missions, Bishop Aquila had a pilot friend of his fly down and take me to see the seminary in Fargo. After a few weeks, I did accept his invitation to serve as formation director at Cardinal Muench Seminary for one year, and that's how I came to live in Fargo. I was still very interested in helping young seminarians as they prepared to receive Holy Orders. That year was challenging as I helped to guide those men in their human, academic, apostolic, and especially their spiritual development. I was grateful for all my involvement with Mother Teresa and her priests, and for the many weeks I had spent giving retreats at Creighton University. Because I was officially retired, I was able to accept the position at Cardinal Muench. I continued doing spiritual direction in Sioux Falls, and when I came back to Scranton in 2005, I moved to St. Paul's parish in Scranton.

As always, though I found the work in Fargo very challenging and fulfilling, I also knew I wanted my primary base to be my home diocese. When I finished that year and moved to St. Paul's parish, I was happy to be able to participate in the life of the parish, but I also enjoyed the freedom to continue other ministries. During that time, I went to Fargo for about a week each month to give spiritual direction to the seminarians there. I was also able to continue my work with the IPF, where I continued to give retreats and spiritual direction as part of the program at Creighton University.

*Father John and Sister Cor at IPF in Creighton*

# The Turn of the Century

## SISTER COR IMMACULATUM

*"All of the people that Father John has met and ministered to over the years call forth from him a 'Jesus response.' He loves people and his immediate response is always a Gospel response. He has a world vision. His missionary work in Peru, with Blessed Mother Teresa of Calcutta in the poorest countries of the world, and in war-torn Lebanon, gave impetus to diocesan missionary work here and abroad. As diocesan director of the Pontifical Society for the Propagation of the Faith and Holy Childhood Association, Father John introduced clergy, adults, seminarians, and students to the poor through providing the opportunity to serve God's neglected and abandoned people through mission trips to the most impoverished nations.*

*"And Father John is father. One of the most beautiful gifts of a father is the gift of generativity. I believe that one of the most significant ways that Father John is fathering future generations is through the most important ministry in the Catholic Church today: the education of seminarians, future priests, formed in the Heart of Jesus. As spiritual director to seminarians at the Institute for Priestly Formation and at Cardinal Muench Seminary in Fargo, and as formation director at St. Pius X Seminary in Dalton, Father John has shared his deep spirituality, wise counseling, and strong guidance with men seeking ordination. As spiritual director to many priests in many dioceses, he has been both father and brother. His love for priests is manifest in the Diocese of Scranton Re-Connections program that has provided former active priests with a prayerful, caring, supportive group of clergy.*

*"Another of Father's John's most enduring examples of fatherhood is his ability to identify, encourage, and affirm the gifts of others to continue the ministries that he initiated. Every ministry that he had the vision, courage, and grace to begin has been passed on to others. The legacy of Father John Esseff is actualized in these persons.*

*"Two roads diverged in a yellow wood ...' Father John 'took the one less traveled by, and that has made all the difference.'"*

Those years were exciting and full of rich experiences for me with God's people. Each day held new challenges, and no day was like another. I went where I felt God wanted me to go and I placed all in His hands. I tried to respond as best I could to the many who asked for my help.

# Brothers & Fathers

In a special way, I must admit, Mother Teresa and her sisters always tugged at my heart. Whenever they asked me to give them a retreat, I felt honored and humbled. Throughout the years, I traveled to many of their convents around the world. Even since Mother Teresa's death in 1997, I have enjoyed a wonderful relationship with the Missionaries of Charity. I continue to see them whenever I can. I received a request from the sisters asking if I would give them a retreat in Lebanon in 2006. With great joy, I accepted that invitation.

# CHAPTER 50

## A NEW HEART

### *George*

Like so many others, I went to school. I did my thing. I got out of school and I made my way. I got kind of lucky in doing what I was doing and I made a lot of money in my business. I didn't feel guilty. I was always generous. I was giving, but I was giving from my excess. It's true that I had a family to care for; but it's also true that, over the years, I had a Rolls Royce and I had an airplane; I had a sport fishing boat in Hawaii; I had four homes at one time—one in Tokyo, one in Hawaii, one at the beach here in California, and our main residence, which changed several times over the years. Before we moved into the house that we're presently in, we lived in a house of approximately 6,200 feet. That house was situated atop Rancho Santa Rosa and offered a fabulous view of the mountain, the valley, and the ocean. We were living very well; but again, I can't honestly say I felt guilty. I did feel blessed and we were always grateful for the gifts God had given us. I felt that we had always tried to be generous.

When I thought way back to my early years in business, I saw myself, in relation to the people who worked for me, as generous in simple ways. I did think of them as my "business family," and I tried to be sensitive to any difficulties they might be faced with. If there was something I could do, especially in times of crisis, I did it. Since 1997 when I turned the business over to my son George, I haven't had that type of giving with the workers at the plant. Now all I have is one employee, and that's my secretary.

> ### LINDA BUTLER
>
> *"I have worked for Mr. Esseff for about twenty-four years as the company bookkeeper and his personal assistant. I can say without doubt that Mr. Esseff is one of God's greatest gifts— truly a kind, good, caring person. He has always treated his employees as if they were family. He took personal responsibility for his employees and wanted to see them do well in their lives. Many times he took me aside to ask me about something*

LINDA BUTLER

*in my personal life and to give me 'fatherly advice.' It was more than a friend's advice—it was family concern.*

*"I remember when he sponsored some Vietnamese people, arranging for them to come to America and providing them housing at a ranch in Ojai.*

*"I remember many, many contributions to worthwhile charities and causes over the years.*

*"I remember his love as he personally helped care for his terminally ill daughter, Denise; his parents; his mother-in-law, who lived with him and his wife. He didn't just provide them care, but personally gave them injections and traveled with them to seek better medical care.*

*"These are just of few of my reflections on this fine man."*

As my business grew, my financial situation changed dramatically. Without any doubt, I began to live the 'good life.' Still, I did reach out in small ways to people I was in contact with. We had extensive gardens at our house in Santa Rosa and we did have a gardener, Javier. He did an awful lot of work for us for about nine or ten years. During that time, I had a mobile home that was quite large. My daughter Kathy and my son George had lived in that mobile home for a time when they lived on an avocado ranch that George took care of. When they no longer needed the mobile home, I decided to sell it. I thought it would be great if Javier could buy it, but I knew he would never be able to afford to buy the home for what it was worth (somewhere between $70,000 and $80,000). Javier had been very faithful to us for so many years, and was a really fine worker. I told him I would be willing to sell him the mobile home for $35,000. I also offered him terms so that he could work off some of the debt and pay the rest. He accepted my offer. Now he still lives in what has become a very beautiful home. He still takes care of George's gardening, and also all the gardening at the plant. I have great respect for Javier and his work ethic, and I was happy to be able to help him purchase a home of his own, to climb up the ladder, and to enjoy greater financial security.

In spite of giving that kind of assistance throughout the years, I knew that within my set of circumstances, there was so much more I could do. More than twenty-five years ago, I came to a point when I made a conscious decision to get rid of some of that wealth, to get rid of a lot of the things I owned. The decision came

# A New Heart

after a quiet reaction to something that was in no way new to me. One Sunday at Mass I heard a Scripture reading—one that I had heard many, many times:

> Then Jesus said to his disciples, "Amen, I say to you, it will be hard for one who is rich to enter the kingdom of heaven. Again I say to you, it is easier for a camel to pass through the eye of a needle than for one who is rich to enter the kingdom of God.
>
> When the disciples heard this, they were greatly astonished and said, "Who, then, can be saved?"
>
> Jesus looked at them and said, "For human beings this is impossible. But for God, all things are possible."
>
> -Matthew 19:23–26

That day was not unlike many others. There wasn't anything unusual about my going to Mass that day—or any other day. (I went to Mass and Communion almost every day of my life.) It wasn't as though I had never heard that message before. Basically, I think that my grandfather, very early on, had instilled those same ideas very deeply in me; but I think that, along the way, I did slide into a comfort zone. I was giving, but I was giving from my excess. That particular day something hit me as I listened to that familiar parable.

I was a rich man. If I wanted to buy a car, I bought a car. If I wanted a house, I bought a house. I could buy anything. When a person gets that way, it's easy to think that he's pretty much in control. Maybe I did slide into that kind of thinking to some degree, thinking that I was in control. And it wasn't that I wasn't doing some good things; I was doing some, but I really wasn't dealing with what I had in any special way. Maybe I wasn't treating everything the way I should. I found myself wanting to talk to someone. So one day, I talked to my brother John about how deeply that reading troubled me.

He told me to remember that everything belongs to God. Whatever we have has been given to us by God. Everything really belongs to God, and we are only stewards of those gifts. If we misappropriate our goods, we're really doing wrong. We can be wealthy. We can live in a nice house; but we have to know in our hearts that everything belongs to God. Those creations do not belong to us—not to me, not to my wife, not to my children. All things belong to God.

# Brothers & Fathers

After I had that talk with John, I made a conscious decision about my responsibilities, and I knew I was going to get rid of 'stuff.' Once I began to act on that decision, I felt a renewed faithfulness to what my grandfather had taught me, and to what I had heard from the gospel all my life.

Before my conscious decision to do things differently, maybe what I was doing was just a kindness—and that was good. Yet I knew I wanted to do more. I wanted to make a genuine response to the gospel. I wanted to respond to those in need as my brothers, and to find my own joy in that.

Previous to my conversion, when I gave things or money away, the value varied. Some gifts were more than adequate, but others were small. One guy who was always appreciative for anything I might give him was my old pal, Frank Hanlon. I remember once sending him a fax machine, and I remember particularly the satisfaction that gave me.

*Dear George and Rosemary,*

*I finally got back to Bolivia and got the fax machine set up yesterday.*

*This fax is wonderful. A short time ago I had an urgent communication with the Holy See. Instead of writing to them a letter that would have taken three weeks to get there, and three weeks for a reply, I sent a fax in nineteen seconds and had the reply in a few hours.*

I'll tell you: his letters were wonderful. Until his death, Frank and I kept in touch. He never lost his ability to make me laugh. Those letters were certainly more of a gift to me than anything I ever sent him.

*"At the Mayo Clinic, the cardiologist, after reviewing all the clinical tests, kept saying, 'Remarkable!' All the tests showed normal except that I have more oxygen in my red blood cells than people in the States. That is because I have been living in higher altitudes. The problem with the back is due to a degenerative disease. They say that in sixty more years, I will be three feet tall.*

*"With the fax machine and our computer we are now in modern times. I sent our fax number to the Franciscan headquarters in New York and, since I have been typing this letter, they sent me a message that we just received a donation of $1,800. So the machine is being very useful in its first full day of operation.*

# A New Heart

*"I hope that you and Rosemary and your children are all well. Take care of your old bones."*

*Your idol,*
*Frank*

I guess I gave Frank things that he needed, and it made me happy to be able to do that. The cost was never the issue. There were others who did not go back as far as Frank and I, and many who were not personal friends, but I would give a thousand, three, maybe even five thousand to individuals or groups who asked me for help. Now that I am thinking back and trying to put things into a more accurate timeframe, I realize what my first big donation was. Previous to any other large contribution, it was my gift to St. Mary Magdalene's Church. I made a response to an appeal from a group of people who wanted to make a downpayment on a home for unwed mothers in Camarillo. At that time, the closest place for unwed mothers to stay was located in downtown Los Angeles; a closer place was needed. I gave the group $25,000. Even with that donation, it wasn't until I made a commitment to really give that I came to the realization that all I had been doing for most of my life was giving from my excess. I was not giving from my substance.

I wanted to change that. In order to facilitate giving the kind of gifts I knew I wanted to give, I started the Esseff Foundation in 1979 in memory of my grandfather, George Abdanour Esseff. According to its documents, the Esseff Foundation is a: non-political, 501(c)(3) non-profit organization dedicated to relieving the sufferings of the poor, both here in America and around the world. In pursuit of that goal, the foundation funnels its resources to those organizations whose track records demonstrate their abilities to assist and house the homeless, feed and clothe the poor, and provide medical care to those in need."

I had to get government approval to set up the Foundation, which took about six or eight months. My attorney did most of that work, but it's a reasonably simple thing to do. It's a 501(c)(3), which means I can give money from the foundation to charitable organizations, and I can put money into the Foundation as a charitable deduction. Rather than just give money to another foundation, I decided to set up the Esseff Foundation, which has really become a family Foundation. By doing that, I could designate which charities would get the money. From then on, I needed to put funds into the Foundation, and I had to determine the best way to do that.

In 1984, I seriously began to liquidate many of our assets. When the opportunity arose, I sold my Rolls Royce, I sold my airplane ... I sold ...

ROSEMARY

*"You sold your toys!*

# Brothers & Fathers

Yes, I did. I sold my toys. All of those things sold within a very short period of time—maybe a year or a year-and-a-half; but I still had a lot of excess to get rid of. I continued to liquidate. I had a collection of Netsuke (pronounced net-skay) from Japan that I had accumulated over a period of years. They were created by Japanese artists and served a very practical purpose. Japanese men, who wore traditional garments which had no pockets, needed a place to keep personal belongings (such as money, tobacco, and medicine). The containers for those items (which might be a pouch, a small woven basket, or a beautifully crafted box) were called sagemono and hung by cords passed behind the obi, the sash holding the man's kimono closed. The fastener that secured the container's cord at the top of the sash was a carved toggle called a netsuke, which served as the counterweight attached to the other end of the cord, preventing the sagemono from falling through the obi. Each netsuke is little and, in western culture, might be compared to a fob (the device that holds a pocket watch). The containers carrying whatever the men wanted to be readily available were at the other end of the netsuke. Netsuke is unique to Japan, and each was carved—usually with reproductions of animals or other figures. Some were carved out of precious woods, others were made from gems or jade or ivory. They are really very beautiful. Over a period of many years, I had collected about sixty of them. I got interested in them when I first began going to Japan. Every time I would go there, I would visit antique shops and pick up a netsuke at a bargain price—maybe somewhere in the area of fifty dollars to one-hundred-and-fifty dollars. In time, they came to be quite valuable, some worth maybe $1,500 to $2,000 apiece. I donated that collection to Marywood College in Scranton, where Sister Cor Immaculatum was the head of the Art department. They still have that collection in their antiquity museum.

> ### ROSEMARY
> ❧
> "Just as he looked for old netsuke in Japanese antique shops, in Europe George would pick up coins—especially from France and Italy."

Now that I'm thinking about the netsuke, I remember that I got rid of all my other collections as well. I had been collecting different things for maybe fifteen or twenty years. I did have a pretty extensive silver coin collection.

I actually got some of those French coins from a Japanese gold trader in Japan. They were original Napoleonic coins from the 1800s, and they were all gold. Most of the things I would become intrigued by had a history to them. I find a lot of that kind of stuff very interesting. Anyway, I think I gave that collection to my son George. Nonetheless, we were rid of them; but even now, we still have some things we want to get rid of. As we're working down, we still have the exclusive antique necklace and bracelet that I bought from a shop in Canada. It was the one I spoke about that was made by the French jeweler for Napoleon. I didn't buy those pieces the first time we saw them; I haggled the shop owner for quite a while until he finally decided to sell them to me at a much more reasonable price than he was originally asking. They're the pieces I gave to Rosemary as an anniversary gift. I think I paid about $1800 for them, and Sotheby's recently appraised them at $15,000.

## ROSEMARY

*"If I liked something, if I enjoyed it artistically, I would buy it. My choices were not based on the money value of the item. When it came to our purchases, there was an interesting dynamic in place. George's possessions were his possessions and he could do whatever he liked with them. When it came to my possessions, they were also his. It was taken for granted that anything that belonged in the house was his and he could do whatever he wanted, without regard to—Did I like it? Did I want to get rid of it? Those questions were never asked, and I pretty much went along with that—until it came to the lamp. For all the beautiful things we have had over the years, my absolute favorite, without any doubt, is still the hurricane lamp that I bought in Scranton for fifty cents. I've managed to hang on tenaciously to that, and to some other pieces that I treasure for sentimental reasons."*

Whenever Rosemary wanted to buy something, generally she would choose it because of its aesthetic value. When she bought something, she didn't buy with the same idea I had. She never worried about what its value might be if we decided to sell it in the future.

I'm sure that lamp will be the last thing to go. And I'm very sure it'll bring more money in than we bought it for. How could we get less than fifty cents for it in this day and age?

Seriously, I think that we went through a period when we had enough money that we could buy whatever we liked, things that most people can't buy. For example, we have a set of crystal that we bought. It was really beautiful. But I have to admit, it was a fantastic deal. It was crafted by a glass cutter who worked for one of the most famous glass cutting houses in the world. He was almost 90 years old and the set we bought was one of the last sets of hand-cut crystal that he made. He also signed every piece that he did for us.

> ### ROSEMARY
> ⇒≍⇐
>
> *"When we had the opportunity to buy that set of crystal, Bill Nasser said that this would be a good deal.*
>
> *"I said, 'Well, they're beautiful. Just think of the work that went into each piece.' And I was thinking about how this elderly man was still able to create such beautiful pieces even in the last years of his life. I knew I would love to have some of his work and I asked George, 'Are we able to afford to buy this?' Without hesitation, he said, 'Yes, buy it!' So we did buy the crystal, and we used it for quite a long time. I still have some of those pieces, but others were smashed during the earthquake in 1992.*
>
> *"We still have the other pieces that survived and we still use them to this day."*

I don't think we ended up buying anything we didn't use. Even the Netsuke, we had on display at our house for years, where people could see and appreciate them as art.

When it came to buying, I have to admit: I was unlike Rosemary. I found that I liked the process. I liked to get things at a good price. I bought the Rolls Royce, again, only after the owner came down in price and accepted my offer. I didn't jump at the chance to buy it. I didn't really want it, but I bought it for $45,000 and sold it for about $55,000 six years later. By then, we had put only 5,000 miles on it, so it was a good deal for me and also for the guy who bought it. But I did make a profit!

> ### ROSEMARY
> ⇒≍⇐
>
> *"I remember being asked if I drove it. Who would go to a Pick and Save in a Rolls? Or to Von's Market in a Rolls? You must be kidding. I drove it when absolutely necessary— when I didn't have my own wheels."*

Now that I think about it, getting anything at a bargain price was, I guess, the fun of buying for me. Just like in the market when I was a kid, I got a kick out of buying cheap and selling high. Anyway, these were some of the kinds of things we eventually sold or are still hoping to sell—but, of course, not Rosemary's lamp!

What I have already done is sell a lot of things and then put the money into the Esseff Foundation. The money I got from the Rolls Royce went into the Foundation. I also put money that I got from land I sold, and stocks that had big, big gains.

# A New Heart

Recently, in 2005, I put two pieces of property into the Foundation that amounted to about $500,000. I'd put that money into the Foundation and I wouldn't have to pay taxes on those gains. The Foundation got the benefit of the total amount; those monies could then be given to charities. All of these ventures took place over time.

The general idea was to get rid of things we didn't need—sell them and put the money into the Foundation. Then it was my hope that we could sell, not what we didn't need, but from our substance. It was then that Rosemary and I decided to sell our home in Santa Rosa. That decision came in 1998 after a lot of

*Home in Santa Rosa*

prayer. We had bought that house when our children were starting to have their own children and we lived there for about twelve years. The house was located on twenty-five acres of land in Camarillo, in the Santa Rosa Valley—a very prestigious area. It had six bedrooms and six-and-a-half baths. The main house was accented by a circular motor court, a view gazebo, and a lighted volleyball court. It also had an indoor swimming pool for the kids. There was a guest cottage and a separate staff apartment on the site. It was a place where a lot of wonderful memories were made.

It was from that house that Denise had been married. Mary Ellen, Kathy, and George Jr. could visit or bring their children there to stay whenever situations called for that. The grandchildren were able to invite their friends and they had a lot of great times there.

*George and Rosemary with their children and grandchildren at the house in Santa Rosa*

## KIMBERLEY SPENCER

*"I remember the house in Santa Rosa. In fact, it's the only one of my grandparents' houses that I have any memory of. We (the grandchildren) would always go to the third floor because the TV was up there, and we were always hoping to see an episode or two of the Teenage Mutant Ninja Turtles. But if the TV didn't grab our attention, we had a lot of other things we could do. One of our favorites was to play dress-up and be silly. My grandmother had a chest up on the third floor filled with a whole bunch of silly stuff just for us to play with: wigs, jewelry, and crazy dress-up clothes of all kinds. There was a bright orange wig, a pigtail wig, a black one, and a purple one. We weren't the only ones who had fun dressing up. One time, my mom's brother, Uncle George, went up to the third floor for some reason, grabbed the bright orange wig, put it on, and came downstairs. Uncle George started acting like a woman and said, 'I'm Aunt Susie.' For some reason, (s)he had a southern accent. That was the day our 'Aunt Susie' was born, and whenever Uncle George felt like being silly with us kids, Aunt Susie would join us. We had a lot of fun with that.*

*"We would also have a lot of fun with our cousins, the Esseff boys—whose mom was the only girl in that house. We insisted on dressing them up too! We'd put the big fake pearl necklaces and the big gaudy jewelry on them. That was fun—at least for us, maybe not for them.*

*"When we gave up playing dress-up, we'd just normally go upstairs and mess around or just play basketball in the front or swim or play volleyball or whatever. If anyone couldn't find something fun to do, it was their own fault.*

*"At one point, a big change occurred. One day, when we arrived, Gidue was sitting in the living room, and there was a big poster and a marker sitting on an easel. So everyone was asked to come into the living room. The TV's off, and we're kind of like, 'OK, what's going on?' And Gidue began. I was pretty young at the time, but my oldest sister, Michelle, was very aware of what was really going on."*

# A New Heart

## MICHELLE SPENCER BURNS

"For a few months during my teenage years, my grandfather went on a crusade for his children and grandchildren. After three major heart attacks and two major strokes, George Esseff wanted to make sure of what all parents wish to be assured of: that their children and grandchildren are good, honest, and wholesome people. He just went about determining this in a slightly different way.

"He gathered all eleven of us grandchildren to his house for a series of meetings. He would bring up controversial topics facing children today: sex, drugs, and the role of religion in our lives. I don't remember a great deal about those meetings other than, mostly, my cousins, siblings, and I were in shock. Sex, drugs, and Rock 'n Roll—these were not common topics in the Esseff household we knew! As my grandfather pulled out terms that are just not 'grandfather things' to say, we looked at each other out of the corners of our eyes; siblings made eye contact of disbelief with one another. I was the oldest of all the grandchildren; my siblings and my cousings looked to see how I would react, and also how the oldest in each of their families would react. Knowing our places, each one of us kept incredibly silent and tried to pretend as though this wasn't the most uncomfortable family meeting ever. When it came to the topic of religion and how God worked in our lives, I felt relif. Gidue talking about using pot and about 'sex everywhere on that damn TV,' was alient o us; discussing God in this house was certainly not. As he continued, we listened about how we must always stay close to God. Though I can't quite recall his exact words, the basic idea was that George Esseff made it a daily goal to act in a way that would get him to Heaven, and he wanted to make sure all of his children and grandchildren were there in Heaven by his side.

"At first, I thought this whole ida was crazy. Whose grandparent does this? I took an informal survey of my friends to find out if, as I suspected, mine was the only one. Once I got over the teenage embarrassment of the whole ordeal, I began to consider why he would do such a thing. Well, you don't have a man who has accomplished all my grandfather has by following the crowd. Once again, George Esseff was an original! While other grandparents might sit, worry, complain, and pray about what their grandchildren may or may not be into, George Esseff was facing this concern head-on. Basically, these meetings were his way of acting instead of remaining idle. He might succeed, he might ruffle some feathers, he might even fail, but he would do what he thought he should.

## MICHELLE SPENCER BURNS

*"We never know when we're going to have a 'priceless moment.' At one of those meetings, I saw Gidue cry. And it was only then that I had the maturity or the perception or the need to realize something that had never crossed my mind: My grandfather, the holder of patents, the founder of companies, the probing adventurer around the world, the fearless chairman or member of the board was scared to death about what might happen to all of us. It was the first time I looked at him, not as a figure, but as a man. Like any other really good man, his love and concern for his family knew no bounds and would take him to any extreme to protect them.*

*"Though these memories of the 'Santa Rosa Meetings' were not as warm and cuddly as my earliest remembrance of Gidue (who used to wear a teakettle cozy on his head ot make me smile), they are probably even more precious. In a photograph I still have that captures one of those 'teakettle cozy' moments, his arms are folded across his chest—as always—and his face reveals there is nothing out of place, nothing out of the ordinary. This, we might believe, was what he always wore. I am pointing at him, a smile from ear to ear across my face. That, too, is my grandfather—though I didn't know it at that time, a man of many surprises and even more hidden truths."*

In time, all of our children had homes of their own. Our home in Santa Rosa, like all of our other homes, served us very well at a particular time. But once Rosemary and I made up our minds that we should sell it, we went out and looked for a place to rent. I had a lot of equity in that house and so, under normal circumstances, when both Rosemary and I die, that asset would go to our children. Instead of doing that, I sold the house and netted out just over a million dollars from the sale of the house. We don't own a home now; we rent a beautiful home which fills our needs very well.

## ROSEMARY

*"At that time I wasn't feeling very well, and by that time we had made up our minds that we didn't want to own any house; we wanted to rent. It was better to rent rather than to buy something else because then we could put the money from the house into the foundation. So we started to look for a rental, and for a while nothing turned up. Finally, we did learn about the house that we live in now."*

# A New Heart

We were at a wedding and Rosemary was discussing with one of the women from the Legatus group that we were looking for a house to rent. It was just a casual comment and the woman she was talking to said, "We have been living in a house we rented in Westlake, but recently we bought a home of our own. I don't know if the owners might rent that house to you, but you might want to look into that." The woman gave Rosemary the name of the people who owned the house, and suggested that we might call them to see if we could take a look at the house. Well I did make that call, and they called back. They told me, "We just don't rent to anybody, but if we can interview you first, then we will let you look at the house." That was the deal. We couldn't even look at the house until they interviewed us. So I said that would be fine. The owner and his wife, came to our house in Rancho Santa Rosa to interview us. When they arrived at the gate, they had to ring the doorbell, which they did, and I pressed the button and opened the gate. They drove the 800 feet to the door of our house. The first thing that came into view was a big grotto where we had placed statues of the Blessed Mother, the Sacred Heart of Jesus, and St. Michael the Archangel. When the couple came to the door, after greeting us, the husband said, "Why did you call us to rent a house? How could you leave this house?" We told them we were looking for something smaller. Before we went into the house, I showed them the outdoor Stations of the Cross that were about five-hundred feet long. By the time they came inside the house, they were pretty convinced that we were very strongly Catholic and, in no time, they said that they would like us to rent their house if it would meet our needs.

We made arrangements to see their place and, when Rosemary and I walked in, we saw one of the most gorgeous homes we had ever seen. I heard Rosemary say, "This is a home I could love. It was ideal. One of the main reason we wanted to move was that Rosemary's knee was really bothering her and she was having a lot of difficulty going up and down the stairs. In this new home, the master bedroom was on the ground floor. There was an upstairs with several rooms and a full bath, but everything we needed was on the first floor. She loved the house as it was, and I told them we'd be very happy to rent it. I didn't even ask them what the price was. When the time came for them to tell us how much it would cost us, I could have fallen through the floor: They wanted $2,800 a month, and this was clearly a place that could have easily been rented for $6,000 a month.

# Brothers & Fathers

### ROSEMARY

*"I asked if they had a timeframe for the rental because I didn't want to move in and then have to pick up and leave within a short period of time. Jean said, 'As long as you want to stay, you can stay, regardless of months or years. It's up to you.'*

*"The next words out of my mouth were, 'Well, you have your renter.' That was 2002, and we have been in this house ever since. We're very happy here. It's close to church and close to town, and I don't need to drive far. It's close to a hospital and, in so many ways, just really convenient for me. The house is also really very beautiful. And the owners are wonderful to deal with. Every time I see him, the husband says, 'Thank God, you're here.'"*

In a short while, I really thought we were taking advantage by renting the place so cheaply. Rosemary and I went out to dinner with the owners and I told Frank that I felt that I would really like to pay more rent. He said, "You keep your mouth shut. If you don't keep quiet, I'll reduce the rent." That was the end of that. We're happy here; they're happy; and hopefully we can stay here as long as we need to—or maybe as long as we live. The owners originally built the house for Jean's parents and they didn't live in it too long before they passed away. Frank and Jean have a house of their own, but they want to keep this house in the family.

Once our house was sold, we moved into their rental house, which is about 4,000 square feet. We had the equivalent of a house full of furniture to get rid of. There were some things our children and our grandchildren needed or wanted, and so they took those items. Some other things we gave to charities to auction off. And still others we sold. Again, we put all those funds we earned into the Foundation.

I guess I should clarify one other thing. I've taken care of Rosemary and the children and the grandchildren. The children all received their funds—during our lifetime. I've made sure that all those family matters are in order. Those details took years to work out and were quite an undertaking. No matter how much planning I've done, I can be doing the wrong thing. But I did what I thought was right. I measured everything out in terms of what I hoped would guarantee that all of them have enough to help them, but not so much that it would take care of them for the rest of their lives. I want to let them earn their own way in building their lives. I watched children from other rich families waste their lives away with craziness. I would rather see my children and grandchildren develop their gifts and talents and work towards some focal point of value in their lives.

I feel my own family is adequately cared for. As for Rosemary and me, we live off a trust called the "charitable remainder." Now we live off the interest from that trust, and I'm hoping that we can die broke. That's what I'm hoping. I hope that we measure everything in such a way that it comes out that we leave the charitable remainder trust when we die. We'll be gone and through the trust, money will be given to charities that we have designated. And that means we won't have anything—and that's the way I'd like it to be.

I honestly still believe that everything we have was given to us by God, and we are now the stewards of dispersing it properly. As long as we do that, I think we're doing the right thing. We always got more back than we gave. I used to worry about my reason for giving because every time I gave, I got back so much it was unbelievable—even financially. On many occasions, I found that I got something I never expected; something would come unexpectedly, and it wasn't a small sum—not like I got a thousand dollars. I remember one time when I got $100,000 in some venture that I had never even thought about. It was totally unexpected; it just came.

At this point in my life, I don't feel as capable as I was twenty years ago. I really have lost a lot of my abilities to do the kinds of things that I was always able to do. After my stroke, I lost some of my capacity for getting things done, but I still want to do those things—and I still try. Right now, I'm trying to market a casket made of titanium. In a few years, if I keep giving at the rate I've been giving, the Foundation will be at a point where the funds will pretty much be depleted. That's why I am hoping that I will be able to raise some money by doing this new project, which is a very long-term thing. Usually I jump to each new task and get something done. This time, I'm not jumping, and not getting it done as fast as I'd like it to; but it'll happen, I hope, and maybe it will generate enough funds to continue the Foundation forever. If that doesn't happen, I have to believe that's the way it's meant to be. I've discussed the entire situation with George Jr. He will take over the Foundation because I think he'll do well, and he'll continue to be able to give to charity. He likes the idea of the Foundation and he and his wife Sherrie have contributed very heavily to it already. I think they'll continue to do that. Before too long, I'll probably make him president of the Foundation.

Even before we sold our last home, I had been working with Many Mansions, a non-profit housing organization based in Thousand Oaks. An obsolete motel in Thousand Oaks, known formerly as the Village Inn Motel, was the property that

Many Mansions wanted to buy to turn into a shelter for homeless people. The project was in the works for about four years. When I sold the house, I put the money from the sale of the house into the Foundation; I awarded a million dollars to Many Mansions to help renovate the building and use it as affordable housing for the formerly homeless. The complex consists of 50 one-room efficiency apartments that rent for between $200 and $420 a month, depending on the occupant's income. The complex also includes a large community room with a TV, comfortable seating, open space, and other amenities for socializing. Another room provides space for education classes and social services. There is also a storefront bike patrol which is manned by the Thousand Oaks Police Department. The facility is called Esseff Village, named and dedicated to my grandfather, George Abdanour Esseff, "whose life was devoted to religion, family, and generosity to the poor," and to our daughter Denise, "whose brief life was an example of creativity, joy, and love for the elderly."

Potential residents are referred to Esseff Village by Many Mansions, which has partnered with four other agencies: Lutheran Social Services, Ventura County Behavioral Health, Villa Esperanza, and the County of Ventura Homeless Outreach Program. Residents include the developmentally disabled, mentally ill, and previously homeless adults. Esseff Village was formally opened in January of 2002, although the complex was fully occupied since October 1ˢᵗ of 2001. It has been a wonder-

## Esseff Village Apartments

# Dedication Ceremony

Saturday
January 12, 2002
10:30 a.m. until 1 p.m.

1423 East Thousand Oaks Boulevard
Thousand Oaks, California

*Esseff Village*

ful involvement for us as a family, and a way of trying to live our stewardship in accordance with the gospel.

Although I get a lot of happiness from helping people, I don't like to give to 'bricks and mortar.' I did make something of an exception, however, when I responded to the building campaign run by King's College, my alma mater in Wilkes-Barre. I have always been grateful to the Holy Cross fathers for what I still consider a first-rate education, and I would like to see them able to continue their good work, especially in teaching the faith. In the early eighties, King's ran a five-year campaign in an attempt to reach its goal of approximately $19.5 million. At that time, I was able to give one million dollars to The Campaign for King's, as were two other donors, both of whom were also graduates. Rosemary and I offered that gift in memory of the two people I always think of when I think of service to the poor and care of the frail and elderly—Gidue, my grandfather, and our daughter Denise. I was also very happy when five of my grandchildren opted to

## King's grad now Calif. executive donates $1 million to King's College

WILKES-BARRE — A recent $1 million gift to the Campaign for King's College from George Esseff and his wife, Rosemary, has increased the total amount raised to more than $14.3 million. The campaign, a five-year effort to raise $19.5 million, has reached 73 percent of its goal.

Esseff, a 1952 graduate of King's College, is president and executive officer of Supra Alloys in Camarillo, Calif. He also owns two patents in titanium development.

"Rosemary and I offer this gift in memory of two persons who have exemplified service to the poor and care of the frail and elderly — my grandfather, George Abdanour Esseff, and my daughter, Denise Esseff Ortiz," said Esseff.

The Rev. Laurence Olszewski, vice president for external affairs at King's and director of the Campaign for King's, said the Esseffs' gift is the third seven-figure contribution to the campaign. Altogether 150 gifts have been received. In addition to three gifts of at least $1 million, three were of $500,000, five of $250,000 or more, and 21 of $100,000 or more.

"George Esseff is an extraordinary individual who has a deep commitment to helping others. His gift to King's is greatly appreciated, and is a major step toward reaching the goal of the Campaign for King's," said the Rev. James Lackenmier, president of King's.

After graduating from King's, Esseff, a Wilkes-Barre native, joined the U.S. Corps of Engineers Research and Development Laboratories before going into business for himself in 1955.

Esseff majored in biology and chemistry and minored in physics

**"**George Esseff is an extraordinary individual who has a deep commitment to helping others. His gift to King's is greatly appreciated...**"**

**The Rev. James Lackenmier**
President of King's

and philosophy at King's.

For nearly 20 years, he traveled an average of 250,000 miles a year throughout the world — including 115 trips to Japan — to coordinate his business operations. He is now semi-retired.

He also has supported 20 orphans in Lebanon, where his grandparents are from and has helped bring Lebanese to the United States for educational study. He has helped finance a home for unwed mothers in Los Angeles, and a rectory in Castilla, Peru.

He established the Esseff Foundation in honor of his grandfather to help people in Lebanon. The foundation also helped establish a scholarship for the needy at King's.

*Donation to King's College*

get their degrees at King's College. Mary Ellen's daughters Michelle, Stephanie, and Kim all finished from there. Two of George's sons, Tim and Andrew, eventually chose King's as well. My granddaughter Stephanie gave Tim a tour when he went to visit his cousin. Her great reviews of King's influenced Tim's choice to go there years later.

# Brothers & Fathers

## STEPHANIE SPENCER

Esseff Hall, King's College

"When Michelle finished high school, Gidue made a proposal to her. If she would go to King's College, his alma mater, he would assist her in paying for her education. When I graduated, I was given the same offer and, like Michelle, I also accepted. It was the best gift I could have been given. I loved King's. I got a good education there and I was able to play volleyball and flag football. I lived in Esseff Hall on the fourth floor, and I worked for King's as head waitress in the college dining room. In time, I got to see all of the places that I had heard about all my life. I saw the house where Gidue and Father John had grown up with their Gidue. I saw St. Anthony's Church and so many other places that were part of their history.

Stephanie playing volleyball

"As great as those years were, there was still another fantastic gift I received from Gidue and Framma—my graduation present: a two-week vacation to Lebanon. During the time I was there, Dima Istambouli was married. I was the tallest woman at the wedding, dancing with the oldest man in Lebanon, who fell in love with me! I also sat with General Michel Mir, the head of the Northern Army in Lebanon. With his wife's permission, I got to dance with him. I had a wonderful time, and the days that followed were just as exciting and filled with so much fun.

"I can never repay them for such an amazing gift. I learned so much about my family through the larger family in Lebanon. I understood so much about the culture I grew up in within my own family. I experienced the warmth, the hospitality, the generosity, and the love I had been blessed to live in all my life. It was truly a spectacular gift, and one I will never forget."

Stephanie dancing with the oldest man in Lebanon!

# A New Heart

I like to give to the poor and the needy, but it's not always easy to know just who or which group is most in need at any given time. I've turned the answer to those decisions over to prayer. I've asked God to place in front of me those that I can best help. Very seriously, I've never necessarily gone out looking. Almost everyone I'm involved with now has been those who have just somehow come in front of me. They just seem to present themselves at the right time. Many of them are people or groups who don't require a whole lot of money—maybe ten or fifteen thousand dollars, and to many people those sums are windfalls. Other needs are greater because they serve a broader group of people. Those needs require prayerful consideration as well. These are some of the works that Rosemary and I have dedicated time and thought to over the years, and we certainly hope to be able to continue in the way God guides us.

Besides these endeavors on the home front, there have also been causes outside of this country that have come to our attention and demanded a response. One notable project that we became involved in was feeding the poor in Haiti, the poorest country in the Western Hemisphere. That Haitian effort was an opportunity for me to develop an even deeper understanding of how difficult it is to get gifts into the hands of the poor. When corruption is rampant and there are so many needy people, many hands reach out. Many are the hands of those who aren't looking to help, but instead are hoping to get a lucrative return from goods they have stolen from the poor. Very often, the poor never receive what has been sent for them. Their hands are just as empty after the gifts are given as before.

When I began to have real concerns for the people of another country, I knew I wanted to help in the most direct way possible. I approached them respectfully, and slowly decided who and how I might help.

# CHAPTER 51

## My Journey to Lebanon

### *George*

hen my brother John took on his mission to Lebanon to serve as the director of the Pontifical Mission for Palestine in Beirut, I was eager to support him in whatever way I could. Although I had traveled hundreds of thousands of miles all over the world for my business, I had never been to Lebanon. In fact, in spite of my ethnic background, I had never given any serious thought to going there. When I went to visit John in Lebanon, a new chapter opened in my life.

Although he began his mission in September of 1984, I didn't visit John until December. I visited him as often as I could and, when I did, we stayed in Beirut. I hadn't been with John the first time he went to the village and met our family, so when I went to the village with him, he had already announced my visit and was eager to introduce me to everyone. On my many visits to Lebanon, whenever it was possible, we would go up to the village on weekends. During those visits, we were able to cement the relationship between us and our relatives who, until that time, we actually didn't know existed.

### JOHN

*"One of the first people I met was Antonius (Tanious Assaf) who was Leon Istambouli's grandfather. Leon was the young boy who gave me figs from the 'famous fig tree' of our great grandfather when I first went to the village. When I saw Antonius, I was amazed because he looked so much like my dad. I came to learn that he had two sons and three daughters. One of his sons, Joseph, had showed up at my father's door in Wilkes-Barre looking for relatives, and eventually I met him and his son in Australia, and my brother George met him in Hawaii. His other son, George, also lived in Australia. In the village, I met Antonius's three daughters. One other cousin emerged when he arrived in my office in Beirut and told me that his mother and my mother*

# Brothers & Fathers

> ## JOHN
>
> *were first cousins; his name was George El Koury. In the course of a short time, both my brother George and I became connected with these and many other members of our extended family."*

I find it interesting how both John's involvement in Lebanon and my own played out over the years. John certainly initiated the connection, and I sort of traipsed around behind him for a long time. I saw the work he was doing as the director of the Pontifical Mission and, in time, realized the scope, the intensity, and even the intrigue of that work. After John had finished his work as the director of the Pontifical Mission, both of us still remained willing and eager to help the Lebanese people, who had experienced so much suffering over many years of war. From home, together we established the Mission for Lebanon, and through that organization hoped to deliver direct care to

*Father John and George visit a convent in Lebanon*

those we wanted to help. When that endeavor met with the same kind of political and clerical intrigue that John had experienced as the director of the Pontifical Mission, we knew that we had to abandon that project—and we did. It was then that John signed off and pretty much made up his mind that he wasn't going to go back to Lebanon. As he said, "My Church connections were burnt, and that had to be the end of my involvement there." He returned to America and continued his work in his own diocese. He did return to Lebanon a number of times, mostly to give retreats to the Missionaries of Charity, or to see Marty McDermott or Michele Aboujoude for some special occasion.

On the other hand, my interest continued, and I was still hoping to help the people of Lebanon—no doubt, in part, because they were my

*Father John and George with the President of Lebanon*

grandparents' people. By that time, I knew the best way to do it was to go alone. By that I mean I knew I had to avoid both clerical and political affiliations, and it was best not to align myself with any group. It's no secret how politically involved the people in the Middle East are. In that respect, the Lebanese are equally involved politically and religiously. I could see that there were many who were in need of financial help, and I knew that I could best reach out and help as a private benefactor.

Before I get ahead of myself, I suppose I should start with the family. On my very first visit to the village, I met the family all at one time at a party that took place at Father Deeb's house. Among the young people there was a nephew of Father Deeb. His name was Joseph Deeb and he was a few years older than Leon. Each time I would go to Lebanon, he was one of the people I would see in the village. He was a bright kid, as was Leon, and when he got to be of university age, I offered to send him to college in the United States. I saw the needs his family had, and I thought they could all benefit if Joseph was able to get a college education. He was very interested, and when the time came, he came to America. I established a scholarship for him at King's College in Wilkes-Barre and paid for his room and board. During the summers, I brought him to California and had him work in the factory so he could make some money. I also gave him an old pick-up truck that used to be Sherrie's, so he had transportation to get back and forth to work.

---

### LEON ISTAMBOULI

*"When Uncle George took my cousin Joe Deeb to study in the States I thought that Joe was the luckiest person in the world. I went through high school with the dream of going to the States when I graduated. My parents' protectiveness stopped that from happening. They were haunted by the idea that had survived through generations of Hardinians that America is a kidnapper of the young. It takes them away and gets them hooked on sex and drugs. Because I was the only boy in the family, my parents worried a lot, and had made up their minds that I wasn't going to America; I went to the American University of Beirut."*

---

Besides helping out some other individual people, I did some small things in the village. At one time prior to the beatification of the village saint, Joe Asaf, our cousin from Australia, initiated and funded a renovation of the village center in Hardine. I put some money up to put a new roof on the church there, but that was a little thing in terms of the entire project. Leon was responsible for the renovation of the village center.

*"Fortunately, I graduated from the American University of Beirut as a civil engineer. I worked in that field for two years and I had the privilege of designing and executing the construction and renovation of the church and shrine in honor of a man who has since been canonized a saint of the Catholic Church. I also restored the village square. This work was done before the beatification of Nimatullah Kassab al-Hardini, born Youssef Kassab in 1808 in the village of Hardine. All of us who were from Hardine were filled with pride that one of us had received such an honor. I was happy to be a part of preparing the birthplace where people could visit.*

*"Uncle George was a major donor to that project and, with the availability of resources and support from the Esseff and Assaf uncles in the U.S. and Australia, I was able to finish construction in nine months—two weeks before the beatification ceremony in Rome."*

When the time came for the beatification (and later the canonization), Rosemary and I, as well as John, went to Rome for the ceremonies. We learned that while the canonization was happening, church bells rang throughout all of Lebanon. The entire story of St. Nimatullah Kassab became common knowledge in Lebanon, and most especially in Hardine. In the days of St. Nimatullah, a person's last name typically was derived either form the person's birthplace or from the father's profession. For us in the West, it's a simple thing to hear about St. Francis of Assisi—Francis who came from the town of Assisi. St. Nimatullah Kassab al-Hardini's name follows the same pattern. At the age of twenty, Hardini entered St. Anthony's Monastery and adopted the name of Brother Nimatullah. He was ordained a priest in 1833 at the monastery of Kfifan and chose to live in a monastery rather than in an isolated hermitage. He is described as a man who spent untold hours in adoration of the Blessed Sacrament. He also had a special devotion to Mary and went to confession every day. He was a scholar, and his love of books led him to become an accomplished bookbinder. He served as assistant superior of the Kfifan monastery three times. He had a high regard for the teaching of Syriac, the liturgical language of the Maronite Catholic Church. He urged all those who became priests to learn the language so that they could better appreciate the liturgy. It is also said that he fasted frequently and slept on a blanket made of goat hair. Even with the harsh cold and winds of the mountain in Kfifan, he never wore extra clothing beyond sackcloth. In 1858, he developed pleurisy and died at the age of fifty.

# My Journey to Lebanon

Father Raphael al-Bizaouni, who was a spiritual director to Hardini and gave him the last rites of the Church, reported seeing "brilliant shining rays fill the room when Hardini's soul left his body," and that "an aromatic scent engulfed the entire room for several days." Immediately after his death, people began to visit his tomb seeking blessings and cures. Numerous miracles have been attributed to him. He was canonized on May 16, 2004, and is Lebanon's third saint. Interestingly, St. Charbel Makhlouf, canonized by Pope Paul VI in 1977, was one of Saint Hardini's theology students.

## LEON ISTAMBOULI

*"After the beatification of Nimatullah Kassab al-Hardini, Uncle George invited me to come and visit him in America. My dream visit was about to become a reality. My stay with George & Rosemary started off in what I considered a very strange way. I would go down to Uncle George's company every morning; but before we left, we had to go to Mass. More than that, on our way to Mass, we had to pray a full rosary. It was a nightmare in the beginning, and in one week I had prayed as many rosaries as I had in the last six years. But that nightmare, sooner or later, turned into my refuge and special time with God. For the next three years, I would attend Mass as often as I could (every day for four consecutive months) and, to this day, I pray the rosary any chance I have while I'm driving.*

*"That month in the States with Uncle George turned my life upside down. In that passenger seat in his car, praying and talking was as satisfying as the days when I took my rest with my grandfather under the Abdelnoor fig tree where we prayed and talked.*

*"From that time, Uncle George became a father that I asked for advice; a brother that I spent fun time with, playing cards and talking; a spiritual director that guided me to the right path; and the friend that was there when I needed one.*

*"I remember getting employment at New England Financial in Michigan after spending a year without work in 2000. I was depressed from the job, the weather, and the general climate. I started praying for an answer; I was at the lowest point of stress and depression. I got a call from Uncle George, who asked me if I was interested in working for Supra Alloys. I took the job. I was fortunate to spend five months living with Uncle George and Aunty Rosemary. Usually a person can feel the difference between living with his own parents and distant relatives, but not in my case. I was living with angels that embraced me as one of their own children. I was loved and treated like a son."*

# Brothers & Fathers

I find the story of Saint Nimatullah Kassab al-Hardini very interesting and inspiring. John's good friend, Father Martin McDermott, who has served in Lebanon for almost thirty-five years, was quoted as saying, "Blessed Hardini is a pillar of Lebanese monastic spirituality, which has a long tradition dating back to the fifth century."

When John and I were in Lebanon together, I saw how extensively he dealt with the clergy, and we did see a need for renewal among the Maronite clergy. We often spoke about it and I know I would love to see John do the same kind of renewal work in Lebanon that he is doing for the American priesthood through the IPF. To me, it's kind of ironic because, like John, Saint Nimatullah Kassab was head of formation (at the Maronite seminary), and actually he made it his life's work to renew the Maronite clergy and to develop in them a strong spirituality. A pattern had developed in Lebanon where a priest was just a "Mass" priest. He barely knew more theology than the people he was serving. Priests were being sent out to the villages to offer Mass, and that was just about all they could do. It's hard to know how well prepared even the priests in our own family were, because they were pre-Hardini and his renewal. I think it's ironic that Monsignor John has the know-how and the opportunity to renew the Maronite monks again. I have approached him many times about doing that work; but at this point in his life, he seems dedicated to formation of the clergy here in America. I have never been able to talk John into going to Lebanon to do formation work there.

## JOHN

"Before I left Lebanon in 1986, I went with Father Shiner (a Maronite monk who became a hermit) to his hermitage, where we prayed. Afterwards, I wrote a 15-page document which I sent to the patriarch and the archbishops and bishops who were gathered at the patriarchate at Bkererh to elect a new patriarch. During my time at the Pontifical Misson in Lebanon, I saw the lack of leadership on the part of the bishops and the archbishops, especially in the times of crisis when their people needed their leadership the most. I related many of my experiences that made it clear that most of the bishops and archbishops were out of touch with the needs of their people. They had so many acres of land that could have used to establish homes for young couples, but for the most part they ignored the sufferings of the Lebanese refugees. They were well known for their wealth, which came from funerals that they would attend. I did get a response from the former patriarch, Patriarch Kharishe, who told me, 'You have no authority to lecture us.' I knew that my opinion and my expertise would never be accepted. I still feel that way."

# My Journey to Lebanon

In spite of my brother's refusal to go to Lebanon to do formation work there, I did prevail upon him to talk about his own life of prayer, and he did record that journey as part of our shared autobiography. If it is God's will, it will fall into the hands of those who need it—maybe even the priests of Lebanon. I hope that will be the case.

# CHAPTER 52

## MY JOURNEY IN A LIFE OF PRAYER

### *Father John*

*M*any times, I have been reminded by people that I say certain things: "I received an inspiration from God," or "I really feel that this is how God is encouraging me," or "I heard [something] in prayer. I know what God wants me to do."

I have come to realize that, very often, people find those statements to be quite mysterious. And because some people have challenged me to explain this, and because George has asked me to talk about prayer, I now want to make it clear that what they may perceive as mystery is, as I know it, prayer. It is prayer that they, too, can know.

Having been a priest for more than fifty years, I know what most people expect from me is to be a man of prayer. If I am not a man of prayer, if my profession (as it were) is not to pray, then how else would I describe myself?

"What does this man do?"

Well, primarily, what I am is a man of prayer. I am a pray-er. What I do is pray.

People come to me and ask, "How do you know what God wants of you?"

"I know because I pray."

The next logical questions: "What is prayer? Can you teach us to pray?"

I want to, but, in fairness to those who are searching, I also need to look back at my own life of prayer and share that journey with them.

As a youngster and as an Eastern rite Catholic, I think I did see some mysticism, along with quiet and length of time in prayer; but realistically, I think that prayer was external. There was much vocal prayer, there was incense, there was chanting, there was cantoring, there was a lot of bell ringing. These rituals, along with images of Jesus, Mary, and Joseph that were visible in the church, the Stations of the Cross, the stained glass windows depicting stories of Catholic teachings, and the sounds of choir and music—all of these were helpful. But, none of these things were prayer.

I also remember when I was taught the rosary. I was introduced somewhat later to the meditations and to the lighting of candles. I also remember going to church and serving the Mass. In and through it all, I always thought that prayer was what I was saying to God. It never occurred to me that prayer was what God was saying to me.

So according to the catechism definition of prayer, "the raising up of my mind and heart to God," prayer was about me looking up to God and asking God, through my offering (an offering mostly of things) for His favor. I did do a formula of prayers: adoration, thought of as the greatest prayer that we can pray; contrition, sorrow for sins; thanksgiving; and petition, asking for those things that I wanted or needed.

But at that time, I still don't know whether I was ever brought to an awareness that God was saying something to me, and that my real work was to listen. I think I did not hear that concept in my young life. In seminary, I don't think I heard that concept either. Even as a theologian, and even when I discovered *Mystici Corporis* (and, in so doing, discovered that I was Christ), prayer was pretty much what I was doing, pretty much all about me and what I was saying to God. I did have a spiritual director in the seminary, and after I was ordained, I sought out and consulted another spiritual director.

My journey in prayer led me to the Institute of the Heart of Jesus, which I spoke about earlier. That group sustained me for years in a very wonderful way. I was led to that group soon after my strong and powerful revelation in 1959 in St. John Lateran's in Rome, where Jesus spoke to me of His desire for me to love—charity—and of His desire for me to learn more about Leo XIII who was buried in that chapel. I shared that revelation with a boyhood friend and fellow priest, Father Clem Markowski. Some time later, he and I came to know about the Institute of the Heart of Jesus, a secular institute founded mainly for priests. I became involved and spent a year in novitiate under a novice master who I saw periodically, and to whom I made reports. I told him about my meditation, my rosary, and my prayer. I remember joining the group in 1960 and being very much a part of it throughout 1961, '62, and '63, while I was being refused as an applicant to go to South America to serve the poor there. I also took the vows of poverty, chastity, and obedience in the Institute, even though I had already made the promise of celibacy at ordination.

# My Journey in a Life of Prayer

I was, at that time, very much into wanting to obey all Church authority: my bishop, my pastor, the rules of the Institute. I wanted to live by the rules of the Institute and the rules of the Church in a spirit of obedience. What was new to me was my introduction to taking an inventory of all my property and becoming conscious of the practice of poverty. I remember that, at that time, some of my classmates were buying cottages at nearby lakes. We were making a salary of $60 or $70 a month and eventually it even got to be about $100. But there was more money than just a salary. For myself, I was stationed at a very wealthy parish and people would often give me cash. They would give me gifts. I cataloged all the gifts that I had received and made an inventory of them. I learned accountability for them during the novitiate year. I had to assess how I was using those gifts, and had to ask permission to use the monies that I did have. I had to discern whether each expense was a luxury or a necessity. This examination included my car and all other items that I owned. I really made a serious accounting as to what I was doing with the money and who I was giving it to.

I do believe that the strongest influence during my years with the Institute of the Heart of Jesus was the training and the discipline I received that heightened my awareness of my gifts—what I was receiving materially and how I was sharing those gifts with the poor.

I came to hear the gospel of Matthew in an even deeper way:

> When the Son of Man comes in His glory, escorted by all the angels, then He will take His seat on His throne of glory. All the nations will be assembled before Him and He will separate men one from another as the shepherd separates sheep from goats. He will place the sheep on His right hand and the goats on His left. Then the King will say to those on His right hand, "Come, you whom my Father has blessed, take for your heritage the kingdom prepared for you since the foundation of the world. For I was hungry and you gave me food; I was thirsty and you gave me drink; I was a stranger and you made me welcome; naked and you clothed me, sick and you visited me, in prison and you came to see me." Then the virtuous will say to Him in reply, "Lord, when did we see you hungry and feed you; or thirsty and give you drink? When did we see you a stranger and make you welcome; naked and clothe you; sick or in prison and go to see you?" And the King will answer, "I tell you solemnly, insofar as you did this to one of the least of these brothers of mine, you did it to me."

That very powerful influence in my life, my training with the Institute of the Heart of Jesus, may have prepared me in some small way when I went into my greatest experience in poverty—my years in Latin America. But even with that background, my entry into Peru was a culture shock for me.

And through all these years, I was becoming more aware of the necessity of prayer and the time spent in prayer. I had never abandoned prayer. I always prayed my office. (At that time, we called it the "breviary"—what we now more commonly know as the Liturgy of the Hours.) I had a very strong devotion to the rosary. I also had a very strong devotion to the Passion of Jesus, not only in the Stations of the Cross but also in the Scriptures and in the accounts of Jesus' suffering and death during the liturgical year, especially during the season of Lent. I was very much sustained by my liturgical life. I had a great devotion to the Eucharist and to my hours of adoration before the Blessed Sacrament. Yet during all this time, I did not hear about what I have come to know as prayer.

My awareness of prayer, as I now know it, came with my return to the United States from my mission in Beirut, Lebanon. During the years 1988, '89, and '90, I was continuing a ministry that I had begun in Lebanon when I met Mother Teresa and her sisters, the Missionaries of Charity. Mother asked me to give retreats to her and her sisters and, even after I returned to the States, I continued to travel and give those retreats. I studied the Rule of Life of the sisters, and that was an important spiritual growth for me. As I became more deeply involved in those retreats into prayer, I experienced an ever-growing awareness of the necessity for an ever deeper prayer life and a lifetime of ever deepening prayer. These were key times when I centered in and began to formulate what I can share with you now.

## What is Prayer and How Do We Pray?

When we begin any discussion on prayer, let me say either that you and I are more important than God or that God is more important than we are. The answer is obvious. If God is more important than I am, then what God wants and Who God is certainly is more important than what I want and who I am. Therefore, the attention must be focused on God. Again, what God wants to say to us is more important for us than anything we may have to say to God. God wants to speak to us. God wants to communicate Himself to us. This understanding is fundamental to prayer. When prayer becomes too self-centered, even if it is centered on noble and holy desires—if the focus is on me, I, myself—then we are going in the wrong direction and there is going to be some difficulty. Even as we describe prayer as the "lifting up of my mind and heart to God," we're a little off center there. When we pray, our prayer often becomes too self-centered.

Prayer is a personal *response* to the presence of God. That is very elemental. God is present to every person in the world. So if you want to learn about prayer, then the first movement means you must become aware of God's presence—of God's making Himself present to you. You don't make God present to you; *God* makes Himself present to you. God is the prime mover in our awareness and acknowledgement of His own presence. That is what prayer is. It is what God does to us rather than something—anything—that we do. St. John reminds us that first God loves us—we do not first love God. God *first* loves us and then we, *in response* to God's love, return that love. His love is far more important than our love for Him. He wants and appreciates and is grateful for our love, but since His love for us is more important than our love for Him, His love deserves more of our attention.

As we approach prayer, the pray-er first of all moves to an awareness of God's presence. The pray-er simply acknowledges God's presence; he is able to admit, "Yes, God, my Father, *You* are my life. Yes, You love life and being into me, and all the things that are around me, and into all that comes through my senses. You love talents and longings into me."

The focus is on God and that God is doing these things. When I am praying, the first focus of everything is this: He is present. And from that presence, He then gives me the awareness, the talent, and everything that is around me. God is creating and making all.

Let me make a distinction that I think is very important. When I was in seminary, I was taught about meditation. We were going to meditate on God. Now, when I am thinking about God, when I am thinking about holy things, when I am thinking about Jesus, I am meditating. Likewise, when I am thinking about you, when I am thinking about your qualities, when I am thinking about how good you are or how generous you are, I am meditating. When I am thinking about God, that is meditation. It is all meritorious and good. When I think about Christ, when I think about His life and I think about the meditations that I am having, they are very helpful. But those thoughts are exactly that—meditation. They are not *prayer*.

Prayer begins when I grasp the profound truth that God not only created me but also that each moment He continues to re-create me, that is, He keeps me in existence. It begins to happen when I say, "Yes, God, my Father; *You* love life into me. I am because You have loved me into being, and each moment You *continue* to love me into being."

When I say to *myself*, God loves life into me, that is not prayer. That is a meditation.

Do you see how I am using the words?

Prayer begins when He becomes me. When I say, "Yes, God, my Father; *You* love life into me."

I am not speaking to myself.

When there is a *You–I* relationship with the Father, Son, and Holy Spirit, I call this genuine prayer. If there is a consideration of what He is and does, but not a *You–I* relationship, it may be helpful, good, and holy, but it is not essentially prayer.

There is a difference between persons and things. As I sit and look around me, there are many things that I see. God is present to things. God saturates these things with His Being, with His Presence, because He loves life and being into them. In the room that I am sitting in, with all that is in it, God loves and brings into being everything that is here; but those things cannot acknowledge God as the source of their being—only a person can *respond* to the presence of God. All things are, therefore, incapable of prayer. My chair cannot pray; it cannot respond personally to God's creating it into being. My watch, my desk, my lamp cannot respond. You and I, however, because we are persons, can acknowledge the presence of God, and that is the first step in prayer.

The second essential step for prayer is on the part of the one who is the pray-er.

When I realize that everything I have and that everything I am comes from God, that He brings life into me, that He fills me with all that I am; when I realize what God is to me, what God is to us, what He does for us and how much He loves us, there is only one response. This is the very important second step. The realization of God as the source of all—of me—brings a response that is polite, obvious, and spontaneous.

"Yes, God! Thank You!"

We do more than say, "Yes, You do this, God." We respond, "Thank You, God, my Father, for loving life into me, into my being—for sharing with me Your own, wonderful life. Thank You, Jesus. Thank You, the Son of God, my brother. Thank you, God, the Holy Spirit, for living on in me."

Gratitude is just as obvious, spontaneous, and overflowing as being aware of what God is and what He does. Notice that the "Thank You" is a *response*. The awareness of another and receiving from that other is essential for gratitude.

Think of this: You open a door and you are looking into a strange, dark room; immediately you begin to speak into the dark room just in case there might be someone there. When people want to pray, they sometimes think this way. They just can't sit here and do nothing, so they start speaking, and they think they're praying. What they're actually doing is talking into a dark room. They start, but without any awareness of the Other. We must first be conscious of someone who is there, who looks into our eyes; and then we are able to continue, because we are assured that we are talking to *someone*.

If I have received all of these gifts, if this person who is God has loved all these things into me and I am aware of that person being there, then as I look into His eyes, gratitude is the obvious response.

"Father, I thank You for giving me the gifts and talents You've given me. I thank You for the blessings You have shared with me." It is essential that I am aware that I am talking to a person: this Father, this Son, this Holy Spirit. Without that awareness, if I begin immediately, saying, "I believe in You, I hope in You, I love You, I'm sorry for my sins, please forgive me for failing to keep Your commandments"—all these acts of what I may think of as prayer are simply times of talking into a dark room in which maybe someone is present. But we haven't the certainty. We haven't made contact, eyeball to eyeball; we lack conscious awareness that someone is, in fact, there.

Yet, on the other hand, when I have this awareness of God, this awareness of His having given me all that I am and all that I have, the response can truly and only be, "Thank You, Father; Thank You, Jesus; Thank You, Holy Spirit." That's what prayer is. Even if we spend only a few minutes in this kind of prayer, it is really and truly prayer.

The other kinds of things you are doing may be meditation; you may be talking *about* God. You may be saying things, but there is no contact. Or maybe you're just talking into a dark, empty room.

Prayer demands the communication first: the awareness of God pouring His graces into you, loving you, giving you all that you have; it demands an awareness of Him as the source of all things. As you experience this conscious awareness and make contact with the living God, then you can truly look back at Him, into His face, and say, Thank You, Father; Thank You, Jesus; Thank You, Holy Spirit.

And it is no accident that offering this "Thank You" is precisely what we do in the Eucharist. (The name of our greatest communal act of prayer comes from the word "to give thanks.") In the Eucharist, we come together as Christ's own body, with Jesus really present in our midst; and in the power of the Holy Spirit we say, "Thank You"—for all we have, for all we are, and above all, that You have sent us Your own Son who, "On the night before He died for us ... took bread and said, 'This is my body' ... took the cup and said, 'This is the cup of my blood.'"

For us who *are* the living Body of Christ, what could be more appropriate, more in keeping with who we are as Jesus? In the words of one of our Eucharistic Prayers, we remember that, "At the end of the meal, knowing that he was to reconcile all things in himself by the blood of his cross ... he gave you thanks." Amazing! He gave God thanks. Face-to-face with the betrayal by his friend, he gives God thanks! About to be abandoned by his disciples, he gives God thanks! On the verge of his beating, his imprisonment, his excruciating death on the cross, what does Jesus do? He gives God THANKS! And that is exactly what we do every time we come together to celebrate the Eucharist: WE—who *are* Jesus—give God thanks. From the midst of our joys, our sorrows, our hopes, our fears, our dreams, our disappointments, our sickness—even in the face of our own death—we give God THANKS!

It is good to stop and realize, though, that even this act of thanksgiving that we offer to God is only secondarily our gift to God; *first* it is God's gift to us. For, as we pray to the Father in one of our prefaces at Mass, "You have no need of our praise, yet our desire to thank you is itself your gift. Our prayer of thanksgiving adds nothing to your greatness, but makes us grow in grace, through Jesus Christ, our Lord."

After we acknowledge God's presence and thank Him, then the third and final step is a *loving response*. When we realize that God has loved us into being, then we respond to that love freely. We do not say, "God, I love You," but rather, "God, I love You *too!*" When we say this to God, it implies that we are aware that He loves us first. And, therefore, to say, "God, my Father; Christ, my Brother; Holy Spirit, I love You *too*" is our obvious response to the Other. God's love for us is more important than our love for God. Because He loves us, we can say, "I love You, too." Then there is relationship. Only then can prayer begin.

When we come to God in real prayer, we are aware of Him, His creating us, His loving us, and we respond in gratitude to Him. We respond to His love by loving Him, and then we can ask Him, the source of everything, for many different things. We may ask Him, "Please, God, help me to overcome this disease. Or, "Please help me to find a good job." Or any of a hundred other requests. Each of these is a very profound and beautiful prayer. We know God is there, we are grateful to Him for all that we are and all that we have, and we approach Him as a loving Father with our needs. Jesus told us that we must become as little children and that whatever we ask God He will give us because our God is all powerful and all loving. But asking must begin with this total dependence on God. When we come to God in this posture of prayer, we are aware that God is the one who gives us everything. That awareness is very important. We are aware that, without God, we are nothing, and so we pray from a posture of total dependence. In this way, when we ask God for whatever it is that we want, that request is honoring Him and praising Him and glorifying Him as our Father. As children, we totally depend on Him, and so we say, "God may it please You to give me whatever these gifts are." A child goes to his parent to ask for things. He goes there in total confidence; he knows that he will receive whatever he needs and so honors his father by asking him for the things he needs. He compliments his father as loving and giving. And when we pray for gifts, it is a great big compliment to the Father and the Son and the Holy Spirit. "You, Father, are good. You love me and you fill all of my needs."

When He taught us to pray, Jesus told us to call God, *Abba*. We are to call Him, "Daddy." We are to respond to our Father as any child would. Call Him "Daddy." As His children, we totally depend on Him and so we are saying, "God may it please You to give me what I ask for. You are everything." So this honoring and praising and glorifying God as our Father is prayer. Even the asking, following the awareness of God's presence, is prayer. And our gratitude is prayer, too.

When we engage, then, in intercessory prayer, we honor and praise God. He is one—God. He is everything. He is the one who creates, sustains, loves, forgives. "Merciful Lord, You are everything. You are universal providence. You are the God of all."

So the acknowledgement, as I begin to pray from this posture of total dependence, is that I am the recipient of a gift that I do not deserve, and I am, therefore, filled with gratitude.

The pray-er who thinks that if he does enough 'spiritual push ups,' (be those novenas, triduums, pilgrimages, or whatever other rituals he thinks entitles him to what he seeks), he, this pray-er is not in the dependent, grateful posture of prayer. In short, such a pray-er is not praying.

God longs to communicate Himself to us in prayer. God wants, more than we do, to communicate Himself to us. Why is it, then, that there is so much failure in prayer? I think it's because we are afraid that if we don't do all the talking, then nothing is happening in the prayer. We fail to realize that prayer requires profound listening; it requires silence on the part of the pray-er. God—Father, Son, and Holy Spirit—wants to communicate; that's really what prayer is. It is the Father, Son, and Holy Spirit communicating Himself to me—or to you—personally and uniquely. And that's where the fear comes. Can it be that God is so in love with me, that God has something to say to me personally? And can it be that, if I listen to Him, I will hear Him tell me that He loves me as His son, His daughter? That the Lord Jesus personally loves me? That the Holy Spirit personally sanctifies me?

So each and every one who longs to pray, who longs to hear what God wants to say to him, must be in the posture that allows himself to *listen* to God in the silence, trusting that He will communicate Himself to each of us as His child—personally.

Real prayer is intensely personal. God has an infinite desire to communicate with me, with you, with each one of His children. The virtues that I practice are the activities that come from God's communication with me. I desire to communicate with God and I respond by saying, "I believe in You, I trust in You, I thank You, I love You too." We become involved in a personal communication that might be compared to what happens in radio. Each radio station has a transmitter to send out signals. But there is also a receiver. God has put the power to receive in each one of us, His children. He has given us of His Spirit, with all the capacity to receive His love.

And so the Father is constantly communicating Himself to us, His children. He communicates to me—personally. He wants to pour His love into me. And so I become aware of His being with me and I am aware of that presence. Then—and *only* then—can I communicate in prayer. That communication is, above all, the receiving of His divine love—what He wants to give me because He is the source of it all. What I give back to Him is what I have already received from Him.

Again, my response is "Thank You!"

This communication grows. We have the capacity to grow in the awareness of His presence—of His unique, personal, loving, providential, sanctifying, saturating love, His constant pouring out of more and more of His love upon us. He is our Father. He is a good Father. He continues to speak to us through all the circumstances of our lives—through the Church; through His living Word, the Scriptures; above all, through Jesus, His eternal Word made flesh; through the Holy Spirit who constantly invites us to be His son or His daughter. First, we listen. Then we speak. He wants us to speak to Him and communicate with Him personally.

In my awareness of Him as I thank Him, He tells me, "I love you." The gratitude pours out because I have recognized that He is the source of it all. And with my heart filled with gratitude for all that I am, all that I have, I can only stand in awe of the love that God is. God has loved me into being. My grateful heart is filled with love and I say, "I love You too."

# My Journey in a Life of Prayer

God is consistently saying with everything in my life that He loves me. Even as I approach Him as my loving Father and ask Him for favors, even in that, He is saying, "I love you." And even in my asking Him, I am saying, "I love You, too." There is a communication. I must listen if I am to hear God. And then, I must respond to what I hear. My response is always one of gratitude and love.

In my introduction to prayer as a child, I learned that this kind of prayer was *mystical* and intended for only a few. I am so grateful to God for His not giving up on me.

What a tragedy if even one of us doesn't learn to pray.

What gratitude if even one of us does.

God longs to communicate with every person and to make all of His children ordinary mystics. Yes, God wants normal, ordinary people to be mystics—to engage in mystical prayer. It's not for the few; it's not for someone who is extraordinary; it's not for those whom others think are 'far out.' People may say, "What do you mean, 'God's talking to you? Yeah. Yeah. Right. You must be some kind of nut."

No.

The Father longs to have communication in prayer with every one of His children. He wants all of us to be ordinary, everyday, down-to-earth mystics. He has called us out of darkness into His own wonderful light. He has done this for everyone. That beautiful truth was not communicated to me early in my life, but I would like to communicate it to as many people as possible, as early as possible. I would like to communicate it to *you*. I would like to help you become a person of prayer—an ordinary mystic.

# CHAPTER 53

## THE CONTINUATION OF MY MISSION

## *George*

There were people I was able to help in the village of Hardine, and there were those in the village who were generous to me as well. Leon's parents, Rahme and François, gave me hospitality every time I went to Lebanon after John had left. Sometimes I stayed with them at their home in Jounieh, and other times we stayed in the mountains in the village. They are especially gracious and generous each time I go there, and now that Leon lives in America with his wife and children, they come here once a year to visit him. We always get together on those occasions.

As I began to set my sights on helping with some larger projects, I looked to people I knew could guide me. I had met some individuals through John's office, and also through my family and acquaintances. Some of them became invaluable conduits for delivering help. One of the most important associations that I had was my connection, through John, of a man by the name of Michele Aboujoude.

---

### JOHN

*"Michele was an engineer who used to go out with me on projects. As director of the Pontifical Mission, if I was going to use money to rebuild a particular facility or respond to funding needs from one bishop or another on building matters, I knew I could trust Michele to give me an honest and accurate assessment of the real needs. I had met him very early on as director through my office manager, Hoda Sofi. She and Michele were very good friends and, eventually, he and I developed a really good working relationship. That led to a fine friendship that lasted until his death."*

---

I could see that the people needed a lot of financial help, and I could do some of that. I was even more interested in trying to see what I could do to improve the economy in Lebanon, as well as in the village of Hardine. Any kind of building stimulates the economy. I got involved initially through Michele Aboujoude, when I offered him funding for some low-income housing he was doing.

Long before I went to Lebanon, I was involved with the Salesians of Don Bosco. They are a religious order of priests founded in the late nineteenth century by St. John Bosco and named for St. Francis de Sales. Salesian communities can be found all over the world, primarily operating shelters for homeless and at-risk youths; schools; technical, vocational, and language instruction centers for youths and adults; and boys' clubs and community centers.

Because of my involvement with the Salesians in America, when they learned of my interest in Lebanon, they referred me to the person who was running the technical school in Fidar, Lebanon, and I got to meet that priest. It turned out that he, too, was a very close friend of Michele Aboujoude who had done the original building for the school. At any rate, I was able to respond to several of the needs at the school. I did strongly encourage them to include Muslim children in the program, and they have done that.

## KARLENE WEBSTER

"The Book of Deuteronomy says, 'Give generously to Him and do so without a grudging heart; for the LORD, your God, will bless you for this in all your works and undertakings.'

"I met George Esseff through his generous heart while working at the Salesian missions. The Salesians had schools in Lebanon for poor youth and George had a great interest in helping his Lebanese people. George's generosity enabled the Salesians to complete Don Bosco Technique in Fidar, Lebanon, by giving them sufficient funding to buy all of the windows that they needed for the school. He went on to fund an investigative trip for me and him so that we could write a proposal to expand Don Bosco Technique and build a dormitory to house street children. As God would have it, George himself funded the dormitory and the necessary school buses.

"George had also made a promise to his brother, Monsignor John, to help the people of Haiti. So off we went to investigate possibilities. This trip resulted in providing housing for desperately poor people there.

"Then George's generosity became quite personal to me. I found myself unemployed after 14 years, and he graciously offered to fund a position for me at an international nonprofit organization. God has blessed George in all his works and undertakings because of his great generosity.

# The Continuation of My Mission

There was also a sister by the name of Mother Patrick. I met her because of John and knew that she ran a home for the elderly. She needed money to move the home for the elderly to the mountains. The home was located in downtown Beirut and it had been under heavy bombardment during the war. For reasons of a safer and quieter environment, the move certainly seemed to have merit. Mother Patrick also had strong ties with Michele Aboujoude, who was assisting her in her plans.

A project I undertook in partnership with Joseph Assaf was the construction of the Hotel Hardini, which is close to the village. It is a really beautiful spot, and when the hotel was ready for guests, Rahme and François managed the place. The hotel had a wonderful view and included eighteen rooms, a restaurant, a lounge, and a bar situated in an underground level. I had become interested in the project because I thought it would serve as a convenient place for pilgrims to stay who might be interested in visiting the nearby shrine and the church of the saint of Hardine. The work was actually completed before the beatification of Nimatullah. While that project was underway, I returned at least five times to Lebanon. I did put up three-quarters of a million dollars to facilitate the building of the hotel. I also had another motivation: I wanted to give the local people job opportunities. Actually, we did establish an economy for the village. At one time we had almost 80 or 90 people from all the trades working there. They came from Hardine, from the surrounding villages, and from as far away as Tripoli.

There were other considerations when I wanted to give money to people or projects in Lebanon. Giving money away there is not as simple as giving money in America. I cannot use funds from the Foundation. When I was working with the Salesians in Lebanon, I had to give the money to the Salesian order here in America, and then work through them to help the people in Lebanon. Some of the other endeavors simply had to be funded by me privately from taxable income.

One of the most rewarding ventures I became involved in was getting equipment and other medical supplies to needy hospitals in Lebanon. What I did was buy the necessary equipment from hospitals in the United States. I would have all of those things refurbished, and then pay to have them shipped overseas to be placed in an appropriate facility. I also became involved in buying medications for people with chronic illnesses, and working with doctors to see that the right medications were secured and, in turn, given to those who were most needy.

There is no shortage of things to be done in Lebanon. Many things were possible; others were not. Above all, I knew that I did not want to get embroiled in the politics or the many factions, military and otherwise, that enter into the affairs of everyday life in Lebanon. I do think I was able to avoid that complication on my more than twenty-five trips to Lebanon. Maybe part of the reason was that politics at home kept me busy enough.

# CHAPTER 54

## MY TURN TO WRITE THE NEWS

### *George*

*I*n 2004, I felt the need to vent about the news media. Thinking they only gave the viewpoint of the left, and sometimes didn't give the truth at all, I responded by taking out a full-page ad in The Washington Post. That single page cost me $104,655.60. It's pretty self-explanatory as to how I felt at the time.

### YOU'RE A REPUBLICAN???

*In today's America, ask a growing number of high school and college students; their teachers and professors; the self-anointed media elite and/or hard working men and women of all ethnicities, the question, "What is a Republican?" and you'll be told "... a rich, greedy, egotistical individual, motivated only by money and the desire to accumulate more and more of it, at the expense of the environment ... the working poor ... and all whom they exploit ..."*

*I am a Republican ... I am none of those things... and I don't know any Republicans who are.*

*WHAT I AM ... first and foremost, is a loving husband of some 52-plus years, the father of four, and an American who's proud of his country... and his country's heritage.*

*WHAT I AM ... is the grandson of immigrants who risked everything, including their lives and those of their children, to escape tyranny in search of freedom.*

*WHAT I AM ... is a man who grew up during the Depression and witnessed, firsthand, the effects of the stock market crash and the soup lines that followed. I watched as both my parents and grandparents, who had very little themselves, shared what food they had with a half-dozen other families who had even less.*

# Brothers & Fathers

*WHAT I AM ... is someone who worked his way through college by holding down three and four jobs at a time, and then used that education to build a better life.*

*WHAT I AM ... is a husband who, at age 24, started his own business for the 'privilege' of working 60, 70, and 80 hours a week, risking everything I had, including my health, in search of a better life for myself and my loved ones.*

*WHAT I AM ... is a businessman whose blood, sweat, and tears .... and plenty of them ... made it possible for me to provide a secure living, not only for my family and myself, but also for literally hundreds of my employees throughout the years—employees who, in turn, were able to buy their own homes, raise their own families, and give back to their communities and their country.*

*WHAT I AM ... is a man who believes in God; a God who has blessed this country... and all for which it stands.*

*WHAT I AM ... is someone who knows, if you doubt miracles exist in today's world, you need only to look into the face of those who received them ... and the eyes of those who give them.*

*WHAT I AM ... is an American who's proud that his President embraces a belief in God; proud of a President who understands, as 'politically incorrect' as it may be, that there is evil in this world and that, for the security and safety of all freedom-loving people everywhere, it must be confronted ... and it must be defeated.*

*WHAT I AM... is an American who takes comfort in the knowledge that our President refuses to allow decisions concerning the very safety and security of this nation, to be governed by the political whims of foreign governments.*

*WHAT I AM ... is tired of hearing from leading Democrats who see only negativity in America; racism in her people; class warfare in her society; and 'political incorrectness' in her character.*

*WHAT I AM ... is a former Democrat who now understands that it is the soldier and not the reporter that guarantees us our freedoms of press, speech, and dissent.*

# My Turn to Write the News

*WHAT I AM ... is a man who believes in the sanctity of life; a man who is repulsed by the pandering of the political left for votes at the expense of the unborn.*

*WHAT I AM ... is a husband and father who believes in the sanctity of marriage and the preservation of the family unit.*

*WHAT I AM ... is a movie go-er who is repulsed by those insecure, socially inept, elementary thinking, ego-inflated 'entertainers' who have appointed themselves 'experts' in the fields of national security and geo-politics and then use their forum to attack this nation, its leaders, and its actions .... much to the delight and encouragement of our enemies.*

*WHAT I AM ... is an American who understands the difference between 'censorship' and 'choice.' Evidently, these individuals do not, because when these same 'celebrities' receive public ridicule for their offensive actions, the first thing they yell is "Censorship!" What they seem incapable of understanding is ... the right of free speech and dissent is shared equally by those offended ... as well as those who offend. I support, and will continue to support, those films and performers whom I choose to ... and refuse to support those I don't. It is my right as an American ... a right I will continue to enthusiastically exercise.*

*WHAT I AM ... is a voter, tired of politicians who, every time their voting records are subjected to public scrutiny try to divert attention from their political and legislative failures by accusing their opponents of 'attack ads' and 'negative campaigning' .... and the news media who allow them to get away with it.*

*WHAT I AM ... is a Catholic who loves his God and his faith ... and who's been taught to respect all religions whose teachings are based in love, peace, and charity. As such, I am embarrassed and ashamed of those individuals, in both private and public life, whose decisions and actions are devoid of any sense of character or morals; individuals who are only driven by what's best for them ... rather than what's right ... oftentimes at the expense of many .... including our national security.*

*WHAT I AM ... is a realist who understands that the terrorist attack that murdered hundreds of innocent Russian children could have occurred here, in our heartland. That's why I sincerely believe America needs now, more than ever, a President who sees with a clear and focused vision and who speaks with a voice that, when heard by both friend and foe alike, is understood, respected, and believed.*

*WHAT I AM ... is eternally grateful to Ronald Reagan for having the bravery to speak out against Communism, and for having the courage of his convictions in leading the fight to defeat it; and to George W. Bush for the vision, courage, conviction, and leadership he has shown in America's war on terrorism amidst both the constant and vicious personal and political attacks both he and his family are made to endure.*

*WHAT I AM ... is a human being, full of numerous faults and failures, but a man nonetheless, who, though not always successful, has continually strived to do what's right instead of what's easy; a man who is challenging the religious leaders of all faiths to not only preach to their congregations the fundamentals of 'what's right' and 'what's wrong,' but to also then hold them accountable for their actions in both the public and private sectors.*

*WHAT I AM ... is disgusted with the Courts which, on one hand, call the murder of a pregnant woman a "double homicide" but then refer to the abortion of her baby as a "choice."*

*WHAT I AM ... is someone deeply troubled by a political party which embraces a candidate whose primary 'leadership' qualities center around his protesting of the Vietnam war and his labeling the honorable men and women who fought in it (50,000 of whom gave their lives in that action) as rapists and war criminals. That same political party then stepped forward this year to block the appearance of a true Vietnam war hero, retired Admiral and former United States Senator Jeremiah Denton (a man who spent seven years and seven torturous months in a North Vietnam prison), from speaking before an open session of the California legislature as part of that state's 4th of July celebration. The reason Democrats gave for refusing to allow this American hero to speak before their state legislature was because of the 'conservative' nature of his views. As an American, that troubles me deeply .... as well it should you.*

*WHAT I AM ... is a man who feels the need to spend, $104, 655.60 of his own (tax paid) money to purchase this advertisement in order to set the story straight. Some may say this money would have been better spent feeding the world's poor. At the risk of sounding self-serving, as an American and as a Republican, for the last six decades of my life, I have done exactly that ... and* *more. Following the examples of my parents and grandparents, I have used my earnings to feed the poor, shelter the homeless, provide housing for the elderly and medical care for the sick ... and continue to do so ... and I'm not alone in that work.*

*WHAT I AM ... is someone who is paying for this announcement, at my sole expense, in hopes of opening the eyes of those led blindly by ill-informed elements of our great nation who, through either ignorance or malicious intent, repeatedly attack and belittle those of us who belong to a political party that holds true to the belief that "... the rights of the governed exceed the power of the government." For those interested, I am speaking only as a tax-paying individual who is in no way associated with the Republican National Committee, nor with any of its directors or delegates.*

*WHAT I AM ... is a man who understands that 'the American way of life' is a message of self-empowerment for all.*

*WHAT I AM ... is an American who is grateful that our nation gives each of us the opportunity of self-determination and the right to benefit from the fruits of self-achievement.*

*WHAT I AM ... is an American who wants to preserve that way of life for all who seek it.*

*WHAT I AM ... is blessed to be an American ... and proud to be Republican.*

This commentary was a reaction to months of constant badgering by the Democratic party which stated that Republicans were greedy businessmen who took money from the poor and put it in their own pockets. Day after day, I heard that message in one form or another. Finally, I thought, "I've had it! What can I do about it? I talked to a media guy I know and I told him what I wanted to say, and he really did a nice job of putting it in good order and composing it. We then went ahead and had it put in the Washington Post. I think I was amazed at the reaction to it—much more than I ever thought would happen. It appeared in the paper a week or ten days before the presidential election. By Election Day, there were three-quarters of a million hits on my website. Afterwards, we had another 700,000 hits on the site.

I really didn't want Al Gore to get into the White House. I felt he would have wrecked this country. I was voting for Bush. I really felt after (not quickly after—

41

probably a year later), that I would have preferred saying what I did as an Independent rather than as a Republican. If I had it to do again, I wouldn't have made it as Republican as I did, because there are a lot of good Democrats, and I had a lot of responses from them too. There were many who said, "I believe everything you said, and I'm changing my vote." I also heard from Independents who said the same thing. I honestly believe that this article influenced enough people to change the outcome of the election. I know in my heart, this actually swayed enough voters to put President Bush in office. He got in by the skin of his teeth. I have tons of e-mails from people who said that, if they had the opportunity, they would have said what I said. I got calls from people all over the country who agreed with me. It was well worth doing, and certainly much more effective than giving money to the Republican party for yet another ad.

---

### EDITOR'S NOTE

George subsequently composed and published two other articles. The second, entitled "Let's Get the Record Straight!" was published in The Washington Post on Tuesday, March 13, 2007.

The third, "An Open Letter," was published in The New York Times on Tuesday, September 16, 2008.

---

I was content that I had responded to the many negative comments I had been hearing and reading. I was glad I had spoken my piece and was ready to go back to everyday things.

# CHAPTER 55

## COMING FULL CIRCLE

### *George*

#### THE ORDINARY ...

As I began to travel to Lebanon more frequently, I was eager to have Rosemary come with me, meet the 'family,' and see the country. She was curious and wanted to put faces on the names she had heard me mention time and time again. Of course, she had met Joseph Deeb in California when he came to work for me in the summers; and, in a short time, she became comfortable staying with our 'new' relatives when we traveled to the Middle East.

I also tried to interest John in joining us; but more often than not, those attempts were futile. Through the years as we traveled to Lebanon, Rosemary and I developed some very close ties with the people, and most especially the Istambouli family. Rahme and François were tremendously welcoming and hospitable. They were family and they were friends. They felt very comforted when Rosemary and I were able to connect with their son Leon when he lived and worked in California, and they knew they were always welcome at our home. Besides Leon, the Istamboulis had three daughters: Salome, Dima, and Nada. The youngest of the girls was Nada, and she, like her sisters before her, was making plans to marry. The wedding was to take place in the summer of 2006. Of course, we were all invited.

When the time came to discuss who might be going, I spoke to John. He had actually made plans previously to give the Missionaries of Charity a retreat, and would be unable to attend the wedding. He was open to doing something with the family as Rosemary and I (as well as our three grandsons and several of our nieces) would be there. Joe Deeb would be there and, of course, Leon and his wife and children, along with many of the family that John knew from both Lebanon and Australia. As we discussed what might work, John suggested that the family spend time in prayer, as there were many in the family who had requested prayers. Most especially, we knew we all wanted to pray for one of our cousins, Mary Theresa, who had been diagnosed with cancer, and was hoping to be cured. John said that he would be happy to go to Lebanon earlier with us, conduct a retreat, and then continue to the sisters' convent to give them their retreat.

That was the plan, and it went off pretty smoothly—until an unexpected situation developed. I didn't want to disturb my brother, but I knew I had to call him. It was July 16th, the day before our scheduled return flight home.

## And ... The Extraordinary

The phone call that left John so frustrated when I spoke to him at the retreat house of the Missionaries of Charity on July 16, 2006, had a bit of history behind it. It was also responsible for our decision to write this shared autobiography.

About two weeks before, Rosemary and I had met John in the airport in New York and boarded a plane that would take us to the Middle East. When we arrived in the Beirut airport, we were picked up by François and Rahme and their soon-to-be son-in-law Maroun el Khoury. They took all of us to the Istambouli home in the coastal city of Jounieh, where we visited a little while and then got a good night's sleep. The next day we met others from our family, along with our grandson Andrew, who had already begun his summer-long vacation in Lebanon and was staying in the mountains in the village of Hardine. We joined him and we all went to the nearby Hardini Inn. That was the location for the five-day retreat that John had planned for about thirty family members. Some of those who came were part of the extended family we had come to know during the past dozen years in Lebanon. Some had traveled from America or Australia to be there. The retreat was a time for many graces, and an opportunity for all of the family to pray with John. When the retreat ended, my cousin, Joe Assaf, and I drove John to the convent where the sisters lived in the village of Becharré, probably most famous as the birthplace of the Lebanese poet, Kahlil Gibran. John's retreat for the sisters would begin the following day and last until the following Sunday, July 16. Joe and I returned to celebrate the marriage of Maroun to Rahme and François' daughter Nada. We were looking forward to a wedding celebration, a few days of relaxation, and a visit with Andrew before meeting John and returning to the States on Monday, the 17th. We were the last of the visiting family members still in Lebanon.

During that week, a series of historical events occurred that resulted in massive airstrikes on Lebanon by the Israeli air force. That news was broadcast throughout the world. Although we were unaware of each of the details, we were aware of the bombings as soon as they began because we could hear the planes. We couldn't hear the bombs but we could hear the planes. Though you can hardly hear commercial jets flying overhead, military jets make a very audible, distinctive sound. We knew that they were on a bombing mission not too far away from where we were.

It's important to remember just how small the country of Lebanon is—somewhere around 135 miles by 35 miles. Its shape resembles that of a banana. In order to bomb the selected targets, the jet pilots had to over fly their targets in the south, go north deeper into Lebanon, swing back towards their targets, release the bombs, and then return northward to repeat the same maneuver. Those swings would involve flying at least 35 miles past the targets, most of which were in the South. Syria, like Israel, also borders Lebanon, and the Israeli pilots couldn't fly into Syrian air space or they'd be shot down. So they'd go down to the south, drop the bomb, and come back, always staying over Lebanon or their own country. That's what was going on. We could hear the planes, day and night. When the bombing started on July 12th, Rosemary, my grandson Andrew, and I were staying in Jounieh, which is not very far from Beirut. News of the developing story blared into the living room by way of Lebanese television and CNN. Rather quickly, we knew that Beirut's Rafic Hariri International Airport had been hit. Israel alleged that the airport was being used by the Hezbollah to import the weaponry it was using against the Israelis. In a short time, the Israelis had bombed two runways. They came back the next day and bombed a third runway. Throughout all the days that followed, they never bombed the terminal. The Israelis have the same 'smart bomb' as America; they have the equipment that lets them pick a target, and that's exactly what gets hit. So with the runways out of commission, there was no way any planes were going to get in or out of the airport—no way anyone was entering or leaving Beirut.

The Israelis wanted to curtail all traffic. To ensure that, bridges were also blown out that could take the Hezbollah out of Lebanon and into Syria, or could facilitate getting any kind of weaponry to the Hezbollah. A naval blockade of Israeli ships was also put in place. Actually, just before the blockade started, word was sent to all the ships in the harbor: "Get out of here now or you'll never get out." There were maybe four or five ships that had been in the harbor—freighters and different kinds of ships. They all went out to sea at the same time. In a very short time, the Lebanese civil infrastructure was severely damaged and a ground invasion of southern Lebanon was underway.

I have to interject what my angels did for me during that time. While I was in Lebanon, I had plans to visit three hospitals. I was making plans to send refurbished medical equipment to all of them. One of those hospitals was in Tyre, in the

South of Lebanon. That week, I was supposed to go down there and check things out. I probably would have been there when the bombing started—except that the people I was going with said, "We have another hospital up here, not far from Hardine. We'd like you to take a look at that one first, and then we can go to Tyre and see the hospital there later." That's what we did. If I had followed the original plan, I would have been in Tyre when the bombing began in that area. I thank my angels for taking care of me yet again.

As the conflict escalated, announcements were made via television concerning evacuation. The United States was advising all Americans to leave. Because it was the height of the tourist season, there were many people from various other countries in Lebanon who also might want to leave. We learned that Americans interested in getting out had to register at the American embassy in Beirut, since there was no getting out by air. What alternatives they might offer, we weren't sure—but we were going to register. In order to do that, each person had to submit his or her passport number, the date and place of birth, and any other information listed in the passport. Of course, we had all that information; but John had his passport with him. So François, who speaks excellent English, waited until after eight o'clock in the evening, hoping John might answer his phone. He did reach John, got the information from him, and then Rahme took all the information and sent it via e-mail to the American embassy. When that was done, I asked François what he had told John about what was going on, and he said, "Nothing." I had no idea what John was thinking. Maybe he thought we needed the information for our tickets; but François told him nothing and, of course, John had no way of knowing anything because of the silent retreat. He and the sisters had no access to radio and TV. I knew that I had to do something. John needed to know what was going on because he was counting on leaving Lebanon on Monday, and I knew that was absolutely not going to happen. I decided to call him myself.

Before John went on retreat, all of our plans had been made: When he finished the retreat, he would meet us in the village of Hardine on Sunday evening. When he arrived, I planned to take everyone to dinner (as I usually did each time I left the country). Our plane was scheduled to leave at two in the morning, so we had to be at the airport by midnight. Having dinner together was a good way for us to spend the last evening before going to the airport by midnight. Andrew was staying for the rest of the summer, and François would drive Rosemary, John, and me to the airport. That's what John was expecting so, to some degree, I understood his reaction to the news I gave him. Personally, I wasn't experiencing his sense of urgency and I tried to get him to relax. I told him, "Have some faith. Try to rely on the angels." I really knew just how frustrated and angry he was when he came back with, "What the hell kind of angel is going to get us out of here?" He wasn't in the mood for smart remarks. "I'll meet you in Hardine tonight!"

That conversation was over.

# CHAPTER 56

## LONGING TO GO HOME

### *Father John*

After I spoke to George, I left the convent and took the half-hour drive to the Hardini Inn. When I arrived there, Francois's nephew, a young man by the name of Hatum, was at the hotel, along with Joe Assaf's three children. The sister who dropped me off was disappointed because she had been hoping to see George to thank him for a lectionary and a sacramentary he had sent the sisters for their new house in Becharré. But George wasn't there, and the sister had to get back to the convent. Hatum drove me to the village.

When I was reunited with the family, and as I slowly began to get the picture, I realized that George had been right about the situation we were faced with. I think that we could agree in retrospect that, without a doubt, I certainly did not want to stay, and I continued to find it very difficult to believe that we might *have* to stay. Yet, it seemed quite certain that there was no way we were going to get out of there without the help of the American government. Every single day, I kept thinking, "We've got to get out of here," because I really thought the situation was going to escalate and then we'd be there indefinitely. The chaos of the moment was not unfamiliar to me. We were there, but we really didn't know what was going to happen. We could only speculate as to how long this situation was going to continue. I remember before leaving the retreat house, when I first told the sisters about what had happened, one of them (who took this kind of chaos in stride) said, "Wonderful! You can stay here with us a month. This is Divine Providence."

So we were each reacting in our own way.

By the time my family was all together, and with the situation the way it was, we had trouble knowing where to go or what to do. We had to talk about those things. In other words, should we stay in Hardine, where we were pretty safe from the bombings (that were mostly in the South, but as far north as Jounieh); or should we go to Jounieh, where we could be closer to the seaport in the event we had the opportunity to leave?

After a lot of discussion, we finally decided we should go to the Istamboulis' home in Jounieh.

Eventually, things began to work out—in large measure due to the efforts of another one of François and Rahme's daughters, Salome. She worked in the Australian embassy as a personnel director and was able to get in touch with a man named Simon, who obviously had some connection with the American embassy. All the negotiations for getting us out of Lebanon were going on between Salome and Simon—and whoever else could make things happen. That was all we knew. It seemed there was nothing we could do but wait. We could only hope Simon and Salome would be able to help, and that we would be among those who were allowed to leave. We could only pray that there would be a solution to the situation that seemed to go on and on.

# CHAPTER 57

## DEALING WITH DETAILS

### *George*

*I*knew my medications, and probably John's, were going to run out. I decided to go to a doctor to try to get the medications we needed. Francois's daughter Salome was taking me into town and, shortly after we left the house and were driving down the hill towards the doctor's office, she got a call from Simon who told her, "Get them up to the American embassy by one o'clock. That was good news. But it was already late morning and the American embassy was thirty-five minutes away. We had to go back home, pack our clothes, and be certain we didn't have more than 15 kilos to carry on with us. Fortunately, earlier that morning Rosemary and Salome had gone out and bought blankets and all the stuff that anyone hoping to be evacuated was expected to bring. All those types of details were being broadcast on TV. We found out later that only people who were going out by ship needed those things; anyone flying out didn't need those supplies.

We did get to the embassy on time. There were a lot of people in and around the embassy, adding to the confusion of the moment. Children were crying; tensions were high; but people were helping one another. We didn't have much to eat, but we were given some rations to eat or to take with us. We had thought at first that they were going to bring in a ship to take people out, but the helicopters came in off the aircraft carrier Iwo Jima before that happened. Later, Australian military ships did come in to evacuate people. We waited at the embassy for about six hours until we were given a spot on a military chopper. We boarded the first Marine helicopter on the heliport on the embassy grounds in Beirut, and were airlifted to Larnaca in Cyprus. There were about forty-five people on that flight.

In Cyprus, we met a man and I was telling him who we were and what had happened. He invited us to stay at a small hotel that was off the beaten path. We went with him and had a dinner of meat, rice, and salad. It was July 19. We took time to celebrate Andrew's 18th birthday and to remember our daughter Denise, whose birthday he shared. We stayed at that hotel overnight. As we were leaving the hotel the next morning, we saw the first ship coming into Larnaca from Lebanon. It was a commercial ferry boat—the kind people can drive a car onto. It was helping in the evacuation effort, and came into port after taking a much longer route because it had to weave in and out of the blockade that the Israelis had set up.

We went by taxi to the airport in Larnaca, which is within twenty minutes of the port where people continued to arrive. There were a lot of people in the airport who were in the same position as we were, all hoping to get flights home. The ships that had come from Beirut to aid in the evacuation continued to arrive in Larnaca, and those who came ashore were swelling the crowd. There was a lot of confusion and fear.

I went to the Cyprus Airways desk, and waited in line to see what Middle East Airlines would do for us in terms of honoring our tickets. It was taking so damn long, I said to myself, "I'm not waiting any longer. I'll just go and buy four new tickets out of Cyprus." I wanted to make sure that we each had a seat. I went to the woman at the counter and she said she could get us four seats. I said I'd take them and she handed the tickets to me. I paid for them, and as I was about to go back to tell John that I had four tickets, the same woman told me, "If you have MEA tickets, someone over there should be able to stamp them. Bring them back to me and I'll give you credit. I won't charge you for three flights; I'll only have to charge you for your grandson." That made sense; Andrew didn't have a ticket because he had originally planned to stay in Lebanon for the entire summer. I hurried back to MEA and ran in. There was still a line there. I went to the head of the line and asked the clerk, "Could you do me a favor and stamp these tickets?" She did. Then I went back and got the credit, and each of us had a ticket. Since we had left Beirut on the first helicopter, we were ahead of the really heavy crowds that eventually came. We had our tickets and we were ready to go to Paris.

All things considered, we were glad to be on our way, but we knew we had no flight booked out of Paris. We had missed the flights that we had originally booked to go home. So when we arrived in Paris, we didn't know when we could get a flight, because all the flights were booked. That's pretty typical: Every flight going in or out of the Middle East in the summer is booked with tourists. The recent events in Lebanon had intensified the problem. I remember hearing that, just before the bombing had started at the Beirut airport days before, there were four Middle East Airline planes on the ground. In minutes of learning of the situation, MEA pilots had their wheels up and flew empty planes to Amman, Jordan. I'm sure those empty flights added even more confusion throughout the network.

# Dealing with Details

In Paris, Rosemary, John, and I had our original round-trip tickets to negotiate with, but again Andrew didn't. I was trying to arrange a flight for the next day. I explained our situation to the clerk at the desk. My grandson Andrew was with me and I couldn't leave him in Paris. By then, I had confirmed Rosemary's ticket and mine. However, Andrew still had no ticket. I decided I would stay; Rosemary would go and I would arrange to have Andrew go home on my ticket. The man working security knew the situation and he called his supervisor over. I explained the situation again. He told me that he'd get Andrew on the flight with Rosemary and me. He told me to follow him to the ticketing booth. I did. The airline was treating us as evacuees, and they were buying people off their flights because they were so overbooked. They were paying $800 to anyone who would accept the offer. I had business-class tickets originally and that was the reason I was even able to connect to this point. One line had three to four hundred people waiting. There wasn't anyone in line for business class. The clerk said, "You can go; you have tickets." I told him again that I was very grateful that we could all go together and I needed to buy the ticket for Andrew from Paris to Los Angeles. The man said, "You don't want to do that. A one-way ticket will cost $7500. I'll give you a round-trip ticket for $2500 and, if he wants, he can come back to Paris sometime." Andrew never did that, but I hope he kept the ticket for a souvenir. I was grateful for the attendant's concern, and for the bargain he arranged—oddly enough, that ticket saved me $5000.

By that time, John had also gone through MEA and had his ticket honored for his trip back to New York. He was flying with a different outfit, but we all boarded the bus together to get to the right terminals. They dropped John off first, and I blessed him on his way, hoping that the rest of the journey would be fine for him. We continued to a different terminal.

We thought everything was in order. But when we went to board the airplane and the attendant put one ticket in the turnstile, it wouldn't go through. He tried it again. The same thing happened. I remember thinking, "Something's wrong." The attendant went to the computer, entered something, and all the time I was thinking, "We're not going to make this flight." At that moment, two new tickets popped up—for first class! Evidently, the other guy told this attendant to bump us up to first class.

The flight to California was comfortable and uneventful, and that was a blessing. Rosemary and I were in the house for just about twenty minutes when the phone rang. John was calling to tell us he was in New York. It was Thursday, July 20, 2006.

# Brothers & Fathers

We were all safely home.

Home—something of a mystical word, isn't it? It's the place where all our journeys begin, the place we continually long for, the haven we seek for ourselves and those we love.

About a month after our return to America, Rosemary, John, and I took time to be together and to remember, not just our last venture to Lebanon, but our long journeys through lifetimes of blessings.

Each of us has much to ponder—and much to be grateful for. God willing, we will remain mindful of one of many questions in the Psalms as we continue on our way:

*How can I repay the Lord for all the good He has done for me?*

I hope we will respond to God's grace each day to search for that answer and do His will.

# Chapter 58

## Safely Home

### *Father John*

*W*hen we think of home, we think of a place where we can rest. As I look back on my life, the only time I could say "Hello" was after I said "Goodbye." And the only time I could say "Goodbye" was after I had said "Hello." We always have to say "Goodbye" to those places we have been in order to say "Hello" to where we're going. When I said "Goodbye" to Wilkes-Barre, I could then say "Hello" to the seminary. When I said "Goodbye" to America, I could say "Hello" to Peru. When I said "Goodbye" to Lebanon, I could say "Hello" to America. Looking back, it seems I have spent more time on the journey than at home.

But as Dad used to say, always in Arabic, "Everything in its time is beautiful." How true that has been for me—and, I think, for my brother George. I think both of us have learned that there is truly a time for everything under the sun.

It's always been good to remember that and think of all the 'times' we have had, and those we have yet to enjoy.

> *There is an appointed time for everything,*
>
> *and a time for every affair under the heavens.*
>
> *A time to be born, and a time to die;*
>
> *a time to plant, and a time to uproot the plant.*
>
> *A time to kill, and a time to heal;*
>
> *a time to tear down, and a time to build.*
>
> *A time to weep, and a time to laugh;*
>
> *a time to mourn, and a time to dance.*
>
> *A time to scatter stones, and a time to gather them;*

*a time to embrace, and a time to be far from embraces.*

*A time to seek, and a time to lose;*

*a time to keep, and a time to cast away.*

*A time to rend, and a time to sew;*

*A time to be silent, and a time to speak.*

*A time to love, and a time to hate;*

*A time of war, and a time of peace.*

*—Ecclesiastes 3:1−8*

And after all these 'times,' what is Heaven?

Heaven is the only place we will say "Hello" and never have to say "Goodbye"—the place where we will finally be able to say, "We are safely home."

# CHAPTER 59

## EPILOGUE: LEBANON REVISITED

## *Ellen Franco*

*W*hen George Esseff offered me the opportunity to go to Lebanon, I must say I did hesitate, thinking perhaps such a decision would be less than prudent. After some soul searching, careful consideration of my responsibilities, and, I must admit, my sense of curiosity and adventure, I said I would go.

When I announced that I was going to Lebanon for a visit with George and his brother, Monsignor John Esseff, I got mixed reactions from the members of my family and from my friends. There were some raised eyebrows, some trepidation, and some point-blank exclamations of, "Are you crazy?"

Like most people who live in America, I had a 'newspaper photo gallery' of Beirut and the rest of Lebanon. The photos, dating back to the 1980s, were mostly ones that captured car bombings, aerial attacks, or random explosions on film. If war wasn't in full bloom, there was at least a pretty good imitation going on. I also had a lot of communication with Monsignor Esseff while he served in Beirut from 1984 to 1986. During his stay there, he sent me many taped reflections on what was happening. There were many stories which told of ongoing human tragedies. How the lives of the Lebanese people were affected was brought home to me when, after his return to America, Monsignor asked if my family and I would give hospitality to a Lebanese man and his wife who had arrived in America. They were hoping to have their child born in this country so that the child would have American citizenship in the event of even greater chaos at home. The couple did live with us for several months. About a month after Sandra was born, the family left to visit some of their family in England.

Other insights I gained throughout those years were the result of examining Islam with Monsignor Esseff. When he returned from the Middle East, some aspects of Islam were very troubling to him—especially those that dealt with the concept of Jihad. He worked for many months trying to express what he witnessed as Jihad. As he saw it, much of the fighting in Lebanon had more to do with extremism stemming from the fundamentalist Islamic propagation of Jihad than civil war among the Lebanese people. After he returned to America, in time, he had several works published that spoke of the threat of Jihad. Many people considered what he said to be an attack on Islam when, in fact, the articles were intended to explain how Jihad is understood and carried out by those who adhere to that radical fundamentalist belief.

Much of what Monsignor saw and commented on was considered a prejudicial theory by many. On the other hand, in retrospect, the events of 9/11 translated that theory into something of an unheeded, but nonetheless prophetic, warning. Subsequent events in other parts of the world seemed to add credence to those same statements which he made in the late 1980s.

That, in a nutshell, was the aura that emanated from Lebanon for me. Now that I can look at those words, the reactions I had to my going to such a place are very understandable.

Because of the length of the flight and the time difference, we arrived in Lebanon at night. It was quite a sight as we began our descent. Lights, more yellow than white, decorated the coastline that seemed to end in a field of black. By the time we landed, I was excited and full of curiosity as to what lay ahead. We were among the first people to step off the plane at the airport in Beirut. George showed his passport and went on through. I showed mine and did the same. Monsignor Esseff showed his passport and was detained for what turned out to be almost an hour while George and I waited. I noticed a lot of men in uniforms—different kinds of uniforms. Some were obviously airport personnel, but others were wearing various kinds of military camouflage, not all the same. I wasn't sure what it all meant; but really, I had more of a sense of security than a sense of fear. I had become used to a tight sense of security in any airport. Why would the Beirut airport be any different?

Finally, Monsignor came through the gate (although he never really found out what the delay was about). We were met by relatives of their family who had had a long wait. I can't help but say both George and Monsignor could have passed for natives in the crowd. Me—never in a million years! But I went through without a hitch. It was Monsignor who was detained, and I chuckled as I remembered my son-in-law saying, "Are you sure you want to go? You know those two can fade into the crowd. How about you?"

I felt safe.

# Epilogue: Lebanon Revisited

About two in the morning, we arrived at the home of François and Rahme Istambouli and were given our rooms. I was asleep in an instant.

On that first morning in Lebanon, I woke up under a quilt with patches of Mickey Mouse and his friends. That was familiar and comforting, but I couldn't help but think I had put some little people out of their beds. I could see a brilliant blue panorama that grabbed my attention through the glass door leading to the balcony. I was on my feet. In a matter of seconds, I was looking out at the brilliance of the sky that merged into the Mediterranean Sea, not more than a mile away from my balcony. The view was breathtakingly beautiful. 'Beautiful' was not a word that I had ever before associated with Lebanon.

But as the days passed, 'beautiful' was the operative word.

The Istamboulis live in Jounieh, about 15 kilometers north of Beirut. Like the homes of most other people around them, their home is in a white high-rise cement building. There they own the eighth floor. Their daughter Salome, who works in the Australian embassy (and who was so involved with the evacuation of the American Esseffs) lives with them. While we were there, François and Rahme's daughter Dima (Barakat) was also living with them. Dima's husband Jad was still working in Australia, and would be returning to Jounieh soon. They have three beautiful daughters: Sharleez, Lindzy, and Zoey who, like all kids under five, kept everyone busy. Dima had left her architectural position in Australia and was preparing a new home for her family on the second floor of the building. On the third floor of the same building were Dima's sister, Nada; her husband, Maroun el Khoury; and their son, Joe. Their brother Leon and his family live in Detroit, Michigan.

I enjoyed spending time with the girls, who wanted me to see so many things. Nada and Dima took me shopping, and Salome and her friend George took me out to dinner. I also enjoyed the children, so much like my own grandchildren, and hours and hours of conversation. I even learned a few words in Arabic. Although everyone spoke English, and some spoke French, the native language was undeniably Arabic. I remember one day asking a question that I had often wondered about: Why is it that Lebanese people do not refer to themselves as Arabs? There was a lot of discussion about that; but generally speaking, the end result was that those in the family held a pretty common belief. In their minds, 'Arab' seems synonymous with 'Muslim,' and they always want it to be clear that they are Christians.

I became a part of that family for the entire time we lived there. We shared meals, prayers, stories, children, and friends; and, as the days passed, we came to know and enjoy each other. Their hospitality was boundless, and in and from the comfort of their home, I experienced Lebanon.

# Brothers & Fathers

Very soon after our arrival, a Dr. Maroun Ghabash came to see George and Monsignor at our 'home' in Jounieh. Long involved in philanthropic work in Lebanon, George had purchased thousands of dollars worth of medicines to be distributed among the poor in the area. Dr. Ghabash is one of several doctors with whom George has been in contact. They discussed the arrival of those medicines and the distribution of them—a project that was well under way before we left Lebanon. Besides discussing practical matters, Dr. Ghabash spent a lot of time that evening with Monsignor and George, expressing his desire to live his Christian faith by serving the poor. Sometimes he sounded more like a priest than a doctor. But then I realized: Healing is the main concern of both. He said he liked to think of himself as a 'warrior of peace.'

George was eager to visit the hospitals and doctors in Beirut to see what progress had been made in his latest endeavors. On the second day after our arrival, George, Monsignor, and I went to visit the hospital where Dr. Ghabash and his wife, both anesthesiologists, worked pro bono one day a week. He took us to visit the maternity section of the hospital. There were birthing tables, incubators, and cribs for newborns filling the nursery that was ready to open. With George's help, the equipment had all been gathered from hospitals in America, refurbished, and sent to Lebanon. Dr. Ghabash was obviously happy about the recent improvements in the hospital's physical plant and was eager to get the medicines that would soon be in Lebanon, ready for distribution. He made a careful assessment of the medicines that George had made available, and he told George which ones he could use and which would be better sent elsewhere to serve other people's needs. During the days that followed, George had other meetings with ministers of the Parliament to ensure that the medicines for chronically ill patients in Lebanon would continue to be made available through that project.

Perhaps, for my benefit, the doctor then took us to another area of the hospital that was not in view, located behind the area we had visited. There were enormous holes in the sides of the hospital, left from the bombings of years before—sad reminders of what had halted or interrupted continuing advancement in hospital care in that facility. That was the only remnant of the years of war in Lebanon that I saw. There were no bombed out sites evident as I rode through the city. There was, however, much talk about the disparity that existed among hospital facilities and available medical care throughout the country.

On each of our trips into Beirut, we took the autobahn through the city. It looked like any other major highway that cuts through a big city, bordered on both sides by businesses of all kinds, and advertisements for just about anything. The

# Epilogue: Lebanon Revisited

city was very modern and there was new construction everywhere. There were differences too. I saw no speed limits posted anywhere and, though the autobahn could easily accommodate five lanes of traffic, there were no signs or lines indicating a delineation of lanes. People etched in and out as they drove past one another, cutting ahead with usually no variation in the speed of the car. I remember seeing only one 'Stop' sign and one traffic light in Beirut. Yet all the time I was there, I never saw an accident or any kind of traffic altercation. The people I met liked it that way and were adverse to having too many laws. There seemed to be a lot of personal freedom in those areas in spite of a heavy military presence throughout the city.

Nowhere was that military presence more pronounced than when we went to visit the residence of a man I was told was General Aoun. That visit was connected to some of the work George was doing in the local hospitals. When we approached the area, we passed many soldiers who were fully armed. I was amazed at how young those soldiers looked—younger than all my children. Before we could drive close to the home, the car was stopped and scanned for bombs.

In the past, General Aoun had served as the President of Lebanon and also as the head of the Lebanese Army. In the midst of ongoing conflicts, he had left Lebanon and lived for years in exile in France. He was now a minister of Parliament and received us very graciously. He is a Christian and seemed a very peaceful man, interested in doing whatever has to be done to promote peace. There is also talk of his running again for the presidency. It was an honor to meet him. His concerns were primarily for the people of Lebanon, and he was grateful to George for the work he had been doing to help the Lebanese people. Throughout the entire visit, he held his rosary in his hand.

The political machines were still grinding away, but, it seemed to me, in subtler ways. Without question, there were many, like Dr. Ghabash, working to make the lives of the people better, who also regarded themselves as 'warriors of peace.'

Another place I visited with George and Monsignor was Don Bosco Technique, a school that George has financed generously over many years. The school, an impressive structure set in the hills of Fidar, Lebanon, offers young Lebanese students professional specialization in a multitude of trades, including refrigeration, air conditioning, auto mechanics, computers, electronics, and interior design. We met priests there who had taken on the training of the young by enlisting well-qualified professors from local universities. There was ongoing classroom instruction as well as hands-on work in well-equipped, sophisticated workshops. We saw a car some of the students were building that was powered by solar panels. The building itself was a full facility offering dormitory accommodations to those who needed them. The staff was hoping for an increase in enrollment (primarily through financial support that would make it possible to offer scholarships to prospective students in need). George was ready to continue his support through that type of assistance.

During that same visit to Don Bosco Technique, George met with a representative of IRD (International Relief and Development). It is the stated mission of the group "to reduce the suffering of the world's most vulnerable groups and provide tools and resources needed to increase their self-sufficiency ... in regions of the world that present social, political, and technical challenges." Like us, IRD's representative was impressed by what he saw, and seemed eager to advocate for the cause of Don Bosco Technique.

In the course of the many days that followed in the home of François and Rahme, many members of the extended family (as well as other people) visited George and Monsignor. The high regard that was felt for both men was very evident. Monsignor spent many hours listening to and counseling those who came with their concerns. George continued to investigate the many areas where he thought he could be of some assistance to the people of Lebanon whom, I began to realize, he considers extended family.

Besides the serious work to which both Monsignor and George dedicated themselves, there was also time for visiting many very beautiful places in Lebanon. On one of our first days in Lebanon, looking out of the window on the opposite side of the house from my bedroom on the upper floor, I could see what seemed to be cable cars, similar to what might be seen at a ski resort. When I asked about them, Rahme told me it was the telepherique, the quickest way to get to the top of the mountain to the Shrine of Our Lady of Lebanon, towering over the village of Harissa. The shrine was built to commemorate the fiftieth anniversary of the proclamation of the dogma of the Immaculate Conception by Pope Pius IX on December 8, 1854. The imposing statue of Mary stands on the highest hill of Harissa, atop a pedestal base of one hundred steps that leads pilgrims to stand at Mary's feet. Although the site is a central point of worship for Catholic communities in Lebanon, many whom we saw there were dressed in traditional Muslim garb. I learned that Muslims have a great devotion to Mary and are always among those at the shrine. It was nearing Ramadan, and there were many Muslims at the shrine, at the telepherique station, and throughout all of Jounieh.

Another place we visited was nearby Byblos, an amazing site that presents the architectural ruins said to cover more than seven thousand years of history. Origi-

# Epilogue: Lebanon Revisited

nally the area was a simple fishing village, dotted with huts. The discovery of those ruined huts placed their construction in Neolithic times before 3800 B.C. Numerous archeological excavations have revealed the work of Phoenicians, as well as that of other cultures. Stories of Byblos as an important shipping center conjure up the excitement of men selling cedar for shipbuilding, trading in gold or linens, building temples to pagan gods, and creating baths and other public buildings for Romans or Greeks to use. When I climbed the stairs of the castle there and looked out on the remains of great temples, I was as close to antiquity as I had ever been and it was hard to believe that such towering pillars could ever have been buried. As I walked around the town and through the shops, I had one foot in the 21st century but the other could readily step into any one of those thousands of years of history.

One morning, after several days in Lebanon, I went downstairs to find George and Leah el Khoury with their two daughters, Sandra and Carla, sitting on the balcony with Monsignor, George, and the Istamboulis. This was the couple who had lived with my family and me in the late 1980s. Sandra, a beautiful college senior who, years before had been born in Scranton, stood before me. The last time I had seen her, I could hold her in my arms; she was only weeks old. We had a wonderful reunion and George and Leah invited Monsignor and me to join them on a day-long excursion through Lebanon. We accepted the offer. A few days later, we began our tour by driving to the area south of Beirut. We visited the ancient towns of Sidon and Tyre. In Tyre, we saw the necropolis or 'city of death' that contains an amazing array of tombs dating back to the Roman and Byzantine periods, between the 2nd and 6th century A.D. In any discussion of the city of Tyre, references to the Phoenicians, Alexander the Great, the Persians, the Romans, Jesus Christ, Islamic conquests, and the hippodrome are very likely to surface. It was difficult to wrap my head around the idea of how many extraordinary people may have stood mesmerized by the beauty of the sea—as I was that day.

We drove back to Beirut and continued our journey through the Chouf mountains and on towards the Beiteddine Palace, which is a very impressive example of Lebanese architecture. The palace took more than thirty years to build (1804–1840), and includes museums, mosaics, and artifacts of people who once lived there. The skill and artistic talents of so many people who were responsible for the beauty of the buildings speak volumes about the never-ending flow of talent among peoples of the world. I could imagine a troop of cavalry passing in review in the massive courtyard as the leader of the moment sat on the balcony and reviewed his troops.

# Brothers & Fathers

We continued our auto tour through the mountains and drove through the Bequaa Valley, rich in crops of all kinds. I recalled the tragic story that Monsignor had sent to me years before. A young Jesuit he knew had been tortured and murdered, and later found in a well in the Bequaa. It seemed impossible that Father Nicholas Kluiters could have been murdered in such a beautiful valley that seemed to generate only new life.

We continued through the lush valley and finally arrived at Baalbek. There, I found myself walking not only in ancient history but also in ancient theology. I marveled at the ingenuity of men who built massive temples to gods I don't believe in. To contemplate how such enormous temples were put in place without the kind of equipment we have today is to sit bewildered and in awe of man's capabilities. We stayed as long as we could; but as the day came to an end, we began our journey home.

The trip left me filled with a great sense of appreciation. Just this short time was making it clear to me that people can't live in Lebanon without feeling a tie to the ancient world, without hearing about diversity in cultures, thinking, theology, politics, economy, and everyday living. It's a country packed with ancient ruins, and also one that abounds in natural beauty.

Besides the sea and the mountains, perhaps the most amazing natural wonder we saw on another day was Jeita, an underground crystalline cave in the Keserwan region north of Beirut. The slow-moving water carved out sculptures over centuries that attest to the magnificence of the hand of nature. Discovered in 1836, the caves defy adequate description. There is an upper grotto filled with astounding formations that we enjoyed from a dry pedestrian path. There is also a lower grotto that meanders deep into the ancient caves. We traveled through that area by boat and the spectacle continued to fascinate all of us. We saw more statue-like forms, figures the water had sculpted, and rock formations that looked like flowing curtains, melting whipped cream, or petrified waterfalls. There are photographs to be had, but the beauty and majesty of the caves challenge even the most talented professional photographers. It's just one of those places that demand the cliché: "It has to be seen to be believed."

In the midst of the beauty of the physical country were certainly the Lebanese people themselves. The Istambouli family was the embodiment of hospitality, and accommodated all of us in so many ways. They were not only eager to share their home with us, but also their country and their traditions. To do that, they took us for several days to the mountain village of Hardine, from where both the Esseff

# Epilogue: Lebanon Revisited

and Sahd families had emigrated. I had heard about the village years before when Monsignor initially visited there in 1984. He was hailed as a returning hero when he entered the village for the first time under a banner that read, "Welcome Home, Monsignor." The pictures I had in my head were replaced by the reality of the family home, the village, and the surrounding area.

The house itself was very beautiful and, to me, surprisingly modern. Again, from my room on the upper floor, there was a spectacular view. In the lower part of the house, Rahme showed me stored potatoes, on- ions, fruits, figs, and pine nuts. There were barrels in which arrack, a favorite mid-eastern alcoholic drink, was fermenting. Each day, there were three elaborate meals which consisted of traditional Lebanese dishes. More often than not, the immediate family was joined by family, neighbors, and friends.

There was a village church where a priest who seemed to be living a hermetic life presided at Mass each day. The design, construction, and renovation of that church and the nearby village square were com- pleted under the direction of François and Rahme's son Leon, a civil engineer. There were at least three other churches, an outdoor shrine that was very old,

*Father John, Ellen Franco and George in Lebanon*

and a newly discovered cave church in the mountains that had been there for—who knows how long. We also attended Mass there.

Near the Istamboulis' house was a tiny store. American as I am, I couldn't help but think of it as the 7/11 of the village. Anyone could buy a cup of coffee there, or canned goods, or candy bars, or cleaning products, or other household items that people sometimes run out of and want to replace quickly. However, there

were also bottles of whiskey, mostly scotch, for sale. A Snickers candy bar or Dewar's whiskey: It was so Lebanon. Much like the absence of speed limits, there didn't seem to be any law concerning such things as the sale of alcohol. I saw a culture where people were comfortable with a call to personal responsibil- ity.

*The Hardine village store*

# Brothers & Fathers

One day while we stayed in the village of Hardine, Dima drove us farther into the mountains to visit the wadi, the caves in the mountains where Christians hid during persecutions. Some would say the roads there were treacherous, barely able to hold two passing cars, and without any guardrails. But cars moved along quickly, and horns were used much more frequently than brakes. At one hairpin curve, there was a sign picturing a car going over an embankment—a gentle reminder of what might happen, but no directive as to what a safe speed might be.

*Driving in Lebanon*

Staying in the village of Hardine was perhaps the best taste of Lebanon that I had.

In Hardine, I did what was most natural to me. Zooey was sometimes tired and ready for a nap. I took her for a walk in her stroller, not once but many times. The road I walked revealed a Lebanon that I never heard a word about in the papers. As I wandered around the village, I saw all kinds of growth. There were walnut trees, fruit trees, grapes, squash, and olives. I saw the olive trees, laden with their fruit, both green and black. (Now I know the green ones are not fully ripe but the black ones are.) The land itself seems to sustain the people with an abundance of fruits, vegetables, nuts, oil from the olives, and breads of all kinds. It also provides the materials for building their homes and work places. Cement, marble, and granite are plentiful throughout the country. It's easy to see why the people have such a love for a country that is so bountiful.

Another thing that was interesting was the size of the country—about the size of the state of Connecticut. I tried to imagine all of the diversity of America in such a small area. No doubt, the size of the country adds to the intensity that exists in the diversity. And diversity there is! We all got along as best we could in Arabic, French, or English, and there was nothing more delightful than hearing the children move from one language to another.

One of the most interesting days unfolded after a night of intense rain. On the night of the rain, all power went out and we had to use candles until the generator could be turned on. Power outages were not all that uncommon an occurrence in the village, or anywhere in Lebanon. In the morning, we were told we had brought a blessing with us: the blessing of rain. It would ripen the olive crop. It was the first rain of the season.

# Epilogue: Lebanon Revisited

That day after the rain stopped, I took Zooey for a walk. I walked down the road, all the way to the entrance of the village. Just as I was about to turn around, I saw a good-sized snail slowly crossing the road. It looked like a cartoonist rendition, with its little snail horns protruding from its head. I don't think I had ever actually seen a snail like that. I started back up the hill. I met one of the neighbors, Mr. Deeb, whom I had met the day before at lunch at the Istambouli home. He offered me some walnuts from the tree in his front yard, which he broke open with his bare hands. I ate them. He was trying to tell me something in Arabic—I understood nothing. I spoke to him in French—he understood nothing. We seemed to be at a stalemate, but he kept looking down by the side of the road and I thought maybe he was looking for a flower or something of interest that grew by the side of the road. We continued to walk up the road toward the Istambouli home where, my guess was, Mr. Deeb was headed to play cards. It was then we came upon the same children I had passed on my way down the road. Each of them was carrying a bag and looking just as intently at the road as Mr. Deeb was. I really don't know how I knew, but it slowly dawned on me that they were all out looking for snails—the very kind I had seen at the end of the road. After some inquiry, I learned later that the snails did, in fact, come after the first steady, drenching rain. Everyone ran to gather them. The snails would be put in pails with sand and kept for several weeks until they were clean enough to eat. They were a delicacy—a gift of the first rain of the season, eaten only once a year. We didn't stay in Lebanon long enough to eat them, but I'm sure they were served with great fanfare after we left.

One day, Dima was eager to show us more of the country, and we headed deeper into the mountains. We stopped in the village of Becharré so Monsignor could visit the Missionary of Charity sisters for whom he had often conducted retreats, one of which had been in 2006. (It was that time when he, George, Rosemary, and Andrew had to be evacuated from Lebanon by helicopter.) After our visit, Dima suggested that we stop at the museum of Kahlil Gibran, the Lebanese poet and author of so many well-known books of poetry. This very same village was Gibran's birth place. We went through the museum where, along with his books, we saw many of his original drawings and paintings, and I began to remember thoughts he expressed so eloquently in his poetry.

His words are known and loved throughout the world. A favorite of mine is his chapter on children. There I was in this beautiful little country that has experienced the sorrow of seeing so many of its children leave, but has also experienced the happiness of seeing how much they have contributed to the world at large.

# Brothers & Fathers

I was reminded of how often George and Monsignor have given great tribute to their grandfather, Gidue. He was one such child of Lebanon who left. I thought how fitting it was that his grandsons could return to minister, each in his own way, to the Lebanese people.

*Your children are not your children.*

*They are the sons and daughters of Life's longing for itself.*

*They come through you but not from you,*

*And though they are with you yet they belong not to you.*

*You may give them your love but not your thoughts.*

*For they have their own thoughts.*

*You may house their bodies but not their souls,*

*For their souls dwell in the house of tomorrow, which you cannot visit,*

*not even in your dreams.*

*You may strive to be like them, but seek not to make them like you.*

*For life goes not backward nor tarries with yesterday.*

*You are the bows from which your children as living arrows are sent forth.*

*The archer sees the mark upon the path of the infinite, and He bends you with*

*His might that his arrows may go swift and far,*

*Let your bending in the archer's hand be for gladness;*

*For even as He loves the arrow that flies,*

*So He loves also the bow tha is stable.*

*—Kahlil Gibran: The Prophet*

What a blessing that George Abdanour Esseff left Lebanon. What a blessing that his children and his children's children have gone "swift and far." In his own way and in his own time, George Abdanour Esseff voiced so many of the other words of his countryman, Gibran:

*You give but little when you give of your possessions.*

*It is when you give of yourself that you truly give …*

*There are those who give little of the much which they have—and they give*

*it for recognition and their hidden desire makes their gifts unwholesome. And*

*there are   those who have little and give it all …*

# Epilogue: Lebanon Revisited

*These are the believers in life and the beauty of life, and their coffer is never empty ...*
*There are those who give with joy, and that joy is their reward.*

*—Kahlil Gibran: The Prophet*

Both George and Monsignor have served the memory of their grandfather well.

It was truly a delight to see them enjoy the beauty of Lebanon together—a special delight for me to see that beauty with them. I am grateful for my visit to Lebanon.

It was a wonderful gift.

It was a gift of beauty.

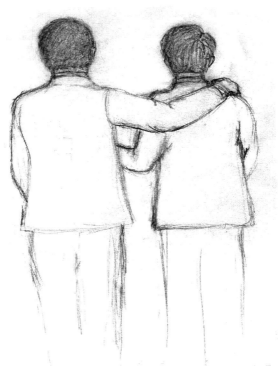

*Mary Ellen's sketch of her dad and Father John*

# INDEX

## A

Abad, Alfredo, 242
Abbott, Sr. Nancy, I.H.M., 258, 293
Abdelnoor, 360, 517
Abe's Deli, South Main St., Wilkes-Barre, PA, 28, 29
Aboujoude, Michele, 514, 533-535
Abraham family, 359
absolution, 173
ADD/ADHD, 320
addiction, 300
Addis Ababa, Ethiopia, 392
adoration (of the Most Blessed Sacrament), 28, 147, 487-488, 515, 522, 524
advent, 137
advocate, 281, 287
Africa, 392-393, 427-428
Agnes Flood (1972), 264-265, 267, 275, 278
Ain Saadeh, Lebanon, 382
Ajami, John, 348-349, 353, 356-357, 370, 373
AlAnon, 295
Alaska, 288
Albania, 366
Alcoholics Anonymous (AA), 166, 297-298, 324, 484, 488, 489
alcoholism, alcoholic, 131, 140, 165, 204, 260, 275, 277, 295, 296, 324, 484
Aleppine, 356
Alexander the Great, 563
Alexandria Hospital, 178
Alexandria, VA, 179
Alina Lodge, NJ, 295
altar, 8, 14, 15, 26, 28, 36, 56, 126, 131, 134, 142, 144, 373, 390, 429, 440, 470, 488
altar boys, altar servers, 13, 14, 15, 26, 28, 35, 36, 56, 131, 295
Altemose, Sheriff Jake, 217
aluminum, 120-121, 188, 199
ambition, 346,

American, 35, 37, 101, 102, 162, 202, 207, 221, 225, 226, 227, 228, 233, 235, 237, 240, 242, 250, 288, 348, 349, 355, 356, 358, 359, 360, 364, 366, 367, 369, 373, 374, 375, 376, 380, 391, 392, 395, 396, 428, 432, 471, 494, 497, 514, 515, 517, 518, 534, 535, 537, 538, 539, 539, 541, 546, 551, 557, 565
American University of Beirut, 515-516,
Amman, Jordan, 552
Ammons, Chris, 258, 296
Amos and Andy, 40
Amsterdam, the Netherlands, 221-222
Analomink, PA, 170
anawim, 259, 426
Anaya, Lebanon, 349,
Anderson, Terry, 379, 382
Androlas, Grace, 357,
angel, 145, 329-330, 335, 336, 517, 523, 545, 546-547
Angel Memorial Clinic, Boston, MA, 209
Angeloni, Archbishop, 351
angelus (prayer), 164
anger, angry, 42, 52, 65, 164, 165, 167, 168, 222, 248, 250, 297, 454-455
anodize, 120-121, 122, 201
anoint, anointing, 173-174, 438-439, 470, 471, 476, 485
Anointing of the Sick, Sacrament of the, 173-174, 485
Anthracite Mining Company, 208
Aoun, General, 561
apostle, 147
apostolate, 278
Aquila, Bishop Samuel, 489-490
Aquinas Institute of Theology, Dubuque, IA, 426,
Arab, 559
Arabic, 5, 46, 71, 97, 114, 175, 345, 349, 354, 355, 359, 360, 363, 364, 370, 371, 559, 566, 567,
Arafat, Yassir, 350
Aramaic, 175

# INDEX

Arbez, Father, 97
archbishop, 97, 217, 347, 360, 362, 393, 518
Archdiocese of Baltimore, 429
Archdiocese of Los Angeles, 339, 482
Archdiocese of Washington, 97, 429
Arizona, 122
Armenian, 328
Armstrong, Coach Bob, 87, 88
Army, 166, 186, 190, 208
Army Corps of Engineers, 95, 100, 101, 117,
    119-123, 156, 157, 158, 178, 179,
    183, 201, 478
Arpaia, Frank, 324-325, 479
Arrack, 565
ascetic, 74
Aschenbrenner, Alice, 488
Aschenbrenner, George, 488
Aschenbrenner, Rev. George S.J., 434
Asia, Asian, 202, 221, 227, 335
Assaf family, 359, 549
Assaf, Antonius (Tanious), 513
Assaf, Joseph, 513, 515, 535, 544
Assisi, Italy, 516
assistant pastor, parochial vicar, 129, 133,
    169, 217, 256
Associated Press, The, 380
Assumption of the Blessed Virgin Mary, 244
Astrolite, 272
Athens, Greece, 375
Atlanta, GA, 208
Aubrey, Father, 148
Aunt Lizzy, 178
Aunt Mae, 165
Aunt Marian, 3, 19, 43, 116, 173, 303, 401,
    404
Aunt Sarah, 3, 22, 43, 116, 173, 303, 401,
    404, 421
Australia, 394, 399, 421, 466, 513, 515-516,
    543, 544, 550, 551, 559
authority, 62, 63, 64, 68, 69, 135, 137, 141,
    260, 379, 408, 518, 523,
auxiliary bishop, 290
awe, 27

## B

Baalbek, 564
Back Mountain area, PA, 39, 53
Badger Pass, 406
Baio, Scott, 326
Baltimore, MD, 38, 43, 47, 56, 73, 74, 78,
    80, 81, 84, 234, 290
Bambera, Bishop Joseph, 431
Banick, Rich, 435
Bank of America, 327,
baptism, christening, 135, 152, 181, 182,
    214, 247, 285, 424-426, 428, 469
Barakat, Dima Istambouli, 510, 543, 559,
    565, 567
Barakat, Jad, 559
Barakat, Lindzy, 559
Barakat, Sharleez, 559
Barakat, Zoey, 559, 568-569
Baranco, Peru, 233
Barbacane, Jeanette, 258
Barbario family, Wilkes-Barre, PA, 35
Barqa, Lebanon, 376
Barrett, Msgr. Francis, 133, 135, 138, 141,
    145, 169, 171, 172, 217
basilica, 142
Basilica (Cathedral) of St. John Lateran,
    Rome, 142, 143, 522
Basilica of St. Mary Major, Rome, 142
Basilica of St. Paul Outside the Walls,
    Rome, 142
Basilica of St. Peter, Rome, 142
Bass, Dr. Steve, 412
beatification, beatify, 515-517, 535
Beaupre, Lawrence K., 435, 437, 443
Becharré, Lebanon, 1, 544, 549, 567
Beckman Dickinson, 327
Beirut, Lebanon, 342-399, 513, 524, 535,
    545, 546, 551, 552, 557-563
Beiteddine Palace, 563
Belgium, 202
belief, 164, 166
Benediction (of the Most Blessed
    Sacrament), 14, 15, 127, 147

# INDEX

Benestad, Dr. Brian, 258

Beqaa Valley, Lebanon, 367-369, 377, 379, 564

Beverly Hills, CA, 415

Bible, scripture, 8, 97, 281, 286, 290, 311, 432, 489, 495, 524, 530

bilocation, 144

Bing Crosby Stables, 306

biretta, 80, 140

Birkbeck College Summer Institute, University of London, 405

bishop, 73, 77, 80, 126, 129, 130, 133, 217, 242, 251, 256, 257, 259, 260, 277, 280, 290, 301, 347, 350, 353, 362, 363, 374, 382, 392, 422, 425, 434, 473, 478, 479, 489, 518, 523, 533

Bishop Emeritus, 474

Bizaouni, Rev. Raphael Al, 517

Bkerke, Lebanon, 351

Black, Dr., 415-416

bless, blessing, 57, 67, 70, 85, 109, 117, 125, 126, 127, 144, 146, 147, 148, 151, 153, 179, 193, 203, 210, 215, 217, 249, 257, 258, 282, 299, 304, 349, 354, 369, 388, 417, 419, 424, 430, 432, 442, 466, 470, 476, 482, 493, 510, 517, 527, 534, 535, 538, 541, 553, 554, 566, 568

Blessed Sacrament, 28, 29, 142, 143, 144, 147, 365, 488, 515, 524

Blessed Sacrament chapel, 142, 143, 488

Blessed Virgin Mary, Blessed Mother, 26, 164, 369, 505, 562

Blood of Christ, 397

Body of Christ (Church), 98, 99, 100, 139, 527-528

Body of Christ (Eucharist), 126, 397, 527

Bogotá, Columbia, 330-331

Bohr, Msgr. David A., 430, 439-440, 478, 479

Bolivia, 233, 246-247, 331, 496

Bonfanti, Toni, 392

Borek, Ray, 129, 131

Boston, MA, 209, 217-219, 233, 397

Bowery, Wilkes-Barre, PA, 11, 29, 30

Boylan, Rev. Martin, 436

brain tumor, 409, 412, 415, 421, 445

Brodhead Creek, 170

Bronx, NY, 436

Brooklyn, NY, 214

Brown, Dr., 46

Brown, Rev. Raymond, 97

Buckingham Palace, London, 223

Burbank, CA, 286

Burns, Michelle Spencer, 70, 71, 72, 406, 502, 503-504, 509-510

Burti, Carol, 470-471, 484

Bush, President George W., 540, 541, 542

Bushkill, PA, 133, 134, 140, 172

business, 101, 158, 178, 181-191, 195, 198, 199, 200, 201, 202, 203, 221-226, 246, 263, 272-274, 303-313, 315-329, 412, 422, 457, 493

Butler, Linda, 493-494

Byblos, Lebanon, 562-563

## C

Cairo, Egypt, 363, 375

Calcutta, India, 365, 366, 419

Califa Street, Van Nuys, CA, 197

California, 116, 187, 188, 190, 191, 195-204, 205, 210, 211, 219, 232, 247, 253, 254, 255, 260, 263, 265, 272, 286, 303, 317, 325, 327, 328, 330, 337, 349, 399, 401, 406, 411, 413, 414, 421, 423, 424, 440, 446-447, 461, 467, 472, 479, 515, 540, 543, 553

Callahan, Msgr. Francis, 290

Calle Arroyo, 232, 267, 310, 311

Calle Yucca, 310-311, 410

Calle, Dr. Fabio, 242

Camarillo, CA, 319, 337, 340, 497, 501

Cambodia, 300

Camp St. Andrew, Tunkhannock, PA, 75-78

Campaign for Human Development, 294

# INDEX

Campbell, George, 484-486

Canada, 114, 124, 223, 287, 481, 499

Canaya Homeless Assistance Program, 338

cancer, 162, 329, 373, 431, 544

canon, canon law, 85, 134

canonization, canonize, 516-517

Cappelloni, Rev. Thomas A., 265, 278, 481

cardinal, 233, 347, 360

Cardinal Muench Seminary, Fargo, ND, 490, 491

Carlin, Father, 77

Carmelite, 382

Carmella's Newspaper Stand, East Stroudsburg, PA, 138

Carrigan, Rev. Neil, 481

cassock, 14, 28, 36, 80

Castilla district, Peru, 234

catechesis, 259

catechism, 522

cathedral, 79, 80, 125, 126, 233, 390, 393

Catholic Charities, 302, 339-340

Catholic Light, The, 435

Catholic Near East Welfare Association (CNEWA), 343-345, 374, 393-395

Catholic Relief Services (CRS), 344, 355, 373, 393

Catholic Social Services, 392

Catholic University of American (Washington, D.C.), 80, 97, 100, 101, 103, 104, 110, 115, 136, 215

Catholic, catholicism, 26, 35, 36, 93, 126, 134, 141, 146, 147, 153, 206, 216, 217, 239, 244, 277, 278, 285, 291, 295, 297, 301, 363, 397, 422, 423, 425, 428, 429, 442, 476, 482, 483, 491, 505, 516, 521, 522, 538, 562

Catonsville, MD, 73

Cawley, Msgr. Thomas, 217, 423-424

celebrant, 397

celibacy, celibate, 182, 214, 242, 243, 345, 522

Central Intelligence Agency (CIA), 119, 355

chalice, 172

Chamberlain, Margretta, 296

Chamseddine, Sheik Mohamad Medi, 354-355

chancery, 259, 290, 344, 347, 422

chaplain, 215

charity, 142, 539

Charles in Charge, 326

chastity, 522

chasuble, 26

chemist, chemistry, 119

Chesapeake Bay, 99

Chicago, IL, 290

Chico State University, 305, 310, 311

Chimbote, 234, 236, 248

china painting, 211

china, pottery, 210-211

Chinatown Connection, 325-326

Chinchilla, PA, 438, 441

Chouf mountains, 563

Christ the King Parish, Dunmore, PA, 259, 280, 281, 288, 299

Christ, Christus, 98, 157, 259, 379, 388, 429, 442, 473, 527-531, 563

Christian, 97, 104, 278, 291, 297, 351, 354, 366, 367, 375, 382, 388, 398, 486, 559, 560, 565

Christie's, New York, 224

Christmas, 88, 137, 140, 141, 173, 209-210, 372, 373, 410, 413

Chrysler, 185, 186

Church (building), 7, 8, 13, 14, 15, 29, 25, 36, 56, 61, 110, 126, 133, 134, 137, 138, 139, 141, 145, 164, 166, 172, 235, 245, 247, 250, 256, 280, 359, 360, 377, 379, 393, 416, 425, 485, 506, 515-516, 521, 535, 565

Church (universal or parish community), 26, 36, 56, 68, 73, 97, 98, 110, 131, 138, 141, 147, 166, 168, 214, 216, 217, 218, 219, 241, 249, 250, 257, 260, 277, 278, 280, 284, 291, 298, 299, 311, 337, 347, 358, 382, 391, 422, 424-426, 429, 430, 436, 437, 470, 472, 475, 476, 480-482, 487, 491, 514, 516, 517, 523, 530

# INDEX

Church of Mar Shina (St. Shina), 360
Cincinnati, OH, 330
Citizen Watch Company, 327
Civil Air Patrol, 171
cladding, clad, 273, 342
Clarks Smmit, PA, 438
Clarks Summit State Hospital, 300
Clarks Summit, PA, 476, 486
Clearfield, PA, 102
clergy, 290, 388, 425, 426, 430, 473, 518
cloister, 178, 246
CNN, 545
coal, 54
coal region, 20
Coal Township, PA, 91, 110
Cold War, 335
College Miseracordia, Dallas, PA, 51, 89, 91, 93, 95, 119, 246
Columbia County, PA, 285
Communism, communists, 221, 540
Conaboy, Judge Richard, 282
Conboy, Joe, 77
concelebrate, concelebration, 126, 144, 291, 416
concubinage, 242
Conejo Valley, California, 232, 272, 304, 306
confession, 128, 134, 140, 144, 145, 147, 163, 173, 214, 365, 469, 487, 515
confessional, 173
Confirmation, Sacrament of, 396, 428, 466
Confraternity of Christian Doctrine (CCD), 134
Conmy, Rev. Anthony (Tony), 38, 125
Connecticut, 77, 355
consecrate, consecration, 126, 144, 216, 370
consolation, 142
Continental Rack, 188, 197, 199
convent, 71, 134, 215, 216, 302, 365, 492, 514, 544, 549
conversion, 26, 79, 80, 134, 168, 206, 469, 496
Cooke, Terence Cardinal , 354, 355
Cordiano, Richard, 488

Cosmos Minerals, 272, 313, 315, 340-342
Costello, Msgr. Francis (Frank), 127
County of Ventura Homeless Outreach Program, 50
Crabtree, Frank, 296
Cramer, Rev. David, 481
creation, 27, 243, 259
creator, 236
Creighton University, 432, 478, 479, 481, 489, 490
Crespi High School for Boys, San Fernando Valley, CA, 254, 480
cross, crucifix, 28, 233, 354, 373, 528
Crucible Steel, 120, 121, 158
crucifixion, 28, 398
Cuba, 287
Cummings family, 215
Cursillo, Cursillista, 242, 291
Curtin, Dr., 181
Cushing, Richard Cardinal, 217, 233
Cyprus, 383-384, 551, 552

## D

Dallas, PA, 51, 89, 95
Dalton, PA, 296, 429-432, 438, 440, 485-487, 491
Damascus, Syria, 375
Dana Street, Wilkes-Barre, PA, 17
Dannemiller, Father, 97
Danville, PA, 96
"Dark Night of the Soul" (St. John of the Cross), 372
darkness, spiritual, 148
Davis, Tony, 30
deacon, diaconate, 7, 110, 125, 434
dean, 146
death, dead, dying, 18, 24, 28, 45, 102, 103, 104, 105, 106, 161-169, 170, 171, 172, 173-175, 190, 213, 215, 217, 242, 244, 247, 248, 255, 269, 275, 322, 331, 348, 349, 350, 361, 365, 376, 382, 397, 398, 408, 411, 416, 418, 421, 423, 424, 437-438, 442,

445, 447, 451, 462, 464, 465, 517,
  524, 528, 533, 563
Debayeh Palestinian Camp, 356
Deeb, Joseph, 515, 543, 567-569
Deeb, Rev. Daniel, 358-360, 515
Delaney, Geraldine O. ("G.O.D."), 295
Delano Street, Van Nuys, CA, 197
Delaware River, 169
Delaware Valley, 169
Democrat, 538, 540, 542
demon, 477-478
Densevich, Charles (Chick), 475-476
Densevich, Dolly Marie, 475-476
Denton, Senator Jeremiah, 540
Denver, CO, 463
depression, 8
detox, 296
Detroit, MI, 223, 330, 559
Devil, Satan, 139, 148
devote, 62, 442
devotion, devout, 15, 26, 65, 140, 144, 147,
  148, 168, 295, 329, 414, 485, 515,
  524
*Diakonia*, 426
diamond, 222-223
Diocesan Mission Board (Diocese of
  Scranton), 429
diocese, 75, 98, 129, 133, 134, 242, 256, 257,
  285, 300, 301, 363, 374, 422, 425,
  426, 428, 429, 437, 441, 473, 476,
  481, 491, 514
Diocese of Allentown, 429
Diocese of Altoona-Johnstown, 475-476
Diocese of Piura, Peru, 234, 235, 239
Diocese of Scranton, 73, 75, 125, 217, 247,
  258-261, 274, 276, 302, 346, 425,
  426, 429, 472, 473, 474-476, 489,
  490, 491
discernment, 101
discernment of spirits, 433
Discovery Channel, 326
divine, 98
Divine Redeemer, 98
Divine Word Fathers, 148

Dodson School, Wilkes-Barre, PA, 46
dogma, 562
Dolan, Rev. Kenneth (Ken), 126
Dominican, 259
Dominican College of St. Rose of Lima,
  Dubuque, IA, 426
Don Bosco Technique, Fidar, Lebanon,
  534, 561-562,
Doolittle, Clifford, 283
Dorning family, 111, 114
Dorning, Agnes, 110, 111, 114, 177, 189,
  267
Dorning, Joseph (Doc), 92, 93, 111, 113,
  114, 115, 153, 177, 180, 190, 198,
  204, 206-210, 221, 230, 263, 267-
  269, 271, 303, 308-309317, 401, 438,
  494
Dorning, Julia, 207
Dorning, Lillian Madara (Diamond Lil),
  111, 113, 114, 115, 153, 178, 180,
  190, 193, 198, 204, 206, 208-209,
  210, 221, 230, 263, 267-269, 271,
  303, 308-309, 317, 410-411, 438, 494
Dorning, Robert, 91, 93, 111, 112, 114, 177,
  189, 193, 267
Dougherty, Bishop John M., 290
Druze, 388
Dubka, 362
Dubuque, IA, 259
Dunmore, PA, 259, 280
Durante, Jimmy, 40
Dutch, 367
dysentery, 241

*E*

earthquake, 248-249, 250
East Beirut, Lebanon, 364, 366, 370, 373,
  375
East end, Wilkes-Barre, PA, 38
East Stroudsburg State College, 134, 215,
  217
East Stroudsburg State Hospital, 133

# INDEX

East Stroudsburg, PA, 133, 134, 135, 136, 141, 146, 148, 167, 172, 174, 182, 211, 216, 233, 275, 426

Easter, 28, 29, 141, 287, 394

Eastern Group, 259

Economation, Inc., 446

ecstasy, ecstatic prayer, 142

Ecuador, 429

ecumenical movement, 259

ecumenical, ecumenism, 277, 278, 285, 300, 337

Egypt, 224, 231, 363, 375

Elias, Anthony (Tony), 53, 54, 55, 96, 129, 130, 151, 216, 218, 247, 255

Elias, Marlene Esseff, 3, 4, 7, 11, 37, 50, 54, 55, 95, 110, 115, 130, 139, 140, 151, 161, 163, 213, 216, 218, 247, 248, 255

Elias, Theresa, 139

Emmanuel, Bill, 488

Emmanuel, Billy, 488

Emperor of Japan, 229

emphysema, 253

encyclical, 97, 217, 258

England, 201, 221, 239, 249, 263, 275, 557

English, 348, 349, 354, 358-359, 364, 386, 404, 546, 559, 566

Enthronement of the Sacred Heart of Jesus, 139, 140, 143, 300

epilepsy, 405

episcopacy, 475

Episcopalian, 259, 476

Equador, 233

Eritrea, Ethiopia, 392-393

Esseff, Anthony (Uncle Tony), 3, 116

Esseff family, 36, 37, 55, 111, 114, 115, 149, 459, 565

Esseff Foundation, 480, 497, 500-501, 504, 506-508, 535

Esseff Village, 339, 508

Esseff, Mae Ann, 13, 103, 106, 130, 156, 161-169, 190, 197, 247, 275, 276, 416, 418

Esseff, Andrew John, 1, 411, 509, 544, 546, 551-553

Esseff, Cecilia Oblen (Grandma, Sithue), 3, 4, 7, 19, 26, 28, 61, 62, 67, 68, 69, 70, 103, 104, 105, 106, 116, 126, 515, 537, 541

Esseff, Celia Sahd (Mom), 3, 4, 7-8, 12, 13, 15, 16, 19, 22, 23, 26, 28, 29, 36, 37, 43, 56, 64, 65, 67, 68, 70, 74, 102, 103, 104, 106, 111, 114, 115, 126, 129, 130, 136, 139, 145, 156, 162, 164, 167, 168, 168, 173, 174, 187, 189, 190, 191, 198, 204, 210, 214, 218, 230, 247, 253, 255, 256, 263-265, 275, 282, 320, 360, 362, 397, 401, 412-413, 421, 423, 424, 438, 494, 537, 541

Esseff, George Abdanour (Gidue), 1-11, 19, 21, 22, 26, 29, 32, 36, 37, 43, 56, 59-60, 61, 67, 86, 101, 103, 105, 107, 116, 126, 161, 173-175, 177, 213, 320, 343, 345-346, 358, 361, 395, 460, 495-496, 497, 508, 509, 515, 537, 541, 567-569

Esseff, George Jr., 70, 152-156, 158, 175, 177, 178, 180, 181, 182, 189, 193, 205, 206, 210, 213, 254, 263-265, 304-307, 311, 312, 316, 321, 330, 336, 337, 342, 401, 402, 405, 414, 416, 450, 455, 457-460, 494, 498, 501, 502, 507

Esseff, Joseph (Dad), 3, 7, 8, 11, 13, 15, 16, 17, 21, 23, 26, 27, 28, 30, 31, 32, 33, 36, 37, 39, 40, 42, 43, 45, 46, 47, 48, 49, 50, 51, 52, 53, 56, 60, 61, 62, 63-66, 67, 68, 69, 70, 75, 100, 101, 102, 103, 104, 105, 106, 111, 114, 116, 126, 129, 130, 131, 135, 136, 137, 145, 153, 156, 161, 162, 163, 164, 165, 167-169, 174, 186, 187, 189, 190, 191, 197, 198, 204, 210, 314, 219, 230, 247, 253, 255, 256, 263-265, 275, 282, 297, 319, 320, 322, 361, 397, 401, 412, 437-438,

# INDEX

446, 449, 451, 453, 454, 494, 513, 537, 541, 555

Esseff, Joseph Jr. (Joe), 16, 55, 64, 65, 78, 130, 161, 165-166, 172, 190, 214, 219, 255, 297-298, 328, 329, 422, 437, 440-441, 450-451, 455, 477

Esseff, Joyce (Aunt Joyce), 116

Esseff, Mary (Aunt Mary), 116

Esseff, Moses, 174, 361

Esseff, Patty (Sr. Patrice Kenny), 293-294, 297, 328, 422, 423, 437, 477

Esseff, Peter (Uncle Peter), 3, 116, 161

Esseff, Rosemary Dorning, 1, 65, 66, 89, 90, 91-96, 100, 105, 109-110, 111-117, 123, 130, 149-156, 157, 158, 159, 161, 175, 177-180, 181, 182, 185, 186, 187, 188, 189, 190, 193, 197, 198, 203, 204, 205-212, 213, 218, 219, 221-232, 246, 253, 254-255, 260, 263-265, 267-269, 271, 274, 303-313, 316, 317, 319, 324, 328, 329, 330, 331, 334-335, 336, 385, 399, 401-402, 403-404, 405, 410-411, 413, 415, 416-417, 418-419, 421, 422, 438, 447-450, 451, 453-455, 461-462, 464-466, 482-483, 496-498, 499-501, 504-507, 509-511, 516, 517, 535, 543, 544, 546, 551-554, 567

Esseff, Sherrie, 311, 312, 407, 408, 411, 416, 417-418, 507

Esseff, Tim, 509

Esseff-Arpaia Poductions, 446

Ethiopia, 375, 392

Eucharist, 36, 134, 142, 144, 145, 168, 170, 172, 177-180, 391, 425, 469, 474, 524, 527-528

Europe, 141, 145, 201, 202, 221, 260, 263-264, 271, 316, 362, 450, 498

evangelize, evangelization, 425

evil, 106, 478, 538

exorcise, exorcism, Rite of Exorcism, 477

extraordinary prayer, 244

Extreme Unction, "Last Rites", 173, 215, 279, 438, 470, 517

## F

faith, 71, 147, 152, 154, 189, 193, 214, 311, 373, 405, 408, 417, 424, 427-428, 442, 460, 486, 539, 540, 546, 560

faithful, 98, 163

Family Theater, South Main St., Wilkes-Barre, 18

Family Therapy Institute, Rockville, MD, 289

famine, 392

Fargo, ND, 476, 489-490, 491

fast, fasting, 134, 516

fatherhood, 59, 69

Fatima Center, Dalton, PA, 297, 438, 473, 474

Federal Pacific, 183

Fidar, Lebanon, 534, 561

Fides House, Washington, D.C., 98, 127

Finland, 201

First Friday, 279, 439

Fitzpatrick, Huey, 280

Flannery, Joseph X., 284, 388

Flood of 1955, 169-172, 213

Flores, Raphael, 242-243

Florida, 122, 141, 292, 441

Flukt, Rev. Theo, 364-365

Flynn, Rev. George, 255

Foccia, Italy, 221

Food for the Poor, 436

formation, 78, 213, 295, 367, 430-434, 471-472, 476-483, 489-491, 518-519

Fort Belvoir, Virginia, 95, 100, 101, 115, 117, 119, 156, 177, 178, 179, 205, 478479

Forty Hours Devotion, 145

Forty-Fort, PA, 187, 188, 189, 190

Foster, Msgr. Ed, 348, 352, 353, 354, 357-360

Four County Migrant Ministry Committee (Union, Northumberland, Montour, & Columbia Counties, PA), 285

France, 102, 201, 208, 224, 356, 498

Franciscan, 85, 140, 178, 246, 373, 496

# INDEX

Franco, Ellen, 235, 236-239, 343, 367, 369, 376, 389-391, 424-425, 542, 557-569
Frank, Rev. Richard (Dick), 125
freedom, 288, 381, 430, 537, 538, 561
Freeman, Lee, 277
French, 102, 349, 364, 498, 499, 559, 566, 567
Fresno, CA, 328
Friendship House, Scranton, PA, 288
Frost, Robert, 299
fundamentalism, 422
funeral, 175, 177, 416, 418, 420, 442
Futura Titanium, 200, 201, 202, 203, 231, 272, 311, 315, 342

## G

Gabuzda, Rev. Richard, 431-434, 477, 479
Galligan, Rev. Robert, 141-145, 217
GAR High School, Wilkes-Barre, PA, 53
*Gaudium et Spes* (Pastoral Constitution on the Church in the Modern World), 216
Gaza, 343
geisha, 226
Gemayal, President Amine, 351, 353, 355, 365, 514
General Motors (GM), 322, 324
Georgetown University, 90
Georgia, 208
Gere, Rev. Paul, 258, 278, 293, 296
Germany, German, 120, 201, 230, 362, 405, 413, 421
Ghabash, Dr. Maroun, 560-561
Gibran, Khalil, 408, 544, 567-568
Glendale, CA, 198
glory, 127
God, 9, 17, 24, 27, 56, 62, 64, 65, 68, 71, 74, 76, 79, 96, 98, 100, 106, 114, 116, 125, 127, 128, 129, 131, 138, 142, 143, 151, 153, 156, 163, 164, 166, 168, 174, 175, 178, 189, 193, 213, 214, 215, 216, 217, 234, 236, 241, 243, 244, 248, 249, 255, 256, 257, 267, 269, 272, 277, 284, 293, 294, 295, 297, 298, 317, 319, 320, 321, 327, 330, 335, 336, 340, 354, 355, 372, 373, 376, 377, 379, 383, 387, 391, 396, 398, 399, 05, 416, 419, 424, 425, 430, 431, 432, 433, 434, 435, 438, 442, 443, 445, 448, 460, 462, 466, 468, 476, 477, 482, 483, 484, 485, 486, 487, 488, 490, 491, 493, 495, 503, 506, 507, 511, 519, 521-531, 534, 535, 538, 539, 554
golf, 406
Good Friday, 28, 29
Gore, Vice President Al, 541
Goshen, NY, 208
Gospel, 136, 236, 238, 256, 259, 260, 277, 427, 485, 491, 496, 509, 523
grace, 141, 145, 147214, 216, 257, 297, 340, 364, 366, 399, 417, 442, 469, 471, 476, 544, 554
Grady, Sr. Maureen, 394
gratitude, 315-342
Greek Orthodox, 388
Greeks, 563
Greeley, PA, 130
grief, 103, 106, 164, 165, 167, 190, 247, 255, 269, 440, 443, 464
Guam, 288
Guggenheim brothers (Little Guggi and Big Guggi), 52, 53
guilt, 395, 396, 397
Guinea, 427

## H

habit (religious), 84, 85
Hafey, Bishop William J., 73, 125, 126, 133
Hahn family, Wilkes-Barre, PA, 35
Haiti, 428, 434, 437, 511
Handley's Diner, Wilkes-Barre, PA, 264
Hanlon, Rev. Frank, 45, 49, 50, 55, 81, 82, 83, 84, 85, 86, 92, 104, 177-178, 246-247, 331, 496-497

# INDEX

Hannan, Bishop Jerome D., 133, 134, 205, 217

*Happy Days*, 326

Hardine, Lebanon, 1, 2, 353, 358-362, 515-516, 533, 535, 545-547, 549, 564-566

Harissa, Lebanon, 349, 562

Harris, Rev. Michael, 436

Harrisburg Steel, 342

Harrisburg, PA, 41, 287, 441

Harrity, Rev. Vincent, 217

Harrod's, London, 223

Harry, Bill (Uncle Bill), 103, 106

Harry, Billie, 18

Harry, Eddie, 18

Harry, Mae Esseff (Aunt Mae), 103, 106

Harvey, Doc (St. Mary's Seminary), 79

Harvey's Lake, Dallas, PA, 39, 41, 53, 135

hatred, 168

Hawaii, 317-318, 394, 399, 411, 412, 421, 464, 493, 513

Hazard, Wilkes-Barre, PA, 30

Hazle Street, Wilkes-Barre, PA, 11, 13, 18, 30, 39

Hbu-Hamara, Rev. John, 388

healing Mass, healing service, 470, 485

heart attack, 329

Heaton, Sr. Miriam, R.G.S., 258, 293

Heaven, 15, 103, 104, 106, 503, 556

Heffernan, Cor Immaculatum, I.H.M., Sister, 215-217, 218, 247, 256, 257, 258, 298-300, 434, 472, 478, 483, 490, 491, 498

Hell, 106

hepatitis, 253, 258

Hermel, Lebanon, 376

hermitage, 349, 515, 518

Heverline, Miriam, 427-428

Hezbollah, 1, 377, 396, 545

hierarchy, 141, 216, 348, 352

Hilltop Manor, Scranton, PA, 260, 277, 292, 298

Hinger, Rev. George, 215

hippodrome, 563

Hodgkin's disease, 162

Holland, 201, 202, 364, 367, 376, 378

Hollywood, CA, 188, 325

Holmes, Bob, 287, 289

Holmes, Joan, 287-289

Holy Childhood Association, 427, 491

Holy Communion, 26, 168, 169, 174, 214, 285, 370, 388, 419, 469, 495

Holy Cross Fathers, 81, 84, 509

Holy Father (pope), 217, 354, 355, 358

Holy Land, 343, 438

holy oils, 173

Holy See, 496

Holy Thursday, 28

holy water, 127

Holy Week, 26, 379

holy, holiness, 69, 98, 102, 107, 175, 257, 362

homeless, 287, 301-302, 337-339, 367, 460, 483, 497, 508, 534, 541

homily, sermon, 26, 27, 127, 136, 137, 360, 371, 486

homosexual, 243, 472

honesty, 229

Hong Kong, 231, 327

Horn, Rev. John S.J., 431-434, 478, 479, 481, 482

Hospice St. Joseph, Port au Prince, Haiti, 428

Hospital Militar, Piura, Peru, 245

hostage, , 380

house of detention, 275

House of Joy, Becharré, Lebanon, 1

housing, 287

housing project, 259-260, 275-276

Hubert, Dr., 447-448

Hudak, Rev. Cyril, 125

humility, 139

Hunehan, Rev. John, 363

Hurricane Connie (1955), 169

Hurricane Diane (1955), 169

# INDEX

## I

Ike, 30, 31
Immaculate Conception of the Blessed Virgin Mary, 139, 562
Immaculate Conception parish, Scranton, PA, 181
Immaculate Heart of Mary (IHM) Sisters, 139, 141, 215, 216
immigrant, 61, 256, 207, 300, 322, 336-337
immigration, 348
incarcerated, incarcerate, imprison, 277, 279, 281, 282, 285, 367, 528
incense, 36, 521
India, 333-334, 373
Indian, 240, 244
Indiantown Gap, PA, 287, 288
Infra-Temp, Inc., 446
injustice, 100, 363-364,
inmate, 279, 282, 283, 291
Institute of Priestly Formation (IPF), 432-434, 478, 479, 480-483, 489-491,
Institute of the Heart of Jesus, 148, 522-523,
International Relief and Development (IRD), 562
invent, inventor, invention, 122
investiture, 291
Iowa, 259
Ireland, 248, 263-266
Irish, 535
Islam, Islamic, 343, 373, 422, 557-558, 563
Israel, Israeli, 1, 201, 350, 356, 375, 544, 545, 552
Istambouli family, 543, 564-565, 567
Istambouli, François, 533, 535, 543, 544, 546, 549, 550, 559, 562, 565
Istambouli, Leon, 360-361, 513, 515-516, 517, 533, 543, 559, 565
Istambouli, Rahme, 533, 535, 543, 544, 546, 550, 551, 559, 562, 565
Istambouli, Salome, 543, 550, 551, 559
Italy, 221, 498
Ivory Coast, 427

## J

Japan, 37, 202, 203, 224-230, 272-273, 311, 316, 317, 319, 331, 333-335, 341, 404, 446, 498
Japanese, 203, 225-227, 273, 305, 327, 332, 340, 341, 404, 405, 446, 498
Jefferson Hospital, Philadelphia, PA, 155, 156, 162
Jeita, 564
Jenco, Rev. Larry, 344, 372-374, 380, 382
Jerusalem, 343, 356, 364
Jesuit, Society of Jesus, 343, 364, 367, 376, 381, 564
Jesus, 23, 28, 29, 97, 139, 140, 141, 142, 144, 238, 239, 251, 258, 259, 275, 276, 287, 290, 291, 293, 297, 300, 347, 354, 371, 372, 390, 391, 393, 398, 425, 429, 430, 432, 469, 470, 473, 478, 484, 485, 487, 488, 491, 495, 521, 522, 524, 525, 527-531, 563
Jewish, Jew, Judaism, 278, 281, 337
Jihad, Holy War, 373, 396, 557-558,
Joan, Sister (College Miseracordia, Dallas, PA), 92
John Paul II, Pope, 350, 355, 422, 429, 433
John XXIII, Blessed Pope, 217
Jolliet, IL, 344
Jolson, Al, 40
Jordan, 350, 375, 552
Joseph, Johnny, 53, 54
Josephine, Empress, 224
Jounieh, Lebanon, 348, 349, 375, 383, 544, 545, 549-550, 559, 560, 562
joy, 99, 100, 125, 126, 164, 175, 211, 214, 217, 415, 492, 496
Judas, 147, 148
jujitsu, 211
Jung, Carl, 259
justice, 347, 430
Juventud in Marcha, 242, 243, 244

# INDEX

## K

Kairos ministry, 292
Kanavy, Kathleen, 434, 478, 479
karaoke, 225
Karas, Speedy, 41
Kaschenbaugh, Father Arthur, 79, 80
Kassab, Youssef (St. Nimatullah Kassab al-Hardini), 361, 516-518, 535
Katzenjammer Kids, 51
Kelly family, 116
Kelly, Ann Esseff (Aunt Ann), 3, 4, 66, 110, 116, 134, 324
Kelly, Jack (Uncle Jack), 66, 110, 116, 134, 324
Kelly, Maria, 134135
Kennedy, Rev. Michael, 217
Kenny, Sr. Patrice, R.S.M., 258, 299
Kensington Gardens, London, 223
Keserwan, 564
Kfifan Monastery, Lebanon, 516
KGB, 334
Khairche, Msgr., 353
Kharishe, Patriarch, 518
Khoury, Carla El, 563
Khoury, Catherine (Aunt Catherine—Grandma's sister), 66, 106, 264
Khoury, George El, 424-425, 463
Khoury, Joe El, 559
Khoury, Leah El, 424-425, 463
Khoury, Maroun El, 544, 559
Khoury, Nada El, 543, 544, 559
Khoury, Sandra El, 424-425, 463
Kim, 84
kimono, 225, 228-229, 230
kindness, 175
King's College, Wilkes-Barre, PA, 56, 78, 80, 81-90, 91, 93, 94, 97, 100, 103, 199, 446, 509-510, 515
kingdom, 346, 425, 483, 495
Kirby House, Mountaintop, PA, 297
Kitty's, Wilkes-Barre, PA, 31, 39
Kluiters, Rev. Nicholas, 367-369, 376-379, 382, 564

Knights of Columbus, 205, 206
Kopacz, Msgr. Joseph, 431, 489
Koran, 343
Korea, 96, 119, 214
Korean conflict, 119, 120, 190
Koury family, 359
Koury, Father, 14, 15, 27, 28, 29, 42, 43, 56, 125
Koury, George El, 358, 514
Kovatch, Deacon Gene, 436
Kreish, Rev. Albert, 357
Krissinger family, 153
Kuhns, Gary, 277-278,

## L

La Reina High School for Girls, San Fernando Valley, CA, 254, 304, 307
Lackawanna County, 259, 285, 292
Lackawanna County Housing Authority, 292
Lackawanna County Jail, 259, 275, 276, 279, 280-284, 290, 291
Lackawaxen, PA, 130
Lackenmier, Rev. James, 509
Lady (the horse), 306
laicizatin, laicize, 475-476,
laity, lay, 216, 281, 427, 429, 434,
Lane, Rev. T.J. (King's College), 83, 84
Lantanzi, Dr., 412
Larnaca, Cyprus, 348, 375-376, 383, 386, 551, 552
Latin America, 133, 217, 234, 246, 247, 253, 336, 425, 427, 523
Latin American, 286
Latin rite of the Roman Catholic Church, 35, 40, 73, 84, 110, 126, 350, 371, 382
Latino, 247
Lavin, John, 38, 41, 45, 425
Lavin, Tom, 45
Lavine, Bernice, 158
Lavine, Sid, 158
Lebanese, 9, 12, 19, 20, 35, 36, 37, 38, 47, 67, 70, 93, 101, 102, 105, 107, 112,

114, 127, 134, 345, 352, 353, 354, 356, 357, 358, 359, 366, 369, 371, 382, 395, 398, 399, 408, 422, 423, 518, 534, 535, 544, 557, 561, 563, 564, 565, 568

Lebanon, 1, 2, 19, 61, 93, 102, 105, 125, 127, 288, 326, 335, 343-399, 413, 421-443, 422, 423, 424, 425, 430, 432, 421-443, 446, 467, 472, 492, 510, 513-519, 524, 533-536, 543-546, 550-554, 555, 557-569

Lee, Bruce, 325

Legatus, 505

Lemay Street, Van Nuys, CA, 198

lent, 28, 141, 524

Leo XIII, Pope, 143, 522

Leukemia, 155

lewisburg, PA, 292

Lima, Peru, 233, 234, 246, 331,

liturgy, 36, 215, 216, 291, 376, 390, 397, 398, 420, 436, 484, 516, 524

Liturgy of the House (Divine Office, Breviary), 23, 524,

*London Times*, 264

London, England, 201, 221, 223, 263

Lord, 63, 125, 142, 143, 175, 193, 217, 244, 260, 289, 302, 329, 355, 375, 386, 390, 391, 405, 411, 417, 467, 484, 529, 534, 554

Los Angeles, CA, 340, 387, 404, 467, 497, 553,

Los Robles, CA, 447

Loss, 161, 167, 168

Louisiana, 287, 336

Lourdes, France, 141, 145

love, 9, 5759, 60, 63, 65, 67, 69, 73, 84, 85, 93, 94, 95, 98, 101, 106, 116, 117, 126, 130, 134, 136, 139, 142, 143, 145, 146, 164, 167, 168, 175, 178, 182, 198, 203, 210, 211, 214, 216, 217, 218, 222, 223, 227, 249, 250, 255, 277, 288, 289, 300, 306, 307, 310, 313, 316, 328, 345-347, 357, 358, 361, 363, 364, 365, 366, 372,

373, 378, 381, 389, 390, 391, 396, 408, 415, 417, 418, 419, 424, 425, 441, 442-443, 458, 460, 466, 469, 470, 478, 486, 487, 491, 494, 505, 510, 515, 517, 522, 525-531, 539, 556, 567

Lowenstein, Bro. Joseph, 351, 352, 354, 356

Lowman, Marita, 435

Lubac, Henri de, 97

Lustig, Julius, 39, 56

Lustig's Market, 39, 42, 43, 49, 56

Lutheran, 259, 278

Lutheran Social Service, 338, 508

Luzerne County, PA, 285, 292

Ly, Bruce, 325

Lybia, 396

lymphoma, 162

## M

MacIntyre family, 215

Madara, Grandmother, 210-211

Magnificat, 365

Mahanoy City, PA, 207

majesty, 27, 142

Majors, Lee, 325

Majors, Lee II, 325

Malta, 481

Many Mansions, 339, 507-508

market, 27, 29, 30, 31, 32, 33, 39, 48, 86, 101, 137

Markowski, Rev. Clem, 125, 148, 522

Maronite Patriarch, 350, 351, 352, 354, 357, 358, 394, 518

Maronite Patriarchate, Lebanon, 352-353, 518

Maronite, Maronite Rite, Maronite Church, 7, 35, 51, 73, 84, 85, 101, 110, 125, 126, 127, 351, 357, 359, 363, 364, 371, 376, 473, 516, 518, 521

Marquette University, Milwaukee, WI, 95, 96

# INDEX

marriage, 63, 65, 67, 92, 95, 109, 115, 117, 140, 151, 152, 153, 178, 182, 190, 208, 213, 214, 469, 475, 476, 481

Martha (Aunt Martha), 3

Martin, Sister (St. Mary's School, Wilkes-Barre, PA), 83

Martino, Bishop Joseph F., 474, 489

martyr, 142, 376

Marworth, 296, 300

Mary Health of the Sick, Thousand Oaks, CA, 340, 401

Mary, Blessed Mother, Blessed Virgin Mary, 139, 366, 372, 393, 485, 515, 521

Maryknoll, 38

Maryland, 43, 472

Marywood College, Marywood University, 215, 259, 296, 498

Mass, 1, 7, 8, 14, 15, 21, 26, 27, 36, 40, 46, 56, 88, 126, 127, 131, 133, 134, 135, 137, 138, 140, 144, 147, 148, 166, 168, 171, 173, 174, 188, 215, 218, 221, 225, 244, 245, 247, 248, 256, 281, 282, 285, 291, 296, 337, 349, 350, 359, 360, 364, 366, 370, 371, 373, 376, 388, 393, 395, 416, 424, 426, 429, 430, 435, 440, 442, 447, 470, 478, 484, 485, 486, 487, 495, 517, 518, 522, 528, 565

Massachusetts, 84

Mayo Clinic, 496

McAndrew, Sr. Martha, I.H.M., 258, 287, 293

McCarkle family, Wilkes-Barre, PA, 35

McCauley, Mother, 302

McCormick, Bishop J. Carroll, 217, 256, 258, 280, 290

McDermott, Rev. Martin, 364, 514, 518

McDermott, Rev. Martin S.J., 343

McGarry, Msgr. James, 439-440

McGowan, Bill, 83

McHugh, Msgr. Connell ("The Old Man of the Mountain"), 146, 147, 217

MCI, 83

McIntyre, Michael, 312-313, 408, 412

McIntyre, Clifton, 412

McIntyre, Kathy Esseff, 69, 181, 182, 189, 205, 206, 213, 254, 263-265, 306-308, 310, 311-313, 316, 401, 405-408, 409, 412, 494, 501

McKernan, Rev. Leo, 431-432

McLaughlin, Rev. Thomas, 481

McLaughlin's Funeral Home, Wilkes-Barre, PA, 21

McMahon, Dr., 162

McNelis, Dr., 136

Meals on Wheels, 339, 340

medical school, 85, 90, 92, 119, 178

meditation, 522, 525

Mediterranean Sea, 559

Mehri, Bishop Joseph, 363, 375

Melchite, 364

Mellon family, Wilkes-Barre, PA, 35

mercy, 98, 469

Mercy Hospital, Wilkes-Barre, PA, 136, 164

Mercy School of Nursing, Scranton, PA, 288

Mercy sisters, 84, 92, 136, 293, 302

mesallurgist, metallurgy, 119, 222

Mestizoes, 240

Methodist, 277

Methodist Mission Board, 278,

Mexican, 286

Mexico, 366, 428, 436,

Meyers, Atty. Morey, 281

MGM, 322

Michigan, 517

Mickey (the horse), 306-307

Middle East, 1, 351, 357, 358, 374, 378, 380, 391, 394, 481, 515, 543, 544, 552, 557

Middle Eastern, 102

Midland, MI, 330

migrant worker, 260, 285-286, 300, 426

Mike family, 36, 106

Mike, Jake, 135

Miller, Jimmy, 39

mines, mining, 207, 208

minister, ministry, 59, 99, 100, 115, 143, 146, 147, 148, 149, 213, 214, 216, 217, 237, 249, 250, 251, 256, 257, 258, 259, 260, 265, 275, 276-278, 280, 285, 290, 292-293, 295, 300, 302, 340, 345, 358, 395, 425, 426, 428, 430, 433, 434, 439, 472, 475-477, 490-491, 568

Ministerium, 300

Mir, Gen. Michel, 510

miracle, 152, 156, 171, 310, 336, 385, 391, 412, 468, 469, 517, 538

miraculous medal, 145

misery, 234, 250

mission club, 245

Mission for Lebanon (MFL), 422-423, 514

Missionaries of Charity, 1, 343, 364, 366, 428, 431, 471, 492, 514, 524, 543, 544, 567

Missionary Sisters of the Sacred Heart of Jesus (Cabrini sisters), 256

missionary, mission, 38, 129, 134, 172, 178, 217, 232, 233-251, 253, 255, 263, 271, 291, 294, 302, 343-399, 424-429, 430, 431, 434, 435, 436, 441, 478, 480, 490, 491, 524, 533-536, 534, 562

monastery, monastic, 125, 143, 144, 178, 216, 516, 518

monk, 356, 518

mononucleosis, 156

Monroe Avenue, Scranton, PA, 181

Monroe County, 133, 276, 442

Monroe County Hospital, 133, 136

Monroe County Jail, 133, 175, 276

Montessori, 143

Montour County, PA, 285

Moorpark Junior College, 305, 313

moral, 8, 454, 484

Moscow University, 334

Moscow, Russia, 331-332, 334

Moses, 23

Moses Taylor Hospital, Scranton, PA, 181

Mother Superior, 247

Mother Teresa of Calcutta, Blessed, 1, 365, 366, 369, 393, 419, 427, 432, 471-472, 488, 490, 491, 492, 524

Mount Pocono, PA, 146

Moyallen Street, Wilkes-Barre, PA, 11, 13, 16, 17, 18, 23, 29, 30, 32, 46, 114, 164, 190

Mrs. Snoopy, 11, 39

Mt. Huascaran, 248

Mufti, 354, 373

Mullally, Rev. Gerald, 481

Muncy, PA, 276

Murphy, Dr., 153

Murray, John Courtney, 97

Murray, Mrs., 439-443

Murray, Thomas, 439-443

Muslim, 351, 354, 365, 366, 382, 398, 559, 562

mystery, 27, 214, 239, 243, 267, 346, 390, 391, 397, 521

mystic, mysticism, 521, 531

Mystical Body, 98, 214, 257

Mystical prayer, 531

*Mystici Corporis* (Encyclical of Pope Pius XII), 97, 99, 141, 142, 522

## N

Nabha, Lebanon, 379

Nagoya, Japan, 229, 272

Namoor (the dog), 27

Nanticoke, PA, 99

Napoleon, 224, 499

Nasser, Bill (Uncle Bill), 66, 116, 181, 183, 500

Nasser, Catherine Esseff (Aunt Catherine), 66, 105, 116

National Honor Society (NHS), 404

National Security Administration (NSA), 66

Native American, 240, 242

nativity, 373

Necropolis, Tyre, 563

neoprene, 83

# INDEX

Neville, Rev. Joseph S.J., 478
New England Financial, 517
New Jersey, 292, 295, 484
New York, 91, 129, 148, 214, 224, 292, 296
New York Athletic Club, 344,
New York City, 263, 330, 342, 344, 346, 348, 350, 352, 363, 369, 372, 382-383, 385-386, 392, 394, 496, 544, 553
*New York Times, The*, 542
Newman Club, 134, 215
Nicholson, PA, 431
Nicosia, Cyprus, 382-384, 387
Nigritos, Peru, 242, 243
Nissho Iwai, 203, 342
Nixon, President Richard M., 269
Nolan, Msgr. John, 353, 375, 392-394
Nolan, Tommy, 52
North Carolina, 363
Northumberland County, PA, 285
Northumberland, PA, 23, 24, 27
Norway, 201
Notre Dame University, Notre Dame, IN, 81, 83
Novak family, Wilkes-Barre, PA, 35
Novak, Msgr. Leonard, 424
novena, 8, 26, 36, 148, 414, 529
noviatiate, novice, 84, 85, 94, 522
nun, 50, 216, 246-247, 248, 340, 376, 383
nuncio, papal, 347, 350, 393

## O

O'Boyle, Patrick Cardinal, Archbishop of Washington, 97
O'Connor, John Cardinal , 290, 301, 346-347, 354, 374-375, 392-394
O'Dea, Dick, 296
O'Hara, Father (King's College), 81, 82, 84
oasis, 339
obedience, obey, 74, 129, 130, 137, 138, 141, 522, 523
Oblen family, 36
Oblen, Arthur (Uncle Art), 62, 64

Oblen, Catherine (Aunt Catherine), 3, 19, 62
Oblen, Eddie, 104
Office of Urban Ministry, Diocese of Scranton, 259, 290, 291, 295, 300, 301, 343, 426
Ohio, 328
Ohio State University, 332,
Ojai, CA, 311, 336, 405, 494
old world, 102, 103
Omaha, NE, 432, 478, 481
ordination, ordain, 63, 100, 106, 110, 123, 125-128, 129, 130, 133, 144, 151, 161, 163, 167, 177, 213, 246, 295, 429, 472, 473, 475, 476, 482, 491, 516, 522
organized crime, 185
original sin, 139
Ornish, Dr. Dean, 461-467
Ortiz, Denise Esseff, 69, 205, 206, 213, 254, 263-265, 267, 268, 303, 304-307, 310, 312, 313, 316, 319, 339, 342, 399, 401-420, 421, 438, 443, 445, 450-451, 455, 461, 464, 465, 494, 501, 508, 509, 551
Ortiz, Joseph, 414, 415, 417, 421
Our Lady of Guadalupe, 217
Our Lady of Guadalupe, 483,
Our Lady of Lebanon Shrine, Harissa, Lebanon, 349-350, 562
Our Lady of Snows parish, Clarks Summit, PA, 289
Our Lady of the Abingtons parish, Dalton, PA, 483, 484, 486-489
Our Lady of the Sacred Heart, 186
Our Lady of the Snows parish, Clarks Summit, PA, 439
oxide, oxidation, 120-121
Oxnard, CA, 327, 339, 340

## P

painting, 210, 211
Paita, Peru, 242, 243

# INDEX

Palestine, Palestinian, 346, 350, 351, 356, 357, 366, 388

Palestinian Liberation Organization (PLO), 350, 377

Pan American Highway, 241

papal, papacy, 142, 143, 258, 349

parenthood, 151

Paris, France, 145, 332, 335, 447, 552-553

parish, 7, 9, 13, 28, 25, 43, 56, 98, 110, 126, 129, 130, 131, 133, 135, 136, 140, 147, 167, 168, 169, 173, 205, 206, 211, 214, 217, 218, 233, 234, 235, 237, 238, 241, 242, 246, 248, 249, 251, 254, 256, 257, 259, 260, 261, 275, 280, 282, 290, 301, 337, 340, 367, 377, 394, 423-427, 430, 431, 437, 439, 475, 479, 484-488, 490, 523

parishioner, 141, 147, 172, 260

parliament, 560

Parsons, PA, 246

passion, 524

pastor, 27, 43, 110, 127, 129, 130, 131, 133, 134, 135, 136, 137, 138, 139, 140, 141, 146, 169, 171, 173, 217, 236, 256, 260, 280, 289, 295, 340, 423, 424, 431, 439, 470, 479, 481, 489, 523

pastoral, 146

*Pastores Dabo Vobis* of Pope John Paul II, 433, 477

Pat's Barber Shop, Wilkes-Barre, PA, 30, 31

patent, 122, 156, 157, 199, 327

Patriarch (family), 62

Patrick, Mother, 535

Paul VI, Pope, 517

Paxinos, PA, 23

Paye, Sr. Ann, 302

peace, 105, 126, 163, 164, 175, 208, 215, 238, 391, 417, 478, 486, 488, 539, 556, 561

Peach Tree Street, Atlanta, GA, 208

Pearl Harbor, 37

Peckville, PA, 487

pedophilia, 249

penance, 173

Pennsylvania, 7, 41, 91, 100, 102, 125, 177, 184, 189, 205, 216, 234, 237, 264, 268, 277, 285, 286, 287, 300, 301, 303, 330, 343, 485

Pennsylvania State Prison for Women, Muncy, PA, 276, 279

Peoria, IL, 126

Perry, Rev. Carmen, 481

Persian, 563

Peru, 217, 219, 232, 233-251, 254, 258, 259, 302, 357, 363, 427, 428, 432, 442, 491, 523, 555

Peruvian, 234

Peyton, Father, 26

Philadelphia, PA, 23, 25, 155, 156, 162, 168, 290

Philippines, 288

Phillips, Helen, 428, 437

philosophy, 27, 79, 85, 94

Phoebe Snow, 138

Phoenicians, 563

Pico, Juan, 242

piety, 26, 29,

Pike County, PA, 129, 133

Pilgrimage, 98, 145, 343, 373, 438, 529

Pittsburgh, PA, 40, 41, 234, 330

Pittston, PA, 131

Piura, Peru, 246, 250, 253, 255, 330, 331

Pius IX, Pope, 562

Pius XII, Pope, 97, 98

Plymouth, PA, 54

Pocono Catholic High School, 215

Poconos, Pocono Mountains, 137, 146, 169-172, 357

Poland, Polish, 383

Polednak, Rev. John, 430-431

Pontifical Mission for Palestine, Beirut, Lebanon, 2, 342-399, 422, 513-514, 518, 533

Pontifical Mission in Jerusalem, 351,

Poor Clare Sisters, 140, 246

poor, poverty, 8, 26, 59, 69, 97, 98, 99, 140,
143, 217, 234, 237, 239, 240, 241,
242, 243, 246, 250, 256, 257, 258,
259, 260, 275-302, 345-348, 350,
355, 362, 363, 364, 373, 375, 378,
387, 399, 426, 428, 430, 434, 435,
436-437, 460, 472, 483, 491, 497,
511, 522, 523, 540, 541, 560
pope, 97, 143
Port au Prince, Haiti, 428
Portsmouth, England, 263
praise, praising, 127
pray, prayer, 8, 15, 23, 26, 56, 65, 67, 95,
101, 105, 107, 126, 127, 138, 142,
143, 147, 148, 152, 156, 164, 166,
167, 173, 174, 175, 189, 191, 215,
229, 230, 236, 243, 244, 247, 277,
282, 290, 300, 320, 345, 346, 347,
354, 363, 364, 365, 373, 377, 378,
388, 389, 390, 391, 395, 405, 408,
414, 417, 418, 420, 427, 429, 431,
434, 438-439, 442, 460, 473, 474,
478, 480-482, 484-488, 489, 491,
501, 511, 517, 518-519, 521-531,
543, 544, 550, 559
prayer life, 148, 433
preach, preaching, preacher, 127, 130, 134,
136, 144, 425, 437, 540
Precious Blood, 98, 126
pregnancy, pregnant, 151, 170-171, 177,
181, 190, 191
prelate of honor, 290
Presbyterian Seminary, Dubuque, IA, 259
President of the Republic of Lebanon, 351-
352, 354
President's Advisory Council, 199
Presidential Palace, Beirut, Lebanon, 351
Preventive Medicine Research Institute,
Sausalito, CA, 461-465
priest, priestly, 26, 27, 41, 43, 51, 56, 59,
73, 75, 79, 85, 94, 98, 99, 110, 125,
126, 127, 129, 130, 133, 134, 136,
141, 143, 144, 146, 148, 151, 152,
161, 163, 165, 175, 213, 216, 217,
218, 219, 233, 236, 242, 246, 247,
251, 255, 256, 261, 278, 281, 285,
291, 293, 297, 300, 301, 344, 345,
347, 353, 359, 361, 363, 364, 367,
372, 373, 374, 376, 377, 379, 381,
382, 388, 389, 392, 394, 396, 416,
424-426, 430-432, 434, 436, 470,
472, 474-479, 483, 484, 486, 488,
489, 490, 515, 519, 521, 522, 560,
561, 565
priesthood, diocesan, 98, 148, 167, 233,
357, 425, 429, 430, 431-432, 472,
474, 481-482, 518
priesthood, presbyterate, Holy Orders, 56,
73, 75, 97, 100, 125, 128, 133, 145,
146, 151, 214, 217, 218, 256, 257,
281, 282, 299, 300, 345, 347, 376,
390, 397, 425, 429-433, 439, 469,
471-488, 490
Primary Health Care Center, 300
Prince of Peace, 373, 560
prison ministry, 275-277, 280-284, 290-
292
prison, prisoner, jail, 258, 259, 260, 275,
276, 277, 278, 280-284, 287, 290-
295, 296, 298, 300, 435, 483, 488,
523
procession, 14, 393
prophetic, prophecy, 218
Prospect Street, Wilkes-Barre, PA, 3, 4, 11,
32, 36, 68, 103, 173, 174
Protestant, Protestantism, 277, 278, 337,
340
protocol, 350, 351, 352, 356,
provincial, 433
Pueblo Nuevo, Peru, 242
Puerto Rico, 340
Purgatory, 163
Pyle, Mary, 143, 144

## Q

Quebec, 114
Queones, Dr. Raphael, 412, 417

# INDEX

Quesada, Francine, 442-443
Quinn, Rev. Michael, 280, 289

# R

R.O.T.O.R., 325
Raheb, Dr., 356
Ramadan, 562
Rancho Santa Rosa, CA, 493, 501, 504-505
Ray family, Wilkes-Barre, PA, 35
Raymond, Rev. Maurice, 256
Reagan, President Ronald, 540,
real estate, 197, 322, 324, 341
Reardon, Father, 110
reconciliation, 145, 174, 290, 373, 473, 474, 484
Re-Connections, 473-475, 491
rector, 84, 85, 104, 430, 431, 439, 478
rectory, parish house, 126, 131, 133, 135, 137, 138, 139, 140, 141, 145, 146, 148, 169, 174, 182, 216, 234, 235, 236, 237, 241, 249, 250, 255, 260, 290, 368, 424, 472
Red Cross, 365, 388
redeemer, 98
Redemptorist Center, NY, 297
reflection, 259
Reform in the Correctional Institutions in the State of Pennsylania" (Pastoral Letter of the Pennsylvania Bishops), 277
refugee, 286-287, 336, 350, 518
rehabilitation, 295, 484
religion, 56, 97, 106, 298
Rembrand House Museum, 222
renew, renewal, 431-432, 436, 480, 518
Republican, GOP, 537-542
resurrection, 103, 244, 438
retreat, 1, 2, 125, 148, 168, 215, 242, 291, 295, 297, 300, 343, 365, 366, 394, 428, 431, 434, 472-475, 477, 478, 481, 484, 489, 490, 492, 514, 524, 543, 544, 545, 546, 549, 567
revelation, 259, 522

reverence, 360, 436
Rijksmuseum, Amsterdam, 222
ritual, rite (liturgical), ceremony, 14, 36, 110, 112, 125, 126, 141, 174, 214, 230, 247, 291, 521, 529
Robe Company, 158
Robert Morris School, Scranton, PA, 288
Roche, Rev. Edward, 249
Rochester, NY, 342
Rockville, MD, 289
Rolls Royce, 322-324, 493, 497, 500
Roman Catholic, 35, 59, 217, 473
Roman family, 41
Roman, Tony, 162-163
Romans, 563
Rome, Italy, 141, 142, 143, 221, 263, 348, 365, 366, 393-394, 489, 516, 522
Roosevelt, Franklin Delano (FDR), 37
rosary, 26, 55, 1051, 148, 349, 485, 517, 522, 524, 561
Rue de Bac, 145
Russel's, Wilkes-Barre, PA, 18
Russia, Russian, 119, 331-335, 392, 393, 539

# S

sacrament, 173, 214, 215, 297, 345, 377, 469, 470, 471
Sacred Heart of Jesus, 139, 140, 143, 300, 505
Sacred Heart Parish, Greeley, PA, 130
Sacred Hearts of Jesus and Mary parish, Scranton, PA, 424-425
sacrifice, 244, 397, 426
sacristy, 15, 144, 247, 373, 390
Safi, Hoda, 348, 351, 352, 354, 358, 533
Sahd, Charles (Uncle Charlie), 23
Sahd, Frank (Uncle Frank), 23, 106
Sahd, Joseph (Uncle Joe), 23, 24, 25, 362
Sahd, Mamie, 102
Sahd, Rev. Stephen, 127
Sahd, Sadie Elia (Grandma Sahd), 25, 362

# INDEX

Sahd, Samuel (Grandpa Sahd), 23, 24, 25, 27, 67, 79, 362

Sahds, Sahd family, 23, 102, 359, 565

Saigon, 288

saint, 221, 247, 297, 379, 486, 487, 516-517, 535

Saints & Sinners, St. Paschal's, 311-312, 405

Salesians, 534, 535

Salvation Army, 30, 79, 80, 301

San Fernando Valley, 205, 206, 232254, 306, 308, 404, 479

San Giovanni Torondo, 143, 221

San Martin de Porres parish, Talarita, Peru, 234-235, 236-239, 244, 249, 251

Sanbetti family, Wilkes-Barre, PA, 35

sanctuary, 125

Sandbourne Stree, Wilkes-Barre, PA, 255

Santa Ana, 218

Santa Barbara, CA, 415

Santa Monica, CA, 324, 415

Santa Rosa Valley, CA, 447, 501

Santa Rosa, CA, 494, 504

Sausalito, CA, 461

savior, 98, 256

Sayre Hospital, Sayre, New York, 91

Scanlon, Sean, 486-487, 488

Scott, Rev. Edward, 436

Scranton Primary Health Care Center, 287

Scranton Times, The, 376, 435, 437, 443

Scranton, Gov. William, 296

Scranton, Mary, 282, 296

Scranton, PA, 75, 79, 97, 116, 125, 133, 138, 181, 182, 183, 184, 185, 186, 187, 197, 205, 211, 216, 217, 253, 257, 258, 259, 260, 261, 264, 265, 279, 281, 288, 290, 292-293, 296, 300-302, 330, 343, 344, 346, 349, 356, 357, 362, 363, 366, 367, 392, 396, 424, 429, 431, 435, 440, 475, 479, 490, 497, 499, 563

Scrantonian, The, 391

Scribner, Dr. Robert, 253, 268, 271-272, 309, 322, 447-450, 461, 466

Scribner, Margaret, 271, 450

Seattle, Washington, 200

seminarian, 72, 73, 74, 75, 78, 98, 99, 104, 260, 278, 429, 478, 490, 491

seminary, 38, 41, 43, 47, 55, 56, 73, 74, 75, 76, 78, 81, 84, 88, 93, 94, 99, 101, 116, 125, 134, 142, 177, 234, 259, 265, 429-433, 439, 440, 471, 473, 475-478, 481-488, 522, 555

semitics, 97

Serra Club, Serrans, 205, 326, 478-482,

Serra, Padre Junipero, 326, 478

servant, 346

service (liturgical), 14

service (ministerial), 15, 216, 244, 357, 377, 426, 432, 474

sex, 225

sexton, 7, 280

sexual misconduct, sexual impropriety, sexual abuse, 217, 423-424, 431, 473

Sfeir, Patriarch Nasrallah Pierre, 395

Shamokin, PA, 91, 93, 95, 110, 112, 115, 180, 189, 208, 209, 267

Shanahan, Rev. James, 234-235

Shaver Lake 805, LLP, 446

Shaver Lake, CA, 328-329, 450

Shavertown, PA, 413, 424

Sheen, Archbishop Fulton J., 97

shelter, 171, 287, 301-302, 337

Shields, Eleanor, 258, 293

Shiite, 354, 355, 366, 375

Shiner, Father, 518

Shintoism, 228

Sho Sho (the dog), 4, 310

Shohola, PA, 129, 130, 131, 133, 134, 141, 161, 295, 426, 488

shrine, 148, 229-230, 349, 361, 516, 535, 562, 565

Sidon, 563

signal corps, 183

silence, 1, 28, 74, 76, 92, 105

Simon, Charlie, 17

Simon, Ms., 46

sin, 217

# INDEX

Singing, 127

Sioux Falls, SD, 490

sister (religious), 84, 137, 140, 215, 216, 217, 256, 293, 299, 362, 364-365, 366, 369, 370, 383-384, 427, 428, 429, 434, 471, 483, 492, 524, 535, 544, 546, 549, 567

Smith, Billy, 41

Sobringki, Mary, 215

Sobrinski, Joe, 215

Sobrinsky family, 215

social justice, 138, 143, 258,

Society for the Propagation of the Faith, 217, 290, 424-430, 432, 434, 437, 438, 441, 483, 484, 491

Sofia University, Tokyo, Japan, 404

Sotheby's, New York, 224, 499

soul, 98, 116, 148, 517

South America, 140, 217-218, 221, 233-251, 256, 263, 285, 330, 471, 484, 522

Spain, 201, 231

Spanish, 233, 237, 285, 307, 417, 478

Spencer, David, 70, 84, 30-310, 406, 411, 453

Spencer, Gladys, 309

Spencer, Kimberly, 502, 509

Spencer, Mary Ellen Esseff, 69, 70, 179, 180, 181, 182, 189, 205, 206, 210, 254, 263-265, 268, 305-310, 312, 315-317, 401, 402-403, 406, 407, 408, 409-410, 411, 412, 414, 415, 417, 418, 448, 453, 501, 509, 569

Spencer, Stephanie, 84, 509-510

Spirit, Holy Spirit, 379, 380, 391, 425, 432, 526-531

spiritual director, 84, 142, 430-434, 481, 484, 489, 490, 491, 517, 522

*Spiritual Exercises* of St. Ignatius Loyola, 433, 481

spiritual father, 145, 214

spirituality, spiritual, 95, 116, 145, 148, 152, 168, 214, 295, 296, 297-298, 300, 408, 417, 419, 427, 433, 434, 443, 482, 491, 518, 524, 529

Springfield, VA, 179, 181

Ss. Peter and Paul parish, Scranton, PA, 489

St. (Mar) Charbel Makhlouf, 349, 361, 517

St. (Mar) Shina, 360

St. Ailey's Orphanage, Beirut, Lebanon, 369

St. Aloysius, Wilkes-Barre, PA, 127

St. Ann's Maronite Church, Scranton, PA, 181

St. Ann's Monastery, Scranton, PA, 125, 257, 301

St. Ann's Parish, Shohola, PA, 129, 130, 133

St. Anthony, 36, 62, 127, 164, 174

St. Anthony's Monastery, 516

St. Anthony's parish, Wilkes-Barre, PA, 14, 28, 25, 36, 42, 53, 126, 130, 173, 510

St. Catherine Labouré, 145

St. Charles Seminary, Baltimore, MD, 41, 43, 56, 73, 78, 79, 84, 213

St. Dominic's, Parsons, PA, 246

St. Don Bosco de Sales, 534

St. Elizabeth's Parish, Van Nuys, CA, 205, 206, 479

St. Francis Church, Beirut, Lebanon, 373

St. Francis of Assisi, 516

St. Francis Parish, Scranton, PA, 260, 275

St. Francis X. Cabrini, 256

St. Gabriel's Retreat House, Clarks Summit, PA, 297, 474, 476

St. Ignatius Loyola, 433, 481

St. James Society, 217-219, 233, 234, 236, 242

St. John Neumann, 145

St. John of the Cross, 372

St. John the Evangelist, 525

St. John's Church, Bushkill, PA, 133, 134, 140, 172

St. John's Parish, Scranton, PA, 259-260

St. Joseph, 521

# INDEX

St. Joseph's Church, Coal Township, PA, 110

St. Joseph's Hospital, Scranton, 288

St. Joseph's University, Beirut, Lebanon, 343

St. Jude, 95, 96

St. Lucy's Parish, Scranton, PA, 256, 257, 258, 259

St. Luke's Church, Stroudsburg, PA, 133, 134, 140

St. Mark's Church, , 133

St. Maron, 35

St. Mary Magdalene's Church, Camarillo, CA, 340, 497

St. Mary's Parish, Mount Pocono, PA, 146

St. Mary's Parish, Wilkes-Barre, PA, 27, 127

St. Mary's School, Wilkes-Barre, PA, 9, 26, 29, 36, 37, 38, 40, 41, 42, 45, 46, 55, 56, 73, 84, 125, 166

St. Mary's Seminary, Baltimore, MD, 27, 56, 78, 79, 80, 81

St. Matthew's Parish, East Stroudsburg, PA, 133-149, 155, 163, 167, 169, 173, 174, 182, 212, 213-219, 275, 295, 423, 426, 488

St. Michael the Archangel, 148, 505

St. Nicholas School, Wilkes-Barre, PA, 41, 42, 54

St. Nimatullah Kassab al-Hardini (Youssef Kassab), 516-518, 535

St. Paschal's Church, Ojai, CA, 311, 337, 407, 416,

St. Paul, 142

St. Paul Prison Guild, 290

St. Paul's parish, Scranton, PA, 490

St. Peter, 142

St. Peter's Cathedral, Scranton, PA, 125, 301

St. Petersburg, FL, 292

St. Pio Adoration Chapel, 488,

St. Pio of Pietrelcina, 143-145, 221, 417

St. Pius X Seminary, Dalton, PA, 429-432, 434, 438, 473-477, 483, 489, 491

St. Theresa, 414

St. Theresa's parish, Shavertown, PA, 413, 423-424

St. Therese of Lisieux, 145

St. Thomas Aquinas, 79

St. Anthony, 8,

Stahurski, Rev. Thomas, 265, 278, 481

Standard Oil of Ohio, 342

Stations of the Cross, 139, 505, 521-522, 524,

Stavoy, Rev. Stephen, 436

Stedelijk Museum, Amsterdam, 222

stigmata, 143, 144

stipends, 15

stole, 125

streetcar, 54, 99

Stroudsburg, PA, 133, 134, 136, 172, 295

Studio City, 324

subdeacon, 126

suffering, 28, 69, 98, 100, 130, 133, 172, 234, 244, 257, 259, 260, 275, 285, 296, 354, 364, 382, 388, 395, 397, 398, 416, 443, 473, 497, 518, 524

Sugar Notch, PA, 52

*Summa Theologica* (St. Thomas Aquinas), 79

sumo wrestlers, 226

Sunni, 354

superior, 249, 362, 365, 395, 396

Supra Alloys, 342, 405, 446, 455, 517

surplice, 28, 36

surrender, 164

Susquehanna River, 99, 186, 264

Sweden, 201

Sweeney, Doc, 215

Sweeney, Kathy, 215

Swoyersville, PA, 38

Sydney, Australia, 399

Syracuse, NY, 477-478

Syria, Syrian, 359, 374, 375, 377, 545

Syriac, 97, 360, 516

Syrian Orthodox, 127

# INDEX

## T

tabernacle, 172
Taffera, Rev. Mark, 289
Taiwan, 226
Talarita, Peru, 234, 236
Tanzania, 429
Targett, Rev. Lionel, 234-239, 241, 246,
    248, 249, 250, 254, 263, 331, 442
Team Ministry, 258, 260, 278, 287, 293-294,
    296, 298-299
telepherique, 562
Telespond , 292-294, 298-300
Ten Commandments, 298
Teranova, Frank, 382
Terranova family, 382
Terranova, Darlene Sahd, 382
Terranova, Joseph, 387
Thailand, 373
The Farm, Dalton, PA, 300
*The Scranton Times*, 138
*The Scranton Tribune*, 283, 437, 443
Theological College, Washington, DC, 97
theology, theological, 94, 97, 99, 259, 433,
    564
Theresa Clare, Mother, 139
Thomas Aquinas Seminary, Dubuque, IA,
    259
Thomas, Johnny, 69
Thousand Oaks, CA, 232, 254, 263, 319,
    322, 401, 408, 507-508
Ti-Core, 199, 200
Tijuana, Mexico, 432
*Time* magazine, 415
Timlin, Bishop James C., 290, 366, 422,
    423, 429, 432, 434, 473-475, 488
titanium, 120-121, 122, 157, 158, 178,
    182, 183, 184, 187, 188, 199, 201,
    202, 203, 204, 211, 221, 226, 231,
    272-274, 315, 321, 322, 331, 335,
    341-342, 445, 460
Tokyo, Japan, 202, 229, 331, 404, 493
Tradition (Church belief and practice), 518

tradition (custom), 67, 102, 110, 111, 112,
    127, 564
travel, 221-232, 263
Treskauskas, Rev. George, 130
Tri-County Migrant Committee (Wyoming,
    Lackawanna, & Luzern Counties,
    PA), 285
triduum, 529
Tripoli, 535
tuberculosis, TB, 240
Tunkhannock, PA, 75
twelve steps, 295
Tyre, 545-546, 563

## U

U.S. Department of Agriculture, 208
U.S. Embassy, Beirut, Lebanon, 344, 348,
    382, 384, 386, 546, 550, 551
U.S.S. Eisenhower, 375
Ubaldi, Dr., 258
UCLA, 415
Uganda, 481
Ukai, cormorant fishing, 230
Ukraine, 481
Under One Roof, 338
Union County, PA, 285
Uniontown, PA, 23
United Kingdom (U.K.), 116
United States government, 119, 120, 122,
    157, 158, 179, 180, 183, 184, 202,
    208, 258, 295, 497, 549
United States, America, USA, 1, 37, 61,
    201, 202, 217, 233, 236, 245, 246,
    247, 250, 253, 258, 273, 277, 327,
    331, 336, 337, 341, 343, 344, 355,
    362, 363, 369, 372, 373, 382, 386,
    388-389, 391, 421, 424, 515-517,
    524, 536, 540, 544, 545, 546, 554,
    555, 557, 560, 566
University of California, Northridge, 319,
    404, 410
University of London, 319, 405
University of Pennsylvania, 90, 181, 207

# INDEX

University of Piura, 242
University of Scranton, 258, 275
University of Southern California, 319, 339, 404

## V

VA Hospital, Wilkes-Barre, PA, 135
Valley View Terrace, Scranton, PA, 259, 260, 278, 292, 298
values, value, 56, 101, 107, 202
Van Gogh Muesum, 222
Van Loon, Msgr. Neil J., 290
Van Nuys, CA, 197, 205, 325,
Vatican, 348, 355, 375, 383,
Vatican Council II, 97, 144, 173, 216, 217, 247
Velechi, Bill, 488
Velechi, Zora, 488
Ventura County Behavioral Health, 508
vestment, 26, 144, 245
victim, 424
Vietnam, 286, 288, 289, 296, 300, 327, 336, 540
Vietnam War, 242, 540
Vietnamese, 287-288, 289, 327, 336, 337, 494
Villa Esperanza, 508
Virginia, 95, 100, 115, 119, 130, 149, 172, 178, 182, 183, 189, 190, 475, 478
vocal prayer, 521
vocation, 56, 134, 216, 256, 478, 482
Vocation Director, 215, 216

## W

wadi, 565
Wal*Mart, 327
Walsh, Rev. Jeffrey, 431
Walsh, Rev. John, 215, 217
Walton, Rev. Bill, 278
Walton, Rev. William, 258, 293, 296

war, 1, 9, 32, 37, 38, 83, 185, 208, 350, 354, 364, 377, 388, 392, 395, 396, 426, 442, 491, 538, 540, 556, 560
Wartburg Lutheran Seminary, Dubuque, IA, 259
Warunek, Sharon, 427-428
*Washington Post, The*, 537, 542
Washington, D.C., 80, 97, 100, 110, 115, 127, 154, 155, 178, 179, 234, 289, 292, 347, 352, 366
wealth, wealthy, 226
Webby, Rev. George, 51, 125
Webster, Karlene, 534-535
West Bank, 350
West Beirut, Lebanon, 354, 365, 366, 369, 370, 373, 375, 392
West Chester, NY, 216
West Lake, CA, 304
West Side Hotel, Scranton, PA, 281
West Virginia, 479
Westlake, CA, 505
White House, 541
Wilkes College, Wilkes-Barre, PA, 93
Wilkes-Barre, PA, 3, 4, 11, 18, 27, 31, 35, 38, 39, 46, 51, 52, 54, 59, 73, 78, 80, 81, 88, 95, 99, 101, 112, 114, 115, 119, 125, 126, 129, 131, 134, 133, 135, 164, 168, 173, 174, 185, 187, 199, 218, 240, 246, 254, 255, 263, 264-265, 267, 271, 301, 413, 440, 509, 513, 515, 555
Williamsport, PA, 427,
Wilms, Peter, 201-202, 221, 272
Wincovitch, Sheriff Joseph, 282, 283
Windsor Castle, 223
Windsor, Canada, 223, 224
Wing, Marcella, 211
Wisconsin, 215
wonder (of God), 27
Word of God, 372, 530
World War I, 208
World War II, 116, 120
worship, 562
Wuellner, Rev. Francis (Frank), 126

# INDEX

Wyoming County, PA, 285
Wyoming Valley, PA, 265
Wyoming, PA, 38

## *Y*

Yarrrish, Rev. Bernard, 290
Yemen, 373
yoga, 462-466
Yosemite, 406
Yoshimoto, Ricky, 203, 226, 341-342
youth group, 311
Yungay, Peru, 248-249

## *Z*

Zateeny family, 215
Zimbar, Genevieve, 217